Family Violence
in the United States

2
edition

Family Violence

in the **United States**

2 edition

Defining, Understanding, and Combating Abuse

Denise A. Hines
Clark University

Kathleen Malley-Morrison
Boston University

Leila B. Dutton
University of New Haven

Los Angeles | London | New Delhi
Singapore | Washington DC

Los Angeles | London | New Delhi
Singapore | Washington DC

FOR INFORMATION:

SAGE Publications, Inc.
2455 Teller Road
Thousand Oaks, California 91320
E-mail: order@sagepub.com

SAGE Publications Ltd.
1 Oliver's Yard
55 City Road
London EC1Y 1SP
United Kingdom

SAGE Publications India Pvt. Ltd.
B 1/I 1 Mohan Cooperative Industrial Area
Mathura Road, New Delhi 110 044
India

SAGE Publications Asia-Pacific Pte. Ltd.
3 Church Street
#10-04 Samsung Hub
Singapore 049483

Acquisitions Editor: Kassie Graves
Editorial Assistant: Elizabeth Luizzi
Production Editor: Astrid Virding
Copy Editor: Janet Ford
Typesetter: C&M Digitals (P) Ltd.
Proofreader: Barbara Johnson
Indexer: Jean Casalegno
Cover Designer: Anupama Krishnan
Marketing Manager: Erica DeLuca
Permissions Editor: Adele Hutchinson

Printed in the United States of America

Library of Congress Cataloging-in-Publication Data

Hines, Denise A.

Family violence in the United States : defining, understanding, and combating abuse / Denise A. Hines, Kathleen Malley-Morrison, Leila Dutton. — 2nd ed.

p. cm.
Includes bibliographical references and index.

ISBN 978-1-4129-8900-8 (pbk.)

1. Family violence—United States. I. Malley-Morrison, Kathleen. II. Dutton, Leila. III. Title.

HV6626.2.H56 2013
362.82'920973—dc23   2012032639

This book is printed on acid-free paper.

Certified Chain of Custody
Promoting Sustainable Forestry
www.sfiprogram.org
SFI-01268
SFI label applies to text stock

14 15 16 17 18 10 9 8 7 6 5 4 3 2

Contents

Detailed Contents

Preface and Acknowledgments

My friend went out with a boy who tried to control what she did. He would say he hated her.

I had a former female friend who tended to be very domineering. She would never resort to physical violence, but she used guilt-manipulation and yelling to control her boyfriends.

My best friend was in an abusive relationship. Her boyfriend used to push her around and try to control her appearance, activities, and friendships.

My boyfriend and I were fighting and he tried to go to sleep, so I punched him in the chest to wake him up.

These descriptions of aggressive relationships are quotes from college students, just like most of you who are reading this book right now. They describe the typical type of aggression occurring between partners in relationships—what some researchers call "minor violence" (Straus, 1990a) and others call "situational couple violence" (Johnson, 2008). Indeed, most aggression in relationships, both intimate relationships and other family relationships, is not the type that we see on the news or in most of the case studies presented in this book. Such cases are extreme examples; they are meant to capture our attention and spur research into, and resources for, people involved in highly abusive situations.

People involved in extremely abusive family relationships are the ones most in need of intervention services such as those offered by domestic violence agencies, Child Protective Services, medical professionals, and mental health professionals. They are also the ones who tend to receive the most research attention. However, most cases of family aggression involve psychological aggression and occasional minor violence. In fact, according to dozens of studies on dating aggression in college students and young adults (e.g., Hines & Saudino, 2003; Sabina & Straus, 2008), about one third of the students reading this book right now are involved in dating relationships in which at least some violence (e.g., slapping, pushing, shoving) has occurred. Some researchers argue that prevention services need to focus on these types of relationships because preventing minor violence in intimate partner and family relationships will result in a large improvement in social and psychological health (M. Straus, personal communication, March 4, 2004). Compared to people not involved in aggressive relationships, men and women in relationships in which minor violence has occurred suffer from more depression, psychological distress, and psychosomatic symptoms (e.g., Stets & Straus, 1990). Because at least one third of the population have been involved in these types of relationships, eliminating even minor violence from close relationships, Straus argues, would result in vast improvements in mental health. We focus in this Preface on dating aggression because many of you are involved in such relationships; however, consider how much social and psychological health would improve if violence and aggression are eliminated from all forms of family and intimate relationships.

Family and intimate partner aggression, in the form of minor physical violence or psychological aggression has touched most of us. Most of us have witnessed it, experienced it, and/or used it in our lifetimes. In order for us to eliminate aggressive and abusive behaviors from relationships, we must be willing to confront our own experiences with these behaviors. All aggression matters, whether it is extreme or minor, verbal or physical, committed by men or women, by ourselves or someone else. How often have you been victimized by someone else's cruel words or actions? More important, how often have you done or said something that could harm another person (e.g., boyfriend or girlfriend, brother or sister, mother or father) either emotionally or physically? Because most of us have been socialized to view aggression and abuse as something outside of ourselves, confronting our own abilities to behave aggressively and abusively is a crucial first step in understanding and eliminating aggression and abuse from our lives and the lives of others in this country (Mills, 2003).

Because the bulk of the research on family violence has focused on those most in need of intervention services, much of the research and many of the case examples presented in this book involve individuals subjected to severe forms of family violence. We also present as much research as possible on population-based studies, which include cases of minor violence and psychological aggression as well. As you read this book, consider the quotes at the beginning of this Preface and this discussion of the impact of even minor aggression on people's psychological and social health. Consider also your own life and the lives of your loved ones—how many of them have been involved in relationships in which aggression occurs? How much better do you think your life and/or their lives would be if aggression were not present in your or their closest relationships?

This book addresses all types of family aggression. For most of the chapters, we limit our discussion to relationships in which some type of close, long-term commitment is involved (e.g., parent-child relationship, sibling relationship, husband-wife relationship; committed intimate partner relationship, even if not married). However, we do have a chapter focusing on maltreatment in college student relationships which might not be long-term or intimate, but in which aggression may still occur (Chapter 7). In addition, in both the chapter on maltreatment of male partners (Chapter 6) and maltreatment in lesbian/gay/bisexual/transgender/queer/intersex (LGBTQI) relationships (Chapter 8), we also consider some of the research on dating violence. Our decision to do this reflects two issues: (1) there is a dearth of research on these populations of victims in general because the bulk of the research, practice, and policy attention has focused on female victims of men, and (2) for the LGBTQI population, in most states, gays and lesbians are denied the right to marry; consequently, we were forced to concentrate on violence in their nonmarital intimate relationships, and research typically does not distinguish between committed versus non-committed intimate relationships in this population. Because the types of aggression discussed in these two chapters occur at rates at least equal to those of men's maltreatment of female partners (Chapter 5), we consider it important to devote a chapter to each of them, even though systematic research is still developing in these two areas and is certainly not as extensive as research on the maltreatment of female partners.

In the first chapter of this book, we focus on a discussion of the problems and controversies surrounding the process of defining family violence and abuse. We also discuss the different perspectives that can be found in the legal, medical, and social service professions, and the differences between these professional points of view and lay opinions. We then introduce a cognitive-affective-ecological conceptual approach, which provides a unifying framework for the book.

In Chapters 2–10, we discuss specific types of aggression in family relationships. Chapter 2 is devoted to child physical maltreatment, Chapter 3 to child sexual maltreatment, and Chapter 4 to child neglect and psychological maltreatment. Although research shows that these forms of maltreatment typically overlap, we chose to discuss them separately for ease of presentation. However, we provide a discussion of the co-occurrence of many of these types of child maltreatment and the implications for the child's adjustment. In Chapters 5 through 8, aggression within adult intimate relationships is discussed. Specifically, we provide a discussion of the maltreatment of female partners by men, of male partners by women, within college student dating relationships, and within the LGBTQI community. In Chapter 9, the maltreatment of older adults is discussed, followed by a discussion of the maltreatment of family members with disabilities, an under-researched area. In Chapter 10 we provide the limited information available on two "hidden" types of family violence: violence against siblings and parents by children and adolescents. In all these chapters, we begin with illustrative case studies, then address definitional issues and provide a discussion of the prevalence of the particular type of aggression. Next, predictors and correlates are discussed, structured according to our conceptual model, followed by information on the possible consequences of each type of aggression. Finally, efforts at preventing and intervening in family violence are presented. Within these chapters, we also provide information on the most extreme type of family violence, that of homicide of family members. Most chapters also have a "special issues" section addressing a specific issue related to that particular type of family violence.

Our book concludes with three chapters focusing on placing family violence into the larger cultural context of the United States. Chapter 11 discusses the contemporary and ecological context of family violence in the United States today, including the role of culture in contributing to, maintaining, and providing rationalizations for violence in interpersonal relationships. In Chapter 12, we provide a brief discussion of family violence in various racial and ethnic communities in this country, and consider how each group's context may play a role in varying rates of family violence. Chapter 13 addresses another specific cultural context, that of religious affiliations and values, in tolerance or intolerance for violence in families.

Our decision to write the first edition of this book was a result of writing our first book with Sage Publications. When writing that book, *Family Violence in a*

Cultural Perspective, we became so involved in the research that we could not contain everything we wanted to write in just one book. Our editor at the time at Sage, Jim Brace-Thompson, noticed the problem and suggested the possibility of a second book, a possibility we had already thought of but had not yet mentioned to him. We were thrilled that all of us were on the same page, and we would like to thank Jim for giving us the opportunity to write the first edition of this book. We were delighted with its reception in the field and the feedback we received from people who read it or used it in their classes. When Kassie Graves, our current editor at Sage, approached us to update the book for a second edition, we were happy to do so. We would like to thank Kassie for her patience and suggestions as we updated this book, and we would like to thank her assistant, Elizabeth Luizzi, for her assistance in putting together the manuscript. We would also like to thank four reviewers for their valuable suggestions on how to update the book, many of which we incorporated, such as more tables, end-of-the-chapter discussion questions, and two new chapters. These reviewers are Elwood W. Hamlin II from Florida Atlantic University, Margie L. Kiter Edwards from the University of Delaware, William Curcio from Montclair State University, and Phil Davis from Georgia State University.

Members of the Family Research Laboratory and the Crimes Against Children Research Center at the University of New Hampshire, including Murray A. Straus, David Finkelhor, Theodore Cross, Kimberly Mitchell, Kathy Becker-Blease, Emily Douglas, Wendy Walsh, Janis Wolak, Lisa Jones, Melissa Holt, and Glenda Kaufman Kantor, provided excellent feedback on several chapters in the previous edition of this book, which have been incorporated into the current edition as well.

Several of Denise's students provided valuable research for this edition, including Stephanie Henderson, Alexa Chu, Emily Corbett, Claire Hunt, and Julia Kelley-Vail. A number of her students also provided assistance with the new tables in many of the chapters and with the development of the end-of-the-chapter discussion questions, including Michelle Collett, Dani Dimitrova, Gayatri Khosla, and Ashley McCartney. Hayley Rogers provided invaluable assistance in the development of the References section for this book and did research on a few of the case studies that appear. Some of Kathie's students provided much needed help with tracking down sources, doing Internet searches for important documents, and putting together references. They include Heidi Niederhausen, Xiaofei Jalette, Candace Cantrell, Erin Anderson, Linh Phuong Vu, Elan Parker, Nikki Pelezza and Rina Beyda. Many thanks go to four University of New Haven students—Victoria Baker, Jennifer Nolan, Corrianne Dionne, and Marisa Auguste—who helped Leila by obtaining articles, conducting Internet searches, and assembling references.

Denise would like to acknowledge the support of her many family members and friends through the years. Her partner, Matthew Kelleher, remains a constant source of support and encouragement in all of her work. Her parents especially have supported her and expressed much pride and love at every step along the way. Likewise, Kathie extends her appreciation to her family and to her friends Eli and Carolyn Newberger. Leila would like to also thank Cynthia Dutton, Elizabeth Dutton, and Tracy Tamborra for their support in all of her endeavors, including this project.

PART I

Defining and Understanding Abuse

Issues in the Definition of Family Violence and Abuse

Women can verbally abuse you. They can rip your clothes off without even touching you, the way women know how to talk, converse. But men . . . weren't brought up to talk as much as women do . . . So it was a resort to violence, if I couldn't get through to her by words . . . On some occasions she was the provoker. It didn't call for physical abuse . . . [but] it did call for something. You know, you're married for that long, if somebody gets antagonistic, you want to defend yourself. (Ptacek, 1998, p. 188)

What are your views on this case? If this man struck his wife when she antagonized him, has he been abusive? How about his wife? If she verbally attacked him, put him down, tried to antagonize him with her words, was she also guilty of spousal abuse? Is one form of abuse (e.g., physical aggression) more abusive than another form (e.g., verbal aggression)? What is the basis for your judgment? Does abusive behavior by one spouse justify retaliatory aggression?

I was married when I was 20-years-old and after a week, there was a violent episode. He didn't hit me, but he tore up things in the household, and it was all due to, he didn't like what I was cooking for supper. But by the end of the following week, which was two weeks into the marriage, he put a loaded gun to my head. I had never felt that kind of scaredness before. (Anderson, 2010, p. 11)

Would you identify the woman who reported this experience as a victim of domestic violence, wife abuse, and/or maltreatment? At what point in the scenario might you call her husband's behavior abusive? When he started tearing up the household? If he had worked hard all day and had asked his wife to have steak and beans ready for him when he came home, and she had forgotten to prepare supper and just offered him a sandwich, would he have been justified in his anger? What reasons might she have had for staying with him after that incident? Would you be reluctant to call his behavior abusive until he actually threatened her life? What kinds of options might have been available to her as the violence escalated?

> His hand on my throat, pressing me into the bed . . . I never called it . . . rape. I called it rough sex. Forcing himself on me. Being selfish and inconsiderate, a beast, a monster. He called it getting what he wanted. What he was entitled to. (Letellier, 1999, p. 10)

Does this appear to be a case of marital rape? A definite case of domestic assault? The victim in this case is a gay male. Does that affect your judgment of the case in any way? If so, how? How likely is it that the victim in this case will be able to find appropriate support services to help him deal with this relationship and its effects on him?

> When my son was a toddler . . . he would often attempt to squeeze past the front door where stone steps awaited his fall. Verbal reprimands and redirecting his attention else-where were fruitless, as he attempted time and again to get out . . . Rather than allow him to experience for himself the consequences of wandering too close to those steps, I swatted him smartly a couple of times on his diapered behind . . . ! It took two more swattings before he became convinced of the certain connection between trying to get out the front door and the painful consequences, but after that, he needed no more reminders! (Newberger, 1999, p. 79)

The woman who told this story did so proudly, pleased with her ability to discipline her son. What is your view? Is corporal punishment an appropriate response to self-endangering behaviors in a toddler? Is it appropriate in other circumstances? Or, is it possible that there are always better methods for dealing with child behavior that is considered undesirable?

> After being hospitalized with a broken hip, 80-year-old Mr. Jaffin began living with his daughter and son-in-law. His daughter repeatedly berated him for not being able to clean his room and began referring to him as their third child. Reminding him what an avid golfer he'd been before the accident, she ridiculed him for now being unable to go to the mailbox without his walker and assistance from a family member. Within a month, Mr. Jaffin began to feel worthless and withdrew from his family and friends. He spent the day in his room sleeping or watching television, no longer socializing with or even phoning old friends. (Humphries Lynch, 1997)

What are your views of Mr. Jaffin's situation? His daughter and son-in-law have taken him in, provided him with his own room and television, presumably keep him warm, safe, and well fed, and try to motivate him to be the active man he once was. Given these circumstances, would you say he is being maltreated in any way? Should the medical personnel who are overseeing his recovery from the broken hip intervene in the family situation? If so, how?

In the United States, one can expect considerable disagreement on the answers to these questions. Consider the first case. The problem of domestic violence against women has received a great deal of attention for years as an important social problem, but only recently has there been acknowledgment of the extent to which much partner violence may be reciprocal and symmetrical—that women can be as abusive toward their partners as men can; indeed, Straus (2010) has argued that many academics have deliberately concealed, denied, and distorted relevant evidence documenting violence against their partners by women. The Violence Against Women Act (VAWA) of 1994, expanded in 1998 and 2002, was designed to provide women with broad protections against violence in their communities and in their homes, but society has been slower to provide protections for male victims of intimate abuse. In 2005, the Violence Against Women and Department of Justice Reauthorization Act was created, yet there were still no pieces of legislation concentrating specifically on men (as of this writing, VAWA 2012 was still in committee, with little movement toward any focus on men). Some people assume that cases where women abuse their partners are so rare there is no need to provide shelters for their victims. Others believe that shelters for men are unnecessary because they assume that most women, such as the woman portrayed in Case 1, are only verbally abusive, or assume that verbal aggression such as name-calling is in poor taste but calling it abusive is a misuse of the term. What do you think are the implications of such arguments when there are many men who are being verbally and physically maltreated by their partners?

Consider the other cases. Does marriage—or cohabitation, for that matter—entitle individuals to engage in sexual behavior with their partners whenever and however they want? Although there was resistance for decades to the idea that rape could occur within a marriage, as of 2005, all 50 states have removed marital rape exemptions from their criminal statutes. However, before 2005, 30 states did not include marital rape as a valid form of punishable sexual violence (Monson, Langhinrichsen-Rohling, & Taft, 2009).

Historically, many shelters did not consider cases of marital rape to fall within their domain because it is not life threatening, and many rape crisis centers did not want to deal with female domestic violence victims. Consequently, battered women who had also been sexually assaulted were left unaided, sometimes shuffled back and forth between facilities (see Malley-Morrison & Hines, 2004, Chapter 15), which is perhaps one reason why women who have been sexually as well as physically assaulted are less likely to seek help (Flicker et al., 2011).

For many decades after the public recognition of child abuse and wife abuse as serious social problems, members of the gay/lesbian community, fearing additional stigmatization, were reluctant to admit that abuse took place within their relationships. Only recently have victims of intimate violence in those communities begun to speak out, although services are still limited. As of June 2009, gay marriage is legal in Massachusetts, Connecticut, Iowa, Vermont, Maine, and New Hampshire (Vestal, 2009, April 8), and many gay/lesbian couples are raising children. In response to these developments, many researchers have begun studying violence in gay/lesbian relationships. In a 2010 Internet study of 402 men who have sex with men, 11.8% of the total sample reported physical violence from a current male partner and 7% reported perpetrating violence against a male partner (Stephenson, Khosropour, & Sullivan, 2010).

The extent to which corporal punishment should be considered abusive is very controversial. Although the percentages of adults who approve of corporal punishment may be declining, a majority of parents in the United States spank their children and consider spanking appropriate and necessary (Gershoff, 2008) despite the fact that many professional organizations, such as the American Psychological Association and the American Academy of Pediatrics, have issued statements recommending that children not be subjected to corporal punishment. One 2004 study conducted in Hawaii showed that 95% of 270 parents sampled had hit a 3-year-old child in the past year (Duggan, 2004, cited in Straus, 2010). On the other hand, there is evidence that the rate of physical punishment is declining (Zolotor, Theodore, Runyan, Chang, & Laskey, 2011).

Finally, should we view Mr. Jaffin's feelings and behavior simply as inevitable outcomes of the medical and other problems associated with aging, or is he a victim of elder maltreatment? He is not being physically abused. Nobody is trying to hurt or exploit him. But is he being emotionally abused? If so, how should he be helped? When he went to his orthopedist for a follow-up on his hip, he was referred to a psychologist who diagnosed him as clinically depressed. This psychologist began seeing him and his overwhelmed daughter regularly and helped them both work out a better way of dealing with their circumstances (Humphries Lynch, 1997). Given that elder abuse is a reportable offense, should the hospital personnel have notified Adult Protective Services rather than privately initiating the counseling program?

Definitional Issues

At the heart of many of the debates concerning whether particular behaviors are abusive are inconsistencies in the definitions of terms. Definitions of abuse, for example, have varied in the extent to which they incorporate assumptions about causes (e.g., people who hurt the ones they love are "sick"); effects (e.g., abusive behaviors are those that cause harm); motivations (e.g., abusive behaviors are intended to hurt rather than discipline); frequency (e.g., slapping is abusive only if it is chronic); and intensity (e.g., hitting is abusive if it is hard enough to cause injury). Such definitions, which vary in their inclusiveness and differ within and across fields, influence the likelihood that individuals subjected to unwanted behaviors within domestic settings will receive interventions from the legal, medical, and/or social service communities. In one study of social workers in military Family Advocacy programs, these clinicians reported that existing definitions of wife and child maltreatment were ambiguous and needed further operationalization; in making their own determinations concerning whether or not maltreatment had taken place, these clinicians often overrode the official definitions and followed their own judgments (Heyman & Smith Slep, 2006).

Efforts to distinguish among terms such as violence, abuse, and maltreatment have not led to any consensus. Definitions continue to vary in their inclusiveness (how broadly the construct is defined) and their abstractness (the extent to which they focus on specific behaviors or define one abstract construct in terms of another). For example, Levesque (2001) held that "family violence includes family members' acts of omission or commission *resulting in* physical abuse, sexual abuse, emotional abuse, neglect, or other forms of maltreatment that hamper individuals' healthy development" (p. 13, italics added). Emery and Laumann-Billings (1998) distinguished between two levels of *abuse—maltreatment* (i.e., minimal or moderate forms of abuse, such as hitting, pushing, and name-calling) and *violence* (i.e., more violent abuse involving serious endangerment, physical injury, and sexual violation). Here, *abuse* is the broader term, and *maltreatment* and *violence* are considered subtypes of abuse, varying in level of intensity.

According to the American Academy of Family Physicians (2004),

> Family violence can be defined as the intentional intimidation or abuse of children, adults, or elders by a family member, intimate partner or caretaker to gain power and control over the victim. Abuse has many forms, including physical and sexual assault, emotional or psychological mistreatment, threats and intimidation, economic abuse and violation of individual rights. (para. 7)

Thus, the Academy defined family violence as abuse, emphasized the intention of power and control, and included "mistreatment" as a form of abuse. Finally, Straus, in his early work (Straus, Gelles, & Steinmetz, 1980), distinguished between *socially accepted violence* (e.g., spanking) and *abusive violence*, defined as an "act which has a high potential for injuring the person being hit" (pp. 21–22).

One of the biggest debates in the field is whether corporal punishment should be considered inherently abusive. Recently, Straus (2010) defined corporal punishment as "the use of physical force with the intention of causing [bodily] pain, but not injury, for purposes of correction or control of the child's behavior" (pp. 1–2)—thus emphasizing both intent and expectations concerning outcomes. He went on to explain, "Examples include spanking on the buttocks, hand slapping, shoving, grabbing or squeezing hard, ear twisting, pinching, and putting hot sauce or soap on a child's tongue (for example, for cursing)" (p. 2), and noted that substantiated cases of physical abuse have indicated that in at least two thirds of the cases, the abusive incident began as ordinary corporal punishment, then escalated. If child abuse is defined as behaviors that put children at risk for injury, and both psychological and physical injuries are considered, then there is a basis for considering corporal punishment abusive because of the demonstrated negative effects of corporal punishment. Knox (2010) strongly contended that "[h]itting children is an act of violence and a clear violation of children's human rights" (p. 103).

There has been considerable resistance to a ban on corporal punishment among professionals as well as laypeople. Box 1.1 provides a sampling of major social science perspectives on the issue. Each of these authorities presents empirical data in support of his or her position, yet there are no signs that the differences will be resolved soon.

Box 1.1   Is Corporal Punishment Abusive?

"The Study [the UN Secretary-General's Study on Violence against Children (UNSG)] should mark a turning point—an end to adult justification of violence against children, whether accepted as 'tradition' or disguised as 'discipline.' There can be no compromise in challenging violence against children. Children's uniqueness—their potential and vulnerability, their dependence on adults–makes it imperative that they have more, not less, protection from violence." (Pinheiro, 2006, p. 1)

"...a two-swat nonabusive spanking is one of the most effective disciplinary tactics when 2- to 6-year-olds respond defiantly to milder disciplinary tactics, such as time out." (Larzelere & Kuhn, 2007, p. 2)

"Authoritative parents endorse the judicious use of aversive consequences, which may (but certainly need not) include spanking...The prudent use of punishment within the context of a responsive, supportive parent-child relationship is a necessary tool in the disciplinary encounter." (Baumrind, 1997, p. 330)

"Spanking is not a very effective strategy. It does not teach children new behaviors or what to do in place of the problem behavior. It is also not useful in suppressing the problematic behavior beyond the moment. Research indicates the rate of misbehavior does not decline, in fact, the problem behavior returns, even if the parent escalates the punishment." (Kazdin, 2010, p. 1)

Another perspective comes from Emery (1989), who holds that "calling an act 'abusive' or 'violent' is not an objective decision but a social judgment, a judgment that is outside of the realm of responsibility of social scientists" (p. 322). Similarly, Zuriff (1988) argued that

> the definition of psychological maltreatment is not a task appropriate for psychologists as scientists or researchers . . . [The] problem of defining "maltreatment" is one of determining a point on a set of continua at which the psychological effects of parental behavior are to be designated "harmful." I suggest this is not an empirical question . . . [Psychologists] should leave the determination of good and evil, benefit and harm, to the law, ethics, and religion. (p. 201)

While agreeing that terms like maltreatment represent social constructions and value judgments, we disagree that psychologists and other social scientists cannot aid in the definitional process by means of scientific data and scientific thinking. Social and medical scientists are in some ways uniquely qualified to provide evidence concerning the harmfulness of particular behaviors for the well-being of their recipients, others with whom those recipients interact, and even the larger community within which the recipients of those behaviors must function. Indeed, in considering the kinds of behaviors and interactions that may be harmful to members of families (broadly defined to include gay/lesbian relationships and cohabiting couples), we prefer the term *maltreatment* to the other commonly used terms, in part because of the explicit value judgment built into the prefix "mal."

Our term *maltreatment* embraces *corporal punishment* as well as *abuse, family violence, wife beating, domestic violence, child abuse, spousal abuse,* and *elder abuse,* as these are commonly defined. We acknowledge that some forms of maltreatment are more serious than others. Children who receive a single slap on the hand or the buttocks during childhood are not being maltreated to the same degree as a child who is raped, or beaten every day, or constantly criticized and humiliated. However, we view all these behaviors as forms of maltreatment, and not beneficial ways for individuals to treat each other, inside or outside of families. As Straus has repeatedly pointed out, even acts that seem like relatively minor forms of maltreatment (e.g., spanking) are risk factors for negative outcomes for individuals and society (Straus & Kaufman Kantor, 2005). Although our conceptual preference is for the term *maltreatment,* most researchers in family violence study the more extreme forms of maltreatment, and therefore, throughout this book, we generally use the term that the researchers used to describe the particular form of maltreatment of interest to them.

Definitions of terms such as maltreatment are embedded in broader perspectives on human beings, families, and intimate relationships. During the second half of the 20th century, new perspectives emerged within the international community, including the view that the more vulnerable members of the human race (particularly women, children, the elderly, and people with mental and physical disabilities) have an inherent right to freedom from exploitation and abuse. Concurrent with the evolution of that perspective, many countries criminalized forms of family aggression that had a long history of normative acceptance—for example, the beating and rape of wives and children. Accompanying the criminalization of such behaviors has been a *medicalization* of their effects (Newberger & Bourne, 1978). *Medicalization* refers to perceiving a behavior, such as child maltreatment, as a medical problem or illness, and expecting the medical profession to treat the problem. The medical communities in many countries, including the United States, have increasingly been given and/or have assumed the responsibility not just to heal intentional burns, set broken bones, and mend bruised and battered skin, but to alert legal and social service agencies about behaviors now deemed abusive.

Just as the concept of "family" has been broadened to include nonmarital cohabiting relationships and same-sex intimate relationships, legal protections against spousal abuse have increasingly been expanded to include nonmarital relationships. Also, because most definitions of abuse emphasize negative outcomes, the social science community has directed intensive efforts at providing a scientific basis for defining, studying, and intervening in situations of family violence and abuse. In the next sections, we provide a brief introduction to major perspectives on maltreatment in family settings. Many of these perspectives reflect assumptions held before individuals selected a profession, or assumptions developed as part of their professional training and experience. These perspectives, which may guide important decisions concerning the current or future well-being of victims of family maltreatment, may or may not have a solid theoretical or empirical basis. This section is followed by an overview of several theories of familial maltreatment. During the past several decades, increasing work has been done to empirically test such theories in order to improve our understanding of the predictors and consequences of maltreatment and to provide a foundation for intervention and prevention efforts.

Perspectives on Maltreatment

The Human Rights Perspective

One major view on human rights is that they are privileges granted by people in power to those who are less powerful. For much of human history, women and children were seen as having no rights separate from those that men offered them—and such rights were generally extremely limited. A second major view is that human rights are *inherent* in being human. From this latter perspective, in the words of Amartya Sen (1998), human rights are, "entitlements of every human being" (para. 1). This second view is embodied in the United States Declaration of Independence: "We hold these truths to be self-evident, that all men are created equal, that they are endowed by their Creator with certain unalienable Rights that among these are Life, Liberty and the pursuit of Happiness." It is also embodied in international human rights agreements promulgated by the United Nations and other nongovernmental organizations (NGOs).

Emerging from the horrors of World War II, wherein "disregard and contempt for human rights have resulted in barbarous acts which have outraged the conscience of mankind," the newly born United Nations adopted the task of establishing a lasting peace. One of its first accomplishments (1948) was the Universal Declaration of Human Rights, which proclaimed "all members of the human family" have "equal and inalienable rights" and that recognition of these rights is "the foundation of freedom, justice and peace in the world" (United Nations, Universal Declaration, Preamble, para. 1). Article 5, which is most relevant to family maltreatment, states, "No one shall be subjected to torture or to cruel, inhuman or degrading treatment or punishment."

Since the passage of the Universal Declaration, the United Nations has promulgated other international treaties addressing the rights of individuals to freedom from maltreatment, even within their own families. The Convention on the Rights of the Child (Office of the High Commissioner for Human Rights, 1989) specifies that member states

> shall take all appropriate legislative, administrative, social and educational measures to protect the child from all forms of physical or mental violence, injury or abuse, neglect or negligent treatment, maltreatment or exploitation, including sexual abuse, while in the care of parent(s), legal guardian(s) or any other person who has the care of the child. (Article 19)

According to this Convention, assuring such rights to children is necessary in order to rear them "in the spirit of the ideals proclaimed in the Charter of the United Nations, and in particular in the spirit of peace, dignity, tolerance, freedom, equality and solidarity" (Preamble, para. 7). Thus, the international promulgators of this document, like many social scientists in the United States, recognize a connection between eschewing violence in the home and promoting international peace.

Child advocates in many countries have argued that corporal punishment violates the United Nations Convention on the Rights of the Child. The European Network of Ombudsmen for Children (ENOC, 2001) urged the governments of all European countries, as well as NGOs concerned with children, to work to end all corporal punishment. In their view, "eliminating violent and humiliating forms of discipline is a vital strategy for improving children's status as people, and reducing child abuse and all other forms of violence in European societies" (para. 2). ENOC concurred that no level of corporal punishment is compatible with the Convention on the Rights of the Child and that legal and educational steps should be taken to eliminate it. The United States is one of only two countries (the other being Somalia, which has no central government) that have not ratified the Convention on the Rights of the Child, and parents in the United States appear to be very resistant to the notion that corporal punishment may violate a child's rights.

Another important declaration adopted by the United Nations General Assembly was the Declaration on the Elimination of Violence Against Women, endorsed by all member states of the United Nations. According to this Declaration, "violence against women means any act of gender-based violence that results in, or is likely to result in, physical, sexual or psychological harm or suffering to women, including threats of such acts, coercion or arbitrary deprivation of liberty, whether occurring in public or in private life" (United Nations, Declaration on the Elimination of Violence against Women, 1993, Article 1). Other NGOs taking a stand against maltreatment in domestic settings include Amnesty International, which in 2001 released a statement asserting that violence against women is a human rights issue, and that if a government fails to "prevent, prosecute and punish" acts of violence, those acts should be considered forms of torture—and therefore a violation of the United Nations Declaration on Human Rights. As of 2011, the United States is the only country that has signed but not ratified the Convention. Other governments that have not ratified the treaty include Iran, Somalia, Sudan, and Tonga (Blanchfield, 2011). Although late in 2011, President Obama had a list of UN treaties to be ratified, including the Convention of the Rights of the Child (CRC) and the Convention on the Elimination of All Forms of Discrimination against Women (CEDAW), it was not clear when these treaties might actually go to the Senate for approval or whether they could get two thirds of the votes, as required by the U.S. Constitution for passage of a treaty.

The international human rights perspective emphasizes the relationship between social justice and individual rights to freedom from abuse, and between peaceful resolution of conflict in the home and peaceful resolution of conflict in the international community. Proponents of a human rights perspective are often critical of *systemic* or *structural* abuse—that is, abuse of individuals by the very systems or structures responsible for protecting them (e.g., Ellsberg, Jansen, Heise, Watts, & Garcia-Moreno, 2008). One human rights advocate has argued that attention to international human rights principles can help Americans "move away from practices and assumptions that condone, encourage, and improperly respond to family violence" (Levesque, 2001, p. 17).

Legal/Criminal Justice Perspectives

Although the United Nations Convention on the Rights of the Child has some legal status in international law, its main function has been to establish a universal standard that the international community has agreed to adopt rather than to enforce children's rights judicially or to criminalize violation of those rights. To our knowledge, the World Court has not tried any cases of family maltreatment. However, the European Court of Human Rights, established by the European Convention on Human Rights and Its Five Protocols, has addressed cases of family violence originating in a number of different European countries.

In general, the legal approach to family maltreatment in the United States has been to criminalize it. The focus is on both punishment and deterrence. Criminalization has involved mandating members of medical and social service professions to report suspected cases of abuse and imposing criminal penalties on perpetrators of acts identified as abusive. Although the United States has not ratified the Convention on the Rights of the Child, it has ratified the Declaration on the Elimination of Violence against Women and has criminalized abuse of children, domestic partners, and the elderly. According to the federal Child Abuse Prevention and Treatment Act (CAPTA),

> child abuse and neglect is, at a minimum, any recent act or failure to act on the part of a parent or caretaker which results in death, serious physical or emotional harm, sexual abuse or exploitation of a child (individual under the age of 18) and any act or failure to act which presents an imminent risk of serious harm. (42 U.S.C. 5106g)

However, each state has its own set of laws, and, in contrast to the stance taken in many European countries, corporal punishment by parents is legal in every state.

Passed in 1994 as part of an Omnibus Crime Bill, modified in 2002 and 2005, and as of this writing, in committee in 2012, the Violence Against Women Act (VAWA) was revolutionary in its provisions for addressing violence against women, including wife abuse. The International Violence Against Women Act of 2010, introduced in Congress in 2010, which focused on prevention efforts and targeted countries with severe levels of violence against women and children (H.R. 4594 2010), was approved by the Senate Foreign Relations Committee in December of 2010, with caveats limiting the funding that would be permitted for the act if it passes (Aroon, 2010).

The federal Older Americans Act provides definitions of elder abuse and authorizes expenditure of federal funds for a National Center on Elder Abuse but does not fund adult protective services or shelters for abused older persons. Every state has its own set of statutes criminalizing abuse of women and elders and its own procedures for investigating complaints and prosecuting violators. Actual practices often fall far short of the intent of the law; however, there has been enormous change since the days when the criminal justice system saw itself as not concerned with any violence short of murder that took place behind the closed doors of the family home (Iovanni & Miller, 2001). Nevertheless, although there are laws addressing family violence against children, wives, and the elderly, no legislation deals specifically with family violence against siblings or husbands, who are also frequent victims of maltreatment in the family.

Although physical assault of wives has received increasing attention over the years, *marital rape* has been a virtual oxymoron until very recently. The so-called "marital rape exemption," mandating that forced sex of a wife by a husband could not be considered a form of rape, had its basis in English common law, according to which wives, by virtue of the marital contract, gave themselves willingly and irrevocably to their husbands. The nature of the marital contract was interpreted as negating the possibility of marital rape and ensuring the husband's right to have his desires satisfied by his wife (Bergen, 1998). Consistent with this perspective, rape was traditionally defined as a male's "sexual intercourse with a female, not his wife, by force and against her will" (Finkelhor & Yllo, 1985, p. 1). It was not until July 5, 1993, that all states had enacted legislation to criminalize the rape of wives; however, many laypeople are unaware that wife rape is now considered a crime, and still others do not believe it can or should be a crime (Malley-Morrison & Hines, 2004). There are still no laws against sexual assault of husbands, although we know that this form of sexual aggression takes place.

Although the principal legislation relating to domestic maltreatment provides funding for educational and social service programs, the legal perspective emphasizes the criminal justice system response to violation of federal and state statutes. Studies using legal definitions of abuse typically report the number of cases of identified child, spouse, or elder abuse reported to protective service agencies. Such reports provide a vast underestimation of the actual frequency of maltreatment in families because many cases are never reported to any agency. Moreover, many statutes related to maltreatment have exemptions. For example, in every state, the child abuse statutes have exemptions allowing parents to use "reasonable force" for purposes of child discipline and control. Legal definitions of physical abuse reflect cultural norms concerning what exceeds reasonable force, but the boundaries between physical abuse and corporal punishment have been generally left to the discretion of the legal and criminal justice systems (Straus & Runyan, 1997). Moreover, many states still have exemptions from prosecution for a husband raping his wife (Rennison, 2002), such as when he does not have to use force to make her have sex (e.g., if she is physically or mentally impaired and unable to give consent).

Medical Perspectives

Maltreatment in families has been recognized not just as a human rights and a legal issue but also as a medical issue. On an international level, the World Health Organization (WHO, 2005) identifies domestic violence as a pervasive problem that demands a response. Within the United States, professional organizations such as the American Academy of Family Physicians (2004) have also noted that family violence is a public health issue of epidemic proportions. The medical perspective on maltreatment tends to focus on recognizing symptoms, identifying causes, and providing treatment. Medical practitioners frequently emphasize the causes of maltreatment having a biological component (e.g., substance abuse, psychiatric disorders). Recent neuroscience research indicates that partner abusive men may have a number of contributing medical problems (e.g., traumatic brain injury) and have recommended a number of biomedical interventions designed to alleviate the symptoms of these conditions and thereby, presumably, reduce aggression against the partner (Howard, 2011).

From this medical perspective, perpetrators are often viewed as victims themselves and more in need of treatment than of criminal prosecution. For this and many other reasons (including assumptions that the social welfare system does not always respond appropriately), medical personnel often do not report the cases of maltreatment they are mandated to report (Zellman & Fair, 2002) (see Chapter 2). Nevertheless, some of the medical consequences of abuse have been identified in recent years. For example, a 2009 study identified diminished prefrontal cortical gray matter volume in young adults who had experienced "harsh corporal punishment" (HCP) as children (Tomoda et al., 2009, p. T66); gray matter volume was reduced by as much as 19.1% in HCP victims compared to controls.

Social Service Perspectives

The social service system has generally had a much broader perspective on family violence than the medical or legal systems, traditionally viewing maltreatment within family settings as a symptom of family crisis and a need for services. The social service system has been more concerned with ameliorating conditions that give rise to maltreatment than with promoting the prosecution of offenders or providing medical treatment of victims. Much of the emphasis on acts of omission (neglect) in definitions of child and elder maltreatment is derived from social service perspectives. Workers within the field have often emphasized the role of external forces—for example, poverty and discrimination (Beckett, 2003)—in contributing to family maltreatment.

Need for Multidisciplinary Cooperation

In many cases of family maltreatment, representatives of the legal, medical, and social service professions all become involved. A coordinated approach of these various services is often hard to achieve because of the differing definitions and perspectives within these professions. Members of the legal profession want to pursue prosecution of the perpetrator if they believe they can "win" their case. Medical practitioners are more concerned with providing treatment for victims and perhaps perpetrators, but typically see it as beyond their purview to address any problems of poverty, community violence, and despair besetting the family. Social service personnel may believe that any focus on helping, prosecuting, or changing individuals is shortsighted, and emphasize the need to find better housing and employment for family members and address substance abuse problems. Perhaps in part because of the very breadth of their perspective, social service systems have been overwhelmed by family violence cases in recent decades and are not always able to respond appropriately. A number of legal cases have been brought against local social service agencies for maltreating their clients.

Box 1.2	Brief of *DeShaney v. Winnebago County Department of Social Services*, 1989

Born in 1979, Joshua DeShaney was placed in his father's custody when his parents divorced a year later. Joshua's father's second wife and neighbors reported that Joshua was frequently abused by his father. Following a police report and hospital treatment of Joshua's bruises and abrasions in January 1983, the local Department of Social Services (DSS) obtained a court order to keep Joshua in the hospital's custody. However, a child services protective team returned Joshua to his father three days later when his father agreed in writing to enroll Joshua in Head Start and enter counseling himself. A few weeks later DSS was informed that Joshua had again been seen at the hospital but concluded there was no evidence of abuse.

(Continued)

(Continued)

During 1983, a social worker visited the father's home five times. Although she observed that Joshua had bumps and scrapes on several occasions and that the father was not adhering to the terms of his agreement, she took no action. There was also no action taken when the hospital reported in November 1983 that Joshua had again been treated for suspicious injuries. When the social worker visited the home in January 1984, she was told she could not see Joshua because he had the flu. When she tried again to see him in March, she was told that he had recently fainted, but she did not request to see him. The next day Joshua's father beat him severely, causing brain damage and permanent retardation. A medical examination revealed evidence of multiple previous injuries to Joshua's head and body.

SOURCE: Adapted from online news reports.

Consider the case of Joshua DeShaney in Box 1.2. How did the differing perspectives of the various relevant agencies play out in his case? At what points in the process did systems fail him? Do any of the systems seem particularly culpable? After the final critical beating, Joshua's father was arrested, indicted, tried, convicted, and sent to jail for child abuse. Subsequently, Joshua's mother and Joshua (represented by a guardian ad litem) sued the county Department of Social Services (DSS) for depriving Joshua of "his liberty interest in bodily integrity, in violation of his rights under the substantive component of the Fourteenth Amendment's Due Process Clause" (*DeShaney v. Winnebago County Department of Social Services*, 1989, p. 1). Their argument was that by failing to intervene in a way that protected Joshua against his father's violence, the DSS violated the Fourteenth Amendment statement that "no State shall . . . deprive any person of life, liberty, or property, without due process of law." Joshua and his mother lost their case and appealed ultimately all the way to the Supreme Court, where they again lost. In a dissenting opinion, Justices Brennan, Marshall, and Blackmun argued, "The most that can be said of the state functionaries in this case . . . is that they stood by and did nothing when suspicious circumstances dictated a more active role for them. [We] cannot agree that respondents had no constitutional duty to help Joshua DeShaney" (*DeShaney v. Winnebago County Department of Social Services*, 1989, p. 17). In recent times, more cases have been brought against social service agencies. Does that appear to be the best way to deal with the staggering problems of maltreatment in society today? What other approaches might be better?

Disrespect for each other's professions may often hamper cooperation among representatives from different agencies. For example, although several United States Supreme Court decisions in the post–World War II years (e.g., *Brown v. Board of Education of Topeka*, 1954; *In re Gault*, 1967) provided some recognition that juveniles have rights protected by the Constitution, more recent decisions by a more conservative Supreme Court have eroded some of these rights, in part because of a decreased willingness to attend to social science data (Walker, Brooks, & Wrightsman, 1999). For example, "Justice Scalia consistently has considered social science studies to be irrelevant when deciding on constitutional law; for him, the only 'empirical' materials of relevance . . . are legislation and jury decisions" (Walker et al., 1999, p. 11).

Ecological Models of Maltreatment

Many theories have been formulated about various forms of family violence, and most of these theories reflect broader views (paradigms) about human nature. Theories are useful both to organize and integrate knowledge and to guide research (Baltes, Reese, & Nesselroade, 1977). Paradigms are more abstract and general. Recognizing the place of theories within paradigms can help reduce the confusion that can come from trying to understand and evaluate what may seem like an overwhelming morass of theories about family violence. The dozens of competing theories concerning the causes of child, intimate partner, and elder maltreatment can all be incorporated into an ecological paradigm—which we do in the sections that follow.

In general, the prevailing ecological paradigm within the field of family violence derives from the work of Bronfenbrenner (1979), who argued that human development and behavior should be analyzed within a nested set of environmental contexts or systems. The *microsystem* consists of the relations between developing individuals and their immediate settings (e.g., the home). The *mesosystem* consists of relations among the settings in which the developing individual is involved (e.g., between home and school). The *exosystem* includes the larger neighborhood, the mass media, state agencies, and transportation facilities. Finally, the *macrosystem* consists of broad cultural factors, including views about the role of children and their caretakers in society. In an important modification of the theory, Belsky (1993) argued that the ecological system includes an *ontogenetic* or *individual/developmental* level—that is, the unique biological/genetic characteristics that exist even before birth and that individuals bring to every interaction. These biological/genetic characteristics change during the process of development under the influence of both nature and nurture. Building on the Bronfenbrenner/Belsky model, researchers have identified causes of child maltreatment (e.g., Begle, Dumas, & Hanson, 2010), spousal abuse (e.g., Dutton, 1985; Goodlin & Dunn, 2010) and elder abuse (e.g., Schiamberg & Gans, 2000) at different ecological levels. Inherent within an ecological perspective is the dictum that, to understand how so many people can maltreat family members or other intimates, we need to understand many factors: the genetic endowments of those individuals; the microsystem in which they grew up; the microsystem in which they are currently embedded; characteristics of the neighborhood within which their family functions (including the availability of social support and social services, and relationships between the community and the criminal justice system); and the larger society that embraces all the separate neighborhoods. From this ecological perspective, maltreatment is the product of the genetic endowments, behaviors, cognitions, and affects of the individual at the center of the nested set of ecological contexts, as well as the genetic endowments, behaviors, cognitions, and affects of the other actors at each ecological level.

There have been and continue to be single-factor or single-process theories of maltreatment that focus on causes at just one level of the ecological framework. Empirical research addressing hypotheses concerning causes of maltreatment has confirmed that there are identifiable risk factors at every ecological level. Table 1.1 provides a brief

Table 1.1 Major Theories of Family Violence within an Ecological Paradigm

Theory	Supportive Study	Focus	Key Assumptions and/or Findings
BIOLOGICAL INDIVIDUAL/DEVELOPMENTAL THEORIES			
Behavioral Genetics	Hines & Saudino (2004)	Intergenerational transmission of intimate aggression	Intergenerational transmission of intimate aggression is due to shared genes. Genetic influences account for approximately 20% of the variance in physical and psychological intimate aggression
Other Biological Theories	Pinto, Sullivan, Rosenbaum, Wyngarden, Umhau, Miller, & Taft (2010)	Literature on biological correlates (head injury and neuropsychology; psychophysiology; neurochemistry, metabolism, and endocrinology; and genetics) of intimate partner violence perpetration	In abusive males, the combination of decreased serotonin levels, increased testosterone levels, reduced hypothalamic activity, and reduced cortical and subcortical structural activity (which aids in mediating fear-related aggression) results in a predisposition to reacting violently to perceived or actual threats from their partners
	George, Phillips, Doty, Umhau, & Rawlings (2006)	Biological abnormalities, behaviors, and psychiatric diagnoses in perpetrators of intimate partner violence	Perpetrators of domestic violence experience abnormalities in testosterone and serotonin metabolism, resulting in increased sensitivity to environmental stimuli, anxiety, and conditioned fear. Lack of cortical input to the amygdala impairs the abuser's ability to control reactions to these stimuli
	Klinesmith, Kasser, & McAndrew (2006)	Gun interaction and its effect on testosterone levels and aggressive behavior in males	In males, gun exposure increases acts of interpersonal aggression in part by increasing testosterone levels
NONBIOLOGICAL INDIVIDUAL/DEVELOPMENTAL THEORIES			
Attachment	Shurman & Rodriguez (2006)	Females leaving domestic violence relationships	Preoccupied attachment style and high emotional arousal predict a victim's self-reported general preparedness to terminate an abusive domestic relationship with her partner

Theory	Supportive Study	Focus	Key Assumptions and/or Findings
	Rodriguez (2006)	Victims of domestic violence and their child abuse potential	Emotional difficulties and insecure attachment styles of domestic violence victims were significantly positively correlated with child abuse potential
	Volz & Kerig (2010)	Adolescent dating violence	Adolescents with anxious attachment who also perceive aggression as justifiable in relationships may engage in abusive behavior to coerce the maintenance of the relationship
	Grych & Kinsfogel (2010)	Adolescent dating violence	Anxious attachment style often results in adolescent partners who are clingy and over-dependent, which serves as a risk factor for the intensifying of aggressive attitudes and difficulties with anger regulation
	Goldenson, Geffner, Foster, & Clipson (2007)	Female domestic violence perpetrators	Female domestic violence offenders are more likely to exhibit insecure attachment styles and psychopathologies than their non-offending counterparts
	Briere & Jordan (2009)	Implications of child abuse	Early attachment experiences serve as intervening factors between the experience of abuse in childhood and a range of later psychological problems, including relationship problems
Social Information Processing (SIP)/ Cognitive Behavioral	Crouch, Risser, Skowronski, Milner, Farc, & Irwin (2010)	Differences in accessibility of positive and negative schema in parents with high/low risk of child physical abuse (CPA)	Parents at high CPA risk were slower to classify both positive and negative words when primed with faces portraying the opposite "affective valence" and responded more slowly to positive words following priming with negative faces
	Farc, Crouch, Skowronksi, & Milner (2008)	CPA risk status and hostility-related schema activation	High CPA risk parents were more likely to judge pictures of ambiguous children as hostile, which may increase attributions of hostile intent and aggressive behaviors toward children

(Continued)

Table 1.1 (Continued)

Theory	Supportive Study	Focus	Key Assumptions and/or Findings
	Rodriguez & Richardson (2007)	Cognitive schemas, stress, anger and the child maltreatment potential of parents	External locus-of-control orientation (viewed as a preexisting schema in the SIP model) was significantly positively associated with harsh discipline, physical aggression, and child abuse potential
Social Learning	Wareham, Boots, & Chavez (2009)	Social learning and intergenerational transmission of intimate partner violence (IPV)	Experiencing physical maltreatment was associated with an increase in the odds of IPV, while exposure to high levels of corporal punishment from fathers (or father-figures) was associated with an increase in the odds of minor IPV only. Corporal punishment by mothers (or mother-figures) was significantly negatively associated with IPV.
	Gómez (2011)	Cycle of violence; child abuse and adolescent dating aggression as predictors of IPV	Data analyses of three waves of the National Longitudinal Study of Adolescent Health (also known as the Add Health study) showed that child abuse and adolescent dating violence predicted IPV victimization and perpetration in both men and women.
MICROSYSTEM THEORIES			
Systems Theory	Moore & Florsheim (2008)	Interpartner conflict prior to child-birth and later risk for child abuse	Interpartner aggression predicted later physically punitive behaviors in young fathers but not mothers; interpartner hostility before child birth predicted later father hostility toward child.
Stress Theory	Guterman, Lee, Taylor, & Rathouz (2009)	Neighborhood conditions, parental stress, personal control, and risk for child physical abuse/neglect	Perceived neighborhood processes had a significant indirect role in predicting CPA through parental stress and personal control pathways. For parents, stress level played the clearest direct role in predicting both child physical abuse and neglect.

Theory	Supportive Study	Focus	Key Assumptions and/or Findings
	Roberts, McLaughlin, Conron, & Koenen (2011)	Adult stressors, childhood adversity, and risk of IPV	For males who had experienced a high level of childhood adversity, recent stressors were associated with heightened risk to commit an act of IPV (as compared to men with low levels of childhood adversity). For women, high levels of childhood adversity and recent stressors were associated with increased IPV risk. For both men and women, there is a high stress sensitization effect, in which recent stressors and histories of childhood adversity are associated with an elevated risk of committing acts of IPV.
	McCurdy (2005)	Support, stress, and maternal attitudes	Increased stress negatively affected maternal attitudes regarding physical punishment, while increased support resulted in positive effects. For women experiencing stress with job change, home visits (formal support from such organizations as Healthy Start) resulted in less harsh maternal attitudes.
EXOSYSTEM THEORIES			
Ecological Theory	Freisthler, Gruenewald, Ring, & LaScala (2008)	Population and environmental characteristics and childhood injuries resulting from accidents, assaults, and abuse	Child abuse, accidents, and assaults among children occurred at higher rates in Zip codes with larger percentages of African American residents, female-headed households, and more off-premise alcohol outlets.
	Goodlin & Dunn (2010)	Single victimization (one victim only), repeat victimization (same victim, more than one incident of violence), and co-occurring (more than one victim) patterns of domestic violence victimization	In households in which family violence occurred, the number of individuals within the household was significantly positively correlated with repeat and co-occurring forms of victimization. Victims without a high school diploma were significantly more likely to live in a household with co-occurring forms of victimization than a household where the same victim suffered from multiple violence incidents, and those victimized by ex-spouses, parents/stepparents, siblings, and other relatives were more likely to live in co-occurrence households than those victimized by current spouses.

(Continued)

Table 1.1 (Continued)

Theory	Supportive Study	Focus	Key Assumptions and/or Findings
	Merritt (2009)	Neighborhood conditions and child abuse potential	Parents' potential for abuse increased when they were male, lived in impoverished communities, or felt burdened by demands relating to childcare; abuse potential decreased when they were married, working full time, had a high school diploma (or higher), enjoyed a decent income, and received social support.
Sociocultural Theories	Bryant-Davis (2010)	Physical, mental, and social correlates of IPV across cultures and ethnicities	Though African American women are at greater risk for severe intimate partner violence, they report lower rates of post trauma symptoms; a sense of personal empowerment serves as a protective factor for African American women. Asian Americans and Pacific Islanders exhibit a low rate of formal help-seeking, leading some to falsely assume that IPV is not a problem within their communities. Among Latinas, lack of help-seeking is due in part to gender role ideologies, traditional beliefs about marriage, familism, taboos against talking about sex, respect for authority, lack of community resources, and fear of violence.
	Wright, Perez, & Johnson (2010)	African American female victims of IPV and empowerment	In African American women victimized by IPV, personal empowerment mediated the relationships between race and PTSD and between race and depression. This suggests African American women may demonstrate greater resiliency when faced with IPV because of their internal coping methods.
MACROSYSTEM THEORIES			
Feminist Theory	Yllo & Straus (1990)	Analysis of survey data and census tract data	Patriarchal ideology was positively correlated with wife beating, especially in states with high levels of structural inequality between men and women.

summary of the basic assumptions of several current theories of maltreatment in families. It also indicates the ecological level being addressed by each theory, and an example of at least one empirical study addressing hypotheses associated with that theory.

Individual/Developmental Theories

Biological Theories

Studies linking biology to the perpetration of intimate partner violence generally fall into one of four major areas: head injuries; psychophysiological processes; neuro-chemistry, metabolism and endocrinology; and genetic factors (Pinto et al., 2010). According to Pinto et al. (2010), "Rates of head injuries among abusers, ranging from 40% to 61%, have been significantly higher than those found in the general popula-tion" (p. 390). Moreover, there is evidence linking temporal lobe dysfunctions to sexual offenses, specifically incest and pedophilia. Sexual activity is related to activity in the temporal lobe, and changes in sexual functioning are related to damage to that lobe (see Hucker et al., 1988). Incest offenders and pedophiles show abnormalities within the temporal lobes, abnormalities that do not characterize any other types of offenders studied (e.g., Hucker et al., 1986; Hucker et al., 1988; Langevin, Wortzman, Dickey, Wright, & Handy, 1988; Wright, Nobrega, Langevin, & Wortzman, 1990).

Testosterone has been linked to two different types of family aggression: IPV against women and incest. Among military servicemen and low-income, culturally diverse groups of men, higher levels of testosterone were related to both physical and verbal aggression against wives (Booth & Dabbs, 1993; Soler, Vinayak, & Quadagno, 2000). However, because these are correlational studies, we do not know which came first— the high testosterone or the aggression—and aggression has been shown to lead to increases in testosterone (e.g., Gladue, Boechler, & McCaul, 1989; van Anders, Goldey, & Kuo, 2011). In studies linking testosterone to incest, castration significantly reduces recidivism rates (Wille & Beier, 1989), suggesting that testosterone levels and sexual aggression are related. What may be the problem, though, of concluding from these studies that high testosterone *causes* sexual aggression?

Furthermore, most of the recent studies in humans linking aggression to testoster-one levels show that the links are neither simple nor direct (Englander, 1997). There appear to be many contextual variables that play a role in what may be, at most, a weak positive link between testosterone levels and aggression. For example, Klinesmith, Kasser, and McAndrew (2006) found that the presence of a gun led to both increases in testosterone and aggressive behavior—with the testosterone par-tially mediating the relationship between handling a gun and then acting aggressively. Moreover, recent studies have indicated that testosterone is related to aggressiveness in women, and that levels of testosterone in women are related to aggression by their partners (Hermans, Ramsey, & van Honk, 2008). George, Phillips, Doty, Umhau, and Rawlings (2006) suggest that it is abnormalities in testosterone metabolism that may contribute to an overreactivity to environmental cues like "slights" that produce feel-ings of threat and even paranoia. Based on their review of the psychophysiological studies of batterers, Pinto et al. (2010) suggest that although the results across studies show some inconsistencies, there is some evidence that batterers may experience irregularities in autonomic nervous system functioning that lead to problems in emotion regulation and thereby to intimate partner violence. The neurochemical studies on the role of excessive testosterone and reduced serotonin activity in batterers appear to indicate that these factors may contribute to rapid responding to rage- or fear-producing stimuli and interfere with a more cognitive and non-violent response to such situations (Pinto et al., 2010).

It has also been shown that child abusers have large increases in physiological reactivity in response to stressful and nonstressful mother-child interactions, as measured by skin conductance and heart rate (Wolfe, Fairbank, Kelly, & Bradlyn, 1983). In addition, child abusers are more physiologically reactive to a child's cry and smile, suggesting that they find both of these aversive (Frodi & Lamb, 1980).

Behavioral Genetics. A defining goal of behavioral genetic research is to estimate the extent to which genetic and environmental factors contribute to variability in selected behaviors in the population under study. This involves decomposing phenotypic (observed) variance of a trait or behavior into genetic and environmental components. Heritability is the proportion of phenotypic variance attributable to genetic factors. The remaining variance is attributed to environmental factors, including both shared environmental influences (common to all members of the family) and nonshared environmental influences (the ones unique to each individual that operate to make members of the same family different from one another). Nonshared environmental influences include microsystem factors such as differential parental treatment; differential extrafamilial relationships with friends, peers, and teachers; and nonsystematic factors such as accidents or illness (Hines & Saudino, 2002; Plomin, Chipuer, & Neiderhiser, 1994).

To date, only one empirical study has specifically addressed the issue of genetic influences on family violence (Hines & Saudino, 2004). In this twin study, genetic and nonshared environmental influences were the only significant contributors to individual differences in the use and receipt of both physical and psychological aggression in romantic relationships. These findings, which supported the hypothesis that familial resemblance in intimate partner aggression is due to shared genes, not shared environments, are consistent with those of many other studies showing that genes and nonshared environments influence the use of aggression in general (e.g., Carey & Goldman, 1997; DiLalla & Gottesman, 1991). This study further showed that many of the same genes and environments influencing the receipt of physical aggression also influence its use. Thus, there appear to be genetic and nonshared environmental influences on a tendency to get involved in aggressive romantic relationships, and aggressive people tend to choose aggressive partners (Hines & Saudino, 2004).

The statement that behaviors are genetically influenced means that certain people, due to their genotype, may be more likely to commit aggressive acts in their relationships than people who do not have that same genotype. In other words, genetic influences are *probabilistic,* not deterministic. Genetic influences on aggression in family relationships must be seen as a predisposition toward aggression, not as destiny (Gottesman, Goldsmith, & Carey, 1997; Raine, 1993). The environment and manipulations in the environment can be very successful in reducing aggressive behaviors and preventing the full expression of any genetic predisposition (Hines & Saudino, 2004; Hutchings & Mednick, 1977; Raine, 1993).

As we have shown, behavioral geneticists are not the only theorists interested in the role of biology in family violence, although research on biological factors is sparse. A possible reason for this lack of research is the assumption that if aggression in the family has a biological component, nothing can be done to ameliorate it—an assumption that is incorrect. Although biological factors contribute to family violence, the environment also plays a large role and most likely interacts with biological traits. Identifying people who are biologically at risk for behaving aggressively, and altering their environments, may help reduce family violence.

Attachment Theory

The basic assumption of attachment theories (e.g., Bowlby, 1969/1982, 1973) is that early experiences with caregivers contribute to the development of internal prototypes of human beings and human relationships. According to this perspective, individuals who develop a secure attachment style have positive feelings toward self and others, whereas individuals who develop an insecure attachment style have negative feelings toward self and others. In relation to family violence, the basic propositions tested are that child abuse leads to an insecure attachment style and that an insecure attachment style leads to family violence. The representative studies presented in Table 1.1 are among those providing some support for these theoretical propositions. For example, in a study examining the cycle of violence perpetuated by victims of intimate partner abuse, insecure attachment styles as well as anxiety and depression were significantly positively correlated with child abuse potential (Rodriguez, 2006). Although Bolen (2005) warned against overinterpreting the results of studies of the relationship between attachment style and relationship aggression, Briere and Jordan (2009), based on their review of the literature on the outcomes for women of childhood maltreatment, identify early attachment experiences as a contextual factor that can intervene between the experience of abuse in childhood and a range of later psychological problems, including relationship problems.

There is also evidence that an insecure attachment style is itself a risk factor for abusing an intimate partner. According to Grych and Kinsfogel (2010), adolescents who are anxiously attached often become clingy and overdependent, placing them at risk of abuse by their intimate partner. Another study (Volz & Kerig, 2010) indicated that in an effort to maintain an intimate relationship by coercion, anxiously attached youths who perceive aggression as justifiable in relationships and who fear that their partners want to terminate the relationship may engage in violent and abusive behavior. Insecure attachment style and antisocial, borderline, and dependent psychopathologies have also been implicated in cases of both male and female perpetration of domestic violence (Dutton, 2007; Goldenson, Geffner, Foster, & Clipson, 2007). Finally, although studies of attachment style in relation to readiness of a domestic violence victim to terminate an abusive relationship are scarce and evidence is mixed, Shurman and Rodriguez (2006) found that the more preoccupied the female victim was in her attachment style, and the more depressed, hopeless, and anxious she felt, the more ready she felt to end the abusive relationship.

Social Information Processing Theories

Social information processing (SIP) theories, and cognitive behavioral theories, place much greater emphasis than other theories on social cognitive processes in individuals who maltreat others. These theories emphasize that it is the perpetrator's judgments about the behaviors, thoughts, and feelings of family members and their limited response repertoire for dealing with frustrations, disappointments, and negative emotions that lead to a reliance on aggression. These theories are important in their emphasis on the role of cognitive processes in family maltreatment; indeed, it is likely that most abusers do not see their behavior as abusive but as an appropriate response to the inappropriate behavior of family members. In one study based on an SIP model, Farc, Crouch, Skowronski, and Milner (2008) built on earlier work indicating that people whose thinking is dominated by hostility-related schema have a heightened tendency to make hostile interpretations of the behaviors of others and to behave aggressively. They found that parents at high risk of committing child physical abuse (CPA) were more likely than parents at low risk to judge ambiguous photos of children as hostile. According to Farc et al. (2008) hostility-related schema activation in parents is additive, which may increase attributions of hostile intent and aggressive behaviors directed toward children. Furthermore, Crouch, Risser, Skowronski, Milner, Farc, and Irwin (2010) found that parents who were at high risk for CPA were slower to classify both positive and negative words when they were primed with faces portraying the opposite "affective valence." They concluded that parents with high and low CPA risk differ in how they process "affectively incongruent" information (Crouch et al., 2010).

In another social information processing study, Rodriguez and Richardson (2007) examined the role of both preexisting cognitive schemas (including locus of control, perceived attachment, and empathy) and contextual variables (stress and anger) in predicting risk of child maltreatment. They found that both external locus of control and perceived attachment to the child were predictive of child abuse potential, and that empathic perspective-taking ability was negatively related to overreactive discipline (i.e., a harsh, angry disciplinary style).

Social Learning Theory

One of the most popular explanations for family violence comes from social learning theory, which posits that individuals learn "appropriate" situations and targets for aggression the same way they learn everything else—that is, through the patterns of reinforcements and punishments that they experience and through observing both the behaviors of significant others and the consequences of those behaviors. Thus, social learning theorists predict children who observe interparental violence or experience violence at the hands of their parents are likely to repeat this behavior in their own family relationships as adults. Considerable support for such suppositions comes from extensive research on the intergenerational transmission of family violence, which clearly indicates that violence in the family of origin, either witnessing and/or experiencing it, is predictive of violence in later close relationships. However, there are two major caveats for this support: (1) there is also strong evidence that not everyone who grew up in an aggressive family will become aggressive

(Kaufman & Zigler, 1987); and (2) intergenerational continuity in aggression can also be due to the genes, not just the environments, that family members share. Support for a cycle of violence hypothesis in which social learning is considered to be of critical importance comes from Gómez (2011), who found that both child abuse and dating aggression were significant predictors of perpetration of and victimization by intimate partner violence in adult men and women.

Microsystem Level Theories

Systems Theory

Systems theorists emphasize the importance of analyzing families as dynamic, adaptive social systems with feedback processes taking place among family members in ways that maintain the stability of the system (Kazak, 1989). Systems theorists typically view influences in families as bi- or multidirectional; for example, children influence parents as well as parents influence children; interactions between husbands and wives can influence the interactions of both with elderly parents; how a husband treats a wife may be related to how she treats their children. From this perspective, maltreatment in families is not a simple matter of one disturbed family member harming an innocent victim; rather, it results from everyday stresses and strains on the family system that produce conflicts, accommodations, and various responses, sometimes including violence. In some family systems, wives may tolerate maltreatment from their husbands because the husbands are providing a home for their children, or may sacrifice a daughter to the incestuous behaviors of their husbands to protect themselves from his aggression; or husbands may stay with violent wives to try to protect their children. Systems conceptual frameworks have been valuable in highlighting the complexity of most forms of family violence but have been consistently challenged by feminists, who view family violence—particularly wife abuse—as a gendered problem; that is, a problem residing in men due to patriarchal norms. In one longitudinal family systems study, Moore and Florsheim (2008) examined the extent to which the relationship between young mothers and fathers was associated with their child-rearing behaviors and attitudes. They found that (a) high rates of intra-couple hostility prior to birth of the child predicted later father hostility toward the child, and (b) low levels of intracouple warmth during a conflict resolution task was predictive of higher levels of later physically punitive behavior toward the child.

Stress Theory

Stress theorists have identified stressors at many levels of the ecological context in which individuals develop and family interactions take place. Stress is typically defined as the experience individuals have when the demands of the situation exceed their ability to deal with it. Within the family microsystem, common stressors may be too many children, not enough income, absence of one parent, and marital conflict. In particular, poverty is a risk factor for various forms of family maltreatment (e.g., Berger, 2005; Caetano & Cunradi, 2003; Merritt, 2009), particularly child neglect (Carter & Myers, 2007). Although there is considerable evidence of a relationship between poverty and maltreatment, a recent analysis of child maltreatment and economic data from the Current Population Survey from the Bureau of Labor Statistics revealed small and inconsistent relationships between poverty and child abuse rates (Millett, Lanier, & Drake, 2011). Millett et al. conclude that the relationship between poverty and child maltreatment may be more complex than has been assumed.

Abuse of one parent by another may result from one stressor—for example, the victim's substance abuse—but also constitutes a stressor for other members of the family, leading, for example, to the victim's abuse of the children. There is considerable empirical evidence supporting a link between stressors and family violence, but stress does not necessarily lead to violence. Although Straus (1980) found that the greater the number of stressors parents were experiencing, the higher their level of child abuse, he also found that stress did not lead to child abuse except within the context of several other variables—specifically, growing up in a violent family, low attachment to the marital partner, a dominant role for the husband, and isolation from social support.

Events or changes that overwhelm the resources of the individual and send reverberations into family life often take place outside the home. A family member may lose his or her job, face discrimination because of a handicap, be arrested for drunk driving, or seek affordable mental health services and be unable to find them. The impact of such stressors appears to be particularly destructive when the individual lacks social support. For example, Garbarino and Sherman (1980) found that neighborhoods characterized by greater social isolation and "social impoverishment"—that is, neighborhoods where isolated families compete for scarce resources rather than assisting each other—had higher rates of child maltreatment. The interaction of exosystem characteristics of the neighborhood with characteristics of the families can exacerbate or ameliorate the conditions leading to maltreatment.

Exosystem Level Theories

Ecological Theories

In this book, we follow the contemporary practice of using the term *ecological paradigm* to refer to a broadly integrative conceptual framework that encompasses theories addressing factors at different levels of the human ecological system. Among others, Zielinski and Bradshaw (2006) have argued that given the diversity of outcomes in children known to have been maltreated, it is essential to take an ecological approach to determine how and to what extent the contexts in which the maltreated child develops influence the outcome for each child. However, the label *ecological theory* has also been applied more narrowly to theoretical frameworks (e.g., Garbarino & Kostelny, 1992; Merritt, 2009) focusing on neighborhood variables such as social cohesion and social isolation. Proponents of this approach emphasize the importance of paying attention to neighborhood variables when addressing problems of family violence. Freisthler, Gruenewald, Ring, and LaScala (2008) found that children living in poorer neighborhoods that had larger percentages of female-headed households with children and more off-premise alcohol outlets had more injuries from child abuse as well as from accidents and assaults.

Sociocultural Theories

Although social support has frequently been identified as a factor that can reduce the likelihood of violence as a response to stress (Milner, 1994), there is also evidence that norms within an individual's peer group and community can contribute to the likelihood that violence will be viewed as an acceptable solution to difficulties within the family (Straus, 1980). Men's peer groups may support rigid sex role norms designed to ensure a superior status for men and subordination in women and children. Religious groups may endorse corporal punishment of children and encourage women to stay within abusive marriages in order to keep the family together. Evidence of differences among religious groups and in different areas of the country in tolerance for and use of aggressive tactics within the family supports the view that local norms play a role in the sanctioning of some forms of maltreatment. Also of importance are findings that the effects of abuse may vary based on the cultural values and contexts of the survivor of the abuse; for example, there is evidence that although African American women may experience more intimate partner violence than White women, they often suffer less psychological distress and exhibit higher levels of empowerment (Wright, Perez, & Johnson, 2010).

Macrosystem Level Theories

Feminist Theory

At the heart of a variety of feminist perspectives is the assumption that domestic violence, or violence within the family, is a *gendered* problem; moreover, feminists generally concur that characteristics of perpetrators, victims, and interactions among perpetrators and victims, as well as expectations about families and society, are all profoundly influenced by gender and power (Yllo, 2005). From these perspectives, use of terms like *domestic violence* and *intimate partner violence* is inappropriate because of their gender-neutral quality. This gender neutrality fails to place the responsibility for *family terrorism* where it belongs: on men operating within a global patriarchal system that denies equal rights to women and legitimizes violence against women, children, and the elderly (Hammer, 2003).

Patriarchy, defined by Loseke and Kurz (2005) as "the system of male power in society," has been identified by feminists as one of the most powerful forces contributing to wife abuse in the United States and in most other countries. In patriarchal societies, men have more social, economic, and political power and status than women. They consider themselves superior to women and children and feel entitled to use force if necessary to maintain dominance in family decision making. Men's sense of entitlement, gender inequality, and patriarchal values are seen as causes of wife abuse (Barnett, 2000), femicide (Smith, Moracco, & Butts, 1998), media portrayals of sex and rape (Bufkin & Eschholz, 2000), and sexual abuse of children (Candib, 1999).

Violence against women and children has been connected to patriarchal norms around the world (Levinson, 1989). Moreover, within the United States, there is evidence that the greater the social inequality between men and women, the higher the levels of wife assault (Straus, 1994). Male dominance within the family has been found to predict not just wife beating but also physical child abuse; moreover, the higher the level of husband dominance in the family, the stronger the likelihood of child abuse (Bowker, Arbitell, & McFerron, 1988). On the other hand, in a meta-analysis of studies addressing the link between wife assault and maintenance of a patriarchal ideology, Sugarman and Frankel (1996) found that the only component of patriarchal ideology that consistently predicted wife assault was the perpetrator's attitude toward violence. Pleck (2004) has pointed out that patriarchal theories are not helpful in explaining domestic violence in gay, lesbian, bisexual, and transsexual relationships, nor can they adequately explain partner violence by women toward men (Hines & Douglas, 2011a).

Summary

As was illustrated in Table 1.1, there is some empirical support for each of the major theories of family violence, but there are also limitations to the empirical support. None of the individual theories can account for all forms of family violence, nor can any single theory fully explain even one type of family violence. Essentially, research designed to test the validity of the theories has been effective in identifying risk factors for maltreatment at each of several different levels of the ecological systems in which development takes place. Conversely, the reciprocal of many of these risk factors can serve as protective factors against maltreatment or the negative impact of maltreatment. For example, social support within the micro- and exosystem has long been recognized as an important protective factor, along with higher income and higher education.

Even what may seem like a simple and clear-cut case of maltreatment of one family member by another is likely to have multiple causes. For example, a father may commit incest on his prepubertal daughter because of his sexual inadequacies with adult women, *and* his wife's overt contempt for him, *and* his wife's unconscious denial that her husband is doing to their daughter what her father did to her, *and* the norms of his peer group that a man's home should be his castle, *and* his personal belief that his family should be obedient to him, *and* society's tolerance for pornography, *and* the lack of availability of appropriate services within the community, *and* inadequate funding for intervention programs for incest offenders.

In a previous book (Malley-Morrison & Hines, 2004), we provided an extensive analysis of family violence in ethnic minority communities in the United States. In the current book, we focus more on family violence in the majority White European American community. We begin by describing the major forms of child maltreatment (physical maltreatment, sexual maltreatment, neglect and psychological maltreatment) in Chapters 2, 3, and 4; then, in Chapters 5 through 10, we review the research in the United States today on intimate partner violence, including violence in gay/lesbian relationships, and the research on other forms of family maltreatment (maltreatment of older family members, disabled family members, siblings, and parents). In the final section of the book, we focus on the historical and ecological context of family violence in the contemporary United States, including the role of culture in contributing to, maintaining, providing rationalizations for, and providing protection against violence in close relationships as well as religious influences on family violence. As you read these chapters, consider the different perspectives that individuals from the different relevant professions (e.g., psychology, law, social work) would bring to their interpretation of the findings and the particular recommendations they might make for interventions into various forms of family maltreatment. Also consider how the findings would be interpreted within the different theoretical frameworks described here. Finally, consider your own experiences of maltreatment as well as your views and values concerning various forms of maltreatment. Which, if any, of the forms of maltreatment seem worse in their consequences? For example, is the abuse of children worse than the abuse of adults? Is physical abuse worse than psychological abuse? Consider your answers to these questions. Now, does it surprise you to learn that women staying in shelters because they have been beaten by their husbands often say that it was his psychological abuse that was more damaging (Follingstad, Rutledge, Berg, Hause, & Polek, 1990)? Even though the number of domestic violence refuges today is still not enough to support every victim, community-based shelter programs can now provide resources such as emergency shelters, 24-hour crisis hotlines, support groups, counseling, advocacy, and children's programs (C. M. Sullivan, 2006). Do such resources seem adequate to the different forms of violence taking place in relationships? What do you see as the best approaches to ending maltreatment in families?

Discussion Questions

1. What factors in our culture make us more tolerant of women physically abusing their partners and less tolerant of males physically abusing their partners?

2. Picture a scenario where a man is abusing his nonabusive partner. Picture a scenario where a woman is abusing her nonabusive partner. Picture a male and a female partner mutually abusing one another. Do you react differently to each scenario? Why? What factors in our culture make each scenario more or less OK?

3. When, if ever, is corporal punishment OK? Does the age of the child matter? Does the gender? Does it matter *where* the child is hit or spanked? If differences in child age or gender or the location of a hit matter, why is that so? Why might some of these characteristics make corporal punishment seem more OK than others? What experiences or viewpoints in our society or culture influence your judgment?

4. Is verbal abuse less severe or traumatizing than physical abuse? Do you associate one gender more than another with either of these types of abuse? How do your views on gender differences in the use of particular forms of aggression influence your opinions on abusive relationships and the extent to which men and women are likely to be either victims or both victims and perpetrators?

5. How would you react to an individual forcing his or her partner to have sex? Would you react differently if you found out that this couple was married? Married for 20 years? Does rape seem less wrong if a couple is or has been married? What kinds of circumstances are likely to influence views on marital rape? Rape in other intimate relationships?

6. Is hitting someone only once abusive? Is hitting someone every day abusive? Does it make a difference if one individual is hitting another as a form of discipline (for example, a parent disciplining a child or if the hitting is motivated by a desire to hurt) Does it matter if the physical aggression leaves a bruise or injury? Is the physical aggression less abusive if it doesn't bruise or injure? How much does motivation, frequency, and intensity matter to the appropriateness of labeling an event as abusive? Why?

7. Do you think there should be different laws for maltreatment or mild to moderate abuse, and violence or severe abuse? What about for physical versus mental/verbal abuse? Why? Is one form of maltreatment more or less traumatic than another? If so, why? If not, why do some people assume that one form of maltreatment is more traumatic than others?

8. The United States is one of two countries that are resistant to the notion that corporal punishment may violate a child's rights. In this culture, behavior that would be deemed abusive if done to a partner or an equal (i.e. slapping, hitting, etc.) is seen as adequate punishment for a child. In what way may the assumption that corporal punishment is appropriate for children be detrimental for a child at the time it occurs? What could be the long-term consequences of using corporal punishment?

9. People have a hard time accepting the idea that forced sex or rape can occur in a married couple because of the belief that a man has a right to his wife's body, as his property. Marital rape laws were created to counteract this misconception; however, there are still no laws that address a situation in which a husband is being sexually assaulted or abused by his wife. Why is sexual aggression by females against their partners harder to accept, culturally and in our legal system? How is sexual abuse of a husband equally detrimental or harmful as sexual abuse of a wife? Why is it important that we have equal and all encompassing laws?

10. There are many agencies (e.g., legal, medical, social, etc.) that get involved in cases of abuse and violence. Some agencies are interested in helping both the perpetrator and the victim while others concentrate solely on the victim and turn away perpetrators. Which, if any, is the better method? What are the consequences of helping both victims and perpetrators in the same place, simultaneously? What are the consequences of turning away perpetrators and focusing only on victims?

11. Biological studies show that abnormal levels of testosterone and serotonin predict higher levels of risk in battering behavior. Does "blaming biology" help or hurt how we see victims and perpetrators of domestic violence and abuse? Which perspective (e.g., biological versus psychological or social work) is the "best" lens to use in looking at violence and abuse?

12. Studies show that demographic and individual factors such as a low income, loss of a job, and low education level are correlated with perpetration of violence and abuse. Why is it incorrect to say that an individual with one or a few of these factors will inevitably perpetrate abuse? What, if anything, predicts abusive and violent behaviors? Why are these predictor factors not causational?

PART II

Child Maltreatment

2

Child Physical Maltreatment

Kayla, a painfully shy six-year-old, lived with her biological father and stepmother. One day, a family friend noticed that Kayla had two black eyes and several other bruises. This friend insisted they take Kayla to the local emergency room, where both the father and Kayla said she had sustained the bruises from a bicycle fall. After discovering that Kayla also had internal bleeding and a broken nose and doubting the bicycle story, the doctor asked a nurse to call the Florida Department of Children and Families (DCF). A DCF worker interviewed everyone involved. At a court hearing, the judge found no reason to doubt the bicycle story, and Kayla was sent home. Although her case was supposed to be monitored by a private agency hired by the DCF, neither the agency nor the DCF ever followed up on it. Over two weeks later, Kayla appeared in school with heavy makeup covering facial bruising. A few weeks later, she had even more bruises and said she had fallen off her bicycle again. Her teacher called DCF, who sent someone to visit Kayla's father. The worker insisted he take Kayla to a doctor, who found large bruises on her back, stomach, and head, and said she exhibited symptoms of chronic physical abuse. Kayla's father admitted that on occasion he spanked her with a paddle because she was a difficult child. Kayla returned home with her father and was monitored by DCF. She came to school two more times with bruises on her face and body, which she said were the result of being pulled down the stairs by the family dog. Because of the huge lump on her forehead, Kayla's teacher called DCF again and discovered the case had been closed (Russ, 2003).

K ayla's story is a notorious case from the DCF files in Florida. It clearly displays the signs and symptoms of children who are physically maltreated. What types of physical maltreatment did you identify in this case? What factors may have caused the maltreatment? Kayla's father, Richard, had a history of violent criminal behavior and had served jail time for assault and other crimes (Associated Press, 1998). How could this history have contributed to his behavior toward his daughter? What were the consequences of the maltreatment? The ultimate consequence for Kayla, unfortunately, was death. Within several weeks of the last report to the DCF, Kayla's body was found buried in a shallow grave in a national forest. Her father, Richard, beat her to death in a fit of rage because she soiled her underwear. When her body was found, it was discovered that her skull was fractured, four ribs were broken, her lung was punctured, her liver was split in three places, and her back and buttocks bled internally, so much so that her muscles were saturated with blood (Bickel, 2000). Richard's punishment was life imprisonment with no chance of parole. What could the system have done to prevent such a tragedy from happening?

Systematic research into child maltreatment in the United States began four decades ago with the publication of Kempe and colleagues' 1962 article on the battered child syndrome (Kempe, Silverman, Steele, Droegemueller, & Silver, 1962). Since that time, researchers have become increasingly concerned with the ways in which child maltreatment can manifest itself, the extent to which children suffer at the hands of their parents, the possible causes and correlates of child maltreatment, the consequences for children of victimization, and the ways in which we can intervene in abusive families or prevent maltreatment from happening. We have learned much in all of these areas, but it is questionable how much we have succeeded in ameliorating the problem of child maltreatment in the United States. Official statistics in the United States are clear that most forms of child maltreatment have been declining since the early 1990s (Sedlak et al., 2010; U.S. Department of Health and Human Services, 2011). At the same time, as more research is conducted, we understand better the complex and subtle ways that children can be maltreated.

In this chapter, we discuss studies in the most-researched area of child maltreatment: physical maltreatment. In the following chapters, we discuss sexual maltreatment, neglect, and psychological maltreatment. Although the major types of child maltreatment tend to overlap, with victims of one type of maltreatment likely to be victims of at least one other type as well, we follow the most common pattern of discussing each type separately. However, in Chapter 3 we discuss the issue of multiple types of child maltreatment, or what has been called "polyvictimization" (Finkelhor, 2008). As you read the current chapter, keep Kayla's case in mind and consider what factors may have contributed to her death.

Scope of the Problem

Exact rates of the physical maltreatment of children are hard to pin down, in part because studies vary in their definitions of the problem. Even within the same study, data may be reported from several sources using different definitions. For instance, states have different statutes for the definition of physical abuse, and Child Protective Services (CPS) workers have their own biases and interpretations of the cases they investigate. Nevertheless, each CPS agency and each state provide data to the government for physical abuse rates, data that are used by both the National Child Abuse and Neglect Data System (NCANDS) and the National Incidence Studies (NIS).

One aspect of the definitional problem is that the lines between physically abusive versus sub-abusive versus non-abusive behaviors are blurred; there is no consensus on the exact severity, frequency, or duration of physical aggression that is necessary for a behavior to be deemed abusive. Consider Kayla's case again.

Although several people assumed that she was physically abused, her physical maltreatment may never have been substantiated by the state, and therefore, she would not have been counted in national statistics on physically abused children. Consider also the case in Box 2.1 below. Even this case might be hard to substantiate, especially if Jacinta's mother did not admit that her husband physically maltreated the child. Also, must injury occur in order for a behavior to be labeled physically abusive? Is risk of injury enough? What if no physical injury ever occurs, but the child is slapped on a daily basis for no apparent reason? What if the child was punched "only" once with no lasting injury? Is a precise and universal definition of physical abuse possible?

Box 2.1	Case of Physical Maltreatment by a Caregiver

Jacinta was five weeks old when she was first examined at a local hospital. She had many unexplained injuries, including a torn frenulum (tissue that connects the tongue to the mouth), lacerated and infected gums, a fractured nose and upper jaw, and burns to the buttocks and thigh. The hospital staff decided to do a full skeletal x-ray to investigate whether there were any other injuries, and they discovered a fractured forearm that was approximately two weeks old.

Sally, Jacinta's mother, explained that the burn to the buttocks occurred when her 17-year-old niece gave Jacinta a bath and allowed her to roll over and come into contact with an electric heater. The thigh burn occurred when Peter, Jacinta's father, accidentally spilled hot milk on Jacinta. Sally explained that the facial injuries occurred when Sally was carrying Jacinta over her shoulder, tripped over the family dog, and fell such that she landed on Jacinta's face. Finally, she stated that the fractured arm must have occurred when the hospital staff held Jacinta's arm too tightly to collect blood.

Sally herself arrived at the hospital with a large bruise on her cheek, but she denied any violence by her husband toward either her or the child, and stated that the bruise was actually a birthmark that had always been there. A child welfare team investigated Jacinta's case and decided to place Jacinta in foster care. They informed Sally that court papers had been filed to make Jacinta a ward of the state. Sally then confessed that Peter abused both Jacinta and Sally, and that Jacinta's facial injuries occurred when Peter punched her.

SOURCE: Oates, Ryan, & Booth, 2000

According to the U.S. Department of Health and Human Services (USDHHS; 2011), the rates of substantiated physical maltreatment reported from CPS agencies reveal that physical maltreatment is the second most prevalent form of child maltreatment, comprising 17.6% of all maltreatment cases in 2010, second only to neglect cases. Reports also indicated that that rates of substantiated physical maltreatment declined 56% between 1992 and 2010 (Finkelhor, Jones, & Shattuck, 2011). In 2010, approximately 121,380 children were physically maltreated by their parents. Physical maltreatment was not the form of maltreatment most likely to lead to death (neglect resulted in more fatalities). In all, there were an estimated 1,560 child maltreatment fatalities in 2010, for an estimated rate of 2.07 children per 100,000; 22.9% of maltreatment fatalities were due exclusively to physical maltreatment, and an additional 22.2% of fatality cases were due to physical maltreatment in combination with neglect (USDHHS, 2011).

According to the Fourth National Incidence Study of Child Abuse and Neglect conducted in 2005–2006 (Sedlak et al., 2010), the NCANDS data reported by the DHHS underestimate the number of children physically maltreated in this country. The rates of physical maltreatment found in the NIS-4 analysis are higher than the NCANDS rates, probably because the investigators had access to more sources of data than just CPS agencies. The four NIS studies (conducted in 1980, 1988, 1993, and 2005–2006) solicited information from community professionals mandated to report child abuse cases, specifically professionals from schools, hospitals, law enforcement agencies, and welfare offices. These mandated professionals were asked to report all cases of child maltreatment with which they had come in contact and to indicate which ones they had reported to CPS. The NIS investigators also solicited reports from CPS agencies, so that they could compare the cases reported by the professionals with the reports received by CPS from either professionals or nonprofessionals, such as neighbors, family members, and friends. In identifying maltreatment cases as physical, sexual, and emotional abuse, and physical, emotional, medical, and educational neglect, the NIS respondents were instructed to use a definition of maltreatment emphasizing deliberate acts or marked inattention to the child's basic needs that could result in foreseeable and avoidable injury or impairment to a child, or worsen an existing condition.

The most recent NIS survey (NIS-4) contains a nationally representative sample of over 10,790 professionals in 1,094 agencies serving 126 counties. Like the NIS-2 and 3 surveys, the NIS-4 used two sets of standardized definitions of abuse and neglect. Under the *Harm Standard,* the only standard in NIS-1, children were identified as maltreated only if they had already experienced harm from abuse or neglect. Under the *Endangerment Standard,* added to NIS-2, -3, and -4, children were included in the maltreatment group if they had experienced abuse or neglect that put them at risk of harm (Sedlak et al., 2010). According to the Harm Standard, more than 1.25 million children—or 1 in 58—were maltreated in 2005–2006. Of these, more than 323,000 children—or 58% of the abused children—were physically abused, a 15% decrease from the previous survey in 1993. According to the Endangerment Standard, nearly 3 million children—or 1 in 25—were maltreated in 2005–2006, with 476,600 physically abused, a 22% decrease from the previous survey year.

Another older, but nonetheless informative source of data suggests that actual rates of physical child maltreatment are even higher than indicated in reports on identified cases. Straus, Hamby, Finkelhor, Moore, and Runyan (1998) administered the parent-child version of the Conflict Tactics Scales (CTS-PC) to a national population-based representative sample of parents who self-reported how often they used specific physical acts (e.g., hitting, beating up) to discipline their children. The instructions for the CTS-PC tell participants that parents and children use many different ways to settle differences and that following is a list of the things that they may have done when they have had a disagreement with their child. They are then instructed to indicate the number of times in the past year they did each of the things listed, which range from non-violent disciplinary acts (e.g., discuss an issue calmly), to psychologically aggressive acts (e.g., insulted or swore at the child), to physically aggressive acts (e.g., slapping, kicking, hitting with a fist).

According to this survey, almost two thirds of parents hit their children at least once in the previous year (Straus et al., 1998). Moreover, nearly 5% of the parents reported using one of the behaviors on the Severe Physical Assault Index in the previous year (example items include hitting the child with a fist, kicking the child, and throwing or knocking down the child). The researchers consider the items on this scale to be the best indicators of physical abuse, which means that the rates of physical abuse are actually nearly 11 times greater than the DHHS findings and five times greater than the NIS findings. Table 2.1 presents the divergent results that these national studies have found for the extent of child physical maltreatment.

Predictors and Correlates

Since large numbers of children are being physically maltreated by their caregivers each year, it is important to identify the risk factors influencing parents to maltreat their children. The identified risk factors reflect every level of the ecological theory discussed in Chapter 1. Furthermore, many researchers (e.g., Newberger, Hampton, Marx, & White, 1986; Straus & Smith, 1990) have found that it is the *combination* of risk factors, not any single risk factor alone, that puts children at risk for physical abuse. Table 2.2 summarizes these risk factors for each level of the ecological model.

Macrosystem

Economic Indicators

Families suffering from unemployment and/or low income seem to be at a higher risk for physically maltreating their children than their more economically successful counterparts (Gillham et al., 1998; Sedlak et al., 2010; Straus & Smith, 1990), especially if the parents are dissatisfied with their standard of living (e.g., Straus & Smith, 1990). Also, less educated parents engage in more maltreatment than more highly educated parents (Jackson et al., 1999). It is important to note that although these economic indicators do predict the physical maltreatment of children, the rates of child physical maltreatment have been steadily declining—even through the Great Recession. With the exception of neglect, this decline is also evident in all other types of child maltreatment (Jones & Finkelhor, 2009; USDHHS, 2011), intimate partner violence (Catalano, 2007), and criminal behavior in general (Federal Bureau of Investigation, 2010a), which means that the association between economic indicators and child physical maltreatment is much more complex than it appears. More research is needed to understand how exactly these economic indicators are related to these types of maltreatment.

Table 2.1 Prevalence Rates of Physical Maltreatment of Children

Study	Description of Sample	Measure/Definition of Maltreatment	Rates of Maltreatment
U.S. Department of Health and Human Services (2011), *Child Maltreatment 2010*	An estimated 3.3 million referrals, involving the alleged maltreatment of approximately 5.9 million children in 2010	Cases that have been referred to Child Protective Services (CPS) in 2010	• Physical abuse comprised 17.6% of all maltreatment cases in 2010 • 121,380 children physically abused by parents in 2010 • 22.9% of maltreatment fatalities (N = 1,560) were due to physical abuse; an additional 22.2% were due to physical abuse in combination with neglect
Sedlak et al. (2010), Fourth National Incidence Study of Child Abuse and Neglect (2005–2006)	A nationally representative sample of over 10,790 professionals in 1,094 agencies serving 126 counties	• *Harm Standard*—requires that an act or omission result in demonstrable harm in order to be classified as abuse or neglect • *Endangerment Standard*—a sentinel thought that the maltreatment endangered the children or a CPS investigation substantiated or indicated their maltreatment	• *Harm Standard*: More than 323,000 children—or 1 in 58 children—were physically abused • *Endangerment Standard*: Nearly 3 million children—or 1 in 25—were maltreated in 2005–2006, with 476,600 physically abused
Straus, Hamby, Finkelhor, Moore, & Runyan (1998)	1,000 households in a national population-based representative sample of parents	Conflict Tactics Scales, Parent-Child Version	• 61.5% of parents hit their children at least once in previous year • 89.9% reported hitting their children ever • 4.9% of parents reported using behavior on Severe Physical Assault Subscale in past year

Table 2.2   Predictors of Physical Maltreatment of Children

Level of the Ecological Model	Specific Predictor	Examples of Studies
Macrosystem	Unemployment/Low Income	Gillham et al. (1998); Sedlak et al. (2010); Straus & Smith (1990)
	Lower Educational Level	Jackson et al. (1999)
	Cultural Acceptance of Parents' Use of Physical Punishment	Gershoff (2002); Straus & Stewart (1999)
Exosystem	Social Isolation	Bishop & Leadbeater (1999); Coohey (2000b); Straus & Smith (1990)
	Poor Neighborhood Quality	Drake & Pandey (1996); Garbarino & Kostelny (1992); Korbin, Coulton, Chard, Platt-Houston, & Su (1998); Zuravin (1989)
Microsystem	Younger Children	Jackson et al. (1999); Straus & Smith (1990)
	Child's Difficult Temperament/ Development Abnormalities	Belsky & Vondra (1989); Sullivan & Knutson (2000a)
	Single Parent Homes or Homes with a Nonbiological Parent	Gillham et al. (1998); Sedlak et al. (2010); Straus & Smith (1990)
	Chaotic Home Environment	Mollerstrom, Patchner, & Milner (1992)
	Other Types of Violence Within the Family	Appel & Holden (1998); Coohey (2000b); Jackson et al. (1999); Kelleher, Chaffin, Hollenberg, & Fischer (1994); Straus & Smith (1990)
Individual/ Developmental	Violence in the Family of Origin	Jackson et al. (1999); Kaufman & Zigler (1987); Straus & Smith (1990)
	Maternal Mental Illness	Brown, Cohen, Johnson, & Salzinger (1998); Whipple & Webster-Stratton (1991)
	Parental Substance Abuse	Besinger, Garland, Litrownik, & Landsverk (1999); Reid, Macchetto, & Foster (1999)
	Limited Parenting Skills	Azar & Siegel (1990); Dopke & Milner (2000); Milner (2003); Simons, Whitbeck, Conger, & Wu (1991)

Level of the Ecological Model	Specific Predictor	Examples of Studies
	Poor Parental Coping Strategies	Caliso & Milner (1992); Cantos, Neale, & O'Leary (1997); Dolz, Cerezo, & Milner (1997); Nayak & Milner (1998); Reid, Kavenaugh, & Baldwin (1987); Whipple & Webster-Stratton (1991)
	Parents' Gender (mothers) and Age (younger)	Brown et al. (1998); Milner (1998); Sedlak et al. (2010); Straus, Hamby, Finkelhor, Moore, & Runyan (1998)

Cultural Values

The occurrence and perpetuation of physical child maltreatment seem to be supported by a culture in the United States that is accepting of violence and reluctant to get involved in family matters. Although the general cultural context of violence in the United States will be discussed at length in Chapters 11–13, there are aspects of the community and broader society that have particular relevance to physical child maltreatment in the majority culture.

Parenting has traditionally been viewed as a private matter in this country, and the government has been reluctant to interfere in parents' rights to raise their children as they see fit (Harrington & Dubowitz, 1999). Although several laws have been passed since the early 1960s prohibiting excessive parental violence against children, there continues to be, in actuality, considerable tolerance for aggression against children. Such aggression may not be characterized as abusive by the average person, but is considered maltreatment by many researchers (e.g., Straus, 1994). For example, the laws in this country support the use of physical punishment for children. Although physical abuse is illegal in all 50 states, all states allow parents to physically discipline their children (Davidson, 1997). Furthermore, as of 2010, teachers in 19 states are allowed to use corporal punishment on their students (Center for Effective Discipline, 2010), and the Supreme Court upheld the right of teachers to use corporal punishment on children, even those with disabilities (*Ingraham v. Wright*, 430 U.S. 651, 1977; Lohrmann-O'Rourke & Zirkel, 1998). Moreover, while most professionals having contact with children are required to report suspected cases of child abuse (Davidson, 1988), some of these regulations are being undermined by the federal Welfare Reform Act of 1996. This act weakens the definition of child abuse and may exclude many less severe cases of maltreatment; in addition, this act indicates that parents are not required to get necessary medical care for their children if it interferes with their religious beliefs (Harrington & Dubowitz, 1999).

This acceptance of violence can perpetuate the physical maltreatment of children. Cultural norms allow parents and teachers to aggress against children, and most parents accept physical punishment as an acceptable and even desirable method of child rearing (Harrington & Dubowitz, 1999; Straus & Stewart, 1999). The cumulative impact of ordinary physical punishment on the social and psychological health of this nation may be even greater than the cumulative impact of acknowledged forms of child physical abuse; thus, our goal should be eliminating all forms of physical punishment (M. Straus, personal communication, March 4, 2004). Studies have shown that both physical child abuse and corporal punishment are associated with criminal behavior (e.g., Gershoff, 2002). Straus argues that although the association with criminal behavior is larger for physical abuse than for corporal punishment, many more people experience corporal punishment than experience physical abuse. Thus, eliminating all forms of physical discipline would result in a drastic reduction of criminal behavior in this country.

Exosystem

Families characterized by physical maltreatment seem to be more socially isolated than those families where maltreatment does not occur (e.g., Coohey, 2000; Straus & Smith, 1990). Furthermore, they tend to have fewer sources of social support than non-maltreating families. For example, in one study, mothers who engaged in physical maltreatment reported fewer friends and less contact with their friends than their demographically matched controls (Bishop & Leadbeater, 1999). Moreover, these mothers rated their friendships as lower quality than the non-maltreating mothers, and both relationship quality and social support were independent predictors of maltreatment.

Several studies have assessed neighborhood quality as a predictor of child physical maltreatment. For instance, neighborhoods with a high percentage of single-parent families (Drake & Pandey, 1996), evidence of social deterioration (Garbarino & Kostelny, 1992), inadequate social resources (Zuravin, 1989), impoverishment, child care burden, and instability (Korbin et al., 1998) have all been shown to have higher levels of child physical maltreatment than their counterparts. However, one study showed that many of these neighborhood influences (e.g., concentrated disadvantage and neighborhood crime) no longer influenced child physical maltreatment after controlling for family composition and family socioeconomic status (Molnar, Buka, Brennan, Holton, & Earls, 2003). The only neighborhood-level variable that still predicted child physical maltreatment after controlling for other influences was immigrant concentration, in that a higher immigrant concentration was a protective influence on child physical maltreatment rates (Molnar et al., 2003).

Microsystem

Characteristics of the Victim

Age is probably the most well-researched, child-level risk factor for physical maltreatment; younger children are more likely to be maltreated than older children, and as children age, their risk for being physically maltreated continually declines (e.g., Jackson et al., 1999; Straus & Smith, 1990). Other child-level risk factors are difficult temperament and behavior problems, and medical, developmental, or intellectual abnormalities (e.g., prematurity, low birth weight, low IQ or mental retardation, physical disability) (Belsky & Vondra, 1989; Sullivan & Knutson, 2000).

If such characteristics of children put them at risk for physical maltreatment, does that mean the children are somehow responsible for their own maltreatment? Or, must responsibility for child maltreatment always lie in the parents and/or the eco-logical systems in which the parent-child interactions take place? A reasonable argu-ment is that if the parents' dispositions are such that their child's traits lead them to behave in an irritable and punitive manner, it is still ultimately the parents' fault for the physical maltreatment (e.g., Harrington & Dubowitz, 1999; Kolko, 2002). Indeed, children's traits do not predict their own physical maltreatment above and beyond the parent's traits (Ammerman, 1991).

Characteristics of the Family

Several characteristics of the family seem to put a child at risk for physical mal-treatment. For example, if there is only one parent or if one of the parents is nonbio-logical (i.e., a stepparent), the children in that family are at a greater risk for being physically maltreated (e.g., Gillham et al., 1998; Sedlak et al., 2010; Straus & Smith, 1990). Maltreating families also seem to be quite chaotic. They often appear to have limited cohesion, limited communication, and high conflict (Mollerstrom, Patchner, & Milner, 1992). In addition, the extent of the family violence may be quite perva-sive. That is, mothers and fathers who physically and/or verbally maltreat their spouses are more at risk for physically maltreating their children, and parents who verbally maltreat their children are more at risk for physically maltreating them, too (e.g., Appel & Holden, 1998; Jackson et al., 1999; Straus & Smith, 1990). These family dysfunctions may also generalize: physically maltreating parents tend to report more interpersonal problems outside of the family, including social isolation, limited support from extended family and friends, and loneliness (Coohey, 2000; Kelleher, Chaffin, Hollenberg, & Fischer, 1994).

Individual/Developmental

Family History of Aggression

One of the most consistent parental risk factors for the physical maltreatment of children is the parents' own childhood history of family violence—through either being victimized by child maltreatment (even just repeated corporal punish-ment) or witnessing interparental violence in childhood. Although not all children who grow up in violent homes go on to maltreat their own children, it is estimated that about 30% will, and those who were exposed to violence in their families of origin are at significantly greater risk for physically maltreating their own children than those who were not (e.g., Jackson et al., 1999; Kaufman & Zigler, 1987; Straus & Smith, 1990).

Psychopathology and Alcohol/Drug Abuse

Parental psychopathological problems have also been implicated in parents' tendencies to physically maltreat their children. Mothers who are depressed and/or anxious (e.g., Whipple & Webster-Stratton, 1991) or sociopathic (e.g., Brown, Cohen, Johnson, & Salzinger, 1998) are at higher risk for physically maltreating their children. Parents who abuse alcohol or drugs are also at greater risk for maltreating their children (e.g., Besinger, Garland, Litrownik, & Landsverk, 1999). Indeed, it has been estimated that substance abuse accounts for approximately two thirds of child maltreatment fatalities in this country (Reid, Macchetto, & Foster, 1999).

Emotions and Cognitions

Physically maltreating parents also differ from non-maltreating parents in the way they think about, feel about, and interact with their children. Physical maltreatment often occurs in the context of parental perceived child noncompliance, which suggests that physically maltreating parents have limited parenting skills. For instance, physically maltreating mothers, in comparison to non-maltreating mothers, believe that using physical discipline is an appropriate way of rearing children and have higher expectations for their children's behavior (Simons, Whitbeck, Conger, & Wu, 1991). Perhaps because their children cannot possibly live up to these high expectations, maltreating mothers perceive their children more negatively than non-maltreating mothers do (Azar & Siegel, 1990), are hyperaware of their children's noncompliance, are more likely to view their children's behavior negatively, and are less apt to see their children's positive behaviors (Milner, 2003). Moreover, in comparison to non-maltreating mothers, physically maltreating mothers tend to perceive a noncompliant child's behavior as being more intentional, stable, and global, more difficult to control, and more stressful (Dopke & Milner, 2000).

Negative cognitions about their children then translate into negative interactions between maltreating mothers and their children. Maltreating mothers have few positive interactions and many negative interactions with their children (Caliso & Milner, 1992; Dolz, Cerezo, & Milner, 1997) and even respond aversively to any prosocial approaches by their children (Reid et al., 1987). In addition, when faced with the inevitable misbehavior of their children, physically maltreating mothers tend to use emotion-focused rather than problem-focused strategies to resolve the situation (Cantos, Neale, & O'Leary, 1997). Perhaps these strategies are why maltreating mothers' child-rearing styles seem to be inconsistent, critical, hostile, and eventually aggressive (Whipple & Webster-Stratton, 1991), and why they score lower on measures of problem-solving ability, conceptual skills, and cognitive flexibility (Nayak & Milner, 1998).

Other Demographic Predictors

Younger, single, and/or nonbiological parents are more likely to physically maltreat their children than their counterparts (Brown et al., 1998; Milner, 1998; Straus et al., 1998). Furthermore, female parents are more likely to physically maltreat their children than male parents (e.g., Sedlak et al., 2010). Consider these findings. Why would younger parents be more likely to maltreat their children? What kinds of situations and stresses confront single parents that might increase their risk for maltreating their children? Why would nonbiological parents be more likely to maltreat a child than a biological parent? And finally, why would mothers be more likely to maltreat their children than fathers?

Application of the Ecological Model

Box 2.2 provides more information about the case of Jacinta, introduced in Box 2.1. As you read about the characteristics of her parents, consider how many of the risk factors you have just read about apply to her case. If you were a child protective worker involved in her case, what would your recommendations be? Would you allow Jacinta to return to the care of her mother? Would you allow her to live with her paternal grandmother? What do you think would be the best approach to keeping Jacinta safe from further maltreatment? The decision made by the professionals in this case was to place her in foster care. Do you agree with that decision?

Box 2.2	Jacinta's Parents

The investigation into Jacinta's case revealed several important facts about her parents, Sally and Peter. In high school, Sally had attended a special class for slow learners. She had been very unhappy in school, had felt teased and picked on by other children, and had become quite wild as a teenager, unable to keep herself from getting involved with abusive males. While Jacinta was in the hospital, the nursing staff observed that Sally did not seem to have the skills or intellectual competence to care for Jacinta adequately. Her parents were supportive of her, but were retired, in ill health, and unable to provide the necessary care for their granddaughter.

As a child, Peter had been removed from his parents' care because of abuse, and spent many years in juvenile correctional institutions. He had a long history of increasingly violent crime. Although he did not have a formal psychiatric evaluation during the case review process, professional observers believed he had all the characteristics of a psychopathic personality. At the time Sally married him, he was an unemployed truck driver. His mother insisted that he was just a victim of circumstances and was willing to take Sally and Jacinta into her home.

SOURCE: Oates et al., 2000

Consequences

Both short- and long-term consequences of child physical maltreatment have been found in almost every area of human functioning. However, the link between child physical maltreatment and its consequences is not necessarily straightforward or direct. In fact, many aspects of the maltreating situation itself and other areas of the child's life can moderate the impact of physical maltreatment on a child's adjustment. For instance, the perpetrator's gender and relationship to the victim can be important: One study showed that physical maltreatment by mothers may be associated with worse outcomes than physical maltreatment by someone else (Herrenkohl, Herrenkohl, & Toedter, 1983), whereas another showed that among women, violence by a father but not violence by a mother was predictive of low self-esteem (Herrenkohl, Herrenkohl, Egolf, & Russo, 1998). Furthermore, the combination of more than one maltreating caretaker and/or more maltreatment types (e.g., physical maltreatment in combination with neglect and/or sexual maltreatment) can result in more severe outcomes (Brown & Anderson, 1991; Finkelhor, 2008; Herrenkohl et al., 1983). Other aspects of the maltreatment situation, such as the timing, frequency, severity, and duration of the maltreatment may also aggravate negative outcomes (Brown & Kolko, 1999; Keiley, Howe, Dodge, Bates, & Pettit, 2001; Manly, Kim, Rogosch, & Cicchetti, 2001). The more chronic, frequent, and severe the maltreatment, the more severe the outcome. Physical maltreatment during the preschool period is particularly risky for negative outcomes such as internalizing and withdrawn behavior (Manly et al., 2001), and physical maltreatment prior to the age of five has been associated with more negative outcomes than later physical maltreatment (Keiley et al., 2001). Overall, the family environment, such as level of poverty, high levels of stress, and parental psychopathology may also make outcomes worse (Augoustinos, 1987; Kurtz, Gaudin, Howing, & Wodarski, 1993; Malinosky-Rummell & Hansen, 1993; Walker, Downey, & Bergman, 1989).

Protective Factors

Although various studies show differing results, certain child characteristics, such as gender and age, may have a moderating effect on the extent or types of negative outcomes that a child experiences as a result of physical maltreatment (Malinosky-Rummell & Hansen, 1993). Several researchers have found that child characteristics, such as a relationship with a supportive non-maltreating caregiver, a high IQ, some genetic factors, and how children think about their maltreatment experiences (Brown & Kolko, 1999; Herrenkohl, Herrenkohl, Rupert, Egolf, & Lutz, 1995; Herrenkohl, Herrenkohl, Egolf, & Wu, 1991; Kashani, Daniel, Dandoy, & Holcomb, 1992) can lessen the impact of child physical maltreatment. For example, children who blame themselves for the maltreatment have worse outcomes (Brown & Kolko, 1999). In a study looking specifically at the role of support networks on children's adjustment, Ezzell, Swenson, and Brondino (2000) found that peer support was particularly helpful in reducing internalizing behaviors, such as depression and anxiety, in a sample of physically maltreated adolescents whose cases were substantiated by CPS, while family support was associated with less depression. Teacher support was not associated with any adolescent outcomes, nor were any of the types of support (family, peer, or teacher) related to a decrease in externalizing or aggressive behaviors (Ezzell et al., 2000). This study addressed teacher, peer, and family support. Can you think of any other sources of support that may serve as a protective factor against the effects of child maltreatment?

Short-Term Consequences

Physical Injuries

In the short term, the most obvious outcome of child physical maltreatment is physical injury. Skin lesions—including bruises, abrasions, lacerations, burns, and bites—are the most common type of injury seen by medical personnel in cases of child physical maltreatment, with burns accounting for approximately 10% of all physical maltreatment cases. The next most common injury is most likely fractures; physical maltreatment accounts for anywhere between 11% and 55% of fractures in children, and as much as 70% of fractures in infants under the age of one (Reece, 2011).

One of the most widely discussed types of injuries in infants is shaken baby syndrome. Babies have large and poorly supported heads, and when they are shaken back and forth, the brain moves in the opposite direction. Consequently, brain tissue and blood vessels are sheared. Infants under one year of age who present to medical personnel with shaken baby syndrome suffer from central nervous system damage, and may present with seizures, failure to thrive, vomiting, hypothermia, bradycardia (slow heart rate), hypotension, respiratory irregularities, or coma (C. F. Johnson, 2002). Approximately 15% to 25% of these infants will die from this type of head trauma, and of those who survive, 80% to 90% will have varying degrees of learning disabilities, paralysis, blindness, seizure disorders, and/or remain in a persistent vegetative state (Bonnier, Nassagne, & Evrard, 1995). Further issues of child fatalities due to child maltreatment are discussed in Box 2.3.

Box 2.3   Child Maltreatment Fatalities

According to the most recent statistics released by the U.S. Department of Health and Human Services (2011), an estimated 1,770 child deaths in the year 2009 were a result of child maltreatment, which is a rate of 2.34 per every 100,000 children in the population and represents a continuation of the increase in the rate of child maltreatment fatalities over the previous five years. The majority of fatalities were due to either physical abuse or neglect. More than one third of these fatalities were due to neglect alone, with 66.7% due to neglect or neglect in combination with some other form of maltreatment; 44.8% of deaths were due to physical abuse alone or in combination with another form of maltreatment. In over 75% of the cases, the perpetrator of the maltreatment was a parent, and in the majority of cases (88.1%), these families had no contact with CPS in the five years prior to the death of the child. In other words, the families in which children died or were killed because of maltreatment were not currently under any maltreatment investigation.

Perhaps one reason for the lack of involvement of CPS was that the majority (~81%) of the child victims were under the age of four years, and over 46% were under the age of one (USDHHS, 2010). Death due to maltreatment during infancy is particularly problematic. Children under the age of one are at the highest risk for death due to traumatic brain injury (Rorke-Adams, Duhaime, Jenny, & Smith, 2009), which is most often caused when an infant is violently shaken (Christian, Block, & Committee on Child Abuse and Neglect, 2009).

Therefore, an infant is at a high risk for homicide victimization; however, a newborn is at an even higher risk. According to the Centers for Disease Control and Prevention (2002), the risk for being murdered on the first day of life is ten times greater than at any other time throughout the life cycle. Although theories as to why parents murder their newborns abound (e.g., an unmarried teenage mother is ashamed of her sexual activity and is afraid to tell her parents that she is pregnant), there exists only one population-based study of neonaticide to date, and this study seems to refute the stereotype of the type of person who kills her newborn. Herman-Giddens, Smith, Mittal, Carlson, and Butts (2003) reviewed all death cases of infants

(Continued)

(Continued)

under four days of age in North Carolina from 1985 through 2000. In all the cases in which the perpetrator could be determined, the perpetrator was the mother. They found that 34 newborns were killed or discarded by their mothers, which projects into 2.1 per 100,000 newborns per year. Males (58.8%) were significantly more likely than females (35.3%) to be murdered, and Black newborns were over-represented (52.9%) as cases in comparison to their representation in the overall population of newborns (28%). The age of the mothers ranged from 14 years to 35 years, and the average age was 19.1 years. Approximately one fifth of the mothers were married. Mothers received prenatal care in just under one half of the cases, and eight mothers denied having been pregnant (Herman-Giddens et al., 2003).

Particularly poignant in this analysis was the description of the methods that the mothers used to kill their newborns. In just over 50% of the cases, the mothers either left the newborns in the trash or other waste disposal area (e.g., landfill, dumpster) or in the toilet in which they had given birth. In addition, in just over 50% of the cases, the newborn was strangled or drowned, or died from exposure to the elements. Although not included in the analysis because the babies had never been born, these researchers also found that three mothers had shot their fetuses in utero, and two mothers' fetuses died because of self-induced abortions (Herman-Giddens et al., 2003).

Although all of these statistics on child fatalities due to maltreatment are disheartening, it is important to further note that these numbers are widely believed to underestimate the rate at which children die because of maltreatment. For example, the numbers that the USDHHS collects are based on widely divergent measurement criteria among individual states. The states vary widely in their definitions of abuse and neglect, in terms of which child fatalities they accept for further investigation for maltreatment, and in the extent to which they classify, report, and track child maltreatment fatalities (Chance, 2003). Therefore, the numbers presented here are conservative estimates of the extent to which our children, infants, and newborns are dying because of maltreatment. What is also uncertain is how many of these child fatality cases were intentionally perpetrated by the parents. That is, how many parents intentionally killed their children versus how many child fatalities were the result of physical abuse or neglect getting out of hand? It is impossible to know for sure.

What is being done to prevent child maltreatment fatalities in this country? One step that has been taken in at least 49 states is the Safe Haven laws that are supposed to prevent neonaticide (Child Welfare Information Gateway, 2010). According to these laws, parents can anonymously drop off an unwanted newborn to certain authorities, such as hospitals and fire stations without being charged with abandonment (Herman-Giddens et al., 2003). To improve our ability to detect child maltreatment fatalities, child death review teams (CDRTs) now exist in all 50 states. It is their job to obtain comprehensive information from multiple sources when a child fatality is referred to them from CPS, law enforcement, or medical examiners (Chance, 2003). However, even though these teams exist in all 50 states, there is still no uniform system for reporting child fatalities to the CDRTs or for deeming a child fatality as due to maltreatment (Block, 2003).

Psychological Injuries

In addition to sometimes experiencing physical injury, physically maltreated children also suffer socially, emotionally, and cognitively. For instance, physically maltreated children tend to develop an insecure attachment to their parents that has been labeled disorganized/disoriented attachment (e.g., Barnett, Ganiban, & Cicchetti, 1999). This insecurity in relating to parents seems to carry over into other social relationships. As toddlers and preschoolers, physically maltreated children notice distress in their peers, but are less likely than their non-maltreated counterparts to show empathy or concern. Furthermore, they are more likely to show fear or anger at another's distress, but rarely sadness, and they may even strike or withdraw from distressed peers—a behavior that replicates their parents' way of dealing with a distressed child (Klimes-Dougan & Kistner, 1990; Main & George, 1985). As schoolchildren, physically maltreated children tend to display less friendly, less positive peer interactions, in comparison to non-maltreated children (Kaufman & Cicchetti, 1989). They have limited social competence (Feldman et al., 1989) and are less cooperative and more disturbed in their interactions—they tend to display fewer prosocial and more antisocial behaviors (Salzinger, Feldman, & Hammer, 1993). Indeed, their play is often marked by fights, war, and conflict (Harper, 1991).

These negative ways of interacting with peers may account in part for why physically maltreated children are often rated as the most disliked children in their classes (e.g., Dodge, Pettit, & Bates, 1994) and why they have problems making friends (Gelles & Straus, 1990). Dodge, Bates, and Pettit (1990) theorized that physically maltreated children's problems in interacting with their peers may stem from inappropriate cognitions about social behaviors resulting from their own experiences of maltreatment. In their study, maltreated children tended to attribute hostile intent to their peers' ambiguous behaviors; for example, if a peer accidentally bumped into them in a hallway, maltreated children would be likely to think that the behavior was intentional. Moreover, the maltreated children had a limited capacity to generate alternative solutions to social problems, focused only on negative solutions, believed in the appropriateness of violence as a problem-solving technique, and had little ability to identify nonaggressive solutions to social problems.

Traditionally, family violence researchers have assumed that family members, including maltreated children, behave aggressively because they view aggressive behavior as morally justifiable, normal, and acceptable (Astor, 1994). However, research comparing non-maltreated to maltreated children on moral judgments of hypothetical and actual transgressions reveals no differences in the children's judgments of the severity or wrongness of the following acts: (1) aggression against another child; (2) psychologically harming another child; and (3) conflicts over objects with another child (Smetana et al., 1999). All children viewed these acts as deserving of punishment and as wrong whether an authority figure witnessed the acts or not. The only differences between maltreated and non-maltreated children's responses to these transgressions were in their affective responses. Physically maltreated boys were less angry at being victimized than boys who had not been physically maltreated, and the normally observed gender differences in children's responses to others' distress (i.e., girls feel greater distress and concern for another's hurt feelings) were not observed in physically maltreated children.

Difficulties in other areas of cognitive functioning identified in physically maltreated children include problems in motivation and task initiation (Allen & Tarnowski, 1989), lower intelligence (Erickson, Egeland, & Pianta, 1989), and receptive and expressive language problems (McFayden & Kitson, 1996). Some cognitive problems have been shown to be due to head injuries caused by the physical maltreatment (Lewis, Shanok, & Balla, 1979), but others have been attributed to lack of communication and stimulation in the home environments (Augoustinos, 1987).

In addition to social and cognitive problems, physically maltreated children also tend to have higher rates of emotional difficulties. In a large community sample of children, physically maltreated children were more likely than non-maltreated children to suffer from major depression, conduct disorder, oppositional defiant disorder, agoraphobia, overanxious disorder, and generalized anxiety disorder, even after controlling for potential confounds, such as income, family history of psychiatric disorder, and perinatal problems (Flisher et al., 1997). Other studies confirm that physically maltreated children and adolescents tend to have higher rates of internalizing symptoms, such as depression, hopelessness, and low self-esteem (e.g., Keiley et al., 2001; Mahoney, Donnelly, Boxer, & Lewis, 2003). Clinical studies have shown that physically maltreated children display suicidal behaviors (Fantuzzo, delGaudio, Atkins, Meyers, & Noone, 1998), although this outcome was not found in community samples (Flisher et al., 1997). Moreover, up to one third of physically maltreated children develop post-traumatic stress disorder (PTSD) (Saunders, Berliner, & Hanson, 2003), with up to 81% presenting partial PTSD symptoms (Runyon, Deblinger, & Schroeder, 2009).

Perhaps the most-researched, short-term consequence of physical child maltreatment is in the area of externalizing symptoms. Physical maltreatment during the preschool period is predictive of externalizing and aggressive behaviors (Keiley et al., 2001; Manly et al., 2001), and the more severe the maltreatment, the more severe the symptoms (Brown & Kolko, 1999). In a study of clinic-referred abused adolescents, severe parental aggression toward the adolescents predicted greater externalizing problems, even after controlling for witnessing interparental aggression (Mahoney et al., 2003). Externalizing problems tend to display themselves as oppositional defiant disorder or conduct disorder when they are severe enough to be diagnosable (Famularo, Fenton, & Kinscherff, 1992; Flisher et al., 1997), but at the subclinical level, physically maltreated children tend to have problems with aggression and other forms of antisocial behavior. That is, physically maltreated children are more at risk than non-maltreated children for poor anger modulation (Beeghly & Cicchetti, 1994), increased rule violations, oppositionalism, and delinquency (Flisher et al., 1997; Malinosky-Rummell & Hansen, 1993; Walker et al., 1989). They are more likely to commit property offenses and be arrested, and more likely to drink, use drugs, and smoke cigarettes (Gelles & Straus, 1990; Kaplan, Pelcovitz, Salzinger, Mandel, & Weiner, 1998). Moreover, they are more likely than non-maltreated children to commit a serious antisocial act (Lewis, Lovely, Yeager, & Femina, 1989; C. S. Widom, 1989).

Long-Term Consequences

In the long term, people with histories of childhood physical maltreatment have been shown to have problems in their financial, social, emotional, marital, and behavioral functioning. Again, the most researched forms of long-term effects have been aggressive and other antisocial acts. These studies indicate that people with histories of childhood physical maltreatment are at increased risk for being arrested for a violent crime and for being chronically involved in criminal behavior (Widom, 1989). They are also more likely to enter prostitution (Widom & Kuhns, 1996) and engage in other sexual risk taking behaviors (Herrenkohl et al., 1998). Both women and men with histories of childhood physical maltreatment may also abuse drugs and alcohol, although the association is stronger in women than in men (Langeland & Hartgers, 1998). Both men and women are at higher risk for being diagnosed with antisocial personality disorder (Luntz & Widom, 1994). Antisocial behavior tends to spill over into family life: People with histories of childhood physical maltreatment are at increased risk for physically maltreating their children and significant others (e.g., Coohey & Braun, 1997; Kalmuss, 1984; Kaufman & Zigler, 1987; Marshall & Rose, 1990; Straus & Smith, 1990; Widom, 1989). In addition, they are at increased risk for becoming the victim of intimate partner violence (e.g., Cappell & Heiner, 1990). Which of these outcomes are descriptive of Peter, Jacinta's father?

People with histories of childhood physical maltreatment may have other problems in their lives that have nothing to do with the perpetration of aggressive behavior. For instance, adult survivors of child physical maltreatment may have lower intelligence and reading ability than their non-maltreated counterparts (Perez & Widom, 1994). They may also be at increased risk for health problems (Lesserman et al., 1997), including chronic pain (Goldberg, Pachas, & Keith, 1999). In a 17-year longitudinal study of a community sample, people who had been physically maltreated were at an increased risk for depressive and anxious symptoms, emotional-behavior problems, and suicidal ideation and attempts (Silverman, Reinherz, & Giaconia, 1996). Longitudinal studies also show increased risks for personality disorders, major depressive disorder, dysthymia, and PTSD (Cohen, Brown, & Smailes, 2001; Horwitz, Widom, McLaughlin, & White, 2001; C. Widom, 1999); however, some of these associations largely disappear after other stressful life events are considered (Horwitz et al., 2001). Given findings such as these, would you want to see Jacinta receive mental health services in foster care?

Special Issue: Corporal Punishment

Although all of the above studies have been concerned with the consequences of what many call physical "abuse," several researchers have pointed out that physical disciplinary practices need not be labeled abusive in order for them to have negative consequences (e.g., Straus, 1994, 2011). Corporal punishment (i.e., spanking) is viewed by some researchers (e.g., Baumrind, 1997) as an effective and desirable method of raising children. The public tends to agree with this assertion; close to 95% of parents have used physical discipline on their children at some point in time (Straus & Stewart, 1999), on average three times per week (Giles-Sims, Straus, & Sugarman, 1995). Although parents usually use corporal punishment when their children are under the age of three, nearly 25% of 16-year-olds were found to be subject to corporal punishment by their parents (Straus & Stewart, 1999).

Straus (2011) has argued that even this socially approved form of discipline can have long-lasting negative effects because it teaches children that violence is an appropriate way of dealing with problems and weakens the child's bond with the parents. In a meta-analysis of corporal punishment and its associated child behaviors, Gershoff (2002) concluded that corporal punishment is strongly associated with many negative behaviors, including less moral internalization; more aggression; more delinquent, criminal, and antisocial behavior; poorer quality of parent-child relationship; poorer mental health; greater likelihood of abusing one's own spouse or child; and greater likelihood of being a victim of physical abuse by the parent. These effects were greatest for middle school children. Moreover, the association between corporal punishment and aggressive or antisocial behavior was stronger for boys than for girls. Finally, the association between corporal punishment and aggression became increasingly stronger as the age of the children increased.

Although the results of Gershoff's (2002) meta-analysis are strong and striking, she pointed out several limitations inherent in her analysis. First, all of the studies reviewed were correlational; thus, corporal punishment may not *cause* the negative outcomes. The direction of causation could be reversed, or some third variables, such as inconsistent parenting style may be causing both the corporal punishment and the poor outcomes. Furthermore, her study does not give any indication as to which conditions may make these negative outcomes more likely. Not all children will display these negative behaviors, but the exact combination of factors that produce each outcome still needs to be discovered.

Straus (2011) provides some further analysis and counterpoints to the limitations that Gershoff (2002) mentioned. He analyzed the correlation/causation issue in several ways. For example, although child misbehavior was influential in predicting whether a parent would use spanking, it predicted only 9% of the variation in spanking behavior, whereas parents' approval of corporal punishment was a much stronger predictor (Winstock & Straus, 2011). Moreover, longitudinal studies show that children who were not spanked improved their behavior over a two-year time period, whereas those who were spanked got worse (e.g., Straus, Sugarman, & Giles-Sims, 1997). Other analyses showed that the effects of spanking on antisocial behavior in children remained whether the spanking was done in a context of positive or negative parenting (Straus, 2011). Finally, Straus presented some new data that showed that spanking even had a significant negative influence on the development of intelligence—the more spanking the children experienced, the lower their IQ four years later (Straus & Paschall, 2009). These authors argued that the mechanisms that link spanking to lower IQ included the fact that parents who spank do less explaining, which leads to a smaller vocabulary in children, which then leads to a lower IQ. Straus (2011) argues that based on available data, by eliminating spanking as a parenting practice, we could reduce antisocial behavior by 1.54 million cases—a ten times greater reduction than would be achieved by reducing physical abuse alone—and overall, we would have better behaved children, be better parents, have less physical abuse, less delinquency, less crime, less partner violence, and children who are less depressed, do better in school, and ultimately achieve better economically in the future.

Do these results on the possible consequences of corporal punishment influence your views on whether it should be considered a form of maltreatment? Do you think that, as discussed in the section on macrosystem influences, the cumulative impact of corporal punishment on the social and psychological health of this country could be worse than that of physical child abuse? Why or why not? Could eliminating corporal punishment and other forms of "minor" aggression against children result in reduced social ills?

Prevention and Intervention in Child Maltreatment

In considering the community response to child maltreatment, we begin by discussing the history and laws that led to prevention and intervention programs being implemented in the first place. We also discuss how Child Protective Services (CPS) generally work, and consider some of the special issues related to the criminalization of child maltreatment. We then end by giving considerable attention to programs that have been designed to prevent child maltreatment in general, and child physical maltreatment in particular.

Child Abuse Laws and CPS Procedures

In 1962, following publication of the landmark work by Kempe and colleagues on the battered child, the U.S. Children's Bureau adopted the first laws mandating physicians to report any known cases of child abuse to social service agencies. The logic behind the laws was that because children are often not able to speak for or defend themselves, professionals who deal with children have the obligation to protect them from abuse. If physicians report any child maltreatment cases they see to social service agencies, appropriate services and protection could be offered to these children and their families. Within five years, all states had passed child abuse reporting laws for physicians, and care was taken to ensure that any professionals reporting such cases would be exempt from civil or criminal liability (Davidson, 1988; Nelson, 1984; Zellman & Fair, 2002).

As research into child maltreatment expanded, an increased understanding of the problem led to a broader definition of acts constituting child abuse; by the 1970s, sexual maltreatment, emotional maltreatment, and neglect were also included in the definition. In addition, it became evident that several other types of professionals were sometimes in a position to detect child maltreatment. By 1986, virtually every state required that nurses, social workers, other mental health professionals, teachers, and school staff, as well as physicians, be mandated reporters of child abuse (Fraser, 1986; Zellman & Fair, 2002).

Perhaps the most influential child abuse law ever passed in this country was the Child Abuse Prevention and Treatment Act (CAPTA, Public Law 93–247) in 1974. This law freed millions of federal dollars to support state child protection agencies; however, in order to receive this federal funding, the states' child abuse reporting laws had to conform to the federal standards. The states also had to create policies and procedures for reporting and investigating alleged child abuse, and had to offer treatment services for these families. CAPTA also gave states the power to remove children from homes if the children were deemed to be in danger (Myers, 2002; Zellman & Fair, 2002).

In 1980, the federal government passed the Adoption Assistance and Child Welfare Act, which required that states do everything they could (*reasonable effort*) to prevent the removal of children from their families, and to do all they could to reunite children with their families in the event of a removal. In 1997, the government clarified the "reasonable effort" phrase in the Adoption and Safe Families Act: "in making reasonable efforts, the child's health and safety shall be of paramount concern" (42 U.S. Code § 671(a)(15)(A)) (Myers, 2002, p. 306). In February 2001, President Bush called for a $200 million increase in funding for the Promoting Safe and Stable Families program. This funding was to be used for helping states to ensure the safety of abused children by enabling them to be quickly adopted into safe, stable homes when efforts to keep the family together had failed (Carter, 2001). Later in 2001, Congress reauthorized the Promoting Safe and Stable Families (PSSF) program (P.L. 107–133), including the additional money requested by the president (Child Welfare League of America, 2001). Under the federal regulations, the job of CPS is to receive incoming calls concerning potential child abuse cases, investigate these cases, deem if abuse has occurred, and then take appropriate action. CPS workers tend to collaborate with local law enforcement and other child professionals in medicine, mental health, education, and law to determine what the appropriate action should be. Most cases do not go to court unless the maltreatment is very serious, probably because the U.S. Supreme Court declared in 1987, "child abuse is one of the most difficult crimes to detect and prosecute, in large part because there often are no witnesses except the victim" (*Pennsylvania v. Ritchie*, 1987, p. 60). Therefore, the majority of cases are referred for tertiary intervention (Myers, 2002).

The Processing of Child Maltreatment Cases

Although all states have laws concerning the reporting of child maltreatment, there are no common guidelines for assessment, substantiation, and processing of these cases; however, in general, reports that are substantiated by the state's CPS agency are referred to juvenile rather than criminal courts. The hearings are dependency hearings designed to determine the extent to which the child is safe in the family home rather than to determine the guilt of a parent. In rare cases, typically sexual maltreatment cases, where there is also a goal of punishing the perpetrator rather than merely protecting the child, the case may go to criminal court (DePanfilis, 2011).

Cases typically go through seven steps. First is intake and screening. Calls regarding suspected cases of child maltreatment are usually made to a state hotline or local CPS program, and the CPS worker asks certain questions to determine whether the case meets guidelines for child maltreatment and/or the urgency with which CPS should respond. If a response is necessary, it is typically made within 24 hours for high urgency cases, and between 24 hours and 2 weeks for less urgent cases (DePanfilis, 2011), with an average response time of 2.9 days in 2009 (USDHHS, 2010).

The initial assessment or investigation is the second step. This step is typically done by a CPS worker alone or in conjunction with law enforcement or another community service provider (although if only an assessment is done, this is sometimes done alone by a community service provider). Interviews are conducted with the child, siblings, parents, other caregivers, and any others who may have information regarding the alleged maltreatment. Child safety is assessed to determine whether the child is in immediate danger of serious harm, and if so, immediate steps are taken to ensure the child's safety, such as out-of-home placement. The likelihood of future maltreatment is also formally assessed in order to help develop a service plan (DePanfilis, 2011).

For families that continue with services, the third step is conducting a family assessment. The CPS worker conducts a thorough family assessment to identify, consider, and weigh factors that affect the child's safety and well-being. The family's strengths, risks, and needs are evaluated, and these all help to determine the fourth step: service planning. At this step, ideally, the correct mix of services, intervention, and treatments are tailored for the child and family. At the fifth step, the services are provided, and it is the responsibility of CPS to arrange, provide, and coordinate the services for the child and family. More and more, states are working toward making sure that evidence-based practices are used at this step (DePanfilis, 2011).

The sixth and seventh steps involve the continued evaluation of the child and family's progress and case closure. At step six, progress is evaluated on a regular basis, ideally every 3 months, to make certain that the child is safe and the family is achieving desired outcomes, goals, and tasks. If the families have achieved the desired outcomes and goals and the effects of maltreatment have been addressed, then the child is determined to be safe and the family's case is closed by CPS. Sometimes, however, cases are closed because the family discontinues services and CPS does not have the legal authority to refer the case to juvenile court (DePanfilis, 2011).

Unfortunately, the social service and criminal justice systems are flawed. When the child abuse laws were first enacted back in the 1960s, it was thought that maltreatment of children was very rare and that prevention would be a low-cost venture (Nelson, 1984). However, it soon became clear that the vast numbers of child abuse referrals were overwhelming for CPS agencies short on funds, staff, and time. In reaction to the unmanageable caseloads, CPS agencies have been forced to narrow their definitions of abuse so that only the most serious cases get attention. Unfortunately, this process means that many families needing services fall through the cracks of the system because the abuse is just not severe enough to receive CPS attention (Zellman & Fair, 2002).

Recently, as part of child welfare reform, several states have enacted what are variously called dual track, alternative response, or multiple track systems. Such systems allow CPS agencies to accept certain reports of child maltreatment without formally logging them as a CPS report that must be investigated (Shusterman, Hollinshead, Fluke, & Yuan, 2005). If the case is severe, an investigation—perhaps in conjunction with law enforcement—will be conducted. However, if the case is less severe, an investigation will not be conducted; rather, a comprehensive assessment will be done to determine an appropriate match with community services (Goldman &

Salus, 2003). As a result of such dual track systems, anywhere between 20% (Oklahoma) to 71% (New Jersey) of reports of child maltreatment are diverted to this type of alternative response, with the cases reflecting less immediate safety concerns more likely to generate an alternative response and cases of child sexual abuse more likely to generate an investigation (Shusterman et al., 2005).

Because CPS is so overwhelmed in their caseloads, many "mandated" reporters have chosen not to report certain cases of child abuse. This fact is evident in the fourth National Incidence Study (NIS-4), which collected data from both CPS agencies and professionals who dealt with children. The NIS-4 revealed that in 2005–2006, only 32% of abused children under the Harm Standard and 43% of abused children under the Endangerment Standard received CPS attention. These percentages represent an increase from the previous NIS study; however, it is unknown whether these figures are attributable to the majority of maltreated children not being investigated because they are being screened out by CPS, or because possible cases are not being reported by mandated professionals to the designated authorities (Sedlak et al., 2010). It is likely to be a combination of these two factors; thus, it is worth understanding why some mandated reporters may not report to CPS when they suspect a child is being maltreated.

Zellman and Fair (2002) conducted a study to determine how many professionals failed to report cases and why. They found that 40% of mandated reporters decided not to report a case of suspected child abuse at some point in their careers. Child psychiatrists were the professionals most likely *not* to report a case of suspected child abuse. Their main reason was their belief that reporting would not help the child or family because it would not help them see the seriousness of the problem or stop the maltreatment. Professionals who failed to report were also concerned that a report would disrupt the treatment of their client and/or family, and some believed they could help the family better than the CPS agency. Many respondents believed that in some cases, reports to CPS agencies would only hurt matters, not help them—especially the more mild cases of maltreatment that would probably be screened out by CPS agencies anyway. Moreover, reporting such cases to CPS would carry a risk that the family would terminate treatment, and therefore, even the child professional would not be able to monitor the child's safety (Zellman & Fair, 2002).

The study by Zellman and Fair adds to the considerable evidence that the CPS system is overburdened and unable to carry out the goals imposed by law. Child professionals realize this fact and are therefore less likely to report certain types of maltreatment to the authorities, even when they are legally mandated to do so. One implication of this practice is that if child abuse is not reported to the authorities, then appropriate statistics on the extent of this problem cannot be obtained, and funding may consequently be cut (Finkelhor, 2005). However, overreporting of abuse may also be a problem. According to Besharov (2005), requiring professionals and encouraging laypeople to report "suspected" cases of abuse is part of what overburdens the system; too much time is spent investigating cases of unfounded maltreatment, and victims who truly need help are being ignored because there are simply not enough resources to find and help them. What do you think? Does it seem likely that overreporting is what interferes most with the process of protecting children from abuse, or is underreporting the more likely problem? Or could both underreporting and overreporting be problems? What are the implications of these problems? What can be done to solve them?

Prevention and Intervention Programs

Over the past 40 years, hundreds of child abuse prevention programs have been implemented with the goals of improving parenting skills and knowledge, increasing social supports, and altering child-rearing norms (Daro & Connelly, 2002). Generally, these prevention and intervention programs fall under three types: primary, secondary, and tertiary. *Primary prevention programs* are programs aimed at the general population, usually in the form of media campaigns, with the goal of educating the public about the nature of the problem and ways to prevent it. *Secondary prevention programs* are more focused: They tend to target populations at high risk for abusing their children. These programs are designed to increase parents' child-rearing skills and knowledge so that abuse may be prevented *before* it begins. *Tertiary prevention programs,* which in comparison to primary and secondary prevention receive the lion's share of funding in this country, are aimed at families that have come to the attention of CPS because they have already experienced abuse. These families are either referred for services by CPS or ordered by the courts to get help to ensure the safety of the child. The tertiary programs generally assess the families' strengths, weaknesses, and needs, so that an appropriate intervention can be set up to address the child's individual needs and safety (Harrington & Dubowitz, 1999; USDHHS, 2001). These programs are usually offered not only for the problem of physical abuse, but also for all the other types of child maltreatment. In the following sections, we discuss each type of program and evidence regarding the extent to which they actually achieve the goal of preventing child physical abuse.

Primary Prevention

Primary prevention programs for child physical maltreatment were popular in the 1970s and 1980s, and came in the form of public service announcements on television and radio, and news coverage of the most egregious cases of child abuse (Daro & Connelly, 2002). Research on these programs in those early years—specifically between 1975 and 1985—showed that public recognition of child maltreatment as a public safety issue increased from 10% to 90%, and that there was a steady reduction in the use of corporal punishment and verbal maltreatment among parents (Daro & Gelles, 1992). Furthermore, by providing information on how to get help, they educated adults as to how they can assist children who are severely abused in their neighborhood (Daro, 1991).

The shaken baby syndrome public awareness campaign is the most thoroughly evaluated of these primary prevention campaigns. One program, tested in eight counties in western New York, provided information on shaken baby syndrome to all parents of newborns at hospitals in those counties. This program showed high retention rates of information among the parents and a 47% reduction in the rates of abusive head injuries among infants in those counties (Dias et al., 2005).

Similarly, the *Period of Purple Crying* program, which helped parents understand and cope with normal infant crying, showed that in comparison to mothers who did not participate in the program, mothers who went through the program were more likely to walk away from a situation in which an infant was inconsolably crying (Barr et al., 2009).

Secondary Prevention

Secondary prevention programs are those aimed at parents who are deemed to be at greatest risk for abusing their children. These programs often target pregnant women or women with young children whose circumstances match those of parents who have abused their children. The most popular type of secondary prevention programs comes in the form of home visiting. The six most common programs serve 550,000 children each year in the United States (Gomby, 2005).

The most widely cited home visitation project was conducted in Elmira, New York (Olds et al., 1997; Olds, Henderson, Chamberlin, & Tatelbaum, 1986). The purpose of this study was to investigate whether intensive nurse home visitation was an effective way of preventing abuse by mothers considered to be at high risk (i.e., poor, unmarried teenagers). The mothers were recruited before the birth of their first child. One group was offered the intensive nurse home visitation program during pregnancy and the first two years of the child's life, in addition to the developmental screenings and transportation to prenatal and well-child care that the other groups were given. The early reports showed that only 4% of the high-risk mothers in the intensive home visitation program abused their children, compared to 19% of the other high-risk mothers. These short-term benefits seemed to be sustained; 15 years later, the mothers who had received the home visitation still had lower rates of child abuse (Olds et al., 1997; Olds et al., 1986).

Home visitation programs are thought to work because they prevent the problem of maltreatment before it has the chance to occur. Mothers who are pregnant or just starting to parent are less likely to be offended by someone providing guidance in child care than mothers who have been reported for abuse. Moreover, by coming into the privacy of the parents' homes, the service provider is able to evaluate and make changes in the home environment and work with the parents at attaining healthy interactions with their children. In addition, they are able to educate the parents about appropriate child-rearing techniques and child development on a flexible schedule (Daro & Connelly, 2002).

Other home visitation programs have shown similar successes. For instance, in the Healthy Start Program in Hawaii, which also recruited high-risk mothers, no child abuse was reported in 99% of the program families. This rate was significantly different from that of the high-risk families not enrolled in the program. Moreover, at two years of age, the children in the program had more positive developmental outcomes and improved health status in comparison to the controls (Wallach & Lister, 1995). The success of this program led to the development of a national program disseminated by the National Committee to Prevent Child Abuse and Neglect entitled Healthy Families America (HFA) (Wallach & Lister, 1995). As Daro and Harding (1999) found in their analysis of 29 evaluations of HFA:

Healthy Families America (HFA) home visitation programs documented notable change among participant families, particularly in the area of parent-child interaction and parental capacity. Most families receiving these services appear better able to care for their children; access and effectively use health care services; resolve many of the personal and familial problems common among low-income, single-parent families; and avoid the most intrusive intervention into their parenting, namely, being reported for child abuse and neglect. (Daro & Connelly, 2002, p. 436)

Later evaluations of 60 (Sweet & Appelbaum, 2004) and 43 (Geeraert, Van den Noorgate, Grietens, & Onghena, 2004) home visiting programs have shown significant reductions in child abuse reports and injuries to children. These programs seem to work best when mothers are enrolled during their pregnancies (DuMont et al., 2008), when delivered by nurses rather than paraprofessionals (Olds et al., 2002), and when partnered with other early interventions and specialized supports (e.g., Ammerman et al., 2009). To date, more than 40 states have invested in quality home visitation programs (Johnson, 2009).

Tertiary Prevention

Tertiary programs, aimed at preventing re-abuse in families already substantiated for abuse, are the most common type of prevention/intervention services. According to the USDHHS (2010), approximately 60% of child maltreatment victims—or about 594,000 children—received tertiary prevention services in 2009. This means that a sizable minority of child abuse victims do not receive tertiary services, even though their cases were substantiated. Consider the case of Kayla at the beginning of this chapter. She was one of the children who never received any tertiary prevention. What were the ultimate consequences for her lack of services? Do you think service intervention could have prevented her death?

It is not quite clear how policies within each state's social service agencies influence which children get the needed care (Kolko, Seleyo, & Brown, 1999), but several factors have been identified in earlier reports of the USDHHS (e.g., 2001). Consider which of these factors may have been present in Kayla's case. In comparison to their respective counterparts, victims were more likely to receive services if they (1) had multiple forms of maltreatment; (2) were physically abused or neglected (i.e., not sexually abused); (3) had a prior history of maltreatment; (4) were non-White or non-Hispanic; (5) were reported by medical personnel rather than social or mental health professionals; (6) were under the age of four; and (7) were maltreated by their mothers. Many of these families have long histories of multiple forms of maltreatment, and dysfunctional methods of dealing with stress have been firmly established within the family relationships (Browne & Herbert, 1997). Moreover, because these are the most severe cases, many of these families are also characterized by severe depression, substance abuse, and interparental violence (Daro & Cohn, 1988). What are the implications of these findings? How might their situations affect their willingness and ability to receive help?

Because substantiated cases are generally from the most violent families with the most dysfunction, these families are the least likely to show improvements in treatment. Often, there is no change in behavior, no matter how much treatment they receive (Ayoub, Willett, & Robinson, 1992; Willett, Ayoub, & Robinson, 1991). Approximately one third of families receiving tertiary services and half of service completers have a recurrence of abuse (Malinosky-Rummell, Ellis, Warner, Ujcich, Carr, & Hansen, 1991). In addition, tertiary programs are characterized by problems with initial engagement and compliance and high dropout rates (Cohn & Daro, 1987). Up to 66% of families receiving these tertiary services drop out before completion (Warner, Malinosky-Rummell, Ellis, & Hansen, 1990). Telephone and in-person engagement tends to increase attendance and completion rates (e.g., McKay, Stoewe, McCadam, & Gonzales, 1998), and some programs are trying strategies such as motivational enhancement sessions (e.g., Chaffin et al., 2004) and increasing cultural sensitivity (e.g., Baumann & Kolko, 2005).

Most tertiary programs are neither comprehensive nor built on an integrative conceptual framework (Daro & Connelly, 2002). Many of these programs focus on the parents; their aim is to teach abusive parents alternative techniques for raising their children. Almost a million families in the United States each year participate in parent training programs, most often as a result of CPS involvement (Barth et al., 2005; Johnson et al., 2008). This is the primary intervention that child welfare services relies on, and the parents' clearance from the child welfare system or reunification with their children is typically contingent on their completion of such training (Barth et al., 2005). Such programs are typically completed in 6 to 10 sessions, and may be somewhat successful immediately following their completion. However, the long-term success of parent training programs is questionable because the sessions all take place within an office setting, there are few sessions, and the training relies solely on a group format with no individualized treatment (Johnson et al., 2008).

Overall, the parent training programs that are relied on heavily by CPS have little evidence to show that they either improve parenting or decrease child maltreatment (Barth et al., 2005). Some reasons why such programs may not be beneficial are that:

- They do not consider the multiple problems that families involved in child welfare may have, including substance abuse, intimate partner violence, serious mental health problems, and trauma, all of which have substantial influences on the ability of a person to parent.
- Parents who are still with their children are combined in one group setting with parents whose children are in out-of-home care, even though the two sets of parents have very different levels of functioning, needs, motivations, and expectations.
- There is no assessment of the individual needs of each family.
- There is no flexibility in the content or length of the program.
- There is no in-home, reality-based training.
- Parents of children of varying ages are grouped together in one group, even though children of different ages require different parenting techniques. (Barth et al., 2005)

Experts argue that instead of offering a generic short-term parent training program to almost every family in the child welfare system, it would be better to assess each family and offer more intensive programming only to families that really need it (Barth et al., 2005).

One such program that has helped some abusive parents and families improve in functioning is Project SafeCare, which addresses the behavioral deficiencies of abusive parents (Gershater-Molko, Lutzker, & Welsh, 2003). Some programs also specifically address the needs of the abused child, who most likely will have therapeutic needs following abusive episodes. Two types of programs have been shown to help abused children. First, therapeutic day programs, which offer developmentally appropriate and therapeutic activities, have led to improved intellectual and language abilities in abused children at a one-year follow-up (Oates & Bross, 1995). Also, an intensive, group-based treatment program for abused children designed to offer supportive peer relationships to abused children and help them recognize their feelings through play, speech, and physical therapy, led to increased cognitive functioning, peer acceptance, maternal acceptance, and developmental skills (Culp, Little, Letts, & Lawrence, 1991).

Some experts argue that focusing only on the parent or only on the child in a treatment program is shortsighted because there tends to be an ongoing, negative, and hostile relationship between the child and parent that needs to be addressed at the family level. As Runyon and Urquiza (2011) argue, "effective treatment needs to address: (1) parenting skills, (2) distorted cognitions/attributions, (3) development of adaptive and nonviolent coping strategies, and (4) development of greater affective regulation" (p. 197). They point toward three programs—Parent-Child Interaction Therapy (PCIT), Alternatives for Families (AF-CBT), and Combined Parent-Child Cognitive Behavioral Therapy (CPC-CBT)—all of which include both the parent and the child and use a cognitive-behavioral therapy (CBT) framework. A CBT framework for child maltreatment evaluates the antecedents and consequences of physical abuse and other more adaptive forms of parent-child interactions, and tends to have three foci: (1) teaching parents various cognitive, affective, and behavioral skills to help them manage their emotions when faced with stressful situations, (2) teaching children a variety of healthy coping skills to help them cope with their past abusive experiences and any future life stressors, and (3) helping both parents and children work together to create a safety plan for when stressful events occur (Runyon & Urquiza, 2011).

PCIT has shown reductions in child problem behaviors and improvements in their compliance, and lower rates of physical maltreatment among the parents, along with improved parent-child interactions (Timmer, Urquiza, Zebell, & McGrath, 2005). AF-CBT has shown evidence of improvements in the parent-child relationship—for example, there was more family cohesion and less conflict, physical abuse, and parental distress at a one-year follow-up (Kolko, 1996). Finally, CPC-CBT has shown reductions in parents' anger and use of physical punishment, and reductions in child behavioral problems and PTSD symptoms (Runyon et al., 2009).

Because a primary goal of CPS is family reunification, one of the major initiatives of CPS agencies is intensive family preservation programs. Intensive family preservation programs are short-term intensive and supportive intervention programs for the parents and children, either in their home or another location that is familiar to the child. The focus tends to be on anger management, stress reduction, and instruction of child development and parenting skills. However, overall, evaluations of such programs show that they are ineffective in protecting children, reducing out-of-home placement, or improving parental behavior (Gelles, 2000; Lindsey, Martin, & Doh, 2002; USDHHS, 2002). Thus, many experts argue that family reunification should no longer be the primary goal of CPS (e.g., Gelles, 2005).

Because not all suspected cases of maltreatment are reported to or even investigated by CPS and the empirically supported treatment programs discussed above are not available to all CPS agencies, it means that even though we have programs available to help abused children and their families, the majority of abused children and their families will not receive any services at all or any kind of treatment that can actually help them. What is the impact of the lack of services on the future of these children and the future of child abuse in this country? What are the costs of child abuse and insufficient or ineffective services to society as a whole?

Summary

In sum, it is difficult to ascertain exactly how many children in this country are physically maltreated each year. Self-report statistics suggest that nearly 5% sustain severe physical violence in any given year, and official statistics from CPS agencies suggest that only a minority of these children are referred for state intervention. In addition, only a fraction of the families who are reported for child physical abuse receive any services from the state. Thus, millions of children each year are being physically maltreated by their parents and yet receive no help, as was the case with Kayla, the young girl who died at the hands of her father even though her case was reported to the state. The short- and long-term consequences for these children can be debilitating, and some researchers provide evidence that even minor physical maltreatment, in the form of corporal punishment, can also lead to maladjustment. It is imperative that we encourage parents to use nonphysical means to discipline their children; that we encourage those who are physically maltreating their children to get help; and that we also ensure that the children who are physically maltreated get the help they need. Existing research into the various predictors of child physical maltreatment shows that we have substantial knowledge concerning which families and children are most at risk for abuse. These risk factors come at every level of the ecological model, and thus, we have the knowledge to target and refine our prevention and intervention efforts to those who need it most.

Discussion Questions

1. Why do some cases of child physical maltreatment get lost within the system? Is there anything that can be done to prevent cases from becoming lost?

2. Many studies have shown that rates of child physical maltreatment have declined within the past 10 to 15 years. What are some reasons for this decline?

3. Discuss ways to prevent victims of child physical maltreatment from suffering from psychological injuries.

4. Studies have shown that physical punishment (i.e., spanking) of children causes long-term consequences such as delinquency, lower IQ, and behavioral problems. Do you believe that eliminating physical punishment of children would benefit society? Why or why not?

5. Although there are numerous laws that require physicians, teachers, social workers, and others who work with children to be mandated reporters, we still have many cases of child abuse that are never reported. Why?

6. How can prevention programs protect children from maltreatment in generations to come? How would they affect CPS agencies? What are some prevention and intervention programs that help reduce child abuse? What other approaches can you think of that might help prevent child abuse?

7. How can treatment that focuses only on the victim of maltreatment both benefit and harm the child victim? What about treatment that focuses only on the parents?

8. Discuss how intensive family preservation programs can help victims of child abuse. Are there ways these programs may harm the victim and/or the family?

9. The short- and long-term consequences for victims of child physical maltreatment can be debilitating, and some researchers suggest that even minor physical abuse, in the form of corporal punishment, can also lead to maladjustment. What are some ways we can encourage families not to use physical punishment to discipline children?

3

Child Sexual Maltreatment

A good man leans his weight upon my back, breathes in my ear, wraps his arm in affection high on my chest, near my neck. He means well, and whispers words of healing neither he [n]or I have ever heard said to us. "I'm glad you're here, son. I'm glad you're a boy." Memory floods and overwhelms me, rushing me back to a bedroom of a tenement on the South Side of Chicago . . . My father's arm is tight across my throat, arching my back. He is exhaling hard, in rhythm, as he shows me why he is glad I am his son. Twenty years since I found his body, dead by his hand. I rage that he is not alive today, so I could strangle him with my own hands. I hunger for a dish of vengeance, a repast of revenge . . . My predatory, molesting grandmother died in her sleep. The neighbor lady, at 32, seduced me at 14. Two months later, she ate a .22. The coach who groomed me drowned in alcohol. The apostate priest who raped me now lives down south, troubled only by the knowledge that his secret is broken. My mother . . . lives a mile from me. She shares a dilapidated apartment with my brother. He is forty years old, and still lives with her. He has never married. She has never remarried. No need to. She raised her sons to be her husbands. None of these baby-raping monsters will ever spend a day behind bars. None will pay a penny of recompense. None will know the thump of my fist, the crack of my boot . . . I have not been avenged. I shall never be avenged. Vengeance is the Lord's . . . I hope. But it is my experience that He leaves justice to mere mortals, and His servants have done a lousy job (Abraham, 1997, pp. 1–3).

This extreme example of child sexual abuse (CSA) described by the victim, Scott, portrays the myriad perpetrators who have been known to victimize children sexually. Scott was sexually maltreated by his father, mother, grandmother, a neighbor, a priest, and a coach. In addition to these perpetrators, other family members such as grandfathers, uncles, aunts, and siblings have all been implicated in the sexual maltreatment of both girls and boys. The current chapter deals solely with the sexual maltreatment of children by adult family members, but the majority deals primarily with the most-researched type of CSA: father-daughter incest. However, we also give consideration to other types of incest, including incest perpetrated by mothers and sustained by boys.

Consider Scott's case. From what consequences, both physical and psychological, do you think he suffers as an adult? He was probably first sexually victimized by his parents and grandmother, and later by a neighbor, priest, and coach. Do you think this pattern of revictimization might be common among survivors of CSA? Why? Scott is very angry because his perpetrators were never held responsible for what they did to him. Sexual maltreatment, in some instances, can leave physical evidence (e.g., sexually transmitted diseases, pregnancy, physical injuries such as vaginal or anal tears), but it is often less detectable than physical maltreatment, in part because the child victims may not reveal the evidence. How often do you think children are willing to reveal their maltreatment, and how often do you think they are believed? What particular circumstances would dictate both the disclosure of CSA and whether or not the child victims are believed? With the possible exception of the priest, Scott's abusers were never held accountable, and in the case of his mother, it seems as if the incest is ongoing. Perhaps one of the reasons his perpetrators were never prosecuted was because the CSA occurred at a time when people did not discuss or even acknowledge that the problem existed. How often do you think child sexual abusers are held accountable these days? What circumstances do you think mitigate whether they are held accountable? The questions posed here are among the issues we discuss in this chapter. Think about your answers to these questions as you read the sections on the prevalence, predictors, and consequences of CSA, and approaches to intervention.

Scope of the Problem

Before we discuss the incidence and rates of CSA by family members, it is important to define exactly what CSA is. This is not easy, as researchers have been unable to formulate a consistent definition. Most studies have, as one criterion for judging sexual acts as abusive, an arbitrary age difference of at least five years between the victim and perpetrator (e.g., Finkelhor, 1979); however, this criterion does not take into consideration that siblings with less of an age discrepancy can be perpetrators of sexual abuse. Furthermore, there is no consensus on what acts constitute abuse. Sometimes *noncontact* acts such as voyeurism, exhibitionism, and exposure to pornography are included in operational definitions (i.e., measures) of sexual abuse, which leads to very high incidence rates. If only *contact* sexual abuse is included (e.g., fondling; oral, anal, vaginal intercourse), rates are lower. Most studies do not specify the frequency or duration of sexual contact necessary for it to be considered abuse, although many workers indicate that just one instance of sexual contact (or noncontact) is enough to label an act abusive. When we consider the causes and consequences of CSA, a child intentionally exposed once to pornography is going to differ dramatically from the children who experienced the abuse described in Box 3.1.

| Box 3.1 | Case of Child Sexual Maltreatment |

The sexual maltreatment of Ann and Marie by their father began around the same time, when Ann was five and Marie was four. At the time of their evaluation by a psychologist, both were adolescents, and Marie was the one who had reported the maltreatment. Ann had mixed feelings about the fact that Marie had disclosed the maltreatment—she was happy that at least now the maltreatment would stop because her father would get help, but she was also upset that her father was in trouble.

Ann reported that, most commonly, her father would fondle her in the breast area and between the legs. At different stages of her life, he would perform different sexual acts on her, which she and Marie would discuss on occasion. The most extensive abusive act Ann experienced was what the girls called the "full treatment." This consisted of the father's undressing her, fondling her, and lying in bed with her back to his chest. He would roll her around his genital area and touch her on her breasts and vaginal area. During the course of the interview, Ann related many incidents of this type being perpetrated against her, almost on a weekly basis during certain periods of her life … Marie described the same type of fondling as Ann … As Marie got older, the father would perform oral sex on her as well. In describing this, Marie became quite tearful and felt guilty and "dirty" because of this particular abuse. She wondered if it was her fault and if she should be blamed for not stopping her father sooner.

SOURCE: Cohen & Mannarino, 2000, pp. 212–214

Major studies assessing prevalence rates for CSA are summarized in Table 3.1. The first source of data is the official National Child Abuse and Neglect Data System (NCANDS) statistics provided annually to the U.S. Department of Health and Human Services (USDHHS). All states have laws prohibiting the sexual abuse of children (Myers, 1998), but each state has its own definition of what is considered sexual abuse and therefore what is prohibited. Because sexual abuse statutes vary from state to state, the official statistics need to be interpreted with caution. Generally, though, adult sexual contact with a child under the age of 14 is illegal, as is any kind of incest. According to the 2010 NCANDS statistics, 9.2% of all substantiated maltreatment cases were CSA cases, and nationwide 63,527 children were victimized by sexual abuse (USDHHS, 2011). Although these rates of substantiated cases of CSA are high, they reflect a decrease of 62%—from approximately 23 cases per 10,000 children to approximately 8.6 cases per 10,000 children—from 1990 rates (Finkelhor, Jones, & Shattuck, 2011). The majority of perpetrators were relatives of the children because Child Protective Services (CPS) generally does not get involved in cases of extrafamilial child sexual maltreatment (Finkelhor, 1994).

The Fourth National Incidence Study (Sedlak et al., 2010; see Chapter 2), based on child maltreatment cases reported to CPS as well as cases known to community professionals, shows a similar picture of CSA in the United States. According to the Harm Standard, the number of CSA cases declined 38% from 3.8 per 1,000 children in 1993 to 1.8 per 1,000 children in 2005–2006. Similarly, according to the Endangerment Standard, the number of cases declined 40% from 4.5 per 1,000 children

Table 3.1 Prevalence Rates of Child Sexual Maltreatment

Study	Description of Sample	Measures/Definition of Maltreatment	Rates of Maltreatment
U.S. Department of Health and Human Services (2011), *Child Maltreatment 2010*	An estimated 3.3 million referrals, involving the alleged maltreatment of approximately 5.9 million children, in 2010	Cases that have been referred to Child Protective Services (CPS)	• 9.2% of all reported maltreatment cases were CSA cases • Nationwide, 63,527 children were victimized by CSA (8.6 cases per 1,000 children)
Sedlak et al. (2010), Fourth National Incidence Study of Child Abuse and Neglect (2005–2006)	A nationally representative sample of over 10,790 professionals in 1,094 agencies serving 126 counties	• *Harm Standard*—requires that an act or omission result in demonstrable harm in order to be classified as abuse or neglect • *Endangerment Standard*—a sentinel thought that the maltreatment endangered the children or a CPS investigation substantiated or indicated their maltreatment	• *Harm Standard:* 1.8 per 1,000 children in 2005–2006 • *Endangerment Standard:* 2.4 per 1,000 children in 2005–2006 • 37% of the children were abused by their birth parents, 23% by a nonbiological parent or partner, and 40% by some other person
Finkelhor (1994)	Results calculated from 19 studies of data from about 150,000 confirmed cases of CSA reported in the United States to welfare authorities	Determination varies by survey; in most cases using legal terms and definitions of child abuse/sexual abuse/neglect to determine maltreatment of child	• Lifetime CSA rate for women was about 20% to 25% and for men about 5% to 15% • Parents were the perpetrators 6% to 16% of the time, any relative 1/3 of the time • Perpetrators known to child victim 85% to 95% of the time
Finkelhor, Ormrod, & Turner (2009); Finkelhor, Turner, Ormrod, & Hamby (2009)	Population based samples of children and their parents, cross-sectional telephone survey (4,549 children sampled, ages 0 to 17)	Phone interview conducted with parent; if child between 10–17 years old, interview also conducted with child. Used enhanced version of Juvenile Victimization Questionnaire	• Annual incidence of CSA estimated at 6%, and lifetime prevalence at 9%

in 1993 to 2.4 per 1,000 children in 2005–2006. According to NIS-4, cases of CSA were 4 to 5 times more likely to involve girls than boys. Overall, 37% of the children were maltreated by their birth parents, 23% by a nonbiological parent or partner, and 40% by some other person (Sedlak et al., 2010).

Although official statistics are very informative, Finkelhor (2008) points out that most CSA is not reported at the time it occurs; in fact, the majority of CSA is often never reported. In addition, sexual maltreatment perpetrated by a family member is even less likely to be reported to officials than extrafamilial CSA (Hanson, Resnick, Saunders, Kilpatrick, & Best, 1999). Consequently, more accurate sources for an estimate of the prevalence of CSA may be retrospective reports of CSA in nonclinical populations (Berliner & Elliott, 2002). In a review of these studies, a lifetime CSA rate of 20% to 25% for women and 5% to 15% for men was estimated (Finkelhor, 1994). This CSA included both intra- and extrafamilial contact sexual abuse. The age range of victimization was from infancy through 17 years, with a peak age range of 7 to 13 years, and a mean of 9 years. In the general population, parents were the perpetrators 6% to 16% of the time, and any relative was the perpetrator in one third of the cases. Strangers accounted for only 5% to 15% of the cases; thus, 85% to 95% of the perpetrators were known to the child victim (Finkelhor, 1994). Recent surveys on population-based samples of children and their parents estimate a 6% annual incidence of CSA and a lifetime prevalence of 9% (Finkelhor, Ormrod et al., 2009; Finkelhor, Turner et al., 2009). However, because parents were involved in the surveying, this may have lowered the reported rates; indeed, few children reported intrafamilial CSA in these surveys.

These self-reported rates of CSA in nonclinical samples are dramatically lower than rates found in clinical samples. People who seek help from mental health practitioners because of a history of CSA probably have had more severe maltreatment experiences, and the data confirm that supposition. Participants in clinical samples have identified 25% to 33% of CSA perpetrators as parents, and any relative as the perpetrator in half of the cases. Three fourths of the clinical victims experienced multiple episodes of maltreatment, as opposed to approximately 50% in nonclinical samples (Saunders, Kilpatrick, Hanson, Resnick, & Walker, 1999); and in the great majority of the cases, the multiple episodes consisted of completed or attempted oral, anal, and/or vaginal intercourse (Elliott & Briere, 1994; Ruggiero, McLeer, & Dixon, 2000).

In the recent research literature on CSA, more attention is given to girl victims than to boy victims—possibly because, given the likely social stigma and social mores, boys are less likely to report maltreatment and less likely to label what happened to them as an abusive sexual experience. The reported cases do provide some evidence of differences in CSA experiences, based on the gender of the victim. Boys are more likely to be older when their maltreatment begins, to have a nonfamily member as the perpetrator, and to have a woman as their perpetrator (Holmes & Slap, 1998).

Predictors and Correlates

Predictors of intrafamilial CSA exist at every level of the ecological model, as shown below and summarized in Table 3.2. However, it is important to note that although we are able to identify a variety of predictors of CSA, we are unable to predict with much accuracy exactly who will sexually maltreat the children in their families.

Table 3.2   Predictors of Intrafamilial Child Sexual Maltreatment at Each Level of the Ecological Model

Level of the Ecological Model	Specific Predictor	Studies
Macrosystem	Unemployment	Sedlak et al. (2010)
	Low socioeconomic status	Sedlak et al. (2010)
	Indirect link between pornography and sex offending	Simons, Wurtele, & Heil (2002)
Exosystem	Living in rural areas	Sedlak et al. (2010)
	Social isolation	Dadds, Smith, Weber, & Robinson (1991)
Microsystem	Gender (girls)	Finkelhor, Hotaling, Lewis, & Smith (1990); Sedlak et al. (2010); USDHHS (2010)
	Age (7–12 years)	Finkelhor (1993); Ruggiero, McLeer & Dixon (2000); Saunders, Kilpatrick, Hanson, Resnick, & Walker (1999)
	Having a nonbiological father-figure living in the home	Finkelhor (1984); Sedlak et al. (2010)
	Living without natural mother, or having an emotionally unavailable mother	Finkelhor (1984); Finkelhor, Hotaling, Lewis, & Smith (1990)
	Mother's drinking behavior	Vogeltanz et al. (1999)
	Families that are disorganized, disrupted, or dysfunctional in some way	Brown, Cohen, Johnson, & Salzinger (1998); Dadds et al. (1991); Elliott (1994); Fleming, Mullen, & Bammer (1997); Hoagwood & Stewart (1989); McLaughlin et al. (2000); Madonna, VanScoyk, & Jones (1991); Mannarino & Cohen (1996); Mullen, Martin, Anderson, Roman, & Herbison (1993); Mullen, Martin, Anderson, Romans, & Herbison (1994)
	Lack of intimacy between parents, marital problems or instability, and role reversal between mother and daughter	Hubbard (1989); Lang, Langevin, Van Santen, Billingsley, & Wright (1990); Ray, Jackson, & Townsley (1991)

(Continued)

Table 3.2 (Continued)

Level of the Ecological Model	Specific Predictor	Studies
	Natal fathers out of the home frequently or less involved in caregiving	Parker & Parker (1986)
Individual/ Developmental	Gender (male)	Sedlak et al. (2010)
	Psychopathology	Herkov, Gynther, Thomas, & Myers (1996)
	Arrested psychological development	Groth, Hobson, & Gary (1982)
	History of child sexual victimization	Bard et al. (1983); Langevin, Handy, Hook, Day, & Russon (1983); New, Stevenson, & Skuse (1999)
	Masturbation to pornography; negative early sexual experiences; self-reported likelihood of raping a woman	Briere & Runtz (1989)
	Poor social skills	Finkelhor (1984)
	Narcissistic personality disorder, self-centeredness, and lack of empathy for victims	Ganzarain (1992)
	Poor impulse control, multiple major life stressors, alcohol and drug abuse, and psychosis	Cohen et al. (2002); Hermin (1981); Marshall & Norgard (1983); Peugh & Belenko (2001)
	Cognitive distortions	Kubik & Hecker (2005); Segal & Stermac (1990)

Macrosystem

Economic Indicators

According to NIS-4, various economic indicators are risk factors for CSA. For example, the employment status of the parents puts a child at risk, in that the rate of sexual maltreatment of children whose parents were not in the labor force was 3.7 per 1,000 children, which stands in contrast to 0.9 per 1,000 for children of employed parents and 1.1 per 1,000 for children of unemployed parents. Furthermore, children in low socioeconomic status (SES) families (see Chapter 2 for NIS-4's definition of low SES) were about three times more likely to be sexually maltreated than children not in low SES families (Sedlak et al., 2010).

Cultural Values

The sexualization of children in the media and elsewhere, the view of children as property, and male entitlement have all been implicated as providing cultural sanctions for the sexual maltreatment of children (e.g., Russell, 1995), although an empirical link has yet to be established. The availability of child and adult pornography may lead to adult sexual interest in children (Russell, 1995); however, the link between pornography and CSA appears to be indirect at best (Knudsen, 1988). One study showing this indirect link looked at incarcerated sexual offenders; the offenders who reported experiencing sexual abuse as children and early exposure to pornography displayed less empathy toward abused children and had more child victims (Simons, Wurtele, & Heil, 2002). Furthermore, the percentage of pornographic images displaying children and adolescents on the Internet appears to be on the rise (Mehta, 2001), as is the arrest of online child pornography possessors. One longitudinal study shows that in 2000, there were 1,713 arrests for Internet-related possession of child pornography, which increased to 3,672 in 2006 (Wolak, Finkelhor, & Mitchell, 2011).

Exosystem

Children living in rural areas are significantly more likely to be sexually maltreated than children living in urban areas (Sedlak et al., 2010). This finding could be due to the relatively greater social isolation experienced by families in rural areas, and social isolation is a risk factor for CSA (Dadds et al., 1991).

Microsystem

Age and gender are salient predictors of CSA victimization. The mean age of CSA victimization seems to be somewhere between the ages of 7 to 12 years (Finkelhor, 1993; Ruggiero et al., 2000; Saunders et al., 1999), and girls are significantly more likely to be victimized than boys (Finkelhor et al., 1990; Sedlak et al., 2010; USDHHS, 2010). However, male victims are less likely to disclose CSA, which is evident from anonymous self-report surveys that show a higher rate of male victimization than official reporting statistics do (Larson, Terman, Gomby, Quinn, & Behrman, 1994). What do you think contributes to such under-reporting in male CSA victims?

The majority of research on predictors of CSA has focused on the microsystem level, specifically on problems and dynamics within the family and the specific relationship between the perpetrator and the victim. Possibly the most researched family structure implicated in CSA is the stepfamily. Finkelhor (1984) found that a stepfather was five times more likely to sexually maltreat a daughter than a natal father. In addition, girls with stepfathers were more likely to be sexually maltreated by other men than girls who live with both natural parents or only their mother. The NIS-4 report showed that the highest rates of CSA occur among children who lived in homes with stepparents (4.3 per 1,000 children, according to the Harm Standard) or with the cohabiting partner of their biological parent (9.9 per 1,000 children), particularly in comparison to children living with both biological parents (0.5 per 1,000 children)

(Sedlak et al., 2010). Related predictors of intrafamilial CSA are death, imprisonment, hospitalization, abandonment, and divorce of a child's parents (Kim & Kim, 2005).

Relationships with mothers may also play a role in risk for CSA. According to Finkelhor (1984), if a girl ever lived without her natural mother, she is three times more likely to be sexually maltreated than girls who always lived with their mothers. Moreover, if the mothers are perceived as unavailable (e.g., emotionally distant, often ill, or unaffectionate), girls are also at increased risk (Finkelhor, 1984; Finkelhor et al., 1990). Finally, in families in which both biological parents are present, CSA is most likely to occur if the father is a nondrinker but the mother drinks (Vogeltanz et al., 1999); the mother's drinking behavior may lead her to be unavailable to her daughter, which may leave the girl emotionally needy and more vulnerable to the advances of a sexual predator.

In addition to the relationships between the child victim and her parents, other dynamics within the family are also predictive of CSA. Less cohesive families that are disorganized and generally dysfunctional, with perhaps other forms of child maltreatment, are more vulnerable to having a child victimized by sexual maltreatment (Alaggia & Krishenbaum, 2005; Cyr, Wright, McDuff, & Perron, 2002; Elliott, 1994; Kim & Kim, 2005; Madonna, VanScoyk, & Jones, 1991; Mannarino & Cohen, 1996; Mullen, Martin, Anderson, Romans, & Herbison, 1994). These families may also be subject to much disruption, such as parental separation, absence, and conflict, frequent moves (Mullen et al., 1994), and interparental violence (Kellogg & Menard, 2003). Moreover, the parents may be characterized as uncaring, overcontrolling, and rejecting (Fleming, Mullen, & Bammer, 1997; McLaughlin et al., 2000; Mullen et al., 1993). These dysfunctional families have been profiled as headed by a young mother who has had many negative life events and an unwanted pregnancy (Brown, Cohen, Johnson, & Salzinger, 1998); the mother may also have mental health problems (Brown et al., 1998; Fleming et al., 1997). Furthermore, the families may lack emotional closeness, cohesiveness, and flexibility; have problems with communication; and be socially isolated (Alaggia & Krishenbaum, 2005; Dadds et al., 1991; Kim & Kim, 2005).

It is important to note that perpetrators of CSA do not molest every child with whom they come into contact. Rather, they select children who are vulnerable in some way—for example, passive, quiet, shy, unhappy, needy, and/or living in such a home as described above. Once they identify a vulnerable child, predators tend to engage in a grooming process. This grooming process is a gradual process of sexualizing the relationship over time, and consists of a calculated plan for how to approach the child, how to introduce sexual touching and other sexual behaviors into the relationship, how to maintain the child's cooperation, and how to prevent the child from reporting the abuse (Elliott, Browne, & Kilcoyne, 1995). Often, these latter two goals are achieved through bribes, force, threats, or fear (Saunders et al., 1999).

Much research has been done on the types of incest described in Box 3.1: father-daughter incest. As in the case described here, families with father-daughter incest tend to be characterized by very traditional family values. Now read Box 3.2, a clinical description of the family from Box 3.1. What do you notice about this family? What characteristics do they have that may distinguish them from more functional families?

| Box 3.2 | Ann and Marie's Family |

Ann and Marie's family did not interact or communicate in a healthy manner, which allowed the father's sexual abuse of the girls to commence and continue for many years. The family members were overdependent on each other and emotionally enmeshed, such that if something threatened the family's stability, each person's survival was at stake. The family was also characterized by an unhealthy marriage and the parentification of the children (i.e., the children were given adult responsibilities). The family members did not want to confront issues that were threatening to family stability; and therefore, their communication was vague and served to placate issues rather than to constructively resolve problems. Therefore, it is not surprising that Ann and Marie stated that they were afraid of reporting their father's sexual abuse because they feared the family would disintegrate, and thus they also felt an overwhelming sense of responsibility to hold together this dysfunctional family unit. Their mother's attitudes and behaviors contributed as well: She told the girls that she would fully support them during this time, but also stated that she could not choose her daughters over her husband. In other words, she could not support her daughters over her husband. Ann and Marie subsequently began displaying signs of empathy toward their father.

SOURCE: Cohen & Mannarino, 2000

Consistent with the family described in Boxes 3.1 and 3.2, families characterized by father-daughter incest tend to be patriarchal in structure, with the children subservient to the adults (Alaggia & Krishenbaum, 2005; Alexander & Lupfer, 1987; Wealin, Davies, Shaffer, Jackson, & Love, 2002). Role reversal between the mother and daughter is also characteristic of father-daughter incest families (Ray, Jackson, & Townsley, 1991), probably because there is a lack of intimacy between the parents (Hubbard, 1989) and marital problems, marital instability (Lang, Langevin, Van Santen, Billingsley, & Wright, 1990), or intense marital discord (Alaggia & Krishenbaum, 2005). Examples of some marital problems that incest offenders often have include mistrustfulness, lack of mutual friends, lack of shared time together, low mutual give-and-take in disagreements, tendency to not confide in each other, poor quality of sexual relations, and being lonely within the marriage (Lang et al., 1990). Alcohol problems seem to be characteristic of both parents (Nelson et al., 2002).

In father-daughter incest families, there is role and boundary confusion, affective enmeshment, and poor adaptation and problem-solving skills (Hoagwood & Stewart, 1989; Kim & Kim, 2005). When natal fathers are the abusers, they tend to have been out of the home or infrequently in the home during the daughter's first three years. If the abusing natal fathers were in the home during those years, they tended to be less involved in caregiving. Possibly because there was no opportunity for early bonding, there was no insulation from sexual desires for the daughter (Parker & Parker, 1986). In addition, sexual problems between the father and his wife may lead him to seek sex from his daughter as a surrogate source of affection (Ganzarain, 1992).

Individual/Developmental

According to NIS-4 (Sedlak et al., 2010), the majority (87%) of the CSA perpetrators are male; however, the perpetrator is much more likely to be male when the perpetrator is a nonbiological parent (97%) versus a biological parent (80%). Nonetheless, the vast majority of research that has been conducted on the individual/developmental contributions to CSA has been done on male perpetrators. The research that follows has been done solely on male sexual abusers, and we address female sexual maltreatment of children in a later section.

Finkelhor (1984) posed four questions that need to be answered at the individual/developmental level in order for CSA to be understood more fully:

(1) Why does a person find relating sexually to a child emotionally gratifying and congruent?

(2) Why is a person capable of being sexually aroused by a child?

(3) Why is a person blocked in efforts to obtain sexual and emotional gratification from more normatively approved sources?

(4) Why is a person not deterred by conventional social inhibitions from having sexual relationships with a child? (p. 17)

In answer to the first question concerning why a person would find relating sexually to a child emotionally gratifying and congruent, research indicates that incarcerated child sex abusers have higher rates of psychopathology than other incarcerated individuals and that increased psychopathology is associated with increased sexual deviancy (Herkov, Ginther, Thomas, & Myers, 1996). Moreover, the majority of sex offenders develop these deviant sexual interests prior to adulthood (e.g., Abel & Rouleau, 1990; Caldwell, 2002). However, incarcerated child sex abusers represent a very small minority of child sex abusers and probably are not representative of the offenders who are never reported or caught; this latter group probably has fewer detectable psychological abnormalities (Finkelhor, 1984).

It has been suggested that child sexual abusers have arrested psychological development, such that they experience themselves emotionally as children and can therefore relate better to children (Groth, Hobson, & Gary, 1982). However, arrested psychological development does not explain why adults would be sexually aroused by a child. In answer to Question 2, it has been shown that there is more childhood sexual victimization in the backgrounds of child molesters than in several comparison groups (e.g., Bard et al., 1983; Langevin, Handy, Hook, Day, & Russon, 1983), and that the families of child sexual abusers may be characterized by sexual abuse through the generations (New, Stephenson, & Skuse, 1999). This history of CSA is theorized to lead to a sexual interest in children. For example, one theory posits that offenders learned through modeling that people can use children for sexual gratification (e.g., Veneziano, Veneziano, & LeGrand, 2000). However, only about 28% of child sexual abusers report being sexually abused as children, and not all sexually abused children will become child sexual abusers; therefore, the relationship between childhood victimization and adult perpetration does not appear to be straightforward (Hanson & Slater, 1988).

Exposure to child pornography, especially when child sex is mixed with adult sex, may also lead to sexual interest in children. In partial support of this conjecture, Briere and Runtz (1989) found that masturbation to pornography was predictive of college males' sexual interests in children. Among those male students, 21% had experienced some sexual attraction to small children; 9% at some time had fantasies about sex with a child; 5% had masturbated during fantasies about sex with a child; and 7% stated it was at least somewhat likely that they would have sex with a child if there was no likelihood of detection or punishment. Along with masturbation to pornography, variables predicting attraction to children included negative early sexual experiences and self-reported likelihood of raping a woman.

Even if there is a relatively high rate of sexual attraction to children, the variables associated with this attraction do not explain why some men act on it while others do not. In answer to Question 3 as to why some men are unable to get their sexual and emotional needs met in adult relationships, it has been found that child sex abusers tend to be "timid, unassertive, inadequate, awkward, even moralistic types with poor social skills who have an impossible time developing adult social and sexual relationships" (Finkelhor, 1984, p. 43). It has also been suggested that sexual abusers suffer from narcissistic personality disorder, and they display low self-esteem, lack of empathy for their victims, and self-centeredness (Ganzarain, 1992). In addition to these personality traits, some family-level characteristics, such as marital instability, may contribute to the men's inability to gain emotional and sexual satisfaction in adult relationships (Finkelhor, 1984).

Finally, even though all of these characteristics may exist, they do not explain why some men overcome the societal taboos against sex with children and/or incest. Several individual-level factors contribute to this disinhibition, including poor impulse control (e.g., Cohen, Gans et al., 2002), multiple major life stressors (e.g., Hermin, 1981), alcohol and drug abuse (e.g., Peugh & Belenko, 2001), and psychosis (e.g., Marshall & Norgard, 1983). Although poor impulse control and psychosis have been implicated in some cases, alcohol and drug abuse seems to be the disinhibitor in a majority of cases (e.g., Greenfeld, 1996). Another common disinhibitor seems to be cognitive distortions, whereby the offenders rationalize their behavior by thinking that teaching children about sex is good for them and that children need to be liberated from repressive sexual bonds of society (e.g., Kubik & Hecker, 2005; Segal & Stermac, 1990).

Consequences

In addition to being correlates of CSA, many of the variables already discussed also moderate the consequences of CSA. Factors such as poverty, family dysfunction, parental psychopathology, and parental alcohol or drug abuse can serve to worsen the consequences of CSA (Fitzgerald et al., 2008). Other moderating factors that serve to worsen outcomes are longer duration of maltreatment, greater intensity of maltreatment, closer relationship of the child to the perpetrator, greater frequency of maltreatment, the use of force, injuries (e.g., Kendall-Tackett, Williams, & Finkelhor, 1993; Ruggiero et al., 2000), and higher levels of self-blame and feelings of shame on the part of the victim (Feiring, Taska, & Lewis, 1999).

In addition to moderating factors that can make outcomes worse, other factors, such as age and gender, can contribute to the outcome. Maltreated younger children tend to have more sexual and nonsexual behavior problems than maltreated older children, who have more internalizing problems (e.g., Ruggiero et al., 2000). Maltreated boys tend to have more externalizing problems than maltreated girls (e.g., Holmes & Slap, 1998). Other factors such as attributional style, coping strategies, and level of cognitive functioning have been implicated as moderating factors for outcomes (e.g., Mannarino & Cohen, 1996; Shapiro, Leifer, Martone, & Kassem, 1992; Spaccarelli, 1994). For example, children who blame themselves, feel shame, perceive themselves as different from other children, and view their maltreatment experiences as threatening tend to have worse adjustment.

One of the most important moderators seems to be maternal belief in the child's disclosure of CSA and her subsequent support of the child (Bernard-Bonnin, Hebert, Daignault, & Allard-Dansereau, 2008). Although the majority of parents do believe and support their children, several factors appear to have an influence on maternal disbelief (Sirles & Franke, 1989). In one study, a younger victim was believed more often than an older victim; the more severe the maltreatment (e.g., intercourse versus fondling), the less likely the mother was to believe the child; if the mother was home during a CSA incident, she was less likely to believe the child; if the perpetrator was a stepfather, only 56% of the mothers believed their children, but if he was a biological father, 86% believed their children; if the perpetrator was another relative, 92% believed their child's disclosure; if the child was also physically maltreated, the child was less likely to be believed; and if the perpetrator abused alcohol, the child was less likely to be believed (Sirles & Franke, 1989). Think about the logic behind these findings: Why might a mother be less likely to believe her child in the above instances? What would be the implications for her existence, family life, and well-being if she were to believe the child? On the other hand, think of the effects on the child: If a child is less likely to be believed when there is physical maltreatment and alcohol abuse on top of the sexual maltreatment, what are the implications of this "quadruple whammy" (not being believed, being sexually and physically maltreated, and living in a home with an alcoholic) on the child's mental health?

Short-Term Outcomes

The effects of CSA are pervasive; the mental health outcomes can negatively affect almost every aspect of functioning, including brain functioning (Cohen, Perel, DeBellis, Friedman, & Putnam, 2002). In the short term, CSA has been found to affect a child's emotional, behavioral, cognitive, and interpersonal health. For instance, sexually maltreated children are more depressed, anxious, suicidal, and aggressive than nonmaltreated children (e.g., Boney-McCoy & Finkelhor, 1995; Brodsky et al., 2008; Deblinger, Mannarino, Cohen, & Steer, 2006; Hotte & Rafman, 1992; Lanktree, Briere, & Zaidi, 1991). They have lower self-esteem, suffer more often from post-traumatic stress disorder (PTSD), and engage in a range of sexual behaviors that are developmentally inappropriate (Deblinger et al., 2006; Friedrich, 2001; Ruggiero et al., 2000). Cognitively, they do not achieve as well in school, perceive themselves as different from their peers, blame themselves for negative events, and distrust others (e.g., Mannarino, Cohen, & Berman, 1994). They are also less socially competent (Mannarino & Cohen, 1996). Overall, the two most common short-term outcomes of CSA are sexualized behavior and PTSD (Kendall-Tackett, Williams, & Finkelhor, 1993).

Long-Term Outcomes

Usually, children's symptoms in reaction to CSA improve over time; however, sometimes symptoms do not abate and may actually worsen into adolescence and adulthood (Kendall-Tackett et al., 1993). Individuals whose symptoms persist are more depressed and suicidal than nonmaltreated adults (Briere & Runtz, 1987; Browne & Finkelhor, 1986). They seem to suffer from more anxiety disorders, including PTSD, than the general population (Saunders et al., 1999; Stein, Golding, Siegel, Burnam, & Sorenson, 1988). They also tend to be more violent, angry, self-mutilating, and irritable than their nonmaltreated counterparts (Briere & Gil, 1998; Briere & Runtz, 1987; Duncan & Williams, 1998). In addition, they may suffer from self-blame, low self-esteem, a negative attributional style, low self-efficacy, helplessness, and hopelessness (Jehu, 1988). They may externalize their emotional distress through such activities as self-mutilation (e.g., cutting, burning, hair pulling), heightened sexual activity, binge eating and purging, and alcohol or substance abuse (Briere & Gil, 1998; Briere, Woo, McRae, Foltz, & Sitzman, 1997; Piran, Lerner, Garfinkel, Kennedy, & Brouillette, 1988), and may engage in a range of risky sexual behaviors, resulting in multiple sex partners, unwanted pregnancies, and sexually transmitted diseases (Noll, Shenk, & Putnam, 2009; van Roode, Dickson, Herbison, & Paul, 2009). Finally, a history of CSA can greatly affect adult intimate relationships: Women with a history of CSA are more likely to divorce or never marry; they have fewer friends, are less satisfied with their relationships, and are more interpersonally sensitive than women without a history of CSA (Elliott, 1994; Gold, 1986; Russell, 1986). Moreover, a history of CSA increases one's risk for revictimization in adolescence and adulthood (Brown, Cohen, Johnson, & Smailes, 1999; Widom & Brzustowicz, 2006).

Although all these possible consequences of CSA have been observed in adulthood, very few studies consider that many mediating factors, such as other aspects of family functioning could also be contributing to the negative outcomes. In one study of the consequences of CSA, researchers compared the outcomes of twins who had been sexually abused as children with their co-twins who had not been abused (Nelson et al., 2002). They found that the nonabused co-twins of sexually abused twins functioned more poorly than those twin pairs in which neither twin had been abused, suggesting that many of the family background factors associated with CSA, namely parental alcohol abuse, physical and emotional maltreatment, and childhood neglect contributed to negative outcomes. However, the nonabused co-twins fared better than their abused twins, suggesting that the CSA had an independent effect on the abused twins' poor outcomes. The outcomes for the sexually abused twins included increased risk for major depression, attempted suicide, conduct disorder, alcohol dependence, nicotine dependence, social anxiety, rape after the age of 18, and divorce (Nelson et al., 2002).

Dissociation

One controversial outcome that has been attributed to CSA is dissociation. *Dissociation* has been defined as the mind's ability to remove itself from the reality of an abusive situation, and the thoughts, feelings, and memories that go along with the abuse. Although several researchers have found a relationship between CSA and dissociation (e.g., Chu & Dill, 1990; Elliott & Briere, 1992; Zanarini, Ruser, Frankenburg, Hennen, & Gunderson, 2000), other researchers (e.g., Pope, Hudson, Bodkin, & Oliva, 1998) have argued against the existence of dissociation and do not believe that a person can forget traumatic events. In one review of the relevant literature, Joseph (1999) argued that there is significant neurological support for the reality of dissociation as a phenomenon, and that it exists as a possible consequence of CSA. In the review, Joseph presented evidence that memory deficits of emotionally traumatizing events are due to disturbed hippocampal activation and arousal. An emotionally traumatizing event can cause the release of corticosteroids, which suppress neural activity associated with learning and memory and can cause hippocampal atrophy. Because the hippocampus is involved in memory processes, it is possible that emotionally traumatizing events will not be remembered.

There is also anecdotal evidence that memories of CSA can be forgotten but later remembered. Consider the case in Box 3.3 of a woman who, in adulthood, remembered an incident of CSA. What is unique about this case is that the offender admitted to sexually abusing her; in most cases of this type, the offender denies the abuse, and therefore, it is unknown whether the recovered memory of CSA is true or not, as there is also evidence that false memories can be induced in people (see e.g., Loftus & Ketcham, 1994).

Box 3.3   Can People Forget and Later Remember CSA?

David A. Hoffman, a former child psychologist...pleaded guilty in April [1994] to gross sexual exploitation...Hoffman was charged with the crime after a woman remembered being sexually abused during a two-year period, beginning when she was 8 and living in Columbus with her mother...The woman is now 26 and lives in Michigan. She had no recollection of the abuse until July 1992, said detective John Harris..."She worked in a probation office in Grand Rapids, Michigan typing reports," Harris said. "Her first memory of the abuse came when she was typing a report regarding a sexual abuse case. Then, whenever she had to type reports involving sexual abuse, she would become very distraught." ...The woman sought therapy. She called Harris after her psychologist urged her to file a police report. In 1993...[Hoffman] "admitted committing the molesting offenses," Harris said.

SOURCE: Medick, 1994, as cited in Freyd, 2002, p. 139

Several questions arise in regard to this case. One, why would individuals forget such traumatic memories? Two, how do they forget? And three, how do they later remember? In answer to the first question, it has been theorized that children forget incidences of CSA because not remembering the abuse by a trusted caregiver is necessary for survival (Freyd, 2002). Children need to preserve their relationships with their caregivers for their security and survival, and to admit that their caregivers are betraying them would lead to a disruption in that relationship and a probable disruption in their security. Indeed, studies show that children are more likely to forget abuse by a trusted caregiver than they are to forget abuse by a stranger (e.g., Williams, 1994). How does the child forget and later remember the CSA? One mechanism through which children forget is the neurological changes in response to traumatic events mentioned previously. Another means is through selective attention—that is, during a CSA experience, children can focus their concentration on other events that are occurring simultaneously, such as music playing in the background. Concentrating on the music allows the child to avoid completely processing the traumatic event; however, because some of the event will necessarily be processed, cues—such as the same music playing again in the future—can prompt a child to later remember the CSA (Freyd, 2002). Consider again the case in Box 3.3. How did these factors play into (1) why the woman forgot her abuse; (2) how she forgot; and (3) how she remembered?

Not only is there anecdotal evidence of forgotten episodes of CSA, there is also empirical evidence. In one study, a group of 129 girls originally brought to an emergency room because of sexual abuse were interviewed 17 years later. Among the issues addressed were questions regarding childhood histories of sexual abuse (Williams, 1994, 1995). Of these women, 38% reported no recollections of CSA. An additional 10% reported periods of forgetting and later remembering the abuse (Williams, 1994, 1995). Thus, close to one half of this group of women, in which there was documented evidence of CSA had periods of time in which they forgot the CSA. Although women who were younger at the time of the abuse were more likely to forget it, 26% of those who were 11 to 12 years old, 31% who were 7 to 10 years old, and 62% who were 4 to 6 years old at the time of the CSA had no memories of the abuse (Williams, 1994).

Does CSA Really Have Negative Consequences?

Another controversy surrounding the consequences of CSA comes from the contentious article published in 1998 by Rind, Tromovitch, and Bauserman. They argued that (1) the majority of studies on the consequences of CSA are based on clinical samples, and therefore, the findings cannot be generalized to the population as a whole; (2) there is no evidence of a direct link between CSA and adult psychopathology, nor is there evidence that everyone who experiences sexual abuse as a child will suffer psychologically or socially; and (3) clinical studies suffer from a possible flaw of "effort after meaning." That is, when people seek clinical help for their current functioning and search for reasons for their problems, they may pick out an event such as sexual abuse that happened earlier in their lives. To support their criticisms, Rind and colleagues (1998) conducted a meta-analysis of 59 CSA studies done with college students. They found that although students who had a history of CSA functioned less well than those who did not report such a history, the effects were only slight. That is, non-CSA students were only slightly better adjusted than CSA students, and the sexually abused men showed fewer negative reactions to their experience than the sexually abused women.

The Rind et al. (1998) report created a huge public controversy in the United States. Their results were lauded by pedophiles, subjected to intense criticism in the media, and condemned by Congress. Because of this backlash, several researchers (e.g., Dallam et al., 2001; Ondersma et al., 2001) have reassessed the conclusions made by Rind et al. For instance, Ondersma et al. (2001) pointed out that the effect sizes that Rind and colleagues found for the relationships between CSA and 17 negative outcomes are similar to the effect size between smoking and lung cancer, but the smaller effect size between smoking and lung cancer does not lead people to assume that smoking has nothing to do with lung cancer, or to smoke more because there are no negative outcomes. This analogy can be taken one step further: Smoking is associated with more than just lung cancer (e.g., emphysema, heart disease, etc.); not every person who smokes will get lung cancer, but is at risk for one of a whole host of outcomes. Similarly, CSA is associated with not just one particular negative outcome and not every person who is victimized by CSA will suffer from one particular outcome, but is at risk for a whole host of outcomes.

Furthermore, Dallam et al. (2001) pointed out many inherent flaws in the 1998 Rind et al. analysis, including (1) exclusion of other relevant outcomes shown to be highly related to CSA but not systematically studied in college students, such as PTSD, antisocial behavior, substance abuse, early and risky peer sexual experiences, and revictimization of sexual abuse in adulthood; and (2) the generalization of the results from studies of college students to the general population, even though college students are a highly functioning group of people, and fewer victims of CSA who have debilitating outcomes would be found among them, as CSA victims tend to suffer from academic difficulties and are less likely to finish high school.

Special Issue: Polyvictimization

In recent years, an important advance has been made in the study of childhood victimization—researchers have begun to move away from studying the impact of a single victimization and have moved toward studying the impact of multiple types of victimizations and adversities on children (Finkelhor, 2008; Finkelhor, Ormrod et al., 2009). This line of research has been key in explaining why some children seem to be unaffected in both the short and long term by CSA and other forms of child victimization (Bonanno & Mancini, 2008), while others are severely affected.

Research on polyvictimization—or victimization from more than one type of childhood trauma and adversity—shows that 22% of child victims have four or more different types of victimizations in a single year (Finkelhor, Ormrod et al., 2009). It is these children who suffer from polyvictimization who are at risk for the most severe negative outcomes (Turner, Finkelhor, & Ormrod, 2006), and this risk increases for each additional adverse childhood experience (Dong et al., 2004). Thus, it is the cumulative trauma burden rather than any particular type of trauma itself, that predicts poor outcomes (Finkelhor, 2008). This is not to say that CSA is a neutral experience for those children who have no trauma burden—it can still be very painful, upsetting, and frightening—but these children tend to recover quickly, as long as they do not experience any subsequent victimizations. It is important to note that a single CSA experience does increase the risk for subsequent victimizations (Fargo, 2009). However, research on CSA victims in treatment does support this notion that it is the cumulative trauma that is associated with poor outcomes; indeed, clinical samples show that a majority of victims who present for treatment have at least one additional traumatic experience (Deblinger et al., 2006).

Special Issue: Female Sexual Abuse of Children

Most of the above literature focused on one type of CSA: adult male to female child. This type of CSA was the first to come to public attention back in the 1970s and 1980s, when adult females victimized as children started coming forward. Then male victims of CSA also began to talk about their sexual victimization by men, and it seemed that young boys were at almost equal risk as young girls for CSA from adult males (Elliott, 1993). Currently, there is growing attention to another, hidden perpetrator of CSA: that of the female child sexual abuser. Traditionally, it has been assumed that women cannot and would not sexually maltreat children. Female-perpetrated CSA goes against our long-held, cherished views of women as nurturers of children; if women can and do sexually maltreat children, it undermines our views of how women relate to children. Female-perpetrated CSA also stands in direct contrast to our traditional explanations for male-perpetrated CSA, those of male power and aggression: If women are also sexual abusers, then male power and aggression do not lie at the heart of CSA (Elliott, 1993).

It has been argued (e.g., Hetherton, 1999) that women, particularly mothers, perpetrate CSA much more than believed, and that they may "hide" their CSA in the guise of maternal caretaking acts, such as bathing and dressing the child—for instance, during such acts mothers may fondle the child's genitals. Sometimes women's perpetration of CSA can become much more severe and overt, as is described in Box 3.4. Acts that have been reported include the insertion of objects into the anus and vagina; the rough handling of boys' penises in an attempt to get them erect; oral sex and masturbation of the child and forcing the child to reciprocate; forcing the child to watch adults having sex; and bestiality (Longdon, 1993).

Box 3.4   Female-Perpetrated Child Sexual Abuse

My father was absent most of the time due to his work. Mother slept with me nearly every night as far back as I can remember. The initial memories of abuse were that of being fondled, which probably began in infancy. By the time I was three years old, Mother was having me touch her as well. Later I was introduced to oral sex. This sort of behaviour occurred almost nightly until I was twelve years of age. This in itself was horrible enough; but by the time I entered school, Mother started torturing me in sexual ways.

(Continued)

(Continued)

The first time I remember being sexually tortured was when Mother took me into a wooded area and fondled me, had oral sex with me, and inserted her fingers into my vagina. I cried and screamed because of the severe pain. This only made Mother angry; so to shut me up and to threaten me, she picked up a large stick and shoved it inside my vagina. This incident taught me the lesson of silence and to turn off feelings of pain.

—Lynne Marie, now 40 years old

SOURCE: Elliott, 1993, p. 131

How common is female-perpetrated CSA? The current statistics indicate that almost 90% of CSA perpetrators are men (Sedlak et al., 2010). Two things need to be considered when interpreting these statistics: Before CSA itself became known as a social problem, it was assumed that one in 1 million children were the victims of CSA. Now that we are able to acknowledge that children can be sexually maltreated, we know that the numbers are closer to one in five children. Once we acknowledge that women can sexually maltreat children, we may see a rise in reports of female-perpetrated CSA (Elliott, 1993). Moreover, if we accept that the current statistics are correct (that one in five children is sexually maltreated and that of those, 10% are maltreated by women), then over 6 million people in the United States today were, are being, or will be sexually maltreated by women.

Several researchers have tried to address the problem of female-perpetrated CSA by studying mother-son incest cases. In one of the first studies on this issue, the mother-son incest experienced by the eight men studied were typically cases where the mother attempted to satisfy her own emotional and physical needs for intimacy and security (Krug, 1989). She would seek out her son, in many cases when she was in conflict with the adult male in her life; in some cases, she made overt sexual overtures toward her son. Consider the case of mother-son incest in Box 3.5. What types of sexual acts occurred? Why do you think the mother perpetrated the act? What were the effects on this man's life?

Box 3.5   A Case of Mother-Son Incest

A 29-year-old, lower middle-class white male, named Bob*, who was in a methadone maintenance program, entered psychotherapy because of symptoms of depression that were not related to the methadone treatment. During treatment, Bob revealed incidents of sexual abuse by his mother, who was on the faculty of a prestigious university, had divorced his father when he was two years old, and never remarried. During his childhood, Bob served as both his mother's confidant and her advisor, and from the time of the divorce until Bob was in his mid-teens, Bob's mother continually slept with him. Starting when Bob was seven years old, his mother insisted that they have intimate sexual contact, which on some occasions included sexual intercourse. At 10 years of age, Bob started using recreational drugs, and by age 15, he began using heroin. At age 18, Bob married and left home, but the marriage lasted only three years, as both Bob and his wife were heavy drug users.

SOURCE: Krug, 1989

NOTE: *This name has been fabricated to facilitate the telling of the story.

Krug (1989) found that the eight men in his study suffered many problems in adulthood that could be related to their mother-son incest experiences. Specifically, most were anxious, depressed, had extra-relationship sexual contacts, and abused substances. Kelly, Wood, Gonzalez, MacDonald, and Waterman (2002) reported similar symptoms in their clinical study of 17 cases of mother-son incest. They found that men who were abused by their mothers experienced more adjustment problems than men whose perpetrators were not their mothers, even though the abuse experiences were somewhat subtle (e.g., genital fondling) and possibly difficult to distinguish from normal caregiving.

The mother-son incest victims in the Kelly et al. (2002) study experienced more sexual problems, dissociation, aggression, and interpersonal problems than the father-son incest victims. Moreover, these problems were moderated by their initial perceptions of abuse: If they initially perceived the sexual maltreatment as nonabusive, they were more likely to report PTSD symptoms and aggression. If they had any positive feelings about the maltreatment at the time it occurred, they were more likely to suffer from later aggression and self-destructiveness. Why is it that these positive feelings might be associated with more maladjustment? Might it be that experiencing incest as somewhat pleasurable might lead to a later strong reaction of shame, guilt, and disgust? Is it possible that the victims may not understand how they could experience something so wrong as remotely pleasurable, and therefore might perceive themselves as being even more deviant for having these feelings? As an example of such a dynamic, consider this victim of mother-son incest:

One male survivor described feeling that his most intense orgasm occurred at age 13 while having intercourse with his mother, who immediately ridiculed and verbally abused him after he ejaculated. He recalled running into the bathroom and scrubbing his genitals in a manic attempt to wash away the incest. He then cried and vomited when he realized he could not wash it away. In therapy, he stated that the abuse would have been less harmful if he had not experienced pleasure, because "I am now associated with something that is disgusting that I liked. I have incest tendencies. I am a part of the incest. I am as screwed up as my mother. I am as tainted, I am as damaged, I am as dirty as she is . . . The incest has cheapened and dirtied my manhood." (Kelly et al., 2002, p. 437)

Consider this case further. What role do you think the mother's ridicule and verbal abuse played in his response to the experience?

Several researchers and victims argue that female-perpetrated CSA may be more harmful than male-perpetrated CSA (e.g., Elliott, 1993), although there is currently no empirical support for this proposition. One basis for this argument is that the experiences of survivors of female-perpetrated CSA are often silenced. Consider this victim's story:

> My mother and grandmother sexually abused me from the time I was four. I hated going home and spent most of my time figuring out how to get out of the house . . . I begged my aunt to let me live with her. In my life I have taken most drugs, been alcoholic, had a nervous breakdown and have never had a happy relationship with a man or woman. Yet, I have managed to hide the real reason from everyone. I felt that I must be a complete freak of nature for this abuse to have happened to me. No one is sexually abused by a woman. I must be crazy. (Elliott, 1993, p. 1)

In addition, if survivors of female-perpetrated CSA do speak out, they may not be believed, even by their own therapists. In fact, one study showed that 78% of the victims of female-perpetrated CSA were not believed when they disclosed their abuse experiences (Elliott, 1993). To receive help, many of these victims, both male and female, fabricated their CSA experiences and said that the perpetrator was male (Longdon, 1993). Therefore, the consequences of the CSA in and of itself are compounded by the fact that no one takes their experiences seriously (Longdon, 1993). Consider how these victims' experiences influence our current estimated rates of female-perpetrated CSA. In what way would our estimates be affected?

Finally, some survivors report that female-perpetrated CSA is worse than male-perpetrated CSA because it goes against the stereotype of what a mother is supposed to be. Survivors of female-perpetrated CSA experience the same consequences as discussed in the previous section of this chapter. Although there are no systematic studies, it has been documented that victims of female-perpetrated CSA have suffered from substance and alcohol abuse, suicide attempts, gender identity problems, difficulties in maintaining relationships, unresolved anger, shame, guilt, self-mutilation, eating disorders, depression, and agoraphobia (Elliott, 1993).

Why would women sexually maltreat children? Although empirical studies are rare, a few studies give some indication as to the dynamics of female-perpetrated CSA. Women tend to use violence less frequently than male perpetrators, and instead resort to coercion. Women are more likely than men to know their victims, and they tend to have fewer victims than men. It appears that, like male perpetrators, women maltreat girls more often than they maltreat boys. However, this last finding may be merely a result of reporting bias—that is, because of certain social mores, males are less likely to report any type of abusive experience, and this tendency may be compounded when the perpetrator is female (Jennings, 1993). In fact, at least one study shows that women sexually maltreat girls and boys at approximately the same rate (McCloskey & Raphael, 2005).

There is an association between a past history of CSA and women's offending and between substance abuse and offending. Moreover, female sexual abusers seem to be particularly dependent on men's attention for their self-esteem and their survival (Jennings, 1993). However, none of these traits fully describes every female sexual abuser, and some researchers have attempted to create typologies of abusers. One particularly interesting typology was created by Matthews (1993) from her experiences as a therapist to female sexual abusers. She postulates that there are three types of female sexual abusers: (1) *the teacher/lover offender,* who sees her victim as her partner and believes that the experience is a positive one for both of them; this type of abuser tends to be psychologically a child herself, but responds very well to therapy; (2) *the predisposed offender,* who generally has a history of being sexually abused herself; these women act alone in their abuse and generally abuse family members; they have very deviant sexual fantasies and have problems with self-destructive and suicidal behaviors because they hate themselves and believe they were born evil; these women are often very hard to treat; and (3) *the male-coerced offender,* who is coerced into abusing children by her male partner(s); these women are often passive and powerless in their relationships, and fear violence and abandonment if they do not participate in the abuse; they do not feel loved or lovable, and stay in these relationships in order to avoid being alone; many times and for whatever reason, they will initiate the sexual abuse of children themselves, though. Through her work with treating female sexual abusers, Matthews (1993) has found that the best interventions occur when long-term treatment is combined with short-term incarceration.

Prevention and Intervention

Criminal Justice Involvement

One of the most difficult obstacles to effective prevention and intervention for CSA is disclosure. Victims often delay disclosure—with a large majority never disclosing—and the closer the perpetrator is to the child, the less likely it is that the child will disclose, particularly if that perpetrator is living in the same household (London, Bruck, Ceci, & Shuman, 2005; London, Bruck, Wright, & Ceci, 2008). Moreover, even if the victims do eventually disclose, their recantation rates for substantiated abuse are also high, particularly if they were maltreated by their parents (London et al., 2008). In one study, children who recanted cases of substantiated abuse were more likely to have been abused by a member of their household, had a non-perpetrator parent who expressed disbelief or was unsupportive, and were more likely to be under the age of 10 (Malloy, Lyon, & Quas, 2007).

What inhibits CSA victims from disclosing? The most common factors seem to be embarrassment and shame, expectation that they would be blamed for their own maltreatment, belief that they would not be helped, not wanting to upset anyone, and wanting to protect the perpetrator (Anderson, Martin, Mullen, Romans, & Herbison, 1993; Fleming, 1997). Moreover, among victims who said that they did eventually disclose their abuse to someone, less than 10% say that their abuse was reported to authorities (Mullen et al., 1993; Smith et al., 2000).

Nonetheless, of all of the types of child maltreatment discussed in this book, CSA—when disclosed and reported to authorities—is the most likely to involve the criminal justice system. In a meta-analysis of 24 studies with samples involved in criminal prosecution of child maltreatment, 79% involved only sexual abuse cases and the remaining 21% involved a combination of physical and sexual abuse cases (Cross, Walsh, Simone, & Jones, 2003). The great majority of the child abuse cases referred to prosecutors (approximately 72%) was carried forward without dismissal. Among the cases carried forward, plea rates averaged 82% and conviction rates 94%. In comparison to national data on felony dispositions, child abuse was less likely to lead to the filing of charges and to incarceration than most other felonies, but more likely to be carried forward without dismissal. In addition, rates for diversion, guilty pleas, and trial and conviction for the child abuse cases were essentially consistent with those for all violent crimes (Cross et al., 2003). Although perpetrators·of CSA seem to be treated similarly to other felons in criminal court, the profile of the perpetrators is quite different. Compared to other felons, child sexual abusers are more likely to be employed, to have been married, and to be mostly non-Hispanic Whites—characteristics that are also in sharp contrast to the child maltreatment cases heard in juvenile court (Cullen, Smith, Funk, & Haaf, 2000).

Although studies show that reporting to the police is more likely when the perpetrator is a stranger (Hanson et al., 1999), most of the studies of the adjudication of child sexual abuse cases in criminal court do not separate intrafamilial from extrafamilial abuse. However, in one study focusing specifically on the prosecution of CSA cases where the alleged perpetrators were family members, Martone, Jaudes, and Cavins (1996) examined state attorney office records addressing 451 allegations of intrafamilial sexual abuse between 1986 and 1988. They found that 72% of the cases showed probable cause of sexual abuse. The complaints filed in these cases included 77 felony charges, 29 misdemeanors, and 30 juvenile charges against 136 alleged family perpetrators. Although 51% of the alleged perpetrators ended up in court, only 17% of the original 451 allegations were prosecuted for a felony. Only 36% of the victims had to appear in court. Of the 77 felony complaints filed, 48 (62%) ended in convictions and 43 of these individuals served time (average 6.8 years). Thus, relatively few of the perpetrators for whom probable cause of sexual abuse was demonstrated actually served time in prison for their crimes, and this rate itself would be even lower when we consider all of the perpetrators of sexual abuse who were never even taken to court.

The adjudication of CSA cases in criminal courts adds additional levels of complexity to the already complex process of adjudicating a child maltreatment case. Testifying in court can be a terrifying experience for the child victim (Somer & Szwarcberg, 2001), who may also be subjected to multiple and embarrassing interviews about the abusive events (Ghetti, Alexander, & Goodman, 2002). Medical testimony is important, but most sexually maltreated children have no specific or diagnostic medical evidence of sexual contact (DeJong, 1998). There are controversies over the role of expert witnesses (Allen & Miller, 1995) and the competency of children to testify in criminal cases (McGough, 1997). In addition, when the child is too young or too disturbed to testify, there are issues surrounding the acceptability of hearsay evidence (McGough, 1997; also see Golding, Alexander, & Stewart, 1999).

Many modifications have been recommended concerning the processing of criminal child maltreatment cases, with the specific goals of reducing the stress for the child and increasing the number of convictions of perpetrators. There has been much research, including mock trial research on many of these innovations, which range from simple procedures such as familiarizing child victims with the courthouse prior to the beginning of the trial and "vertical prosecution" (i.e., having the same attorney work on a case throughout its prosecution) to procedures diverging more dramatically from traditional criminal practices—for example, videotaping of the children's testimony in a room away from the alleged perpetrator; allowing hearsay evidence concerning the abused children's report of their abuse rather than making them testify directly in court; using anatomically detailed dolls to allow children to show exactly what was done to them; and allowing the children to have a support person (e.g., a non-offending parent) with them in court (e.g., Goodman, Quas, Bulkley, & Shapiro, 1999; McGough, 1997).

What is known about the extent to which innovations are used and their effects on the successful prosecution of cases? Evidence from a survey of prosecuting attorneys in 41 states revealed that the most common types of cases involving child witnesses were child sexual abuse/sexual assault cases (88%) (Goodman et al., 1999). The types of innovation most commonly used by the reporting prosecutors were vertical prosecution, the presence of a support person in the courtroom, and a tour of the courtroom for the children—all of which were relatively easy and inexpensive to implement. Much less frequently used were videotaped testimonies and interviewing child witnesses behind one-way mirrors—which were seen as too expensive, not necessary, and jeopardizing the case because they contribute to jurors' distrust of the child testimony. Similarly, the use of anatomically detailed dolls to elicit children's testimony was seen as harmful to the case and not necessary. Regarding outcomes, the increased use of vertical prosecution and faster trials were both associated with increases in guilty pleas and in guilty verdicts. By contrast, using one-way mirrors in an interview room was negatively associated with both guilty pleas and convictions.

Box 3.6	The Processing of the Ann and Marie Case

When Marie first disclosed her father's sexual abuse to a counselor, she experienced a great deal of pressure from her sister Ann to keep quiet and then refused to repeat her claims during a CPS investigation. Consequently the case was closed as unfounded. Later, when Marie disclosed the abuse to a counselor, CPS was again called, and the father was arrested. The girls' mother was very ambivalent about pressing legal charges against the father for his incestuous behavior with his daughters. She was particularly anxious to avoid the public shame that would come with having her husband's sexual abuse as part of the public record. A probation officer interviewed both girls to determine both the extent of the harm they had experienced and the further trauma that might accompany the outcome of a trial. Ann, the 14-year-old daughter, said she would feel guilty about sending him to prison but

(Continued)

> (Continued)
>
> also felt he should not get away with what he had done. Marie, the 13-year-old, initially felt much less ambivalence, asserting that her father should go to jail. She later backed down from this desire, saying he had shown improvements in therapy. It is not clear whether she had really changed her mind or was again experiencing excessive pressure from her family.
>
> SOURCE: Cohen & Mannarino, 2000

Consider the disposition of the case of Ann and Marie in Box 3.6. At the time that the report describing their case was published, the case against the father was still pending. What do you think the court experience is likely to be like for each girl? What kind of accommodations might be made to make the experience less traumatic?

Treatment of CSA Victims

As you may have discerned from this discussion of CSA, many of the victims and perpetrators are in great need of some sort of therapeutic intervention. Experts in the field think that several issues need to be addressed in treatment, including feelings of self-blame and shame (Feiring & Taska, 2005), processing of CSA-related cognitive distortions that could be associated with PTSD and depression symptoms (Hayes et al., 2009), sexual behavior problems and dysfunctions that seem to be uniquely related to the trauma of CSA (Deblinger, McLeer, Atkins, Ralphe, & Foa, 1989), and instruction in personal safety skills to decrease the likelihood of revictimization (Kenny, Capri, Thakkar-Kolar, Ryan, & Runyon, 2008; Runyon & Deblinger, 2008).

Some workers in the field (e.g., Cohen & Mannarino, 2000) believe that the entire family of incest victims should undergo therapy. Most such programs for intervention combine several, if not all, of the following elements: group therapy for the perpetrator; group therapy for the spouse of the perpetrator; group therapy for the child victim; dyadic therapy for the nonperpetrating parent and the victim; individual therapy for the victim; and eventual family therapy for the perpetrator, victim, nonperpetrating spouse, and any siblings. However, if the perpetrator is unwilling to admit to the abuse and/or if the nonperpetrating parent is unwilling to adequately protect the children from the perpetrator, families will not qualify for these programs. Unfortunately, this is the problem for the majority of CSA cases (Cohen & Mannarino, 2000).

Several approaches have been developed for CSA victims and their families, including play therapy, psychodynamic approaches, family treatment, and cognitive behavioral approaches; however, few of these interventions have been subjected to rigorous evaluations. In this chapter, we focus on play therapy and cognitive-behavioral therapy. Play therapy was perhaps the earliest therapeutic intervention developed, and it is typically designed to reduce the child victim's emotional distress and remove obstacles to healthy development through symbolic play (Webb, 1999).

The most beneficial of play therapies seems to involve a combination of both directive (i.e., the therapist directs the child's play in an effort to get them to process CSA-related memories) and nondirective (i.e., letting the child play the way she or he wants) play, which balances the drawbacks and benefits of each kind of play. The child is not permitted to avoid the trauma itself, which can happen in nondirective play, but the therapy does not overfocus on the trauma either, which can happen in directive play (Gil, 2006). One model of this is Trauma-Focused Play Therapy, a therapeutic intervention that has been deemed "promising and acceptable" by the Office for Victims of Crime, based on the limited evaluation research that has been conducted thus far (Saunders, Berliner, & Hanson, 2003).

The most empirically validated treatment program for children who are victims of CSA is trauma-focused cognitive behavioral therapy (CBT) (Saunders et al., 2003), which involves psychoeducation (educating the child and non-offending caregiver about sexual abuse and the therapy procedure); parenting skills training; anxiety management (how to use relaxation and cognitive and emotional strategies to reduce anxiety-provoking thoughts about the abuse); exposure (talking, drawing, and writing about the abuse experience to reduce negative emotions and avoidance); cognitive therapy (challenging cognitive distortions about the event and the consequent negative thoughts about the self and others); conjoint parent-child sessions to enhance communication; and enhancing future safety and development (e.g., teaching safety skills) (Cohen, Mannarino, & Deblinger, 2006). This type of treatment involves the non-offending caregiver in an effort to help the caregiver cope, communicate with the child, and assist with any behavioral problems (King et al., 2000). Such caregiver involvement has been shown to be critical in reducing depression and behavior problems in the child victims (Deblinger, Lippmann, & Steer, 1999).

Over 14 studies have provided evidence of the efficacy of trauma-focused CBT for the reduction of maladaptive symptoms in child victims. Such evidence includes reductions in symptoms of PTSD, depression, and anxiety (Cohen, Deblinger, Mannarino, & Steer, 2004; Deblinger, McLeer, & Henry, 1990), improvements in sexualized behavior and internalizing symptoms (Cohen & Mannarino, 1997), improvements in social competence (Cohen, Mannarino, & Knudsen, 2004), and reductions in sexually inappropriate behavior (Cohen, Mannarino, & Knudsen, 2005).

Treatment of CSA Offenders

The most common treatment method for CSA offenders is CBT combined with relapse-prevention, usually in a group format (McGrath, Cumming, & Burchard, 2003). Such programs typically target deviant sexual arousal and the internal factors believed to be related to reoffending, such as distorted cognitions and inappropriate attitudes related to sexual deviance, denial and minimization of their sexual offending, social skills deficits, poor interpersonal relationships, inability to empathize, impulse control issues, emotional regulation problems, and substance abuse. Sex education, relationship skills, communication skills, anger management, emotion regulation, relaxation training, and problem-solving techniques are typical program components. Relapse prevention focuses on understanding the chain of events that leads to the offending, and then helping offenders develop skills and techniques to break that chain.

A meta-analysis on the effectiveness of CBT-based treatment approaches provides evidence that they reduce recidivism. In addition, recent programs show even more promising results, with a sexual offense recidivism rate of 9.9% (compared to 17.4% in comparison groups) and a non-sexual offense recidivism rate of 32% (compared to 51% in comparison groups) (Hanson et al., 2002). Nonetheless, there are limitations to these programs, and experts argue that treatment should be more individualized to meet the offender's needs and specific triggers (Hanson & Morton-Bourgon, 2005), and should be more intense for higher-risk offenders (Harkins & Beech, 2007).

Prevention of CSA

Although treating the victims of CSA is necessary, a more effective approach to ending the suffering associated with it would be to prevent it from happening in the first place. All states, as mentioned previously, have laws against CSA; however, these laws are obviously not enough to deter potential perpetrators. The most widely used, and somewhat controversial CSA prevention programs in this country are programs that target children and aim to change their behavior. These programs began in the 1980s and have been integrated into many schools' curriculum or other children's groups (e.g., Boy Scouts). These programs teach children about good, bad, and questionable touches, and the rights of children to control who touches them. They also provide children with various service options and referrals, and other strategies for what to do if anyone does touch them inappropriately. Evaluations show that these programs have been successful in providing children with the safety information and the skills to avoid or lower their risks of being sexually maltreated (Berrick & Barth, 1992; Daro, 1994; MacMillan, MacMillan, Offord, Griffith, & MacMillan, 1994; Rispens, Aleman, & Goudena, 1997). They have also been able to provide sexually maltreated children with the skills necessary to get the help they need and reduce their risk of revictimization (Hazzard, 1990; Kolko, Moser, & Hughes, 1989).

The controversy surrounding these programs stems from the fact that they were modeled on sexual assault programs for women, which sought to empower women by educating them about sexual assault and how to protect themselves in the event of an assault (Berrick & Gilbert, 1991). Therefore, these programs try to empower elementary school students by educating them about what sexual abuse is and ways in which they can ward off an assault (Reppucci, Haugaard, & Antonishak, 2005). The problem is this: Are all children developmentally mature enough to understand the distinctions of "good" versus "bad" touches and by whom and when can they be touched in private places? To give an example, can a four-year-old understand the following: "A good touch is when someone close to you gives you a hug. A bad touch is when someone touches you in a private place. Someone close to you can touch you in a private place and it may not be bad, such as when they are touching you there to clean you. However, someone close to you can touch you in a private place and it can be bad even if it is when they are bathing you."

If we find that some children, particularly older ones, are capable of understanding the intricacies of CSA, as some (but not all) have been shown to be, should we then also be giving them the responsibility of protecting themselves? This seems to be the major question here. What are some of the implications of placing this responsibility on children? Is it possible that if they do subsequently become the victims of CSA, the normal self-blame reaction that tends to follow an abusive experience may be compounded by their perception that they were supposed to have protected themselves? Can you think of ways to improve programs designed to help children protect themselves without giving them developmentally inappropriate responsibilities?

In response to such criticisms about typical prevention programs, Plummer (2005) countered that such programs have had a positive influence on the prevention of CSA. Millions of people, including adults, have become educated as to the extent and nature of the CSA problem, and children are now more willing to come forth and disclose sexual abuse that occurred to them. These certainly are positive results, but do not resolve the problem of putting the responsibility of protection solely on the child. As Finkelhor and Strapko (1992) recommend, we should call these programs *disclosure programs* instead of *prevention programs*. Furthermore, as both sides emphasize (Plummer, 2005; Reppucci et al., 2005), parents should be brought into these programs as the primary protectors of their children. Indeed, many parents want to be, and they have been shown to be effective in teaching their children about appropriate touching and self-protective measures, particularly when they are given specific instructions for how to talk with their children about these issues (Burgess & Wurtele, 1998).

Summary

Child sexual maltreatment by caregivers is a major problem in this country; however, its exact rate is difficult to ascertain because the research is plagued with controversy as to which acts should be considered abusive. Our best estimates suggest that as many as one fourth of women and one fifth of men may have experienced sexual maltreatment as a child, but not all of this maltreatment was perpetrated by a family member. Predictors of CSA come at most levels of the ecological model, but it is factors at the individual/developmental level that may be most important in figuring out why adults would find sexual gratification in children, particularly children who are related to them. CSA can have devastating consequences to its victims, both in the short and long term, and these victims (as well as their perpetrators and their families) are in need of psychological help. Most of the research and resources have focused on father-daughter incest; however, current research shows that mothers can also sexually maltreat their children at a rate that is probably much higher than we expect. Future research should be directed toward not only males-as-perpetrators, but females-as-perpetrators as well. Recall Scott in the case that opened this chapter. He was sexually maltreated by many members of his family, including both his mother and father. Do you think that each of his parents had different reasons for sexually maltreating him? What were those reasons? What were the consequences for Scott?

Discussion Questions

1. What circumstances help influence whether a child is believed when she or he reports CSA? Why are children sometimes not believed? What does this say about society? The courts? The children's parents?

2. The majority of child sexual abusers are relatives of the child. Why do you think this is? Does this fact contradict what you believed prior to reading this chapter? Why are the perpetrators not usually strangers?

3. How does being victimized as a child contribute to a greater chance of perpetrating abuse as an adult?

4. Males are less likely to report victimization than females. What in society makes it less okay for males to report CSA or more okay for females to report CSA?

5. Research shows that a father is more likely to perpetrate CSA if he was frequently away or less involved in his daughter's first three years of life. How and why does this distance make a difference?

6. Why do you think some people—but not others—are deterred from perpetrating CSA by conventional social norms or inhibitions?

7. Why are traumatic memories of abuse forgotten? Why do they sometimes resurface later? How does this affect a child's believability?

8. For a long time, it was believed that women did not and could not sexually maltreat children. Do you think the consequences are different for a child if he or she is maltreated by his or her mother or his or her father? In what ways?

9. The court experience of testifying against a perpetrator can be very traumatizing and confusing for a child. What accommodations can the court system make to make this experience less traumatic and less confusing for a child?

10. CSA prevention programs are aimed at changing behavior of children. How might this place responsibility and blame on children in the eyes of society? What could be a better model for a prevention program?

4

Child Neglect and Psychological Maltreatment

In October of 2003, Raymond and Vanessa Jackson were arrested for starving four adopted children in their home in New Jersey. The Jacksons had seven children altogether, but only the four boys, ages 9 to 19, were on the brink of starving to death. The case came to the attention of authorities when a neighbor found the eldest boy rummaging in their garbage at 2 a.m., looking for food. It was later revealed that the boys had been locked out of the kitchen and survived on a diet of uncooked pancake batter, peanut butter, and dry cereal. The boys said they sometimes gnawed on wallboard and insulation to stave off hunger. None of the boys weighed more than 50 pounds. Neighbors assumed the oldest boy, who was only four feet tall, was 10 years old, not 19. When the children were taken into state custody, the three youngest were put into foster care, and the oldest was hospitalized in a cardiac unit. What is particularly alarming is that the Jacksons had been visited 38 times over the previous two years by social workers for the state. How did these workers not notice the starving children? Did they see the children when they came to the house? Did they not ask for the children's medical records? How did these children go unnoticed by a state that had this family under surveillance? These questions were among those posed by reporters, legislators, and child advocates in the weeks following this horrific discovery (McAlpin, 2003; Usborne, 2003).

This notorious case received widespread attention as an example of the failure of Child Protective Services (CPS) to adequately protect children from the horrendous behaviors that parents can sometimes perpetrate on their children. Only one year prior to this case, New Jersey's CPS came under fire because of their inadequate response to a family in which a seven-year-old boy, dead from starvation, was found in a plastic box in the basement, with his twin and four-year-old half brother alive, but emaciated, in an adjoining room. As a result of that discovery,

New Jersey spent millions of dollars revamping their CPS system, only to have the Jackson story emerge one year later. New Jersey is not the only state to have failures come to light. The question that must be asked is why the system is unable to protect children from such terrible neglect. Is it possible that neglect is particularly difficult to identify, especially when it occurs behind closed doors? What warning signs might there be that a child is being neglected?

Like neglect, psychological maltreatment can be extremely difficult to detect. In Chapters 2 and 3, we discussed definitional problems that have plagued the literature on physical and sexual maltreatment of children; such definitional problems are even more pronounced for the two types of maltreatment discussed in this chapter. Consequently, arriving at prevalence statistics for neglect and psychological maltreatment has been difficult, and results of studies are sometimes widely divergent. Despite these difficulties, research on the predictors and consequences of these behaviors has proliferated.

Neglect

Scope of the Problem

Only in relatively recent decades have the profound negative consequences of neglect led to its public recognition as a severe form of child maltreatment. But what exactly is neglect? How should it be defined? Do we need to see immediate psychological damage to the children in order for their parents to be considered neglectful? What if the psychological consequences do not appear until later in life, when people are cognitively able to realize the neglectful practices of their parents? Should intentions be taken into consideration? Does it matter whether a child is neglected because stressors in the parents' lives made them unable to provide proper care for the child? Should the omission of adequate care be considered neglect only if parents deliberately—perhaps through actual hostility—ignore the care of their child? Would your opinion change if you knew that there is research that shows that the harm to the child can be just as serious whether the parent was intentional in their neglect, or merely careless, ignorant, depressed, or overwhelmed (Greenbaum et al., 2008)?

Neglect is commonly viewed as parental failure to meet a child's basic needs (Greenbaum et al., 2008); unlike physical and sexual abuse, neglect refers to acts of omission rather than of commission. Even though this is a commonly accepted definition, there are arguments over what exactly constitutes a child's basic needs. Nonetheless, several different forms of neglect have been identified (Erickson & Egeland, 2011). *Physical neglect,* the most obvious and well-known form of neglect, occurs when parents fail to provide for the basic physical needs of their child, such as feeding, bathing, and providing shelter, or when they fail to protect the child from harm and danger. *Psychological or emotional neglect* occurs when parents fail to attend to their child's basic emotional needs. Examples are not picking up or attending to a crying infant and not comforting children when they are hurt; however, there is considerable controversy over exactly what a child's basic emotional needs are, and cultures vary in their views on emotional neglect. For instance, Korbin (1980) points out that the Western middle class practice of giving infants and young children their own rooms to sleep in at night would be considered emotionally neglectful by the standards of other cultures. Despite these cultural differences, it appears that in its more severe forms, emotional neglect can lead to a medical condition called nonorganic failure to thrive (i.e., retardation in the rate of growth) and other serious long-term consequences (Erickson & Egeland, 2011).

Medical neglect is failure to address the basic medical needs of the child, such as routine checkups, immunizations, recommended surgery, and prescribed medicine. As noted in Chapter 13, this type of neglect has been at the root of considerable controversy in regard to several religious communities in the United States. *Mental health neglect* is the failure to provide mental health treatment to a child who obviously suffers from serious emotional and/or behavioral disorders; this type of neglect is not widely acknowledged as a form of maltreatment. Finally, *educational neglect* occurs when parents do not comply with state ordinances for the attendance of their children in school. Often, professionals also consider a parent's failure to cooperate or become involved in the child's education to be a form of educational neglect (Erickson & Egeland, 2011). Overall, at the core of conceptions of neglect is the assumption that parents are responsible for protecting their children from known hazards. As more hazards become known, the definition of neglect and its different forms will continue to evolve (Garbarino & Collins, 1999).

One of the basic problems facing scholars concerned with neglect is that research and public attention for it has lagged far behind that of physical and sexual maltreatment of children, even though the consequences may be just as—or even more—serious (Erickson & Egeland, 2011). Consequently, problems that may be due specifically to neglect often are ignored, perhaps because our culture is more preoccupied with violence and acts of commission than it is with things that cannot be so readily seen (acts of omission). Severely beaten children attract more attention because the wounds are evident, but the emotional scars suffered by neglected children may be more insidious and traumatic (Garbarino & Collins, 1999).

It is ironic that physical maltreatment grabs so much of the public's attention, because official statistics indicate that neglect is much more common than physical maltreatment. Table 4.1 summarizes the major national studies assessing the prevalence of child neglect. According to the U.S. Department of Health and Human Services (USDHHS) (2011), neglect is by far the most common type of child maltreatment—78.3% of all maltreatment cases substantiated by CPS in 2010 were cases of neglect. In addition, as opposed to the 56% and 62% declines we have seen from 1990 to 2010 for child physical and sexual maltreatment, respectively, child neglect has remained relatively stable over that time period, with a modest 10% decline, according to USDHHS figures (Finkelhor, Jones, & Shattuck, 2011).

Data from the Fourth National Incidence Study (NIS-4) (Sedlak et al., 2010, see Chapter 2) reinforce the findings from the USDHHS—neglect is the most prevalent type of maltreatment in this country. However, as opposed to the relatively stable, but slight decrease in the rate of neglect reported by the USDHHS between 1990 and 2010, NIS-4 showed increases in the incidence of neglect between 1986 (NIS-2) and 2005–2006 (NIS-4). These increases were significant when neglect was considered under the Endangerment Standard, and only marginally significant when

Table 4.1 Prevalence Rates of the Neglect of Children

Study	Description of Sample	Measures/Definition of Neglect	Rates of Neglect
U.S. Department of Health and Human Services (2011), *Child Maltreatment 2010*	An estimated 3.3 million referrals, involving the alleged maltreatment of approximately 5.9 million children, in 2010	Cases that have been referred to Child Protective Services (CPS) in 2010	• 78.3% of all maltreatment cases in 2010 were cases of neglect • 32.6% of maltreatment deaths were due to neglect • 35.5% of fatalities were due to neglect combined with physical abuse
Sedlak et al. (2010), Fourth National Incidence Study of Child Abuse and Neglect (2005–2006)	A nationally representative sample of over 10,790 professionals in 1,094 agencies serving 126 counties	• *Harm Standard*—requires that an act or omission result in demonstrable harm in order to be classified as abuse or neglect • *Endangerment Standard*—a sentinel thought that the maltreatment endangered the children or a CPS investigation substantiated or indicated their maltreatment	• *Harm Standard*—771,700 children were neglected, at a rate of 10.5 per 1,000 children in the United States • *Endangerment Standard*—2,251,600 were neglected, a rate of 30.6 per 1,000 children

considered under the Harm Standard. The increases from 1993 (NIS-3) to 2005–2006 (NIS-4) were not significant. Overall, under the Harm Standard, the number of neglected children rose between 1986 and 2005–2006 from 474,800 to 771,700, for a rate of 10.5 neglected children per 1,000 in the United States; under the Endangerment Standard, the numbers rose from 917,200 to 2,251,600, a rate of 30.6 neglected children per 1,000 and an increase of 245%. Physical neglect was the most often reported type of neglect (295,300 in 2005–2006 under the Harm Standard; 1,192,200 under the Endangerment Standard), but emotional neglect was also a significant problem (193,400 in 2005–2006 under the Harm Standard; 1,173,800 under the Endangerment Standard) (Sedlak et al., 2010).

Despite the great wealth and resources of the United States, neglect is a grave problem for children in this country. Moreover, even though it is commonly thought that children are at greater risk for fatal physical abuse, children are more likely to die from neglect than from any other form of maltreatment. According to the USDHHS (2011), in 2010, 32.6% of maltreatment deaths were due to neglect, and an additional 35.5% of fatalities were due to neglect combined with physical maltreatment. Moreover, the rates of fatalities due to neglect may be even higher than these statistics show because they are more difficult to investigate than fatalities due to physical maltreatment. There is also considerable controversy over how to define and assess fatalities due to neglect (Bonner, Crow, & Logue, 1999; Lung & Daro, 1996). Take the examples in Box 4.1. Which of the fatalities would you attribute to neglect?

Box 4.1   Possible Cases of Fatal Child Neglect

1. A 4-month-old infant died from massive trauma after being ejected from the front seat of a car in a traffic collision. The child was not secured in an infant car seat (p. 156).

2. A 6-year-old boy fatally shot his 4-year-old brother with a handgun he found in the pocket of a coat hanging in the closet. The parents were in the next room watching television (p. 156).

3. A mother was giving a bath to her 2-year-old son, Bob. She left him in the tub and went to the kitchen for 10 minutes. She then sent her 8-year-old in to check on Bob, who was lying face down in the tub. Bob was taken to the hospital, where he was unresponsive with a temperature of 90°F. After treatment, Bob began breathing again, and he was admitted. After 9 days in the pediatric intensive care unit, Bob had minimal brain functioning and was unresponsive to any stimuli. He died two days later. The cause of death was deemed to be pneumonia with anoxic brain injury after a near-drowning. The CPS worker told the mother that 10 minutes was too long to leave a 2-year-old unattended in a tub, and the mother replied that she did it all the time.

4. A 7-month-old infant named Roger was brought to a local ER by his parents because of respiratory problems. The police were called to the ER because of a fight between the parents, and the parents left before the infant saw a doctor. Roger was then brought to the ER the next day by his grandfather, and had to be hospitalized because of severe respiratory distress and malnutrition. Roger was the size of a newborn. A CPS investigation found that both parents abused drugs and alcohol and that Roger's mother had used crack, marijuana, and alcohol while she was pregnant with Roger. There were also outstanding warrants for both parents' arrests, and both had been in prison at least once previously. Roger died five days after admission because of multiple organ dysfunction and pneumonia.

SOURCE: Bonner et al., 1999

As these examples indicate, the determination of "fatality by neglect" may be in the eye of the beholder. Many such cases may not be determined to be neglect related; even if neglect is seen as the cause, the determination would not necessarily be noted on the death certificate (McClain, Sacks, Froehlke, & Ewigman, 1993). For all these reasons, neglect fatality rates should be assumed to be much higher than the reported figures indicate. Furthermore, although fatalities can result from a failure to provide supervision, protection, medical care, or nutrition (Bonner et al., 1999), where exactly do we draw the line between a momentary lapse in supervision and chronic neglect? And, does this distinction necessarily make a difference when determining whether neglect was involved in a child fatality? Are any of the neglectful acts in Box 4.1 more egregious than the others? Can any be associated with merely a lapse in supervision, or do they all appear to reflect chronic neglect? Is there any sure way to tell the difference between momentary inattention and chronic neglect in any or all of these cases?

Special Issue: Prenatal Exposure to Alcohol and Drugs

Consider the last case in Box 4.1 that presented the example of the mother who used drugs while she was pregnant. Although not without controversy, prenatal drug exposure has been deemed a form of neglect because these mothers often neglect the well-being of their fetuses through lack of prenatal care and through their continual use of drugs during infancy. The most recent statistics from the National Institute on Drug Abuse (2011) show that more than 15% of pregnant women between the ages of 15 to 17 used illicit drugs, over 6% of 18- to 25-year-old pregnant women did, and about 2% of 26- to 44-year-old pregnant women used illicit drugs. Moreover, the number of infants born prenatally exposed to alcohol far exceeds this estimate and cannot readily be determined, and issues of pregnant women abusing prescription drugs are becoming more widely recognized.

The reason why some consider prenatal exposure to substances as an issue of child neglect has to do with the potentially devastating effects prenatal exposure can have on the developing embryo, fetus, and child. The effects on infants of prenatal exposure to substances may vary depending on the substance used. In addition, because mothers who use and abuse substances during pregnancy often also have chaotic home environments, poor nutrition, and little-to-no prenatal care, and because they often abuse multiple substances, it can be difficult to tease out the direct impact of any particular substance on the developing child. Moreover, the postnatal home environment is typically stressful and marked by continued parental substance abuse, further complicating efforts to ascertain the specific influence of different substances on a child's development (Kelley, 2002).

What is clear is that of all drugs, it is the legal drug—alcohol—that has been shown to have the direst consequences for prenatally exposed infants. Moreover, it is the only substance of abuse that has been shown to have irreversible negative effects, such as mental retardation, neurological deficits, facial malformations, and growth retardation (Kelley, 2002). The most serious effects of prenatal alcohol exposure fall under the label fetal alcohol syndrome (FAS). Approximately 12,000 infants each year are born with FAS (Kelley, 2002). This syndrome is characterized by pre- and postnatal growth retardation, microencephaly, abnormal facial features, mental retardation, and other possible behavioral problems, such as hyperactivity and poor motor coordination, which are indicative of central nervous system dysfunction (Day & Richardson, 1994). Less serious effects from alcohol exposure fall under one of two categories: alcohol-related birth defects (ARBD) and alcohol-related neurodevelopmental disorder (ARND). The extent to which infants and children suffer from these disorders is unknown because the criteria for each are not always clear (May & Gossage, 2001). Children with ARBD have alcohol-related physical abnormalities of the skeleton and some organ systems, without the facial abnormalities. Children with ARND exhibit retardation or learning difficulties, and other behavioral problems (May & Gossage, 2001).

At least 15 states in this country have laws that label prenatal exposure to drugs as child abuse, while many other states require notification of CPS if an infant is born exposed to substances (Christian, 2004). The Keeping Children and Families Safe Act of 2003 encourages all states to develop policies requiring notification of CPS for substance-exposed infants; certain child welfare funds are contingent on the development of such policies. From a child welfare perspective, it is noteworthy that the environment into which these infants are born is fraught with risks for their development. The behavioral problems of drug-exposed infants often lead to them being "hard to parent"; that is, these infants exhibit irritability, frequent crying, poor feeding patterns, poor consolability, frequent startles, and frantic sucking (Schutter & Brinker, 1992). This situation would be difficult to handle for even the best of parents, as these children tend to elicit parenting reactions that are punitive, hostile, or ignoring (Cuskey & Wathey, 1982). However, when the mother is a substance abuser, the situation becomes even worse. Substance abusing mothers tend to be rigid and over-controlling of their children. They display little emotional involvement or responsiveness, and they receive little pleasure from interacting with their children (Burns, Chethik, Burns, & Clark, 1991). They also tend to have low self-esteem and few positive social supports or parenting models (Cuskey & Wathey, 1982). It should come as no surprise, then, that these children are significantly more likely to be abused and neglected than demographically matched controls (Jaudes, Ekwo, & Voorhis, 1995; Kelley, 1992). In one study, as many as 60% of drug-exposed children were the subject of subsequent substantiated reports of child maltreatment (Kelley, 1992).

Given the risks for maltreatment to these children, it is not surprising that a significant portion of them are removed from their homes. In one study, as many as 42% of cocaine-exposed children had been placed in foster care (Kelley, 1992). Moreover, these children do not fare well in the foster care system: Children prenatally exposed to drugs are more likely to require multiple foster care placements than other children, and they tend to remain in foster care for longer periods of time (Curtis & McCullough, 1993).

Is taking the baby away immediately following birth in the best interests of the child? There are at least two main elements to the controversy over the removal of the child from a woman who abused drugs during pregnancy: (1) Although early medical studies seemed to indicate that exposure of unborn infants to illegal drugs carried significant risks for the fetus, later research has illustrated just how difficult it is to separate effects due to the exposure of one particular drug from effects due to smoking, alcohol use,

poor nutritional status, poor health, sexually transmitted diseases, and inadequate prenatal care—all associated with poverty; (2) The women whose babies are taken from
them are disproportionately single mothers from minority groups who are unemployed,
undereducated, and poor (Sagatun-Edwards & Saylor, 2000).

In a California study of how drug-exposed infants were processed in the social
service and juvenile justice systems following a positive toxicology screen
(Sagatun-Edwards, Saylor, & Shifflett, 1995), there was an overrepresentation of
Black and Latino cases and an underrepresentation of White and Asian cases as
compared to their relative distributions in the urban county covered by the court.
Only 22% of the women were married, and most were unemployed and had not
finished high school. The baby's father was incarcerated or awaiting a hearing in
criminal court in 25% of the cases. During the process of the court hearings, a
total of 52 cases (~20%) were ultimately returned home—34 cases following
reunification services and 18 at the initial dispositional hearing. A study addressing ongoing dispositions of drug-exposed infant cases in California indicated that
although minority cases were disproportionately represented and rated as at a
higher risk than White cases in the initial (dispositional) hearing, when controlling
for other risk factors, it was the mothers' compliance with court orders and attendance at hearings that significantly predicted subsequent court decisions (e.g.,
whether the child could be reunified with the mother or was placed into a perma-
nency planning program aimed at adoption) (Sagatun-Edwards & Saylor, 2000).

Box 4.2   Deirdre

At the age of 19, Deirdre was the mother of three and pregnant with her fourth
child. Her first child was born positive for cocaine and placed with Deirdre's mother.
Her second child was also born positive for cocaine, and a judge ordered Deirdre
to enter drug treatment or lose that child as well. A local treatment center evaluated Deirdre and recommended a two-year residential program, but there were no
openings in the program at that time. Deirdre waited six months for an opening to
become available and then entered the program. Her child was placed in foster care,
and was shuttled back and forth through several foster homes over the next few
years. Deirdre left the drug treatment program after three months, and became
pregnant again. Fearful that her third baby would be taken away because she was
still using drugs, she did not seek prenatal care. However, when she was six months
pregnant she was arrested for shoplifting, and the judge ruled that to protect her
unborn baby, she had to finish her pregnancy in jail. Following the birth of her third
child, she entered a day treatment program that provided neither transportation
nor child care. Because she could not find anyone to take care of her child, she
dropped out of the program. This was a violation of her parole, so the judge ordered
her back to jail and had her son removed from her care. Pregnant again, Deirdre
requested drug treatment, but because she had lost custody of her child, she was
no longer eligible for Medicaid and could not afford the program.

SOURCE: Whiteford & Vitucci, 1997

Consider the case of Deirdre described in Box 4.2. From an ecological perspective, what factors contributed to the fetal abuse that ultimately resulted in the removal of her children? In your view, to what extent was removal of her children in the best interest of those children? What alternatives are there to the criminal justice approach that might better serve Deirdre and her children? As Whiteford and Vitucci (1997) point out, sometimes the only way that poor minority women can get desired treatment for their addictions is to get pregnant and/or arrested. Are there better solutions?

Predictors and Correlates

The majority of research on predictors of child neglect focuses on the mother. Such predictors come at every level of the ecological model and are summarized in Table 4.2.

Table 4.2   Predictors of Neglect at Each Level of the Ecological Model

Level of the Ecological Model	Specific Predictor	Studies
Macrosystem	Poverty	Sedlak et al. (2010)
Exosystem	Social isolation and poor social networks	Dubowitz (1999); Polansky (1979); Polansky, Chalmers, Butenwieser, & Williams (1981); Polansky, Gaudin, Ammons, & Davis (1985); Williamson, Borduin, & Howe (1991)
	Poor relationships with extended family	Coohey (1995); Giovannoni & Billingsley (1970)
	Absence of fathers or poor relationship with fathers	Brown et al. (1998); Coohey (1995); Dubowitz et al. (2001)
Microsystem	Age of child	Scannapieco & Connell-Carrick (2002); Sedlak & Broadhurst (1996)
	Irritable or fussy children; disabled or premature children	Jaudes & Mackey-Bilaver (2008); Sedlak et al. (2010); Thomas & Chess (1977)
	Households with single parents with a cohabiting partner	Sedlak et al. (2010)
	Households with four or more children	Sedlak et al. (2010)
	Single-parent families	Dubowitz (1999)

(Continued)

Table 4.2 (Continued)

Level of the Ecological Model	Specific Predictor	Studies
	Domestic violence in the home	Slack, Holl, Altenbernd, McDaniel, & Stevens (2003)
	Mothers who have a greater number of children during their teen years and who were younger at the birth of their first child	Zuravin & DiBlasio (1992)
Individual/ Developmental	Gender of parent (female)	USDHHS (2010)
	Poorly educated, young, angry, dissatisfied, hostile, an external locus of control, and low self-esteem.	Brown, Cohen, Johnson, & Salzinger (1998)
	Psychopathology	Altemeier, O'Connor, Vietze, Sandler, & Sherrod (1982); Brown et al. (1998); Schumacher, Slep, & Heyman (2001)
	Substance abuse	Smith & Fong (2004)
	A history of childhood abuse or neglect	Pianta, Egeland, & Erickson (1989)
	Lack of empathy	Shahar (2001)
	Poor coping mechanisms	LaRose & Wolfe (1987)

Macrosystem

Studies consistently show that poverty is the largest contributor to neglect in this country. For example, the NIS-4 report showed that children in the lowest economic category (i.e., household income was below $15,000 a year, parents' highest education level was less than high school, or any household member participated in a poverty-related program) had over 8 times the rate of physical neglect, 4 times the rate of emotional neglect, and 7 times the rate of educational neglect, than all other children. In addition, NIS-4 showed that of all types of maltreatment, neglect was the most clearly associated with poverty (Sedlak et al., 2010). Why might there be such a strong relationship between income and neglect? Could it be that children who are in poor families are also more likely to be reported for neglect because there is a bias that poor families are inherently more neglectful of their children? Can you think of any other reasons for such a strong association? Recall that poverty is associated with unemployment, limited education, social isolation, large families with many children, and teenage pregnancy. What role might these factors play in neglect?

It is important to note that most children who are raised in poverty are not neglected. Nonetheless, the associations between neglect and poverty are so strong that some researchers (e.g., Black & Krishnakumar, 1999) have argued that we should coin another term: "societal" or "collective" neglect. Researchers also argue that eliminating poverty is essential to eliminating child neglect (e.g., Crittenden, 1999; Hamburg, 1992) and noted that the inability of the United States and/or its unwillingness to provide adequate health care, child care, education, and policies to help all families and children in this country contributes to the epidemic of child neglect. Indeed, even in the research domain, this country suffers from "neglect of neglect" (Dubowitz, 1999). However, it is also important to note that eliminating poverty may not completely eliminate child neglect, as wealthy families are also known to neglect their children, particularly emotionally (Crittenden, 1999). Thus, having an abundance of resources is not sufficient to ameliorate the inabilities of some parents to appropriately address their children's needs.

Exosystem

Although poverty imposes enormous stresses on families, not all poor families neglect their children. As a matter of fact, the majority of poor families do not neglect their children; thus, poverty is neither a necessary nor sufficient cause of neglect. The majority of families throughout human history have been poor, and by historical and cross-cultural standards, most poor U.S. families would not be considered impoverished. Therefore, as Crittenden (1999) suggested, a lack of material goods cannot be reason enough for parents to neglect their child; she proposed that to understand the nature of neglect more thoroughly, we must compare those poor families who do not neglect their children to poor families who are neglectful.

In Crittenden's (1999) view, there must be a third variable that causes both poverty and neglect in poor families that neglect their children. She postulated that the problems of being unemployed, unmarried, and socially isolated may be the key variables that separate poor neglectful families from poor nonneglectful families. According to her formulation, most parents throughout human history had to work for their resources, had to stay committed to each other for the family's survival, and had to live and raise their children in communities where other families were doing the same. If many of today's poor, neglecting families are unable to do what humans throughout history have done, Crittenden argued that they must suffer from an inability to form and maintain enduring, successful, and productive human relationships.

There is evidence to support Crittenden's conceptualization of the neglectful poor. First, neglectful families tend to relocate a lot, which contributes to their sense of social isolation (Polansky, 1979). Compared to nonneglectful mothers, neglectful mothers often have no social networks (Dubowitz, 1999) or feel surrounded by unsupportive people (Polansky, Gaudin, Ammons, & Davis, 1985). Neglectful mothers also perceive themselves as receiving less material aid, guidance, and support from the social networks they do have, and they feel like they are not being included in social activities (Williamson, Borduin, & Howe, 1991). Neglectful mothers may also have poorer relationships with their own mothers than nonneglectful mothers (Coohey, 1995). Even when neglectful mothers maintain ties with their mothers and rely on them for help with child care and money, they neither perceive them as a source of emotional support, nor give much support in return. Thus, these relationships are characterized by a low level of exchange because the neglectful mothers perceive their mothers in a negative light (Coohey, 1995). Furthermore, the absence of fathers in these homes contributes to the mothers' inability to provide adequate care for their children (Dubowitz et al., 2001).

In addition to perceiving little support from their own mothers, neglectful mothers seem to have poor relationships with their extended families (Giovannoni & Billingsley, 1970), and their interpersonal relationships may be characterized by pervasive feelings of futility, emotional numbness, clinginess, and loneliness (Polansky, Chalmers, Butenwieser, & Williams, 1981). Also, neglectful parents are more likely to be single parents, have a poor quality marriage (e.g., Brown, Cohen, Johnson, & Salzinger, 1998), not live with their partners, and have shorter relationships with their partners (Coohey, 1995). In addition to these problems, or perhaps due to them, several researchers have found that neglectful families tend to be the poorest of the poor (e.g., Bath & Haapala, 1993), and often suffer from unemployment (Dubowitz, 1999).

Microsystem

Characteristics of the Child. What kinds of characteristics might children have that could contribute to poor relations with their parents and thereby lead to neglect? Age appears to be one factor, with children under 3 being the most vulnerable to neglect and to its more severe consequences (Scannapieco & Connell-Carrick, 2002), probably because older children have fewer needs than younger children. However, older children may be more at risk for emotional neglect (Sedlak & Broadhurst, 1996).

It also appears that irritable or fussy children (e.g., Thomas & Chess, 1977), and disabled or premature children (e.g., Jaudes & Mackey-Bilaver, 2008; Sedlak et al., 2010) are more likely to suffer from neglect than other children. Brachfield, Goldberg, and Sloman (1980) assert that ultimately it is the parents' responsibility to respond to their children in a sensitive manner, regardless of any difficulties the children may have. What is your view of this issue? Can you think of child characteristics that may make child care difficult? Should parents who do not cope well with those characteristics, and thereby neglect their children, be reported for child maltreatment? If so, what would be the best intervention methods for such cases?

Characteristics of the Family. The NIS-4 identified characteristics of the family that may be risk factors for child neglect. The highest rates of neglect occurred in households with single parents with a cohabiting partner, and in households with four or more children (Sedlak et al., 2010). Why do you think these associations exist? Why might children from single-parent families with cohabiters and children from large families be more likely to be reported for neglect than their counterparts? Other research shows that families without a supportive social network, particularly single-parent families, are at higher risk for neglect (Dubowitz, 1999), as are households characterized by domestic violence (Slack, Holl, Altenbernd, McDaniel, & Stevens, 2003). Finally, mothers who have a greater number of children during their teen years and who were younger at the birth of their first child showed an increased risk of neglect (Zuravin & DiBlasio, 1992).

Individual/Developmental

Mothers are significantly more likely to be reported as neglectful than fathers (USDHHS, 2010), which may be a reflection of the fact that single-parent households tend to be headed by women and a reflection of stereotypes holding that women are responsible for childcare (Turney, 2000). Indeed, even in two-parent families, it is not uncommon for only the mothers to be labeled neglectful (Azar, Ferraro, & Breton, 1998). Thus, most of the research on characteristics of neglectful parents tends to focus on mothers.

Neglectful mothers tend to be poorly educated, young, angry, dissatisfied, and hostile, and to have an external locus of control (i.e., a belief that outside forces determine their circumstances) and low self-esteem (Brown et al., 1998). They are more likely to suffer from some sort of psychopathology, including depression (Schumacher, Slep, & Heyman, 2001), poor impulse control, especially under stress (Altemeier, O'Connor, Vietze, Sandler, & Sherrod, 1982), and even sociopathy (Brown et al., 1998). Neglectful fathers are more likely to show little or no warmth, and to suffer from psychopathology or sociopathy (Brown et al., 1998; Schumacher et al., 2001). Neglectful parents are also more likely to abuse substances (Smith & Fong, 2004).

In addition to problems affecting their ability to respond to their children, many neglectful parents have a history of abuse or neglect in their own childhood. Pianta, Egeland, and Erickson (1989) suggested that neglectful mothers are trying to resolve their own issues of trust, dependency, and autonomy—issues that are related to their history of abuse and neglect. They also argued that rather than trying to meet their children's needs, these mothers are seeking to satisfy their own needs through their relationship with their children, and unrealistic expectations of their children probably led to an unhappy parent-child relationship. Of all types of maltreating mothers, neglectful mothers seem to have the most negative interactions with their children (Burgess & Conger, 1978), and they seem to show the least empathy (Shahar, 2001). Neglectful mothers also tend to have poor coping mechanisms for dealing with problems with their children. For example, instead of confronting their child (as abusive parents tend to do), neglectful parents often do not demand anything from their children and actually avoid them during stressful events (LaRose & Wolfe, 1987). Perhaps because no one is psychologically available to these mothers, they cannot be psychologically available to their children (Garbarino & Collins, 1999).

Consequences

There is some evidence that neglect, in comparison to other types of maltreatment, can have the most pervasive and negative outcomes. Neglected children are the most at risk for fatalities (USDHHS, 2010), and emotional neglect can lead to nonorganic failure to thrive (Greenbaum et al., 2008), which can result in death or pervasive physical and psychological problems. Several investigators have come to the conclusion that neglected children, in comparison to other maltreated children, also suffer the worst effects socially, emotionally, and academically. For example, one longitudinal study showed that at age 24 months, neglected children—in comparison to physically abused and control children—had the least enthusiasm in problem-solving tasks, and were the most angry, frustrated, and noncompliant children (Egeland, Sroufe, & Erickson, 1983). At 42 months, they had the worst impulse control, the least flexibility and creativity, the lowest self-esteem, the most incompetence on school tasks, and the most difficulty coping. They were also the most withdrawn, dependent, and angry of all the groups of children.

Other problems have been identified in neglected children. At two years of age, they are easily frustrated, angered, noncompliant, avoidant, and unaffectionate in their social interactions with their mothers, and by 3.5 years of age, they show poor impulse control, rigidity, little creativity, and more unhappiness than their peers; by 4.5 years, they still have the poor impulse control, and they also show extreme dependence on their teachers and poor adjustment in the classroom (Erickson & Egeland, 2011). Overall, neglected children tend to have poor expressive and receptive language skills, a low overall IQ, cognitive dysfunctions, and academic difficulties (Cahill, Kaminer, & Johnson, 1999; Culp, Little, Letts, & Lawrence, 1991; Gowan, 1993). In social interactions, they tend to be passive, withdrawn, and unaffectionate; they tend to initiate interactions less frequently than other children (Crittenden, 1992), and they tend to display mostly internalizing, withdrawn, and aggressive behaviors (Erickson, Egeland, & Pianta, 1989; Manly, Kim, Rogosch, & Cicchetti, 2001).

The low IQ and poor academic performance characteristics of these children (Eckenrode, Laird, & Doris, 1993) can extend into adulthood. At age 28, even after controlling for several possible confounds, adults who had a childhood history of neglect still had a lower IQ and poorer reading abilities (Perez & Widom, 1994). The problems of social incompetence, depression, withdrawal, and other behavior problems also seem to continue throughout the childhood of neglected children (Aber, Allen, Carlson, & Cicchetti, 1989; Herrenkohl, Herrenkohl, Egolf, & Wu, 1991).

When neglected children become adolescents, they have a higher likelihood than control subjects of being aggressive, delinquent, and engaging in violent crime (Kotch et al., 2008; Merskey & Reynolds, 2007; Widom, 1989; Zingraff, Leiter, Johnson, & Myers, 1994). Neglected children are also at risk for running away from home and becoming prostitutes (Kaufman & Widom, 1999; Widom & Kuhns, 1996), and for developing personality disorders and psychological problems such as depression, anxiety, self-mutilation, and suicidal ideation (Johnson, Cohen, Brown, Smailes, & Bernstein, 1999; Johnson, Smailes, Cohen, Brown, & Bernstein, 2000; Lipschitz et al., 1999). As adults, individuals with a history of neglect are at higher risk of engaging in violence against an intimate partner (White & Widom, 2003), and they may neglect their own children; several researchers have found that some neglectful parents report a history of neglect in their own childhoods and many report a history of feeling unwanted or unloved as children (Gaudin, Polansky, Kilpatrick, & Shilton, 1996; Polansky et al., 1981).

Consequences of Neglect in Combination with Other Forms of Maltreatment

Although these studies show that neglected children are at risk for many developmental problems, the results are subject to debate on a number of methodological grounds. For one, many investigators failed to distinguish between the various types of neglect. Second, because there is no consensus in the literature on the definition of neglect, most investigators study only neglected children whose neglect was substantiated by CPS. The problem here is that because CPS is an overburdened institution, only the most severe cases get substantiated (Gaudin, 1999), and it may be only these very severe cases that show the most negative outcomes. Third, as with other types of maltreatment, the outcomes of neglect depend on a variety of moderating factors. Several factors that may impact the outcome, particularly poverty, were discussed in the previous section on predictors and correlates of neglect. The more severe and more frequent these factors, the more likely the child will have a poor outcome. Other factors, such as the age of the child and the chronicity and severity of the neglect, have also been found to influence outcomes (English et al., 2005). If the neglect begins when the child is an infant, the child is more likely to become developmentally disabled. In one study, children who were neglected as infants, in comparison with those whose neglect began in early childhood, performed less well cognitively; were less confident, assertive, and creative; and had poorer self-esteem and emotional health (Erickson et al., 1989).

The combination of neglect with other forms of maltreatment also seems to contribute to negative outcomes. As mentioned in Chapter 3, most forms of child maltreatment do not occur in isolation, and the consequences of experiencing multiple forms increases the risk for poor outcomes (Finkelhor, 2008). For instance, in comparison to either type of maltreatment alone, neglect in combination with sexual abuse has been associated with poorer reading and math skills, more suspensions from school, and increased delinquency (Eckenrode et al., 1993; Gaudin et al., 1996). Neglect in combination with physical abuse appears to be related to poorer English skills (Eckenrode et al., 1993).

Consequences of Neglect in Comparison to Other Forms of Maltreatment

As can be seen from the discussion thus far, neglect and physical maltreatment are conceptually and experientially different acts with potentially different consequences. Some studies, such as those done as part of the Minnesota Longitudinal Study of High Risk Parents and Children (e.g., Erickson et al., 1989), attempted to address these possible differences by comparing neglected children not only to nonmaltreated controls, but also to physically abused children. After all, neglect and abuse are two different phenomena—one involves acts of commission, the other involves acts of omission. In addition, these researchers further divided the neglected children into those who were physically neglected and those who were emotionally neglected. Overall, they found that all maltreated children performed poorly in comparison to the control group, and that there was a high incidence of anxious attachment among them (Erickson & Egeland, 2011). They also found some interesting differences between groups.

The Minnesota study (Erickson & Egeland, 2011) showed how problematic emotional neglect can actually be: At 1.5 years of age, the emotionally neglected children were the most anxiously attached of all the children; in addition, they showed a steep decline in their intellectual functioning between the ages of 9 months and 2 years. At 2 and 3.5 years, they displayed little positive affect, were angry and noncompliant, and showed no persistence. At 4.5 years, in addition to other problems displayed by neglected children (e.g., noncompliance, impulsivity, dependence on teachers), emotionally neglected children displayed nervous signs and self-destructive behavior. During their elementary school years, these children were rated by their teachers as being low in peer acceptance and overall emotional health; they were more aggressive than their peers and performed significantly worse on tests of achievement. During their teen years, emotionally neglected children had a higher number of social problems, were more delinquent, more aggressive, and more suicidal than their peers, and the majority of them had at least two psychiatric disorders, with almost all having one (Erickson & Egeland, 2011).

The Minnesota study also shows that in comparison to physically abused and nonabused children, both physically and emotionally neglected children are more passive, withdrawn, avoidant, and isolated in their peer and other relationships (e.g., Erickson et al., 1989). In addition, they are more aggressive, noncompliant, and uncooperative than non-maltreated children (Erickson et al., 1989), and they tend to display more internalizing and externalizing behavior problems (Erickson & Egeland, 2011). Consequently, they tend to be unpopular with their peers (Erickson et al., 1989). They have more problems with regulating their own emotions; are less able to discriminate the emotions of others; are more hopeless in stressful situations; have poorer coping strategies; display less agency, ego control, self-esteem, positive effect, and sense of humor; and they display more dependency and negative affect (Egeland & Sroufe, 1981; Egeland et al., 1983; Erickson et al., 1989; Pollack, Cicchetti, Hornung, & Reed, 2000). Moreover, their teachers rank both groups of neglected children as inferior academically and unable to cope with the everyday demands of school. As teenagers, those who had been physically neglected displayed poor academic achievement, delinquency, relatively high dropout rates from high school, high rates of alcohol use, and relatively high rates of expulsion (Erickson & Egeland, 2011).

Prevention and Intervention

There is no overarching social policy for the issue of child neglect, and programs that are designed to prevent and intervene in other forms of maltreatment are typically used for neglect as well. However, because neglect can have different causes and consequences than other forms of maltreatment, there is a need to develop prevention and intervention programs that are specific to neglect and informed by neglect research. This issue is becoming more pressing because, as the issue of neglect becomes better publicized, more cases are being reported.

An additional complication is that current CPS policies regarding neglect are quite vague. For example, there are no clear-cut guidelines for what is considered less-than-optimal parenting and what is considered neglect (Gelles, 1999). Consequently, usually only the most extreme forms of neglect are addressed in intervention programs. When intervention programs are mandated for neglectful families, programs tailored for child neglect seem to be effective with fewer than 50% of the families mandated to use them, and the most effective ones are those that are long-term and very comprehensive (Gaudin, 1993; Holden & Nabors, 1999). It is difficult to develop effective programs when the individual/developmental problems that make it difficult for parents to connect with their children are the same problems that make it difficult for parents to connect with service providers. Indeed, experts in the field argue that it is important to reach out to expectant parents—for example, through home visitation programs such as those discussed in Chapter 2—before they have a chance to become neglectful, because trying to secure intervention services for them afterwards is very difficult (Erickson & Egeland, 2011).

Because of the specific problems that neglectful families face, several researchers have forwarded suggestions to improve the effectiveness of intervention programs. For example, DePanfilis (1999) has argued that such programs should be family-based, not individual-based; they should help to create an alliance between the family and agencies or people in their community who are sources of support; they should empower families to manage several co-occurring stressors in their lives effectively in order to solve their own problems without relying on the social service system; and they should work with the families' strengths, instead of trying to fix their weaknesses. DePanfilis (1999) suggested that successful neglect intervention programs should encompass some or all of the following, depending on the families' needs: (1) provision of concrete resources; (2) provision or mobilization of social support networks; (3) developmental remediation, such as therapeutic day care for the neglected child, peer groups at school that are geared toward developmentally appropriate tasks, public health visits to the family with the goal of providing assistance with attachment needs of each family member, mentors for the parents to provide nurture, recreation, and role modeling, and/or individual assistance with parenting skills; (4) cognitive-behavioral therapy to provide instructions about basic child care, social skills training to handle child care tasks, stress management such as relaxation techniques or other coping mechanisms, and cognitive restructuring to address dysfunctional and self-defeating thoughts; (5) individual-focused therapy to help individual family members deal with other related problems, such as alcohol or drug abuse, depression, and developmental delays; and (6) family systems therapy to aid with family functioning, communication skills, roles, home management, and responsibilities. Erickson and Egeland (2011) further argue that such programs need to be empathic and compassionate regarding the parents' experiences, yet hold the parents responsible for their behavior. To what levels of the ecological framework are these goals directed? What will be needed at the macro- and exosystem levels to establish such programs?

Psychological Maltreatment

Scope of the Problem

Table 4.3 summarizes some of the major prevalence studies of psychological maltreatment in this country. According to the USDHHS (2011), psychological maltreatment is the second least prevalent form of child maltreatment (medical neglect is the least prevalent), accounting for 8.1% of all maltreated children. Although the USDHHS identified only 55,405 children as victimized by psychological maltreatment in 2010, the NIS-4 (Sedlak et al., 2010) indicated that 148,500 children (or 2 per 1,000) were emotionally abused according to the Harm Standard in 2005–2006) and 302,600 children (4.1 per 1,000 children) were emotionally abused according to the Endangerment Standard in 2005–2006. Why the differing numbers? Why does one study based on CPS reports find incredibly low estimates for psychological maltreatment, while another study based on cases identified by mandated reporters finds moderately high estimates? Historically, one of the most difficult problems has been defining and conceptualizing the concept of psychological maltreatment within the child maltreatment types. Therefore, it has been very difficult for legal and medical services to provide accurate estimates or services for families suffering from this elusive phenomenon. Where do we draw the line between less-than-adequate parenting and psychological maltreatment? After all, almost all parents at some point in time engage in behaviors that ignore, criticize, or are unsupportive of their children in some way. When are the behaviors just necessary discipline or parenting? Or even just a momentary lapse in good judgment? How do we know when they have crossed the line into psychological maltreatment?

To give an example, imagine what would happen if a child called the police because his parents called him a dirty name. Has he been psychologically maltreated? What is the legal response likely to be? What would your response be? There are states that attempt to define psychological maltreatment, with some requiring serious psychological injury or likelihood of such injury before CPS intervention, but others allowing intervention when a parent fails to provide for their child's emotional and psychological needs (Hart et al., 2011). However, it is rare that a child will be the subject of a CPS investigation when the only form of suspected maltreatment is psychological.

Society has traditionally subscribed to the belief that physical and sexual maltreatment are more harmful than psychological maltreatment (Brassard, Hart, & Hardy, 2000; Kashani & Allan, 1998). However, studies show that the psychological dimensions of all other forms of child maltreatment are the most damaging, and that psychological maltreatment alone is associated with a host of negative outcomes (Hart et al., 2011). Moreover, in early childhood and adolescence, psychological maltreatment—particularly isolation and denying emotional responsiveness—is the most damaging, and in middle childhood, psychological maltreatment—particularly verbal abuse—in combination with physical maltreatment is the most harmful type of maltreatment (Brassard & Donovan, 2006; Hart, Binggeli, & Brassard, 1998). Take, for example, the case in Box 4.3. Do you think the emotional

Table 4.3 Prevalence Rates of the Psychological Maltreatment of Children

Study	Description of Sample	Measures/ Definition of Maltreatment	Rates of Maltreatment
U.S. Department of Health and Human Services (2011), *Child Maltreatment 2010*	An estimated 3.3 million referrals, involving the alleged maltreatment of approximately 5.9 million children, in 2010	Cases referred to Child Protective Services (CPS) in 2010	• 8.1% of maltreated children were psychologically maltreated (55,405 children)
Sedlak et al. (2010), Fourth National Incidence Study of Child Abuse and Neglect (2005–2006)	A nationally representative sample of over 10,790 professionals in 1,094 agencies serving 126 counties	• *Harm Standard*—requires that an act or omission result in demonstrable harm in order to be classified as abuse or neglect • *Endangerment Standard*—a sentinel thought that the maltreatment endangered the children or a CPS investigation substantiated or indicated their maltreatment	• *Harm Standard:* 148,500 children (2 per 1,000) were emotionally abused • *Endangerment Standard:* 302,600 children (4.1 per 1,000 children) were emotionally abused
Binggeli, Hart, & Brassard (2000)	Review of official reports, adults' retrospective reports, and representative surveys of American parents	Definition depends on the study being reviewed	• 15% to 20% of American children experience psychological maltreatment without any other form of maltreatment • 33% of American children are psychologically maltreated in combination with some other form of maltreatment

scars that Cinderella suffered will heal as quickly as the physical scars suffered by the child in Box 2.1 of Chapter 2? What messages were conveyed to Cinderella? How easily can the effects of these messages be overcome?

Box 4.3   Cinderella: A Case of Psychological Maltreatment

The teenage half brother of Cinderella, an emotionally abused child, lived at home with her until she was four years old and recounted a series of maltreatments against Cinderella by her stepmother. Cinderella was never allowed to play outside, while the other kids in the household were. Cinderella was left in the car alone when her stepmother and the other kids went visiting or shopping. Her stepmother called her "stupid" and "ugly" on many occasions. She also yelled at Cinderella a lot and gave her a large share of the household chores. The stepmother spanked Cinderella many times, sometimes even with a spatula or a wooden spoon, and while the other children received little corporal punishment from the mother, Cinderella often had scratches or bruises all over her body.

One major source of conflict between Cinderella and her stepmother was over Cinderella's eating habits. If the stepmother did not feel that Cinderella was eating properly, she would forcefully stuff food into Cinderella's mouth or slap her. Many times she would also be sent to her room for this behavior, and on her way, the stepmother would kick her hard enough to hurt her. Cinderella was kept in her room so often that the bedroom smelled of urine. The other children were rarely sent to their rooms. The half brother recounted that Cinderella cried often, was always very sad, and never smiled. However, after Cinderella was removed from the home and the half brother visited her in her new home, he stated that for the first time, Cinderella was happy, smiling, and affectionate—her entire appearance and demeanor had changed.

SOURCE: Binggeli, Hart, & Brassard, 2001

Several researchers (e.g., Hart et al., 2011) have argued that psychological maltreatment is at the core of all other forms of child maltreatment, including physical and sexual abuse, and neglect. In other words, it unifies all types of maltreatment. According to Binggeli and colleagues (2001):

a) psychological maltreatment is probably embedded in nearly all other acts of abuse and neglect as the psychological meaning of those acts,

b) it appears to be the strongest predictor of the impact of child maltreatment, and

c) psychological maltreatment may have the longest-lasting and strongest negative effects on survivors of child abuse and neglect. (p. 15)

In addition, psychological maltreatment can occur on its own. Thus, as opposed to being one of the *least* prevalent forms of child maltreatment, as reported by USDHHS, it is more likely *the most* prevalent.

In 1995, the American Professional Society on the Abuse of Children (APSAC) attempted to resolve some of the definitional crises plaguing the construct of psychological maltreatment by offering a basic definition and conceptualization. Two of the most widely accepted statements include:

Statement 1: "Psychological maltreatment" means a repeated pattern of caregiver behavior or extreme incident(s) that convey to children that they are worthless, flawed, unloved, unwanted, endangered, or only of value in meeting another's needs. (APSAC, 1995, p. 2)

Statement 2: Psychological maltreatment includes (a) spurning [acts that reject and degrade a child], (b) terrorizing [acts that put the child or a loved one in a dangerous situation], (c) isolating [denying the child opportunities to meet and interact with others outside the home], (d) exploiting/corrupting [acts that encourage the child to develop inappropriate behaviors—e.g., criminal, deviant, etc.], (e) denying emotional responsiveness [ignoring the child's needs to interact], and (f) mental health, medical, and educational neglect. (APSAC, 1995, p. 4)

Take another look at the case in Box 4.3. Does this case fit this conceptualization and definition of psychological maltreatment? Based on the six factors in Statement 2, what types of psychological maltreatment did Cinderella suffer from? Did the perpetrator convey the messages described in Statement 1? How?

Several researchers have attempted to achieve a better estimate of the incidence of psychological maltreatment by either using adults' retrospective reports of behaviors reflecting the above definition of psychological maltreatment or asking parents the types of behaviors they use with their children. Based on a review of the literature that included official reports, adults' retrospective reports of psychological maltreatment, and representative surveys of American parents, Binggeli and colleagues (2000) estimated that 15% to 20% of American children experience psychological maltreatment without any other form of maltreatment, and more than 33% of American children are psychologically maltreated in combination with some other type of maltreatment.

Predictors and Correlates

Little research has been conducted on the specific predictors of psychological maltreatment (see Table 4.4), probably because most cases of psychological maltreatment never become known to the public. The NIS-4 report (Sedlak et al., 2010) provides the most information on predictors of psychological maltreatment, which mainly fall at two levels of the ecological model: the macrosystem and the microsystem. At the macrosystem level, NIS-4 showed that children of the lowest socioeconomic status (household income below $15,000 a year, parents' highest education level less than high school, or any household member participated in a poverty-related program) were 5 times more likely to experience emotional abuse than other children; children whose parents were not in the labor force were more than twice as likely to be emotionally abused as children whose parents were employed; and children from rural areas were more than twice as likely to be emotionally abused as children from urban areas. At the microsystem level, children over the age of 6 were

Table 4.4   Predictors of Psychological Maltreatment at Different Levels of the Ecological Model

Level of the Ecological Model	Specific Predictor	Studies
Macrosystem	Low socioeconomic status	Sedlak et al. (2010)
	Unemployment	Sedlak et al. (2010)
	Living in rural areas	Sedlak et al. (2010)
Microsystem	Age: Children over the age of 6	Sedlak et al. (2010)
	Children living with non-biological parents or with a single parent	Sedlak et al. (2010)
Individual/ Developmental	Mental illness and/or personality disturbance	Lesnik-Oberstein, Koers, & Cohen (1995)
	Physical illness	Lesnik-Oberstein et al. (1995)
	Poor verbal reasoning abilities	Lesnik-Oberstein et al. (1995)
	Engaging in fewer social activities	Lesnik-Oberstein et al. (1995)
	Major depression and/or substance use disorders	Hawley, Halle, Drasin, & Thomas (1995); Radke-Yarrow & Klimes-Dougan (2002)
	Experiencing psychological maltreatment as a child	Hemenway, Solnick & Carter (1994)

more than twice as likely to be psychologically maltreated as children under the age of 6; children living with other married parents and those living with a single parent, whether with or without a partner, were psychologically maltreated at significantly higher rates than those living with two married biological parents, with the highest rate of psychological maltreatment for children whose single parent lived with a partner, which was more than 10 times greater than for children living with two married biological parents.

The other research that assesses predictors primarily focuses on the individual/developmental level. Such research shows that parents who psychologically maltreat their children have increased levels of difficulties with interpersonal and social interactions, problem solving skills, and mental illness. For example, one study showed that in comparison to non-maltreating mothers, mothers who psychologically maltreat their children have more symptoms of mental illness, such as depression, aggression, and hostility; they have more personality disturbances, such as social anxiety, neuroticism, and low self-esteem; they have more physical illnesses; they have poorer verbal reasoning abilities; and they engage in fewer social activities (Lesnik-Oberstein,

Koers, & Cohen, 1995). Parents who psychologically maltreat their children can often be diagnosed with major depressive and substance use disorders (Hawley, Halle, Drasin, & Thomas, 1995; Radke-Yarrow & Klimes-Dougan, 2002). Finally, there seems to be an intergenerational transmission of this behavior as well, with parents who were yelled at frequently as children growing up to be parents who are more likely to frequently yell at their own children (Hemenway, Solnick, & Carter, 1994).

Consequences

More research on the consequences of psychological maltreatment has been conducted than on its predictors and correlates, and the research tends to be more elusive. This is probably due to the fact that a single act of psychological maltreatment is unlikely to cause any damage, but the cumulative effects of psychological maltreatment over time are what results in harm—harm that may be even more serious than that experienced by victims of physical and sexual maltreatment (Higgins & McCabe, 2000; Ney, Fung, & Wickett, 1994). Although not specifically addressed in studies, many moderators probably impact the severity of the adjustment problems of psychologically maltreated children. Factors such as the severity of the abuse, its duration and frequency, child's age, child's gender, and socioeconomic status probably influence how much the child will be affected by the maltreatment. Furthermore, the presence of a supportive adult in a psychologically maltreated child's life can buffer negative consequences (e.g., Rutter, 1985).

Research has shown negative impacts of psychological maltreatment in almost every aspect of a child's life. Furthermore, because this form of child maltreatment is often not reported to authorities, the impacted children may experience the maltreatment throughout their childhood and still feel its effects well into adulthood. The effects of psychological maltreatment are often better and more powerful predictors of negative outcomes than any other form of maltreatment (e.g., Brown, 1984; Crittenden, Claussen, & Sugarman, 1994; McCord, 1983; Ney et al., 1994; Vissing, Straus, Gelles, & Harrop, 1991).

Psychological maltreatment of children has an impact on children's interpersonal lives, their emotional lives, their social competency, their ability to learn, and their physical health (Hart et al., 2011). For example, in early childhood, psychological maltreatment has led children to feel unloved and inadequate. They may suffer from low self-esteem, anxious attachment to their caregivers, negative emotions, hyperactivity, and distractibility. They may lack impulse control, and have difficulty learning and solving problems. Some lack enthusiasm, persistence, and creativity in their schoolwork. Furthermore, many display angry and noncompliant behavior, which frequently leads to physical aggression (Egeland & Erickson, 1987; Egeland et al., 1983; Erickson et al., 1989; Herrenkohl, Egolf, & Herrenkohl, 1997). This aggression has been shown to continue into adolescence, where it is reflected in a higher degree of juvenile delinquency and assaultive behaviors (Brown, 1984; Herrenkohl et al., 1997; Loeber & Strouthamer-Loeber, 1986; Vissing et al., 1991). How many of these effects can you see in the case of Cinderella in Box 4.3? In her case, do you think it is possible to separate the effects of the physical maltreatment from those of the psychological maltreatment?

Along with a higher rate of juvenile delinquency and aggressiveness, adolescents with a history of psychological maltreatment also seem to have problems with their interpersonal relationships (Vissing et al., 1991). These problems may result from negative perspectives on their possibilities for enjoyment in life, purpose in life, prospects for a future life, chances of having a happy marriage, and expectations for being good parents (Ney et al., 1994). These adolescents also have higher rates of conduct disorders, attention problems, anxiety and withdrawal, psychotic behaviors, and motor excesses (Crittenden et al., 1994).

As college students, individuals with a history of psychological maltreatment have higher rates of anxiety, depression, interpersonal sensitivity, dissociation, low self-esteem (Briere & Runtz, 1988, 1990), and bulimia (Rorty, Yager, & Rossotto, 1994). As adolescents and adults, people with histories of being verbally abused by their mothers are more likely to develop a range of personality disorders, including narcissistic, borderline, obsessive-compulsive, and paranoid personality disorders (Johnson, Cohen, & Smailes, 2001).

Adults with a childhood history of psychological maltreatment are more likely to physically abuse their children and spouses (DeLozier, 1982; Dutton, 1995). Outside their families, adult men with childhood histories of psychological maltreatment have been shown to have higher rates of criminal behavior, emotional instability, and substance abuse (McCord, 1983). Other studies attest to the range of difficulties that adults with a history of childhood psychological maltreatment display, including low self-esteem, anxiety, depression, and interpersonal sensitivity (Downs & Miller, 1998; Kent & Waller, 2000; Langhinrichsen-Rohling, Monson, Meyer, Caster, & Sanders, 1998; Mullen, Martin, Anderson, Romans, & Herbison, 1996). To what extent do these outcomes seem to be the same as the outcomes of the other forms of maltreatment? How would you account for any differences in outcomes associated with psychological maltreatment as compared with the outcomes of the other forms of maltreatment? In what ways can the similarities in outcomes be accounted for?

Special Issue: Children Witnessing Interparental Aggression

Many researchers conceptualize the witnessing of interparental aggression as a form of psychological maltreatment. Some judges have ruled it as a form of neglect (Myers, 2005), and there have been cases where men have been prosecuted for assaulting their female partners in front of children (e.g., *People v. Johnson*, NY Int. 116, 2000). Such incidents have prompted research into the possible consequences that this type of exposure can have on child witnesses, and the majority of research has focused on children of battered women (Wolak & Finkelhor, 1998). Indeed, the majority of children of battered women have witnessed severe violence against their mothers (Graham-Bermann, Gruber, Girz, & Howell, 2009); however, it is important to note that the majority of children of maltreated men have also witnessed the violence (Hines & Douglas, 2010a), and thus, their adjustment should be evaluated as well. Consider the case of Maria presented in Box 4.4. How do you think she might be affected in the short run by witnessing the abuse of her mother? How might she be affected in the long run?

| Box 4.4 | **Children Witnessing Interparental Aggression** |

Once married, conflict between Mr. and Mrs. P. increased dramatically as a result of Mr. P.'s infidelities and verbal abuse, and worsened with the birth of their first child, Maria. The first violent incident occurred three months after Maria was born and involved Mr. P. pushing, slapping, and hitting his wife. The second incident occurred four months later in which Mr. P. repeatedly punched his wife's face with his fists. Following this, Mrs. P. was battered severely every few months with considerable family tension between incidents. Each battering incident left Mrs. P. with bruises on her face or torso and necessitated calling in sick to the hospital where she worked as a nurse. Their second and third children were born at intervals of two years, and although each child was planned and ostensibly desired by both parents, Mr. P.'s beatings were especially severe shortly after each birth. Maria [now age seven] witnessed the most extensive violence between her mother and father, but there were times when Mr. P. would force all his daughters to watch while he beat their mother.

SOURCE: Rosenberg, Giberson, Rossman, & Acker, 2000, p. 261

It is estimated that approximately 15.5 million children are exposed to interparental violence annually, and that 7 million are exposed to more severe violence, such as seeing a parent being beaten up, threatened with a gun or knife, stabbed, or shot (McDonald, Jouriles, Ramisetty-Mikler, Caetano, & Green, 2006). In a review of studies on children exposed to interparental violence, Wolak and Finkelhor (1998) found that most of the research involved children of battered women in shelters. Most, if not all, of these children had frequently witnessed very severe violence by their fathers against their mothers; moreover, these children were not just passive viewers of the violence—they often interceded in the violence or were victims of violence themselves. Wolak and Finkelhor's review revealed that such children tend to have problems in five areas of functioning: (1) *behavioral*—they tend to be more aggressive and delinquent than children not exposed to violence, to be cruel to animals and truant from school, and to suffer from attention deficit hyperactivity disorder more often than non-exposed children; (2) *emotional*—they tend to be more anxious, angry, depressed, and withdrawn than non-exposed children, to suffer from lower self-esteem, and to have symptoms of post-traumatic stress disorder (PTSD); (3) *social*—they tend to have poor social skills, be rejected by their peers, and have an inability to empathize; (4) *cognitive*—they may suffer from language and other developmental delays, and have academic problems; and (5) *physical*—they may suffer from difficulty sleeping and eating, have poor motor skills, and display psychosomatic symptoms (e.g., bed-wetting). More recent research confirms Wolak and Finkelhor's conclusions (Gewirtz & Edelson, 2007; Graham-Bermann et al., 2009; Graham-Bermann & Seng, 2005; Kilpatrick et al., 2003; Lieberman & Knorr, 2007; McDonald, Jouriles, Briggs-Gowan, Rosenfield, & Carter, 2007).

One recent meta-analysis showed that between 40% and 60% of school-aged children who witnessed interparental violence score in the clinical range for a variety of both internalizing and externalizing behavioral problems (Wolfe, Crooks, Lee, McIntyre-Smith, & Jaffe, 2003). Moreover, because child witnesses are also at higher risk for sustaining other types of child maltreatment in the home (Daro, Edelson, & Pinderhughes, 2004; Graham-Bermann et al., 2009; Osofsky, 2003), this accumulation of types of maltreatment can lead to even more severe outcomes (Finkelhor, 2008).

Children may suffer both direct and indirect effects from witnessing interparental violence. Direct effects include dealing with the immediate physical danger and emotional problems resulting from witnessing a traumatic incident, as well as learning violent behaviors modeled by parents. Indirect effects may occur when the negative impact of violence on the mother's emotional and physical health results in poor parenting skills (e.g., inconsistency, distraction, irritability, unresponsiveness or neglect, and/or abuse), which in turn can affect the psychological functioning of her children (Dehon & Weems, 2010; Wolak & Finkelhor, 1998). Whatever the pathways, the negative effects of witnessing parental violence seem to follow children into adolescence, when they are at greater risk for running away and using drugs and alcohol (Goldblatt, 2003; Wolak & Finkelhor, 1998) and for behaving aggressively toward their peers (Moretti, Obsuth, Odgers, & Reebye, 2006). As adults, former child witnesses of interparental violence are more likely than nonwitnesses to exhibit trauma symptoms, anxiety, depression, low self-esteem, aggression, poor social skills, stress, and alcohol and drug problems (Wolak & Finkelhor, 1998). Furthermore, they are more likely to perpetrate spousal and child maltreatment in their own families, and are more likely to be victimized by spousal aggression (Milletich, Kelley, Doane, & Pearson, 2010; Wolak & Finkelhor, 1998).

There is increasing recognition that child maltreatment and intimate partner violence are tightly intertwined. Based on a review of the relevant literature, Appel and Holden (1998) concluded that the rate of co-occurrence of child abuse and interparental violence across the United States population is approximately 6%; however, they also concluded that within samples of homes that are identified as violent by professionals, the co-occurrence rate appears to be about 40%, with others arguing that it is as high as 60% (Daro et al., 2004). Even when children are not physically maltreated by either of their parents, there is increasing concern that merely observing interparental violence can have deleterious effects on children. Consequently, in increasing numbers, children are being removed from the custody of mothers who are staying with or returning to their batterers. Some researchers argue that one aspect of this child removal policy seems to be an assumption among child welfare workers that mothers are the primary caregivers of children and that any trauma to the children is more the mother's fault than the father's, even if the trauma stems from the father beating the mother (Mills, 2000). Moreover, critics argue that many child welfare workers seem to believe there is only one acceptable way for battered women to respond to their perpetrator's violence, and that is to leave the abusive partner permanently. If battered women fail to respond to this mandate, some child welfare workers have argued that their children should be removed permanently from their custody (Magen, 1999; Mills, 2000).

Not surprisingly, this trend has generated much controversy. Advocates for battered women view the policy as adding another layer of abuse to the lives of battered women—specifically, abuse at the hands of a CPS system that takes their children away from them, instead of providing adequate assistance in the process of their trying to escape from their batterers (Fleck-Henderson, 2000). In addition, adding another type of maltreatment to the laws can cripple an already overburdened CPS. Doing so increases the number of referrals that CPS must investigate (Kantor & Little, 2003). Minnesota, for example, had to repeal a law mandating reporting of all intimate partner violence exposure cases because it overwhelmed the CPS system. Moreover, such laws put victims of intimate partner violence in a precarious position—if they were to seek help from the systems that were available to them, those systems would be mandated to report them to CPS for child abuse (Jaffe, Crooks, & Wolfe, 2003).

Box 4.5	Child Maltreatment and Intimate Partner Violence

The Department of Social Services (DSS) became involved with the Smith family after Joe assaulted Sandra with a knife, inflicting several wounds. Joe was arrested and a criminal case against him was initiated. Sandra, who reported to the caseworker that she feared for her life, obtained a restraining order; however, she refused to testify because she did not want him to go to jail. Joe was given three years probation and mandated to attend a batterers' treatment program. Sandra's caseworker helped Sandra and her two small children enter a shelter, but Sandra, who was the only person of her racial/ethnic background in the shelter, was soon asked to leave. She was then unable to find a place that would take her and her children, so she returned home. Shortly after that, Joe rejoined the family.

SOURCE: Fleck-Henderson, 2000

Consider the case described in Box 4.5. If you were a CPS worker assigned to this family, what would your reaction be? Do you think the children should be removed from the home? If you were a battered women's advocate, what would your response be? Would you want to remove the children from the home? Are there other possibilities? In this particular case, the DSS worker, the intimate partner violence specialist, and a trained consulting team ultimately agreed that the risk of danger to the children was too high, and had them moved to foster care (Fleck-Henderson, 2000). Do you agree with their decision?

Given that millions of children are exposed to interparental violence in this country, increasing efforts have focused on developing effective intervention strategies. The general consensus is that to be optimally effective, the intervention program must include both the children and their parents (Graham-Bermann & Hughes, 2003; Ziegler & Weidner, 2006), and consider the parents' reactions to the violence and how those reactions may be impacting the children (Ziegler & Weidner, 2006). Several such programs have been proposed, such as Ziegler and Weidner's (2006) family-based debriefing methodology, in which parents undergo their own personal debriefing, and then listen and emotionally support their children as they work with professionals to be empathetic and help their children explore their own experiences in a way that makes them feel validated and safe.

Graham-Bermann and Hughes (2003) offer three specific programs they consider to be exemplary intervention strategies. The Learning Center and Advocacy program is a 16-week program for battered women and their children, in which the mothers are provided with advocates who work with them for an average of 9 hours a week so that the mothers can acquire education, transportation, housing and other services; this program seems to increase children's feelings of self-competency and mothers' social support. Project SUPPORT is specifically for child witnesses who have been diagnosed with aggressive behavioral problems. The children and mothers have weekly home visits from the staff, in addition to 60 to 90 minute weekly therapy sessions for the mothers, where the mothers are coached on effective parenting to rebuild their parenting skills. Their children are mentored by other adolescents who model appropriate behaviors. This intervention appears to be effective in reducing aggressive behavioral problems in the children and in improving mothers' parental competency. Finally, the Kids Project is a 10-week long, small-group program focused on reducing the fear and worries and increasing the social skills of child witnesses. Children are educated on family violence and are taught to develop positive attitudes about family and gender, while their mothers get parenting support to reinforce the children's education. This program has been shown to reduce children's internalized problems and symptoms of PTSD.

Prevention and Intervention

Legally, psychological maltreatment is difficult to prosecute. Although many Americans realize the harm that psychological maltreatment can inflict, they do not consider this type of maltreatment to be worthy of legal intervention. It is rare for a court to consider a case of psychological maltreatment, unless other forms of maltreatment—such as the ones discussed previously in this book—are present. In addition, because of the difficulty in coming to a consensus on what constitutes psychological maltreatment rather than just inadequate parenting, CPS is limited in its ability to intervene and provide services to psychologically maltreated children (Hart, Brassard, Binggeli, & Davidson, 2002).

To our knowledge, there is no literature addressing prevention and intervention efforts that are specific to psychological maltreatment. There may be several reasons for this. First, for reasons discussed previously, some researchers have found that CPS agencies are reluctant to pursue cases of psychological maltreatment in the absence of other forms of maltreatment (especially physical or sexual maltreatment). Second, for agencies in most states to substantiate cases of psychological maltreatment, they must have evidence of both the parental behavior and mental injury to the child (Brassard et al., 2000). Furthermore, there is a lack of federal funding opportunities for investigating psychological maltreatment, and consequently, research into its prevention and intervention is lacking (Binggeli et al., 2001). Nonetheless, CPS investigators are increasingly being trained to look for signs of psychological maltreatment when investigating other forms of child maltreatment (Trickett, Mennen, Kim, & Sang, 2009).

The only treatment programs that are available for intervention in psychological maltreatment consider this problem only tangentially. These programs include some of the treatments discussed in Chapter 2, including Parent-Child Interactive Therapy. Others are concerned with treating either externalizing behaviors (e.g., Incredible Years Teacher Training Series) or internalizing behaviors (e.g., Primary Mental Health Project) that can be observed in psychologically maltreated children, but are not specific to psychological maltreatment itself (Hart et al., 2011).

It is possible that because no prevention or intervention effort has explicitly targeted psychological maltreatment, any efforts to address it in the context of other maltreatment types have failed. In fact, psychological maltreatment appears to be the most resistant to intervention efforts (Daro & Cohn, 1988). In one study, psychological maltreatment had the highest recidivism rate: 75% of parents continued to maltreat their children in this manner, and 10% of clients actually became more abusive of their children. In addition, clients' compliance with treatment did not relate to their success rates (Ney et al., 1994). What are your thoughts about the best ways to reduce or end psychological maltreatment of children? Can anything be done to persuade parents that calling their children names, putting them down, or swearing at them as a response to behaviors that they do not like may not be the most effective means of fostering healthy development?

Summary

This chapter covered the two most elusive—but the two most prevalent—types of child maltreatment: neglect and psychological maltreatment. The study of both has been plagued with definitional problems. Researchers argue that psychological maltreatment is at the core of all types of child maltreatment, and official statistics show that neglect is the most common type of maltreatment. In addition, it is likely that all studies with data on the prevalence of these two types of maltreatment are underestimating their true extents. Possibly because neglect and psychological maltreatment are difficult to spot, children such as the Jackson boys and Cinderella are slow to receive intervention efforts. However, even if their families do receive intervention, such interventions are usually not tailored to these two types of maltreatment, and parents who maltreat their children in these ways are notoriously resistant to treatment. What do we do to help these children, then? As this chapter has shown, both neglect and psychological maltreatment may have the worst consequences of all types of maltreatment; therefore, it is important to understand why parents neglect or psychologically maltreat their children so that we can properly intervene. Research on the predictors of neglect shows that the causes of these behaviors come at every level of the ecological model, and include such variables as poverty, social isolation, unemployment, certain child characteristics, and parental psychopathology and substance abuse. Perhaps if we target these predictors, we can ameliorate the problem of child neglect in this country. The situation, however, for psychological maltreatment is much more complex. Probably because of the difficulties in defining this behavior, little research has been done on its predictors. Therefore, because of the limited knowledge we have of this elusive phenomenon, we are unable to properly treat either the perpetrators or the victims.

Discussion Questions

1. Why do the media and the public pay so much attention to physical and sexual maltreatment rather than neglect and psychological maltreatment when the latter two are much more common?

2. What is the controversy surrounding the act of taking a child away from a mother who was abusing drugs during pregnancy? Is taking the baby away immediately following birth in the best interests of the child?

3. Will ending poverty eliminate child neglect?

4. How are poor families who neglect their children different from poor families who do not neglect their children?

5. Why are children under the age of three most vulnerable to physical neglect and why are older children more at risk for emotional neglect?

6. Why are mothers significantly more likely to be reported as a neglectful parent than fathers?

7. Why might parents who have a history of neglect in their own childhood perpetrate neglect on their own children? How can we stop this cycle?

8. What would be the advantages of having programs for neglectful families that are family based rather than individual based?

9. Why is psychological maltreatment the most damaging form of child maltreatment?

10. Do you think that witnessing interparental aggression is a form of psychological maltreatment? Why or why not?

PART III

Intimate Partner Maltreatment

5

Maltreatment of Female Partners

> *I met Mr. Wonderful on May 1st and he moved in on May 31st. Two weeks later he tore the earlining to my right ear. After repeatedly hitting me, forcing a broom handle up inside me and spitting in my face I finally had him arrested. Oh yes, he lit my hair on fire and put lit cigarettes on my face and arms, too . . . [A]fter three marriages and divorces I didn't want another failure so when he got out of jail after six months and came to see me I let him in the house. He hit me again but the District Attorney dropped the charges I made against him this time, even though he had broken probation and harassed me* (Account of Nan G., from Norwood, 1988, p. 98).

Consider the above case of intimate partner violence (IPV). What factors do you think contributed to the violence Nan experienced? How common do you think such violence is for women in this country? Why do you think the district attorney dropped the charges in the latest incident? What could be done to help Nan get out of this relationship? The current chapter deals with these types of issues, as we consider the incidence of IPV against female partners and less physically violent relationships, including those characterized by psychological maltreatment, sexual maltreatment, and stalking. We also consider the vast research done in the previous few decades on the predictors and consequences of maltreatment of women by their male partners and review several types of prevention and intervention efforts aimed at helping female victims and changing the behaviors of perpetrators.

During the 1960s, the women's movement enlightened the general public in the United States on the problems of sexism and male domination. This public education was followed in the 1970s by an anti-rape campaign dramatizing the extent to which women could be the direct victims of male violence. These women's movement initiatives led to the establishment of networks where women could share their victimization experiences (Stacey, Hazlewood, & Shupe, 1994). Shelters for battered women began to open in the mid-1970s, in the face of opposition from much of the public and the government. Nonlethal IPV was thought to be characteristic of the poor, mentally ill, and socially deviant, and therefore not worthy of funds. Moreover, IPV was often attributed to the women's movement, with the implication that the female victims got what they deserved (Straus, 1980). Fortunately, researchers in this area did not always agree with government officials. In 1974, starting with Richard Gelles's groundbreaking study on the incidence and possible causes of IPV, the systematic study of IPV began. Before reviewing the research on physical IPV of women, it is important to note that abusive relationships often involve more than one type of maltreatment, including physical assault, psychological maltreatment, sexual assault, and stalking (Baum, Catalano, Rand, & Rose, 2009; Black et al., 2011; Brewster, 2003; Finney, 2006; Krebs, Brieding, Browne, & Warner, 2011; Logan, Cole, & Shannon, 2007; Logan & Walker, 2010). For example, a national population-based study found that among women who had experienced physical IPV, 93% also experienced psychological aggression, 30% experienced stalking, and 30% experienced sexual assault by that same partner (Krebs et al., 2011). The National Intimate Partner and Sexual Violence Survey (NISVS) similarly found that among female victims of physical violence, sexual violence, and stalking by a current or former male intimate, 14.4% had experienced physical violence and stalking, 12.5% experienced rape, physical violence, and stalking, and 8.7% experienced rape and physical violence (Black et al., 2011). Thus, to focus only on one type of maltreatment prohibits a complete understanding of the nature of IPV. The physical maltreatment of women by men is what initially brought public attention to the issue of IPV (Stark, 2007) and has garnered the most research attention; thus, it will be discussed first.

Physical Maltreatment

Scope of the Problem

The physical maltreatment of female partners has been the most extensively studied form of adult maltreatment, and Table 5.1 presents some of the major population-based studies that have been conducted since the 1970s on this form of maltreatment. These studies use different methodologies and define IPV in different ways, and thus, specifying precise rates of physical IPV against women is difficult. Generally speaking, studies that frame physical IPV against women as a criminal issue (e.g., Catalano, Smith, Snyder, & Rand, 2009; Truman & Rand, 2010) show the lowest rates of IPV against women, probably because of a reluctance of women to define these acts by their male partners as crimes. The highest rates come from studies (e.g., Caetano, Vaeth, & Ramisetty-Mikler, 2008; Kessler, Molnar, Feurer, & Appelbaum, 2001; Straus, 1995; Straus & Gelles, 1988) that use the Conflict Tactics Scales (CTS) (Straus, Hamby, Boney-McCoy, & Sugarman, 1996), which defines physical IPV as a family conflict issue and asks people to think about conflicts they have had with their partners and report the number of times the given tactics were used to resolve those conflicts, including physically, psychologically, and sexually aggressive tactics. Studies that use a combination of these methodologies (e.g., use CTS items, but frame them in the context of safety issues) tend to find rates in between the criminal studies and the family conflict studies (e.g., Black et al., 2011; Tjaden & Thoennes, 2000a).

Table 5.1 Selected Studies on the Prevalence of Physical IPV Against Women

Study	Description of Sample	Measures/Definition of Maltreatment	Rates of Physical Maltreatment by an Intimate Partner
Black et al. (2011) National Intimate Partner and Sexual Violence Survey (NISVS)	Representative sample of 9,086 women and 7,421 men 18 years or older in the United States	10 items covering a range of behaviors from slapping, pushing, and shoving to being beaten, kicked, and burned on purpose	32.9% of women experienced some type of physical IPV in lifetime 24.3% of women experienced severe physical violence in lifetime 4.0% experienced some type of physical IPV in last 12 months
Truman & Rand (2010) National Crime Victimization Survey (NCVS)	Nationally representative sample of 134,000 individuals from 77,200 households Self-report survey based on reported and unreported crimes	Among the questions asked are: "Has anyone attacked or threatened you in any of these ways: a) with any weapon, for instance, a gun or knife; b) with anything like a baseball bat, frying pan, scissors, or stick; c) by something thrown, such as a rock or bottle?" Respondents are also asked if they have been grabbed, punched, choked or threatened, and whether anyone has raped or attempted to rape them or committed any other form of sexual attack or unwanted sexual act against them If they report any of these incidents, they then identified their relationship with the perpetrator	4.1 per 1,000 women experienced physical IPV in past year

Study	Description of Sample	Measures/Definition of Maltreatment	Rates of Physical Maltreatment by an Intimate Partner
Brieding, Black, & Ryan (2008) Behavioral Risk Factor Surveillance System	Representative sample of over 70,000 adults 18 and older drawn in 2005 from 18 U.S. states and territories	Four questions assessed threats, attempted physical violence, physical violence, and unwanted sex	20.2% of women experienced physical IPV in their lifetime 1.4% experienced physical IPV and/or unwanted sex in last 12 months
Caetano, Vaeth, & Ramisetty-Mikler (2008) National Couples Survey	1,136 couples interviewed face-to-face in their homes Multistage area probability sample representative of married and cohabiting couples from the 48 contiguous United States "Oversampled" Blacks and Hispanics	Conflict Tactics Scales (CTS) (see Straus, 1995) in the past year	Approximately 8% of couples reported mutual violence Approximately 4% reported the perpetration of violence by the male partner only
Kessler, Molnar, Feurer, & Applebaum (2001) National Co-Morbidity Survey	Nationally representative household survey of 8,098 people in the age range of 15–54 that was fielded between September 1990 and March 1992 Respondents were sampled using a multistage area probability design Sample included 1,738 married or cohabitating men and 1,799 married or cohabitating women	CTS (see Straus, 1995) in the past year	17.4% of women reported being victims of minor physical violence 6.5% of women reported being victims of severe physical violence

(Continued)

Table 5.1 (Continued)

Study	Description of Sample	Measures/Definition of Maltreatment	Rates of Physical Maltreatment by an Intimate Partner
Tjaden & Thoennes (2000a) National Violence Against Women Survey (NVAWS)	Representative sample of 8,000 women and 8,000 men 18 years old or older in the United States conducted in 1995–96	Survey incorporated items from the original CTS concerning whether any other adult had slapped or hit them, kicked or bit them, choked them, hit them with an object, beaten them up, threatened them with a weapon, or used a gun, knife, or other weapon on them If they indicated that an aggressive behavior had been perpetrated against them, they were asked about their relationship with the perpetrator	20.4% of women were victims of a physical assault by current/former partner ever 1.4% of women were victimized within the last 12 months
Hale-Carlsson et al. (1996) 1994 Behavioral Risk Factor Surveillance System	Population-based, random digit-dialed telephone survey of the noninstitutionalized New York State population aged greater than or equal to 18 years; 692 women and 546 men, ages 18 to 44	Seven questions addressing physical assault from an intimate partner, including slapping, kicking, punching, being beaten, threatened, and/or assaulted with a knife or a gun	5.6% of women reported IPV, of whom 42.3% reported more severe forms of violence (i.e., kicked, bitten, punched, or beaten or threatened/ assaulted with a knife, gun, or other object)
Sorenson, Upchurch, & Shen (1996) National Survey of Families and Households	Multistage probability sample of 10,000 households that was supplemented by an oversample of 3,000 households of Blacks, Hispanics, absent-parent households, and recently married couples; 53% of the sample (n = 6,779) was married and completed a self-administered survey on IPV	How many fights resulted in their spouse hitting, shoving and throwing things at them Whether they were cut, bruised, or seriously injured in a fight with their spouse	3.2% of women reported that their spouse had hit, shoved, or thrown something at them in past year 1.1% of women reported being cut, bruised, or seriously injured as a result of IPV in past year

Study	Description of Sample	Measures/Definition of Maltreatment	Rates of Physical Maltreatment by an Intimate Partner
Straus (1995) National Alcohol and Family Violence Survey	National probability sample of 1,970 married or cohabitating couples interviewed face-to-face in 1992	CTS in the past year Participants were told they were answering questions about their intimate relationships, were told that different couples utilize different methods of resolving conflicts, and were asked about both their own and their partners' behaviors Severe violence operationalized as having a high probability of causing injury (e.g., kicking, punching, using weapons or objects)	Minor assault of women by men was 95 per 1,000 women Severe assault of women by men was 19 per 1,000 women
Straus & Gelles (1986) National Family Violence Surveys of 1975 and 1985 (NFVS)	1975 survey: Nationally representative sample of 2,143 married couples, conducted via face-to-face interview 1985 survey: Nationally representative sample of 6,002 married and cohabiting couples interviewed via telephone	CTS (see Straus, 1995) in the past year	Minor assault of women by men • 1975: 121 per 1,000 • 1985: 113 per 1,000 Severe assault of women by men • 1975: 38 per 1,000 • 1985: 30 per 1,000

Perhaps because of widespread attention to the problem in both the scientific community and the media, the major prevalence studies have shown steady declines in physical maltreatment of female partners from the 1970s, even though these different methods of assessing the prevalence of physical IPV sometimes lead to vastly different estimates. For example, according to the U.S. Department of Justice (DOJ), in 2008, there were 477,080 reported cases of women who were the victims of physical IPV (Catalano, Smith, Snyder, & Rand, 2009), which was a decline from the 1993 estimate of 1.1 million women. These numbers represent a 53% decline, from 9.4 women per 1,000 to 4.5 women per 1,000. In 2009, those numbers dropped again to 4.1 per 1,000 women (Truman & Rand, 2010).

These DOJ statistics reflect only the incidents of physical IPV against women deemed criminal by the respondents; another survey obtaining physical IPV rates from a nationally representative sample of couples answering questions on various tactics used to resolve conflicts shows similar declines. In the 1975 National Family Violence Survey (NFVS), 12.1% of wives reported that they had been the victims of some sort of violence (e.g., slapping, pushing, punching, beating up) from their husbands within the previous year. Nearly 4%, or 2.1 million wives nationwide, reported that they had been the victims of severe violence (Straus & Gelles, 1986). In the 1985 resurvey, there was a 27% decrease in the rate of severe violence by husbands, which projected to 432,000 fewer cases of severe violence against women and a national incidence rate of 1.6 million wives (Straus & Gelles, 1986).

The NISVS, a nationally representative telephone survey of 9,086 women and 7,421 men conducted in 2010, did not examine changes in IPV over time, but provides detailed and current information about physical IPV, psychological maltreatment, sexual violence, and stalking among adults in the United States (Black et al., 2011). Results revealed that 32.9% of the women experienced some type of physical violence from an intimate partner in their lifetime and 4.0% had experienced it in the past 12 months. Further, 24.3% of women reported experiencing severe physical violence (e.g., beaten, burned, choked) by an intimate partner at some point in their life. The prevalence rates reported in all these studies show that despite the apparent decline in rates of physical IPV of women over the past few decades, such IPV continues to be a major social problem in the United States.

Gaining an understanding of the problem of physical IPV against women is complicated by the fact that there seem to be different types of IPV. One attempt at differentiating IPV comes from M. P. Johnson (2008) who asserts that there are four types: *intimate terrorism, situational couple violence, violent resistance,* and *mutual violent control.* The central feature of *intimate terrorism* is that violence is one tactic in a general pattern of control of one member of the couple over the other. The IPV is frequent, unlikely to be mutual, likely to involve serious injury, and involves psychological maltreatment. Johnson argues that men are the perpetrators in the vast majority of intimate terrorism cases. *Situational couple violence* is IPV that is perpetrated by one or both partners. The IPV typically involves reciprocal low-level violence that occurs infrequently (Johnson & Leone, 2005). *Violent resistance* occurs when victims use violence against a partner in response to IPV they have sustained (M. P. Johnson, 2008). According to Johnson (2008), women are the majority of perpetrators of this type of IPV. The fourth type of IPV is *mutual violent control,* which is relatively rare and is characterized by both partners attempting to control the other through the use of violence. Laroche (2008) tested Johnson's distinction between *intimate terrorism* and *situational couple violence,* and found support for the existence of the two distinct types of IPV, but not that men are predominantly the perpetrators of intimate terrorism.

It is difficult to come by exact estimates of intimate terrorism, but in comparison to situational couple violence, it is quite rare. As mentioned in the Preface, relationships characterized by low to moderate levels of reciprocal aggression are much more common than those characterized by extreme violence on the part of one of the partners. However, intimate terrorism has been the fascination of the public and researchers alike, and thus, more research has been conducted on this type of IPV. Consider the case of intimate terrorism presented at the beginning of this chapter. Does it sound like ones you have heard about in the media? What dynamics do you perceive? Given the information presented, what are possible causes of such types of IPV? What are possible consequences?

Predictors and Correlates

Studies on the predictors and correlates of physical IPV against women have come at every level of the ecological model but focus primarily on the characteristics of the woman and the male partner (Table 5.2). The studies focusing on predictors have all been correlational—thus, we do not know for certain whether the risk factor preceded the IPV, the IPV preceded the risk factor, or a third variable caused both the risk factor and the IPV.

Macrosystem

Poverty. Low income, particularly poverty, seems to be a major risk factor for physical IPV against women in this country. According to statistics from the DOJ, physical IPV against women is highest in the poorest income category and becomes lower as income increases (Rennison & Welchans, 2000; Rennison & Planty, 2003). In fact, low income is consistently viewed as one of the major and most important risk factors for physical IPV against women (e.g., Brieding, Black, & Ryan, 2008; Hotaling & Sugarman, 1986; Straus, 1990b). Also, it is not just income that predicts IPV against women but also having few economic opportunities (Follingstad, Wright, Lloyd, & Sebastian, 1991), a low occupational status (Straus, 1990b), a poor work history (Bassuk, Dawson, & Huntington, 2006) and low educational attainment (Brieding et al., 2008; Hotaling & Sugarman, 1986; Kessler et al., 2001).

Attitudes. Several researchers have studied attitudes that may be related to the physical maltreatment of women, particularly those concerning traditionalism and the approval of violence against women. It appears that in marriages characterized by physical IPV against women, both husbands and wives are more traditional and conservative in their belief systems (Follingstad, Wright et al., 1991; Rosenbaum & O'Leary, 1981). The belief that husbands should be dominant in marriage, whether held by the wife or the husband, can lead to IPV against women if the marriage is

Table 5.2   Predictors of Physical IPV Against Women

Level of the Ecological Model	Specific Predictor	Studies
Macrosystem	Low income/socioeconomic status	Brieding, Black, & Ryan (2008); Hotaling & Sugarman (1986); Kessler, Molnar, Feurer, & Applebaum (2001); Rennison & Welchans (2000); Rennison & Planty (2003); Straus (1990b); Thompson et al. (2006)
	Perpetrator's poor work history	Bassuk, Dawson, & Huntington (2006)
	Few economic opportunities	Follingstad, Wright, Lloyd, & Sebastian (1991)
	Low educational attainment	Brieding et al. (2008); Hotaling & Sugarman (1986); Kessler et al. (2001); Thompson et al. (2006); Walton-Moss, Manganello, Frye, & Campbell (2005)
	Low occupational status	Straus (1990b)
	Traditional/conservative beliefs	Follingstad, Wright et al. (1991); Rosenbaum & O'Leary (1981)
	Approval of violence in interpersonal relationships	Kaufman Kantor & Straus (1990)
	Need for power in a relationship	Straus, Gelles, & Steinmetz (1980); Yllo & Straus (1990)
	Stress	O'Leary (1988); Straus (1990b)
Exosystem	Neighborhood poverty	Cunradi, Caetano, Clark, & Schafer (2000)
	Social isolation	Follingstad, Brennan, Hause, Polek, & Rutledge (1991); Straus (1990b)
	Community violence	Rhagavan, Mennerich, Sexton, & James (2006)
	Living in a rural area	Murty et al. (2003)
Microsystem	Younger age of the victim	Black et al. (2011); Brieding et al. (2008); Fagan & Browne (1994); O'Leary et al. (1989); Rennison & Welchans (2000); Suitor, Pillemer, & Straus (1990); Vest, Catlin, Chen, & Brownson (2002)

Level of the Ecological Model	Specific Predictor	Studies
	Victim's exposure to aggression in family of origin	Cappell & Heiner (1990); Cascardi, O'Leary, Lawrence, & Schlee (1995); Kessler et al. (2001); Lipsky, Field, Caetano, & Larkin (2005); Whitfield, Anda, Dube, & Felitti (2003)
	Mental health problems of the victim	Cascardi et al. (1995); Ehrensaft, Moffitt, & Caspi (2006); Vest, Catlin, Chen, & Brownson (2002); Walton-Moss et al. (2005)
	Woman's alcohol abuse	Kaufman Kantor & Asdigian (1996); Kilpatrick, Acierno, Resnick, Saunders, & Best (1997)
	Victim is a single mother	Thompson et al. (2006)
	Couples who cannot communicate or resolve conflicts in rational, nonjudgmental ways	Douglas (1991)
	Use of psychologically aggressive tactics within the couple	O'Leary, Malone, & Tyree (1994)
	Marital dissatisfaction	O'Leary (1988); Stith, Green, Smith, & Ward (2008)
	Cohabitation	Kessler et al. (2001)
	Physical IPV prior to marriage	O'Leary et al. (1989)
	Being separated or divorced	Catalano (2007); Rennison & Welchans (2000); Vest et al. (2002); Walby & Allen (2004); Walker (2009)
Individual/ Developmental	Alcohol/substance abuse	Fals-Stewart (2003); Gondolf (1988); Gondolf & Foster (1991); Hamberger & Hastings (1991); Hotaling & Sugarman (1986); Kaufman Kantor & Straus (1990); Kessler et al. (2001); Murphy, O'Farrell, Fals-Stewart, & Feehan (2001); O'Farrell, Fals-Stewart, Murphy, & Murphy (2003); Saunders (1992); Stith, Crossman, & Bischof (1991)

(Continued)

Table 5.2 (Continued)

Level of the Ecological Model	Specific Predictor	Studies
	Exposure to violence in the family of origin	Ehrensaft et al. (2003); Godbout, Dutton, Lussier, & Sabourin (2009); Holtzworth-Munroe & Stuart (1994); Hotaling & Sugarman (1986); Kalmuss (1984); O'Leary et al. (1994); Roberts, Austin, Corliss, Vandermorris, & Koenen (2010); Straus (1990b)
	Borderline personality traits	Dutton, Saunders, Starzomski, & Bartholomew (1994); Holtzworth-Munroe & Stuart (1994)
	Antisocial personality traits/ aggressive personality	Dutton et al. (1994); Holtzworth-Munroe & Stuart (1994); Hotaling, Straus, & Lincoln (1990); Murphy et al. (2001); O'Leary et al. (1994)
	Mental illness	Kessler et al. (2001)

under stress (Straus, 1990b). Moreover, traditional and conservative beliefs lead both men and women to be less assertive with each other, which is also related to IPV against women (Follingstad, Wright et al., 1991; Hotaling & Sugarman, 1986; Rosenbaum & O'Leary, 1981). Men who are physically aggressive toward their female partners are also more likely to approve of violence in interpersonal relationships (Kaufman Kantor & Straus, 1990). They view violence toward women as a legitimate means of interaction (Straus & Gelles, 1990b), so much so that the belief that hitting a female partner is appropriate behavior has been deemed as one of six major risk factors for IPV against women (Straus, 1990b).

Power and Stress. Although it is commonly believed that men have all the power in relationships characterized by IPV against women, some researchers have shown that this is not always the case. In fact, status incompatibilities, wherein *either* the man *or* the woman holds all the power, may predispose the couple for IPV as a means to either legitimize or regain power in the relationship (Straus, Gelles, & Steinmetz, 1980; Yllo & Straus, 1990). One study found that male perpetrators scored significantly higher on a measure of powerlessness (e.g., feeling unfairly treated, feeling that bad things always happen to them) than men in nonviolent relationships, those in mutually violent relationships, and male victims of IPV (Caetano et al., 2008). These men may have a great need for power (Dutton & Strachan, 1987) and feel little control over the events in their lives (Prince & Arias, 1994); thus, if the woman is the more powerful partner, the man may use violence to take that power away from her.

All the risk factors discussed so far have one thing in common: stress. Poverty, attitudes regarding marriage and violence against women, and status incompatibilities would not necessarily directly lead to violence if stress were not underlying all of them. In fact, stress, particularly when it is combined with feelings that the marriage is unimportant (Straus, 1990b), is one of the strongest predictors of a husband hitting his wife (O'Leary, 1988).

Exosystem

Several variables have been the focus of research on exosystem level predictors of IPV against women. Neighborhood poverty (Cunradi, Caetano, Clark, & Schafer, 2000) and neighborhood violence (Rhagavan et al., 2006) are significant predictors. Moreover, the more isolated a family is (e.g., lives in a rural area) (Murty et al., 2003) and the less social support the family receives, the greater the likelihood of IPV against women (Follingstad, Brennan, Hause, Polek, & Rutledge, 1991). One of the six factors that put men in the NFVS at risk for hitting their female partners was social isolation—men who had sources of support tended not to be violent, even if they were under a great deal of stress (Straus, 1990b).

Microsystem

Characteristics of the Victim. Research on characteristics of women that make them vulnerable to maltreatment is controversial because it may appear to be a form of "blaming the victim." However, it is important to make the distinction between causation and blame. Whether a victim's behavior played a causal role in a victimization incident is a scientific question. Whether the victim's behavior is blameworthy is a moral question for the legal system and public opinion (Felson, 2002). It is important for social scientists to investigate causality in incidents, whereas the determination of blame is a matter for the courts.

Research on victim-level characteristics associated with IPV against women focuses primarily on demographic characteristics. An individual's youth seems to be a particularly strong risk factor in community samples (e.g., Fagan & Browne, 1994; O'Leary et al., 1989; Suitor, Pillemer, & Straus, 1990; Vest, Catlin, Chen, & Brownson, 2002), in samples of battered women (e.g., Rennison & Welchans, 2000), and in national population based studies. These studies consistently show that the peak age of victimization for women is 18 to 24 years of age (Black et al., 2011; Breiding, Black, & Ryan, 2008), with risk steadily declining thereafter (Breiding et al., 2008; Rennison & Welchans, 2000). Additionally, lower education among victims is associated with higher rates of IPV victimization, as is being a single mother (Thompson et al., 2006).

Another, more controversial victim-level predictor is the intergenerational transmission of physical IPV victimization. Several studies have shown that women exposed to aggression in their families of origin, either through witnessing or experiencing it directly, were more likely to become victims of IPV (e.g., Cappell & Heiner, 1990; Cascardi, O'Leary, Lawrence, & Schlee, 1995; Lipsky, Field, Caetano, &

Larkin, 2005; Whitfield et al., 2003). Other victim-level risk factors include physical and mental health problems (e.g., depression) (Ehrensaft, Moffitt, & Caspi, 2006; Cascardi et al., 1995; Vest et al., 2002; Walton-Moss, Manganello, Frye, & Campbell 2005). A woman's alcohol use may also be a risk factor. Clinical samples of alcoholic women show that there is often a history of violent victimization in relationships (Kaufman Kantor & Asdigian, 1996); however, longitudinal studies suggest that women are using alcohol to cope with their IPV experiences (Kilpatrick, Acierno, Resnick, Saunders, & Best, 1997).

Characteristics of the Relationship. Couples who are unable to communicate or resolve conflicts in rational, nonjudgmental ways are at risk for IPV against women (Douglas, 1991). The use of psychologically aggressive tactics predisposes couples to physical maltreatment of women; that is, couples tend to attack each other's vulnerabilities prior to an episode of physical IPV. It is these types of interactions that may lead to marital discord, which correlates with psychological maltreatment of women, which in turn predicts later physical maltreatment of women (O'Leary, Malone, & Tyree, 1994). Such interactions can also result in marital dissatisfaction, another strong predictor of physical IPV against women (O'Leary, 1988; Stith, Green, Smith, & Ward, 2008).

Physical IPV of female partners occurs not only when couples live in the same household but also prior to marriage (see Chapter 7) and when couples are separated or divorced. Compared to women who are married, those who are cohabiting with a male partner are at increased risk for severe physical IPV (Kessler et al., 2001). As many as 30% of dating college students and young adults are involved in a physically aggressive relationship (Hines & Saudino, 2003; Sabina & Straus, 2008), and physical aggression prior to marriage is a strong predictor of aggression during marriage (O'Leary et al., 1989). Being separated or divorced from one's perpetrator is a major risk factor for being physically assaulted (Catalano, 2007; Rennison & Welchans, 2000; Vest et al., 2002; Walby & Allen, 2004). The most dangerous time for a battered woman appears to be after she leaves her batterer (Walker, 2009).

Individual/Developmental

Alcohol and Substance Use. An important individual/developmental level predictor of IPV against women is the perpetrator's alcohol and substance use. A high percentage of male batterers evidence alcohol problems (Gondolf, 1988; Hamberger & Hastings, 1991; Hotaling & Sugarman, 1986; Saunders, 1992), and a high percentage of male alcoholics have problems with IPV (Gondolf & Foster, 1991; Murphy, O'Farrell, Fals-Stewart, & Feehan, 2001; Stith, Crossman, & Bischof, 1991). When male alcoholics abstain from using alcohol, their rates of IPV perpetration mirror those of population-based samples (O'Farrell, Fals-Stewart, Murphy, & Murphy, 2003). Fals-Stewart (2003) found that the odds of physical aggression among domestically violent men were 8 to 11 times higher on the days they drank. Alcohol use is characteristic not only of men who use terroristic violence but also of men who engage in situational couple violence. In the National Comorbidity Study, alcohol dependence was a significant predictor of minor violence perpetration (Kessler et al., 2001), and the 1985 NFVS showed that alcohol was involved in half of the violent couple interactions, with a man's use of alcohol putting him at 2 to 3 times the risk for hitting his wife (Kaufman Kantor & Straus, 1990).

Arguments abound about whether alcohol and substance use *cause* IPV (e.g., Flanzer, 2005; Gelles & Cavanaugh, 2005; Leonard, 2005). Some argue that alcohol abuse causes IPV against women because the physiological effects of alcohol (e.g., lowering inhibitions) lead a man to aggress against his female partner (e.g., Flanzer, 2005). However, approximately 80% of the heaviest drinkers do not hit their female partners, and studies have shown that alcohol is involved in only approximately one half of battering incidents; thus, alcohol use is neither a sufficient nor necessary cause of IPV against women. Even among batterers with drinking problems, their use of alcohol during battering incidents is variable; that is, they may use a lot of alcohol during one incident, some in another, and none in still another (Walker, 2000). On the other hand, research shows that the probability of a man assaulting his wife during a drinking incident is as much as 11 times greater than when he has not been drinking (Fals-Stewart, 2003). Some researchers have found that a third variable, such as impulsiveness or an abuse-prone personality, is responsible for both the alcohol abuse and the IPV against women (e.g., Collins & Messerschmidt, 1993). One study of possible third variable effects showed that male alcoholics who were partner violent showed significantly higher levels of antisocial personality traits than those who were not partner violent; after controlling for antisocial personality traits, IPV was no longer associated with alcohol use, suggesting that alcohol problem severity was largely redundant with antisocial personality traits (Murphy et al., 2001). This finding has been replicated with a community sample as well (Hines & Straus, 2007).

Intergenerational Transmission. Another individual/developmental risk factor for IPV against women is exposure to violence in the family of origin. Men are at risk for hitting their female partners if either they were maltreated as a child and/or witnessed interparental violence. This has been shown among male perpetrators in therapy (e.g., O'Leary et al., 1994), nationally representative samples of men (e.g., Kalmuss, 1984; Roberts, Austin, Corliss, Vandermorris, & Koenen, 2010; Straus, 1990b), samples of men in the community (e.g., Ehrensaft et al., 2003), and batterers (e.g., Holtzworth-Munroe & Stuart, 1994). In fact, the man's exposure to family-of-origin violence is often considered the strongest and most consistent predictor of IPV against women (Godbout, Dutton, Lussier, & Sabourin, 2009; Hotaling & Sugarman, 1986).

The most common theory to explain this intergenerational transmission is social learning theory (e.g., Eron, 1997); this theory posits that, because aggression against intimates runs in families, children learn how to behave aggressively through watching their parents and being reinforced for their own aggression. However, other research suggests that intergenerational transmission may be at least partly genetically influenced (Hines & Saudino, 2004). That is, children seem to inherit genes from their parents that predispose them to aggressive behaviors; however, their eventual use of these behaviors may not depend on whether their parents behave aggressively (i.e., being exposed to an aggressive familial environment). Instead, children's genetic predisposition to behave aggressively may influence them to seek out aggressive peer groups or to associate with other children in the family who may also be genetically predisposed to behave aggressively. Therefore, their eventual use of aggressive behaviors may have little to do with their parents' actual use of aggressive behaviors but may have everything to do with inheriting a genetic predisposition from their parents and being exposed to aggressive models in their peer groups (Hines & Saudino, 2004).

An important caveat to the intergenerational transmission of violence is that most men exposed to violence in their families of origin do not use IPV as adults (Widom, 1989). Some protective factors against intergenerational transmission have been identified, including older age at first exposure to violence, a less difficult temperament, higher intelligence, and cognitive appraisals of the violence. Examples of the cognitive appraisals that can have a protective influence include not idealizing or protecting the images of violent parents, not choosing sides in parental fights, and having better coping mechanisms to deal with parental violence (Caesar, 1988).

Personality Traits. Another individual/developmental risk factor is the personality characteristics of male perpetrators. Dutton, Saunders, Starzomski, and Bartholomew (1994) found that several personality dysfunctions—borderline, antisocial, aggressive-sadistic, and passive-aggressive personality—are related to men's IPV perpetration. Dutton theorizes that this association is due to long-standing attachment disorders that have their roots in paternal rejection, exposure to maltreatment in childhood, and a "failure of protective attachment." These men seem to have developed a fearful-angry attachment style, which causes them to lash out violently toward their female partners during confrontations and perceived separations.

Similarly, Holtzworth-Munroe and Stuart (1994) found that personality dysfunction predicts male battering and theorized that there are three types of male batterers. Violence by *family-only batterers* results from a combination of stress and low-level risk factors, such as childhood exposure to marital violence and poor relationship skills. On occasion, during escalating conflicts, these men may engage in aggression that typically does not escalate. *Borderline-dysphoric batterers* come from a background involving parental maltreatment and rejection, which leads them to have difficulty forming stable and trusting attachments to an intimate partner. Instead, they are highly dependent on, yet fearful of losing, their female partner. Consistent with this attachment style and their borderline personality traits, these batterers are jealous, lack adequate relationship skills, and have hostile attitudes toward women. *Generally violent-antisocial batterers* resemble other antisocial, aggressive men. They have experienced high levels of family-of-origin violence and associate with deviant peers. They are impulsive, lack interpersonal skills, have hostile attitudes toward women, and view violence as acceptable. Their IPV is part of their general engagement in antisocial behavior, and their female partners are readily accessible victims, but not their only victims.

Even among men who use situational couple violence, a generalized antisocial tendency may account for their use of aggression against their wives. For example, men who hit their wives in the NFVS were more aggressive both outside the home and against their own children (Hotaling, Straus, & Lincoln, 1990). In addition, among husbands in a marital therapy program, both aggressive (i.e., willingness to hurt others, enjoyment of conflicts and arguments, a desire to get even) and defendant (i.e., a readiness to defend oneself, suspicion of others, tendency to be offended easily) personality traits prior to marriage predicted psychological aggression at 18 months after marriage, which in turn predicted physical aggression at 30 months of marriage (O'Leary et al., 1994). Because the association between these aggressive personality traits and IPV against women are so strong, and because they have been shown to fully mediate the association between alcohol use and IPV perpetration (Hines & Straus, 2007; Murphy et al., 2001) some have argued that aggressive personality is a major risk factor for physical IPV against women (e.g., Hines & Straus, 2007; O'Leary, 1988).

Mental Illness/Psychological Disorders. Finally, mental illness is a strong predictor of men's IPV toward women. For example, one large-scale national study of male perpetrators of IPV found that depression, general anxiety disorder, and non-affective psychosis increase the odds of men's perpetrating minor violence whereas dysthymia, adult anti-social behavior, and nonaffective psychosis increased the odds of severe violence perpetration (Kessler et al., 2001).

Consequences

Female victims of physical IPV may suffer numerous consequences (e.g., social, economic, physical, psychological). Physical and psychological injuries will be discussed here because they are the most researched. Because the research on psychological effects is correlational, we cannot make any definitive conclusions that the observed consequences are true effects of the IPV. However, for physical injuries we are better able to make conclusions regarding cause and effect.

Physical Injuries

The National Violence Against Women Survey (NVAWS) of 1996 found that 41.5% of the women who were physically assaulted by an intimate since age 18 were injured during their most recent victimization (Tjaden & Thoennes, 2000a). The NVAWS also showed that victims of intimate terrorism were more likely to be injured than victims of situational couple violence (Johnson & Leone, 2005). The NISVS (Black et al., 2011) found that 14.8% of women who were assaulted, raped, and/or stalked by an intimate partner at some point in their lives suffered an injury. Among women who reported IPV to the DOJ, 50% were injured by their male partners with 4 in 10 seeking medical treatment (Rennison & Welchans, 2000). Methodological differences are likely to account for varying rates of injury between studies, such as differences in how IPV and injury were measured.

In addition to being injured, sometimes seriously, many women are also at risk for being killed by their partners. Furthermore, the flip side is also a possible consequence of IPV against women: That is, sometimes the victimized woman will kill her partner in self-defense. These issues are discussed further in Box 5.1 on intimate partner homicide.

Box 5.1   Intimate Partner Homicide

Although rare in comparison to the rates of physical IPV against women, male intimate partners commit about one third of homicides of women (Catalano, 2007). Based on FBI data, the murder of women by male partners has remained steady in this country since 1976, when 1,587 females were killed by intimate partners; similarly, 1,640 were killed in 2007 (Catalano, Smith, Snyder, & Rand, 2009).

The homicide of intimate partners seems to comprise three different types: (1) an abusive man kills his female partner; (2) an abused woman kills her male partner in self-defense; and (3) an abusive woman kills her male partner. Although abused men have been known to kill their female partners in self-defense, this type of homicide has never been systematically investigated. Further, there is little research on the third type of homicide (i.e., an abusive woman kills her male partner) outside of simply reporting how often it happens.

Most, if not all, of the cases of male-perpetrated intimate homicide involve men who either are afraid that his female partner will leave him or upset that she has, or are jealous that she may be involved with another man (Cazenave & Zahn, 1992). The first motive—that of feared separation—accounts for the fact that men are more likely to kill estranged partners than partners with whom they currently reside (Cazenave & Zahn, 1992). Moreover, fear of separation seems to be more of a problem in homicide-suicide cases than is jealousy. Although homicide-suicide occurs in approximately 15% (Block & Chrisakos, 1995) to 27% (Morton, Runyan, Moracco, & Butts, 1998) of all partner homicides by men, in all cases the men killed their female partners and themselves because their partners had left the relationship (Rasche, 1988, as cited in Saunders & Browne, 2000).

What distinguishes male IPV perpetrators who kill their partners from those who do not? In a review of the literature, Aldarondo and Straus (1994) found that the following individual/developmental level characteristics of the male perpetrator predicted life-threatening violence: dependency, violent behavior outside the home, exposure to violence in the family of origin, possession of weapons, and killing or abusing pets. Characteristics of the IPV situation also predicted life-threatening violence, including high frequency of violence, physical injuries, rape, threats to beat or kill, and controlling and psychological maltreatment.

When women kill their male partners, two situations are possible: either an abusive woman kills her male partner or a battered woman kills her abuser in self-defense (Cazenave & Zahn, 1992). The first situation has rarely been systematically investigated; we know little about what distinguishes abusive women who kill their partners from abusive women who do not. Furthermore, we do not know their motives behind killing their partners (e.g., separation, jealousy, as with abusive men who kill), nor do we know any characteristics of the relationship or the abuser that distinguish them. The little research that has been done on this issue will be discussed in the following chapter on the maltreatment of male partners.

We do, however, know some information about battered women who kill their abusers in self-defense. In a review of research on battered women who murder their abusers, Browne (1987) found seven markers that distinguished battered women who kill from those who do not: frequent intoxication of the abuser; drug abuse by the abuser; high frequency of IPV against the women; more severe injuries of the women; being raped or sexually assaulted by the abuser; being subjected to threats of murder by the abuser; and suicide threats by the woman. Thus, the nature of the abuse is different for battered women who kill versus those who do not: Their abuse is more severe, sadistic, and frequent, and it involves sexual assault. These women remark that at the beginning of the relationship, their male partners were the most romantic, attentive lovers they ever had and that the abuse did not begin until after they made some sort of major commitment to one another. At this point, the male partner's attention became an obsession, and he controlled and restricted her behavior. Although the battered women did not report the first battering incident, subsequent attempts to get help from authorities often failed or did not stop the violence. As the violence escalated in these relationships, there occurred a steady decrease in contrition on the part of the male partner—expressions of remorse became less common, and the severity and frequency of the beatings increased. Often, the woman was prompted to kill her batterer because his violence reached a new level: Either he threatened to kill their children or he gave signs that he was ready to follow through on previous threats to kill her (Browne, 1987).

Psychological Effects

Depending on the extent, nature, and duration of abuse, IPV victims can experience a wide range of psychological consequences. Among population-based and community samples of women, we see that 22.3% of female victims of IPV report at least one PTSD symptom (e.g., had nightmares, felt constantly on guard, felt numb or detached) (Black et al., 2011) and that female victims report more depressive symptoms and lower mental and social functioning in comparison to non-victimized women (Thompson et al., 2006).

Most of the research on the psychological consequences of physical IPV against women focuses on samples of battered women. Overall, these studies find that battered women may experience PTSD, anxiety, depression, anger and rage, addictive behaviors, nightmares, dissociation, shame, low self-esteem, somatic problems, suicidality, and sexual problems (Briere & Jordan, 2004; Giles-Sims, 1998; Lipsky et al., 2005; Tuel & Russell, 1998). These reactions are a function of the duration and severity of the IPV they experience, with women whose experiences are longer and more severe suffering more psychological problems (Briere & Jordan, 2004; Follingstad, Brennan et al., 1991; Thompson et al., 2006).

As many as 10% to 35% of abused women may attempt suicide, and as many as 50% may contemplate it (Stark & Flitcraft, 1988). In several studies of battered women, both subclinical and clinical levels of psychological problems have been found (Ehrensaft, Moffitt, & Caspi, 2006; Follingstad, Brennan et al., 1991; Follingstad, Wright et al., 1991). For instance, the majority of battered women in one sample reported feeling angry, emotionally hurt, fearful, and anxious as a result of the IPV; over 25% had symptoms of depression and anxiety, and over 50% presented with symptoms of psychosomatic reactions to stress, including persistent headaches, back and limb problems, and stomach problems (Follingstad, Wright et al., 1991).

Subjective reports of distress by battered women and the extent of the IPV they suffered seem to predict their levels of depression, anxiety, and general psychopathology (Kemp, Rawlings, & Green, 1991). One longitudinal study of female IPV victims found an increase over time in major depression, marijuana dependence, alcohol dependence, PTSD, and generalized anxiety (Ehrensaft, Moffitt, & Caspi, 2006). In a comparison study of battered women from a shelter, battered women from a community sample, and nonbattered women, both groups of battered women were significantly more likely than the nonbattered group to suffer from major depression, psychosexual dysfunctions, phobias, obsessive-compulsive disorders, anxiety, dysthymia, alcohol and drug abuse, panic disorders, and antisocial personality disorders (Gleason, 1993). Most of the battered women were diagnosed with major depression (63%–81%), psychosexual dysfunctions (87%–88%), and phobias (63%–83%).

Although the majority of battered women in Gleason's (1993) study did not suffer from alcohol and drug abuse, a substantial minority did abuse alcohol (23%–44%) and drugs (10%–25%), rates that were significantly greater than the rates for nonbattered women. These associations are likely due to female victims using alcohol to cope with the IPV. Several longitudinal studies of women have shown that sustaining IPV puts them at risk for alcohol and drug abuse rather than vice versa (Kilpatrick et al., 1997; Martino, Collins, & Ellickson, 2005; Salomon, Bassuk, & Huntington, 2002; Testa, Livingston, & Leonard, 2003). PTSD seems to be a mediator in this relationship (Salomon et al., 2002), such that women use these substances to self-medicate the symptoms of PTSD they may experience as a result of IPV.

Battered Woman Syndrome

According to Lenore Walker (2009), many battered women experience clusters of symptoms, which she labeled battered woman syndrome (BWS). Three of these symptom clusters correspond to PTSD and include intrusive recollections of the traumatic event(s) (e.g., flashbacks, nightmares), high anxiety levels and hyperarousal (e.g., exaggerated startle response, hypervigilance to further harm), and avoidance and emotional numbing (as evidenced by denial, minimization, repression, depression, and/or dissociation). What may be specific to BWS are disrupted interpersonal relationships due to the perpetrator's exertion of power and control (e.g., controlling when and if she saw friends/family, restricting her time if she went out by herself, threats to harm the victim's family members), distortion of body image (i.e., dislike of her entire body), somatic or physical complaints (e.g., fibromyalgia, asthma), and issues with sexual intimacy (e.g., was forced to have rough sex, was forced to have sex with his friends, man withheld sex or other forms of physical intimacy).

The existence of a BWS has been the subject of much controversy. One of the primary criticisms is that not all battered women experience the symptoms Walker describes, and the symptoms are not unique to battered women; thus, labeling it a syndrome is problematic (Ferraro, 2003). Critics have also argued that this notion of a syndrome does not encompass the range of issues related to the nature and dynamics of battering, the effects of violence, battered women's responses to violence, and the social and psychological context in which IPV occurs (Briere & Jordan, 2004; Dutton, 1996). Further, Dutton (1996) argues that BWS places the emphasis on pathology by characterizing battered women as damaged or disordered rather than emphasizing her efforts and strengths and the many ways she responds to the battering. However, there has been support for the notion that battered women suffer PTSD-like symptoms: About 30% to 85% of battered women evidence PTSD (Astin, Lawrence, & Foy, 1993; Balos & Trotsky, 1988; Cascardi et al., 1995; Gleason, 1993; Kemp et al., 1991; Saunders, 1994). Even among community samples of women, the level of PTSD symptomatology is higher in women who experience physical IPV than in maritally discordant and happily married controls (Cascardi et al., 1995). Based on this discussion, do you feel that a diagnostic category of battered woman syndrome should exist? If so, why? If not, what would you propose to label the set of symptoms that battered women sometimes experience?

Special Issue: What Prevents Victims from Leaving?

Considering the numerous and serious consequences of being a victim of IPV, many people ask "Why doesn't she just leave?" Assuming that victimized women can simply walk away from their perpetrator ignores the context in which victims live and the effects that IPV have on them, especially those living under the coercive control of a partner. That said, there are two categories of factors that inhibit a woman from leaving an abusive male partner: internal and external (Barnett, 2000, 2001).

Internal inhibitory factors are behaviors and beliefs learned through gender socialization and individual experiences (Barnett, 2001). Women are encouraged to value themselves in terms of their relationships with men. Therefore, many women's self-esteem is tied to being in a relationship. Consequently, some women believe that leaving an abusive partner is worse than occasional physical maltreatment. Alternately, some women's self-esteem is so damaged by the IPV that they believe their perpetrators when they say that no one else will want them. Some women may also not recognize that what is happening is abusive or may believe that violence in relationships is normal. They may blame themselves for the maltreatment, often as a result of the perpetrator's efforts to blame the victim.

Other internal inhibitory factors are because they love their partner, believe that marriage is forever, and/or believe that their perpetrator will change, especially if he enrolls in treatment. The psychological effects of victimization can also contribute to a woman's staying (e.g., anxiety, depression, PTSD). Issues surrounding children are common and range from not wanting their children to be without a father, to the perpetrators threatening to tell Child Protective Services that the mother is abusive or neglectful (Barnett, 2001), to fearing that their perpetrator will get the children in a custody dispute. Many women fear the perpetrator will retaliate if they leave, and rightfully so because they are at the greatest risk for escalating violence and stalking when they have separated from their partners (Langhinrichsen-Rohling, Palarea, Cohen, & Rohling, 2000). Isolation can play a major role in why women stay: Women often isolate themselves because of shame (Dunham & Senn, 2000; Ferraro & Johnson, 1983; Rosen, 1996) and/or because the perpetrator has prohibited her from maintaining her relationships with friends, family, and coworkers (Stark, 2007). Thus, women may have (or believe they have) no one to turn to.

External inhibiting factors pertain to how society is structured (i.e., patriarchy, problems of economic dependency) (Barnett, 2000). Because women make less money than men and are expected to be the primary caretakers of children, women are more likely to be economically dependent on their perpetrator. When they seek help, family members and religious leaders may discourage women from leaving their perpetrator and encourage them to change their own behaviors (e.g., be more submissive, avoid upsetting the husband).

The reasons for why women stay are many and varied, and depend on the unique circumstances of each victim. Most battered women do not want to leave their partner; they simply want the violence to stop, and although many victims stay, most victims actively seek help (Barnett, 2001) and do eventually leave violent relationships (Holtzworth-Munroe, Smutzler, & Sandin, 1997). Advocates argue that instead of asking why women do not leave, a better question to ask is, "Why does he do it?" so that the responsibility for the IPV is placed where it belongs: on the perpetrator.

Psychological Maltreatment

Scope of the Problem

As compared to physical IPV, there is a dearth of research on men's psychological maltreatment of female partners. This is surprising given that: (1) psychological IPV predicts physical IPV in relationships (e.g., Murphy & O'Leary, 1989); (2) psychological IPV tends to co-occur with physical IPV (e.g., Frye, Manganello, Campbell, Walton-Moss, & Wilt, 2006; Henning & Klesges, 2003; Stets, 1990); (3) it often occurs in the absence of physical IPV (e.g., Henning & Klesges, 2003; Stets, 1990); and (4) most battered women, when interviewed about psychological IPV, state that the psychological IPV was much worse than the physical IPV they sustained (e.g., Baldry, 2003; Follingstad, Rutledge, Berg, Hause, & Polek, 1990).

Consider the case in Box 5.2. What types of psychologically aggressive acts did Nancy's husband use? What were the consequences?

Box 5.2   Psychological Maltreatment of Nancy

As someone who suffered abuse throughout a 15-year marriage and beyond, I would like to share what I believe to be some sure signs of emotional abuse. Emotional abuse is more insidious than other abuses and just as damaging. Through this type of persecution, my partner attacked my very soul—using words and mannerisms that caused much pain and suffering. Over time, he systematically eroded my self-confidence and self-worth and created hurt so deep I could no longer bear his presence in my life.

My partner never took responsibility for his own actions. He blamed me incessantly, even for his own abusive behaviour. When confronted, he always had some excuse to justify himself. At his hands, I was subjected to insults, put-downs, shouting, threats and sarcasm. I was criticized, called names, humiliated, intimidated and given ultimatums. Sometimes, he disguised his snide or cutting comments as humour. I found that even his subtlest comment could hurt me as much as his stronger, louder and more obviously denigrating statements. He typically ended his verbal assaults by accusing me of provoking his abuse or telling me that I deserved it. He shunned my explanations and what I might say in my own defense...

[M]y partner habitually chose to walk or stand in front of, rather than beside, me when we were out together. The messages I got were that he couldn't care less about me, was somehow better than me...that I could never be his equal anyway. Often he verbalized these sentiments too...I learned the hard way that living under the cloud of emotional abuse does affect one's health and well being. Because I believe that relationship partners can and should discuss ways to ensure that their words and actions do not inflict discomfort on one another, I made many attempts to alert him to how his words and actions made me feel. Sadly, he rejected them all, telling me repeatedly that whatever I had to say was not worth his time or attention.

SOURCE: Globus-Goldberg, 2001, paragraphs 1–3, 6. Also refer to http://www.springtideresources.org/resource/emotional-abuse-survivors-story-nancy. Reprinted with permission.

There seem to be three reasons for the lack of research on psychological maltreatment: (1) physical IPV and its consequences are much more apparent than psychological IPV and its consequences; (2) there is an implicit (and mistaken) assumption that the consequences of physical IPV are more severe than those of psychological maltreatment; and (3) research on psychological maltreatment has been plagued by definitional problems; indeed, it has been even harder for investigators of psychological maltreatment to come to a consensus on its definition than it has been for investigators of physical IPV (Arias, 1999).

The issue of definitional problems can be illustrated through describing some of the different studies addressing psychological maltreatment. The first measure to explicitly ask about psychological maltreatment was the original CTS administered in the 1975 NFVS. The CTS operationally defined psychological maltreatment with six acts that either verbally (e.g., insulted or swore at other person) or symbolically (e.g., threw, smashed, hit, or kicked something) hurt the other person (Straus, 1990a). Walker (1979), in her study of battered women, determined that in addition to verbal and symbolic hurt, psychological humiliation and verbal harassment were also components of psychological maltreatment. In later work with battered women, Follingstad, Rutledge, Berg, Hause, and Polek (1990) identified six distinct types of psychological maltreatment: (1) verbal attacks (i.e., ridicule, verbal harassment, name-calling); (2) isolation (social and/or financial); (3) jealousy and possessiveness (even with family, friends, and pets); (4) verbal threats of harm, abuse, and/or torture; (5) threats to divorce, abandon, and/or have an affair; and (6) damage and/or destruction of personal property. Murphy and Cascardi (1999) identified five subcategories of psychological maltreatment in their clinical investigations of battered women: (1) isolating and restricting the partner's activities and social contacts; (2) attacking the partner's self-esteem through humiliating and degrading comments; (3) withdrawing in hostile ways; (4) destroying property; and (5) threatening harm or violence. More recently, the NISVS (Black et al., 2011) assessed two categories of psychological maltreatment: (1) *expressive aggression,* which included acting in a dangerous manner, calling the partner names, and insulting or humiliating the partner, and (2) *coercive control,* which involved behaviors used to monitor and control one's partner, such as limiting access to money, interfering in relationships with friends and family, and issuing threats. The varying types of psychological maltreatment found in the research indicate that such maltreatment is highly complex and therefore difficult to operationalize (Kelly, 2004). Table 5.3 presents a summary of selected studies that investigated the prevalence of various forms of psychological maltreatment.

Most of the work on psychological maltreatment indicates that if a woman is physically maltreated she also tends to be psychologically maltreated; however, the reverse is not always true. For instance, the 1985 NFVS showed that in only 0.2% of the cases was a woman physically but not psychologically maltreated, and 65% of the male respondents reported using psychological, but not physical, IPV against their wives (Stets, 1990). Thus, physically maltreated women are likely to be psychologically maltreated, but most psychologically maltreated women are not also physically maltreated.

Rates of psychological maltreatment of women appear to be quite high. Among a large sample of women who had been physically assaulted by a male partner, the percent that experienced psychological abuse ranged from 15% (threatened to kill himself if she ended the relationships) to 67% (raised his voice, yelled, or shouted at her) (Henning & Klesges, 2003). Even higher rates of psychological maltreatment of women were found among couples attending marital therapy: 94% of the men insulted or swore at their wives; 94% did or said something to spite their wives; 90% stomped out of the room, house, or yard; and 97% sulked or refused to talk about an issue (Barling, O'Leary, Jouriles, Vivian, & MacEwen, 1987). The NISVS (Black et al., 2011) found that 40.3% of women experienced *expressive aggression* at least once in their lifetime and 10.4% in the 12 months prior to taking the survey; 41.1% had experienced *coercive control* in their lifetime and 10.7% in the last 12 months. Among women who had experienced any form of IPV (e.g., stalking, sexual abuse, physical assault), the percent who experienced coercive control ranged from 17% (partner prevented the woman from knowing about or having access to family income) to 55% (partner insisted on knowing who the woman was with and where she was at all times).

To measure psychological maltreatment, most studies—with the exception of the NISVS—use the CTS, with its relatively restricted set of psychologically aggressive acts. The few studies that used the most comprehensive psychological maltreatment assessment tool, Tolman's (1989) *Psychological Maltreatment of Women Inventory (PMWI),* suffer from a different problem: They tend to have samples restricted to battered women. Among a sample of 207 battered women, over 75% said their partners had perpetrated the vast majority of the 58 behaviors listed in the scale within the past six months, with being kept from medical care the least reported behavior (29%) and being sworn at (95%), not permitting his partner to talk about her feelings (95%), and acting insensitively to her feelings (98%) the most frequently reported (Tolman, 1989).

Table 5.3 Summary of Selected Studies of the Prevalence of Psychological Maltreatment

Study	Description of Sample	Measures/Definition of Maltreatment	Rates of Psychological Maltreatment by an Intimate Partner
Black et al. (2011) National Intimate Partner and Sexual Violence Survey (NISVS)	Representative sample of 9,086 women and 7,421 men 18 years or older in the United States	*Expressive aggression:* 5 items; e.g., told you that you were a loser; insulted, humiliated, of made fun of you in front of others *Coercive control:* 13 items; e.g., destroyed something that was important to you, tried to keep you from seeing or talking to your family or friends, kept you from having money for yourself	Expressive aggression • 40.3% experienced some form in their lifetime • 10.4% experienced some form in the past 12 months Coercive control • 41.1% experienced some form in their lifetime • 10.7% experienced some form in the past 12 months
Frye, Manganello, Campbell, Walton-Moss, & Wilt (2006)	427 women who had experienced any form of IPV (e.g., physical assault, stalking, sexual assault)	Five items assessing coercive control (four drawn from the Canadian Violence Against Women Survey and one from Tolman's 1989 Psychological Maltreatment of Women Inventory)	• 55% insisted on knowing who the woman was with and where she was at all times • 35% tried to limit the woman's contact with family and friends • 31% were jealous and didn't want woman to talk to other people • 30% controlled most or all of the woman's daily activities • 17% prevented woman from knowing about or having access to family income, even if she asked

(Continued)

Table 5.3 (Continued)

Study	Description of Sample	Measures/Definition of Maltreatment	Rates of Psychological Maltreatment by an Intimate Partner
Barling, O'Leary, Jouriles, Vivian, & MacEwen (1987)	187 couples attending marital therapy	Conflict Tactics Scales (CTS)	• 94% of the men insulted or swore at their wives • 94% did or said something to spite their wives • 90% stomped out of the room, house, or yard • 97% sulked or refused to talk about an issue
Henning & Klesges (2003)	3,370 adult women entering the criminal justice system after an incident of domestic abuse perpetrated by a male partner	Eight items adapted from the Psychological Maltreatment of Women Inventory	• 67% raised his voice, yelled, or shouted at her • 64% called her names, cursed at her, or insulted her • 58% got jealous or suspicious of her friends • 47% checked up on her (listened to her phone calls, etc.) • 33% tried to keep her from having independent activities • 28% threatened to kill her or her kids if she ended the relationship • 15% threatened to kill himself if she ended the relationship
Tolman (1989)	207 women at intake for domestic violence program	Psychological Maltreatment of Women Inventory	• 98% acted insensitive to her feelings • 95% swore at her • 90% blamed her for his violence • 89% ordered her around • 86% called her names • 85% insulted her in front of others • 85% monitored her time • 79% did not allow her to socialize with friends

Predictors and Correlates

Even though the majority of research on the psychological maltreatment of women has been conducted with battered women, the limited research on predictors has been done with community samples and concentrates on only two levels of the ecological model: microsystem and individual/developmental. On the microsystem level, psychological maltreatment has been associated with increased marital conflict and dissatisfaction and fewer children in the home (Stets, 1990; Straus & Sweet, 1992). At the individual/developmental level, the psychological maltreatment of women is associated with several characteristics of the male perpetrator, including higher frequency of alcohol intoxication, the use of verbal aggression outside of the home, and younger age (Stets, 1990; Straus & Sweet, 1992). Furthermore, there is evidence for the intergenerational transmission of psychological maltreatment (Hines & Malley-Morrison, 2003; Hines & Saudino, 2004).

Consequences

The bulk of the research on psychological maltreatment of female partners has been on its consequences, and the majority of this research has focused on battered women. Of six types of psychological maltreatment assessed in 234 battered women, jealousy/possessiveness and isolation were the most frequent types; however, verbal attacks and verbal threats of harm, abuse, and torture were the most painful types (Follingstad et al., 1990). The women who felt that the psychological maltreatment was worse than physical IPV experienced particularly severe consequences, including higher passivity; greater social isolation; greater fear, shame, and depression; lower self-esteem; and greater acceptance of responsibility for the maltreatment.

Greater psychological maltreatment is also associated with more serious and chronic illnesses, more visits to a doctor, more use of mental health services, more use of psychotropic medicines, lower relationship satisfaction, fewer feelings of power and control in the relationship, and more attempts to leave the relationship (Marshall, 1996). In one community sample of women, psychological maltreatment by male partners was associated with both depression and problem drinking in the women (Arias, Street, & Brody, 1996, as cited in Arias, 1999).

Most research on psychological maltreatment of battered women has assessed the relative impact of physical and psychological maltreatment on psychosocial functioning. For instance, among battered women, psychological maltreatment—not physical IPV—predicts a woman's intent to leave her partner (Arias & Pape, 1999), marital dissolution (Jacobson, Gottman, Gortner, Berns, & Shortt, 1996), low self-esteem (Aguilar & Nightingale, 1994), psychological maladjustment and distress, alcoholism (Kahn, Welch, & Zillmer, 1993), and PTSD (Arias & Pape, 1999; Kahn et al., 1993). One study found that women who are psychologically maltreated suffer the same incidence and severity of depression, anxiety, PTSD, and suicidal thoughts as those who are both physically and psychologically maltreated (Pico-Alfonso et al., 2006). Another study shows that psychological maltreatment contributes uniquely to the prediction of PTSD and depression among female victims after controlling for the influences of physical IPV, injuries, and sexual coercion (Mechanic, Weaver, & Resick, 2008). Still another study shows that psychological maltreatment (i.e., jealous control, ignoring, ridiculing traits, criticizing behavior) is a stronger predictor than physical IPV of fear among battered women; each IPV type contributes equally to low self-esteem, and even though physical IPV contributes more to depression, psychological maltreatment is still a significant predictor (Sackett & Saunders, 2001). Overall, these studies show that among battered women, the consequences of psychological mal-treatment may be more severe than the consequences of physical maltreatment. Moreover, the psychological maltreatment of battered women seems to impede them from seeking help for their relationship problems because it instills fear, increases dependency on the perpetrator, and damages self-esteem, which in turn lessens the strength that is necessary to end a relationship (Murphy & Cascardi, 1999).

Sexual Maltreatment

Scope of the Problem

Sexual maltreatment of female intimate partners has been the least studied type of IPV against women. This inattention is likely to due to a lack of realization until recently that husbands can sexually assault their wives. To this day, there are many people whose conceptions of sexual maltreatment exclude the possibility of sexual maltreatment in marriage. Another reason for this inattention to the sexual maltreat-ment of female partners is problems with defining it. Consider the cases presented in Box 5.3. Which would you consider "sexual abuse"? Are there any cases that you do not consider to be sexual abuse? Why?

Box 5.3   Possible Cases of Sexual Maltreatment of a Female Partner

1. *Mrs. Fisher:* "It happens very often. If I refuse he will go to other women. Then it would be my fault and a sin. Whether I like it or not I have to give in" (Russell, 1990, p. 83).

2. *Mrs. Carter:* "Sometimes when I didn't want to have intercourse and he did, he pushed it. He used verbal tactics. He laid guilt trips on me. Like when we would go for a long time without any sex he would demand it, and I would feel like I had to have sex though I didn't want it. I'd just be passive and let him have his way. I felt I had no way out" (Russell, 1990, p. 77).

3. *Mrs. Morgan:* "He wanted me to have sex with him when I didn't want to. I had no desire. I didn't want him to touch me, so he forced me. He said I was his wife and I had to do it...He said he was going to beat me. He called me names. He said I was his wife and he had a right to sleep with me when he wanted to" (Russell, 1990, p. 44).

4. *Mrs. Palmer:* "One time I had the flu and I didn't feel like having sex, but he forced me to anyway. He used his arms and body to pin me down so I couldn't move.

> With all of the violence that had occurred before—him beating me all the time—I was afraid of him when he told me I better not move …After the incident when I had the flu he only had to talk to me, to use verbal force, because I was afraid of him" (Russell, 1990, p. 94).
>
> 5. *Mrs. Atkins:* "We had come back from a party and he had drunk too much …When we got home I went to bed immediately. He came in, got in bed, and wanted to make love. I wasn't in any mood to do that. He forced himself, by using his strength to pin my arms down. He started kissing me, touching me, aggressively grabbing me, all the time holding my arms down …I fought him for a long time. I tried to free my arms, but I couldn't. I yelled abuse at him, told him to leave me alone and to stop it. Finally, because it was obvious I wasn't going to get my way, I ended up just lying there" (Russell, 1990, p. 165).

Over the years, research on sexual maltreatment has expanded from examining husbands' rape of their wives to men's rape of their female partners. Also, there has been expanded investigation into sexual coercion, which the NISVS (Black et al., 2011) defines as "unwanted sexual penetration after being pressured in a non-physical way" (p. 2). Sexually coercive behaviors can range from emotionally coercing one's partner into having sex to physically forcing them to have sex with other people, animals, and objects (Bergen & Bukovec, 2006). Just as male perpetrators often engage in various types of physical and psychological IPV, they often engage in multiple forms of sexual aggression as well.

The best estimates of the prevalence of sexual maltreatment of female partners come from the NISVS, NVAWS, and a large-scale national telephone survey of U.S. adults. According to the NISVS (Black et al., 2011), approximately 1 in 5 women report experiencing sexual coercion by an intimate and 9.4% recount being raped by an intimate partner at some point in their lifetime, with 6.6% reporting completed forced penetration, 2.5% attempted forced penetration, and 3.4% completed alcohol/drug facilitated penetration. Although it did not assess the other types of sexual violence, NVAWS reported similar findings for the lifetime prevalence of rape by an intimate partner: 7.7% (Tjaden & Thoennes, 2000a). In addition, a study using a national probability sample revealed that 7% of the unmarried women reported having been raped by a current partner, and 17% had been raped by a partner at some point in the past; 9% of married women reported being raped by their current spouse, and 20% reported rape by a former partner or spouse in the past (Basile, 2002).

When looking at samples of battered women, between one third and two thirds of the women report experiencing partner rape (Campbell & Soeken, 1999; Frieze, 1983; McFarlane & Malecha, 2005; Shields & Hanneke, 1983; Walker, 2009). One study looking specifically at sexual assault among a sample of battered women found that 68% of battered women also reported sexual assault; 79% of these sexually assaulted women reported repeated episodes of forced sex (McFarlane & Malecha, 2005). In addition, 40% of men enrolled in a domestic violence intervention program reported emotionally pressuring their partner to have sex, 17% had sex with their partner when she was asleep, 8% threatened to withhold money, 6% forced her to look at pornography, and 4% coerced her to enact what they had seen in pornographic material (Bergen & Bukovec, 2006).

As with other types of IPV, for several reasons these figures are considered underestimates of the actual rate of sexual maltreatment. First, some victims do not disclose sexual assault to researchers because of shame and fear of being blamed (Bennice & Resick, 2003; Russell, 1990). Second, surveys do not include women who are homeless or residing in some sort of institution (e.g., hospital, mental health facility, jail, shelter) and who may be at an increased risk for having experienced partner rape (Russell, 1990). Third, some women believe that it is their wifely duty to submit to sex; thus, because these women do not feel that they can say no, they are in a sense "unrapeable" (Russell, 1990). Russell (1990) therefore proposed that a better way of estimating the prevalence of marital rape would be to calculate the percentage of women who were forced into having sex, but also felt that they had the right to refuse.

This last point is important to consider. According to Finkelhor and Yllo (1983), men use four types of coercion during marital rape: (1) social coercion, in which the wife feels it is her duty to submit; (2) interpersonal coercion, in which the husband uses threats to leave, cheat on, or humiliate his wife to get her to submit; (3) threats of physical force; and (4) actual physical force. Several researchers (Basile, 2002; Bergen & Bukovec, 2006; Logan, Cole, & Shannon, 2007) have documented additional forms of sexual coercion, such as bribery, bullying, and begging. One study of women sexually coerced by their partners found that women had sex with a current spouse when they "really did not want to" because they thought it was their "duty" (61%), after a romantic situation (e.g., back rub) (27%), after the partner begged and pleaded (19%), in return for a partner's spending money on them or taking them out to dinner (30%), and after their partner said things to bully or humiliate them (12%) (Basile, 2002).

Reread the cases in Box 5.3. Which cases in Box 5.3 illustrate which types of coercion? Does it matter to our definitions of rape which type of coercion a man uses to get his female partner to have sex with him? Is Mrs. Fisher "unrapeable" because she accepts societal mores obligating wives to have sex with their husbands as part of the marriage vows? What happens if a woman does not physically resist her male partner because she knows that either she will lose the battle or that if she resists she will be hurt worse, as is the case with Mrs. Morgan? Does her lack of resistance mean that the act is not "rape"? Consider the account of Mrs. Atkins. If she passively gave in to her husband's demands in the future because of her experiences in this particular instance, can her future submissions be considered "rape"?

Although the prevalence rates of partner rape extrapolated from the existing research may be underestimates, research indicates that rape of a female partner is almost three times as likely as stranger rape (Finkelhor & Yllo, 1985; Russell, 1990). A study with a large representative sample of women found that the more intimate the relationship between the perpetrator and the victim, the more likely the rape was to succeed and the more frequently the victim was raped (Russell, 1990). Indeed, 33% to 50% of wives who are raped are raped more than 20 times during their marriages (Finkelhor & Yllo, 1985; Russell, 1990). In the majority of cases

(58%), the husband uses only the minimal force necessary to carry out the rape, but in many instances more severe force is used. For instance, in 17% of the cases in one representative sample (Russell, 1990), a weapon was used; in 16%, the male perpetrator hit, kicked, or slapped his partner, and in 19% of the cases, he beat or slugged his partner.

Studies of battered women also reveal high rates of rape: As many as 59% of battered women may also be raped (Campbell & Alford, 1989). Because battered women are at higher risk for rape by their partners than nonbattered women, most of the research on the predictors and consequences of female partner rape, as well as on prevention efforts, has been done with battered women who were also raped. When you read the next sections, keep in mind that most of this research—other than the representative surveys by Russell (1990), Finkelhor and Yllo (1985), and Basile (2002)—was conducted on battered women, usually those living in shelters. What are the implications of this fact for the generalizability of the results?

Predictors and Correlates

Macrosystem

Four macrosystem level influences on partner rape have received the most attention, although the evidence is mixed: poverty, ethnicity, religion, and attitudes toward partner rape. For example, although one earlier study (Finkelhor & Yllo, 1985) showed that women who did not complete high school, who were unemployed, and who made under $10,000 per year were at greater risk for partner rape than their counterparts, a more recent study (Basile, 2002b) found that income did not predict seven types of sexual coercion, including behavior that would legally be defined as rape. Religious affiliation seems to predict partner rape, in that women who are or were raised Protestant (Finkelhor & Yllo, 1985; Russell, 1990) or have no religious affiliation (Finkelhor & Yllo, 1985) are at greatest risk for partner rape, whereas Catholic and Jewish women seem to have the lowest risk (Finkelhor & Yllo, 1985; Russell, 1990). Church attendance, however, does not predict sexual maltreatment (Basile, 2002). There are similar mixed results with respect to ethnicity as a predictor of sexual maltreatment. One study (Russell, 1990) found that Asian women were at the lowest risk, Black women at the highest risk, and Whites and Latinas did not differ from the other races in their risk for partner rape, whereas another (Basile, 2002b) found that race did not predict any of seven types of sexual coercion, including rape. Results from the NVAWS indicated that Alaskan Native and American Indian women report higher rates of rape by a partner than other races (Tjaden & Thoennes, 2000a).

In assessing the motives behind partner rape, Bergen (1996) found that many of these men use rape to punish their female partners and to assert power and control over them. Furthermore, many of the husbands believed it was their conjugal right to have sex with their wives whenever they wanted. If that right was threatened, such as when his wife could not have sex for medical reasons (e.g., she just had a baby or was sick, as with Mrs. Palmer in Box 5.3), a husband's sense of entitlement might be threatened and he may ultimately force her to have sex with him. In fact, nearly half (46%) of women staying in a domestic violence shelter reported being forced to have sex after being discharged from a hospital, most often after childbirth (Campbell & Alford, 1989).

Microsystem

Age seems to be an important victim-level predictor of partner rape. In comparison to nonraped women, women who are under 30 or over 50 are more likely to be raped by their male partners than women between 30 and 50 (Finkelhor & Yllo, 1985). Prior sexual victimization also appears to be a risk factor. Some studies have found childhood physical and/or sexual violence is associated with marital rape victimization (Shields & Hanneke, 1983; Tjaden & Thoennes, 2000c; Russell, 1990). Also, female victims of partner rape are more likely to have experienced rape or an attempted rape by someone other than their current male partners (Painter & Farrington, 1998; Russell, 1990) and to have had unwanted sexual experiences with a woman and/or a non-blood relative (Russell, 1990). Consider why some of these associations may be occurring. Why are women who are under 30 and over 50 at greater risk for partner rape? Why would having a history of sexual assault make a woman more vulnerable to partner rape?

Individual/Developmental

On an individual/developmental level, a number of studies have found a relationship between a perpetrator's alcohol use and rape of a partner. Women who experience partner rape often report that their perpetrators have a drinking problem. One study of female IPV victims found that the perpetrator's problem with alcohol or drugs was the strongest predictor of the woman being physically and sexually assaulted (Coker, Smith, McKeown, & King, 2000). In a representative sample in San Francisco, 20% to 25% of the male partners were drinking at the time of the rape (Russell, 1990), as was the case with Mrs. Atkins in Box 5.3. Further, in comparison to men who only batter, batterers who also rape have more drinking problems and are more violent both in and outside the home (Frieze, 1983).

Finally, there is some evidence of an intergenerational transmission of sexual maltreatment, although research findings are not consistent (Martin, Taft, & Resick, 2007). For example, one study found that men who raped their partners tend to come from homes in which there was physical IPV against a spouse and/or sexual dysfunction (Bowker, 1983).

Consequences

Consider what you have read so far about partner rape, including the cases in Box 5.3. Now think about the possible consequences of partner rape, especially in comparison to other victimized women such as those who are "just" battered and those who experience rape from a stranger. Who do you think experiences the worst psychosocial consequences—the victim of partner rape, stranger rape, or battering? Consider Mrs. Atkins's case in Box 5.3. What if the perpetrator in that case was a man she just met at the party? Might the rape result in different psychosocial outcomes? The popular belief seems to be that partner rape victims will not suffer as much as stranger rape victims. Do you agree? Consider this quote from Karen, a partner rape survivor:

> It was very clear to me. He raped me. He ripped off my pajamas, he beat me up. I mean, some scumbag down the street would do that to me. So to me it wasn't any different because I was married to him, it was rape—real clear what it was. It emotionally hurt worse [than stranger rape]. I mean you can compartmentalize it as stranger rape—you were at the wrong place at the wrong time. You can manage to get over it differently. But here you're at home with your husband, and you don't expect that. I was under constant terror [from then on] even if he didn't do it. (Bergen, 1996, p. 43)

Several researchers have found that victims of partner rape suffer *worse* psychologically than victims of stranger rape. For example, in Russell's (1990) study, 77% of the partner rape victims reported being very or extremely upset about the rape, and 49% stated that it had a great effect on their lives. These reactions were much more severe than those reported by victims of stranger rape. Moreover, women raped and beaten by their male partners had more severe anxiety, paranoia, and psychoticism, and were less likely to enjoy sex, than women raped by strangers. Partner rape may be worse than stranger rape for several reasons: The woman's ability to trust is disturbed, which leads her to feel more isolated and powerless, and even worse, she has to live with her rapist. Because she must live with her rapist, she is prone to being victimized again and again, and, as shown previously, men who rape their female partners are more likely to complete the rape and more likely to rape repeatedly than other kinds of rapists (Russell, 1990). Further, one study found that sexual assaults committed by current or former spouses or boyfriends were characterized by more physical trauma and injury severity than those committed by strangers and acquaintances/dating partners (Stermac, Del Bove, Brazeau, & Bainbridge, 2006).

Partner rape victims experience a wide range of outcomes, including physical (vaginal stretching, unwanted pregnancies, miscarriages/stillbirths, bladder infections, infertility, soreness, bruising, genital injuries, muscle tension, headaches, fatigue, and nausea and vomiting) and psychological ones (anxiety, shock, stress, intense fear, depression, PTSD, dissociation, and suicidal tendencies) (Adams, 1993; Campbell & Alford, 1989; McFarlane, 2007; Russell, 1990; Temple, Weston, Rodriquez, & Marshall, 2007). Partner rape victims may suffer from severe, sometimes prolonged depression and suicidal ideations; experience flashbacks and nightmares of the incidents; have an inability to trust other men and a fear of intimacy; and have long-term sexual dysfunctions (Bergen, 1996).

In assessing possible consequences of partner rape, not only have researchers compared women who have been raped by their intimate partners to victims of stranger rape, but they have also compared women who are both battered and raped by their male partners to those who are battered only. Women who are both battered and raped are more likely than "just" battered women to use violence on their own children (Frieze, 1983), score significantly higher on scales measuring anxiety, paranoia, and psychoticism, and are less likely to enjoy sex (Shields & Hanneke, 1983). Further, women who are both battered and raped by their male partners, in comparison to battered women, have more severe injuries, are at greater risk for being murdered or of murdering their husbands, are at greater risk for being beaten during pregnancy, and have significantly more health problems (e.g., sexually transmitted diseases, urinary tract infections, decreased sexual pleasure and desire, and other gynecological problems). In addition, they have lower self-esteem and a worse body image (Campbell & Alford, 1989).

Intimate Partner Stalking

Ever since we separated, it's been getting really bad. It has got to the point where I was forced to get a restraining order because he has been constantly following me, spying on me, calling at my place of employment, and giving me a lot of problems. Even after I obtained the restraining order, when I go home from work I find him near my house watching me. When I get up in the morning, I see him right across from my house in his pickup. He calls me at work and follows me everywhere I go. (Dunn, 2002, p. 46)

Scope of the Problem

The above case study illustrates stalking that occurred after a woman separated from her male partner. This section will discuss the most common type of stalking, relational stalking, which was experienced by this victim. Although there is little agreement among experts on how to define stalking (Sheridan Blaauw, & Davies, 2003; Tjaden, 2009), it generally involves "a harmful course of conduct involving unwanted communications and intrusions repeatedly inflicted by one individual on another" (Pathe, Mullen, & Purcell, 2000, p. 191). To meet the criteria for most anti-stalking laws, the behaviors must be repeated and unwanted, committed to intentionally place the victim in fear or cause extreme emotional distress, and cause the victim (or a reasonable person) fear or extreme distress (Cupach & Spitzberg, 2004). When occurring within the context of an intimate relationship, stalking is considered to be a variant or extension of IPV (Burgess et al., 1997; Logan, Leukefeld, & Walker, 2000; Spitzberg & Hoobler, 2002; Spitzberg & Rhea, 1999), with more severe stalking being related to higher levels of other types of IPV (Logan, Cole, & Shannon, 2007; Norris, Huss, & Palarea, 2011). When occurring in the context of a male perpetrator and female victim, stalking often commences after a woman leaves her abusive partner, as in the case study above, but in one out of five cases, it begins while the relationship is still intact (Tjaden & Thoennes, 1998). It is one of many methods that perpetrators use to exert control over a current or former partner (Johnson, 2008; Stark, 2007).

Although relational stalking is often not perceived as seriously by the criminal justice system as other types of stalking, relational stalkers engage in more frequent stalking behaviors (Mohandie, Meloy, McGowan, & Williams, 2006), a wider array of such behaviors (Logan & Walker, 2010), and more violent behaviors (Meloy, Davis, & Lovette, 2001) than nonintimate stalkers. Thus, relational stalkers are more dangerous than nonintimate stalkers (Groenen & Vervaeke, 2009; Harmon et al., 1998; Meloy, 1998; Mohandie, Meloy, McGowan, & Williams, 2006; Schwartz-Watts & Morgan, 1998; Zona, Sharma, & Lane, 1993). Why do you think that abusive men who stalk are more likely to be violent? What are the implications for intervening with abusive men who stalk and abused women who are stalked?

Three large-scale representative surveys have assessed the prevalence of relational stalking in the United States: the NISVS (Black et al., 2011), the National Crime Victimization Survey—Supplemental Victimization Survey (NCVS–SVS) (Baum et al., 2009), and the NVAWS (Tjaden & Thoennes, 1998) (see Table 5.4). Results from the NISVS (Black et al., 2011) revealed that 10.7% of women in the United States have been stalked by an intimate partner at some point in their life, with 4.3% reporting being stalked in the 12 months prior to the survey. Similarly, the NCVS–SVS found that 16.7% of women were stalked at some time during their lives and 3% were stalked in the year preceding the survey, with 66% of those perpetrators being current or former intimate partners (Baum et al., 2009). Lower rates were found by the NVAWS: 8% of women were stalked at some time in their life, with just under half (48%) of the perpetrators being current or former spouses or cohabiting partners, and only 1% had been stalked in the year prior to the survey (Tjaden & Thoennes, 1998). The varying rates of stalking are likely to be related to

Table 5.4   Studies on the Prevalence of Relational Stalking of Women

Study	Description of Sample	Measures/ Definition of Stalking	Rates of Stalking
Black et al. (2011); National Intimate Partner and Sexual Violence Survey	Representative sample of 9,086 women and 7,421 men 18 years or older	Eight tactics including watching/ following, approaching, leaving messages and gifts	• 10.7% stalked in lifetime • 4.3% stalked in the previous year
Baum, Catalano, Rand, & Rose (2009); National Crime Victimization Survey— Supplemental Victimization Survey (NCVS–SVS)	65,270 individuals 18 and older from 76,000 nationally representative households	Seven tactics including following/spying, showing up, leaving gifts, spreading rumors	• 1 in 6 women stalked in lifetime (66% by a current or former intimate) • 3% stalked in prior year
Tjaden & Thoennes (1998); National Violence Against Women Survey (NVAWS) (1995–1996)	Representative sample of 8,000 women and 8,000 men	Eight tactics including following/spying, showing up, unwanted calls, stood outside home, left items	• 8.1% of women stalked in lifetime • 1.0% stalked in the previous 12 months • 48% of those stalked were stalked by current or former spouses or cohabiting partners • 14% were stalked by dates or former dates

methodological differences between studies, including how stalking was measured and the context in which questions about stalking were asked. For example, the NVAWS (Tjaden & Thoennes, 1998) used a strict definition of stalking that required victims to experience a high degree of fear as a result of stalking, and relational stalking was limited to marital and cohabiting relationships. For the NISVS (Black et al., 2011), questions about physical health preceded those about IPV, which may have yielded higher disclosure of stalking victimization than if they had been preceded by questions about crimes.

Stalkers engage in a wide variety of harassing and intimidating behaviors, as illustrated by the case study at the beginning of this section. Stalking behaviors include hyperintimate acts (e.g., showering the victim with unwanted gifts, performing unsolicited favors), mediated contacts (e.g., repeatedly contacting the victim by phone or email, leaving unwanted notes), interactional contacts (e.g., showing up places, intruding into conversations), and surveillance tactics (e.g., following, tracking with a Global Positioning System device) (Spitzberg & Cupach, 2007). Other behaviors include those that are invasive (e.g., breaking and entering), harassing and intimidating (e.g., calling nonstop, spreading rumors), coercive and threatening (e.g., threats against loved ones or pets), and physically aggressive or violent (e.g., assaults, attempted rape, homicide) (Spitzberg & Cupach, 2007). Note that many stalking behaviors overlap with the other IPV behaviors discussed in this chapter (i.e., physical, psychological, sexual).

Based on the data from the NISVS (Black et al., 2011), NCVS–SVS (Baum et al., 2009), and NVAWS (Tjaden & Thoennes, 1998), the most common stalking behaviors include receiving repeated unwanted phone calls (78.8% NISVS; 66.2% NCVS; 61% NVAWS), being watched or followed (31% NISVS; 34.3% NCVS; 82% NVAWS), and receiving unwanted letters, emails, or items (30.6% NCVS; 33% NVAWS). Other frequent behaviors include vandalizing property (29%, NVAWS), spreading rumors (35.7%, NCVS), and waiting for the victim (29% NCVS). Less frequent behaviors include sneaking into the victim's home or car (16.6% NISVS) and leaving strange items (9.0% NISVS).

Increasingly, stalkers are using technology. The NCVS–SVS found that 26.1% of stalking victims reported experiencing some form of cyberstalking, such as receiving unwanted emails or instant messages (Baum et al., 2009). Other types of cyberstalking behaviors include installing recording or listening devices to monitor the victim, disabling the person's computer, covertly entering the person's computer files, taking over the victim's persona online (e.g., in chat rooms, on social networking sites), and setting up a website to sully the victim's reputation (Spitzberg & Hoobler, 2004). Current or former intimate partner victims may be particularly vulnerable to certain types of cyberstalking because the perpetrator is more likely to have access to the victim's computer, car, and cell phone, and to know account passwords.

Stalking, by definition, involves repeated behaviors. On average, it occurs on a weekly basis (Cupach & Spitzberg, 2004) and persists for an average of 22 months (Spitzberg & Cupach, 2007). The NCVS–SVS found that 40% of female victims were stalked for six months or less and over 10% were stalked for over five years (Baum et al., 2009). Stalking does not necessarily progress linearly and continuously;

the behaviors may deescalate and then escalate again or cease altogether and restart at a later time (Mumm & Cupach, 2010), which can serve to create a high degree of anxiety in victims. Although patterns can vary, stalking typically escalates over time (Cupach & Spitzberg, 2004).

Predictors and Correlates

Macrosystem

Income and unemployment appear to be associated with stalking, although the research is not specific to relational stalking. The NCVS–SVS found that 31.7% of victims with an annual household income of less than $7,500 were stalked, in comparison to 9.6% of victims having an income of $75,000 or more; rates of stalking consistently declined as income increased (Baum et al., 2009). Unemployment rates among perpetrators are higher than in the general population, ranging from 16% (Brewster, 2002) to 60% (Kienlen et al., 1997). Why would individuals with a lower income be more at risk for stalking and why would unemployed individuals be more likely to stalk?

Microsystem

Characteristics of the Relationship. The breakup of an intimate relationship is a significant risk factor for stalking. The NVAWS found that 26% of stalking began after the relationship ended (Tjaden & Thoennes, 1998). Among women stalked by an ex-partner, 18.7% believed the stalking commenced because of a breakup. Those who are separated or divorced from their partners are more likely to be stalked than those who are married to or living with the perpetrator (Basile, Swahn, Chen, & Saltzman, 2006; Baum et al., 2009; Walby & Allen, 2004). In a sample of female IPV victims, no longer being in a relationship with their perpetrator was associated with experiencing more severe stalking (Melton, 2007). Why do you think the breakup of a relationship compels some men, but not others, to begin stalking their ex-partners? Is it somehow related to their overall use of IPV? We know that the co-occurrence of other forms of partner maltreatment increases women's chances of being stalked (Tjaden & Thoennes, 2000b, 2000c), and that among female IPV victims, prior stalking and the perpetrator's use of controlling behaviors in the relationship predicts more severe stalking (Melton, 2007). Why might this constellation of IPV-related issues predict men's use of stalking once the relationship ends?

Characteristics of the Victim. There are several characteristics of victims that predict whether they are at risk for being stalked. Individuals between the ages of 18 and 29 appear to be at the greatest risk of being stalked (Black et al., 2001; Baum et al., 2009; Tjaden & Thoennes, 1998). Relatedly, college students are at greater risk of being stalked than those who are employed, unemployed, homemakers, or retired (Basile et al., 2006; Budd & Mattinson, 2000). Women who are single, living in privately rented housing, and poor are more likely to be victimized (Budd & Mattinson, 2000).

Individual/Developmental

Little is known about the characteristics of men who stalk their partners, particularly those who are abusive during the relationship (Logan, Cole, Shannon, & Walker, 2006). Most research on stalkers has been conducted with small forensic/court samples, and relational stalkers are not separated from other types of stalkers (Logan et al., 2006). One study of 112 relational stalkers investigated their personality characteristics (Kamphius, Emmelkamp, & de Vries, 2004). As judged by victims, these stalkers were low on agreeableness, moderately low on conscientiousness and emotional stability, insecurely attached, and highly sensitive to rejection, abandonment, and loss (Kamphius et al., 2004). Male batterers who stalk may have an extensive trauma history. One study (Burgess, Harner, Baker, Hartman, & Lole, 2001) found that 30.9% had been in a major car accident, 25.5% had been robbed or mugged, 23% had witnessed a murder or beating, and 12.1% had lost a parent or sibling before the age of 18. Many of the men reported being physically maltreated before (25.5%) and after (27.9%) the age of 16, and 5.5% reported being sexually abused before the age of 16. In what other ways might abusive men who stalk differ from abusive men who do not stalk?

Consequences

Victims experience a wide range of consequences as a result of being stalked. Although an individual act by a stalker is unlikely to cause any lasting impact, the cumulative impact of a stalker's actions over time can produce the effect of intimidation, control, and fear (Babcock, 2000). Female stalking victims have reported long-term changes in their personalities (86% of victims) and symptom levels indicative of at least one psychiatric disorder (75% of victims) as a result of being stalked (Logan et al., 2009). Thus, the impact of stalking can be quite severe.

Based on an analysis of 143 studies of stalking, Cupach and Spitzberg (2004) developed an 11-category typology of the consequences of victimization. Victims can experience *general effects,* which are diverse negative effects on the quality of life, such as PTSD and a disturbance in a sense of well-being. *Behavioral effects* are those that interfere with their normal patterns of behavior (e.g., changing the normal route taken to work). *Affective health effects* are those that involve the emotional quality of life, such as depression, anxiety, sadness, and grief. Changes in the victims' rational quality of life are *cognitive health effects* and can include distrust, lack of concentration, and suspicion. Examples of *physical/ physiological health effects* include sleep disorders, illnesses, and loss of appetite. *Social health effects* involve changes in the quality of relationships, including losing friends and strengthening ties with family members. *Resource health effects* involve changes in the victim's quality of life in terms of economics and resources. Examples include losing money because of lost time at work and purchasing a home security system. Changes in quality of faith-based belief systems are *spiritual effects.* Victims may experience a loss of or increase in faith in a spiritual entity. On a broader level, victims may experience *societal effects,* such as increased fear of crime as a result of being a victim. When victims have mixed feelings about being stalked (e.g., feeling both frightened and flattered), these are *ambivalent effects.* Research indicates that some victims experience little or no effects, or *minimal effects.* The degree to which victims suffer consequences of stalking is affected by numerous factors, including the frequency, duration, and pervasiveness of the stalking and general coping skills (Blaauw, Winkel, Arensman, Sheridan, & Freeve, 2002).

Prevention and Intervention

Criminal Justice Response

Physical assault, sexual assault, and stalking are considered crimes in all 50 states (Bergen, 1996; Buzawa, Buzawa, & Stark, 2011; Stalking Resource Center, 2012). When the battering of female partners came to public attention in the 1970s, the criminal justice system was criticized for not responding appropriately—for example, for not handling "domestic disputes" in a way that prevented future violence and for not responding quickly to women's calls for help. One of the most notorious cases was that of Tracey Thurman of Torrington, Connecticut. Over a period of several years, Tracey was repeatedly beaten and threatened by her husband Charles, who worked in a local diner where he knew and served many of Torrington's police officers. After one encounter when Charles publicly screamed threats at Tracey and broke the car's windshield while she was inside the car, he was arrested for breach of peace, given a suspended sentence of six months and a two-year "conditional discharge," and ordered to stay completely away from Tracey. His threats and intimidation continued, and Tracey's constant appeals to the Torrington Police Department for protection were ignored. Finally, in 1983, when Charles went to the home where Tracey was staying, she again called the police for help. By the time a single officer arrived, Charles had stabbed Tracey numerous times in the chest, neck, and throat. In the presence of the officer, he kicked Tracey in the head twice. Even after three other officers arrived, he was left free to continue to threaten her, and kicked her again in the head while she was lying on a stretcher. Left partially paralyzed and scarred by his attack, Tracey successfully sued the Torrington Police Department for failure to protect her constitutional rights and was awarded $2.3 million in damages. In 1985, Connecticut passed a mandatory arrest law, and police departments around the country began developing better protocols for dealing with domestic assault cases (*Thurman v. City of Torrington,* 1984).

During the past 30 years, the criminal justice response to men's physical assault of their female partners has changed considerably—all states have enacted legislation designed to modify police and court responses to IPV. For instance, most police precincts have adopted mandatory arrest policies in IPV cases, and prosecutors do not necessarily need a victim's consent to press charges against a perpetrator. Although it has been argued that these policies may actually deter victims from calling the police in incidents of battering (because they may not want their partner arrested and prosecuted and/or they do not want to lose further control over the situation), the criminal justice system—and police in particular—appear to have become more concerned and helpful in IPV cases (Buzawa, Hotaling, Klein, & Byrne, 1999; Mills, 1998, 1999, 2003).

There are three main points at which victims of IPV may come into contact with the criminal justice system: (1) when they are seeking protection orders (also called restraining orders) to keep their partners from assaulting or stalking them; (2) when an incident of IPV has led to an encounter with police that can lead to mandatory or discretionary reporting of the IPV; and (3) during and after filing criminal charges against the perpetrator.

Protection Orders. IPV victims can seek protection orders to document that IPV is occurring and to notify perpetrators that if they violate the protection order, they are subject to criminal prosecution (Malecha et al., 2003). Protection orders, which can be either civil or criminal, are intended to prevent violent or threatening acts against, harassment against, contact with, communication with, or physical proximity to, another person (Baker, 2002). The exact status of the individuals who can obtain these orders—for example, whether noncohabiting partners are included—varies somewhat from state to state. Protection orders are a way of trying to end the IPV without having the perpetrator criminally charged or sentenced to jail for the maltreatment; thus, the goal is prevention rather than punishment.

One provision of the 1994 Violence Against Women Act (VAWA; see Chapter 1) was to make protection orders accessible, affordable, and enforceable across state lines, and to establish penalties for individuals who crossed state lines in order to perpetrate IPV, and it seems to be working. Approximately 10 years following the initial enactment of VAWA, an analysis by Eigenberg, McGuffee, Berry, and Hall (2003) found that state laws provided victims greater access to protective orders and expanded eligible populations to include categories (e.g., dating partner, sexual partners, same-sex partners) that were excluded in earlier legislation (i.e., 1988). There was more access to protective orders outside of normal working hours, and states were increasingly willing to use enhanced sanctions for repeat offenders.

Thousands of women, and numerous men, apply for protection orders every year; however, fewer than half of the women who apply for protection orders receive them, primarily because they stop the process. Why might they do this? In one sample of 150 women who applied for protection orders (Malecha et al., 2003), 54% completed the process and 28% decided not to complete it; the remaining women did not complete the process for reasons beyond their control. The only significant differences between the two groups were that women who dropped the protection order process were more likely to currently be in a relationship with their perpetrators and living with their perpetrators three months after their initial application for the protection order. Thus, whether they are still being assaulted or not, women continuing to live with their perpetrators following their efforts to get protection are the ones most likely to discontinue the effort.

Do protection orders actually give the protection they are designed to provide? The data are mixed. An analysis of 40 studies on the effectiveness of restraining orders showed that they are violated an average of 40% of the time and are perceived to lead to even worse events 22% of the time (Cupach & Spitzberg, 2004). A recent analysis by Logan and Walker (2010) showed similar results: About half of women reported protection order violations within six months. However, even among women who experienced a violation, there were significant reductions in violence, and the women were less fearful of future harm from their partner. Nonetheless, victim perceptions of protection order effectiveness are not consistent across time, in that a participant might report at one time point that the order of protection was helpful, and at a later time point report that it was counterproductive (Botuck, Berretty, Cho, Tax, Archer, & Bennett Catteneo, 2009). Overall, however, there is some evidence that recurrence of violence is lessened in the presence of a protection order (Holt, Kernic, Lumley, Wolf, & Rivara, 2002; Holt, Kernic, Wolf, & Rivara, 2003; Logan, Nigoff, Walker, & Jordan, 2002; McFarlane et al., 2004).

What predicts protection order violations? One study found that perpetrator stalking, victims' sustained fear, and victims' lower perceived effectiveness were predictors of protection order violations (Logan & Walker, 2010). Moreover, it is clear that protection orders are less effective against men with a history of violent offenses, and thus, criminal prosecution might be necessary with repeat offenders who are not deterred by the civil protection orders (Keilitz, Davis, Efkeman, Flango, & Hannaford, 1998). Consider the case in Box 5.4. Do you think such a tragedy could occur again today? How can incidents like this be prevented?

Box 5.4   The Pinder Case

On the evening of March 10, 1989, Officer Johnson responded to a call reporting a domestic disturbance at the home of Carol Pinder. When he arrived at the scene, Johnson discovered that Pinder's former boyfriend, Don Pittman, had broken into her home. Pinder told Officer Johnson that when Pittman broke in, he pushed her, punched her, and threw various objects at her. Pittman was also screaming and threatening both Pinder and her children, saying he would murder them all. A neighbor, Darnell Taylor, managed to subdue Pittman and restrain him until the police arrived. Johnson then placed Pittman under arrest. After confining Pittman in the squad car, Johnson returned to the house to speak with Pinder again. Pinder explained to Officer Johnson that Pittman ... had just been released from prison after being convicted of attempted arson at Pinder's residence some ten months earlier. She was naturally afraid for herself and her children and wanted to know whether it would be safe for her to return to work that evening. Officer Johnson assured her that Pittman would be locked up overnight. He further indicated that Pinder had to wait until the next day to swear out a warrant against Pittman because a county commissioner would not be available to hear the charges before morning. Based on these assurances, Pinder returned to work. That same evening, Johnson brought Pittman before Dorchester County Commissioner George Ames, Jr. for an initial appearance. Johnson only charged Pittman with trespassing and malicious destruction of property having a value of less than three hundred dollars ... [and] simply released Pittman on his own recognizance and warned him to stay away from Pinder's home. Upon his release, [Pittman] returned to Pinder's house and set fire to it. Pinder was still at work, but her three children were home asleep and died of smoke inhalation.

SOURCE: *Pinder v. Johnson* (1995), paragraphs 2–4

Arrest. In the early days of the domestic violence movement, police typically took an arrest-avoidance position, which was seen by many feminists as denying battered women equal protection under the law (Walker, 1993). In the famous Minneapolis Domestic Violence Experiment, Sherman and Berk (1984) found that subsequent offending, including domestic assault and property damage, was reduced by nearly half when the offenders were arrested and jailed. In response to this study, the U.S. Attorney General's office recommended that the no-arrest policies of states be replaced, and currently all states except Arkansas and Washington, D.C., have codified mandatory arrest or proarrest policies. All states have passed legislation allowing, and often requiring, police to make warrantless arrests in response to misdemeanor IPV not committed in their presence, and many police departments have adopted arrest-preferred policies in IPV cases (Buzawa, Buzawa, & Stark, 2011; Hirschel, Buzawa, Pattavina, & Faggiani, 2007). Even in jurisdictions with mandatory arrest policies, police generally have some discretion about whether to make an arrest on a domestic disturbance call, but some states have attempted to reduce police discretion by mandating that specific actions be taken when they respond to domestic violence calls. Thus, police discretion varies by state (Hirschel et al., 2007).

Research on the "extralegal" factors that tend to influence arrest practices show that police are more likely to make an arrest on a domestic disturbance call when serious injuries have occurred (Connolly, Huzurbazar, & Routh-McGee, 2000); when the complainant is a White, affluent, older, or suburban woman (Avakame & Fyfe, 2001); or when the assailant is not married to the victim (Buzawa, Austin, & Buzawa, 1995; Fyfe, Klinger, & Flavin, 1997). They are also more likely to make dual arrests (i.e., to arrest both parties) when the alleged victim has been drinking and is confrontational with the police (Stewart & Maddren, 1997).

Does a policy of mandatory arrest operate to reduce IPV? Here again, the evidence is mixed. Results from numerous studies indicate that the use of mandatory arrest does not serve as a deterrent to subsequent violence (Berk, Campbell, Klap, & Western, 1992; Campbell, Klap, & Western, 1992; Dunford, Huizinga, & Elliot, 1989; Garner, Fagan, & Maxwell, 1995; Garner & Maxwell, 2000; Hirschel & Hutchinson, 1992; Maxwell, Garner, & Fagan, 2002; Pate & Hamilton, 1992; Sherman et al., 1992). An analysis of five studies with a total of 4,032 IPV cases involving a male perpetrator and female victim showed that an arrest had a modest deterrent effect in that it delayed the onset of new offending behavior between the same offender and the same victim, resulting in possibly fewer calls that the police had to handle for those cases (Maxwell et al., 2002). A second finding was that there was a subset of offenders for which arrest had absolutely no deterrent effect—these were chronic offenders who had a high rate of repeat offending. A third finding showed that the majority of offenders did not recidivate, whether they were arrested or not. Thus, arrest did not have a deterrent effect on these offenders because no matter what the intervention, if any, they would not have committed the offense again anyway. The researchers thus questioned whether a policy in which every offender is arrested is cost-effective (Maxwell et al., 2002).

Based on their review of the research on the deterrent effects of arrest on perpetrators, Buzawa et al. (2011) concluded that although arrest for the purpose of deterring an offender from future violence does not always work that does not necessarily mean that arrest per se fails to work. In their view, it may be important to bring certain perpetrators into the criminal justice system, where there are at least possibilities of interventions that may reduce recidivism. They also note that some types of offenders may not be influenced by any sort of intervention except incarceration.

One unintended effect of the institution of mandatory arrest laws is dual arrest—where police arrest both parties involved in a domestic disturbance because they cannot determine who the perpetrator is (Hirschel & Buzawa, 2002; Martin, 1997). The rates of dual arrest vary widely by state (e.g., Lawrenz, Lembo, & Schade, 1988; Municipality of Anchorage, 2000; Office of the Attorney General, State of California, 1999; Wanless, 1996; Zorza & Woods, 1994). Due to pressure from domestic violence advocates, some states have attempted to reduce dual arrest through the creation of primary aggressor policies, which specify that in cases where both parties are violent, arrest should be limited to the "primary aggressor" or to the person who initiated the violence (Buzawa et al., 2011). Dual arrest may still occur if police are unable to determine the primary aggressor.

Some observers suggest that the increase in dual arrests shows that frequently the violence is mutual between the partners; however, others argue that the frequency of dual arrests is one more way of blaming the victim and further victimizing women. Some suggest that the overall declines in calls have occurred because women have become afraid that if they call for help, their partners will make accusations that will lead to their own arrests as well as their perpetrators'; others argue that the decline is due to women's fear that their wishes that their partners not be arrested will be ignored because of mandatory arrest policies that do not consider the victim's wishes; and still others argue that the declines reflect actual decreases in the incidence of intimate violence. Thus, the results of these studies can be interpreted in many different ways and cannot be taken as evidence that mandatory arrest policies are having an ameliorating effect on the incidence of intimate violence.

Processing Domestic Violence Cases. Mandatory arrest policies had some consequences that were unanticipated. An increasing number of cases were referred to the prosecutor, without concomitant increases in budgets or staff to handle such cases (Cahn, 1992; Davis, Smith, & Nickles, 1998). For example, in Milwaukee there was a backload of cases, the time to disposition increased, and pretrial crime increased after mandatory arrest policies were instituted (Davis & Smith, 1995). Without adequate resources, prosecutors' offices often were unable to effectively handle the increase in domestic violence caseloads, and the typical response was to reduce charges dramatically. This practice was criticized because it subverted what mandatory arrest laws were trying to accomplish (Ford, 1983). However, prosecutors saw their actions as reasonable, especially given the noncooperation of many victims. In 60% to 80% of domestic violence cases, victims ultimately repudiate the case because they want to drop the charges; often they refuse to appear in court as a witness (e.g., Buzawa & Buzawa, 2003; Rebovich, 1996).

Because domestic violence cases were getting dismissed by prosecutors' offices or dropped by victims, states began to enact "no-drop" policies, which effectively limited the discretion of victims and prosecutors. Under no-drop policies, prosecutors cannot drop cases unless there are documented failures to find evidence that a crime occurred.

In addition, if the victim wants to prosecute, the prosecutor must follow the victim's wishes. For victims, these policies imposed restrictions that limited their ability to drop charges, and in some jurisdictions, if victims refused to testify in court, they could be subpoenaed and held in contempt of court (Epstein, 1999). Studies of sites that instituted no-drop policies have shown some positive impact. For example, in Washington, D.C., the prosecution rates of domestic violence cases began to approximate those of nondomestic misdemeanor cases, and some cities seem to have experienced a decrease in recidivism rates (Hamby, 1998).

An example of the processing of domestic violence cases through criminal court comes from a study of IPV cases in Sacramento County Criminal Court during a one-year period (Kingsnorth, Macintosh, Berdahl, Blades, & Rossi, 2001). Criminal charges were filed in 70.5% of the cases with an uncooperative victim (i.e., who did not want to press charges) and 82.5% of the cases with cooperative victims. The high level of filing charges reflected the no-drop policy in that office. Of all cases, 57.5% were fully prosecuted (i.e., neither rejected nor dismissed); 56.9% of perpetrators pled guilty, and 0.7% (n = 3) went to trial, of whom two were found guilty. Only 6% of the fully prosecuted and convicted cases received prison terms.

In their analysis of the factors that predicted proceeding with a case, Kingsnorth et al. (2001) found that when there were dual arrests, prosecutors were *less* likely to file a case for prosecution. Presumably when both parties are arrested, prosecutors view the likelihood of successfully assigning responsibility as remote. By contrast, the victim receiving hospital treatment and a greater number of witnesses of the IPV were positively associated with the prosecutor's willingness to file charges. As was true of the initial decision to file a case, the defendants who were under the influence of alcohol or other drugs at the time of the offense were more likely to have their cases fully prosecuted, as were those who had inflicted more severe injuries on their victims. Hospital treatment of the victim, the availability of crime scene photos of the victim, and the severity of the attack all contributed significantly to the level of charges filed. Prior prison terms, prior domestic violence arrests, and perpetrator substance abuse were also positively associated with the level of severity of the charges filed (felony vs. misdemeanor).

A number of barriers to successful use of the criminal justice system by battered women have been identified, and these may influence the women's desire to prosecute a case: (1) fear of retaliation by their batterer (or someone else seeking vengeance on his behalf); (2) victim-blaming attitudes among criminal justice personnel; (3) resistance within the criminal justice system to treating domestic assaults as seriously as other assaults of equal impact; (4) poverty and its associated factors (e.g., transportation problems, inability to take time off from work); (5) fear of abandonment by one's religious or ethnic community; and (6) general distrust of the criminal justice system (Epstein, 1999; Hart, 1993). In addition, others have pointed out that the mandatory arrest and prosecution policies of most jurisdictions have the effect of making a battered woman feel ignored, voiceless, faceless, and powerless during the prosecution process (Mills, 2003).

Given such barriers, one might expect that battered women would not be particularly satisfied with their experiences in the criminal justice system. In a national study of victim satisfaction with criminal justice system responses, in comparison to victims of assaults by nonintimates, the victims of IPV were less likely to report feeling satisfied with their experiences with the police officers (65.5% vs. 84.5%), the prosecutors (51.9% vs. 73.4%), the victim assistance staff (67.7% vs. 81.6%), the judges (53% vs. 71.6%), and the criminal justice system overall (37% vs. 52%) (Byrne, Kilpatrick, Howley, & Beatty, 1999). Moreover, when perpetrators entered a guilty plea, significantly more perpetrators of partner assault were allowed to plead guilty to a lesser crime than nonpartner perpetrators.

Efforts are being made to address the challenges in processing domestic violence cases for both the criminal justice system and victims. Increasingly, domestic violence courts are being established. Such specialized courts take a coordinated community approach to domestic violence cases that typically includes cooperation among judges, district attorneys, law enforcement, probation officers, social service providers, and community agencies working together to effectively respond to each case. Such courts provide victim advocates who assist victims in participating in the criminal justice process, thus increasing cooperation. Some increase their focus on perpetrator intervention by imposing alternative sentences, such as mandated counseling, and increasing their oversight of defendants by monitoring their attendance at mandated programs (Tsai, 2000).

Special Issue: Criminal Justice Response to Intimate Partner Stalking

By 1996, all states had enacted laws that criminalize stalking (Tjaden, 2009). Although stalking is often legally considered a separate crime, it is closely related to—and sometimes a precursor—to physical IPV, and thus, some argue, should be included in domestic violence statutes (Buzawa et al., 2011). There are concerns that the implementation of these relatively new statutes is limited, that law enforcement and prosecution agencies lack policies for how to handle stalking complaints, that few jurisdictions have any personnel with expertise in stalking (Mill & Nugent, 2002), and that legal definitions and sentences for stalking and cyberstalking vary widely across jurisdictions (Roberts, 2008).

Overall, there are major problems in the criminal justice system with helping stalking victims. Relational stalking is often not perceived as serious, and many criminal justice professionals do not seem to understand the extent or gravity of the harm caused by this type of stalking (Logan & Walker, 2010). This state of affairs reflects little change from a pessimistic report made to Congress in the late 1990s, and overall, it seems that stalking is still poorly handled and underassessed (Klein et al., 2009). One study of stalking victims (Botuck et al., 2009) revealed that even the few times that victims had contacted criminal justice authorities during their cases, the responses they received were minimal: The criminal justice authorities took no action, referred the victim to court services, or suggested she obtain an order of protection. Overall, victim contact with the criminal justice system had no association with the trajectory of stalking or with the trajectory of perceived safety.

Even if perpetrators are arrested, there is evidence that few cases are prosecuted in court. In fact, dismissal is the most common disposition of stalking criminal cases

(Logan et al., 2006). One study in Kentucky showed that a majority of stalking cases were dismissed or amended and subsequently dismissed, and ultimately, only 19.9% of arrested stalkers were convicted of stalking (Jordan et al., 2003). By comparison, the average conviction rate of domestic violence arrests is 63.8% (Garner & Maxwell, 2008).

Given the current state of affairs regarding relational stalking in the criminal justice system, several experts have provided recommendations. For example, even if law enforcement officers feel that they cannot take action against the stalker until a chargeable offense is committed, they can work with victims to identify evidence that is needed and to help document the stalker's behaviors. Such a "stalking log" can provide evidence of a pattern of suspicious, threatening, and harassing behavior, and such actions by law enforcement show the victim that they are taking the perpetrator's behaviors seriously (Fraser, Olsen, Lee, Southworth, & Tucker, 2010).

Related recommendations are that police jurisdictions develop clear stalking protocols, train all officers in stalking issues, and use a multidisciplinary approach (e.g., with domestic violence shelters, mental health treatment providers, housing associations, schools and colleges, faith-based programs, neighborhood watch programs, victim advocacy programs). Police should deliver warnings to the perpetrators, arrest them when a crime has been committed, conduct a threat assessment, surveil the stalker, help the victim develop an emergency response plan, and use all available means to eliminate threats to the victim, public, and those responding (NCVC, 2004).

Services for Male Perpetrators

The first intervention program for batterers started in 1977. Since then, hundreds of programs have proliferated across the United States. Their popularity has become so widespread that judges often order batterers to enter them as part of their sentences. The majority of clientele are thus court-mandated (Austin & Dankwort, 1998; Hamby, 1998).

The stated goals of batterer programs are to ensure the victim's safety, change the perpetrator's attitudes toward violence, get the perpetrator to assume responsibility for his violence, and teach the perpetrator nonviolent methods of resolving conflicts. Most states have developed a number of mandates for these programs, the most controversial of which include provisions of group intervention, avoidance of individual and couples' interventions, and focus on issues of power and control in program content (Hamby, 1998). These provisions are controversial because there is little evidence that group intervention is better than individual or couples' therapy, and there is very little evidence that using power and control issues as the focus of program content is an effective way to reach the goals of such programs (e.g., Feder & Forde, 2000; Hamby, 1998). An analysis of state standards for domestic violence treatment programs by Maiuro and Eberle (2008) revealed that 95% of states endorse the power and control model, although 27% focus solely on power and control and the remaining 68% combine power and control with a social psychological treatment modality (e.g., addressing violence-condoning attitudes, interpersonal skills, faulty family-of-origin models). Only 5% used evidence-based models that did not incorporate issues of power and control.

These state-mandated program models are organized by the feminist notion that battering is a social problem stemming from the patriarchal organization of society. The male batterer is seen as intentionally committing violence to maintain a patriarchal structure in which he is superior and the woman is inferior within the relationship (Pence & Paymar, 1993). Most programs that focus on power and control issues use the Duluth model, developed in Duluth, Minnesota, by a small group of battered women's activists (Pence & Paymar, 1993). The model is based on their experience with four male batterers and five female victims who completed the Duluth program. The model assumes that the sole cause for all battering is the batterers' need to control and dominate their partners. This issue of power and control is seen as an exclusively male phenomenon, and changing this dynamic is viewed as the key to changing batterers' behavior. All other risk factors for IPV (e.g., alcohol abuse, personality disorders, anger and control issues, impulsivity, communication skills deficits, couple interaction styles, stress) are viewed as excuses. Program developers consider any psychological diagnosis of the male batterer to involve a rationalization for his behavior and thus to be inaccurate (Pence & Paymar, 1993).

How successful are batterers' programs? There is considerable argument as to what should be the criterion of success. Must all physical IPV be eliminated? Or is reduction the goal? If we consider the elimination of violence the goal, how long should the batterer be nonviolent before we consider him a treatment success? One month? One year? A lifetime? What if physical violence is eliminated but is replaced with severe psychological abuse? Should we also take into consideration increases in positive behaviors, such as caring behaviors toward the partner?

Success rates are also difficult to measure because of a lack of comparison groups. Some studies compare men who complete treatment with either those who never show up or those who drop out. Treatment completers, studies show, tend to be better educated, less severely violent, less likely to be unemployed, and less likely to have substance abuse problems or a criminal history than those who drop out (Rooney & Hanson, 2001). An additional problem with evaluating success rates is that most programs do not have any discharge criteria other than attendance. Batterers can come to these programs, not participate, not make any efforts to change, and still be discharged. This method of treating batterers is in stark contrast to treatment methods for alcoholics and people with mental health problems, who are discharged from treatment only after clinical judgments have been made as to their progress in the program. Therefore, if a batterer is discharged from a program just because he attended it, he may be just as violent as when he entered because he did not fully participate or gain anything from it (Gondolf, 1995). Does that mean that the program itself was at fault, or is the batterer himself to blame? Can we fault the program when the batterer refuses to participate?

Studies of the effectiveness of using batterer intervention programs modeled after the Duluth program show that they do not change perpetrators' attitudes or behaviors. There are no differences in recidivism rates, attitudes toward women, or attitudes toward IPV between male batterers who attend these programs and those who do not (e.g., Davis, Taylor, & Maxwell, 1998; Feder & Forde, 2000). Moreover, attrition rates of men who attend an initial batterer intervention program session are between 40% and 60%, even when attendance is mandated as a condition of probation and failure to attend can result in incarceration (Buttell & Carney, 2002).

Dutton and Corvo (2006) argue that by taking an adversarial and judgmental stance against batterers—and by disbelieving or dismissing batterers' often valid claims of alcoholism, mental illness, and mutuality of abuse—Duluth treatment providers preclude any opportunity to form a therapeutic bond with the batterers, which is the strongest predictor of successful treatment outcome. Thus, it is not surprising that Duluth model treatment does not work and leads to high attrition rates.

Programs that focus on psychological issues, anger problems, communication problems, impulse control issues, and couple interaction problems are often shunned by domestic violence advocates and prohibited by state laws. However, there is evidence that such intervention programs work for male batterers and their female partners. For example, couples' therapy that addresses underlying negative interactions that precede violence has shown positive results (O'Leary, Heyman, & Neidig, 1999; Stith, Rosen, & McCollum, 2003), although a recent review of five studies of couple-focused interventions found mixed results (Stover, Meadows, & Kaufman, 2009). The only treatment that yielded reduced recidivism was one that focused primarily on the male partner's alcohol abuse. In other words, programs that focus on the treatment of alcoholism (without addressing issues of battering) have shown substantially greater reductions in domestic violence among alcoholic batterers than do Duluth model programs (O'Farrell et al., 2003).

Despite such evidence, batterer intervention programs that focus on power and control are still mandated by state laws as programs of choice for batterers, whereas programs that are effective are shunned or, worse, specifically prohibited. For example, Georgia law prohibits any batterer intervention program that links "causes of violence to past experiences," includes "communication enhancement or anger management," addresses addiction, or has a systems theory focus (Georgia, 2002). The rationale for such state prohibitions is that the Duluth model guarantees a victim's safety. However, there is no evidence that this program works, so there is little evidence that it is protecting victims' safety better than programs that do work (Dutton & Corvo, 2006).

Many experts recommend tailoring treatment to the type of batterer (e.g., Cavanaugh & Gelles, 2005; Johnson, 2008; Kelly & Johnson, 2008; Langhinrichsen-Rohling, 2005). For example, Langhinrichsen-Rohling (2005) suggests that generally violent/antisocial batterers would be best served by legal interventions rather than psychosocial ones, whereas borderline/dysphoric batterers are likely to be better served by a combination of individual- and relationship-focused treatment components. Family-only batterers are likely to be best served by couple's therapy. Experts also argue that treatment for batterers who are also stalkers should manage any contributory mental illness; understand what is sustaining the behavior; confront self-deceptions that deny, minimize, or justify the behavior; attempt to instill empathy for victim; address stalker's inappropriate social and interpersonal skills; and address substance misuse (Mullen, Pathe, & Purcell, 2009).

Services for Female Victims

Although victims of IPV may use the criminal justice system to try to prevent further IPV at the hands of their perpetrator, there are other options available to them. In the 1970s, after the problem of IPV against women came to public atten-tion, several grassroots movements began founding shelters for battered women and their children. Since the original shelters appeared in the 1970s, these resources have proliferated. By the 1980s and 1990s, domestic violence agencies became institutionalized across the United States and were funded through both private and public means.

There are currently over 2,000 domestic violence programs in the United States for battered women and their children, many of which are part of the National Coalition Against Domestic Violence (NCADV, 2003). The NCADV was formally organized in 1978 and is the only national organization of shelter and service pro-grams for women. Many of these shelters are similar to the Center for Domestic Violence Prevention (CDVP, 2003), which offers the following services: a 24-hour support line; a community support group for abused women; art and play therapy for children exposed to intimate violence; short-term crisis intervention counseling; clinical counseling by trained staff under the supervision of a licensed therapist; and legal assistance in obtaining restraining orders, preparing for court, and attending hearings. Shelter services may continue for 6 to 8 weeks and include individual coun-seling and support groups; assistance with job and permanent housing searches; child care; tutoring and counseling programs for children; emergency outreach in collabo-ration with the local police; and a teen outreach and counseling program for victims and potential victims of dating violence. CDVP also offers transitional housing for up to one year for completers of the shelter program.

Although not all domestic violence programs have as comprehensive a program as the CDVP, they usually offer varying combinations of the above services. Although laypeople normally think that shelters are the most widely accessed portion of these domestic violence programs, they are actually rarely utilized by IPV victims (less than 10% of women who report IPV to authorities) (Harris, Lieberman, & Marans, 2007). Victim legal advocacy programs are more widely utilized by IPV victims.

The main issue here concerns the extent to which these programs help their clients. Do female victims leave their perpetrators as a result of utilizing such services? Or, do they return to their perpetrators or end up with another man who victimized them? Even worse, does the violence increase when the victims seek assistance? Finally, do the women (and children) who utilize them find them helpful? In answer to the question of whether women leave their batterers as a result of these programs, the evidence is mixed. Some studies find that 25% to 50% of women who use the shelter services at these agencies eventually return to their violent homes (Gondolf, 1988; Strube, 1988); those who do not return tend to have a higher economic status and partners who do not seek help for their battering problems (Gondolf & Fisher, 1988). Contact with post-shelter advocates may decrease the likelihood of the woman being further victimized (Sullivan, Tan, Basta, Rumptz, & Davidson, 1992), but many women eventually return to their batterers even after using these services.

Critics argue that an emphasis on the woman leaving the relationship is problem-atic because leaving can increase the likelihood that she will be battered and/or killed and because she may not be psychologically or financially ready to leave (e.g., Hamby, 1998). Women who use only shelters (i.e., not in combination with other legal or social support systems) may actually be at an *increased* risk for IPV from their male partners, probably in the form of retaliation. However, women who combine the use of shelters with other services fare better, at least for the first six weeks after seeking help (Berk, Newton, & Berk, 1986). Overall, studies show that the people who use shelters experience an increase in social support and quality of life, and a decrease in re-abuse (Wathen & MacMillan, 2003), so they do contribute to lowering rates of IPV. Also, victims who use legal advocacy services are more likely to cooperate with prosecutors, which leads to greater conviction rates (Camacho & Alarid, 2008).

Research on whether women perceive the services they receive from shelters as helpful is quite limited. In a study of women who sought services for IPV-related concerns from a domestic violence shelter, 89% believed that they were helped by the services that they received and 84% reported that they felt better because of these services (McNamara, Tamanini, & Pelletier-Walker, 2008). These findings are similar to a study which examined women's impressions of a hospital-based domestic violence support group (Norton & Schauer, 1997). Of the 59 women in this study, 95% reported that they were mostly or very satisfied with the services that they received. Their reasons for satisfaction included that the group leaders were supportive, they were able to hear about other women's experiences with IPV and were supported by them, they received referrals for additional support/services, and they were able to learn about IPV. These findings are consistent with other literature that shows that women are often very satisfied with the services that they have received for IPV (Bowker & Maurer, 1985; McNamara, Ertl, Marsh, & Walker, 1997; Molina, Lawrence, Azhar-Miller, & Rivera, 2009).

Nonetheless, it is important to note that the philosophy that typically guides these agencies has been a feminist-based philosophy. This perspective has been criticized as a White, middle-class female perspective that alienated many other victims of IPV (see Glass, Rollins, & Bloom, 2009, for a discussion) when it became apparent that IPV victims of other races and ethnicities, sexual orientations, genders, and social class backgrounds sometimes felt alienated by the programs offered at domestic violence agencies (Glass et al., 2009).

Summary

Over the past 30 years, the increasing attention to the problem of men's maltreatment of female partners has led to significant decreases in its incidence. However, IPV perpetrated against women is still a major problem in this country, and much work needs to be done to prevent it from occurring and to intervene when it does. In addition, more research and efforts need to address the other problem behaviors discussed in this chapter, namely situational couple violence, psychological maltreatment, sexual maltreatment, and stalking. More women are victims of situational couple violence than of battering, yet the majority of the current research is focused on battered women. Although battered women are certainly in need of more services than female victims of situational couple violence, eliminating situational couple violence would also result in a vast improvement in the psychosocial health of this nation. In addition, many women are the victims of sexual assault by male partners who are not necessarily battering them as well. Much work needs to be done to address the issue of rape of female partners, particularly when it occurs without battering.

Researchers still need to address more fully the problem of psychological maltreatment, a problem that is more pervasive than the physical or sexual maltreatment of female partners. According to our best studies on this issue, at least a substantial minority of women—if not the majority—experience psychologically aggressive behaviors from their partners, and the predictors, correlates, and consequences need to be more fully understood. Finally, women are at the greatest risk of being stalked by a current and former intimate partner than by strangers or acquaintances. Relational stalkers are also more likely to physically assault their victims than men who stalk strangers. Research should also focus on identifying effective prevention and intervention techniques and improving criminal justice responses. Currently, mandatory arrest and no-drop prosecution policies are expensive policies that have little evidence that they decrease IPV or recidivism. Moreover, the type of batterer intervention program mandated by most states also shows little evidence that it is effective. Domestic violence programs for female victims—which are widespread and often comprehensive—do show evidence of effectiveness.

Discussion Questions

1. Consider the overlap between intimate partner physical violence, sexual assault, psychological maltreatment, and stalking. How would you design a primary prevention program that addresses each type of IPV?

2. Rates of physical IPV against women have declined since 1975. Do you believe these rates will continue to decline? Why or why not? Do you think that perhaps psychological maltreatment and coercive control have increased as a result of the decreased public acceptance of physically assaulting a female partner?

3. If a woman tells you that she sometimes experiences minor forms of violence at the hands of her male partner, should you automatically assume that she is involved in a situationally violent relationship? Can women be involved in extremely abusive relationships when severe forms of violence have not been perpetrated against her?

4. Research indicates that factors such as poverty, low occupational status, and low educational attainment are predictors of men's physical maltreatment of female partners. Why might these associations exist? Do you think the associations could be due solely to class-related reporting biases? Are stressors associated with poverty likely to contribute to physical IPV even when possible reporting biases are considered? Could physical IPV be essentially absent in wealthier classes?

5. Social isolation is consistently associated with IPV. To what extent might social isolation cause IPV? To what extent might it be a result? How can prevention and intervention programs reduce women's social isolation in order to reduce the risk of IPV?

6. To what extent should women be "excused" for killing their batterer? What factors, if any, should play into a jury's or judge's decision to find the woman guilty of manslaughter rather than murder, and the decision to give her a reduced sentence (e.g., life instead of death)?

7. Why do many people think it is easy for a woman to leave an abusive partner? How does this belief make it more difficult for a woman to get the support and help she needs to cope with her situation?

8. To what extent do you agree that behaviors such as insulting or swearing at a partner, throwing or kicking something, raising one's voice, yelling, or shouting at a partner should be included in measures of psychological maltreatment? To what extent do you think the context in which these behaviors take place determines the impact on the partner?

9. Considering that battered women sometimes say that being psychologically maltreated was worse than being physically assaulted, should psychological maltreatment be considered a crime? How would you legally define such maltreatment? How difficult would it be for police to enforce such a law?

10. Restraining orders seem to work to reduce subsequent violence and stalking in some cases of partner maltreatment but not in others. Under what circumstances would you recommend a victim of IPV obtain a restraining order and under what circumstances would you advise against it?

11. Some of the criminal justice responses to IPV, such as mandatory arrest, dual arrest, and no-drop prosecutorial policies, are controversial. Should such responses be abolished? Why or why not?

12. Considering that batterers often present with multiple issues (e.g., alcohol/substance abuse, mental health issues), what do you think is the best approach for treating batterers? To what extent should the program incorporate issues of power and control, anger management, alcohol/substance abuse, mental illness, assertiveness training, etc.? Under what circumstances would you keep couples counseling as an option for batterers and their victims, if at all?

13. Some batterers who stalk have extensive histories of trauma (e.g., witnessing a murder, lost a parent before the age of 18). To what extent might such traumatic events explain why these men became batterers and stalkers? What implications does this have for treating these men?

14. How would you design an evaluation study to assess the effectiveness of a batterer treatment program? How would you measure success?

6

Maltreatment of Male Partners

Within the first six months of marriage, Allen's wife starting beating him, calling him names, and attacking him. After four years of constant emotional and physical maltreatment, and subsequent apologies, Allen decided to file for divorce. During the two years of his divorce proceedings, Allen presented evidence of his wife's violence to the judge, who did not act upon the accounts or believe him. The events that occurred during the divorce proceedings and afterwards are testimony to the plight of many men who experience partner violence from their wives. The judge prohibited Allen from entering the state in which the divorce and custody hearings were being held—thus, he could not attend his own hearings. His ex-wife won custody of their children and kept them from him. He was deemed responsible for medical expenses she incurred through a fraudulent workman's compensation claim and other medical claims that she never reported to the insurance company. He was also financially responsible for the mortgage payments and utility bills for a house he was not allowed to enter. On February 18, 1991, after years of bitter legal battles with his ex-wife, Allen killed himself, leaving behind his children, a fiancée, and many friends (Fathers for Life, 2006).

Consider the above case of maltreatment. Based upon the evidence given, would you determine that Allen had been abused by his wife? If so, in what ways? Did anyone else maltreat Allen? Were his experiences with the legal system abusive? Why do you think the judges in his divorce and custody battles ruled the way they did? Why do you think Allen ultimately killed himself?

When we published the first edition of this book nine years ago, we used the above story to illustrate some of the frustrations, hardships, and maltreatment that men who sustain intimate partner violence (IPV) report experiencing in their relationships and later in the legal system. While considering whether to update this story with a new one, the first author of this book received a phone call from a distraught father who reported that his son, who was an IPV victim, had attempted suicide by hanging because his son's wife threatened that if he divorced her, he would never see his child again. That man obviously saw no other way out, and his story illustrates that although we now know much more about male victims of IPV, not all that much has changed in how they are treated in this country.

The issue of male victims has been—and continues to be—one of the most controversial issues in the literature on family violence. Findings on maltreatment of male partners have been challenged by some feminist researchers who argue that violence by women toward men is in self-defense or retaliation (Belknap & Melton, 2005; Dobash, Dobash, Wilson, & Daly, 1992; Loseke & Kurz, 2005; Saunders, 1988). These authors typically argue that because IPV is an issue of men maintaining power and control over their female partners, it is not possible for women to be perpetrators of IPV. Consequently, much of the literature on the maltreatment of male partners by women over the past 30 to 40 years has been primarily an argument over whether it really occurs. Nonetheless, several advances in our understanding of male victims of IPV have been made in the past 10 years.

Physical Maltreatment

Scope of the Problem

The primary concern of many researchers in the field of family violence is that if we deem the maltreatment of male partners a significant problem; we will divert attention and resources away from abused women, who are the real victims of IPV (Mignon, 1998). However, acknowledging abuse by female partners does not necessarily translate into fewer resources for female victims of IPV, and ignoring the existence of male victims does not make it any less real. In addition, if our goal is to eliminate all violence in family relationships, we must consider and acknowledge maltreatment perpetrated by women. Consider the two cases presented in Box 6.1 of men talking about the physical assaults they experienced from their wives. Do you consider these cases abusive? Why or why not? Are the circumstances and dynamics similar in any way to the ones experienced by abused women? For example, do the participants present a simple reversal of the roles played in your picture of the typical case of IPV? Are there ways in which these cases seem different from those of abused women? Are there problems that appear to be unique to men? Are there problems that male victims may never experience but female victims would? What might such problems be? Finally, consider these cases again, but reverse the roles of the perpetrator and victim. Do you now view the cases as more, less, or equally abusive? Why?

Box 6.1	Can Men be Physically Abused by Women?

Richard C., a man working in financial services with an above-average income, says he was attacked 50 to 60 times by his wife in their 14 years together, most of the time while she was drinking: "A lot of times, I would be working on some papers and there would be a coffee cup there, and she would intentionally spill the coffee; she went from that to throwing the coffee, and then throwing the cup and the coffee. She would throw hot scalding coffee in my face. It was a gradual thing that built over a three-year period, until it got to the point where she would physically strike me ... She would physically attack me, tear the glasses off, kick me in the testicles five, six, seven times ... You couldn't control her. A couple of times, I would wrestle her to the ground, pin her arms around her, and wrap my legs around her, and tell her to calm down, calm down. She'd say, 'O.K. I'm calm now, I'm under control now.' And you let her go, and she'd be right back at you, doing it again" (Cook, 2009, pp. 45–47).

Jake T., a six-foot-tall construction worker, married three years to a woman who was five feet, three inches tall: "I think a lot of her problems had to do with the drug use. I mean, I could never tell when she might come unglued. It would happen all of a sudden, usually in the bedroom. For example, one night I was sitting on the side of the bed, taking off my shoes, and she just came at me, kicking and swinging, no warning, nothin.' Just bang, she starts in. That's the way it was with her. She would never say why. One time, she did throw a knife at me; it missed. But most of the time, she would hit with her fists and kick. I'd just either hold her arms, or put up my arms, and then leave, till she had a chance to settle down" (Cook, 2009, p. 54).

The rates of violence by female partners are derived from many of the sources where we obtain rates of violence by male partners (see Table 6.1). First, crime statistics from the U.S. Department of Justice's National Crime Victimization Survey (NCVS) show that in 2009, 0.9 per 1,000 men were assaulted by an intimate partner, most of whom were women; these men represented 18% of IPV victims in 2009 (Truman & Rand, 2010).

Crime surveys, however, are likely to provide underestimates of IPV victimization because many people—both men and women—are unwilling to label the physical violence they sustain at the hands of an intimate partner a "crime." This reluctance may be even more pronounced in men than in women because the man is supposed to be the physically dominant and aggressive partner; consequently, admitting to victimization by a woman and labeling it a "crime" may be viewed as emasculating (Steinmetz, 1977). Indeed, studies show that men are not only reluctant to report assaults by women, but also unlikely to report nondomestic assaults by other men, even when severe injuries result (Henman, 1996). Furthermore, when IPV is conceptualized as a crime in surveys, women are significantly less likely than men to report their use of IPV, and some research shows that women do not report as much as 75% of their use of IPV in crime surveys (Mihalic & Elliott, 1997).

A second source of data on violence by female partners comes from the 1995–96 National Violence Against Women Survey (NVAWS), which showed that 7% of male respondents reported being physically assaulted by a current or former wife, or cohabiting partner over the course of their lifetime, and 0.8%—or approximately 835,000 of the U.S. adult male population—reported being physically assaulted in the previous year (Tjaden & Thoennes, 2000a). This survey may also underestimate the amount of IPV for several reasons. For example, the respondents were first asked if they were assaulted by anyone, and then subsequently asked to identify the perpetrator; however, when thinking about assaults, most people (men and women) neglect to think about violence by family members, which could also lead to underestimates of the true incidence of IPV.

Table 6.1 Studies on the Prevalence of the Physical Maltreatment of Male Partners

Study	Description of Sample	Measures/Definition of Physical Violence	Rates of Maltreatment
Black et al. (2011), National Intimate Partner and Sexual Violence Survey (NISVS)	U.S. nationally representative phone survey of 16,507 adults (9,086 women and 7,421 men) conducted in 2010	How many of your romantic or sexual partners have ever: • Slapped you? • Pushed or shoved you? • Hit you with a fist or something hard? • Kicked you? • Hurt you by pulling your hair? • Slammed you against something? • Tried to hurt you by choking or suffocating you? • Beaten you? • Burned you on purpose? • Used a knife or gun on you?	• 28.2% of men reported lifetime physical IPV victimization • 4.7% of men reported past year physical IPV victimization
Truman & Rand (2010), National Crime Victimization Survey (NCVS)	• Nationally representative sample of 134,000 individuals from 77,200 households • Self-report survey based on reported and unreported crimes	• Among the questions asked are: Has anyone attacked or threatened you in any of these ways: a) with any weapon, for instance, a gun or knife; b) with anything like a baseball bat, frying pan, scissors, or stick; c) by something thrown, such as a rock or bottle? Respondents are also asked if they have been grabbed, punched, choked, or threatened, and whether anyone has raped or attempted to rape them or committed any other form of sexual attack or unwanted sexual act against them • If they report any of these incidents, they then identified their relationship with the perpetrator	• 0.9 per 1,000 men reported IPV victimization

Study	Description of Sample	Measures/Definition of Physical Violence	Rates of Maltreatment
Caetano, Vaeth, & Ramisetty-Mikler (2008), National Couples Survey (NCS)	• 1,136 couples interviewed face-to-face in their homes • Multistage area probability sample, representative of married and cohabiting couples from the 48 contiguous United States • "Oversampled" Blacks and Hispanics	Conflict Tactics Scales (CTS) (see Straus, 1995)	• Approximately 8% of couples reported mutual violence • Approximately 2% reported the perpetration of violence by the female partner only
Kessler, Molnar, Feurer, & Applebaum (2001), National Co-Morbidity Survey	• Nationally representative household survey of 8,098 people in the age range of 15–54 that was fielded between September 1990 and March 1992. Respondents were sampled using a multistage area probability design • The sample included 1,738 married or cohabitating men and 1,799 married or cohabitating women who were asked questions regarding IPV	CTS (see Straus, 1995) in the past year	• 18.4% of men reported being victims of minor physical partner violence • 5.5% of men reported being victims of severe physical partner violence

(Continued)

Table 6.1 (Continued)

Study	Description of Sample	Measures/Definition of Physical Violence	Rates of Maltreatment
Tjaden & Thoennes (2000a), National Violence Against Women Survey (NVAWS)	Nationally representative sample of 8,000 men and 8,000 women collected via a random digit dialing technique	• Survey incorporated items from the original CTS concerning whether any other adult had slapped or hit them, kicked or bit them, choked them, hit them with an object, beaten them up, threatened them with a weapon, or used a gun, knife, or other weapon on them • If they indicated that an aggressive behavior had been perpetrated against them, they were asked about their relationship with the perpetrator	• 7% lifetime rate of physical IPV victimization for men • 0.8% within the past year
Schafer, Caetano, & Clark (1998), National Alcohol Survey	• Multistage probability sample of 1,599 married or cohabitating heterosexual couples in the contiguous United States in 1995 • Face-to-face in home interviews	11 items from the CTS, including throwing something; pushing, grabbing, or shoving; slapping; kicking, biting, or hitting; hitting or trying to hit with something; beating up; choking; burning or scalding; forcing sex; threatening with a knife or gun; using a knife or gun	• Between 6.22% and 18.21% of men had been the victim of IPV
Hale-Carlsson et al. (1996), 1994 Behavioral Risk Factor Surveillance System	• Population-based, random-digit-dialed telephone survey of the noninstitutionalized New York State population, aged greater than or equal to 18 years • 692 women and 546 men, ages 18–44	Seven questions addressing physical assault from an intimate partner ranging from slapping, kicking, punching, being beaten, threatened, and/or assaulted with a knife or a gun	• 6.9% of men reported IPV, of whom 47.7% reported more severe forms of violence (i.e., kicked, bitten, punched, or beaten or threatened/assaulted with a knife, gun, or other object)

Study	Description of Sample	Measures/Definition of Physical Violence	Rates of Maltreatment
Sorenson, Upchurch, & Shen (1996), National Survey of Families and Households	• Multistage probability sample of 10,000 households that was supplemented by an oversample of 3,000 households of Blacks, Hispanics, absent-parent households, and recently married couples • 53% of the sample (n = 6,779) was married and completed a self-administered survey on IPV	• How many fights resulted in their spouse hitting, shoving, and throwing things at them • Whether they were cut, bruised, or seriously injured in a fight with their spouse	• 2.0% of men reported that their spouse had hit, shoved, or thrown something at them in the past year • 0.3% of men reported being cut, bruised, or seriously injured as a result of IPV in the past year
Straus (1995), National Alcohol and Family Violence Survey	National probability sample of 1,970 married or cohabiting couples interviewed face-to-face in 1992	• CTS in the past year • Severe violence is operationalized as having a high probability of causing injury (e.g., kicking, punching, using weapons or objects) • Minor violence offers less of a chance of injury (e.g., slapping, grabbing)	• Minor assault of men by women was 95 per 1,000 men • Severe assault of men by women was 45 per 1,000 men
Straus & Gelles (1986); Straus & Gelles (1990a), National Family Violence Surveys of 1975 and 1985	• Nationally representative sample of 2,143 married couples in the 1975 survey, conducted via face-to-face interviews • Nationally representative sample of 6,002 married and cohabiting couples in the 1985 survey, conducted via telephone	CTS (see Straus, 1995)	• Minor assault of men by women was 116 per 1,000 and 121 per 1,000 in 1975 and 1985, respectively • Severe assault of men by women was 45 per 1,000 in both survey years

A third source of data on violence against men comes from studies using the Conflict Tactics Scales (CTS). In contrast to the NVAWS, the instructions for the CTS prompt the participants to think about their relationships first, and conflicts that may be occurring within those relationships, and then report the number of times specific violent acts were used (Straus, Hamby, Boney-McCoy, & Sugarman, 1996). Studies using the CTS typically show that in a given year about 50% of all victims of IPV are men. For example, after controlling for age and socioeconomic status, the National Family Violence Surveys (NFVS) of 1975 and 1985 and the 1992 National Alcohol and Family Violence Survey showed that minor assaults (e.g., slapping, pushing) by women toward male partners were reported to have occurred at a rate of approximately 75 per 1,000 in 1975 and 1985, and then increased to approximately 95 per 1,000 in 1992. Rates of severe assaults (e.g., punching, beating up) by women toward male partners reportedly remained constant at approximately 45 per 1,000 in all study years. These rates of severe assaults projected into approximately 2.6 million men per year who sustained IPV that had a high likelihood of causing an injury (Straus, 1995; Straus & Gelles, 1986). Moreover, these studies show that in contrast to declining rates of violence by men toward women, violence by women toward men has remained stable over the 17-year period that spans the time between the first (1975) and last (1992) surveys (Straus, 1995). These results have been replicated by dozens of studies since the 1970s (Straus, 1999), including a meta-analysis (Archer, 2000). Overall, estimates of IPV toward men in general U.S. population surveys using the CTS vary from 8.4% to 18.4% for minor violence and from 3.2% to 5.5% for severe violence, with approximately equal rates of male and female victimization (Caetano, Vaeth, & Ramisetty-Mikler, 2008; Hale-Carlsson et al., 1996; Kessler, Molnar, Feurer, & Appelbaum, 2001; Schafer, Caetano, & Clark, 1998; Sorenson, Upchurch, & Shen, 1996; Straus, 1995; Straus & Gelles, 1986).

A final source of data comes from the National Intimate Partner and Sexual Violence Survey (NISVS), which was a U.S. nationally representative phone survey of 16,507 adults (9,086 women and 7,421 men) conducted in 2010 (Black et al., 2011). According to that survey, 28.2% of men reported lifetime physical IPV victimization, with 4.7% reporting past year physical IPV victimization. Overall, 25.7% of men reported lifetime victimization of slapping, pushing, or shoving, whereas 4.5% reported slapping, pushing, or shoving in the past year. And 13.8% reported lifetime severe physical IPV victimization, whereas 2.0% reported past year severe physical IPV victimization (e.g., hair-pulling, hit with fists, beating, burning, choking).

These rates fall between the NVAWS rates and the dozens of studies using the CTS, including the NFVSs, and most likely reflect differences in how the IPV questions were presented and asked of the participants (e.g., the CTS asks about both perpetration and victimization; asks about more types of physical IPV; asks how many times both they and their partner used those acts of IPV within the previous year rather than how many partners have ever used those tactics; and presents the acts within a survey that includes negotiation tactics and directions that normalize family conflict). Data that are unique to the NISVS dataset include the number of lifetime perpetrators and the age at which the participant was first victimized. With regard to number of perpetrators, 73.1% of male victims reported one lifetime IPV perpetrator; 18.6% two lifetime perpetrators, and 8.3% three or more lifetime perpetrators. As for age at first victimization, 15.0% were between the ages of 11 and 17 years; 38.6% were between the ages of 18 and 24 years; and 30.6% were between the ages of 25 and 34 years (Black et al., 2011).

As shown in studies using the CTS, the apparently equal rates of female and male violence in intimate relationships have been the subject of much debate. One major criticism by some researchers is that the CTS do not measure motives and that most of these women, if not all, may be acting out of self-defense or retaliation (e.g., Belknap & Melton, 2005; Dobash et al., 1992; Loseke & Kurz, 2005; Saunders, 1988). This assumption has been refuted by studies assessing women's motives for IPV, which show that although some women report self-defense or retaliation as a motive, most do not (see Hines & Malley-Morrison, 2001b; Medeiros & Straus, 2006, for reviews). For instance, major reasons reported by women for using physical force against their male partners include to show anger, to retaliate for emotional hurt, to express feelings that they had difficulty communicating verbally, to gain control over the other person, to get their partner's attention, because he was not sensitive to her needs, because he was being verbally abusive, because he was not listening, and jealousy (e.g., Felson & Messner, 2000; Fiebert & Gonzalez, 1997; Follingstad, Wright, Lloyd, & Sebastian, 1991; Hettrich & O'Leary, 2007; Rouse, 1990). Moreover, some women report hitting their male partners because they know that their partners either will not or cannot hit them back, and because they did not think they could hurt him (Fiebert & Gonzalez, 1997).

Johnson (1995) attempted to reconcile this controversy by asserting that each side was drawing its conclusions based on nonoverlapping data gathered from two fundamentally different sources. As mentioned in Chapter 5, Johnson theorized that IPV found in community and population-based samples is situational couple violence (SCV), which is characterized by low-level (e.g., slapping, pushing), low-frequency violence in a couple where both members are about equally violent; this IPV is not part of an overall pattern of control of one partner over the other, but is the result of a conflict "getting out of hand." On the other hand, violence found in shelter and other clinical samples is "patriarchal terrorism" or intimate terrorism (IT). The central feature of IT is that the violence is one tactic in a general pattern of control of one member of the couple over the other. The IPV is more frequent than what is found in cases of SCV, is less likely to be mutual, is more likely to involve serious injury, and involves psychological maltreatment as well (Johnson, 1995; Johnson & Ferraro, 2000).

Johnson (1995, 2006; Johnson & Ferraro, 2000) asserts that IT is the almost exclusive province of men and can be explained by patriarchal theories in which men are trying to exert and maintain control over "their" women. However, there is consistent evidence that women use IPV in the context of controlling behaviors at rates that are much higher than Johnson anticipated (e.g., Felson & Messner, 2000; Graham-Kevan & Archer, 2005; Hines, Brown, & Dunning, 2007; Hines & Douglas, 2010a, 2010b; Migliaccio, 2001; Straus, 2008a). Moreover, although no studies have been conducted yet in the United States on rates of IT by women, two population-based studies in other countries—New Zealand (Ehrensaft, Moffitt, & Caspi, 2004) and Canada (Laroche, 2008)—show that women and men commit IT at similar rates. The New Zealand study was a cohort study that encompassed almost the entire population of that cohort, and it showed that the prevalence rate of IT was 9%, with men and women equally likely to be intimate terrorists. In a 2004 survey in Canada, 40% of all male IPV victims were victims of IT, and 36.8% of all victims of IT were men (Laroche, 2008), findings that replicated the 1999 survey (Laroche, 2005).

Although there are no studies in the United States establishing prevalence rates of IT by women versus men, there is one larger-scale study of male IT victims (i.e., not limited to case studies of male victims). This study consisted of 302 men who sustained IT from their female partners within the previous year and sought help (Hines & Douglas, 2010a, 2010b). IT is characterized by controlling behaviors, severe psychological aggression, and physical aggression, and we focus on those results here. Of the 302 men, 93.4% reported that their female partners used controlling behaviors an average of 42.62 times in the previous year; 96.0% reported that their female partners used severe psychological aggression an average of 28.9 times in the previous year; and 100% reported that their partners used physical aggression an average of 46.72 times in the previous year (Hines & Douglas, 2010a). Thus, men sustained physical, severe psychological and controlling IPV on an almost weekly basis. Moreover, the frequency with which the men sustained violence in the previous year was comparable to the frequency of violence sustained in samples of battered women (i.e., IT victims) (Giles-Sims, 1983; Johnson, 2006; Okun, 1986; Straus, 1990a).

Predictors and Correlates

Although not extensively researched, the predictors and correlates of the maltreatment of male partners tend to be very similar in nature to the predictors and correlates of the maltreatment of female partners. In fact, one study showed that there are no gender differences in 21 predictors of IPV at two of the ecological levels: microsystem (e.g., dominance of one partner, communication problems) and individual (e.g., antisocial personality, attitudes approving of violence) (Medeiros & Straus, 2006). Below, we discuss research at several levels of the ecological model, and a summary of these can be found in Table 6.2.

Macrosystem and Exosystem

The most widely studied macrosystem-level predictor of the maltreatment of male partners concerns socioeconomic status. For example, similar to the maltreatment of female partners, low income of both partners (Kessler et al., 2001; Rennison & Welchans, 2000; Straus & Gelles, 1990b) and unemployment of the male partner (Newby et al., 2003; Straus, Gelles, & Steinmetz, 1980) are associated with the physical maltreatment of male partners. Moreover, women who are employed tend to have higher rates of both reciprocal violence and unilateral perpetration (Caetano et al., 2008). In one study of an exosystem-level predictor of female-to-male physical IPV, Cunradi, Caetano, Clark, and Schafer (2000) found that neighborhood poverty was a significant predictor of the physical maltreatment of male partners.

Microsystem

As with male-perpetrated IPV, stressful circumstances seem to also predict female-perpetrated IPV, particularly more severe levels (Medeiros & Straus, 2006).

Table 6.2   Predictors of the Physical Maltreatment of Male Partners at Each Level of the Ecological Model

Level of the Ecological Model	Specific Predictor	Studies
Macrosystem	Low income of both partners	Kessler et al. (2001); Rennison & Welchans (2000); Straus (1990b)
	Male partner unemployment	Newby et al. (2003); Straus, Gelles, & Steinmetz (1980)
	Employed female partner	Caetano et al. (2008)
Ecosystem	Neighborhood poverty	Cunradi, Caetano, Clark, & Schafer (2000)
Microsystem	Stressful situations	Medeiros & Straus (2006)
	Cohabitation	Caetano et al. (2008); Kessler et al. (2001)
	Shorter relationship length	Caetano et al. (2008)
	Relationship conflict, communication problems, dominance of the female partner, the female partner having a negative view of her partner, jealousy of the female partner	Medeiros & Straus (2006)
	Lower relationship and partner satisfaction	Hettrich & O'Leary (2007)
	Young men	Caetano et al. (2008)
	Men victimized as children	Kessler et al. (2001)
	Men with certain mental health problems	Kessler et al. (2001)
	Men with alcohol-related problems	Caetano et al. (2008)
	Male partner's use of IPV	Kessler et al. (2001); Straus (2008b); Whitaker, Haileyesus, Swahn, & Saltzman (2007)
Individual/ Developmental	Younger age	Caetano et al. (2008); Rennison & Welchans (2000); Straus (1990b)
	Avoidance of relationship problems	Swan & Snow (2003)

(Continued)

Table 6.2 (Continued)

Level of the Ecological Model	Specific Predictor	Studies
	Problem controlling anger	Medeiros & Straus (2006); Swan & Snow (2003)
	Approval of violence	Medeiros & Straus (2006)
	Impulsivity	Caetano et al. (2008)
	Feelings of powerlessness	Caetano et al. (2008)
	Anxious attachment style	Orcutt, Garcia, & Pickett (2005)
	History of aggression against others	Giordano, Millhollin, Cernkovich, Pugh, & Rudolph (1999); Malone, Tyree, & O'Leary (1989); Medeiros & Straus (2006); Moffitt, Caspi, Rutter, & Silva (2001)
	Personality traits of defendence, aggression, impulsivity, neuroticism, disagreeableness	Hines & Saudino (2008); O'Leary, Malone, & Tyree (1994); Robins, Caspi, & Moffitt (2002); Sommer, Barnes, & Murray (1992)
	Psychopathology	Swan & Snow (2003)
	Alcohol and drug problems	Hines et al. (2007)
	Borderline and antisocial personality	Medeiros & Straus (2006)
	Exposure to violence in family of origin	Kalmuss (1984); Medeiros & Straus (2006); Swan & Snow (2003)

In addition, several relationship factors and characteristics of the male partner have been shown to predict IPV victimization among men. For example, cohabitation is a risk for IPV victimization among men (Caetano et al., 2008; Kessler et al., 2001), and the highest level of reciprocal and female-only IPV is in relationships lasting 10 years or less, with decreasing levels thereafter and the lowest levels in relationships lasting 30 years or more (Caetano et al., 2008).

When looking more closely at the characteristics of a relationship, researchers have shown that relationship conflict, communication problems, the dominance of the female partner, and the female partner having a negative view of her partner predict *minor* violence by women toward men. Relationship conflict, communication problems, dominance of the female partner, jealousy of the female partner, and the female partner having a negative view of her partner predict *severe* violence by women against men (Medeiros & Straus, 2006). Similarly, the less satisfied the women are with their relationships, the more likely they are to be aggressive, and the more positive views they have of their partners, the less likely they are to be aggressive (Hettrich & O'Leary, 2007).

Young men (Caetano et al., 2008) and men with a history of childhood violence victimization (Kessler et al., 2001) are at increased risk for IPV victimization, as are men with various mental health problems, including agoraphobia, social phobia, alcohol dependence, dysthymia (i.e., mild, chronic depression), and nonaffective psychosis (Kessler et al., 2001). In fact, men with one or more alcohol-related problems are about three times more likely to be victims of IPV than men without any alcohol-related problems (Caetano et al., 2008).

Special Issue: Reciprocal IPV

As with IPV toward women, the strongest predictor of IPV toward men is a micro-system level predictor, namely the recipient's use of IPV toward the other partner. In other words, the dominant pattern found time and again in the literature is reciprocal IPV—that is, both partners use physical IPV to some extent (Kessler et al., 2001; Straus, 2008a; Whitaker, Haileyesus, Swahn, & Saltzman, 2007). In fact, because over 200 studies show that reciprocal violence is the predominant pattern of IPV, with up to 80% of violent relationships showing some level of reciprocity, several researchers have called for more investigation and consideration of this pattern (e.g., Straus, 2006). This research is vital since early indications are that both physical and psychological injuries are more severe among both men and women who experience reciprocal violence compared to those who experience unilateral violence (Hines & Douglas, 2011c; Straus, 2008b; Whitaker et al., 2007).

Moreover, reciprocal violence appears to be the dominant pattern for both minor and severe IPV (Kessler et al., 2001; Straus, 2008a). Even among clinical samples of IPV victims and perpetrators, reciprocal violence is the norm. For example, among a sample of women arrested for IPV perpetration, the female perpetrators sustained an average of 30.2 acts of physical violence from their male partners within the previous year and 3.4 injuries (Stuart, Moore, Gordon, Ramsey, & Kahler, 2006). Among samples of battered women in shelters (Giles-Sims, 1983; McDonald, Jouriles, Tart, & Minze, 2009; Saunders, 1988), 50% to 75% report using some type of violence against their male partners (Giles-Sims, 1983; Saunders, 1988), 50% to 67% report using severe violence (McDonald et al., 2009; Saunders, 1988), 8% report beating up their partners or using a knife or gun, and 12% report threatening their partners with a knife or gun (Saunders, 1988). Among a sample of male IT victims, 55% used some type of violence, with 19.5% using severe violence (Hines & Douglas, 2011c).

The fact that there is such a high rate of reciprocal violence among clinical samples of perpetrators and victims, and that reciprocal violence in this population also leads to higher levels of injuries (Hines & Douglas, 2011c), shows that a nuanced analysis of the context, predictors, and consequences of reciprocal violence is necessary. Among samples of IT victims, the violence that is used by the victims is typically called "violent resistance" (Johnson, 2006) because it tends to be less frequent than the violence that is perpetrated against them (Hines & Douglas, 2010b). However, it is incorrect to assume that all of this violence is perpetrated in self-defense or retaliation, since initial analyses of such violence show that alcohol and drug abuse of the IT victims are strong predictors (Hines & Douglas, 2011c).

Currently, when investigating reciprocal violence, most researchers divide the samples into "one partner only violent" and "both partners violent." Leonard (2011) points out the fallacy of that division. He states there are cases in which one partner is much more violent than the other, and this type of violence, its predictors, and consequences, could differ in substantial ways from cases in which both partners are equally violent and cases in which only one partner is violent. Given the predominance of reciprocal violence and its more severe consequences, it is time that this type of violence is studied in much more detail.

Individual/Developmental

Most of the predictors and correlates that have been researched so far on the maltreatment of male partners can be found at the individual/developmental level. For instance, the younger a female is, the more IPV she perpetrates against her male partner (Caetano et al., 2008; Rennison & Welchans, 2000; Straus & Gelles, 1990b). Women who use aggression in their relationships may tend to avoid coping with problems in their relationships (Swan & Snow, 2003), have problems controlling their anger (Medeiros & Straus, 2006; Swan & Snow, 2003), approve of the use of violence (Medeiros & Straus, 2006), are more impulsive, and have greater feelings of powerlessness (Caetano et al., 2008).

Similar to male perpetrators of IPV, women who perpetrate IPV tend to have an anxious attachment style (Orcutt, Garcia, & Pickett, 2005). Among one sample of women mandated into batterers treatment, the women were overly dependent upon their partners, which directly related to their use of IPV and was an important predictor of treatment completion (Carney & Buttell, 2005).

One of the most robust predictors of women's use of IPV is a history of aggressive behavior perpetration. For example, longitudinal studies show that early delinquency and a history of conduct problems predict women's IPV perpetration, even after controlling for the male partner's use of aggression (Giordano, Millhollin, Cernkovich, Pugh, & Rudolph, 1999; Moffitt, Caspi, Rutter, & Silva, 2001). In addition, there is evidence that women who use IPV are aggressive in other relationships as well, for example peer and other family relationships (Malone, Tyree, & O'Leary, 1989), that women with an angry-self concept and who were viewed as troublemakers in their adolescence are more likely to perpetrate physical IPV (Giordano et al., 1999), and that a history of criminal behavior is a predictor of women's use of IPV (Medeiros & Straus, 2006).

Personality is also a predictor of female-perpetrated IPV. Specifically, when assessed prior to marriage, the personality traits of defendence (i.e., a readiness to defend oneself, suspicion of others, tendency to be offended easily), aggression (i.e., willingness to hurt others, enjoyment of conflicts and arguments, a desire to get even), and impulsivity (i.e., tendency to act on the spur of the moment, volatility in emotional expression) have an indirect association with women's physical aggression toward their husbands at 30 months of marriage (O'Leary, Malone, & Tyree, 1994). Other researchers (Hines & Saudino, 2008; Robins, Caspi, & Moffitt, 2002; Sommer,

Barnes, & Murray, 1992) have found that high neuroticism and low agreeableness contribute to women's use of both minor and severe physical IPV in relationships; in other words, women who tend to be anxious, emotionally unstable, hostile, self-centered, spiteful, and jealous are at higher risk for using physical aggression against their male intimates.

Moreover, there is evidence of elevated levels of psychopathology and alcohol/drug abuse in female perpetrators of IPV. Women who use aggression in their relationships may suffer from anxiety, depression, or post-traumatic stress disorder (PTSD) (Swan & Snow, 2003). Women who use severe physical aggression and controlling behaviors against their male partners may have problems with alcohol and drugs, mental illnesses, and suicidal ideations (Hines et al., 2007). Furthermore, borderline and antisocial personality traits predict IPV perpetration among women (Medeiros & Straus, 2006).

Several studies have assessed levels of psychopathology among women arrested and/or ordered into treatment for IPV perpetration. Although there is no comparison group to make conclusive statements about psychopathology as a risk, these studies (Dowd, Leisring, & Rosenbaum, 2005; Henning, Jones, & Holdford, 2003; Stuart et al., 2006) show that overall: 21% to 39% of the women showed clinically significant levels of anxiety, 11% to 67% showed clinically significant levels of depression, 10% to 18% bipolar disorder, 5% to 44% PTSD, 37% histrionic personality disorder, 33% narcissistic personality disorder, 12% to 27% borderline personality disorder, and 4% to 7% antisocial personality disorder. In one sample (Dowd et al., 2005), 30% of the women reported at least one suicide attempt, 20% had received inpatient psychiatric care, and 87% had received outpatient mental health treatment. These studies also show elevated levels of drug and alcohol abuse; for example, one study found that 43% of female perpetrators showed clinically significant levels of alcohol abuse and 24% of drug abuse (Stuart et al., 2006), while another found 61% reporting ever abusing alcohol and 25% ever abusing drugs (Dowd et al., 2005).

Finally, a consistent predictor for women's use of aggression against their male partners is their exposure to violence or other forms of maltreatment in their family of origin. The experience of both corporal punishment and physical abuse during childhood predict women's use of physical aggression against men (Kalmuss, 1984; Swan & Snow, 2003), as has witnessing interparental violence in childhood or adolescence (Kalmuss, 1984), and there may be genetic influences on this intergenerational transmission of IPV (Hines & Saudino, 2004). Further, there is evidence that a history of neglect and sexual abuse during childhood predicts women's use of severe IPV (Medeiros & Straus, 2006).

Consequences

Physical Injuries

The majority of studies that have assessed the victimization of male partners compare male victims to female victims. Mostly, researchers attempt to ascertain whether female victims experience more physical injuries than male victims. Overall, the studies show that women are at a higher risk for physical injury than men are, particularly given the same physical acts (e.g., Stets & Straus, 1990). This finding is logical, considering the relative size of the average man versus the average woman. Men can inflict more harm with their fists than women can, and they are more able to restrain a violent partner than women are (Straus et al., 1980).

It should be emphasized, though, that these studies also show that male victims are at risk for physical injury. According to NVAWS, for example, female-perpetrated violence against men accounted for 40% of all injuries due to IPV in the previous year, 27% of all injuries requiring medical attention, 38% of all victims who lost time from work, and 31% of all victims who feared bodily harm (Straus, 2005a; Tjaden & Thoennes, 2000a). Thus, although men may cause more bodily harm than women in violent intimate partner relationships, female-perpetrated violence is not insignificant, as it accounts for a large proportion of physical injuries in the United States (Straus, 2005a).

It should also be noted that some studies suggest that men are as likely or perhaps more likely than women to be assaulted with a weapon (e.g., Brown, 2004). In one study of an emergency clinic in Ohio, 72% of the men who were admitted with IPV injuries had been stabbed (Vasquez & Falcone, 1997). Emergency room doctors have reported treating many types of injuries to male victims, including ax injuries, burns, smashings with fireplace pokers and bricks, and gunshot wounds (McNeely, Cook, & Torres, 2001). Burns, in particular, have been shown to be a greater concern for male victims of IPV than for female victims; men comprise a high percentage of IPV victims in burn units because their female partners threw boiling liquids on them (Duminy & Hudson, 1993; Krob, Johnson, & Jordan, 1986), although a more recent study suggests that there are no gender differences in burn injuries as a result of IPV (Vasquez & Falcone, 1997).

Among the only larger-scale study of male IT victims in the United States, 78.5% of men reported some type of injury as a result of IPV in the previous year, with 35.1% reporting an injury that required medical attention (Hines & Douglas, 2010a, 2010b). Reports of men being physically injured at the hands of their female partners are also evident in the literature on community samples of couples. For example, Cascardi, Langhinrichsen, and Vivian (1992) found that 2% of men who reported experiencing physical IPV reported suffering broken bones, broken teeth, and/or an injury to a sensory organ. Other population-based studies found the rates of injuries to be somewhere between 1% and 20% for men, with differences dependent upon how the IPV was assessed (Black et al., 2011; Makepeace, 1986; Morse, 1995; Stets & Straus, 1990).

Box 6.2   When Women Kill

To our knowledge, the only systematic research that addressed women who kill their intimate partners was part of a larger study on women who kill in general. In this study, Mann (1996) researched the details of a representative sample of all known female-perpetrated homicides in six cities (Atlanta, Baltimore, Chicago, Houston, New York, and Los Angeles) between 1979 and 1983. Almost 50% of these homicides were cases in which the women killed an intimate partner. In one third of those cases, the victim was a husband; in another one third, the victim was a common-law husband, and in the remaining one third of the cases, the victim was a lover.

Several characteristics of the male victims of intimate partner homicide were identified. The majority of the victims were African American (83.4%); Whites constituted 8.3% of victims. The average age at death was 37.9 years, and approximately 75% of the victims had prior arrest records, over half of which were for violent offenses. The majority of the victims had been drinking prior to their deaths, and a substantial percentage of the men incited her in some way, either through insults, arguing, or physical means.

Women who killed their partners also had some distinguishing characteristics. On average, female homicide perpetrators were 33.6 years old, and were predominantly African American (84.1%). They were below the national average in educational attainment, were unemployed or working in semiskilled or laborer positions, and had at least one child. Approximately half of the women had a prior arrest record, and one third had been arrested previously for a violent offense. A substantial minority of the women had used alcohol or drugs prior to the homicide, and just over half claimed they killed in self-defense. Furthermore, over half of the female perpetrators premeditated the homicide, and over 95% used either a knife or gun to kill their intimate partners.

In comparison to women who killed other family or nonfamily members, women who killed their intimate partners received, on average, a lower bond, a lighter sentence (if any), and a shorter probationary period. As Mann (1996) stated, the likely assumption in the legal system was that the male homicide victims got what they deserved, and therefore, the female perpetrators received lighter punishment. However, as Mann (1996) also pointed out, the data show that there was seldom any evidence of frequent male-perpetrated violence toward these women, and when violent domestic encounters did occur, the women often were dominant. In addition, because over half of the homicides were premeditated and over half of the women had criminal histories, this study provides preliminary evidence that most women do not kill because they were battered.

Several studies also show that women's violence against men can be lethal. In the case that introduced this chapter, Allen killed himself because of the abuse he sustained at the hands of his wife and the subsequent legal battles. Women also have been known to kill their male partners, and as discussed in Box 6.2, many times these murders are not in self-defense. Take, for example, the case of the "Black Widow Murderer." In 1990, Blanche Taylor Moore was on trial for murdering her longtime lover with arsenic. Blanche had come under suspicion a few months prior after honeymooning with her second husband, an ordained minister named Dwight Moore. Dwight had to be taken to the hospital when he suddenly became sick, and the doctor discovered arsenic in his system. Because this first dose did not kill him, Blanche gave him a few more poisoned milk shakes; however, Dwight managed to survive. When this story broke, people who knew Blanche called the police because they remembered that Blanche's first husband had died from arsenic poisoning and that a longtime boyfriend had "died of a heart attack." When police exhumed the body of her boyfriend, they discovered a toxic dose of arsenic in his system. She was convicted of that murder in 1990 (her second husband testified against her), is now on death row in North Carolina (Farrell, 1993), and has managed to stave off her execution for more than 20 years.

In addition to discovering arsenic in her boyfriend's system, exhumations also revealed toxic doses of arsenic in the bodies of both of her parents, and many people had called the police to report that they had reasons to believe that Blanche poisoned some of their relatives as well. As it turned out, Blanche Taylor Moore was suspected of killing several people over the course of a quarter century, all in the same small community (Farrell, 1993). Why do you think Blanche's murders went undetected for so long? Would Blanche have come under suspicion earlier if she were a man? What could possibly have influenced Blanche to commit these murders? During the trial, it was revealed that Blanche was the victim of sexual abuse from her father. Do you think this sexual abuse experience could be the cause for her killings? Are her murders justifiable because of the abuse she experienced?

Psychological Injuries

As was discussed with respect to the maltreatment of female partners, maltreatment can have psychological as well as physical effects, and several studies show that the physical maltreatment of male partners can have psychological effects. For example, in the wake of physical maltreatment, men report a range of psychological reactions, from anger to emotional hurt to shame and fear (Follingstad, Brennan, Hause, Poleck, & Rutledge, 1991). Men also report fear in their relationships. For example, in one longitudinal study, 9.5% of younger maltreated men and 13.5% of older maltreated men reported experiencing fear in their violent relationships (Morse, 1995). Over half of the male callers to a domestic violence helpline for men expressed fears that their wives would severely abuse them if they found out about the call to the helpline (Hines et al., 2007); and of male IT victims who were unilaterally terrorized in a representative sample of Canadians, 83% feared for their lives (Laroche, 2005). Male victims in both community and clinical samples report higher levels of psychological distress in comparison to their non-maltreated counterparts. For example, in community samples, higher levels of violence are associated with more severe depression (Cascardi et al., 1992; Simonelli & Ingram, 1998; Stets & Straus, 1990), stress, and psychosomatic symptoms (Stets & Straus, 1990). Moreover, among both college men and a population-based sample of men, higher levels of physical IPV victimization were associated with higher levels of PTSD symptoms (Coker, Weston, Creson, Justice, & Blakeney, 2005; Hines, 2007a). PTSD is an issue among men in victim samples as well. In the one larger-scale sample of male IT victims in the United States, 57.9% reported symptoms of PTSD that exceeded the clinical cut-off on the measure of PTSD; this percentage was significantly greater than two other groups: men in a community sample who reported SCV (8.2% exceeded the clinical cut-off for PTSD) and men in a community sample who experienced no physical IPV (2.1% exceeded the cut-off). The type of IPV experienced (IT, SCV, or none) explained 57.3% of the variance in PTSD scores, and among the male IT victims, exposure to childhood physical maltreatment, experiencing physical IPV in the previous year, and experiencing controlling behaviors in the previous year, all independently predicted PTSD scores. Thus, the authors concluded that similar to battered women, PTSD is a major concern among men who experience IT (Hines & Douglas, 2011b).

Community and population-based studies show that men who suffer from physical IPV victimization may also suffer from physical health problems. These studies show that in comparison to non-victims, men who sustain IPV have poorer overall health (Black et al., 2011; Coker et al., 2002; Parish, Wang, Laumann, Pan, & Luo, 2004; Pimlott-Kubiak & Cortina, 2003; Reid et al., 2008) and are at a higher risk for sexual dysfunction (Parish et al., 2004), STIs (Parish et al., 2004), functional disabilities (Black et al., 2011; Black & Breiding, 2008; Carbone-Lopez, Kruttschnitt, & MacMillan, 2006), asthma (Black & Breiding, 2008), frequent headaches, chronic pain, and difficulty sleeping (Black et al., 2011).

Overall, preliminary research shows that men who experience physical IPV at the hands of their female partners are also exhibiting signs of psychological and physical suffering. However, there are several flaws inherent in this research to date. Can you think of what some of these flaws might be? What types of research designs were used in the research described? Were there any longitudinal studies? Can we definitively conclude that the IPV these men experienced *caused* their suffering? Could their suffering have contributed in any way to the IPV they experienced? Alternatively, what third variables could be operating to influence both the distress and the aggression they sustained? In short, we just do not know the temporal nature of the associations found in the available research, and longitudinal studies are needed to figure out what the ultimate causes of the distress are.

Psychological Maltreatment

Scope of the Problem

An even less researched area than the physical maltreatment of male partners is the psychological maltreatment of men. The same definitional issues that plague the study of psychological maltreatment against female partners also plague the study of psychological maltreatment against male partners, which is part of the reason for the dearth of research. Moreover, in contrast to research on the psychological maltreatment of female partners, the psychological maltreatment of male partners, with limited exceptions, is not typically studied within the context of battering relationships; that is, when researchers study the prevalence, predictors, and consequences of the psychological maltreatment of men, they tend to do so in community samples, particularly in college men. Thus, these issues are largely covered in Chapter 7. Overall, the studies estimate that at least half, and as many as 95% of men are the recipients of some type of psychologically aggressive act in their relationships (Hines & Malley-Morrison, 2001a; Hines & Saudino, 2003; Kasian & Painter, 1992; Molidor, 1995; O'Farrell & Murphy, 1995; Simonelli & Ingram, 1998; Simpson & Christensen, 2005). A summary of these prevalence rates can be found in Table 6.3.

Table 6.3 Studies Assessing the Prevalence of the Psychological Maltreatment Against Male Partners

Study	Description of Sample	Measures/Definition of Psychological Maltreatment	Rates of Maltreatment
Black et al. (2011), National Intimate Partner and Sexual Violence Survey (NISVS)	U.S. nationally representative phone survey of 16,507 adults (9,086 women and 7,421 men) conducted in 2010	*Expressive Aggression:* How many of your romantic or sexual partners have ever . . . • acted very angry toward you in a way that seemed dangerous? • told you that you were a loser, a failure, or not good enough? • called you names like ugly, fat, crazy, or stupid? • insulted, humiliated, or made fun of you in front of others? • told you that no one else would want you? *Coercive Control:* How many of your romantic or sexual partners have ever . . . • tried to keep you from seeing or talking to your family or friends? • made decisions for you that should have been yours to make, such as the clothes you wear, things you eat, or the friends you have? • kept track of you by demanding to know where you were and what you were doing? • made threats to physically harm you? • threatened to hurt him or herself or commit suicide when he or she was upset with you? • threatened to hurt a pet or threatened to take a pet away from you? • threatened to hurt someone you love? • hurt someone you love? • threatened to take your children away from you?	• 31.9% of men reported lifetime expressive aggression victimization • 42.5% reported lifetime coercive control victimization • 9.3% reported past year expressive aggression victimization • 15.2% reported past year coercive control victimization • 10.4% reported lifetime control of reproductive or sexual health

Study	Description of Sample	Measures/Definition of Psychological Maltreatment	Rates of Maltreatment
		• kept you from leaving the house when you wanted to go? • kept you from having money for your own use? • destroyed something that was important to you? • said things like, "If I can't have you, then no one can"? *Control of Reproductive and Sexual Health* How many of your romantic or sexual partners have ever . . . • tried to get pregnant when you did not want them to get pregnant or tried to stop you from using birth control? • refused to use a condom when you wanted to use one?	
Simpson & Christensen (2005)	273 couples in California and Washington recruited to participate in a marital therapy study	Revised Conflict Tactics Scales, psychological aggression scale	• 94.9% of men reported psychological aggression victimization • 48.0% of men reported severe psychological aggression victimization
Hines & Saudino (2003)	179 male and 302 female undergraduate college students, mean age 19.1 years	Revised Conflict Tactics Scales, psychological aggression scale	• 86% of women reported using some form of psychological aggression against their male partner, an average of 18.79 times in the previous year
O'Farrell & Murphy (1995)	88 couples where the men were being treated for co-occurring alcohol and marital problems	Revised Conflict Tactics Scales, psychological aggression scale	• 69.3% of men reported "clinically significant levels" of verbal aggression (above the 75th percentile based on national normative levels)

(Continued)

Table 6.3 (Continued)

Study	Description of Sample	Measures/Definition of Psychological Maltreatment	Rates of Maltreatment
Simonelli & Ingram (1998)	70 heterosexual male undergraduate college students, ages 18–50	Psychological Maltreatment of Women Inventory	• 90% of men reported being the recipient of at least one form of partner psychological maltreatment within the past year • 77% experienced jealousy • 77% experienced withdrawal • 63% experienced diminishment of self-esteem • 60% experienced verbal abuse • 49% experienced social and emotional control
Molidor (1995)	631 Midwestern high school students (ages 13–18) (convenience sample)	Modified 15-item *Psychological Maltreatment of Women Inventory*, which included the following subscales: isolation, monopolization, economic abuse, degradation, rigid sex-role expectations, psychological destabilization, emotional or interpersonal withholding	• Male students reported an average of 23.41 acts of psychological maltreatment in their current dating relationship
Kasian & Painter (1992)	868 female and 757 male college students (convenience sample)	*Psychological Maltreatment of Women Inventory*, which had the following subscales: diminishment of self-esteem, verbal abuse, social and emotional control, jealousy, and withdrawal	• 20% of men reported social and emotional control • 15% reported diminishment of self-esteem • 20% reported jealousy behaviors • 10% reported verbal abuse • 10% reported withdrawal

The recent NISVS study (Black et al., 2011) provides our first glimpse of national rates of different types of psychological maltreatment against male partners. Specifically, these researchers asked about lifetime and past-year victimization from three types of psychological maltreatment: expressive aggression, coercive control, and control of reproductive and sexual health. Table 6.3 provides the operational definitions of these constructs. Overall, 48.8% of men (or 55.2 million) reported lifetime psychological victimization from at least one of these types of aggression, and 18.1% reported some type of psychological IPV victimization within the past year. Just over 30% reported lifetime expressive aggression victimization, the most common types of which were being called names like ugly, fat, crazy or stupid, and being told they were a loser, a failure, or not good enough, with 9.3% reporting expressive aggression victimization within the past year. Just over 40% reported lifetime coercive control victimization, the most common types of which were being kept track of by the perpetrator demanding to know where he was and what he was doing, followed by the perpetrator making decisions that should have been his to make, with 15.2% reporting past-year coercive control victimization. Finally approximately 10.4% of men reported lifetime control of reproductive or sexual health, with 8.7% reporting that a partner tried to get pregnant when he did not want to or tried to stop him from using birth control, and 3.8% having a partner refuse to use a condom when he wanted to use one.

Research on the psychological maltreatment of men who are the victims of IT is in its infancy, but anecdotally, like female victims of IT, male victims also report that the psychological maltreatment tends to be worse than the physical maltreatment. Consider the case of Jerry in Box 6.3. If you were Jerry, would you agree that psychological maltreatment is worse than physical maltreatment?

Box 6.3   Psychological Maltreatment of Male Partners: The Case of Jerry

My wife said that I was ugly, skinny, and my jaws were sunken in. She said that I should grow a mustache to hide my ugly upper lip, which she called "the world's ugliest." She wanted me to grow a beard to hide my sunken jaws. She wouldn't walk next to me but would walk ahead or behind because she was ashamed to be seen with me in public. She threatened to kill me during the night or castrate me while I was asleep …She taught my son to call me, "dummy." She called me "dummy" or "wimp." When I wanted to hug her in the afternoon, she accused me of wanting sex. She always put what I did in the worst light, like she'd always try to find something bad about anything I did. When I bought flowers for her out of my "mad" money, she criticized me for not saving the money …She found negative things about whatever I did. If I confronted her, it would escalate and her criticism would get worse and worse. If I said that a criticism about me wasn't true, then she'd say that "everyone thinks that about you." That leads to confusion …She didn't like it when I had friends, like Steve and Laura who helped me with my work. She accused me of having affairs with Steve, Laura, and their teenage daughter.

SOURCE: Smith & Loring, 1994, p. 2

In a sample of 302 male IT victims in the United States, 100% of the men reported that their female partners used minor psychological aggression (e.g., swearing at, yelling) in the past year on average 65 times; 96% reported that their female partners used severe psychological aggression (e.g., destroying something he cares about, threatening him with violence) an average of 28.9 times, and 93.4% reported that their female partners used controlling behaviors (e.g., not allowing him to see family/friends; not allowing him out of the house) an average of 42.62 times (Hines & Douglas, 2010a).

Reports from male callers to a domestic violence helpline for men also show that female partners use controlling behaviors against their male partners. Specifically, at least half of the male callers to this helpline reported that their female partners used at least one of the following controlling behaviors against them: threats and coercion (e.g., threatening to kill themselves or their male partners, threatening to call the police and have the male partner falsely arrested); emotional abuse (e.g., calling him names, making him think he is crazy, humiliating him); intimidation (e.g., making him feel afraid by smashing things, destroying his property, abusing pets, or displaying weapons); blaming the men for their own abuse or minimizing the abuse; manipulating the system (e.g., using the court system to do such things as gain sole custody of the children or falsely obtain a restraining order against the victim); isolating the victim (e.g., keeping him away from his family and friends and using jealousy to justify these actions); controlling all of the money and not allowing the victim to see or use the checkbook or credit cards; and using the children to control him (e.g., threatening to remove the children from the home) (Hines et al., 2007).

Predictors and Correlates

Very few studies have investigated the predictors of the psychological maltreatment of male partners. A summary of these predictors can be found in Table 6.4 and are discussed below.

Microsystem

The only studies to our knowledge that investigated microsystem predictors of psychological maltreatment against men assessed characteristics of the male victim. Specifically, the more a man witnessed his mother emotionally maltreating his father when he was a child, the more psychological maltreatment he sustained at the hands of his girlfriend in college (Hines & Malley-Morrison, 2003). There may be genetic influences for this intergenerational transmission of psychological aggression victimization (Hines & Saudino, 2004).

Individual/Developmental

Several studies have assessed possible individual/developmental characteristics of the women who psychologically maltreat their male partners. These studies show that women who are high on the personality traits of neuroticism, extraversion, and conscientiousness, and low on agreeableness perpetrate more psychological aggression in

Table 6.4 Predictors of the Psychological Maltreatment of Male Partners

Level of the Ecological Model	Specific Predictor	Studies
Microsystem	Witnessed parental IPV as a child	Hines & Malley-Morrison (2003)
Individual/ Developmental	Personality traits of high neuroticism, high extraversion, high conscientiousness, and low agreeableness	Hines & Saudino (2008)
	Preoccupied attachment style	O'Hearn & Davis (1997)
	Anxious and insecure attachment styles	Murphy & Hoover (2001)
	Cold, vindictive, domineering	Murphy & Hoover (2001)
	Psychological aggression in family of origin	Hines & Saudino (2004)

their dating relationships (Hines & Saudino, 2008), and that women who inflict psychological maltreatment tend to exhibit a preoccupied attachment style (O'Hearn & Davis, 1997). Furthermore, women who use restrictive/engulfment psychological maltreatment tend to display anxious and insecure attachment styles; those who use hostile/withdrawal psychological maltreatment tend to be cold, vindictive, and domineering, and may have suffered from separation protest (e.g., are anxious about separating from their partners); those who use denigration tend to suffer from separation protest and compulsive care-seeking and to be vindictive and domineering; and those who use dominance/intimidation also suffer from separation protest (Murphy & Hoover, 2001). Finally, preliminary evidence shows that women's use of psychological aggression tends to run in families, and that this intergenerational transmission may be genetically influenced (Hines & Saudino, 2004).

Consequences

The impact of physical IPV on men has been systematically studied much more than the impact of psychological maltreatment. The bulk of this research has been done with women, and published case studies, such as the one presented in Box 6.3, are rare indeed. What types of psychological maltreatment did Jerry experience? What possible effects do you think these behaviors had on him? According to Smith and Loring (1994), Jerry experienced some severe negative consequences from this psychological maltreatment: He felt frightened for his life, blamed himself for everything, and lost 31 pounds. Why did he stay with this woman? He states, "There were times that she bought me gifts and said she loved me; I occasionally felt a little kindness, and I thought maybe she would change. It was enough to keep me clinging to her" (p. 2). This statement contains an important insight, as the researchers believe that this man suffered from traumatic bonding, in which the perpetrator alternates abusive behavior with kindness, creating a bond that involves intermittent positive reinforcement, a type of bond that is difficult to break.

Although the Smith and Loring (1994) case study is an important contribution to the literature, it does not tell us much about the effects of psychological maltreatment in the general population of men. Only a few studies have provided some indication of the possible psychological effects of psychological maltreatment against men. In convenience samples, psychological maltreatment has been associated with depression (Simonelli & Ingram, 1998; Vivian & Langhinrichsen-Rohling, 1994), psychological distress (Simonelli & Ingram, 1998), stress, alcohol abuse (Hines, 2001), and PTSD symptoms (Hines, 2001; Hines & Douglas, 2011b).

Among male victims of IT, both controlling behaviors and severe psychological abuse victimization are associated with increased symptoms of PTSD, and controlling behaviors contribute independently to the level of PTSD symptoms, even after considering the effects of physical IPV victimization and exposure to physical violence in childhood (Hines & Douglas, 2011b).

These studies show that men suffer psychologically from the psychological maltreatment they receive at the hands of their intimate partners. However, this research is only a first step in determining the effects of psychological maltreatment against men. What other outcomes do you think we need to study in psychologically maltreated men? What other methods do we need to utilize to gain a better understanding of the effects of psychological maltreatment against men? What possible confounds need to be controlled in future studies?

Special Issue: Sexual Maltreatment of Male Partners?

There is preliminary evidence that men can be sexually assaulted by female partners and even more systematic evidence from studies on college students that men are victimized by sexual aggression (see Chapter 7). For example, among male IT victims, 41.1% stated that within the past year, their female partners had insisted on sexual intercourse when the men did not want to, and this occurred an average of about four times that year (Hines & Douglas, 2010a).

The recent NISVS survey provided the most systematic evidence of sexual aggression against men in a population-based sample (Black et al., 2011). This survey was conducted in 2010, and the following reports of lifetime sexual victimization were reported by the men: 1.4% of men reported lifetime rape victimization (where rape victimization for men was defined as completed or attempted forced penetration of the anus or mouth, or completed alcohol/drug facilitated penetration of the anus or mouth); 4.8% reported that they were made to penetrate (through force, threats of force, or incapacitation through drugs or alcohol) someone's vagina, anus, or mouth with their penis, mouth, or other object; 6.0% were coerced into having sex with someone through non-physical means (such as being worn down through verbal pressure, being lied to, threats that the perpetrator would end the relationship or spread rumors, etc.); 11.7% reported unwanted sexual contact, which included unwanted sexual experiences that involved touch but not penetration (e.g., kissing, fondling, groping); and 12.8% reported non-contact unwanted sexual experiences (such as someone exposing him/herself to him, making him watch pornography, etc.).

The NISVS survey also provided information on the relationship of the perpetrator to the men for many of the types of sexual aggression reported. The majority (52.4%) of rape perpetrators were acquaintances of the men, and 93.3% of the perpetrators were men. A large percentage of these rapes (27.8%) occurred when the men were 10 years of age or younger. However, for the remaining types of sexual aggression, a large percentage of the perpetrators were the female intimate partners of the men. For example, of the men who were made to penetrate someone else, 44.8% of their perpetrators were current or former intimate partners and 79.2% of these victimized men had perpetrators who were only women (i.e., if the men were victimized more than once, all of their perpetrators were women). Over two thirds (69.7%) of the perpetrators of sexual coercion were current or former intimate partners, and 83.6% of these victimized men had perpetrators who were only women. Fewer than 25% of the perpetrators of both unwanted sexual contact (22.6%) and unwanted non-contact sexual experiences (21.1%) were current or former intimate partners, and 53.1% and 37.7% reported only female perpetrators, respectively.

Overall, approximate 8% of men (1 in 12, or nearly 9 million U.S. men) have experienced sexual violence by an intimate partner in his lifetime, and 2.5% (or nearly 2.8 million U.S. men) experienced sexual violence by an intimate partner within the previous year (Black et al., 2011). Given these findings, research is needed to understand the predictors and consequences of this form of IPV against men.

Intimate Partner Stalking

The victim and offender are both in their forties, Caucasian, and have a middle class existence. During the positive time of the [intimate] relationship, both lived in separate homes, were socially active, and traveled. Initially, the stalker persisted in a fantasy of regaining the love of the victim. When her behavior failed to regain his love, she retaliated. The stalking activity began with hang up phone calls, unauthorized accessing of the victim's answering machine at work and home, notes and cards, and drive-bys of the victim's residence. When the victim did not respond by resuming the relationship, the stalker's activities escalated to surveillance of the victim from an alley in a car, jogging in front of his home, poisoning his pet, and stealing his mail. The stalker's behavior escalated to the destruction of the victim's boat. The stalker began making workplace visits which provided her with phone numbers of the victim's friends, family, therapists, clients, and investigative agencies that attempted to assist the victim with terminating the stalking. This resulted in phone calls to forty-six second and third party victims. Extreme psychological distress and physiological reactivity became a consistent part of the day-to-day life of the victim. The victim entered a state of chronic PTSD after his initial efforts to control her stalking failed during the first six months of the stalking. (Dupont-Morales, 1998, pp. 227–228)

Scope of the Problem

As mentioned in Chapter 5, the most common type of stalking involves current or former partners (Cupach & Spitzberg, 2004). However, most research on intimate partner stalking has focused on men's stalking of women. Only two population-based studies have examined stalking of men by current or former partners: the

NVAWS and the NISVS. The NVAWS found that 2% of men in the United States have been stalked at some point in their lives, with 0.4% stalked within the previous year. These percentages project to an estimated 2,040,460 and 370,990 men who are stalked during their lifetimes and annually in the United States, respectively. Among the 179 male lifetime stalking victims in the study, 32% were stalked by a current or former intimate partner (Tjaden & Thoennes, 1998); however, the percent of these stalkers who were same-sex intimates was not reported.

The NISVS (Black et al., 2011) specifically examined stalking victimization by intimates and found that 1 in 19 men (5.3%) in the United States have experienced intimate partner stalking at some point in their lives, which projects into an estimated 5,863,000 victims, with 1,419,000 experiencing stalking in the last 12 months. As was the case with the NVAWS, the NISVS did not report the number of men stalked by women versus men. Thus, there are currently no reliable estimates of the rate with which women stalk men in the context of a current or former intimate relationship.

Predictors and Correlates

Very few studies have investigated the predictors and correlates of women's stalking of current or former male partners. Researchers typically analyze data from female victims only or combine data for female and male victims in the analyses. Below are results from one large-scale nationally representative study that analyzed data separately for male stalking victims.

Although not conducted in the United States, the 2001 British Crime Survey (BCS) provides information about a number of predictors and correlates of stalking at different levels of the ecological model (Finney, 2006). At the macrosystem level, the BCS found that men who do not have a degree or diploma were at greater risk of being stalked by a current or former intimate than those who do. At the exosystem level, men who lived in a rural area were at increased odds of being stalked. At the microsystem level, men who had "a limiting illness or disability" (p. 9) were at greater risk of being stalked. Further, men who were separated from their spouses were significantly more likely to report being stalked than women who were separated, whereas divorced men were less likely to be stalked than divorced women. Unfortunately, the BCS did not distinguish between stalking that was perpetrated by a current or former female partner, a stranger, or an acquaintance. Thus, some of the men in the sample were likely reporting on stalking by women and men who were not current or former intimates. Further research is needed to determine if the predictors and correlates identified in the BCS apply specifically to male victims of stalking by a current or former relationship partner. Research also needs to be conducted on characteristics of women who stalk their intimate partners (i.e., at the individual/ developmental level) to ascertain what puts certain women at risk for intimate partner stalking.

Consequences

Although there appears to be no research specifically examining the consequences of stalking in men targeted by current or former female partners, it is probable that male victims are affected in ways similar to female victims. Cupach and Spitzberg (2004) developed an 11-category typology of the consequences of stalking victimization (see Chapter 5 for a more detailed description of the typology). The analyses were based on 143 studies of stalking, which included male victims. Thus, it can be surmised that men can experience all of the different types of consequences that Cupach and Spitzberg identified, including behavioral effects, affective health effects, cognitive health effects, and resource health effects. Consider the stalking case study described at the beginning of this section. What types of consequences did the victim suffer as the result of being stalked by his former female partner? Would a female victim with a male perpetrator have suffered similar consequences?

Prevention and Intervention

> I am in the middle of it right now and have contacted a national abuse hotline via email. I have never hit my wife, but today I came close to doing this. It should be noted she has hit me more times than I can remember and kicked me. I grabbed her arms in self defense and held her to the floor. I am a very big and strong man, my wife is tall but thin, not strong at all. I know I will be the one who goes to jail even though she is the one hitting and kicking. (Hines, 2009, p. 16)

As this quote illustrates, there are several barriers—both societal and internal—to male IPV victims getting help. It is no surprise, then, that prevention and intervention programs for male victims of IPV and female perpetrators are not as organized or systematic as those for victimized women and male perpetrators. In contrast to the well-organized efforts for female victims of IPV, there is no multi-billion dollar Violence Against Men Act, no battered men's defense, and no legislation that empowers male victims of IPV.

In addition to barriers in receiving help, there are also barriers to leaving the relationship that could affect the type of help that male victims need when reaching out. In one of the only studies to assess these barriers, Hines and Douglas (2010a) found that the main reason that men stay in a relationship in which their partner is abusive is concern for their children (reported by 88.9% of the men), followed by commitment to the marriage (80.5%), and love (71.3%). Other barriers reported by at least half of this sample of male victims included fearing he may never see the children again (67.5%), thinking she will change (55.6%), not having enough money to leave (52.8%), having nowhere to go (52.2%), and being embarrassed that others will find out that he is being abused (52.2%).

Criminal Justice Response

The research on male IPV victims and female perpetrators in the criminal justice system has increased in recent years. Overall, the news is not good. According to one source:

> An arrest is not routinely made when the perpetrator is a woman. Why? Police officers occasionally suggest a range of excuses. These run the gamut from "he would be embarrassed" to "she didn't hurt him that badly" . . . There is no readily available law enforcement documentation of the numerous abuse calls where the male is the victim and no action is taken. (Gosselin, 2000, p. 6)

In other words, it seems that law enforcement is lax when it comes to male victims, even when the men are injured (Brown, 2004). Consider the quotes in Box 6.4 from men who called the police when their female partners were being violent. What do you notice about the responses they received? Are they overall positive or negative? Why do you think there is some variability in their responses? Why do you think the criminal justice system responded in the ways they did? What are the possible ramifications of each type of response for the male victim, his partner, and their children?

Box 6.4   Male IPV Victims Call 911

- Always determine that I was a big man and strong enough to take her physical abuse. Would insinuate that I was a wimp, made humiliating comments.
- First time told me there was nothing they could do because it was a civil matter. Second time told me first they'd have to take us both into custody, but after 20 min of negotiation, finally took her in because I was the one with the wounds. Prosecutor dropped charges in the jail.
- I asked them to take pictures of my injuries and write a police report, they escorted her out of the house but never came back in to take pictures or write a report. I went to the police station and asked for her to be arrested. I was told it would go to the district attorney; the district attorney said they would issue an arrest warrant but never did.
- I experienced total discrimination. They saw me as a large male and my girlfriend is a very attractive woman so they immediately took her side. I was at the hospital with bruising and burned eyes from hot coffee thrown in them. They didn't believe that she did this to me and refused to arrest her. Instead they listened to her saying she was defending herself and did not press any charges. The next incident she ran, so when the police got to my house and saw me bleeding they charged her with felony DV [domestic violence] but later dropped it to misdemeanor assault because we are not married and do not live together.
- Police told me I'm lucky that they determined she was the aggressor. Told me to file a continued restraining order before the emergency protective ordered expired. Told me I should get away from her and file for divorce, that abusers rarely change.
- The first response they arrested me, even after she turned on them, they did nothing. Second time they just wrote a scathing report against her but did nothing.
- The police said she was to be charged with domestic assault, they said a felony charge. They asked her to leave the home, not me, when she wanted me kicked out instead. I eventually volunteered to leave the house overnight to save her from being arrested, as she had no place to go. If one of us didn't leave, they would have arrested her. Since I didn't want that, they gave her a break, it being Christmas time. The police still stressed that they had the right to arrest her whether I liked it or not.

- They asked her to confine herself to her bedroom, she was drunk, and asked me to sleep in the baby's room. We did, she passed out and they left.
- They determined she was the aggressor but said since I was a man it was silly to arrest her. I was appalled.
- They had a sheet that stated I was the victim of DV [domestic violence] and that I was entitled to certain services and provided the phone numbers to call. When I called the numbers the women who answered the phones told me they only can by law provide services to women and not men or else they will lose their money. I was left with no place to stay and had to sleep in my car which is a crime in my area.
- They said based on the testimonies of both parties it was clear that they had to take her.
- Told me to get her help. Told me to spend the night in a hotel. Told me that "crazy people don't know they are crazy."

SOURCE: Hines & Douglas, unpublished data

Studies of male victims in the criminal justice system typically show that male victims are not helped by this system. For example, Buzawa, Austin, Bannon, and Jackson (1992) reported that:

> Not one male victim was pleased with the police response. They stated their preferences were not respected by the officers, nor was their victimization taken seriously. The lack of police responsiveness occurred regardless of degree of injury. For example, one male reported requiring hospitalization for being stabbed in the back, with a wound that just missed puncturing his lungs. Despite his request to have the offending woman removed (not even arrested), the officers simply called an ambulance and refused formal sanctions against the woman, including her removal. Indeed, all the men interviewed reported that the incident was trivialized and that they were belittled by officers. (p. 265)

More recently, however, it seems that a minority of male victims are being treated more fairly, although certainly much more work needs to be done. In one study of male victims—the participants of which are quoted in Box 6.4—46% said that they had called the police because of their partner's violence, and 18.7% found the police very helpful. On the other hand, 56% found the police "not at all helpful." In about half of the cases, someone was arrested, and it was equally as likely that the man would be arrested and placed in jail as it was that the female partner would be arrested and jailed. In 54.9% of cases, the partner was determined to be the primary aggressor. Among those men, 41.5% said the police asked the man if he wanted his partner arrested; 21% reported the police refused to arrest the partner; 38.7% indicated the police said there was nothing they could do and left; and 25.4% said the police did nothing, ignored, or dismissed them (Douglas & Hines, 2011).

If such cases reach the district attorney's office, male victims have even further hurdles to overcome. For example, Brown (2004) found that when only the male partner was injured, the female perpetrator was charged in 60.2% of the cases, but when only the female partner was injured, the male perpetrator was charged in 91.1% of the cases. When there were no injuries to either partner, men were charged 52.5% of the time, whereas women were charged 13.2% of the time. Brown also found that when women were charged with domestic violence, the injuries that they inflicted on their male partners were much more severe than the injuries inflicted by men charged with domestic violence. Thus, a higher threshold needed to be reached in order for women to be charged. Further, in cases where there was a severe injury, 71.4% of male perpetrators were found guilty, as compared to 22.2% of the female perpetrators. Henning and Renauer (2005) had similar findings: In 47% of the cases with female perpetrators and male victims, the prosecutor rejected the case; another 16% were dismissed by the judge. Overall, Henning and Renauer found that female IPV defendants with male victims were treated more leniently than either their male counterparts or the female counterparts who victimized other family members.

Male Stalking Victims and the Criminal Justice System Response

Little research has examined male stalking victims' experiences with the criminal justice system (Tjaden & Thoennes, 2000b). Scholars have speculated that men "may be reluctant to present themselves as victims of stalking in the public, formal, male-dominated or "macho" context of law enforcement" (Cupach & Spitzberg, 2004, p. 49). They may expect that their complaints will not be taken seriously by law enforcement personnel (Dupont-Morales, 1999). In fact, law enforcement officials may not let cases involving male victims into the system as readily as those involving female victims (DuPont-Morales, 1999). The NVAWS found that 46.4% of the victims (male and female) in their study did not consider what happened to them to be stalking (Tjaden & Thoennes, 1998). Further, despite identical experiences of victimization, men were less likely to identify themselves as stalking victims than women (Tjaden & Thoennes, 2000b). Why do you think that is the case? Given the identical experiences, why would men be less likely than women to identify themselves as stalking victims? Given the definition of stalking presented in Chapter 5, do you think that the definition of stalking may inherently exclude some male victims? Why or why not?

Not surprisingly, male stalking victims are less likely than female victims to report stalking to the police (Baum, Catalano, Rand, & Rose, 2009; Tjaden & Thoennes, 1998). Results from the NVAWS revealed that when the victim was a man, the police were less likely to take a report, arrest or detain the perpetrator, refer the victim to a prosecutor or court, refer the victim to victim services, or give advice on self-protective measures (Tjaden & Thoennes, 1998). Male victims were less likely to obtain a protective or restraining order, and male victims who did obtain one were more likely to report violation of the order than female victims. Why do you think these differences exist? Why are men less likely to report their stalking victimization or get a restraining order against their stalker? Why is their stalker more likely to violate it? Further, stalkers of men were less likely to be prosecuted, but more likely to be convicted, and more likely to be sentenced to jail or prison than stalkers of women. However, these differences are not statistically significant because of the small numbers of male victims who reached this stage of the criminal justice system.

Services for Female Perpetrators

Because of mandatory arrest policies in cases of IPV, dual arrests have increased dramatically, and thus many more women are being arrested for IPV (Hamberger & Arnold, 1990). If they get sentenced or plea bargain in court, it is likely that they will be ordered into some kind of treatment program. Moreover, some female perpetrators seek out treatment on their own. In response to these issues, several groups of researchers have investigated possible gender differences in male versus female arrestees in IPV cases, in part to ascertain whether female perpetrators should have different treatment programs than male perpetrators.

For example, some gender differences have emerged in the types of violence used. Specifically, male arrestees seem to use more violence during the arrest incident (Busch & Rosenberg, 2004). Overall, men are more likely to have threatened their female partners with either lethal (Henning & Feder, 2004; Melton & Belknap, 2003) or nonlethal harm (Melton & Belknap, 2003); to have attempted to prevent the victim from calling the police; and to have shoved, pushed, grabbed, dragged, pulled the hair of, physically restrained (Melton & Belknap, 2003), strangled (Henning & Feder, 2004; Melton & Belknap, 2003), and sexually assaulted their victims (Henning & Feder, 2004). By contrast, females arrestees were more likely to have hit the victim with an object, thrown an object at the victim, struck the victim with a vehicle, bitten the victim (Melton & Belknap, 2003), and used a weapon against the victim (Brown, 2004; Henning & Feder, 2004; Melton & Belknap, 2003). However, there seem to be no gender differences in the perpetrator's likelihood to have slapped, punched, hit, knifed, or stabbed the victim (Melton & Belknap, 2003); or in the frequency or severity of psychological maltreatment, suicidal threats, or stalking behaviors (Henning & Feder, 2004).

The physical consequences of this violence may have some gender differences as well. Although both Melton and Belknap (2003) and Henning and Feder (2004) found no gender differences in injuries, Brown (2004) found that female arrestees were more likely to have caused an injury than male arrestees. Busch and Rosenberg (2004) found no gender differences in injury rates of the victims; however, when women injured their victims, they tended to use a weapon or object, but when men injured their victims, they tended to use their bodies alone.

There may also be some gender differences in the histories of the male and female arrestees. Male arrestees seem to be more likely to have a history of domestic violence offenses (Busch & Rosenberg, 2004) and to have violated a protective order (Henning & Feder, 2004). Male arrestees are also more likely to have a history of both violent and nonviolent criminal behavior, and to own a gun (Henning & Feder, 2004). However, among arrestees with prior offenses, there are no gender differences in the number of previous arrests or in histories of prior violence outside the home, and the majority of female arrestees have criminal histories (Busch & Rosenberg, 2004). Moreover, there seem to be no gender differences in juvenile arrest rates (Henning & Feder, 2004), childhood experiences, exposure to interparental conflict, and mental health history (Henning et al., 2003).

Finally, within the incident itself, male offenders are more likely to have a victim who fears him and to involve the children (Henning & Feder, 2004). And although one study suggests that male arrestees are more likely to have used substances prior to the incident (Henning & Feder, 2004), another shows no gender differences in substance abuse problems, the use of substances at the time of arrest, or the types of substances that the arrestees abused (Busch & Rosenberg, 2004).

Overall, these studies show the importance of studying the female perpetrator of domestic violence because the services she needs may be somewhat different from male perpetrators. Currently, however, there are few programs that are specifically designed for female perpetrators (e.g., a 36-week-long intervention in Denver that is a modified version of a male batterers' program, and a 20-week-long anger management program at the University of Massachusetts Medical Center that has a strong cognitive-behavioral emphasis). For the most part, if women are convicted of domestic violence, they are sentenced into the same batterer intervention programs designed for male perpetrators, which are mandated to have a strong emphasis on a patriarchal analysis of domestic violence against women (Carney, Buttell, & Dutton, 2007) and have shown little, if any, effects on male perpetrators (Feder & Wilson, 2005). In one pilot study of 26 women sentenced to a traditional batterer intervention program, women were less passive/aggressive and less likely to use physical aggression against their partner by the conclusion of the program, providing preliminary evidence that women can benefit somewhat from a program designed for men (Carney & Buttell, 2004), which is important to know since it is unlikely that female-focused programs will be developed in the near future (Carney et al., 2007).

Services for Male Victims

One survey of male IT victims shows just how difficult it is for men to get appropriate victim services in this country (Douglas & Hines, 2011). This study found that 23% of the men contacted a domestic violence hotline, and only 7.5% found this resource "very helpful;" on the other hand, 68.7% found it "not at all helpful," and the main reason the men cited was that the hotline said that they only helped women, followed by the hotline referring them to a male batterers' program. Almost half (44%) of the men contacted a local domestic violence agency, and again, less than 10% found this agency very helpful, while 65.2% said it was not all helpful, primarily because the agencies appeared to be biased against men, said they did not help male victims, and suggested he was the batterer.

The dearth of resources for male victims of IPV has been attributed to the feminist view of power relationships (Hines & Douglas, 2009). According to feminist theory, men cannot be victimized by women in a society in which men are dominant (e.g., Dobash & Dobash, 1988). Because domestic violence agencies were based on this paradigm, they are unlikely to offer services to male victims. In fact, according to one study of a random sample of domestic violence agency directors in the United States, in comparison to other underserved groups—LGBTs, elderly, adolescents—men were the least likely group to be offered housing services (with the exception of adolescents, who often were excluded due to legal reasons), group mental health and non-residential support group services, transportation services, and employment services (Hines & Douglas, 2011a).

However, there are some services that do specialize in male victims of IPV. Stop Abuse For Everyone (SAFE, 2011) is a program that offers services for all victims of IPV and is particularly sympathetic to male victims. It lists services that are available and responsive to male victims and provides training to law enforcement, health care providers, social services, and crisis lines on how to recognize IPV against men. It also offers a brochure that is specific to issues of male victims.

The first hotline in the United States specific to male IPV victims, the Domestic Abuse Helpline for Men and Women (2011), was developed in Maine in 2000. It offers a 24-hour hotline, referrals to mental health professionals who understand that IPV is not gender-specific, support groups, and advocacy assistance. In addition, Valley Oasis in Lancaster, California, offers shelter and counseling services for both men and women. The Oasis has 11 cottages, and men and women are kept separate, unless the man's cottage becomes full and they need to combine the sexes; the group counseling services are co-ed, as long as there are at least two men available for the group (Ensign & Jones, 2007). Further, Michigan in 1996 and California in 2008 required that domestic violence agencies that receive state funds must provide services to male victims.

One problem is that most male IPV victims probably do not know that they can utilize these programs, because traditionally they have been geared toward women, and often they are located within women's agencies (e.g., YWCA) or have women-oriented names (e.g., Harriett's House). Therefore, even though some male victims are now being served by these traditionally female-oriented programs, still many others do not reach out for the help that is available (Heinlein & Beaupre, 2002). In addition, society is slow to accept the idea of the male IPV victim. Many men do not seek help for fear of being ridiculed, and shame and embarrassment ensure that their victimization remains hidden in this society. Those victims who are willing to seek help either have trouble locating the few resources available or are unlikely to get the legal help they need to escape an abusive home. This situation is compounded when they have children: Many male victims state that they stay with their perpetrator in order to protect the children from her violence. They know that if they left their violent partners, the legal system would most likely grant custody of the children to their violent partners, and that perhaps even their custody rights would be blocked by their female partners as a continuation of the controlling behaviors she used during the marriage (Cook, 2009; Hines & Douglas, 2010a; McNeely et al., 2001).

Services for Male Victims and Female Perpetrators of Intimate Partner Stalking

Not surprisingly, there are few services for male victims and female perpetrators of intimate partner stalking. Treatment for stalkers can focus on specific psychiatric diagnoses that often accompany stalking, such as borderline personality disorder and mood disorders (Cupach & Spitzberg, 2004). It appears that no research has been conducted on the efficacy of such approaches in treating female intimate partner stalkers. Few studies have investigated treatment approaches for intimate partner stalking, and it appears none has focused on treatment for female intimate partner stalkers. Thus, many perpetrators remain untreated.

Most, if not all, services for intimate partner stalking victims are offered through domestic violence agencies, which men may not contact for various reasons (e.g., they believe services are provided only for women, they think they can handle the stalking themselves, they do not want to look weak, fear they would not be believed) or may be turned away from when they do contact these agencies. Thus, many male victims face the intrusive, harassing, and often dangerous behaviors of female stalkers with little support. Do you think domestic violence agencies would not reach out to male victims because they believe men are not victims of female intimate stalking, just as many think they are not victims of IPV? How can this perception be changed?

Summary

The topic of male IPV victims has been the subject of much controversy over the past three decades in this country. In this chapter, we attempted to move beyond the argument over whether or not men can be IPV victims. There is ample evidence in the literature that many men are maltreated by their female partners, both physically and psychologically, and that often this maltreatment is not in self-defense. Men who have experienced IPV have been shown to suffer many physical and psychological consequences, including injuries, fatalities, depression, alcoholism, stress, PTSD symptoms, fear, and distress. In addition, because the legal system and the public are slow to acknowledge their experiences, they may be doubly victimized—they may experience shame and humiliation if they choose to reveal their victimization. Many times, however, male victims choose to either stay in the abusive relationship to protect the children and/or keep silent about the IPV they experience, and thus, they suffer in silence and isolation. If they do choose to seek help for their situation, they may be unaware of any of the few resources that are available to them. Many researchers have acknowledged for decades that men could be victimized by female partners; however, because of the controversial nature of this topic, we are just beginning to understand its dynamics. There is little research on the predictors and consequences of this type of IPV, and only a few services have been established to help these victims.

Research suggests that although women are more likely to be victims of stalking by a current or former partner, the number of men stalked by women is substantial. Male victims are likely to suffer the same consequences of stalking as female victims, including emotional/psychological, financial, and social effects. For a number of reasons, it is likely that male victims are more reluctant than female victims to seek assistance from formal sources, such as the criminal justice system and domestic violence agencies. It appears that there are no treatment programs specifically geared toward female intimate partner stalkers or male victims of stalking.

Discussion Questions

1. The chapter opened by summarizing the case of Allen. How do you think Allen's children have been affected by this situation? How do you think they were affected as the legal battles ensued? After his suicide? In the future, as adults?

2. What is your perception of the feminist view on male IPV victims? Do you agree or disagree with their perspective? Why or why not? Do you believe that female perpetrators may have motives that move beyond self-defense and retaliation?

3. Why do you suppose men and women are unwilling to refer to IPV as a "crime?" What barriers may exist for male victims who do consider IPV a crime, when it comes time to seek help? What can we do to help to eradicate these barriers?

4. When IPV is conceptualized as a crime in surveys, women are less likely than men to report their perpetration of IPV. Why do you think this is?

5. Between 1975 and 1992, male-to-female IPV decreased, while female-to-male IPV remained stable. Why might this be? How might social causes (domestic violence awareness, helping agencies, law enforcement) influence decreases and stability in IPV?

6. Why do you think socioeconomic factors serve as a predictor for the maltreatment of male partners? What barriers do unemployed men face when seeking help for or escape from IPV?

7. Why might reciprocal violence be the most prevalent form of violence in intimate relationships? Should helping professionals treat victims of reciprocal violence any differently than victims of unilateral violence? Why or why not?

8. Why does anxious attachment style increase the likelihood of IPV perpetration among women?

9. The majority of men killed by their female partners are unmarried. Why might they stay in an abusive relationship without legal binding? What barriers (emotional, economic, psychological, physical, etc.) may be in place to keep these men from leaving?

10. Both men and women report that psychological maltreatment is generally more distressing than physical maltreatment. Why might this be?

11. There are relatively few forums for men to receive help for IPV victimization. What are the ramifications of this shortfall? What can be done to remedy it? How might those in the helping professions ameliorate or exacerbate a male victim's distress?

12. Criminal justice officials (e.g., police officers, prosecutors, judges) may take cases of stalking against men less seriously than those involving female victims. Why is this problematic? What can be done to encourage these officials to take such cases seriously?

13. How can men be encouraged to seek formal assistance (e.g., report to police, obtain a restraining order, contact a domestic violence agency) when dealing with a female stalker?

7

Maltreatment in College Student Relationships

> *On May 2, 2010, Yeardley Love, a fourth-year lacrosse player at the University of Virginia, left a popular burger bar and walked home to her apartment. Love left her apartment door unlocked, so it was easy for her ex-boyfriend, George Huguely, to walk right in when he came to her apartment that night, uninvited. Love tried to hide in her bedroom. Huguely punched and kicked down the door, and then shook Love, hitting her head repeatedly against the wall. He left her in an unconscious state on the bed, took her laptop for fear that police would find the threatening emails he had been sending Love, and left. Around 2 a.m., her roommates returned home and found Love, dead (CBSNews, 2010; Sampson, 2012).*

The prior two chapters focused on maltreatment in established, longer-term relationships; however, it is as important to look at maltreatment in relationships before any kind of formal commitment has been made. As shown in the above case, the maltreatment that can occur in these relationships can be very severe and have tragic consequences. Therefore, it is important to acknowledge that even though the victim and perpetrator may not be married or living together, the maltreatment can be severe and difficult to escape. A second reason to be concerned about maltreatment in dating relationships is that studies show that maltreatment at the dating stage predicts maltreatment after a couple gets married (O'Leary et al., 1989). Third, because people today tend to get married later in life, they are dating more and for longer periods of time. Thus, maltreatment in dating relationships is of increasing concern, and the highest rates of maltreatment occur in relationships among adolescents and college students. In fact, the risk of victimization is greatest in adolescence and declines thereafter (Smith, White, & Holland, 2003).

Our focus in this chapter is on maltreatment in relationships among college students, and studies show that a majority of college students experience some type of maltreatment in their relationships. Specifically, when at least three types of intimate partner violence (IPV) are considered (i.e., physical, sexual, psychological), more than half of college students are victims of at least one type of IPV within a given year (Sabina & Straus, 2008). A related issue is that while we typically treat physical, psychological, sexual, and stalking maltreatment separately, they are often intertwined (Hines & Saudino, 2003; Ryan, 1998; Smith et al., 2003). Reports show that Yeardley Love was not only physically assaulted, but she also experienced psychological maltreatment and stalking during her relationship with Huguely and after it ended. This victimization from more than one type of PV—typically called polyvictimization—is a major problem. In fact, in one study (Sabina & Straus, 2008), 53% of victimized college men and 51.5% of victimized college women experienced two or more victimizations within the prior year (psychological, physical, sexual IPV). The most frequent combination was psychological, physical, and sexual victimization for both victimized men (21.3%) and victimized women (21.3%), followed by sexual coercion only for women (21.1%) and psychological aggression only for men (17.4%). Among the severely victimized, about a third of both men and women report more than one type of severe victimization from a dating partner (Sabina & Straus, 2008).

Similarly, in a longitudinal study of college women, Smith et al. (2003) found that co-victimization of physical and sexual aggression were common: 12.9% experienced both in their first year of college, 9.8% in their second year, 8.9% in their third year, and 7.2% in their fourth year. By the time they exited college, 63.5% of women had experienced both physical and sexual victimization (which included childhood and adolescent victimization as well) (Smith et al., 2003). A meta-analysis of 82 studies of stalking, including college student samples, found that 12% of stalking cases involved sexual violence (Spitzberg & Cupach, 2007). Relationships characterized by polyvictimization tend to have higher frequencies of maltreatment than relationships in which there is only one type of maltreatment (Ryan, 1998), and the outcomes for the victims are more severe. For both men and women, polyvictimization of IPV is the strongest predictor of post-traumatic stress (PTS) outcomes, above and beyond any one form of victimization; for women, polyvictimization is also the strongest predictor of depression (Sabina & Straus, 2008).

Physical Maltreatment in Dating Relationships

Scope of the Problem

Makepeace (1981) conducted the groundbreaking study on physical IPV among college students and found that 1 in 5 students on the campus he studied experienced an act of physical IPV within the previous year, with acts ranging in severity from slapping to life-threatening violence. Since then, more knowledge and precise estimates of the extent of physical IPV among college students have been generated; however, unlike studies on IPV in the general population, there are no national population-based studies of physical IPV among college students. Nonetheless, we know that physical IPV generally begins in adolescence (O'Leary, Woodin, & Fritz, 2006); and that it continually declines from adolescence, to the first year of college, to the senior year of college (Graves, Sechrist, White, & Paradise, 2005).

We also know that IPV is much higher in the college-age group than in later age groups (Straus, 2008a). Although measurement of physical IPV among college students suffers from the same problems discussed in Chapters 5 and 6, the most widely used measure is the Conflict Tactics Scales (CTS) (Straus, Hamby, Boney-McCoy, & Sugarman, 1996). Across samples using the CTS, about 30% of college students (see Table 7.1) report physical IPV in their relationships within a given year (e.g., Sabina & Straus, 2008). The comparable rate for U.S. couples with a median age of 40 is about 12% (Straus & Gelles, 1988). Among college students, perpetration ranges from a low of 13% (Shook, Gerrity, Jurich, & Segrist, 2000) to a high of 47% (Straus et al., 1996), and when gender differences in perpetration are found, women are more physically aggressive than men (e.g., Hines & Saudino, 2003; Ryan, 1998; Shook et al., 2000). When only severe physical violence is considered, approximate perpetration rates are 10%, ranging from a low of 7.4% to a high of 15.1% (Cercone, Beach, & Arias, 2005). Patterns for victimization rates tend to mirror perpetration rates, although victimization rates are higher.

What is particularly noteworthy about some of these studies is the distribution of the types of violent relationships. The majority of violent relationships are bidirectionally violent, followed by female-only violence, and then male-only violence (e.g., Hines & Saudino, 2003; Straus, 2008a). For example, in 69.6% of the violent relationships in 19 U.S. colleges, both the male and female partner were violent; 9.7% of the violent relationships were characterized by male-only violence; and in 20.6% of the relationships, there was female-only violence (Straus, 2008a). When we just look at severe violence (i.e., violence that has a higher likelihood of causing an injury, such as punching or beating up), 56.6% of severe assaults were bidirectional; 15.2% were male-only; and 28.1% were female-only. Similarly, Orcutt and colleagues (2005) found that men and women had similar degrees of reciprocity in terms of severity and injury.

Bidirectional violence should be taken very seriously because it is the most common pattern of relationship violence (Hines & Saudino, 2003; Orcutt, Garcia, & Pickett, 2005; Straus, 2008a), the pattern least likely to cease and most likely to escalate (Feld & Straus, 1989), and the pattern most likely to result in physical and psychological injury (Straus & Gozjolko, 2007; Whitaker, Haileyesus, Swahn, & Saltzman, 2007). However, experts argue about whether this bidirectionality is truly reciprocal or if the woman is only using violence to defend herself (see also Chapter 6). According to female college students who use violence, there is an equal likelihood that either gender will initiate the violence (LeJeune & Follette, 1994), and their motivations for using violence include coercion, anger, punishing what they perceive as their partner's misbehavior (Fiebert & Gonzalez, 1997), and poor communication (Hettrich & O'Leary, 2007). In fact, the causes that women cite the least for their violence are self-defense, drugs and/or alcohol, preventing partner from committing an illegal act, and that their partner was forcing them to have sex (Hettrich & O'Leary, 2007). Thus, according to college women's reports, their violence is not in self-defense. Others argue that men use violence to dominate their partner, whereas women do not (e.g., Hamberger & Guse, 2002). However, among U.S. college students, there is no significant gender difference on self-reports of who is the dominant partner nor in the correlation between dominance and the use of physical IPV (Straus, 2008a).

Table 7.1 Selected Studies (since 1995) of Physical Maltreatment

Study	Sample	Measure of Physical Aggression	Rates of Physical Aggression
Perpetration			
Straus, Hamby, Boney-McCoy, & Sugarman (1996)	317 undergraduate students; 36% male, 64% female	Conflict Tactics Scales over previous 12 months	*Men:* 47% perpetrated an average of 12.9 acts of physical aggression *Women:* 35% perpetrated an average of 9.4 acts of physical aggression
Ryan (1998)	245 male and 411 female college students (283 were from a 2-year technical college, 373 were from a 4-year liberal arts college)	Conflict Tactics Scales over previous 12 months	*Men:* 23% reported physical aggression *Women:* 43% reported physical aggression
Shook, Gerrity, Jurich, & Segrist (2000)	572 college students (395 women, 177 men) involved in dating relationship over previous year; large public Midwestern university	Conflict Tactics Scales over previous 12 months	21% of the sample engaged in physically aggressive behavior 23.5% of women were physically aggressive 13.0% of the men were physically aggressive
Straus & Medeiros (2002)	566 undergraduate students (232 men, 334 women from two universities)	Conflict Tactics Scales over previous 12 months	22% of both men and women engaged in minor physical aggression 10% of men and 11% of women engaged in severe physical aggression
Hines & Saudino (2003)	481 undergraduates in a large Northeastern university; 179 male, 302 female	Conflict Tactics Scales over previous 12 months	*Men:* 29% used physical aggression 10.5% used severe physical aggression *Women:* 35% used physical aggression 7.5% used severe physical aggression

(Continued)

Table 7.1 (Continued)

Study	Sample	Measure of Physical Aggression	Rates of Physical Aggression
Cercone, Beach, & Arias (2005)	414 undergraduates (189 men, 225 women) at a large Southeastern university; involved in a heterosexual dating relationship at some point	Conflict Tactics Scales over the course of their relationship	*Men:* 36.0% perpetrated minor physical aggression 7.4% perpetrated severe physical aggression *Women:* 38.7% perpetrated minor physical aggression 15.1% perpetrated severe physical aggression
Hettrich & O'Leary (2007)	446 women in a dating relationship (at least one month in duration) in the past year at a university in upstate New York	Conflict Tactics Scales—Short-Form, perpetration only over the course of their relationship	32% of women had perpetrated physical intimate partner violence (IPV)
Sabina & Straus (2008)	4,533 undergraduate college students (1,473 men, 3,060 women) in 19 sites in 11 states across the United States	Conflict Tactics Scales over previous 12 months	*Men:* 30.6% perpetrated physical assault 11.3% perpetrated severe physical assault *Women:* 28.1% perpetrated physical assault 10.7% perpetrated severe physical assault
Victimization			
Straus et al. (1996)	317 undergraduate students; 36% male, 64% female	Conflict Tactics Scales over previous 12 months	*Men:* 49% were victimized by an average of 15.9 acts of physical aggression *Women:* 31% were victimized by an average of 9.3 acts of physical aggression
Ryan (1998)	245 male and 411 female college students (283 from a 2-year technical college, 373 from a 4-year liberal arts college)	Conflict Tactics Scales over previous 12 months	*Men:* 40% reported physical aggression victimization *Women:* 34% reported physical aggression victimization

Study	Sample	Measure of Physical Aggression	Rates of Physical Aggression
Hines & Saudino (2003)	481 undergraduates in a large Northeastern university; 179 male, 302 female	Conflict Tactics Scales over previous 12 months	*Men:* 30.5% sustained physical aggression 12.5% sustained severe physical aggression *Women:* 24.5% sustained physical aggression 4.5% sustained severe physical aggression
Smith, White, & Holland (2003)	1,569 women entering the University of North Carolina at Greensboro in 1990 and 1991	Modified Conflict Tactics Scales; assessed threatened to hit or throw something, threw something at them, pushed, grabbed, or shoved them, hit or attempted to hit them with a hand or fist, hit or attempted to hit them with something hard	27.2% of women experienced IPV during their 1st year of college 24.3% during their 2nd year 22.7% during their 3rd year 18.6% during their 4th year 77.8% of women experienced at least one of the CTS items by the end of their college career
Cercone et al. (2005)	414 undergraduates (189 men, 225 women) at a large Southeastern university; involved in a heterosexual dating relationship at some point	Conflict Tactics Scales over the course of their relationship	*Men:* 41.8% sustained minor physical aggression 18.0% sustained severe physical aggression *Women:* 34.7% sustained minor physical aggression 12.9% sustained severe physical aggression
Simons, Gwin, Brown, & Gros (2008)	400 undergraduate students at a private metropolitan university in the eastern United States (55% male, 45% female)	Domestic Violence Index (16-item yes/no questionnaire); index score of 5 or more indicates presence of domestic violence (time range—e.g, ever, past year—not provided)	31% of students overall had experienced IPV

Predictors and Correlates

Research on the predictors of physical maltreatment in college dating relationships falls at every level of the ecological model (see Table 7.2). Unless otherwise indicated, these predictors apply across genders.

Table 7.2   Predictors of Physical IPV in College Student Dating Relationships

Level of Ecological Model	Predictor	Studies
Macrosystem	Dominance	Straus (2008a)
	Experiencing stress based on masculine roles	Jakupcak, Lisak, & Roemer (2002)
	Less masculine, more feminine men and women	Burke, Stets, & Pirog-Good (1988)
	Men with egalitarian gender-role ideologies are less violent toward their female partners	Fitzpatrick, Salgado, Suvak, King, & King (2004)
Exosystem	Associating with violent peers	Silverman & Williamson (1997)
	Isolation/lack of social integration	Makepeace (1987); Straus & Medeiros (2002)
	Suspensions/expulsions, multiple firings from jobs	Makepeace (1987)
	Stress	Makepeace (1987); Straus & Medeiros (2002)
	Higher socioeconomic status (for women)	Straus (2008a)
Microsystem	Victim has a history of physical and/or sexual victimization in adolescence	Smith, White, & Holland (2003)
	Longer, more serious relationships	Doumas, Pearson, Elgin, & McKinley (2008); Hines (2008); Straus (2008a)
	Perpetrator is not happy in the relationship	Hettrich & O'Leary (2007)
	Relationship distress	Straus & Medeiros (2002)
	Perpetrator has negative feelings about/is angry at partner	Hettrich & O'Leary (2007); Ryan (1998); Straus & Medeiros (2002)
	Perpetrator blames partner for problems	Ryan (1998)

Level of Ecological Model	Predictor	Studies
	Communication problems	Follingstad, Bradley, Laughlin, & Burke (1999); Straus & Medeiros (2002)
	Victim's self-worth tied to the romantic relationship	Goldstein, Chesir-Teran, & McFaul (2008)
	Perpetrator's jealousy (among women)	Burke, Stets, & Pirog-Good (1988); Straus & Medeiros (2002)
	Perpetrator's attitudes condoning violence in relationships (among men)	Burke et al. (1988); Straus & Medeiros (2002)
	Perpetrator's dependency on partner (among men)	Ryan (1998)
	Other types of maltreatment in the relationship	Ryan (1998)
	Anxious partner with an avoidant partner	Roberts & Noller (1998)
Individual/ Developmental	Growing up with a single parent, being less close to both parents	Makepeace (1987)
	Witnessing violence between parents	Gover, Kaukinen, & Fox (2008); Silverman & Williamson (1997)
	Experiencing physical maltreatment, neglect, and/or sexual abuse as a child	Burke et al. (1988); Shook, Gerrity, Jurich, & Segrist (2000); Straus & Medeiros (2002)
	Insecure attachment	Orcutt, Garcia, & Pickett (2005); Ryan (1998)
	Less likely to engage in rational behaviors	Follingstad et al. (1999)
	Poorer academic achievement	Makepeace (1987)
	Criminal history	Straus & Medeiros (2002)
	Alcohol and drug use	Follingstad et al. (1999); Hines & Straus (2007); Ryan (1998); Shook et al. (2000); Simons, Gwin, Brown, & Gross (2008)
	Antisocial traits	Straus & Medeiros (2002)
	Borderline traits	Hines (2008)

(Continued)

Table 7.2 (Continued)

Level of Ecological Model	Predictor	Studies
	Anger management problems	Follingstad et al. (1999); Straus & Medeiros (2002)
	Mood swings or a temper	Ryan (1998)
	Trait anger	Follingstad et al. (1999)
	Post-traumatic stress symptoms	Straus & Medeiros (2002)
	Neuroticism and disagreeableness	Hines & Saudino (2008)

Macrosystem

At the macrosystem level is research focusing on dominance of one partner over the other. Traditionally, heterosexual relationship violence has been theorized—and often assumed—to be a function of male dominance over women (e.g., Hamberger & Guse, 2002). However, research among college students has consistently shown that whenever there is dominance of one partner over the other, there is an increased risk of violence by the dominant partner in order to maintain that dominance—and by the subordinate partner in order to achieve something that is blocked by the dominant partner or to change the power structure (Straus, 2008a). Indeed, either men's or women's dominance in a relationship predicts men's violence, women's violence, and bidirectional violence (Straus, 2008a).

Often studied is another set of macrosystem-level predictors that has to do with gender role issues, including the stress perpetrators may feel as a result of their expected gender roles, the masculinity and femininity of perpetrators, and their gender-role ideologies. Men who experience stress based on masculine roles perpetrate more physical IPV (Jakupcak, Lisak, & Roemer, 2002). As men's gender-role ideologies became more egalitarian, men are less physically violent toward their female partners and *experience less* physical violence as well (Fitzpatrick, Salgado, Suvak, King, & King, 2004). Contrary to expectations, less masculine, more feminine men and women are more physically aggressive (Burke, Stets, & Pirog-Good, 1988). What are your thoughts on these findings? Why might they be contrary to expectations?

Exosystem

At the exosystem level, we see that associating with peers who are supportive of physical IPV predicts men's use of violence. Specifically, college men's physical IPV against female partners is influenced by their association with male peers who have attitudes supportive of IPV and engage in IPV themselves; that leads to the belief that IPV is justified and to their use of IPV (Silverman & Williamson, 1997). Other exosystem level predictors include isolation/lack of social integration (Makepeace, 1987; Straus & Medeiros, 2002), suspensions/expulsions, multiple firings from jobs (Makepeace, 1987), and stress (Makepeace, 1987), while higher socioeconomic status predict women's use of violence (Straus, 2008a). Why might a *higher* socioeconomic status predict women's use of violence?

Microsystem

At the microsystem level, predictors tend to cluster in two areas: victim's prior history of maltreatment and characteristics of the relationship. In one study of college women, physical victimization in college was significantly predicted by physical and sexual victimization in adolescence. Childhood victimization did not predict IPV victimization in college, unless there was also victimization in adolescence, a pattern that persisted throughout college (Smith, White, & Holland, 2003). What do you think are potential explanations for these patterns?

Relationship length predicts physical IPV as well, with violence being more likely in longer relationships (Doumas, Pearson, Elgin, & McKinley, 2008; Hines, 2008; Straus, 2008a), probably because the longer a relationship, the greater the possibility for conflict and as the relationship grows more serious, issues of control are more likely to surface, raising the risk of IPV (Hammock & O'Hearn, 2002). Supporting this explanation, studies show that physical IPV is more likely in relationships with higher levels of conflict (Straus & Medeiros, 2002) and where the couple is having sexual intercourse (Hines, 2008), an indicator of a more serious relationship.

Violence is also more likely when the perpetrator is not happy in the relationship (Hettrich & O'Leary, 2007), feels distress about the relationship (Straus & Medeiros, 2002), has negative feelings about or is angry with his or her partner (Hettrich & O'Leary, 2007; Ryan, 1998; Straus & Medeiros, 2002), blames the partner for his or her problems (Ryan, 1998), and when there are communication problems within the couple (Follingstad, Bradley, Laughlin, & Burke, 1999; Straus & Medeiros, 2002). When a person's self-worth is tied to the romantic relationship, that person is more likely to be physically victimized within the relationship (Goldstein, Chesir-Teran, & McFaul, 2008). Women who are jealous are more likely to use physical IPV, as are men who have attitudes condoning violence (Burke et al., 1988; Straus & Medeiros, 2002) and who are dependent on their partner (Ryan, 1998). As noted above, physical IPV is also more likely to occur in relationships in which other types of maltreatment are present, including verbal aggression, sexual aggression, and threats (Ryan, 1998).

One final characteristic of the relationship that has been investigated is attachment. Attachment anxiety, in particular, has been shown to be predictive of either partner's physical IPV (see Individual/Developmental section below), and such an attachment style gets activated when there is a threat—either real or perceived—to the closeness or security of the relationship. An individual with high attachment anxiety will escalate security-seeking efforts, experience overwhelming emotions, and may lash out in violence against their partner, particularly if she or he feels that the partner is unavailable (Orcutt et al., 2005). In fact, research shows that there is a particular combination of attachment styles that is predictive of IPV: people who are high in anxious attachment but involved with a partner who is high in avoidant attachment (e.g., unwilling to provide security) are at highest risk of perpetrating IPV (Roberts & Noller, 1998).

Individual/Developmental

Attachment style has also been studied as an individual-level predictor of physical IPV. For example, physically aggressive women have a desire for an exclusive attachment from their partner (Ryan, 1998) and tend to be high in attachment anxiety and low in attachment avoidance (Orcutt et al., 2005). Bidirectionally violent women seem to have the highest levels of attachment anxiety (Orcutt et al., 2005).

Characteristics of the perpetrator's family-of-origin also predict physical IPV. These include growing up with a single parent, being less close to both parents (Makepeace, 1987), and witnessing IPV between parents (Gover, Kaukinen, & Fox, 2008; Silverman & Williamson, 1997). Moreover, experiencing various types of child maltreatment predict the use of physical aggression in college students' relationships as well, including physical maltreatment (Burke et al., 1988; Shook et al., 2000), neglect, and sexual abuse (Straus & Medeiros, 2002). Reflecting back on previous chapters, what are some of the theoretical explanations for why these childhood experiences predict later physical IPV perpetration?

One of the most studied predictors of the use of physical IPV among college students is the presence of other risky behaviors. In fact, perpetrators of physical IPV are less likely to engage in rational behaviors than non-perpetrators (Follingstad et al., 1999), have poorer academic achievement (Makepeace, 1987), and are more likely to have a criminal history (Straus & Medeiros, 2002). Probably the most studied area of risk is drug and alcohol use. Studies show that physical IPV perpetration is associated with alcohol and drug use for both men and women (Follingstad et al., 1999; Hines & Straus, 2007; Ryan, 1998; Simons, Gwin, Brown, & Gross, 2008), with drinking within a few hours of an argument being predictive of physical IPV within that argument (Shook et al., 2000). Hines and Straus (2007) studied the ways in which these risk behaviors are related to one another and found that antisocial traits and behaviors mediate the influence of binge drinking on physical IPV.

In addition to antisocial traits (Hines & Straus, 2007; Straus & Medeiros, 2002), other traits of the perpetrator predict the use of physical IPV for both men and women. These include borderline traits (Hines, 2008), trouble with anger management (Follingstad et al., 1999; Straus & Medeiros, 2002), having mood swings or a temper (Ryan, 1998), trait anger (Follingstad et al., 1999), and PTS symptoms (Straus & Medeiros, 2002). Two other personality traits predicting the use of physical IPV include: (1) neuroticism, characterized by experiencing psychological distress and negative affect more intensely; being more hostile, anxious, depressed, self-conscious, and impulsive; having ineffective coping mechanisms, and being more prone to irrational thoughts and behaviors; and (2) disagreeableness, characterized by a hostile and irritable mistrust of others; acting in ways that snub or exclude people one does not like; feeling a need to attack or punish others; and lacking emotional expression and attachment to others (Hines & Saudino, 2008).

Box 7.1   Predictors in the Yeardley Love case

Consider George Huguely, the perpetrator of the homicide on Yeardley Love that opened this chapter. Huguely was known around campus for his temper, especially when he was drunk. On one occasion, he punched a sleeping teammate, and on another, he assaulted a female police officer while resisting arrest. He had a history of stalking and obsessive behavior toward other women, sometimes sending up to 20 texts an hour when he had been drinking, asking girls if he could come to their apartment. Huguely had a jealous nature, and he and Love were known to have intense fights (CBSNews, 2010; Sampson, 2012; Wertheim, 2010). Looking back to the predictors identified in this section, which ones are evident in this case? Were the warning signs there? At which levels of the ecological model do these warning signs fall?

Consequences

One tragic outcome of physical IPV in college students, as evidenced in the Yeardley Love case, is death, although this kind of outcome is rare. Physical injury is typically the primary concern regarding the consequences of physical IPV among college students, and studies show that anywhere between 5% and 15% of college students will sustain and/or inflict an injury within a given year. For example, Hines and Saudino (2003) found that 6.1% of college men and 6.5% of college women inflicted an injury in the past year. Moreover, 8.4% of men and 5.0% of women sustained an injury. Higher rates were found by Straus and colleagues (1996), who also reported the average number of injuries inflicted or sustained by their participants in the past year: 15% of male college students inflicted an injury (average of 25.1 injuries); 9% of female college students inflicted an injury (average of 3.6 injuries); 16% of male college students sustained an injury (average of 24.7 injuries); and 14% of female college students sustained an injury (average of 6.2 injuries). Why do you think college men report higher rates and frequencies of injuries for both infliction and victimization?

Risky behaviors have also been found among victims of physical IPV, but these studies are correlational, so it is unknown whether the risky behavior predated the IPV victimization or was a consequence of it. Such risky behaviors include smoking, use of amphetamines and other illegal drugs, binge drinking, having multiple sex partners (DuRant et al., 2007), having sex with strangers, and having one-night stands (Simons et al., 2008). Several studies also show psychological injuries that may result from IPV victimization, but again, these studies are correlational and cannot be taken as evidence of a causal relationship. Potential psychological injuries include suicidal ideation and self-harm (Chan, Straus, Brownridge, Tiwari, & Leung, 2008), depression, anxiety, somatization (when a person has physical symptoms that involve more than one part of the body, but no physical cause can be found) (Kaura & Lohman, 2007), and PTS symptoms (Hines, 2007a). Many of these associations remain even after controlling for other covariates (Kaura & Lohman, 2007). Also, Hines (2007a) found that PTS symptoms in male victims were higher on college campuses with higher levels of hostility toward men. Why do you think that higher levels of hostility toward men on a campus would be related to an increase in PTS symptoms among male victims?

Psychological Maltreatment in Dating Relationships

Scope of the Problem

As with other forms of family violence, psychological maltreatment is the most under-studied form of maltreatment within college student dating relationships, partly because of difficulties in defining it. Psychological maltreatment is typically considered to be a combination of various types of behaviors that attack a partner's self-worth and self-concept, including controlling, coercing, denigrating, isolating, dominating, ridiculing, and using recurring criticism, threats, and verbal aggression (O'Leary, 1999; Stets, 1991). Although this definition represents a wide range of behaviors, the typical measure of psychological maltreatment among college students is the CTS, which is narrow in its measurement of psychological maltreatment, including only criticism, threats, and verbal aggression. Table 7.3 includes the few studies that have established prevalence rates, and as shown, all of these studies used the CTS and show one-year prevalence rates of 75% or higher. Severe psychological aggression (i.e., calling partner fat or ugly, destroying something belonging to partner, accusing partner of being a lousy lover, threatening to hit or throw something at partner) (Straus et al., 1996) ranges from about 20% to 30% of college students during a one-year time period.

Predictors and Correlates

Research on predictors of psychological maltreatment among college students has occurred primarily at three levels: macrosystem, microsystem, and individual/ developmental (see Table 7.4). Unless otherwise noted, predictors apply to both men and women.

Macrosystem

Gender role issues play a role at the macrosystem level. Among college men, stress based on masculine role demands predicts their use of verbal aggression (Jakupcak et al., 2002), in particular the stress due to a demand for emotional expressiveness and vulnerability in managing tense relationship situations (Jakupcak, 2003). Men who hold a more egalitarian gender-role ideology are less likely to use psychological aggression or be psychologically maltreated than men who hold a less egalitarian gender-role ideology (Fitzpatrick et al., 2004). For women, the opposite is true: women with more egalitarian gender-role ideologies have a greater likelihood of psychologically maltreating their partners and being psychologically maltreated than women with less egalitarian gender-role ideologies (Fitzpatrick et al., 2004). Why do you think there are opposite findings for men and women with regard to gender-role ideology?

Microsystem

At the microsystem level, relationship issues play important roles. As with physical maltreatment, people in longer and more serious relationships are more likely to perpetrate and experience psychological maltreatment (Hammock & O'Hearn, 2002; Hines, 2008; Straight, Harper, & Arias, 2003). Conflict resolution strategies within a relationship also predict psychological maltreatment. Specifically, women who have an obliging conflict strategy (i.e., constantly concede to the wishes of the partner with little regard for own desires) are more likely to use psychological aggression, and men and women who have either a problem solving conflict strategy (i.e., actively seeking a solution in which needs and wants of both parties are considered) or an avoiding conflict strategy (i.e., avoiding negative encounters with partner) are less likely to use psychological aggression (Hammock & O'Hearn, 2002). Why do you think these associations with these different conflict strategies exist?

Table 7.3 Selected Studies (since 1995) of Psychological Maltreatment in College Student Dating Relationships

Study	Sample	Measure of Psychological Maltreatment	Rates of Psychological Maltreatment
Perpetration			
Straus, Hamby, Boney-McCoy, & Sugarman (1996)	317 undergraduate students; 36% male, 64% female	Conflict Tactics Scales over previous 12 months	*Men:* 74% perpetrated an average of 15.1 acts of psychological aggression *Women:* 83% perpetrated an average of 16 acts of psychological aggression
Ryan (1998)	245 male and 411 female college students (283 from a 2-year technical college, 373 from a 4-year liberal arts college)	Conflict Tactics Scales over previous 12 months	*Men:* 92% reported verbal aggression perpetration *Women:* 95% reported verbal aggression perpetration
Shook, Gerrity, Jurich, & Segrist (2000)	572 college students (395 women, 177 men) involved in dating relationship over previous year; large public Midwestern university	Conflict Tactics Scales over previous 12 months	82% of sample engaged in verbally aggressive behavior 83% of the women were verbally aggressive 80% of the men were verbally aggressive
Hines & Saudino (2003)	481 undergraduates in a large Northeastern university; 179 male, 302 female	Conflict Tactics Scales over previous 12 months	*Men:* 82% used psychological aggression *Women:* 86% used psychological aggression
Cercone, Beach, & Arias (2005)	414 undergraduates (189 men, 225 women) at a large Southeastern university; involved in a heterosexual dating relationship at some point	Conflict Tactics Scales over the course of their relationship	*Men:* 85.7% perpetrated minor psychological aggression 30.2% perpetrated severe psychological aggression *Women:* 89.3% perpetrated minor psychological aggression 26.7% perpetrated severe psychological aggression

(Continued)

Table 7.3 (Continued)

Study	Sample	Measure of Psychological Maltreatment	Rates of Psychological Maltreatment
Sabina & Straus (2008); International Dating Violence Study	4,533 undergraduate college students (1,473 men, 3,060 women) in 19 sites in 11 states across the United States	Conflict Tactics Scales over previous 12 months	*Men:* 34.4% perpetrated psychological aggression 19.5% perpetrated severe psychological aggression *Women:* 34.4% perpetrated psychological aggression 18.8% perpetrated severe psychological aggression
Victimization			
Straus et al. (1996)	317 undergraduate students; 36% male, 64% female	Conflict Tactics Scales over previous 12 months	*Men:* 76% were victimized by an average of 17.2 acts of psychological aggression *Women:* 78% were victimized by an average of 15.1 acts of psychological aggression
Ryan (1998)	245 male and 411 female college students (283 from a 2-year technical college, 373 from a 4-year liberal arts college)	Conflict Tactics Scales over previous 12 months	*Men:* 91% reported verbal aggression victimization *Women:* 90% reported verbal aggression victimization
Hines & Saudino (2003)	481 undergraduates in a large Northeastern university; 179 male, 302 female	Conflict Tactics Scales over previous 12 months	*Men:* 81% sustained psychological aggression *Women:* 80% sustained psychological aggression
Cercone et al. (2005)	414 undergraduates (189 men, 225 women) at a large Southeastern university; involved in a heterosexual dating relationship at some point	Conflict Tactics Scales over the course of their relationship	*Men:* 89.3% sustained minor psychological aggression 30.2% sustained severe psychological aggression *Women:* 86.7% sustained minor psychological aggression 24.0% sustained severe psychological aggression

Table 7.4   Predictors of Psychological Maltreatment at the Levels of the Ecological Model

Level	Predictor	Study
Macrosystem	Stress based on masculine role	Jakupcak (2003); Jakupcak, Lisak, & Roemer (2002)
	Gender-role ideologies	Fitzpatrick, Salgado, Suvak, King, & King (2004)
Microsystem	Longer, more serious relationships	Hammock & O'Hearn (2002); Hines (2008); Straight, Harper, & Arias (2003)
	Conflict resolution strategies	Hammock & O'Hearn (2002)
Individual/ Developmental	Experienced aggression from a parent	Shook, Gerrity, Jurich, & Segrist (2000)
	Adult attachment insecurity	Gormley & Lopez (2010); Murphy & Hoover (1999); O'Hearn & Davis (1997)
	Threat susceptibility	Hammock & O'Hearn (2002)
	Borderline personality traits	Hines (2008)
	Neuroticism	Hines & Saudino (2008)
	Alcohol use	Hammock & O'Hearn (2002); Shook et al. (2000)

Individual/Developmental

College students who experienced aggression from a parent as a child perpetrate higher levels of verbal aggression (Shook et al., 2000). Related to the microsystem level, but studied at the individual level, attachment style predicts perpetration of psychological maltreatment. Specifically, adult attachment insecurity is associated with greater frequency of psychological aggression perpetration (Murphy & Hoover, 1999). When stress levels are high, men and women with an avoidant attachment style are more likely to commit psychological maltreatment, possibly because when they are under a great deal of stress, "they may withdraw and become defensively critical of their partners" (Gormley & Lopez, 2010, p. 215). In addition to avoidant attachment, anxious attachment predicts psychological maltreatment (O'Hearn & Davis, 1997).

Personality traits also predict the use of psychological maltreatment, and include threat susceptibility (i.e., low self-esteem, trait anger, need for interpersonal control, neuroticism, perception of risk in intimacy) (Hammock & O'Hearn, 2002), borderline personality traits (Hines, 2008), and neuroticism (Hines & Saudino, 2008). Finally, alcohol use predicts psychological maltreatment (Shook et al., 2000), although one study showed that this association may only apply to male perpetrators (Hammock & O'Hearn, 2002).

Consequences

Research on the consequences of psychological maltreatment is very sparse and solely correlational, and to our knowledge, has focused on women. Thus, we do not know whether these issues are a consequence of psychological maltreatment and/or predate the maltreatment. Among college women, illegal drug use, physical and role limitations (e.g., cannot go to class), negative health perceptions, and cognitive impairment are predicted by psychological aggression victimization, even after controlling for physical IPV victimization (Straight et al., 2003). Moreover, women with high levels of approach coping (i.e., when efforts are directed at solving or managing the problem that is causing distress) do not experience these outcomes, whereas low approach coping was associated with more binge drinking and negative health perceptions as psychological maltreatment victimization increased. Why would approach coping moderate the associations between victimization and health outcomes?

Sexual Aggression

Scope of the Problem

Understanding sexual aggression in college dating relationships may be even more difficult than understanding physical or psychological maltreatment. First, very few studies assess sexual aggression specifically within the context of a romantic relationship. Second, among those studies that provide information on the relationship between the victim and perpetrator, there is a discrepancy about their relationship, with the majority of perpetrators saying their victims were romantically involved with them in some way (Abbey, McAuslan, Zawacki, Clinton, & Buck, 2001; Thompson, Koss, Kingree, Goree, & Rice, 2011) and victims saying that their perpetrators were most often just friends (Banyard, Ward et al., 2007; Fisher, Cullen, & Turner, 2000; Lawyer, Resnick, Bakanic, Burkett, & Kilpatrick, 2010) or acquaintances (Fisher et al., 2000; Krebs, Lindquist, Warner, Fisher, & Martin, 2007). Thus, it is clear that when sexual aggression does happen in this age group, there is typically some sort of relationship between the victim and perpetrator, whether friendship, romantic involvement, or acquaintanceship, and thus, we will be reviewing studies on sexual aggression between people who know each other and may or may not have prior romantic involvement.

A larger issue is the definition and measurement of sexual aggression within these relationships. Inherent in the definition is the issue of consent, and thus, sexual aggression is typically considered to be sexual contact against one's will or consent. Lack of consent applies to situations in which a person is unable to give consent, such as when they are drinking, drugged, under age, unconscious, asleep, or disabled. Most studies (see Table 7.5) use the Sexual Experiences Survey (SES) (Koss & Dinero, 1989) to measure sexual aggression, which uses this definition of sexual aggression and consent in its content. This survey was originally written to assess various forms of sexual aggression (e.g., coercion, attempted rape, rape) since the age of 14 among women as victims. A separate version was developed to assess perpetration among men. The underlying reason for the development of this instrument is the same as it was for the

CTS: There is a need to ask behaviorally specific questions with regard to sexual aggression; otherwise, we underestimate the true prevalence. This issue became abundantly clear with the administration of the National Sexual Victimization of College Women Study (NSVCWS) (Fisher et al., 2000): They found that among the women who experienced unwanted completed penetration by force or threat of force, only 46.5% said they considered the incident to be a rape.

Although the SES is the most widely used instrument to measure sexual aggression, it has been revised to account for past year sexual aggression (Humphrey & White, 2000), to focus specifically on dating relationships (Himelein, 1995), and to allow for reports of male victimization and female perpetration (Larimer, Lydum, Anderson, & Turner, 1999). Therefore, results may not be comparable across studies that use this measure, and time periods assessed often differ. This makes conclusions as to the true prevalence of sexual aggression difficult.

Above and beyond this issue are the questions on the survey itself, which have been criticized as vague and open to a variety of interpretations, some of which may not be consistent with a definition of sexual aggression (Ross & Allgeier, 1996). The more controversial items focus on the issue of incapacitated sexual assault (e.g., sexual assault when someone is intoxicated), since consent in these situations is often difficult to ascertain and can be ambiguous (Adams-Curtis & Forbes, 2004). Nonetheless, it is important to note that the majority of sexual assaults on college campuses happen within the context of alcohol use on the part of either or both the victim and perpetrator (e.g., Abbey, McAuslan, & Ross, 1998; Abbey, Ross, McDuffie, & McAuslan, 1996; Fisher et al., 2000; Harrington & Leitenberg, 1994; Hines, Armstrong, Palm Reed, & Cameron, in press; Koss, 1988). Thus, disentangling "drunken consensual sex" from "incapacitated rape" is an important area of future research.

A final concern is the nature of the research itself. As can be seen in Table 7.5, the majority of studies focus on men as perpetrators and women as victims. As mentioned before, the most widely used instrument to measure sexual aggression never initially considered the opposite situation or a situation in which the perpetrator and victim were of the same sex. Thus, we have only limited information on relationships in which the man is the victim and a woman is the perpetrator, and even less within same-sex scenarios (see Chapter 8).

It is clear that sexual aggression is a problem among college students in dating relationships. Assessing both genders, Hines and Saudino (2003) found that 29% of college men and 13.5% of college women in dating relationships perpetrated sexual aggression; 24.5% of men and 24.0% of women were victimized by sexual aggression. In another study, Hines (2007b) found that within 13 universities in the United States, between 0% and 7.2% of women reported being victimized by forced sex in their relationships within the previous year, with 17.0% to 46.7% reporting unwanted verbally coerced sexual intercourse. Among the men, between 0% and 12.0% reported being victimized by forced sex by a dating partner within the past year, with 9.3% to 50% reporting unwanted verbally coerced sexual intercourse. In a separate study (Sabina & Straus, 2008) using the same data, 28.7% of men and 27.8% of women perpetrated sexual coercion; 2.5% of men and 2.2% of women perpetrated severe sexual coercion (i.e., used force or threats).

Similar rates have been found among college students when we look at the range of relationships in which sexual aggression occurs. The research is remarkably consistent in showing that 90% of sexual assaults reported by college students are perpetrated by someone they know (Abbey et al., 1996; Fisher et al., 2000; Hines et al., in press; Koss, 1988). The classic study on the extent of sexual aggression experienced by a representative sample of college women was conducted by Koss and her colleagues in the 1980s (Koss, Gidycz, & Wisniewski, 1987) (see Table 7.5). The results showed that 54% of college women had experienced some kind of sexual assault since age 14, with 15% experiencing rape and 12% experiencing attempted rape. Since then, several studies have attempted to replicate the findings of this classic study, the most famous of which is the NSVCWS, conducted in the Spring of 1997 (Fisher et al., 2000). The NSVCWS focused specifically on sexual assault since the beginning of the academic year, which varied based on when the women took the survey but was an average of seven months duration. Overall, 2.8% of college women reported experiencing a completed and/or attempted rape during the current academic year; 15.5% reported experiencing any kind of sexual victimization; 7.7% experienced an incident involving the use of force or threat of force, and 11.0% experienced an incident that did not involve force (Fisher et al., 2000).

More recently, the Campus Sexual Assault Study investigated sexual assault victimization at two large public universities in the South and Midwest (Krebs et al., 2007). This study assessed sexual assault since entering college, with the time frame varying based on the participant. Since entering college, 12.6% of the women reported an attempted sexual assault, 13.7% a completed sexual assault, 5% a forced sexual assault, 3.4% a forced rape, 11% a sexual assault while incapacitated, and 8.5% an incapacitated rape.

A final study gives some indication of the risk of sexual victimization over time for college women. Humphrey and White (2000) followed a representative sample of women in state-supported universities for five years. They found that the women were most at risk of being sexually victimized (i.e., unwanted sexual contact, verbal coercion to engage in sex, attempted rape, and/or rape) prior to entering college, with 49.5% reporting some type of sexual victimization between the age of 14 and entering college and 13.0% reporting rape in this time frame. In each subsequent college year, the rates of sexual victimization declined from 31.3% and 6.4% reporting any type of sexual victimization and rape, respectively, during their first year in college to 24.2% and 3.9% reporting any type of sexual victimization and rape, respectively, during their fourth year. Overall, 69.8% of women reported some type of sexual victimization, and 21.2% reported a rape between the age of 14 and the end of their college careers.

There is some evidence that college and university women are at a greater risk for sexual assault victimization than their non-college-aged counterparts (Fisher et al., 2000; Koss et al., 1987). This finding could be due to the residential college environment in which almost all of one's time is spent with age-mates, and in which social situations often involve heavy alcohol use. Notably, the majority of sexual assaults—at least 50%—on college students involve the use of alcohol (Abbey et al., 1998; Abbey et al., 1996; Harrington & Leitenberg, 1994; Hines et al., in press; Koss, 1988). In fact, among college students, alcohol-related sexual assaults are about five times more common than forcible assaults (e.g., Lawyer et al., 2010). The role of alcohol in such assaults is complex. Sometimes, a perpetrator intentionally gives a person drugs or alcohol in order to render them incapacitated; however, a much more common scenario is when a perpetrator takes advantage of an incapacitated person who drank or used drugs voluntarily (e.g., Krebs et al., 2007; Lawyer et al., 2010).

The first nationally representative survey of college students also assessed perpetration among men. In comparison to the relatively high rates of victimization reported by women, rates of reported perpetration by men were lower: 25% of college men reported committing some form of sexual assault since age 14, with 7.7% committing rape (Koss et al., 1987). Notice that the rates of perpetration tend to be about half the rates of victimization. One of the possible reasons for this discrepancy is repeat offending. Studies consistently show that a minority of college men—5% to 10%—engage in behaviors that are legally considered attempted rape or rape (Abbey et al., 2001; Koss et al., 1987; Lisak & Miller, 2002; Thompson et al., 2011) and that the majority of college men who commit sexual assault, attempted rape, or rape—about two thirds to three fourths—are repeat offenders (Abbey et al., 2001; Koss et al., 1987; Lisak & Miller, 2002) with offenders committing about 3 to 6 sexual assaults, attempted rapes, or rapes before participating in a study (Abbey et al., 2001; Lisak & Miller, 2002; Mouilso & Calhoun, 2011). Consider the case of Elton Yarbrough in Box 7.2. How many assaults did he commit until he was finally caught? Why do you think he was able to assault so many women before being prosecuted?

Box 7.2   Repeat Rape on a College Campus

Elton Yarbrough is currently serving time in a Texas prison for felony sexual assault. Although he was only tried on one assault charge, five women accused the former Texas A&M economics major of sexual assault, all of which took place between 2003 and 2006 under similar circumstances. Each woman had passed out after drinking heavily, only to wake up to find Yarbrough having sex with her without her consent. As Lt. Brandy Norris, the lead investigator on the case said, "He's a serial rapist. He was smart enough to know he didn't have to hide in the bushes and grab them as they were walking by." The first woman to accuse him was a friend of a friend; they had chatted on Facebook and played pool together. During Thanksgiving break in 2004, Yarbrough did not take the hint from her and her roommate to leave their off-campus apartment. They all fell asleep after a night of drinking, and the woman woke up to find him on top of her, having sex with her. She screamed and demanded he leave, and he did. Her roommate called 911. News of his arrest led three other women to testify that Yarbrough had sexually assaulted them prior to this incident. One of them was a friend of Yarbrough's from his hometown who had consensual sex with him once, but on another occasion, when they were playing drinking games together in 2003, told him that she did not want to have sex with him; she passed out after drinking, and when she woke up, she found him assaulting her. A third woman was a friend of one of Yarbrough's friends. She was in her first year of college in 2004 when she got very drunk at a local bar, passed out at

(Continued)

(Continued)

Yarbrough's off-campus fraternity house, and woke up to find him performing oral sex on her. One month following this incident, Yarbrough raped a friend of a fraternity brother's girlfriend. She had been drinking beer and punch made with grain alcohol; she went to sleep with friends in the common room of the fraternity house, only to awake to find Yarbrough having sex with her. The final woman to formally accuse Yarbrough said she was assaulted by him when he was out of jail on bail. She was his coworker at a local restaurant and went to a party at his apartment. After playing drinking games, she passed out on a sofa, and when she woke up, Yarbrough was assaulting her (Peebles & Lombardi, 2010).

The research also shows that men can be victims of sexual aggression, often by female perpetrators, although this situation is not widely recognized, possibly because there are many who believe that men cannot really be the victims of sexual aggression, particularly by women (see Larimer et al., 1999, for a discussion). Rates of reported victimization among college men differ depending on the measure used and the time frame studied, with as little as 3.2% of men experiencing a sexual assault within a 2-month time period (Hines et al., in press), to 8.2% within a 6-month time period (Banyard, Ward et al., 2007), to 3.7% since entering college (Krebs et al., 2007), to 20.7% in their lifetimes (Larimer et al., 1999). Rates of incapacitated rape range from 1.9% within a 2-month time period (Hines et al., in press) to anywhere between 3.7% to 5.7% in one's lifetime (Kaysen, Neighbors, Martell, Fossos, & Larimer, 2006; Larimer et al., 1999). Rates of forced sexual intercourse range from 0.6% in a 2-month time period (Hines et al., in press), to up to 12% within the past year (Hines, 2007b), to 0.6% in one's lifetime (Larimer et al., 1999). Obviously, given some of the contradictory results, more research is necessary to ascertain more precise prevalence rates.

What is clear, however, is that college women also report engaging in perpetration against men. Up to 28.5% of college women have reported engaging in some type of sexual coercion against men (e.g., Anderson, 1998b), with about 5% engaging in sex with someone who did not want to, 0.8% pressuring someone to engage in sex (Larimer et al., 1999), and 1.6% to 7.1% using physical force to engage their male partners in sexual intercourse (Anderson, 1998a). The types of sexual aggression that women reportedly use include verbal persuasion, the use of alcohol, physical force, and threats of force (Anderson & Aymami, 1993; Struckman-Johnson & Struckman-Johnson, 1994). Thus, both women and men indicate that although verbal coercion is the typical means by which college women gain sexual compliance from men, women sometimes use force.

Predictors and Correlates

Predictors of sexual assault among college students can be found at every level of the ecological model, and a summary is presented in Table 7.6. What is important to note is that most of these predictors have been found for situations involving male

Table 7.5 Selected Studies of Sexual Maltreatment Among College Students

Study	Sample	Measure of Sexual Aggression	Rates of Sexual Aggression
Only Women as Victims			
Koss, Gidycz, & Wisniewski (1987)	Representative sample of 6,159 students from 32 colleges	Sexual Experiences Survey (SES), contains 10 behaviorally specific questions to assess women's experiences since the age of 14 with forced sexual contact, verbally coerced sexual intercourse, attempted rape, and rape	• 54% of college women had experienced some kind of sexual assault since age 14 • 15% experienced rape • 12% experienced attempted rape

Himelein (1995)	100 college women were interviewed at incoming student orientation and again 32 months later	Modified Sexual Experiences Survey focusing specifically on dating relationships	• 38% of women had been sexually victimized in dating situations prior to entering college
			  ○ 15% reported unwanted sexual contact
			  ○ 17% reported sexual coercion or attempted rape
			  ○ 6% reported rape
			• 29% of women reported sexual victimization in dating situations since entering college
			  ○ 8% reported unwanted sexual contact
			  ○ 13% reported sexual coercion or attempted rape
			  ○ 8% reported rape

Fisher, Cullen, & Turner (2000),	Nationally representative sample of 4,446 college women attending a 2- or	10 behaviorally specific screener questions regarding completed, attempted, and threatened rape,	• 2.8% of college women reported experiencing a completed and/or attempted rape during the current academic year (avg. 7 months duration)

(Continued)

231

Table 7.5 (Continued)

Study	Sample	Measure of Sexual Aggression	Rates of Sexual Aggression
National Sexual Victimization of College Women Survey	4-year college between Feb. and May of 1997; phone survey	sexual coercion, sexual contact with force or threat of force, and sexual contact without force If yes to any item, incident-specific questions were then asked	• Rate of rape or attempted rape was 35.3 per 1,000 female students • 15.5% reported experiencing any kind of sexual victimization during that academic year (avg. 7 months duration) • 7.7% experienced an incident involving the use of force or threat of force • 11.0% experienced an incident that did not involve force
Humphrey & White (2000)	Demographically representative sample of college women in state-supported universities in the United States (N = 1,569); longitudinal survey with five time points: fall of first year to assess precollege rates; assessed at the end of each Spring semester during their four college years to assess rates	Sexual Experiences Survey For fall of first year, they completed the survey for age 14 through the beginning of college Each spring, they completed it for the past year during each year; women graduated in either 1990 or 1991	*Prior to college:* • 49.5% experienced some form of sexual assault • 14.0% experienced unwanted sexual contact • 15.1% experienced verbal coercion • 7.4% experienced attempted rape • 13.0% experienced rape *First year of college:* • 31.3% experienced some form of sexual assault • 9.6% experienced unwanted sexual contact • 11.5% experienced verbal coercion • 3.8% experienced attempted rape • 6.4% experienced rape *Second year of college:* • 26.8% experienced some form of sexual assault • 7.8% experienced unwanted contact • 11.8% experienced verbal coercion • 2.4% experienced attempted rape • 4.8% experienced rape

Study	Sample	Measure of Sexual Aggression	Rates of Sexual Aggression
			Third year of college: • 25.7% experienced some form of sexual assault • 6.9% experienced unwanted contact • 11.4% experienced verbal coercion • 2.4% experienced attempted rape • 5.0% experienced rape *Fourth year of college:* • 24.2% experienced some form of sexual assault • 7.2% experienced unwanted contact • 11.8% experienced verbal coercion • 1.3% experienced attempted rape • 3.9% experienced rape
Mohler-Kuo, Dowdall, Koss, & Wechsler (2004)	Data from the 1997, 1999, and 2001 College Alcohol Study; random sample of students from 119 4-year colleges; 23,980 college women	Three questions: 1. "Since the beginning of the school year, have you ever had sexual intercourse against your wishes because someone used force?" 2. "Apart from Question 1, since the beginning of the school year, have you had sexual intercourse against your wishes because someone threatened to harm you?" 3. "Apart from Questions 1 and 2, since the beginning of the school year, have you had sexual intercourse when you were so intoxicated you were unable to consent?"	• 4.7% of women experienced any type of rape • 3.4% experienced rape while intoxicated • 1.9% experienced forced rape • 0.4% experienced rape via threats

(Continued)

233

Table 7.5 (Continued)

Study	Sample	Measure of Sexual Aggression	Rates of Sexual Aggression
Lawyer, Resnick, Bakanic, Burkett, & Kilpatrick (2010)	314 female college students from a mid-size college in the Southeast, Spring semester of 2004	Modified version of the Sexual Experiences Survey	• 29.6% reported at least one sexual assault since age 14 • 5.4% reported a forcible sexual assault • 20.7% reported an incapacitated sexual assault (i.e., they had used drugs/alcohol voluntarily) • 3.8% reported a drug-facilitated sexual assault (i.e., used drugs/alcohol at least partially involuntarily)
Only Men as Victims			
Tewksbury & Mustaine (2001)	541 male university students at 12 southern universities in eight states during Fall 1998 academic term	12-item Sexual Assault Scale (Fiebert & Tucci, 1998), time period was within the past 6 months	• 22.2% reported any sexual assault victimization • 8.3% reported serious sexual assault victimization (i.e., involved threats and/or force)
Both Men and Women as Victims			
Ryan (1998)	245 male and 411 female college students (283 were from a 2-year technical college, 373 were from a 4-year liberal arts college)	Sexual Experiences Survey over previous year with current romantic partner	*Women:* 25% reported sexual aggression victimization *Men:* 9% reported sexual aggression victimization
Larimer, Lydum, Anderson, & Turner (1999)	165 male and 131 college students (both male and female) who were pledging a fraternity or sorority at a large West coast, public university	Sexual Experiences Survey, modified to be gender-neutral, over past year	*Women:* • 27.5% reported at least one type of victimization • 8.4% reported unwanted sexual intercourse • 6.1% reported being pressured to engage in sexual intercourse • 4.6% reported being physically forced into sexual intercourse

Study	Sample	Measure of Sexual Aggression	Rates of Sexual Aggression
			• 16.8% reported someone attempted to use alcohol/drugs to get them to engage in sexual intercourse • 6.1% reported someone used alcohol/drugs to get them to engage in sexual intercourse *Men:* • 20.7% of men reported at least one type of victimization • 13.4% reported unwanted sexual intercourse • 7.9% reported being pressured to engage in sexual intercourse • 0.6% reported being physically forced into sexual intercourse • 9.2% reported someone attempted to use alcohol/drugs to get them to engage in sexual intercourse • 3.7% reported someone used alcohol/drugs to get them to engage in sexual intercourse
Kaysen, Neighbors, Martell, Fossos, & Larimer (2006)	Prospective study of a randomly selected sample of 1,238 college students (406 men, 832 women) at three West coast campuses, who participated in three years of data collection	Incapacitated rape: "Have you ever been pressured or forced to have sex with someone because you were too drunk to prevent it?"	*Women:* • 10% ever experienced an incapacitated rape *Men:* • 5.7% ever experienced an incapacitated rape

(Continued)

Table 7.5 (Continued)

Study	Sample	Measure of Sexual Aggression	Rates of Sexual Aggression
Banyard, Moynihan, & Plante (2007)	225 male and 408 female college students at a large university in the Northeast	How many times during the current academic year (past 6 months) did someone have sexual contact with you when you didn't want it? Sexual contact = attempting or actually kissing, fondling, or touching someone in a sexual or intimate way, excluding sexual intercourse	• 19.6% of women reported unwanted sexual contact • 8.2% of men reported unwanted sexual contact
Hines (2007b), International Dating Violence Study	1,602 women and 715 men in 13 U.S. universities; limited to students in heterosexual dating relationships	Sexual Coercion Scale of the Conflict Tactics Scales (Straus, Hamby, Boney-McCoy, & Sugarman, 1996)	*Women:* • Between 0% and 7.2% reported forced sex in their relationships within the past year • 17.0% to 46.7% reported unwanted verbally coerced sexual intercourse *Men:* • Between 0% and 12.0% reported forced sex by a dating partner within the past year • 9.3% to 50% reported unwanted verbally coerced sexual intercourse

Study	Sample	Measure of Sexual Aggression	Rates of Sexual Aggression
Krebs, Lindquist, Warner, Fisher, & Martin (2007), Campus Sexual Assault Survey	6,821 (5,446 female, 1,375 male) undergraduate students, randomly sampled from two large public universities in South and Midwest; anonymous web-based survey administered in Winter 2006	Participants answered the following four gateway questions: 1. "Has anyone had sexual contact with you by using physical force or threatening to physically harm you?" 2. "Has anyone attempted but not succeeded in having sexual contact with you by using or threatening to use physical force against you?" 3. "Has someone had sexual contact with you when you were unable to provide consent or stop what was happening because you were passed out, drugged, drunk, incapacitated, or asleep?" 4. "Have you suspected that someone has had sexual contact with you when you were unable to provide consent or stop what was happening because you were passed out, drugged, drunk, incapacitated, or asleep?"	*Women Since Entering College:* • 12.6% reported attempted sexual assault • 13.7% reported completed sexual assault • 5% reported forced sexual assault • 3.4% reported forced rape • 11% reported incapacitated sexual assault • 8.5% reported incapacitated rape *Men Since Entering College:* • 2.4% reported attempted sexual assault • 3.7% reported completed sexual assault • 0.7% reported forced sexual assault • 3.4% reported incapacitated sexual assault

(Continued)

237

Table 7.5 (Continued)

Study	Sample	Measure of Sexual Aggression	Rates of Sexual Aggression
Hines, Armstrong, Palm Reed, & Cameron (in press)	1,916 students (535 male, 1,381 female) from a small Northeastern university, surveyed anonymously in 2008, 2009, and 2010	Six items to measure unwanted sexual contact and unwanted sexual intercourse, due to excessive intoxication, threats, or physical force, during the first two months of each academic year	*Women:* • 6.6% experienced at least one act of sexual assault • 3.3% were the victims of forced sexual contact • 0.5% were the victims of threatened sexual contact • 3.7% were the victims of sexual contact when too intoxicated to consent • 0.4% were victims of forced sexual intercourse • 0.4% were victims of threatened sexual intercourse • 1.8% were victims of sexual intercourse when too intoxicated to consent *Men:* • 3.2% experienced at least one act of sexual assault • 0.7% were the victims of forced sexual contact • 0.6% were the victims of threatened sexual contact • 1.5% were the victims of sexual contact when too intoxicated to consent • 0.6% were victims of forced sexual intercourse • 0.4% were victims of threatened sexual intercourse • 1.9% were victims of sexual intercourse when too intoxicated to consent
Only Men as Perpetrators			
Koss et al. (1987)	Representative sample of 6,159 students from 32 colleges	Sexual Experiences Survey Men completed only the perpetrator version of the questionnaire	• 25% of college men reported committing some form of sexual assault since age 14 • 7.7% reported committing rape since age 14

Study	Sample	Measure of Sexual Aggression	Rates of Sexual Aggression
Abbey, McAuslan, Zawacki, Clinton, & Buck (2001)	343 male undergraduates at a large, urban, commuter university; median age of 21 years	Modified 12-item version of the Sexual Experiences Survey (2 additional items addressed sexual assault when consent could not be given due to incapacitation)	• 33% reported perpetrating some form of sexual assault • 78% of those who committed a sexual assault committed a sexual assault more than once • 10% reported coerced sexual intercourse • 3% reported attempted rape • 5% reported rape • 100% involved women they knew
Lisak & Miller (2002)	1,882 college men at a mid-sized, urban commuter university, attending school there between 1991 and 1998	Abuse Perpetration Inventory; contains four behaviorally specific questions regarding rape and attempted rape	• 6.4% of men committed rape or attempted rape *Of these:* • 80.8% committed rape or attempted rape on women who were too intoxicated to consent • 17.5% used threats or overt force in attempted rape • 9.2% used threats or overt force in rape • 10% used threats or overt force to coerce oral sex • 63.3% of the perpetrators committed rape and/or attempted rape more than once (average: 5.8) • 76 repeat rapists accounted for 439 rapes or attempted rapes
Krebs et al. (2007), Campus Sexual Assault Survey	6,821 (5,446 female, 1,375 male) undergraduate students, randomly sampled from two large public universities in South and Midwest; anonymous web-based survey administered in Winter 2006	See Krebs et al., (2007) above. Men were asked about both perpetration and victimization; women were asked about victimization only	• 1.8% of men reported perpetrating a completed sexual assault since entering college • All but one of these were incapacitated sexual assaults

(Continued)

239

Table 7.5 (Continued)

Study	Sample	Measure of Sexual Aggression	Rates of Sexual Aggression
Mouilso & Calhoun (2011)	296 men from a large Southeastern university	Sexual Experiences Survey, Male-Perpetrator Version	• 22.6% reported perpetration of some form of sexual assault since age 14 • 4.4% reported committing completed rape
Thompson, Koss, Kingree, Goree, & Rice (2011)	652 men at a large Southeastern university tested at two time periods: March–April 2008 when they were freshmen and again in March–April 2009	Revised Sexual Experiences Survey (Koss et al., 2007); participants were classified according to the most severe type of act they perpetrated	*Wave 1: Between August 2007 and March/April 2008:* • 2.3% reported perpetrating unwanted sexual contact • 3.3% reported perpetrating sexual coercion • 1.2% reported attempted rape • 4.3% reported completed rape *Wave 2: Between August 2008 and March/April 2009:* • 4.9% reported sexual coercion • 1.8% reported attempted rape • 4.9% reported completed rape
Only Women as Perpetrators			
Anderson (1998b)	212 women from three colleges in and around New York City; 249 women from a midsized commuter university in Louisiana	26-item Sexually Aggressive Behaviors Scale Sexual coercion = behaviors that were meant to trick or pressure someone verbally or psychologically to have sex Sexual abuse = using a position of power or authority to induce someone to have sex Physically forced sex = the threat or use of physical force to get someone to have sex Participants were asked if they had *ever* used these behaviors	New York City: • 28.5% engaged in sexual coercion • 21.1% sexual abuse • 7.1% physically forced sex Louisiana: • 25.7% engaged in sexual coercion • 7.3% sexual abuse • 1.6% physically forced sex

Study	Sample	Measure of Sexual Aggression	Rates of Sexual Aggression
Both Men and Women as Perpetrators			
Ryan (1998)	245 male and 411 female college students (283 from a 2-year technical college, 373 from a 4-year liberal arts college)	Sexual Experiences Survey over previous year with current romantic partner	*Women:* 2% reported sexual aggression perpetration *Men:* 10% reported sexual aggression perpetration
Larimer, Lydum, Anderson, & Turner (1999)	165 male and 131 college students (both male and female) who were pledging a fraternity or sorority at a large West coast, public university	Sexual Experiences Survey, modified to be gender-neutral, in past year	*Women:* • 5.3% of women reported at least one type of perpetration • 4.6% reported unwanted sexual intercourse • 0.8% reported pressuring someone to engage in sexual intercourse *Men:* • 10.3% of men reported at least one type of perpetration • 3.7% reported unwanted sexual intercourse • 2.4% reported pressuring someone to engage in sexual intercourse • 0.6% reported using physical force • 4.9% reported attempting to use alcohol/drugs to get someone to engage in sexual intercourse • 2.4% reported using alcohol/drugs to get someone to engage in sexual intercourse
Sabina & Straus (2008), International Dating Violence Study	4,533 undergraduate college students (1,473 men, 3,060 women) in 19 sites across the United States	Conflict Tactics Scales over previous 12 months	*Men:* • 28.7% perpetrated sexual coercion • 2.5% perpetrated severe sexual coercion *Women:* • 27.8% of women perpetrated sexual coercion • 2.2% perpetrated severe sexual coercion

Table 7.6   Predictors of Sexual Assault Among College Students

Level of Ecological Model	Predictor	Study
Macrosystem	Stereotype that rape is committed by strangers	Lisak & Miller (2002); Salter (2003)
Exosystem	College environment that promotes heavy drinking and sexual activity while drinking	Mohler-Kuo, Dowdall, Koss, & Wechsler (2004)
	Associations with peer groups that approve of rape	Abbey, McAuslan, Zawacki, Clinton, & Buck (2001); Seto & Barbaree (1997); Thompson, Koss, Kingree, Goree, & Rice (2011)
Microsystem	Situations involving alcohol	Abbey, McAuslan, & Ross (1998); Abbey et al. (2001); Abbey, Ross, McDuffie, & McAuslan (1996); Fisher, Cullen, & Turner (2000); Harrington & Leitenberg (1994); Hines et al. (in press); Koss (1988)
	Alcohol use by victims	Abbey et al. (2001); Fisher et al. (2000); Hines et al. (in press); Parks & Fals-Stewart (2004)
	Victim's prior history of sexual assault	Hanson & Gidycz (1993); Himelein (1995); Hines (2007b); Humphrey & White (2000); Krebs, Lindquist, Warner, Fisher, & Martin (2007)
	Victim's prior history of dating violence victimization	American College Health Association (2004); Hines et al. (in press); Krebs et al. (2007)
	Younger age and lower year in school	Gross, Winslett, Roberts, & Gohm (2006); Krebs et al. (2007); Mohler-Kuo et al. (2004)
	Nonassertive resistance techniques	Norris, Nurius, & Dimeff (1996)
	Greater number of sexual partners	Krebs et al. (2007)
Individual/ Developmental	Childhood history of abuse	Casey, Beadnell, & Lindhorst (2009); Forbes & Adams-Curtis (2001); Seto & Barbaree (1997)
	Poor relationship with one's father	Lisak & Roth (1990)
	Juvenile delinquency	Casey et al. (2009); Seto & Barbaree (1997)

Level of Ecological Model	Predictor	Study
	Psychopathic, antisocial, and narcissistic personality traits	Kosson, Kelly, & White (1997); Mouilso & Calhoun (2011)
	Anger at and dominance over women	Lisak & Roth (1990)
	Hypermasculinity	Lisak, Hopper, & Song (1996); Lisak & Roth (1990)
	Adversarial sexual beliefs, hostility toward women, gender role stereotypes	Abbey et al. (1998); Abbey et al. (2001); Forbes, Adams-Curtis, & White (2004); Koss, Leonard, Beezley, & Oros (1985); Malamuth, Linz, Heavey, Barnes, & Aker (1995); Seto & Barbaree (1997)
	Early and frequent sexual intercourse and dating experiences	Abbey et al. (1998); Abbey et al. (2001); Craig Shea (1998); Kanin (1985); Malamuth et al. (1995); Mouilso & Calhoun (2011)
	Female perpetrators: Low agreeableness, high conscientiousness, high extraversion	Hines & Saudino (2008)
	Female perpetrators: More aggressive and power-oriented, less gender role traditional	Craig Shea (1998)

perpetrators and female victims. Where relevant, we highlight where a given predictor involves other gendered relationships. As you read through these predictors, think about the Yarbrough case from Box 7.2 and how some of these predictors played out in that situation. Also, consider that Yarbrough maintains his innocence, claims that all of the sexual encounters were consensual, and that he may have been promiscuous, but that does not mean he raped the women. He is quoted as saying, "I was pretty promiscuous in college. I don't know too many people who weren't. I guess when you combine a lot of drinking and partying in college you're going to have a lot of sex going on" (Peebles & Lombardi, 2010).

Macrosystem

On a macrosystem level, one of the largest contributors is the stereotypes that people hold about sexual aggression that allows sexual predators to continue their behaviors. A false stereotype is that sexual assault is primarily committed by strangers who hide in a dark alley or behind bushes and strike a woman who is walking alone (Salter, 2003). However, as this chapter shows, the large majority of people who commit sexual assault are people who know the victim and target that person because she or he is vulnerable in some way (e.g., intoxicated). Because of this stereotype, only a small fraction of people who are sexually assaulted or raped report their victimization to any authorities, partly because they are unable to define what happened to them as sexual assault or rape (e.g., Fisher et al., 2000) and thus, as criminal. In fact, variables that predict whether a rape will be reported include three of the least common factors during rape: a stranger as a perpetrator, an injury to the victim, and no alcohol involvement (Fisher, Daigle, Cullen, & Turner, 2003). The danger of this stereotype is that it allows perpetrators to hide their behavior and continue to repeat their crimes. This pattern is clearly evident in studies of rape perpetrators (e.g., Lisak & Miller, 2002), in which nonstranger rapists committed a wide range and large number of both sexually and nonsexually violent acts against both intimate partners and children.

Exosystem

The college environment is a major contributor to sexual assault on campus. Both heavy alcohol use (Baer, Stacy, & Larimer, 1991) and sexual activity while drinking (Glenn & Marquardt, 2001) are considered normative and socially acceptable behaviors on campuses. The more normative these behaviors are, the more likely it is that the lines between consensual and nonconsensual sexual activity become obliterated, and sexual assault results (Adams-Curtis & Forbes, 2004). In fact, women who attend universities with high drinking rates are at higher risk for incapacitated rape (Mohler-Kuo, Dowdall, Koss, & Wechsler, 2004).

Much of this behavior is blamed on the Greek systems at some universities, and studies show that sorority membership predicts sexual assault victimization (Copenhaver & Grauerholz, 1991; Kalof, 1993; Mohler-Kuo et al., 2004; Tyler, Hoyt, & Whitbeck, 1998), as does living in a sorority house (Mohler-Kuo et al., 2004). Fraternity men drink more frequently and heavily than nonmembers (e.g., Kilmer, Larimer, Parks, Dimeff, & Marlatt, 1999), and also perpetrate sexual assault more often (Lackie & deMan, 1997; Tyler et al., 1998). However, these associations differ depending on the culture of the fraternity. Members of fraternities that are considered "high risk" (e.g., parties had music that was too loud to allow for conversation, with unequal gender distributions, gender segregation, denigration of women) are more likely to engage in sexual coercion and related behaviors in comparison to members of "low risk" fraternities (e.g., friendly parties, with conversation possible, equal gender ratios, and respect for women) (Boswell & Spade, 1996). Also, once researchers control for alcohol use, the association between Greek membership and sexual assault disappears (e.g., Koss & Gaines, 1993).

It is possible that high risk men seek out high risk social groups, which could account for the associations between high-risk fraternities and sexual assault perpetration. Sexual assault is more common among men who experience peer pressure to engage in sex (Thompson et al., 2011), who perceived their peer groups as being accepting of rape (Thompson et al., 2011), whose friends more strongly approve of forced sex (Abbey et al., 2001; Seto & Barbaree, 1997), and who regularly discuss their sexual behavior with each other (Craig, Kalichman, & Follingstad, 1989; Lisak & Roth, 1988). These friendship groups also place a high value on loyalty to the group, which leads to protective behavior against police and campus authorities who may investigate them (Sanday, 1996).

Microsystem

Alcohol Use. Alcohol use as a predictor of sexual assault has been studied in several ways. In comparison to non-victims, victims of sexual assaults report higher past-month alcohol consumption (Lawyer et al., 2010), higher weekly drinking frequency (Larimer et al., 1999), earlier age at first drink (Larimer et al., 1999; Lawyer et al., 2010), greater number of drinks during a single drinking occasion (Lawyer et al., 2010), greater frequency of binge drinking (Hines et al., in press; Lawyer et al., 2010), recent binge drinking (Howard, Griffin, & Boekeloo, 2008), greater frequency of being drunk (Fisher et al., 2000; Krebs et al., 2007; Lawyer et al., 2010), heavier alcohol consumption (Kaysen et al., 2006), greater number of alcohol-related negative consequences (Larimer et al., 1999), more alcohol dependence symptoms (Larimer et al., 1999), and greater number of hours partying and socializing (Hines et al., in press).

Not only is drinking associated with victimization, but it also prospectively and concurrently predicts sexual assault victimization. Among college women, Parks and Fals-Stewart (2004) found that the odds of experiencing sexual aggression were nine times higher on days of heavy drinking and three times higher on days of non-heavy drinking, in comparison to non-drinking days. At least 50% of college student sexual assaults involve alcohol on the part of either or both the victim and perpetrator (Abbey et al., 1998; Abbey et al., 2001; Abbey, Ross, McDuffie, & McAuslan, 1996; Fisher et al., 2000; Harrington & Leitenberg, 1994; Hines et al., in press; Koss, 1988), and in 81% to 97% of alcohol-related sexual assaults, both the victim and perpetrator had been drinking (Abbey et al., 1998; Harrington & Leitenberg, 1994).

Studies of perpetrators show that sexually aggressive men selectively target drinking or intoxicated women, and they intentionally use alcohol to impair a woman's resistance to their advances (Seto & Barbaree, 1997). In fact, one study found that 75% of college rapists stated that they had purposefully gotten a woman intoxicated to have sexual intercourse with her, and one of the most common strategies was having her play drinking games (Johnson, Wendel, & Hamilton, 1998). Moreover, these sexually aggressive men use their own level of intoxication to diminish their responsibility for their actions (Norris & Cubbins, 1992).

In addition to making victims vulnerable to predators that intentionally target intoxicated people for a sexual assault, alcohol has several biological and psychological effects that alter the victim's and perpetrator's perceptions and behaviors, which in turn, contribute to a sexual assault. Alcohol consumption disrupts higher order thinking processes, such as decision-making, planning, problem-solving, and ability to consider long-term consequences, and leads one to focus on only the things that are salient to that person at that time (see Abbey, 2002). For victims, this process can lead to an inability to detect danger cues, and one experiment shows that intoxicated women report decreased awareness of and discomfort with scenarios associated with greater sexual assault risk, which decreases even further if they had some sort of relationship with the perpetrator (Davis, Stoner, Norris, George, & Masters, 2009). On a more severe level, alcohol's effects on motor skills make it difficult for victims to resist any kind of sexual assault (Larimer et al.,

1999), which is why alcohol is more often associated with completed rape, while sobriety is more often associated with attempted rape (Abbey, 2002).

Alcohol also leads to impaired judgments on the perpetrator's part. Men's beliefs that women's friendly behavior is a sign of sexual interest and that a woman's refusal is a sign that he should try harder become intensified when he is drinking (Abbey, 2002). The more frequently a man misperceives a woman's sexual intentions while he is drinking, the more frequently he sexually assaults women (Abbey et al., 1998), and the longer he believes that she is sexually interested in him and that sex will occur, the more likely it is he will justify using force to have sex (McAuslan, Abbey, & Zawacki, 1998). If their victims are drinking, the situation becomes even more risky. Women who drink alcohol are perceived as more sexually available and promiscuous (George, Cue, Lopez, Crowe, & Norris, 1995), and sexually aggressive men are less likely to believe a woman's lack of consent if she has been drinking (Bernat, Calhoun, & Stolp, 1998). It is important to note that all of this research has been done in situations in which a woman is the victim and a man is the perpetrator, so how well this generalizes to the reverse situation or situations in which perpetrators and victims are of the same sex is unknown. However, we do know that drinking is common during sexual assaults in those situations as well (e.g., Hines et al., in press; Larimer et al., 1999).

Other Aspects of the Situation. Apart from drinking, there are other aspects of a situation that predict sexual assault. The vast majority of sexual assaults among college students occur on dates, at parties, or after parties (Abbey et al., 1998; Abbey et al., 2001; Koss et al., 1987; Krebs et al., 2007). For incapacitated assaults, party settings are especially common (Krebs et al., 2007). Sexual assaults usually occur off campus (Banyard, Ward et al., 2007; Fisher et al., 2000; Krebs et al., 2007), after midnight (Hines et al., in press; Krebs et al., 2007), on Friday or Saturday nights (Krebs et al., 2007), in September and October (Krebs et al., 2007), and in an isolated situation (e.g., back room of a party) (Abbey et al., 2001).

Revictimization. Another microsystem level predictor has to do with the characteristics of the victim. For both male and female college victims, a prior history of sexual assault predicts their likelihood of being sexually assaulted again (Hanson & Gidycz, 1993; Himelein, 1995; Hines, 2007b; Humphrey & White, 2000; Krebs et al., 2007). In comparison to women who were never previously victimized, women who experienced a sexual assault before college are anywhere between 3.7 and 7.9 times more likely to experience a sexual assault in college (Krebs et al., 2007). One longitudinal study of college women (Humphrey & White, 2000) found that the risk of being victimized in college is greatest for women with both childhood and adolescent histories of sexual victimization, followed by women with only adolescent histories of sexual victimization. Women who experienced only childhood sexual assault did not have an increased risk. These results were even stronger for rape in comparison to other kinds of sexual assault.

Why does a prior history of sexual assault contribute to an increased likelihood of sexual assault in college? Several mediating mechanisms have been suggested. Some argue that prior sexual assault contributes to low self-esteem, depression, poor psychological adjustment, and alcohol and drug abuse, all of which make one vulnerable to another sexual assault (Humphrey & White, 2000). What are your thoughts on these and other potential reasons for why a history of prior sexual assault makes ones vulnerable to a future assault? How might that impact the way we think about, prevent, and treat this problem?

Other Victim Characteristics. There are several other victim characteristics that predict victimization. Among women, these include increased number of sexual partners (Krebs et al., 2007), being younger (Mohler-Kuo et al., 2004), and being a freshman or sophomore (Gross, Winslett, Roberts, & Gohm, 2006; Krebs et al., 2007). Female victims of sexual coercion are also more likely to use indirect and less effective forms of resistance, but less likely to use more effective techniques, such as assertive verbal protests and physical resistance (Norris, Nurius, & Dimeff, 1996). For both men and women, being in a relationship (Banyard, Ward et al., 2007), and having a history of dating violence victimization (American College Health Association, 2004; Hines et al., in press; Krebs et al., 2007) and other violent victimization experiences (Howard et al., 2008) puts them at risk for sexual assault victimization. Why do you think these associations between these victim characteristics and sexual assault victimization exist?

Individual/Developmental

Individual/developmental predictors of college male perpetration of sexual assault have been studied extensively, and in addition to the alcohol and peer influences discussed above, such predictors include their childhood and adolescent histories, personality traits and attitudes, and sexual interests.

Childhood and Adolescent Histories. Research consistently shows that college men who sexually assault college women have a history of experiencing childhood physical and sexual abuse (Casey, Beadnell, & Lindhorst, 2009; Seto & Barbaree, 1997). This history also includes witnessing verbal and physical aggression between one's parents (Forbes & Adams-Curtis, 2001) and an extremely poor relationship with one's father (Lisak & Roth, 1990). Such men are also more likely to have engaged in juvenile delinquency (Casey et al., 2009; Seto & Barbaree, 1997). In fact, Casey and colleagues (2009) found that experiencing sexual abuse as a child predicts later sexual aggression at age 22 against a romantic partner, which is partially mediated by early sexual initiation; experiencing child physical abuse predicts later sexual aggression at age 22, which is fully mediated by involvement in delinquent activity. However, more than half of the male perpetrators had no childhood abuse experiences, which means that such abuse, even when mediated by these other predictors, cannot fully explain later sexual aggression.

Personality and Attitudes. Other predictors of male sexual assault perpetration include psychopathic, antisocial, and narcissistic personality traits (Kosson, Kelly, & White, 1997; Mouilso & Calhoun, 2011). Such men display little empathy toward their victims and others (Lisak & Ivan, 1995; Seto & Barbaree, 1997), and seem to feel a need to dominate and control women (Lisak & Roth, 1990). Male perpetrators display high levels of anger toward women (Lisak & Roth, 1990), and endorse statements that justify the rape of women (Seto & Barbaree, 1997). Male perpetrators seem to display "hypermasculinity," which is an exaggeration of male stereotypes, such as physical aggression and calloused sexual attitudes (Lisak, Hopper, & Song, 1996) and which may reflect an underlying marked insecurity about their masculinity (Lisak & Roth, 1990). Related attitudes that predict male sexual assault perpetration include adversarial beliefs about heterosexual relationships (i.e., assumptions that heterosexual sexual relationships are exploitative and manipulative), hostility toward women, acceptance of the use of verbal pressure or force to obtain sex, and traditional gender role stereotypes (Abbey et al., 1998; Abbey et al., 2001; Forbes, Adams-Curtis, & White, 2004; Koss, Leonard, Beezley, & Oros, 1985; Malamuth, Linz, Heavey, Barnes, & Aker, 1995; Seto & Barbaree, 1997).

Sexual Interests. Contrary to popular myth, men who commit sexual assault are not men who experience difficulties meeting or having sex with women. In fact, the opposite is true. Men who commit sexual assault tend to have early and frequent dating and sexual experiences (Seto & Barbaree, 1997), begin having consensual sexual intercourse at an earlier age (Abbey et al., 1998; Abbey et al., 2001; Kanin, 1985; Malamuth et al., 1995), have more sexual partners in their lifetimes (Abbey et al., 1998; Abbey et al., 2001; Kanin, 1985; Malamuth et al., 1995), and have sex more frequently than non-perpetrators (Abbey et al., 1998; Abbey et al., 2001). Such men have been shown to have "unrestricted sociosexuality," which means they are comfortable engaging in sex without commitment or closeness, and thus have a greater number of sex partners (Mouilso & Calhoun, 2011). Given these consistent findings, why do you think the myth persists that men who rape are men who "can't get any"? Why do you think that increased sexual opportunities rather than decreased sexual opportunities predicts male sexual perpetration? Do increased sexual interest, motivation, and opportunity help explain these findings?

College Women as Perpetrators. Preliminary studies on the individual-level predictors of sexual aggression by college women show that these women tend to have the personality traits of low agreeableness, high conscientiousness, and high extraversion (Hines & Saudino, 2008). Similar to male perpetrators, they also tend to have lots of dating experience, have sex with their partners very early in relationships, and have relationships that are characterized by violence, game playing (Craig Shea, 1998), and psychological aggression (Hines & Saudino, 2003). Further, they seem to be more aggressive and power-oriented than women who are not sexually coercive, and they are less traditional in their views about women and relationships. Specifically, they feel that women have the right to express their sexual desires, and see relationships as a means of gaining power, not as a means of expressing tenderness and love (Craig Shea, 1998).

Consequences

The majority of studies assessing the consequences of sexual assault among college students tend to be cross-sectional, which means it is difficult to ascertain whether the stated consequence is truly an outcome of sexual assault or just a correlate. However, one outcome tends to be clear: physical injury. In the NSVCWS, about 20% of the female victims reported an injury as a result of completed or attempted rape, most commonly bruises, black eyes, cuts, scratches, swelling, or chipped teeth (Fisher et al., 2000), with lower rates of injuries for victims of any sexual assault. Similarly, Hines et al. (in press) reported that 5.9% of the male and 5.5% of the female sexual assault victims sustained an injury, including an internal injury, torn vaginal/anal wall, and/or bruises, black eyes, cuts, scratches, or swelling. When alcohol is involved on the part of the perpetrator, it is more likely that a sexual assault will involve penetration and injury (Testa, Vanzile-Tamsen, & Livingston, 2004). However, highly intoxicated victims suffer less injury (Abbey, 2002). In fact, victims of physically forced rape are significantly more likely to report an injury than victims of incapacitated rape (18% vs. 3%) (Krebs et al., 2007).

Both penetration and injury can lead to higher levels of PTSD in the victim (Acierno, Resnick, Kilpatrick, Saunders, & Best, 1999). When alcohol is involved, victims are more likely to blame themselves (Koss, Figueredo, & Prince, 2002; Ullman, 1997), which can lead to avoidance coping strategies, intrusive thoughts (Wegner, Schneider, Carter, & White, 1987), and dysfunctional patterns of self-focus (Snyder & Pulvers, 2001). There is also evidence of a reciprocal relationship between alcohol use and sexual assault (Kaysen et al., 2006), with alcohol use putting one at risk for a sexual assault, which then leads to further alcohol use. For example, both men and women who experience sexual coercion use drinking to cope, which increases their consumption of alcohol and the negative consequences of alcohol use (Fossos, Kaysen, Neighbors, Lindgren, & Hove, 2011).

Other potential consequences include an increased likelihood of cigarette smoking, marijuana use, suicidal ideation, experiencing dating violence in a dating relationship, use of diet pills and vomiting to lose weight, and multiple sex partners (Gidycz, Orchowski, King, & Rich, 2008). Messman-Moore, Coates, Gaffey, and Johnson (2008) showed that college female rape victims and verbal coercion victims report higher levels of sexualized distress, sexual shame, and sexual dysfunction. They also had higher rates of indiscriminate sexual activity. Rape victims reported higher levels of dissociation, higher levels of alcohol use, low self-confidence, identity problems, difficulty with interpersonal boundaries, greater depression, self-criticism, and impaired self-reference. Although the authors conceptualize these as potential consequences, these are cross-sectional studies.

Little work has been done on the psychosocial consequences of sexual aggression against men, but it seems as if the effects are less than those experienced by female victims. In one study on the impact of sexually coercive experiences, about one third of the men reported that they were not upset at all about what happened to them (Struckman-Johnson & Struckman-Johnson, 1998). However, there were several important variables that contributed to whether the men became upset, and there were certainly some men who were very upset about the experience. Variables that predicted poorer outcomes included: being drunk at the time of the incident; not being in a romantic relationship with the woman; and the woman using threats or demonstrating the capacity to harm the man (Struckman-Johnson & Struckman-Johnson, 1998).

Stalking

Scope of the Problem

Some argue that stalking is a variant of intimate partner violence rather than a distinct form (Logan, Leukefeld, & Walker, 2000) (see Chapter 5). Indeed, many stalking tactics involve forms of physical, psychological, and sexual aggression. As with other types of IPV, younger adults are at greatest risk of being stalked compared to other age groups (Black et al., 2011; Tjaden & Thoennes, 1998). Simply being a college student is a risk factor for stalking victimization (Budd & Mattinson, 2000). That is, young adults attending college experience higher rates of stalking than those not attending college. High rates of stalking among college students may be explained by

> the relative relational inexperience of the population, the extent to which relationship norms are in constant flux and evolution, as well as the high degree of relational and geographic mobility of the population, [which] combine to create a potentially volatile mix of relationship misunderstandings and conflicts. (Spitzberg, Cupach, & Ciceraro, 2010, p. 261)

Based on an analysis of available stalking studies, including studies of college students, Spitzberg and Cupach (2007) identified eight types of stalking behaviors, including hyperintimate acts, mediated acts, interactional contacts, surveillance tactics, invasion, harassment and intimidation, coercion and threats, and physical aggression and violence (see Chapter 5 for a more in-depth description of the tactics). Although the frequencies with which college students report experiencing and/or perpetrating stalking behaviors vary by study, the most aggressive and threatening behaviors (e.g., destruction of property, threats to harm or kill the victim) are reported the least (e.g., Amar, 2006; Dutton & Winstead, 2006; Langhinrichsen-Rohling, Palarea, Cohen, & Rohling, 2000). The NSVCWS, a national study of 4,446 randomly selected female college students, found that 41% of victims experienced stalking behaviors 2 to 6 times each week, 13.3% at least once daily, and 9.7% more than once daily (Fisher et al., 2000). A more recent large-scale study of college students found that stalking persisted for an average of 12.47 months (Spitzberg, Cupach, & Ciceraro, 2010); thus, victims experienced a frightening campaign of intrusion, harassment, and intimidation for an average of one year.

Across 18 studies of stalking among college students, Spitzberg and Cupach (2007) found that 21% of students were victims; however, they did not report the percent that were stalked by current or former intimates. Results from the NSVCWS revealed that 13% of the female participants had been stalked since the school year began, with 42.5% stalked by a boyfriend or ex-boyfriend. A more recent study of 1,010 female college students found similar rates; with 11.3% reporting being stalked in the past year and 18% stalked at some point while attending the university (Jordan, Wilcox, & Pritchard, 2007). In this study, however, only 15.7% of the stalkers were a current or former intimate partner. Similar to the state of our knowledge on sexual aggression, it remains unclear what proportion of students are stalked by current or former intimate partners.

Predictors and Correlates

Microsystem

Relationship Characteristics. At the microsystem level, studies indicate that a number of characteristics of the intimate relationship are related to stalking. According to victims, relationships characterized by possessive and dependent love are more likely to involve stalking (Langhinrichsen-Rohling et al., 2000). In contrast to research on physical IPV among college students, stalking occurs most frequently earlier in the relationship (Fisher et al., 2000), and the breakup of a relationship also increases the chances of stalking (Davis, Ace, & Andra, 2000; Dye & Davis, 2003), particularly when repeated breakups occur (Davis et al., 2000). Among a small subsample of female victims of intimate partner stalking (n = 27), 85.2% reported that the stalking occurred only after the relationship ended (Jordan, Wilcox, & Pritchard, 2007). One study found that female college students who experienced denigration and controlling behavior during the relationship were more likely to report being stalked after the relationship ended, thus supporting the notion that stalking is a variant of partner violence (Roberts, 2005).

Victim Characteristics. A number of risk factors for stalking victimization have been investigated among college students. Some research indicates that the gender of the victim is not associated with intimate partner stalking or unwanted pursuit victimization (e.g., Davis et al., 2000; Dutton & Winstead, 2006; Langhinrichsen-Rohling et al., 2000; Logan, Leukefeld, & Walker, 2000), whereas other research has found that men are more likely to be perpetrators (e.g., Bjerregaard, 2000; Williams & Frieze, 2005), and still other research indicates that men are more likely to engage in certain types of pursuit behaviors while women are more likely to engage in others (Alexy, Burgess, Baker, & Smoyak, 2005; Sinclair & Frieze, 2000). In a meta-analysis of research among college students on stalking and related behaviors (e.g., harassment, unwanted pursuit), Spitzberg, Cupach, and Ciceraro (2010) found the ratio of female to male victims was approximately 66% to 27%.

Female college students are at increased risk of being stalked if they frequently go to places that serve alcohol, are from a more affluent family background (Fisher et al., 2000), belong to a sorority, are international students, are in the first year of school, and have been a victim of rape or attempted rape while at the university (Buhi, Clayton, & Surrency, 2008). One study found that American Indian/Alaska Native college women were the most likely to be stalked whereas Asian/Pacific Islander women were the least likely (Fisher et al., 2000).

Unfortunately, the research on predictors and correlates of stalking of college students tends to either analyze data from women only, or to combine data from women and men. Thus, little is known about the characteristics of men that are associated with an increased risk for stalking victimization. To what extent do you think that male victims possess risk factors similar to female victims (e.g., frequent places that serve alcohol, belong to a fraternity, international students)? How might their risk factors differ from female victims?

Individual/Developmental

Research on stalking perpetration among college students has examined a number of correlates at the individual/developmental level. According to victim reports, one study found that intimate stalkers were more likely to have antiso-cial, borderline, histrionic, narcissistic, and paranoid personality characteristics than those who were acquaintances or friends (Spitzberg & Veksler, 2007). College student stalkers are more likely to have an insecure attachment (Davis et al., 2000; Dutton & Winstead, 2006; Langhinrichsen-Rohling et al., 2000; Patton, Nobles, & Fox, 2010), have a need for control (Davis et al., 2000; Dye & Davis, 2003), use psychological abuse and verbal aggression (Davis et al., 2000; Logan et al., 2000), be distressed over the breakup (Dutton & Winstead, 2006), and have problems with anger and jealousy (Dutton & Winstead, 2006; Dye & Davis, 2003; Langhinrichsen-Rohling et al., 2000; Patton, Nobles, & Fox, 2010). To what extent are these characteristics similar to those exhibited by people who perpetrate other forms of IPV? Why do some abusive individuals stalk their current or former partners while others do not? Why do some stalkers never engage in other forms of IPV?

Consequences

As a crime of intimidation and psychological terror, victims of stalking often suffer devastating consequences (National Center for Victims of Crime (NCVC), 2007). However, most research investigates the potential consequences of stalking only in female college students. Little research has investigated the consequences that college male victims suffer at the hands of a female stalker; male victims are either not included in the studies or their data are combined with those of female victims.

As discussed in Chapters 5 and 6, the effects of stalking can vary depending on the frequency, duration, and severity of the stalking. Cupach and Spitzberg (2004) analyzed 143 studies of stalking (some of them studies of college students), and identified 11 types of consequences, which include negative effects on the victim's overall quality of life, normal behavior patterns, emotional quality of life, rational quality of life, physical health, social life, economic status, and spiritual life. One recent study of female college students found that stalking victims reported experiencing more mental health symptoms (i.e., somatization, depression, hostility) and poorer perceived physical health status than female college students who were not victims (Amar, 2006). Thirteen percent reported being physically injured by their stalker. The most common injuries reported included scratches; sprains, strains, sore muscles, or pulls; and bruises, welts, black eyes, swelling, or "busted" lips.

The most frequent responses to stalking victimization include avoiding or trying to avoid the stalker (43.2%) and confronting him or her (16.3%) (Fisher, Cullen, & Turner, 2002). Less frequently, victims reported moving their residence (3.3%), dropping a class the person was in (1.4%), quitting their job (0.8%), or changing universities or colleges (0.4%). Nearly 3% sought psychological counseling and 5.6% became less trustful or more cynical of others. Nearly 4% traveled with a companion and 1.9% bought a weapon. This study did not differentiate between the different types of stalkers. Do you think that victims will respond to intimate partner stalkers differently than they would to stranger or acquaintance stalkers? Would they, for example, be more likely to experience psychological distress or physical assaults?

Prevention/Intervention

The majority of prevention efforts for college students focus on issues of sexual assault, although many could be tailored to include issues of physical and psychological maltreatment and stalking as well (Hines & Palm Reed, 2011). This focus is likely due to Title IX regulations that mandate that colleges engage in sexual violence prevention on their campuses.

Issues with Programming for Physical and Psychological Maltreatment. When programming does exist for physical and psychological maltreatment within college student dating relationships, the problem is the same as what we noted in Chapters 5 and 6: They tend to be based on a feminist conceptualization of IPV that has little empirical support, particularly among college students. As we noted above, in this age group, at least half of the maltreatment is committed by women, and bidirectionality is the most common type of violent relationship. Nonetheless, organization, staffing, and funding of almost all college student IPV programs are wedded to the feminist model, and programs that attempt to move beyond this model risk being denied funding and/or ostracized (see Medeiros & Straus, 2006).

Straus (2008a) argues that we need to move beyond the feminist conceptualization of IPV and replace the assumption in prevention/intervention programs that IPV is primarily committed by men against women. He argues that we need to consider issues of bidirectional violence and how it is the most likely to escalate and result in injury, and the least likely to cease. We need to understand the multidimensional and multicausal nature of IPV, the potential contributions of both parties to the violence, and that the predictors of IPV are largely similar across genders. Finally, we need to pay equal attention to both women and men as both perpetrators and victims (Straus, 2008a). Not doing so hampers our efforts to end IPV because we deliberately ignore half of the perpetrators (Medeiros & Straus, 2006). Paying attention to women as perpetrators is vitally important because cessation of violence by one partner is highly dependent on whether the other partner stops using violence (Feld & Straus, 1989; Gelles & Straus, 1988).

Efforts to Address Stalking on College Campuses. Some researchers and advocates argue that college administrators have ignored stalking as a crime that needs to be addressed on their campuses (Fisher et al., 2000; Fisher et al., 2002). Among 2,438 colleges in a 2002 study, 97% did not mention stalking in their policies (Karjane, Fisher, & Cullen, 2002). However, the situation may be improving, according to a more recent study of the websites of 10 Florida universities with enrollments of 10,000 or more students (Truman & Mustaine, 2009). All 10 universities provided information about stalking on their website, and 90% mentioned stalking in the student code of conduct. Seven of the ten universities had victim service units, the majority of which defined stalking and gave advice on what to do if stalked. Eight had information about stalking on their police department or victim services web pages, with varying amounts of information provided about stalking (e.g., what to do if stalked, safety planning, resources). Some universities provided handouts on stalking, often through the campus police or victim services sites. One university published a victim services newsletter that announced Stalking Awareness Month and a "Stop the Stalker" event. The victims' services office of that same university also had stalking information packets available for victims, which include definitions, information on what to do, a sample no-contact statement, and a sample stalking log; these packets, however, were not available online. Results from this study indicate that large universities in Florida are addressing stalking, although the degree to which they do so varies. Do you think you would find similar results at large universities in other states? Do you think smaller universities and colleges are addressing stalking as well as some of the large universities?

Prevention Programs for Sexual Assault. The majority of sexual assault programs focus on providing information, developing empathy, socialization (e.g., gender issues), and/or risk reduction (Anderson & Whiston, 2005). Several meta-analyses have evaluated the overall effectiveness of these programs, and have shown that they have a moderate effect in changing attitudes that support sexual assault (Brecklin & Forde, 2001; Flores & Hartlaub, 1998). In 2005, Anderson and Whiston conducted a more thorough meta-analysis of 69 studies from 1978 to 2002, across a wide range of outcomes, including rape attitudes (e.g., rape myth acceptance), rape empathy, rape-related attitudes (e.g., hostile attitudes toward women, adversarial sexual beliefs), rape knowledge, behavioral intent (e.g., intention to rape or engage in related behaviors), awareness behavior (e.g., changing dating behaviors or volunteering for rape prevention efforts), and incidence of rape. Overall, these programs had the strongest effect on rape knowledge, followed by rape attitudes. Small effects were found for behavioral intent, rape-related attitudes, and the incidence of sexual assault. No effects were found for rape empathy or awareness behavior. These findings also suggested that effects fade over time, and when experimental evaluations are conducted with a treatment control group, the effects may not be that strong in the first place.

In addition to the problems concerning quality of evaluation and limited effectiveness, these programs have been criticized on several grounds, most of which focus on the fact that they typically do not address the developmental stage of college students or the college climate that students are attending. Traditional college-aged students tend to feel invulnerable. Thus, programs that target risk reduction in college women do not consider that most college women feel that they are too smart to get raped, and even though they recognize that getting drunk is a risk factor, they believe they are better at getting drunk than women who have been raped when drinking (Abbey, 2002). The programs also typically do not address some of the college climate issues and norms that contribute to sexual assault discussed previously: drinking heavily and getting drunk, sexual experimentation and engaging in casual sex, that drinking excuses embarrassing behavior, and behaving without inhibition (Abbey, 2002).

A final criticism of these programs is their focus on women as potential victims who are responsible for their own protection or intervention, and men as potential perpetrators whose attitudes and behaviors must be changed. Thus, their message is that only and all men are potential perpetrators, and only and all women are potential victims. These messages create a defensiveness among participants who are resistant to envisioning themselves in their respective roles, which in turn creates resistance to the information being conveyed about sexual assault (Heppner, Humphrey, Hillenbrand-Gunn, & Debord, 1995; Heppner, Neville, Smith, Kivlighan, &

Gershuny, 1999). Moreover, the targeted audience of these programs does not include all potential victims, as many studies (Hines, 2008; Hines & Palm Reed, 2011; Hines & Saudino, 2003) show that both men and women can perpetrate and be the victims of sexual assault, in both opposite-sex and same-sex situations. As a response, community psychologists have argued that we need to adopt approaches that change the system rather than individuals (Swift & Ryan-Finn, 1995), and that target men and women as community members, not as potential perpetrators and victims (Banyard, Plante, & Moynihan, 2004).

One such primary prevention program is the bystander program (Banyard, Moynihan, & Plante, 2007; Banyard et al., 2004; Hines & Palm Reed, 2011). Through mobilization and education of potential bystanders, bystander models focus on wider audiences and aim to change community norms regarding sexual assault. Instead of approaching men as potential perpetrators and women as potential victims, bystander programs approach both as potential bystanders of a sexual assault. Participants are trained in small groups to safely intervene at various stages to prevent a sexual assault from occurring (e.g., when someone makes a sexist joke; when they see someone carrying an obviously intoxicated person upstairs), or to help someone who has been sexually assaulted. Participants are also provided information about sexual assault and programs on campus and in the immediate community to use to help in a bystanding situation. This approach reduces the resistance to sexual assault prevention information of other programs because the participants do not have to picture themselves as perpetrators or victims. They, instead, picture themselves as helpers and allies in reducing the problem of sexual assault (Banyard et al., 2004; Katz, 1994).

Evaluations of bystander programs are promising, with evidence of changes in attitudes toward sexual assault (Banyard, Moynihan et al., 2007; Ward, 2001) and willingness to help (Banyard, Moynihan et al., 2007), increased empathy for the victim (Foubert, 2000; Foubert & Marriott, 1997), and increased knowledge about sexual assault and actual helping behaviors in sexual assault bystanding situations (Banyard, Moynihan et al., 2007). These effects persist over a 12-month period (Banyard, Moynihan et al., 2007). When extending this model to physical IPV prevention, Hines and Palm Reed (2011) found that, in addition to the above findings, the rates of physical IPV on a college campus significantly decreased two years after the institution of a bystander program, while rates of help-seeking among victims increased. Consider again the Yeardley Love case from the beginning of this chapter and the information presented in Box 7.1. Also consider that a former player who knew Love well said that other players were reluctant to intervene in their relationship stating, "I mean, we ate at the same tables, we trained in the same facility, we all hung out together. No one was about to say something" (CBSNews, 2010; Sampson, 2012; Wertheim, 2010). How could a bystander program have helped to prevent Love's murder? Who were the many bystanders who could have intervened long before the night of the murder? What could they have done?

Intervention Issues. One of the reasons the bystander model is a popular approach is because it trains the people who are the potential helpers of a sexual assault victim in how to respond properly. Although the majority of victims do not seek formal help for their victimization experiences, many will tell someone about their assault, often a close friend or roommate (Krebs et al., 2007). Thus, the first line of intervention is someone the victim knows, with the next line being more formal sources of support. Although the majority of victims—about two thirds—do tell someone they know, there is still a sizeable minority who do not (Krebs et al., 2007), with men about half as likely to tell anyone as women (Banyard, Ward et al., 2007).

The next most common source of support for sexual assault victims seems to be more formal psychological or social sources, such as victims' centers or mental health counseling, with forced sexual assault victims being more likely to seek out these sources than incapacitated victims. In one study (Krebs et al., 2007), 15.8% of forced sexual assault victims contacted a victims', crisis, or health care center, in contrast to only 7.5% of incapacitated sexual assault victims; 22% of forced sexual assault victims sought psychological counseling, while 6% of incapacitated victims sought counseling (Krebs et al., 2007). Again, women were more likely to use these services than men, with women also being more likely to state that they know where these centers are located and to access them for programming (Banyard, Ward et al., 2007). Overall, victims seem to be satisfied with these agencies: Of victims who used these types of agencies, 70.3% of forced sexual assault and 83.6% of incapacitated sexual assault victims were satisfied with the way their reporting was handled, while 11.4% of forced sexual assault victims and 0.8% of incapacitated sexual assault victims regretted their report to these agencies (Krebs et al., 2007).

The least likely source of help seems to be law enforcement, with only 5% or less of rape or attempted rape victims in college reporting their assaults to the police (Fisher et al., 2000; Koss et al., 1987). These rates are lowest among victims of incapacitated rape (Fisher et al., 2003; Krebs et al., 2007). Factors that seemed to inhibit reporting of the assault included the feeling that the assault was not serious enough (56%–67%), it was unclear that a crime was committed or that harm was intended (~35%), and the victim did not want anyone to know (29%–42%) (Fisher et al., 2003; Krebs et al., 2007). Moreover, victims seemed to have mixed feelings when they do report to law enforcement. Of the victims of forced sexual assault who reported the assault to law enforcement, 32.1% were satisfied with the way the report was handled, and 17.2% regretted making the report (Krebs et al., 2007). One reason for the dissatisfaction may be that some police officers discourage a victim from reporting by telling the victim that a cross-examination will be grueling or that his or her identity is likely to be leaked during a trial (Campbell, 2009).

Also consider what happened to one of the victims in the Yarbrough case. The day after she was raped, she went to the student health center. As she recounts, "When I went and I did my rape kit, the lady said, 'Well, were you drunk?'—like, 'It's your fault because you were drinking.' It made me feel bad. She gave me a pamphlet, and she said, 'You can go talk to a counselor on campus about this.'" After this experience, the victim told only three other people about the rape. She ended up transferring out of Texas A&M after her grades dropped as a result of the rape, and she says, "I haven't been able to really trust anybody since then" (Peebles & Lombardi, 2010). Such responses are still seen among medical personnel (Campbell, 2008) and exacerbate the psychological consequences of sexual assault victimization (Kaukinen & DeMaris, 2009). As a response to this problem, Sexual Assault Nurse Examiner (SANE) programs have been established across the country. SANE programs use highly trained nurses to gather evidence from sexual assault victims in the hospital, while also attending to the victim's psychological, legal, and other medical needs. Overall, although the response to female sexual assault victims is getting better, most officials still show little concern over male victims' sexual assault experiences (Krienert & Fleisher, 2005).

Similar to rape victims, few stalking victims report their victimization to formal sources of support; research indicates that less than 20% of college student stalking victims report their victimizations to police, campus law enforcement officials, or university officials (Fisher et al., 2002; Haugaard & Seri, 2003; Langhinrichsen-Rohling et al., 2000). Only 3.3% of female victims in the NSVCWS filed a grievance or initiated disciplinary action with university officials (Fisher et al., 2002) and only 3.9% sought a protective order (Fisher et al., 2000). Female victims appear to be more likely to report victimization than male victims (Bjerregaard, 2002). Similar to victims of sexual assault and physical IPV, stalking victims are more likely to turn to informal than formal sources of support. One study found that about half of female stalking victims sought help, and among those who did seek help, 90% of them sought help from friends, 29% from parents, 12.2% from residence hall advisors, and 7.3% from police (Buhi, Clayton, & Surrency, 2008). Victims do not report their victimization to police for a number of reasons, including the belief that their victimization is not a police matter, the behaviors are not serious enough to report, the police would not take them seriously or do anything, and fear that their stalker will retaliate (Fisher et al., 2002; Tjaden & Thoennes, 1998).

What are other reasons that college students, especially men, do not turn to formal sources of support? Do they think they can handle it themselves? Will they try everything they can to get the stalker to stop before turning to school officials and/or police? Indeed, contacting the police appears to be the last response students choose after more informal responses have failed (Spitzberg, 2002). If the perpetrator is someone with whom they were romantically involved, do you think that plays a role in their reluctance to involve officials?

Summary

This chapter focused on physical, psychological, sexual, and stalking IPV among college students. Although the majority of college students are usually not married or living with their partners, they are at a higher risk for perpetration and victimization from any of these types of IPV than the average person in the general population. That risk declines as they go through their college years and exit college, but by the time students leave college, the majority of them will have experienced at least one type of IPV, with a substantial percentage of those experiencing more than one type. Predictors of IPV come at all levels of the ecological model, and particularly for sexual assault, the college environment itself plays a large role in the perpetration and concealment of an assault. Sexual assault is the most researched type of IPV on the college campus and is often the focus of targeted prevention programs. Such programs have been moderately successful at best, but a new model of programming—called the bystander model—is becoming increasingly popular on college campuses, is showing initial successes in reducing many of the problems that can lead to sexual assault, and can be adapted to include the other types of IPV discussed here as well.

Discussion Questions

1. What is it about the 18 to 24 year old age group that makes them particularly vulnerable to intimate partner violence, sexual assault, psychological maltreatment, and stalking? Is it something about their living environment, social activities, and/or inexperience with intimate relationships?

2. Why do you think that the more egalitarian a man's beliefs are the less physically violent he is toward his partner? What could this say about this individual's upbringing and his identified culture? What implications does this have for primary prevention of intimate partner violence?

3. The presence of alcohol is common in sexual assaults. Why do you think perpetrators rely so heavily on alcohol to perpetrate sexual assault? Why do you think the use of alcohol makes them less responsible in their own eyes and the eyes of their peers?

4. Why do you think that women who suffered sexual abuse as an adolescent are more likely to experience further sexual victimization during their college years? What mechanisms seem to be involved that put her more at risk? Do you think the same findings would apply to male victims if we were to conduct such a study?

5. If more extensive empirical data were gathered on intimate partner maltreatment in same-sex relationships, how do you think the results would differ from data on maltreatment among heterosexual couples? To what extent would the contexts in which the maltreatment took place be similar? Would it depend on whether it was two women in a relationship versus two men?

6. What prevents individuals from intervening in a relationship involving maltreatment of an intimate partner? Are people more or less likely to intervene if they are friends with the victim and/or perpetrator? How does people's reluctance to intervene contribute to the isolation of the victim? How can people be encouraged to intervene?

7. Pressure to adhere to traditional gender roles seems to play a large part in predicting psychological and physical maltreatment for men. If rigid gender roles were to become more flexible, do you think this would result in a significant reduction in intimate partner violence?

8. Do you think that intimate partner violence in a marriage varies significantly from intimate partner violence in dating relationships in terms of the type, frequency, and degree of maltreatment and the effects on victims? Do you think maltreatment in marriage is worse? Why or why not? Are there tactics that perpetrators of dating violence can engage in that perpetrators of marital violence cannot or vice versa?

9. Why are college women more likely to report stalking victimization to the police and other officials than college men? To what extent does this pattern have to do with gender socialization?

Maltreatment in Lesbian/Gay/ Bisexual/Transgender/Queer/ Intersex Relationships

Ann is a lesbian with a PhD who works at a major hospital in Massachusetts. Within 2 months of entering a relationship with Jane, Ann found that Jane was becoming very controlling, dictating where Ann could go and with whom she could spend time, and forbidding Ann to have contact with her former friends. Within 4 months, Jane started threatening Ann, screaming at her, and poking her in the chest if she did anything Jane did not like. The aggression escalated to pushing, shoving, and slapping. When Ann escaped the relationship, Jane started stalking and harassing her at home and work, threatening to beat or kill her (Cabral & Coffey, 1999).

James, who is HIV+, contacted NCAVP [National Coalition of Anti-Violence Programs] seeking emergency housing. James had been in a relationship with his partner for seven years, and in the last three years, his partner had become increasingly abusive, after developing a methamphetamine addiction. His partner would often come home, after days away and proceed to scream at James, calling him trash and telling him that he hoped he would die. He would also physically assault James and steal his HIV medications, using his HIV status to control him and the relationship. James had experienced isolation within his relationship because his partner would not let him have friends outside the relationship. He also limited James's ability to leave the relationship by stealing his disability checks, which made James financially dependent on him (National Coalition of Anti-Violence Programs, 2011, p. 10).

Amy is a 25-year-old, self-identified transgender Latina who had met her partner on the internet when she was living on the west coast. . . . After about a year of a long distance relationship, Amy moved to NYC to be with her partner. Amy soon realized that her partner had lied to her about having his own apartment and that he was renting a room with other men. Amy did not have any friends or family in NYC, and she was in love with her partner, so she decided to stay. Soon after moving in, Amy's partner began to verbally abuse her and began calling her names and telling her that she wasn't a "real woman." The name calling, threats, and harassment escalated over time until it was an everyday occurrence. One evening when Amy wanted to attend a trans-Latina support group at the local LGBTQ Community Center, Amy's partner became physically aggressive and struck her, and told her that if she tried to hang out with those "faggots" again that he would kill her. Amy became increasingly afraid of her partner, especially because she knew there was a gun hidden in the house. Over the course of her relationship, Amy's abusive partner increasingly isolated her from the outside world, refusing to allow her to work or spend time with friends. During the last incident of physical violence, her partner made threats to her that if she left he was going to kill her and pulled out his gun. Amy [escaped] to a homeless shelter. Amy did not feel safe at the shelter, reporting that staff was using transphobic language. Amy decided to leave the shelter and slept on the subway that evening. Amy met another woman on the train that night who told her about the New York City Anti-Violence Project (National Coalition of Anti-Violence Programs, 2011, pp. 11–12).

Conceptions of what it means to be a family have broadened considerably in recent decades in the United States. The nuclear family with a father, mother, and two or more children is no longer the majority family form in this country. One family form that is gaining increasing recognition and acceptance is the same-sex couple, with or without children. Laws are constantly changing, but as of March 2012, six states allow same-sex civil unions (Delaware, Hawaii, Iowa, Illinois, New Jersey, Rhode Island) and five permit same-sex marriage (Connecticut, Massachusetts, New Hampshire, New York, Vermont).

Little research has been conducted on intimate partner violence (IPV) in same-sex relationships, primarily because IPV research has been greatly influenced by the feminist perspective. Feminists, as discussed in Chapter 1, attribute considerable responsibility to patriarchy in explaining IPV, and emphasize the attempts of male perpetrators to exercise power and control over their victims. How well does that perspective apply to the three cases presented at the beginning of this chapter? Does a preoccupation with power and control seem to be at the core of these cases, or are other variables (e.g., substance abuse, stress) equally or more important? What are the implications of these cases for the feminist view of intimate violence as a gendered problem—that is, an attempt by men to retain power and control over their partners by any means? Do any of the other theories described in Chapter 1 throw additional light on the dynamics of these cases? Proponents of the view that violence is not a gendered problem, but a human problem, have pointed toward the little research conducted on violence in lesbian and gay relationships to support their view that male privilege is not at the heart of all IPV. Consider the "human problem" view—does violence in LGBTQI intimate relationships challenge the feminist perspective, as they claim? In what ways?

Scope of the Problem

One of the problems in identifying the rates of maltreatment in LGBTQI intimate relationships is a lack of consistency in the terms and definitions used. In this chapter, we use terms and definitions that have been accepted by social science organizations. Typically, the terms *lesbian* and *gay* have become familiar terms that apply to women who have sex with women (WSW) and men who have sex with men (MSM), respectively. The term *bisexual,* referring to individuals who have sex with both women and men, is also familiar. In general, these are the preferred terms today, as compared to the older term, *homosexual,* with its negative connotations. A less familiar term, *transgender,* can be found in the titles of most self-help and social service groups serving sexual minorities, as well as in much of today's literature on individuals who do not fit neatly under the heterosexual label. *Transgender* is sometimes restricted in its use to "individuals who have a persistent and distressing discomfort with their assigned gender" and who "were born anatomically as one biological sex but live their lives to varying degrees as the opposite sex" (Clements-Nolle, Marx, Guzman, & Katz, 2001, p. 917). More typically, it also includes *transvestites* (i.e., cross-dressers) and *intersexed* individuals (i.e., hermaphrodites, born with biological features of both sexes) (e.g., Lombardi, 2001). In this chapter, consistent with the language of organizations in the field, we use the term LGBTQI (lesbian/gay/bisexual/transgender/ queer or questioning/intersex) to refer to the large and diverse group of individuals who have a minority sexual orientation or identity. Although individuals who identify as transgender and intersex are included in this term, very little research has been conducted on their experiences with IPV. Thus, most of the research discussed in this chapter focuses on the experiences of lesbians and gay men.

Although these are the definitions we use in this chapter, it is important to note that different studies use different definitions of LGBTQI when studying family violence. In some studies, participants are asked to self-identify their sexual orientation. In others, participants are considered LGBTQI if they are currently in a same-sex relationship. In still others, participants only need to have been in a same-sex relationship at some point to be considered LGBTQI. Consider how these differing definitions can influence who would be considered LGBTQI in studies on IPV. Someone could currently be in a same-sex relationship, but later consider it experimentation and eventually establish a long-term heterosexual relationship. Someone may self-identify as LGBTQI, but may not yet have been involved in a same-sex sexual relationship. Others may self-identify as heterosexual, but several months or years later realize that they are lesbian/gay/bisexual. Different studies, based on their own definitions of LGBTQI, may include or exclude individuals in each of these scenarios, and this determination can, in turn, influence the estimated rates of IPV in this community. Thus, obtaining accurate data on the prevalence of IPV in LGBTQI individuals is a difficult process.

In addition, as noted in Chapter 1, until recently, members of the LGBTQI community were reluctant to disclose any information about relationship violence because of fears of further stigmatization. As long as there exists a stigma associated with being LGBTQI, an accurate assessment of the prevalence of same-sex IPV is not possible (Renzetti, 1997). Further, as previously mentioned, mainstream family violence researchers typically have not investigated LGBTQI relationships—in part because of prevailing theoretical perspectives not accommodating the idea of women battering other women, and because of the view that violence between male intimates is violence between equals, and therefore not abusive.

Given recent interest, there are a growing number of studies providing estimates of the prevalence of violence within same-sex relationships. All of these studies have serious methodological limitations, thereby compromising efforts to obtain precise estimates of LGBTQI IPV. For example, the National Violence Against Women Survey (NVAWS) (Tjaden & Thoennes, 2000a) provided no direct evidence on the frequency of IPV experienced by individuals in same-sex relationships. Besides the National Crime Victimization Survey (NCVS) and the National Epidemiological Survey on Alcohol and Related Conditions (NESARC), other national data sources are, in general, service agencies with LGBTQI clients or criminal justice system reports, and in both cases the samples are not representative of the LGBTQI community at large—for example, clients who voluntarily seek help may be more open about their sexual orientation and gender identity than other LGBTQI individuals. Finally, most studies providing information concerning the frequency with which different kinds of IPV occur in LGBTQI relationships are relatively small and nonrepresentative. Nevertheless, taken as a whole, the studies provide clear documentation that IPV is just as pervasive in LGBTQI relationships as in other intimate partner relationships—and perhaps even higher.

Rates of Maltreatment in LGBTQI Relationships in National Studies

Two large-scale nationally representative studies (i.e., NVAWS, NCVS) provide some information about maltreatment in LGBTQI relationships. The NVAWS included an item where respondents indicated whether they had *ever* lived with a same-sex partner as part of a couple. Rates of IPV were then compared between respondents with a history of same-sex cohabitation and those reporting only opposite-sex cohabitation. These comparisons revealed significantly more IPV in the same-sex cohabitants than in the opposite-sex cohabitants. However, the victimized women in same-sex intimate relationships were not typically victimized by their same-sex partners. Rather, IPV against both male and female partners was most commonly perpetrated by men (Tjaden & Thoennes, 2000a). The NVAWS also investigated sexual assaults. The results indicated that men were more likely to be raped by strangers and acquaintances whereas same-sex cohabiting women were more likely to be raped by intimate partners, though it was not reported how many of the partners of the same-sex cohabiting partners were of the opposite sex (e.g., former husband, boyfriend). The study also found that 42.9% of female same-sex cohabitants were raped by an intimate partner, compared to 48% of female opposite-sex cohabitants (Tjaden, Thoennes, & Allison, 1999).

Based on NCVS data for 1993 to 1999, each year an average of 13,740 men and 16,900 women in same-sex relationships reported being victims of IPV (Cameron, 2003). Rates of maltreatment found in this study were substantially higher among

LGBTQI participants; 5.8% of women and 4.6% of the men in same-sex partnerships were victims of IPV annually, compared with 0.24% of married women and 0.04% of married men.

One important source of information on reported cases of IPV in LGBTQI relationships is the annual report of the National Coalition of Anti-Violence Programs (NCAVP). Based on information from 15 agencies serving LGBTQI and HIV-affected victims of IPV from the Pacific Coast, West, Midwest, and Northeast regions, the 2010 annual report documented 5,052 cases of LGBTQI intimate violence, a 38.1% increase from 3,659 in 2009 (National Coalition of Anti-Violence Programs, 2010). This increase is attributed to an increase in reports from an agency in Los Angeles, California, that received additional funding for its programming. Of the LGBTQI victims in 2010, 45.7% were female, 36.8% male, 4.2% transgender, and 1.7% "self-identified." This study is valuable because it provides data on the magnitude and relative distribution of IPV in the LGBTQI community; however, the reported numbers are largely a function of evolving programming and organizational capacities, and are not necessarily representative of LGBTQI intimate violence in the United States because the estimates are derived solely from LGBTQI individuals who use these services.

Results from the 2004 to 2005 wave of the NESARC assessed rates of IPV among a nationally representative sample of 34,653 adult U.S. residents (Roberts, Austin, Corliss, Vandermorris, & Koenen, 2010). The study assessed participants' sexual orientation based on three dimensions: identity (heterosexual, lesbian/gay, bisexual), sexual attraction (e.g., attracted only to males or only to females, equally attracted to females and males), and the sex of their lifetime sexual partners. Lifetime IPV victimization was the highest among heterosexual women in same-sex sexual partnerships (23.8%), followed by bisexual women (20.2%) and lesbians (16.1%). None of the bisexual men reported being a victim of IPV, whereas 11.5% of the gay men reported such victimization, which was significantly higher than the percent of heterosexual male victims with same-sex sexual partners (4.0%), heterosexual male victims with no same-sex attraction (2.0%), and heterosexual male victims with same-sex attraction but no same-sex partners (1.5%). Similar to the results of the NVAWS, however, it is unclear to what extent women and men were reporting on victimization by someone of the same-sex.

Table 8.1 summarizes the results from large-scale studies of the prevalence of maltreatment in LGBTQI relationships. To what extent do you think these rates are representative of the extent of IPV in LGBTQI relationships? How could researchers improve the accuracy of these estimates?

In the sections that follow, we focus on findings from more geographically limited studies, which typically have less representative samples, but provide more specific information concerning the extent and nature of IPV in LGBTQI relationships.

Rates of Maltreatment in LGBTQI Relationships in Nonrepresentative Samples

There are four major types of evidence concerning the rates at which LGBTQI individuals experience IPV: (1) studies examining self-reported rates of IPV within samples of WSW; (2) studies comparing lesbians (and sometimes bisexual women)

Table 8.1   Prevalence Rates of Maltreatment in LGBTQI Relationships

Study	Description of Sample	Measures/ Definition of Maltreatment	Rates of Maltreatment
Cameron (2003), National Crime Victimization Survey 1993–1999 (NCVS)	Random sample of 12,381 of adults ages 18 to 59	Murder, rape, sexual assault, robbery, aggravated assault, and/or simple assault committed by current or former spouses, boyfriends, or girlfriends	5.8% of women in same-sex relationships reported IPV 4.6% of men in same-sex relationships reported IPV
Tjaden & Thoennes (2000), National Violence Against Women Survey 1995–1996 (NVAWS)	Representative sample of 8,000 women and 8,000 men 18 years old or older in the United States	Modified version of Conflict Tactics Scales (CTS)	11.4% of women who had ever lived with another woman as a couple reported IPV by a female partner 13.8% of men who had ever lived with another man as a couple reported IPV by a male partner
Roberts, Austin, Corliss, Vandermorris, & Koenen (2010), National Epidemiological Survey on Alcohol and Related Conditions 2004–2005 (NESARC)	Nationally representative survey of 34,653 adults 18 years old or older in the United States	One item assessed partner violence victimization	20.2% of bisexual women, 16.1% of lesbians, 11.5% of gay men, and 0.0% of bisexual men were victims of partner violence

with heterosexual women; (3) studies comparing lesbians and bisexual women with gay and bisexual men; and (4) studies of gay and bisexual men, sometimes compared to heterosexual men. Thus, the majority of the studies on this issue concentrate on violence in lesbian relationships. Of the available studies, some involve community samples, and some involve lesbians who were recruited precisely because they were victims or perpetrators of relationship aggression. Each study type has limitations, although in the aggregate, the studies provide a useful supplement to the limited national probability sample and criminal report data. They also provide valuable information on the incidence and dynamics of several different types of aggression in LGBTQI intimate relationships, including physical, psychological, sexual, and stalking maltreatment.

Rates of Physical and Nonphysical Maltreatment in Lesbian Relationships

Studies of physical and verbal aggression in lesbian samples yield a broad range of estimates (West, 2002). More than half of the lesbians recruited at music festivals and through other forms of convenience sampling say a female partner has physically and/or verbally maltreated them (Lie & Gentlewarrier, 1991; Lockhart, White, Causby, & Isaac, 1994; McClennen, Summers, & Daley, 2002). Reports of verbal and psychological maltreatment are sometimes as high as 80% or 90% (Lockhart et al., 1994; Turell, 2000; West, 2002). In a nationwide self-selected sample of 100 battered lesbians, aggressive acts that they frequently or sometimes experienced included being pushed and shoved (75% of the women); hit with fists or open hands (65%); scratched or hit in the face, breasts, or genitals (48%); verbal threats (70%); demeaning comments in front of friends or relatives (64%); having eating or sleeping habits disrupted (63%); and having property damaged or destroyed (51%) (Renzetti, 1989).

Rates of Physical and Nonphysical Maltreatment in Gay Male Relationships

Only two published studies provide information about physical and nonphysical aggression in male same-sex relationships. In a study of 817 MSM, 32.4% of the men reported IPV in a current or past relationship (Houston & McKirnan, 2007). Approximately 20% reported verbal maltreatment, 19.2% reported physical violence, and 18.5% reported unwanted sexual activity. Results also indicated that over half (54%) of the men who reported any history of maltreatment (i.e., physical, verbal, sexual) reported experiencing more than one type.

Using a randomly selected community sample of 69 gay and bisexual men, Stanley, Bartholomew, Taylor, Landolt, and Oram (2006) conducted telephone interviews with gay and bisexual men who reported experiencing at least one episode of violence. They found that 28% reported being the sole recipient of physical violence in their relationship. Fifty percent reported that, at some point in the relationship, both they and their partners had been violent. In some cases, men who were first victimized by their partners became aggressive in response to the violence. One man stated, "After the first year I fought back, but at first, I thought it was my place to be abused" (Stanley et al., 2006, p. 35). Twenty-two percent reported being the sole perpetrator of violence in the relationship. All participants reported experiencing at least some form of emotional maltreatment (e.g., yelling, using harsh language) from their partner, whereas only two participants indicated that they had not perpetrated such maltreatment. The data revealed that participants increased their use of emotional maltreatment as their partner's emotional maltreatment escalated, thus engaging in reciprocal maltreatment. Participants reported a wide range of emotionally aggressive acts; serious ones included destruction of furniture and threats to cause physical harm. When both victim and perpetrator reports were considered, physical and emotional maltreatment were strongly correlated; those who were more violent toward their partner were more likely to use emotional maltreatment as well. Also, the more severe the emotional maltreatment, the more severe the physical violence. Results from this study illustrate the complex nature of IPV in LGBTQI relationships. To what extent do you think IPV is similarly complex among heterosexual couples?

Rates of Sexual Maltreatment in Lesbian and Gay Relationships

Although the general public has long recognized that men are capable of sexual assault, and that some men sexually assault other men as well as women, there has been considerable resistance to the idea that women can sexually assault their partners. Yet women are clearly capable of violent sexual coercion. Consider Maureen's story concerning her partner's jealousy over a male friend of Maureen's:

> On several occasions her jealousy was out of control and she took it out on me sexually, by holding me down on the bed, grabbing my breasts, and trying to force something into my vagina, insisting that "this is what you want from him" or words to that effect. (Girshick, 2002a, pp. 1502–1503)

In contrast with results from the NVAWS, studies of small nonclinical samples indicate that rates of sexual aggression within lesbian relationships may be as high, or higher than, rates of sexual aggression in heterosexual relationships. In a study of sexual assault victimization among college students, 30.6% of lesbians, as compared to 17.8% of heterosexual women, reported having been forced to have sex by a partner against their will (Duncan, 1990). In other samples, between 12% and 48% of lesbians have reported being victims of forced sex, or sexual aggression, by their current or most recent partners (Renzetti, 1992; Turell, 2000; Waterman, Dawson, & Bologna, 1989).

The limited findings on the intimate relationships of gay men suggest that gay men are subjected to forced sex by their partners more often than heterosexual men. For example, among college students, approximately 12% of gay men, as compared to 3.6% of heterosexual men, reported having been forced to have sex by a partner against their will (Duncan, 1990; Waterman et al., 1989). Other estimates of forced sex in gay male relationships range from 12% in past or present intimate relationships (Turell, 2000) to more than 33% over a lifetime (Craft & Serovich, 2005; Houston & McKirnan, 2007; Kalichman et al., 2001).

The risk of HIV/STDs within the LGBTQI community adds another dimension to sexual maltreatment within same-sex relationships. Among a sample of HIV-positive gay men, 27.5% of the men reported sexually coercing a partner, and 33.3% were victims of sexual coercion (Craft & Serovich, 2005). Heintz and Melendez (2006) surveyed 58 LGBTQI victims of partner violence (72% of whom were MSM) and found that 41% reported being forced to have sex at least once. Twenty-eight percent (28%) of the participants felt unsafe asking their partners to use protection. Nineteen percent (19%) reported experiencing sexual maltreatment, 21% physical maltreatment, and 32% verbal maltreatment just for asking their partner to use protection.

Some forms of sexual aggression, such as forced unprotected (particularly anal) sex can have side effects that are particularly problematic in the gay community; that is, these practices can result in the spread of AIDS. Some gay men who use coercive sexual tactics already have AIDS, yet insist that their partners submit to unprotected sex, despite the risks. Consider the dilemma of this gay man:

I am HIV positive because Alex insisted that we have sex without a condom. He told me, "If you love me, you'll do this," even though he knew he could easily infect me. I've been going to a counselor for about six months and I've thought about leaving him but I feel trapped because I am HIV positive. (NCAVP, 2000, p. 26)

Rates of physical, psychological, and sexual maltreatment seem to vary according to the type of sample assessed (e.g., convenience vs. nationally representative). Why do you think these differences emerge? Which type of sample do you think is more reliable in producing estimates? Is it possible for researchers to increase the accuracy of data on rates of maltreatment in LGBTQI relationships? If so, how?

Rates of Stalking in LGBTQI Relationships

Although some studies have investigated same-sex stalking (e.g., Pathe, Mullen, & Purcell, 2000; Purcell, Pathe, & Mullen, 2001), very few have been conducted specifically on same-sex relational stalking. The two national studies that could have provided reliable estimates of stalking victimization rates in the U.S. population failed to adequately assess stalking in the context of same-sex relationships. As noted above, the NVAWS did not directly assess sexual orientation; thus, estimates of stalking are based on reports from participants who had ever lived with someone of the same sex as a couple (Tjaden & Thoennes, 2000a). They found that men who had ever cohabited with a man were significantly more likely to have been stalked at some point in their lifetime (7.7%) than those who had never cohabited with a man (2.2%). Thirty percent (30%) of male victims were stalked by an intimate partner, with most of the men stalked by acquaintances and strangers. Women were more likely to be stalked by an intimate partner than men, but the NVAWS did not compare the stalking experiences of women who had ever cohabited with a woman to those of women who had never cohabited with a woman. The NCVS's Supplemental Victimization Survey (Baum, Catalano, Rand, & Rose, 2009), conducted in 2006, examined rates of stalking and harassment in the United States, but unfortunately participants were not asked about their sexual orientation.

Two studies using convenience samples have specifically investigated same-sex relational stalking. One study of same-sex relationship violence found that 23% of lesbians, 19% of bisexuals, and 17% of gay men reported being stalked by a partner (Turell, 2000). The differences in stalking rates across these three groups were not statistically significant, indicating similar rates of stalking among the three groups. Derlega et al. (2011) conducted a study with a sample of 153 lesbians and gay men who had experiences in which one partner wanted to break up and the other did not. They found that 73.2% of the targets reported that the rejected partners monitored their behaviors, 45.1% reported being followed, 40.8% were watched, and 19.7% reported that the partner showed up at places in threatening ways. Rejected partners also reported engaging in these behaviors but at significantly lower rates (i.e., 46.3% reported monitoring the target's behaviors, 17.5% followed them, 31.3% watched them, and 1.3% showed up at places in threatening ways). Further research is needed to provide more accurate estimates of the prevalence of same-sex relational stalking.

Comparisons of Maltreatment Rates in Lesbians and Gay Men

Although the rates vary widely, there is some evidence that within intimate relationships, lesbians are maltreated at higher rates than gay men. In one study, lesbians reported more physical violence, coercion, threats, shaming, and use of children for control than gay men, and bisexuals reported less maltreatment than lesbians or gay men (Turell, 2000). Waldner-Haugrud, Gratch, and Magruder (1997) found that 47.5% of lesbians and 29.7% of gay men reported being victimized by a partner. Thirty-eight percent (38%) of the lesbians and 21.8% of the gay men reported maltreating a partner. Similarly, the NVAWS found that physical violence was more prevalent among female same-sex cohabitants (76.2%) compared to male same-sex cohabitants (35.7%), although an unknown percent of the violence reported by participants was perpetrated by individuals of the opposite sex (Tjaden & Thoennes, 2000a; Tjaden et al., 1999).

Findings on the relative rates of sexual aggression in lesbian versus gay male relationships are not as clear. For example, some studies show that sexual aggression, including unwanted fondling and penetration, is higher in lesbian (30%) than in gay male (12%) relationships (e.g., Waterman et al., 1989), whereas others show equal rates (e.g., Turell, 2000; Waldner-Haugrud & Gratch, 1997). In these studies, rates of sexual aggression reported by both lesbians and gay men ranged from 12% who reported sexual aggression (Turell, 2000), to approximately 33% who reported unwanted fondling, to over 50% who reported unwanted penetration (Waldner-Haugrud & Gratch, 1997).

Intimate Violence and Transgendered Individuals

There are few data on IPV in relationships where at least one of the members is a transgender—perhaps in part because the number of transgendered individuals is relatively small. Consistent with their low numbers, transgendered individuals constitute only a very small share of the cases of LGBTQI intimate violence. In 2010, transgender cases made up 4.2% of the cases of victimization seen at agencies serving LGBTQI and HIV-affected IPV victims (NCAVP, 2011). The forms of maltreatment to which these individuals are subjected may be fairly extreme. For example, data from the Gender, Violence, and Resource Access Survey released in 1998 in Portland, Oregon, by the Survivor Project indicated that 50% of their transgendered and intersexed respondents had been raped or assaulted by a romantic partner (NCAVP, 2003).

Types of Intimate Partner Maltreatment That Are Unique to LGBTQI Relationships

There are some forms of maltreatment that are either unique to or more likely to occur in LGBTQI relationships than in heterosexual relationships. For example, some perpetrators may threaten to "out" the victim to family, friends, colleagues, and/or employers (Speziale & Ring, 2006). Particularly to a person who is not "out" about her/his sexual orientation or gender identity, such a disclosure in the context of a homophobic society can have serious and long-term negative consequences, including effects on the person's mental health, social life, and employment status (Speziale & Ring, 2006). Further, perpetrators may infect or threaten to infect the victim with HIV (Giorgio, 2002; Knauer, 2001; Letellier, 1996). Some perpetrators challenge the authenticity of victim's identities as a form of control. For example, they may accuse the victim of being heterosexual or not "good enough" at their gender identity (Bornstein, Fawcett, Sullivan, Senturia, & Shiu-Thornton, 2006). Perpetrators may also threaten to limit their partner's involvement in the gay community or discourage them from reporting to avoid shaming the community (Balsam & Szymanski, 2005; Miller, Greene, Causby, White, & Lockhart, 2001; Peterman & Dixon, 2003). These forms of maltreatment create additional barriers that prevent LGBTQI victims from seeking help and/or leaving the relationship.

Special Issue: Child Maltreatment in LGBTQI Families

To our knowledge, there are no studies examining the relative rates of child maltreatment in children growing up with at least one LGBTQI parent as compared to children growing up with one or two heterosexual parents. This is a noteworthy gap in the literature, given estimates that between 6 and 14 million children nationwide live with at least one gay parent (American Civil Liberties Union, 1999), an estimate that has likely increased in the past 10 years. The 2010 U.S. Census found that there were 646,464 individuals in same-sex coupled relationships (Gates & Cooke, 2011). Thirty-three percent (33%) of female same-sex couples households and 22% of male same-sex couples households reported at least one child under the age of 18 living in the home (American Psychological Association, 2004b). The 2010 American Community Survey found that 19.4% of same-sex couples households had children under the age of 18 in their home (Lofquist, 2011). Of those who were married to their same-sex partner, 80% were living with their biological children only, 13.1% were living with step or adopted children, and 6.4% were living with a combination of biological and step/adopted children. Among those who were living with a partner but were not married, 67.4% were living with their biological children only, 26.8% with step/adopted children, and 5.7% a combination (Lofquist, 2011).

Some of these children are from previous heterosexual marriages. Increasingly, same-sex couples are having children through surrogate parenting, artificial insemination, and adoption. Four states have laws expressly barring lesbians and gay men from adopting children (Florida's was overturned as unconstitutional in 2008), and 19 states and the District of Columbia permit LGBTQI individuals to petition for second-parent adoption (Family Equality Council, 2012).

There is substantial evidence that growing up with at least one lesbian or gay parent does not have any ill effects on the child's development (Patterson, 2003). There is no research evidence that lesbians or gay men are unfit parents based on their sexual orientation (Armesto, 2002; Patterson, 2000; Tasker & Golombox, 1997). In fact, the results of some research indicate that lesbian and gay parents may possess better parenting skills than heterosexual parents (American Psychological Association, 2004b). For example, studies have found that gay fathers are no different from heterosexual fathers in terms of intimacy and involvement with their children, but were more consistent in setting limits, and more responsive to their children's needs (Bigner, 1999; Bigner & Jacobsen, 1989, 1992). Given the widespread acceptance of corporal punishment in families with heterosexual parents, as well as the prevalence of child maltreatment in this country, it is important to investigate the level of coercive and/or abusive parenting being used by LGBTQI parents.

Predictors and Correlates

Explanations of maltreatment in LGBTQI relationships place considerable emphasis on macrosystem and exosystem homophobia and homonegativity. Attention has also been given to characteristics of victims that enhance their vulnerability to maltreatment within the microsystem, and to individual/developmental characteristics of perpetrators. Most studies have serious methodological limitations, such as omitting a clear definition of maltreatment, relying on retrospective reports of maltreatment within the lifetime, nonrepresentative samples, and not controlling for potential biases; nevertheless, the findings are useful in identifying pathways for future research and intervention. Table 8.2 summarizes the predictors and correlates of IPV in LGBTQI relationships at different levels of the ecological model.

Table 8.2   Predictors of Maltreatment in LGBTQI Relationships

Level of the Ecological Model	Specific Predictor	Examples of Studies
Macrosystem	Homophobia/ heterosexism	Allen & Leventhal (1999); Balsam & Szymanski (2005); Duke & Davidson (2009); Island & Letellier (1991); Renzetti (1998); Russo (1999)
Exosystem	Harassment at school	Kosciw, Greytak, Diaz, & Bartkiewicz (2010)
	Discrimination in the workplace	Allegretto & Arthur (2001); Baumle, Compton, & Poston Jr. (2009); Baumle & Poston (2011); Berg & Lien (2002); Black, Hoda, Makar, Sanders, & Taylor (2003); Blandford (2003)
Microsystem	Younger age	Greenwood et al. (2002); National Coalition of Anti-Violence Programs (2011)
	Substance abuse	Eaton et al. (2008); Klitzman, Greenberg, Pollack, & Dolezal (2002)
	HIV status among gay men	Shelton et al. (2005); Zierler et al. (2000)
	Borderline personality traits	Landolt & Dutton (1997)

Level of the Ecological Model	Specific Predictor	Examples of Studies
	Insecure/anxious attachment orientation	Landolt & Dutton (1997); Stanley, Bartholomew, Taylor, Landolt, & Oram (2006)
Individual/ Developmental	Childhood victimization	Corliss, Cochran, & Mays (2002); Craft & Serovich (2005); Margolies & Leeder (1995); Roberts, McLaughlin, Conron, & Koenen (2010)
	Intergenerational transmission of violence	Craft & Serovich (2005)
	Alcohol/substance abuse	McClennen, Summers, & Vaughan (2002); Renzetti (1998); Schilit, Lie, & Montagne (1990)
	Personality characteristics (e.g., need for control, low self-esteem, jealousy, anger)	Cruz & Firestone (1998); Margolies & Leeder (1995); Miller, Greene, Causby, White, & Lockhart (2001); Renzetti (1992)
	Dependency	Miller et al. (2001); Renzetti (1992)
	Power and control issues	Eaton et al. (2008); Lockhart, White, Causby, & Isaac (1994); Schilit et al. (1990)
	The other partner's violence	Landolt & Dutton (1997); Lie, Schilit, Bush, Montagne, & Reyes (1991)

Macrosystem

As demonstrated throughout this book, the American macrosystem is quite violent. Children, women, men, and the elderly may all be physically, psychologically, and/or sexually victimized within their closest relationships. However, it is also true that members of some groups within the macrosystem may be victimized more than others, and this victimization may lead to higher levels of violence within their families. Among the groups at heightened risk of societal victimization are immigrants, ethnic minority group members (discussed at length in Malley-Morrison & Hines, 2004), and LGBTQI individuals. Although there is no solid empirical evidence linking macrosystem attitudinal variables with LGBTQI intimate violence, there is extensive theoretical and clinical literature postulating this link.

Macrosystem level values in the United States have long included *homophobia* (fear, disgust, anger, hatred, and intolerance in regard to homosexuality), *homonegativity* (negative attitudes toward LGBTQI individuals), and *heterosexism* ("an ideological system that denies, denigrates, and stigmatizes any non-heterosexual form of behavior, identity, relationship, and community," Herek, 2004, p. 316). These values seem consistent with a society that sanctions aggression toward individuals who violate gender roles. Among the ways in which such fears and attitudes are expressed are hate crimes against individuals presumed to be lesbian, gay, bisexual, transgendered, or intersexed.

Hostility toward lesbians and gay men has a long history in this country. Men were executed for sodomy in the colonies as early as 1624, and lesbians and gay men have been subjected for centuries to various forms of institutional violence, including clitoridectomy and castration, forced psychiatric treatment, and dishonorable discharge from the armed services (Herek, 1989). Recently, there existed sodomy statutes in 13 states that punished individuals for engaging in oral and anal sex. Thus, LGBTQI victims would have had to admit to committing the crime of sodomy in order to obtain legal protection against their maltreating same-sex partner (Aulivola, 2004). In 2003, the U.S. Supreme Court struck down anti-sodomy laws on the basis that the government has no right to intrude on the private and personal lives of its citizens (*Lawrence and Garner v. Texas*, 2003).

There is substantial evidence that macrosystem antigay attitudes are associated with pervasive harassment and victimization of LGBTQI individuals, as well as with discrimination (Herek, Gillis, Cogan, & Glunt, 1997). The 2010 Uniform Crime Report indicated that 18.6% of all hate crimes were committed due to bias against sexual orientation (FBI, 2010c). Of those hate crimes, the most frequent types were simple assault (33.2%), intimidation (22.4%), destruction/damage/vandalism (18%), and aggravated assault (16.6%). In a victimized LGBTQI sample, approximately 74% of the victims were male, 22% were female, and 4% were transgendered (Kuehnle & Sullivan, 2001). Almost 45% of the respondents had been victimized by a stranger; about 10% by a family member, ex-lover, acquaintance, or roommate; about 20% by a neighbor, landlord, or tenant; about 12% by law enforcement or security personnel; and about 6% by service personnel. Nearly 50% of the offenses were serious personal offenses. About 18% required outpatient medical treatment, 3% hospitalization, and just over 1% resulted in death.

What does macrosystem antigay hostility have to do with maltreatment within LGBTQI relationships? IPV in LGBTQI relationships is often attributed directly or indirectly to these macrosystem attitudes (e.g., Allen & Leventhal, 1999; Island & Letellier, 1991; Renzetti, 1998; Russo, 1999). One study of lesbian and bisexual women found that experiences of discrimination based on their sexual orientation were correlated with self-reported perpetration of physical, psychological, and sexual aggression against an intimate partner (Balsam & Szymanski, 2005). Three main arguments linking macrosystem homophobia/homonegativity with violence in LGBTQI relationships are: (1) macrosystem homophobia/homonegativity is a weapon used by batterers to intimidate their same-sex partners into enduring their maltreatment and staying within the relationship (Allen & Leventhal, 1999); (2) prior experience with homophobia and homonegativity leads LGBTQI victims to feel there is no alternative to the violence they are enduring (Island & Letellier, 1991); and (3) macrosystem homophobia leads to internalized homophobia, which leads to IPV within LGBTQI relationships (Renzetti, 1998).

This issue of *internalized homophobia* (or *internalized heterosexism*), which represents LGBTQI individuals' internalization of negative attitudes and assumptions concerning homosexuality is frequently cited as a cause of violence in LGBTQI relationships (Duke & Davidson, 2009; Margolies, Becker, & Jackson-Brewer, 1987;

Szymanski & Chung, 2003; Tigert, 2001) and a reason victims do not leave (Bartholomew, Regan, White, & Oram, 2008; Walters, 2011). Research investigating the relationship between internalized homophobia and IPV is mixed. One study found that higher levels of internalized homophobia predicted lower relationship quality among lesbian and bisexual women, which in turn was associated with both IPV perpetration and victimization (Balsam & Szymanski, 2005). In contrast, a study with a small convenience sample of lesbians and gay men did not find a strong association between internalized homophobia and IPV (Kelly & Warshafsky, 1987). Research with lesbians and bisexual women has indicated that the higher their level of internalized homophobia, the greater their depression (Herek et al., 1997; Szymanski, Chung, & Balsam, 2001), distress (McGregor et al., 2001), alcohol consumption (DiPlacido, 1998), dissatisfaction with social support (McGregor et al., 2001; Szymanski et al., 2001); conflict concerning sexual orientation (Szymanski et al., 2001), and the lower their self-esteem (Brubaker, Garrett, & Dew, 2009). All of these symptoms are risk factors for IPV (Szymanski & Chung, 2003). Thus, the relationship between internalized homophobia and IPV appears to be an indirect one.

Renzetti (1998) asserts that, "societal homophobia (a social-structural variable) produces internalized homophobia (a psychological variable), which in turn may generate, among other outcomes, partner abuse in homosexual relationships" (p. 123). Informal support for this position comes from clinicians and social service personnel working with victims. According to Allen and Leventhal (1999),

> The threat of or actual verbal, physical, and sexual violence we face from strangers on the street or family members or acquaintances can also leave us feeling vulnerable for abuse in our relationships. Because violence against us is sanctioned, it may be difficult for those in our communities who are battered not to internalize blame for it . . . When a batterer exploits the very vulnerabilities created by oppression, the victim may not be able to find respite from abuse. (p. 79)

Box 8.1   Norma and Tammy

I'm a 55-year-old gay lesbian woman living in rural Southern Ohio … My new girlfriend Tammy, who's only 35, moved into my trailer very quickly after we got together. Over several months, Tammy took over all of our finances, including my credit cards and monthly disability check … Once, after a big fight during which she hit and kicked me, we made up by going out and getting a puppy that I named Sammy.

During our last fight, Tammy was drunk, she got out her gun, loaded it in front of me, and started calling for the dog. After an hour of begging her to stay away from the dog she pointed the gun at me. I didn't call the police because I don't think they'd know how to handle it. I'm a butch lesbian, I worked in a factory most of my life. Tammy is a tiny little Avon saleswoman. Sammy and I finally got out and went to a friend's house. When we went back to the trailer the next day, Tammy was gone. I'm afraid things will get worse when she comes back.

SOURCE: National Coalition of Anti-Violence Programs, 2003, p. 7

Consider the case of Norma and Tammy in Box 8.1. What is the role of homonegativity—both in the macrosystem and as internalized by Norma—in this relationship? How many forms of maltreatment has Norma experienced? In what ways are these forms of maltreatment similar to those in other family relationships? What contributing factors appear to be operating? To what extent are they different from other cases of IPV? Might some of the circumstances of the case change if Norma and Tammy were living in an urban area where homosexuality is more widespread and accepted?

Exosystem

Although victimization of LGBTQI individuals may be related to macrosystem values, the actual acts of victimization tend to take place within the individual's exosystems and microsystems, such as schools or jobs. For example, among older LGBTQI individuals from LGBTQI support groups and agencies around the United States, 71% of men and 29% of women reported experiences of maltreatment related to their sexual orientation, including verbal and physical attacks or discrimination in housing or employment (D'Augelli & Grossman, 2001). Many LGBTQI college students experience considerable hostility: On one campus, more than 75% of lesbian, gay, and bisexual students had been verbally harassed, usually by other students but sometimes by faculty (D'Augelli, 1992). Almost every respondent had heard derogatory anti-gay/anti-lesbian comments on campus, and approximately 75% said they sometimes feared for their personal safety because of their sexual orientation. More recently, a survey of 7,261 students between 13 and 21 years of age found that 61.1% of LGBT students felt unsafe at school because of their sexual orientation (Kosciw, Greytak, Diaz, & Bartkiewicz, 2010).

Being gay also appears to be associated with discrimination in the workplace, particularly for gay men. Depending on the comparison group, data, and analysis conducted, research has found that the earnings disparity between gay and heterosexual men ranged from 2.4% to 26% (Allegretto & Arthur, 2001; Badgett, 1995; Baumle, Compton, & Poston, 2009; Berg & Lien, 2002; Black, Hoda, Makar, Sanders, & Taylor, 2003; Blandford, 2003; Klawitter & Flatt, 1998). The research on such disparities between lesbians and heterosexual women yields less consistency, with estimates ranging from 2.1% to 30% difference in wages (Baumle et al., 2009; Berg & Lien, 2002; Black et al., 2003; Clain & Leppel, 2001). An analysis of the 2000 U.S. Census data found that gay men who have male partners earned on average 10.7% less than married heterosexual men and about the same as cohabiting heterosexual men (Baumle & Poston, 2011). In contrast, lesbians earned almost 4% more than married heterosexual women and 8% more than cohabiting heterosexual women. Homonegativity in the workplace, like homonegativity in the macrosystem, can operate to keep LGBTQIs in abusive relationships. As one 36-year-old battered gay man explained: "Alan is threatening to out me to my parents and my employer. I know I'll be fired if my employer finds out that I'm gay. I feel very isolated" (NCAVP, 2000, p. 12).

Microsystem

Characteristics of the Victim

Lesbian Relationships. Researchers have examined age, childhood history of maltreatment, and substance abuse as correlates of IPV victimization in lesbian relationships. The NCVAP (2011) found that young adults make up more than one third of cases reported to organizations that work with LGBTQI victims of partner maltreatment. Specifically, 38.9% of survivors who reported IPV were under the age of 30, with the largest proportion (31.6%) between the ages of 19 and 29. With regard to a history of child maltreatment, one national study with a sample of lesbians and bisexual women who had been sexually assaulted by their partners found that 71% were incest survivors (Girshick, 2002b), and among lesbian respondents recruited at a music festival, a history of child maltreatment in the victims of IPV was associated with greater verbal maltreatment in the current relationship (Lockhart, White, Causby, & Isaac, 1994). By contrast, Renzetti (1992) did not find a high prevalence of child maltreatment in the histories of the battered lesbians she studied. As for substance abuse, Eaton et al. (2008) found that lesbians and bisexual women who reported IPV in their same-sex relationships were more likely to have drug and alcohol problems than those who did not report IPV.

Gay Male Relationships. Age, ethnicity, HIV status, substance use, personality, income, the degree to which the men are "out," attachment orientation, a history of family violence, and substance abuse have been investigated as possible victim-level risk factors for IPV among gay men. A study of a probability sample of urban gay men revealed that gay men aged 40 and younger were at greater risk of IPV than gay men aged 60 and over, and gay men who had tested positive for HIV were more likely to be victims of IPV than gay men testing negative for HIV (Greenwood et al., 2002). Contrarily, Houston and McKirnan (2007) found that neither age nor ethnicity was related to reports of maltreatment by gay and bisexual men who were currently or previously involved in a violent relationship. Similarly, Bartholomew et al. (2008) found no correlations between age and IPV victimization in male same-sex relationships. Thus, age is not a consistent predictor of IPV victimization in gay male relationships.

HIV status appears to be related to IPV. In a nationally representative sample of HIV-infected adults, 11% of the gay and bisexual men reported physical harm from a partner or another person close to them since their diagnosis (Zierler et al., 2000). More importantly, among the respondents reporting harm, nearly 45% believed it was their HIV-seropositive status that prompted the physical aggression. One study found that approximately 32% of HIV-infected gay or bisexual men had experienced forced sex by a primary partner, whereas 15% had been subjected to it by a casual partner (Shelton et al., 2005). Additionally, among 700 gay men in the New York City area, ecstasy users were more likely than others to be victims of IPV (Klitzman, Greenberg, Pollack, & Dolezal, 2002). Borderline personality traits and insecure attachment are also characteristic of gay male victims of physical IPV (Landolt & Dutton, 1997).

Characteristics of the Relationship

Dependency and independency issues appear to play a particularly important role in violent lesbian relationships (Miller et al., 2001). Among maltreated lesbians, the greater their wish to be independent and the greater their perpetrator's dependency, the more frequent and varied the maltreatment (Renzetti, 1992). IPV in lesbian couples is also associated with relationship conflicts, including disagreements over who controls or has the most responsibility for the couple's finances, jealousy in both partners, the victim's unemployment, and both the perpetrator's and victim's drug/alcohol abuse (Lockhart, White, Causby, & Isaac, 1994).

Research on maltreating relationships among lesbians and bisexual women has examined issues of power and control. One study with a sample drawn from a gay pride festival found that lesbians and bisexual women who experienced current or previous IPV reported significantly less control and decision-making dominance in their relationship than those who did not experience IPV (Eaton et al., 2008). Controlling behaviors included determining when they engaged in safe sex, with whom they socialized, how they dressed, in which activities they engaged, and major decisions affecting the relationship. Other research on maltreatment in lesbian couples has found that conflicts over alcohol and drug use, unemployment, finances, household responsibilities, emotional intimacy, and sexual behavior contribute to maltreatment (Lockhart et al., 1994; Schilit, Lie, & Montagne, 1990).

Ristock (2003) conducted interviews with 80 lesbians who had been victims of maltreatment by a same-sex partner. Two major themes emerged from the interviews. First, for many of the participants (49%), this was their first relationship and it was frequently with a woman who was older and had been "out" for a longer time period. Some of the interviewees felt that their perpetrators serially abused women who were newly coming out. The second theme was that the maltreatment appeared to occur in a cyclical pattern similar to those found in some abusive heterosexual relationships; however, the patterns sometimes changed over time. Nine percent (9%) reported fighting back with the intent to hurt their partner, 20% fought back in self-defense throughout the relationship, and 11% fought back toward the end of the relationship. One woman reported a role reversal in which she got tired of her partner trying to control her all the time, so she became the primary aggressor within the relationship.

One study indicates that different patterns of maltreatment also occur in gay male relationships. Stanley et al. (2006) conducted interviews with a randomly selected community sample of 69 gay and bisexual men who reported at least one violent episode. When assessing relationship dynamics, they looked to see to what extent the maltreating relationships fell into Johnson's (2001) four-category typology of IPV (see Chapter 5). Stanley et al. (2006) found that 68% of the men described situations in which both men were violent but neither was controlling, corresponding to Johnson's (2001) "common couple violence" category. However, the level of violence among the men in this group as well as the relationship characteristics varied widely, leading the authors to consider this a "catchall grouping" (Stanley et al., 2006, p. 38) rather than representing common couple violence as conceptualized by Johnson. Eight percent of the relationships were labeled as "terroristic" and involved moderately severe violence with one partner who was controlling and violent (Stanley et al., 2006).

Four percent of the relationships were characterized by "violent resistance," with both partners engaging in violence but only one partner exercising control of the other partner. There was only one relationship (1.4%) that was characterized by frequent violence with both men trying to control and dominate the other; this relationship was labeled as "mutually violent."

As is true of other forms of IPV, a major predictor of one partner's violence in LGBTQI relationships is the other partner's violence. For example, among 350 lesbians in Arizona, aggression in intimate relationships was typically mutual; only 30% of the women who had used aggression against a female partner described it as self-defense (Lie, Schilit, Bush, Montagne, & Reyes, 1991). In gay male relationships, the more psychologically and physically aggressive one man is, the more aggressive his partner is (Landolt & Dutton, 1997).

Special Issue: Mutuality of IPV

As just mentioned, one of the strongest predictors of violence in LGBTQI relationships is the other partner's violence. In addition, as shown in regard to IPV in heterosexual relationships, it is often difficult to determine whether a perpetrator and victim can be clearly differentiated or if the violence in the relationship is mutual. Some scholars argue that violence in same-sex couples that involves both partners perpetrating and experiencing aggression is "mutual battering" (Archer, 2000; Dutton, 2005; Johnson, 2001; Katz, Kuffel, & Coblentz, 2002; Robertson & Murachver, 2007; Stanley et al., 2006). For example, one study found that, among a small sample of gay and bisexual men who had experienced at least one violent episode, 50% of the men reported being both the recipient and perpetrator of violence (Stanley et al., 2006).

The principal position of the LGBTQI professional community is that mutual violence in LGBTQI relationships is a myth (e.g., Asherah, 2003; Hart, 1986; McClennen, 2005; McClennen, Summers, & Vaughan, 2002; Merrill, 1998; Peterman & Dixon, 2003; Renzetti, 1992; West, 2002). For example, based on their experiences working with battered gay men, Island and Letellier (1991) argue that when violence is reciprocal in gay male relationships, one partner is consistently the primary aggressor. The main components of their argument are theoretical: (1) calling LGBTQI violence mutual minimizes its significance; (2) the idea that men are trained to be aggressive and consequently can never be victims is a myth; and (3) lesbian women may fight back against their aggressors more often than heterosexual women, but their aggression is self-defense or an expression of rage resulting from earlier victimization.

It has also been argued that because court personnel are still generally unfamiliar with the nature of same-sex battering, they often issue mutual restraining orders even in cases where one partner is the sole perpetrator (Fray-Witzer, 1999). According to Merrill (1998),

> [When] a victim happens to be a man or a perpetrator happens to be a woman, providers, including criminal justice and mental health professionals, are almost always confused about how to proceed. For example, sometimes battered gay and bisexual men who call the police for assistance are mistakenly arrested as perpetrators, and sometimes lesbians who batter are mistakenly referred to battered women's shelters. (p. 130)

To the extent that both parties are seen as equally guilty for the violence without adequate verification, the message is conveyed that what has occurred is "fighting" rather than one party's maltreatment of the other. Moreover, Fray-Witzer (1999) noted that once mutual restraining orders have been issued, if a victim pushes to escape from the maltreatment, the victim becomes vulnerable to the perpetrator's threats of criminal prosecution.

Resistance to the idea of mutual violence is reflected in an effort to reconceptualize the potentially different roles of IPV in same-sex relationships. In a study of 62 lesbians identifying themselves as either victims or perpetrators of IPV, Marrujo and Kreger (1996) distinguished among primary aggressors, primary victims, and participants. From their perspective, lesbian *primary aggressors* (27% of the sample) are similar to heterosexual perpetrators in that they are pathologically jealous, controlling, manipulative, entitled, and have problems with anger. Lesbian *primary victims* (39% of the sample) are clinically similar to victims of heterosexual IPV in experiencing low self-esteem and depression. By contrast, *participants* (34% of the sample) represent a different group, characterized by a repeated pattern of "fighting back" against the primary aggressor with the intention of hurting, injuring, or getting even with that aggressive partner—a response that the authors appear to assume is not itself abusive. The authors also appear to assume that in this last type of relationship, it is always possible to identify a primary aggressor. What do you think?

We noted in previous chapters that there is strong resistance to the notion that women can be perpetrators against their male partners, yet there is considerable empirical evidence that some heterosexual women do behave violently (Hines & Malley-Morrison, 2001b; Straus, 2008b). Given what you have learned about perpetration and victimization in LGBTQI relationships, to what extent do you think people need to reconsider the long-standing assumption that men are almost always the perpetrators of IPV and women are almost always the victims?

Box 8.2 Blake and Trudy

Blake called the Advocates for Abused and Battered Lesbians (AABL) and explained that a court domestic violence advocate had told her to call because she was a lesbian who had been in a fight with her girlfriend over the weekend and had been arrested. Blake explained that she had been with her partner for five months. At first, things had been good between them, but an issue developed because Blake's lover, Trudy, decided that she should make a real woman out of Blake, whom she considered too masculine. Arguments over what Blake should wear when they went out became increasingly loud and usually ended with Blake giving in to Trudy's demands. Blake said she was bigger and heavier than Trudy, and knew she could overpower her, but was nevertheless afraid of Trudy, especially when Trudy started throwing things. In the incident leading to Blake's arrest, Blake had stopped for coffee with a friend after work, and when she got home Trudy threw a mug at her, yelled at her, and accused her of being unfaithful. Blake said she responded by pushing Trudy into the couch, but immediately apologized. Irate,

Trudy started punching Blake, who grabbed her wrists and yelled at her to stop. Trudy broke free and started breaking things, then became calm, walked to the phone, said she was going to call someone for support, but instead called the police, who came and arrested Blake.

When the AABL staff called Trudy to get her side of the story, Trudy described several forms of her own abuse of Blake, but put responsibility for her abuse onto Blake, saying she should be more flexible. Trudy admitted that she insists on sex after a fight because it is a way of making up, but also admitted that Blake does not want to have sex at those times because she is tense. Based on their discussions with Trudy, the staff decided that she is the real abuser, not Blake, and they encouraged Blake to join a support group for battered lesbians.

SOURCE: Goddard & Hardy, 1999

Box 8.2 presents a case provided by Advocates for Abused and Battered Lesbians (AABL) to illustrate the challenge of identifying the victim in cases of lesbian violence. The counselors at AABL believe that identifying the victim is important even in cases where the violence may appear to be mutual; moreover, counselors cannot assume that the individual arrested in such a case is necessarily the perpetrator. In what ways is this philosophy relevant to some of the other cases you have read? From our perspective, the argument that LGBTQI violence cannot be mutual has not been established empirically, and based on the empirical research of heterosexual relationships, it is likely that much of LGBTQI intimate violence is indeed mutual. Nonetheless, in order to determine the type of maltreatment that is occurring in a same-sex relationship, it is imperative to examine the context in which maltreatment takes place, including the perpetrator's intent and emotional reactions after a violent episode (Morrow, 1994), power imbalances in the relationship (McClennen, 2005), characteristics of the partner, and history of maltreatment in the relationship (Rohrbaugh, 2005).

Individual/Developmental

Family History

Macrosystem homophobia may play itself out within the family microsystem of sexually nonconforming girls or boys. In one sample of homeless lesbian and gay youth, several of the respondents reported that their parents had expelled them from home after learning about their sexual orientation; others left because of physical child maltreatment (Mallon, 1998). A study of sexual orientation victimization among 528 self-identified lesbian, gay, and bisexual youth 15 to 19 years old found that only 13% of girls' mothers and 2% of boys' mothers were very supportive of their child's atypical gender orientation (D'Augelli, Grossman, & Starks, 2008). Among the youth with a single parent who knew about their child's sexual orientation, 47% reported that their parents reacted negatively when learning of their child's orientation. Among youth with two parents who both knew about their child's sexual orientation, 31% both responded negatively to learning about the child's orientation (D'Augelli et al., 2008).

Results from the NESARC revealed that lesbian and bisexual women reported experiencing significantly more childhood maltreatment (i.e., physical maltreatment, neglect, witnessing IPV), compared to heterosexual women in the study (Roberts et al., 2010). The strongest data on the relative rates of childhood maltreatment of LGBTQI individuals versus heterosexual individuals come from the National Survey of Midlife Development in the United States (Corliss, Cochran, & Mays, 2002). Compared to heterosexual respondents, gay and bisexual men reported having experienced more childhood emotional and physical maltreatment, and lesbian and bisexual women reported having experienced more severe physical maltreatment. The researchers postulated that there were at least three different pathways by which children with a minority sexual orientation became subject to higher levels of parental maltreatment: (1) they may be punished for directly disclosing their sexual orientation; (2) they may be proportionally more likely to display atypical gender behaviors that anger their parents; and (3) they may be engaging in undesired behaviors such as substance abuse, which could lead to greater conflict with their parents. Whatever the reason, given that childhood maltreatment has often been identified as a major risk factor for later intimate violence, it is possible that the higher levels of childhood maltreatment that LGBTQI youths experience put them at risk for either perpetrating or sustaining IPV in later relationships.

Most of the available evidence suggests that childhood maltreatment is a risk factor for later violence in lesbian relationships. Among lesbian batterers from both urban and rural communities, every batterer had a family history of violence (Margolies & Leeder, 1995). Approximately 70% of these batterers had been sexually maltreated as children, 65% had been physically and/or verbally maltreated, and nearly all had witnessed their mothers being maltreated by their fathers or stepfathers. A history of extensive child maltreatment was also found in a Tucson sample of lesbians who perpetrated aggression in their relationships: Over 80% reported having experienced parental emotional aggression, nearly 60% had been subjected to physical aggression, and more than 25% reported at least one act of sexual aggression (Lie, Schilit, Bush, Montagne, & Reyes, 1991).

The link between childhood maltreatment and current IPV has been rarely studied in gay and bisexual men, and results are mixed. Among a sample of HIV-positive men, witnessing mother-to-father violence was correlated with perpetrating sexual coercion against a partner (Craft & Serovich, 2005). Being a victim of parental violence in childhood was associated with sexual coercion and physical assault perpetration. Further, witnessing violence from mother to father and being a victim of parental violence as a child were both associated with later sexual coercion perpetration. However, one study found no evidence of intergenerational transmission of violence in a sample of gay victims of IPV (McClennen, Summers, & Vaughan, 2002), and another found weak and inconsistent associations between family violence and victimization among gay men (Relf, Huang, Campbell, & Catania, 2004). Thus, the research does not provide consistent evidence supporting the intergenerational transmission of violence among gay men.

Alcohol and Substance Use/Abuse

As shown in Chapters 5, 6, and 7, alcohol and substance abuse are risk factors for IPV, and there is considerable evidence that compared to heterosexuals, LGBTQI individuals abuse alcohol and other substances at higher rates. For example, four population-based studies conducted in the year 2000 indicated that compared to heterosexual women, lesbians and bisexual women were more likely to drink heavily (Gruskin, Hart, Gordon, & Ackerson, 2001). Further, compared to heterosexuals, gay men use significantly more "poppers," sedatives, hallucinogens, tranquilizers, and stimulants (Woody et al., 2001), and transgendered individuals are at higher risk for substance abuse (Lombardi & van Servellen, 2000).

Although there is considerable evidence that LGBTQI individuals are at risk for elevated levels of alcohol and drug use, there is little systematic empirical research examining alcohol or substance abuse as predictors of violence in LGBTQI relationships. However, there seem to be three major themes in the relevant literature: (1) substance abuse may not be a cause of LGBTQI intimate violence, but may be used as an excuse for being abusive (e.g., Island & Letellier, 1991; Renzetti, 1992); (2) lesbians and gay men may drink or use drugs in order to feel more powerful, and, based on their expectations concerning the effects of alcohol or drugs, may behave more aggressively (e.g., Renzetti, 1992); and (3) perpetrators may use drugs or alcohol as part of a coercive pattern; for example, in a sample of almost 300 gay males and lesbians from 14 states, nearly 20% of both the men and women reported that their partners had gotten them drugged or stoned as a sexually coercive tactic (Waldner-Haugrud & Gratch, 1997).

Alcohol/Substance Abuse and Violence in Lesbian Relationships. In one sample of battered lesbians, 39% said that either they or their partners had been under the influence of drugs or alcohol at the time of the battering incident, and an additional 28% said that both had been under the influence (Renzetti, 1998). Frequency of alcohol use is positively associated with the number of different types (physical, emotional, sexual) of aggression both perpetrated and sustained by lesbian participants (Schilit et al., 1990). In this study, over 60% said that they and/or their partners had used alcohol or drugs prior to an IPV incident. On the other hand, among lesbian batterers from urban and rural communities, there was no direct relationship between drug/alcohol abuse and violence (Margolies & Leeder, 1995).

Personality Characteristics

A number of personality characteristics appear to be predictive of physical IPV in lesbian relationships. These include a high need for control and fusion with their partners (Miller et al., 2001); low self-esteem (Margolies & Leeder, 1995); the batterer's dependency (Renzetti, 1992); and the batterer's jealousy (Renzetti, 1992). In gay male couples, perpetration of both physical and psychological IPV appears to be associated with an "abusive personality"—i.e., borderline personality disorder, trait anger, insecure attachment, and recollections of poor parent-child relationships during childhood (Landolt & Dutton, 1997). In a qualitative study of 25 abused gay men, victims attributed the IPV to the perpetrator's jealousy and need for control

(Cruz & Firestone, 1998). Further, gay male perpetrators referred for treatment report having unmet or threatened emotional needs, suggesting an anxious attachment orientation (Stanley et al., 2006).

Applying the Ecological Model

Overall, most of the predictors of maltreatment in LGBTQI relationships appear to be largely similar to predictors of maltreatment in other intimate relationships: A family history of abuse, substance and alcohol use, certain personality traits, and certain types of relationship conflicts are all predictive of aggression in LGBTQI relationships. However, several researchers argue that there are unique stressors that fall at the macrosystem and exosystem levels that may also influence levels of aggression in LGBTQI relationships. These stressors include homophobia, homonegativity, and heterosexism. In addition, the proliferation of HIV in this community provides for additional types of maltreatment and an additional type of disability that may increase one's vulnerability to maltreatment.

Consider now the case in Box 8.3. What forms of maltreatment has Jason experienced? What role do macrosystem, exosystem, and microsystem factors play in the maltreatment Jason has undergone? What individual/developmental factors can you identify that have been shown to be risk factors in other forms of family violence? Are there any features of this case that are unique to LGBTQI relationships?

Box 8.3   Jason, a 16-Year-Old Gay Male

I left home at 16 when my parents found out I was gay. My mother cried a lot and my father called me a "freak of nature," beat me up pretty badly, then told me he no longer considered me to be his son…I couldn't find a job because of my age but some friends…told me how easy it was to turn tricks and make some easy money…Julio picked me up one night…He seemed different than all of the others. He took me to dinner, told me that I was beautiful, asked me questions about myself and seemed really interested in me…Julio asked me to move in with him two months after we met. I knew I was in love with him and couldn't wait to start our life together. He wouldn't give me the keys to his house because…for "security reasons" he didn't want his keys "floating around." When I was home alone though, I felt trapped because the security door would automatically lock behind me when I left. I was also not allowed to use the telephone because he didn't want me to keep in touch with "the other trash from the streets."

Things were going pretty well until Julio and I had our first disagreement. He'd been drinking and was angry at me for breaking a plate when I was washing it. I tried to apologize but he just kept screaming about how inconsiderate and selfish I was. When he told me he was going out to meet his friends, I started crying and told him that I didn't want to be locked in the house alone. He hit me with the door and pushed me away. I grabbed him by the back of his shirt and, when it ripped he fell forward onto the sidewalk. He hit his head and it started to bleed…[He] pushed me away and said he was going to call the police. I got scared and ran away. I went back later that night and things seemed calm. Julio told me everything was going to be okay and I fell asleep in his arms. I was awakened a few hours later by the police who took me away in handcuffs. I was charged with domestic violence, sentenced to three years probation, and mandated to attend a batterers' group for 52 weeks.

SOURCE: National Coalition of Anti-Violence Programs, 2001, pp. 17–19

Consequences

Outcomes of IPV also appear similar across same-sex and opposite-sex intimate relationships. As with other forms of family violence, the most severe outcome of violence in LGBTQI relationships is death. The NCAVP reported the death of six same-sex intimate partners in 2010, six in 2009 (NCAVP, 2011), and 10 in 2008 (NCAVP, 2010). Analysis of the FBI's Supplementary Homicide Reports data revealed that out of 51,007 partner homicides, 0.3% (133) of the victims were lesbians and 1.8% (959) were gay men (Mize & Shackelford, 2008). A U.S. Department of Health and Human Services report on intimate homicides from 1981 to 1998 (Paulozzi, Saltzman, Thompson, & Holmgreen, 2001) revealed that 0.5% of the intimate partner homicides of women were by same-sex partners, and 6.2% of the intimate partner homicides of men were by same-sex partners. These reports do not provide information on the relative proportion of same-sex intimate partnerships in the country during this period, although according to the 2010 U.S. Census Report, an estimated 1.7% of adults are lesbian or gay, 1.6% bisexual, and 0.3% transgender (Gates & Cooke, 2011). Thus, the rate of intimate homicide in lesbian and gay relationships is not disproportionately high relative to their representation in the population.

Some information on nonfatal injuries resulting from IPV among LGBTQI individuals is available from the NCAVP report on data from the year 1999 (NCAVP, 2000). Intake information from 1,175 clients where injury information was recorded revealed that in 60% of the cases, there had been no physical injury. Of the remainder, 29% had received minor physical injuries, and 10% had sustained serious injuries. Much higher levels of injury were reported by a sample of 52 gay and bisexual men recruited from domestic violence programs and AIDS agencies. In this sample, 79% of the men had been physically injured by their partners at least once, and 85% had suffered significant property or financial loss as a direct result of their partner's abuse (Merrill & Wolfe, 2000). Among a sample of 69 gay and bisexual men who had experienced IPV, 22% reported serious injuries, 45% reported minor injuries and 33% reported no injuries; 12% reported receiving medical attention for their injuries (Stanley et al., 2006).

Research concerning the psychosocial correlates of IPV generally cannot establish clearly which ones are risk factors for violence and which are outcomes. Moreover, it is difficult to separate the outcomes of maltreatment in LGBTQI relationships from the effects of other factors, such as societal homonegativity and internalized homophobia. There is some evidence that aggression in LGBTQI relationships, like aggression in heterosexual relationships, is predictive of mental health problems. Gay male victims, for example, were more likely to report mental health diagnoses and depression, but victimization was not associated with lower self-esteem (Houston & McKirnan, 2007). In a sample of both lesbians and heterosexual women, non-physical IPV was predictive of lower self-esteem, and physical IPV was predictive of depression; the gender of the batterer was not a significant predictor of either depression or self-esteem (Tuel & Russell, 1998). Among gay and bisexual men at a gay pride festival, men who were victimized by sexual aggression reported higher levels of dissociation symptoms, trauma-related anxiety symptoms, and borderline personality characteristics. In a study of 817 gay men, substance abuse problems and alcohol intoxication were strongly related to victimization (Houston & McKirnan, 2007). Gay male IPV victims were also more likely than non-victims to report more sexually transmitted infections, unprotected anal sex, and physical health problems.

Prevention and Intervention

A 1998 report from the National Institute of Justice stated that batterer intervention programs for lesbians and gay men were in their infancy—in part because of a lack of theoretical consensus concerning the causes of maltreatment in LGBTQI relationships, and in part because of the reluctance of members of these communities to expose their problems and possibly contribute further to negative stereotypes (Healey, Smith, & O'Sullivan, 1998). Prevention programs are even more limited. Much of the responsibility for education efforts comes from grassroots organizations. Over the past 15 years, increasing attention has been paid to same-sex partner violence and a number of programs aimed at preventing and intervening with LGBTQI partners have developed.

The Social Service System Response

The majority of domestic violence agencies are geared toward helping heterosexual female victims of IPV by a male partner, and are governed by a feminist perspective on domestic violence. Thus, agencies are often ill-equipped to meet the needs of lesbian, bisexual, and transgender women. Further, personnel are frequently uneducated about the characteristics and dynamics of same-sex IPV. In one study, crisis center staff perceived same-sex IPV as less serious than opposite-sex partner violence (Brown & Groscup, 2009). They also thought it was less likely to happen and less likely to worsen over time. Furthermore, some domestic violence advocates and providers are homophobic (Hassouneh & Glass, 2008; Simpson & Helfrich, 2005), including those who are themselves lesbian, gay, or bisexual (Elliott, 1996). This is particularly problematic considering that these crisis workers, advocates, and providers "form the frontline in the fight against domestic violence" (Brown & Groscup, 2009, p. 87).

Just like victims of IPV by an opposite-sex partner, LGBTQI victims need safe places (e.g., safe houses, shelters) available to them (Hart, 1986; Leventhal, 1990; Richards, 1990; Vecoli, 1990). Although there has been an increase in the number of shelters available for battered women in the United States, these shelters are not equally available to all female victims. Sometimes, women who differ from agency personnel (e.g., lesbians, minority women) are seen as inappropriate clients by shelter staff (Loseke, 1992). For example, among personnel from state-funded women's shelters in three southern states, the average client was a young white heterosexual woman with a poor or working class background (Donnelly, Cook, & Wilson, 1999). Personnel from some shelters indicated that they rarely direct outreach efforts at lesbian victims, or even deliberately exclude them, to avoid alienating contributors, important board members, or other residents. LGBTQI victims, especially those who are transgender, may fear violence from both shelter residents and staff (Ray, 2006). "Many mainstream domestic violence shelters are not equipped to house male-identified and/or transgender survivors, and many still have policies that explicitly prohibit [such] survivors from accessing their services" (NCAVP, 2011, p. 27).

In addition to potentially facing homophobic responses from shelter staff and clients, lesbian and bisexual female victims may not be protected from their perpetrator in a shelter. Whereas shelter locations are typically well-guarded from male perpetrators, female perpetrators can more easily obtain this information; they may identify themselves as victims and gain admission into the shelter (Aulivola, 2004). Thus, lesbian and bisexual female victims are at risk of being victimized by their partner even while staying in a shelter.

Domestic violence agencies, in general, have been critiqued as "heterosexist and unwelcoming" to survivors of same-sex IPV (Helfrich & Simpson, 2006, p. 344). NCAVP (2011) found that, in 2010, 44.6% of same-sex IPV victims seeking shelter were turned away. This represents an increase from 34.8% turned away in the previous year. In response to the inadequacy of services for victims of same-sex IPV, Duke and Davidson (2009) identified pioneer agencies with success in achieving LGBTQI affirmative programming and services. Successful strategies used by these agencies included collaborating with other LGBTQI affirmative organizations, posting information about services in public locations, providing 24-hour hotlines, maintaining websites with information about same-sex IPV, and hosting support groups. Duke and Davidson's programming model calls for training of advocates that would dispel myths about same-sex violence (e.g., women cannot rape other women), educate them about barriers to reporting abuse that LGB victims experience (e.g., homophobia, fear of making the gay community look bad), review state laws and their limitations, and establish guidelines for increasing sensitivity (e.g., using inclusive language).

Lesbians and bisexual women have access to domestic violence shelters simply because they are women, but gay and bisexual men usually do not have similar access. Instead of admitting the men into shelters, as with heterosexual men escaping violence by a female partner, domestic violence agencies may provide them with vouchers to stay in a hotel for a short amount of time. The Gay Men's Domestic Violence Project in Massachusetts is an example of one of the rare agencies that specifically helps gay male victims. This non-profit agency provides emergency safe homes for gay male victims. In addition, it provides legal advocacy and accompaniment, a 24-hour emergency hotline, crisis intervention and safety planning, housing and employment advocacy, support groups, and a rent program (Gay Men's Domestic Violence Project, 2011). The project also includes the GLBT Domestic Violence Attorney Program that provides free and sliding-scale legal assistance to LGBTQI victims in Massachusetts.

The economic downturn in the United States in the early 21st century seriously affected the ability of the limited number of existing agencies to provide services to victims and perpetrators of same-sex IPV. NCAVP (2010) reports that, from 2008 to 2009, staff positions in their member programs that provide services decreased by 56% and organizational and program budgets were cut by 66%. Agencies lost staff and experienced severe reductions in provision of direct services, outreach, and community education efforts. Reductions in funding and staff continued in 2010, and in light of a rising number of reported cases to these organizations, this reduction is particularly concerning (NCAVP, 2010).

The Criminal Justice System Response

In 2010, the Department of Justice issued an opinion asserting that "the criminal provisions of VAWA apply to otherwise covered conduct when the offender and victim are the same sex" (Barron, 2010, p. 33). Although the U.S. government has included same-sex victims in the handling of criminal domestic violence cases, the system overall remains ill-equipped to deal with incidents of same-sex IPV (Pattavina, Hirschel, Buzawa, & Faggiani, 2007). The nature of the criminal justice system response to IPV in LGBTQI relationships varies considerably by state and probably even within states. One problem is that some states' domestic violence statutes do not cover same-sex relationships because they specify that the two people involved must consist of a woman and a man (Aulivola, 2004).

Many states with gender-neutral domestic violence statutes do not clearly indicate that the laws cover same-sex couples. Instead, they refer to "household members," "partners," or "cohabitants" (Hodges, 2000; Knauer, 2001). Thus, individual judges, who may be influenced by their own homophobic and heterosexist beliefs, apply these laws at their discretion (Burke, Jordan, & Owen, 2002; Hodges, 2000; Potoczniak, Mourot, Crosbie-Burnett, & Potoczniak, 2003). Gender-neutral statutes can lead to unclear and inadequate protection for same-sex IPV victims (Potoczniak et al., 2003). In addition, states vary by the availability of case law that establishes whether LGBTQI victims are covered.

In all U.S. states, the District of Columbia, and Puerto Rico, when a woman is a victim of IPV by a current or former male spouse, current or former household member, or a man with whom she had a child and/or a sexual relationship, civil protection orders are available (Aulivola, 2004). In contrast, only Hawaii's statute specifically covers current or former same-sex partners (American Bar Association Commission on Domestic Violence, 2008). Three states (Louisiana, Montana, South Carolina) explicitly deny same-sex victims access to civil restraining orders by confining protection to family members of individuals of the opposite sex who are current or former intimate partners; the remaining states have gender neutral language (Kansler, 2011). Only through the courts' interpretation of such language do the laws in Ohio, Illinois, Kentucky, New Jersey, Pennsylvania, and Florida provide same-sex victims with the legal right to domestic violence orders of protection (Kansler, 2011). This means that, in some states, LGBTQI victims cannot obtain protection to prevent IPV, but can only obtain criminal orders of protection after the perpetrator is arrested (Aulivola, 2004).

According to the NCAVP (2011), 3.1% of victims of same-sex IPV in 2010 applied for orders of protection and less than half (45.6%) received them, a decrease from nearly two thirds (65.5%) in 2009. When cases of same-sex IPV result in judges issuing restraining orders, judges often issue unwarranted mutual restraining orders (Hodges, 2000). Such actions by the court make it less likely that victims will turn to the criminal justice system in the future (Pattavina, Hirschel, Buzawa, & Faggiani, 2007).

The Role of Police

There are mixed views on the role of the police as a resource for victims of IPV in LGBTQI relationships. According to one perspective, the police are indifferent to lesbian battering, either because they do not care whether one lesbian beats up another, because they assume beating is part of the lesbian culture, or because they cannot take IPV seriously when there is no man involved (Russo, 1999). In her study of 100 battered lesbians, Renzetti (1989) found that only 19 had ever called the police for help, and 15 of these victims found the police response to be only a little helpful or not helpful at all. Other unhelpful and inappropriate police responses that lesbian IPV victims have experienced include minimizing the problem, arresting both partners for assumed mutual violence, failing to arrest the perpetrator, and failing to intervene at all (Comstock, 1991; Hardesty, Oswald, Khaw, & Fonseca, 2011; Hodges, 2000; Ristock, 2002; Vickers, 1996).

In contrast, some battered lesbians have found the police to be helpful (Hardesty et al., 2011). One lesbian IPV victim commented about the police that "the people I did talk to were very accommodating" (Hardesty et al., 2011, p. 35). Similarly, one battered gay man reported that,

> Overall, my experience with the San Francisco Police as an openly gay male victim of intimate violence was very positive. Only once did I experience blatant homohatred, when two policewomen refused to file an incident report about a restraining order violation and referred to me as "she" and "this woman" to each other and to other officers in my presence. (Island & Letellier, 1991, pp. 21–22)

The NCAVP (2010) study found that reports to police by victims of same-sex IPV have increased, but so have reports of police misconduct and misarrest. The problem still persists that when police officers cannot determine who the victim is, they rely on physical characteristics such as size and appearance (e.g., one looks more "butch") (Aulivola, 2004). Mandatory arrest policies can further complicate matters, especially in situations where an arrest must be made based on the officer's determination of probable cause and the officer is unclear about whom to arrest (Pattavina, Hirschel, Buzawa, Faggiani, & Bentley, 2007). Officers with insufficient training on such special circumstances may incorrectly classify the event as a "mutual fight" (Hodges, 2000; Knauer, 2001; Lilith, 2001; NCAVP, 2002; Vickers, 1996). Further, some officers have ignored standard procedures used to identify the primary aggressor regardless of the physical attributes of the two people involved (Peterman & Dixon, 2003).

Many LGBTQI individuals perceive law enforcement as an inadequate source of assistance because of individual and institutionalized homophobia (Renzetti, 1992; Simpson & Helfrich, 2005). This perception is not without a basis in reality.

One study found a high rate of homonegativity among police officers; 25% of police officers admitted to engaging in at least one of five forms of antilesbian or antigay behavior such as avoiding contact with a lesbian or gay man, objecting to working with a lesbian or gay man, and calling a lesbian or gay man an insulting name (Bernstein & Kostelac, 2002).

Kuehnle and Sullivan (2003) found that lesbian and gay male victims of IPV and bias crimes reported less than half (48%) of the IPV incidents to the police, compared to over 60% of the bias-related incidents. Further, lesbian victims were more likely than gay male victims to report incidents. Whereas some LGBTQI victims will not report IPV to the police for similar reasons as heterosexual victims (e.g., fearing the emotional, physical, financial consequences) (Peterman & Dixon, 2003), it is likely that some do not report because they do not trust the police (Comstock, 1991; Letellier, 1994).

There is some evidence that, in general, police respond to same-sex IPV the same way they respond to heterosexual IPV. Using data from the 2000 National Incident Based Reporting System database, researchers compared police responses to heterosexual and same-sex IPV offenses, examining potential individual (e.g., race, sex), situational (e.g., seriousness of event), and legal factors (e.g., domestic violence arrest policy) that might account for differences in outcomes (Pattavina, Hirschel, Buzawa, & Faggiani, 2007). Overall, they found few differences in police responses to cases involving same-sex couples versus heterosexual couples. For example, they found that arrests were made as often in same-sex incidents as in heterosexual incidents. One difference they found was that in states with mandatory arrest policies, police were more likely to make an arrest when the two individuals were women than when they were men. The researchers suggested that the existence of a mandatory arrest policy might have had the effect of convincing officers that women can indeed be victimized by other women (Pattavina, Hirschel, Buzawa, & Faggiani, 2007).

San Diego's City Attorney Domestic Violence Unit engages in promising practices pertaining to same-sex IPV cases (Aulivola, 2004; Dell'Anno, personal communication, February 6, 2012). The Violence Unit employs a full-time advocate who is assigned exclusively to same-sex IPV cases. The advocate assists victims with safety planning, accompanies them to court appointments, and refers them to LGBTQ-friendly domestic violence services (Gonzales, personal communication, February 6, 2012). All attorneys and police officers associated with the unit are provided extensive and ongoing training on the dynamics of same-sex IPV (Dell'Anno, personal communication, February 6, 2012).

Box 8.4   Criminal Justice Experiences

In 2010, The Network/La Red [in Boston] worked with Sheila, a transgender woman of color who was experiencing harassment and stalking from her abusive ex-partner. Sheila had been with her partner for 7 years. Sheila was in the relationship for 4 years before she started transitioning. She said, "My partner had always been a bit jealous and controlling, but that got worse as I started to transition." Sheila left her partner in 2010, after a fight in which her partner had strangled her. She called The Network/La Red seeking support around filing for a restraining order. During our initial conversations Sheila disclosed experiencing physical, emotional, sexual and identity abuse as well as harassment and stalking after breaking off the relationship. We helped Sheila connect to a LGBTQ domestic violence attorney who would help her with the restraining order process. At the hearing, Sheila was denied the restraining order. The judge told her that she was too big to be afraid of anyone. Sheila has not been able to get an appeal approved and continues to experience harassment and stalking from her ex-partner (NCAVP, 2010, p. 13).

He knocked me down and repeatedly kicked my knees and ribs. I attempted to call 911, but he ripped the phone out of the wall. They called back and he told them everything was OK, but they dispatched a car anyway...The police lieutenant said, "You guys need to get your shit together or someone is going to jail tonight." After the police left, I...quietly left the house. I called 911 from my cell phone and got a gay operator, who was sympathetic to my needs. He convinced me to go home and wait for the police to arrive...The police interviewed me outside the house and checked my injuries. They went upstairs, and not finding any injuries on my boyfriend, arrested him for domestic violence assault. They asked me to sign the arrest warrant. That was the hardest thing I have ever done. I endured several weeks of legal proceedings. Although I got an "Order of Protection," when it came down to it, I dropped the charges. By that time, I had already moved and just wanted it to be over (40-year-old gay white male) (NCAVP, 2003, p. 21).

For the next two years, Robert beat me up on several occasions and finally broke my jaw. I got a restraining order against him...He called to apologize three days after it had been served. He was being so nice that I let him back into the house and...he became abusive again. He broke the dishes and called me a "faggot spic." I called the police and they arrested him. Later, Robert called me from the police station and said that since I got him arrested, I should bail him out. I did bail him out but I didn't let him come home with me. Several days later, I returned to court to request a year's extension on the restraining order...[The] judge told Robert that he would be arrested again if he came near me (34-year-old gay Latino male) (NCAVP, 2001, pp. 10–11).

Box 8.4 presents the stories of several LGBTQI survivors describing their experiences with the criminal justice system. As can be seen, their experiences are quite varied. What factors do you think might account for the variations in their experiences? To what extent do you think that the experiences of victims of IPV in heterosexual relationships also vary widely?

Summary

The prevalence of IPV in LGBTQI relationships seems to be at least as great as in heterosexual relationships. Similarly, some of the risk factors are the same as those found in other family relationships—for example, family history of maltreatment, substance abuse, and dependency. Others appear to be more unique to LGBTQI relationships—for example, societal homonegativity, internalized homonegativity, and AIDS—yet these factors can be conceptualized under the general category of "stressors," which, as shown previously, are influential risk factors for other types of family violence. There is very little research on outcomes specific to IPV in LGBTQI relationships, although death, physical injuries, and some psychological injuries are possible consequences. The development of intervention and prevention programs addressing LGBTQI partner violence is in its infancy, and currently many shelters and state laws do not have provisions for IPV in LGBTQI relationships. However, many states have gender-neutral language in their domestic violence laws, and although not always the case, the criminal justice response to incidents of violence in LGBTQI relationships has been shown to be helpful in at least some situations. As you read in other chapters about the response of the criminal justice system to other forms of family violence, consider the extent to which particular adjustments need to be made to the system to accommodate problems associated with IPV in LGBTQI communities.

Discussion Questions

1. How does violence in same-sex intimate relationships challenge the feminist perspective?

2. Why is the LGBTQI community fearful of revealing information about relationship violence? How does concealing this information affect LGBTQI victims?

3. Considering that most studies found that in lesbian and gay relationships women suffered higher rates of victimization, why did one study find that victimization was more noticeable in men than in women?

4. Why do you think that gay and bisexual men who have experienced sexual maltreatment are at higher risk of becoming HIV positive, illegally having sex for money, and taking sex-related drugs?

5. Why are lesbian relationships more researched than gay or bisexual relationships or those involving transgender and intersex individuals?

6. Why do you think gay men are forced to have sex by their partners more often than heterosexual men are forced to have sex with their partners?

7. What are the unique kinds of maltreatment that victims in same-sex relationships experience?

8. What does macrosystem anti-gay hostility have to do with maltreatment within LGBTQI relationships?

9. How does the internalization of negative attitudes about homosexuality affect someone in a same-sex relationship?

10. What are some characteristics of victims in lesbian and gay relationships?

11. Why do so many studies regarding LGBTQI communities have such serious methodological limitations?

12. What is the link between childhood maltreatment and current IPV in lesbians, gay men, and bisexual men and women? Is this link methodologically sound?

PART IV

Other Types of
Family Maltreatment

9

Maltreatment of Older Adults and People with Disabilities

The 70-year-old woman ran to her bedroom, slammed the door, and called 911. Even though he was shouting, "Get out of my face, or I'll kill you!" the drunken man chased her, kicked in the door, grabbed her, threw her against a dresser, and wrung her neck with her necklace until the necklace snapped. Then he grabbed her again, dragged her, and yelled, "Come out and see the damage I did to your house, bitch!" She told him that she had called the police; in response, he told her that she better leave fast. When the police came, they found her outside, and then took the man—her 37-year-old son—into custody (Doege, 2002a).

The above case is an example of one of the many forms that maltreatment of older adults can take. In this case, an older woman was physically attacked by the son who lived with her. Other older individuals have reported maltreatment by other family members, including spouses, daughters, and grandchildren. Further, as with other types of maltreatment, maltreatment of older adults can be of many types; in addition to physical maltreatment, older adults can suffer from neglect, sexual maltreatment, psychological maltreatment, stalking, abandonment, and financial exploitation. Determining when an older adult is the victim of maltreatment, however, is not always as clear-cut as in the above scenario. In the first part of this chapter, we consider definitional issues in maltreatment of older adults, as well as research addressing its prevalence, predictors, consequences, and prevention/intervention efforts.

Being a human unable to talk back, or less able to talk back, or less able to filter information, means you have less ability to change certain ways you are being treated. A mother or father can go through years of their life innocently and lovingly describing their son, now a teenager, now an adult, as "having the mind of a 2-year-old child" and "utterly incapable of thought," and he might be able to do very little to stop them. (Amanda, 2006, para. 23)

Amy is 42. She works as a party planner. She raised two children, worked to help support her family and has recently left her abusive husband. In addition to hitting his wife, her husband used her low vision as a means to undermine her authority with their children, by telling them they needed to "keep an eye on their mother." (Gesson, 2004, para. 7)

Ben is 26. He was an assistant casting agent before his spinal cord injury. Now, he is an advocate for people with disabilities. Ben's wife has withheld his wheelchair to immobilize him and terrorized him by covering his mouth and nose, as if she was going to suffocate him. (Gesson, 2004, para. 8)

A 90-year-old once prominent California judge married his stepdaughter, who was impersonating her mother/his deceased wife. She spent huge amounts of his money without his consent; when asked why he was letting her spend so much of his money, the former judge said, "I think she's my wife." (Rathbun, 2010, p. 228)

What do you think of these cases? Do they sound very different from other cases you have read in this book? Does the fact that each victim has some form of disability affect your view of the case? To what extent do you think their disabilities played a role in their victimization? The relationship between disability and maltreatment is complex. A physical or mental disability in either the victim or the perpetrator can be a risk factor for maltreatment, and physical or mental disabilities in victims can also be an *outcome* of maltreatment; unfortunately, the lack of a universal definition of "disability" creates variations in research findings and statistics (Sullivan, 2009). In regard to child maltreatment and disability, it is often difficult to determine whether the maltreatment was antecedent to the disability or the disability was a result of prior maltreatment; probably in many cases, maltreatment has led to disability (physical, intellectual, or emotional) and the child's disability has led to further maltreatment. There is considerable evidence of co-occurrence of disability and maltreatment. For example, in a recent study of substantiated child maltreatment cases in Minnesota, 22% of the children had disabilities, and nearly 30% of the maltreated children who were over the age of 5 had disabilities (Lightfoot, Hill, & LaLiberte, 2010). In the second part of this chapter, we focus on victims of maltreatment whose disabilities appear to be *antecedent* to the maltreatment.

Maltreatment of Older Adults

Scope of the Problem

Definitions and Prevalence Rates of Maltreatment of Older Adults

The "discovery" of maltreatment of older adults occurred in the 1970s. After Suzanne Steinmetz introduced the concept during a congressional hearing in 1978, more systematic research into its prevalence and dynamics began (Anetzburger, 1987). As is also the case with research on many of the other types of maltreatment discussed in this book, research on maltreatment of older adults has been plagued with problems. Although researchers agree that family members sometimes maltreat older members, there have been numerous debates over definitions and dynamics of maltreatment of older individuals (e.g., Pillemer, 2005; Steinmetz,

2005); consequently, research on the effects of maltreatment of older people and ways to prevent or intervene in this problem are still quite limited.

Definitional problems in the area of maltreatment of older people by a family member include issues related to neglect of older individuals and whether financial exploitation is abusive. For instance, although neglect is considered a common form of *child* maltreatment, is it possible to neglect an *adult* in ways that should be considered abusive? Adults are usually self-sufficient and self-determining, unless they are in some ways impaired. Therefore, how can they be "neglected"? Or, how impaired must they be in order for us to apply the label "neglect" meaningfully? How about the label "self-neglect," which can be found in many studies on maltreatment of older individuals, and refers to cases in which older adults neglect to eat properly, fail to practice good hygiene, etc.? If an older person neglects his or her own well-being, should we say that person is being abused? Or should we reserve such labels for acts committed (or omitted) by someone other than the individuals themselves? Finally, many researchers argue over whether financial exploitation should be considered abusive. An example of financial exploitation is when family members use the older person's income for their own benefit. The controversy surrounding this type of maltreatment concerns cultural differences in perceptions of family obligations. That is, many cultures would not consider this type of financial exploitation to be abusive because family members have an obligation to share their resources with one another.

For the purposes of this chapter, we discuss the various types of maltreatment identified by the National Center on Elder Abuse (NCEA), which conducted the first National Elder Abuse Incidence Study (NEAIS) in 1996 (NCEA, 1998). According to the NEAIS, maltreatment of older people perpetrated by family members can be of the following types:

(1) *Physical abuse,* which "is the use of physical force that may result in bodily injury, physical pain, or impairment. . . . The unwarranted administration of drugs and physical restraints, force-feeding, and physical punishment of any kind are . . . examples of physical abuse";

(2) *Sexual abuse,* which "is nonconsensual sexual contact of any kind with an elderly person";

(3) *Emotional or psychological abuse,* which "is the infliction of anguish, emotional pain, or distress";

(4) *Neglect,* which "is the refusal or failure to fulfill any part of a person's obligations or duties to an elder. . . . Neglect typically means the refusal or failure to provide an elderly person with such life necessities as food, water, clothing, shelter, personal hygiene, medicine, comfort, personal safety, and other essentials included as a responsibility or agreement";

(5) *Abandonment,* which "is the desertion of an elderly person by an individual who has assumed responsibility for providing care or by a person with physical custody of an elder";

(6) *Financial or material exploitation,* which "is the illegal or improper use of an elder's funds, property, or assets"; and

(7) *Self-neglect,* which "is characterized as the behaviors of an elderly person that threatens his/her own health or safety." (NCEA, 1998)

Table 9.1 summarizes the data on the prevalence of various forms of maltreatment of older adults. Results from these studies vary because of the different ways

Table 9.1 Studies on the Prevalence of Maltreatment of Older Adults

Study	Description of Sample	Measures of Maltreatment	Rates of Maltreatment
Lifespan of Greater Rochester (2011), New York Elder Abuse Prevalence Study (NYEAPS)	4,156 community-residing individuals over 59 years of age	Neglect by a caretaker; financial exploitation; verbal, physical, and sexual maltreatment (Conflict Tactics Scales)	85.5 per 1,000 experienced verbal maltreatment 41.5 per 1,000 experienced financial exploitation 22.6 per 1,000 experienced physical or sexual maltreatment 19.0 per 1,000 experienced neglect
Acierno, Hernandez-Tejada, Muzzy, & Steve (2009), National Elder Mistreatment Study	Nationally representative sample of 5,777 community-residing adults 60 years or older and 813 proxy respondents	Emotional mistreatment; physical mistreatment; sexual mistreatment; potential neglect; financial exploitation	5.2% experienced financial exploitation by family member 5.1% experienced potential neglect 4.6% experienced emotional mistreatment 1.6% experienced physical mistreatment 0.6% experienced sexual mistreatment
Laumann, Leitsch, & Waite (2008), National Social Life, Health, and Aging Project	Nationally representative sample of 3,005 adults between 57 and 85 years of age	Verbal mistreatment; financial mistreatment; physical mistreatment	9% experienced verbal mistreatment (42.5% of perpetrators were family members) 3.5% experienced financial mistreatment 0.2% experienced physical mistreatment by family member

(Continued)

Table 9.1 (Continued)

Study	Description of Sample	Measures of Maltreatment	Rates of Maltreatment
Teaster et al. (2006), National Center on Elder Abuse Study	Cases substantiated by Adult Protective Services in all states, DC, and Guam; 60 years of age or older	Self-neglect; caregiver neglect; emotional maltreatment; financial maltreatment; physical maltreatment; sexual maltreatment; other maltreatment	37.2% self-neglect 20.4% experienced caregiver neglect 14.8% experienced emotional, psychological, or verbal maltreatment 14.7% experienced financial maltreatment 10.7% experienced physical maltreatment 1.0% experienced sexual maltreatment 1.2% experienced other maltreatment
National Center on Elder Abuse (1998), National Elder Abuse Incidence Study of 1996 (NEAIS)	Sample of 20 nationally representative counties with information from two types of sources: (1) reports of domestic abuse of older adults to Adult Protective Services (APS) agencies, and (2) *sentinel agencies* (i.e., agencies that regularly work with older adults), including financial institutions, law enforcement agencies, hospitals, and care providers; these agencies are sometimes mandated (depending on the state) to report cases of abuse to APS	Physical abuse; sexual abuse; emotional or psychological abuse; neglect; abandonment; financial or material exploitation; self-neglect	11.3 per 1,000 older adults experienced some form of maltreatment (excluding self-neglect) Of these maltreatment incidents, 16% were reported to APS for investigation

they measured maltreatment and collected data, and results must be viewed with caution because many maltreatment victims do not disclose the maltreatment (Acierno, Hernandez-Tejada, Muzzy, & Steve, 2009; Bulman, 2010; Catalano, 2007; Klein, Toban, Soloman, & Dubois, 2008). As with other types of family violence, it is difficult to establish reliable estimates of the prevalence of maltreatment of older individuals.

Recently, two large-scale studies were conducted to establish rates of maltreatment of older individuals. One was a national survey of Adult Protective Services (APS) agencies in all 50 states, the District of Columbia, and Guam (Teaster et al., 2006); the other was the New York Elder Abuse Prevalence Study (NYEAPS) that surveyed agencies that work with older adults (e.g., APS, law enforcement, domestic violence programs) (Lifespan of Greater Rochester, Weill Cornell Medical Center of Cornell University, & New York City Department for the Aging, 2011). Results indicated that 14.8% to 47% of abuse cases involved emotional/psychological/verbal maltreatment; 14.7% to 32.7% financial exploitation; 10.9% to 20.4% caregiver neglect; and 10.7% to 38.6% physical maltreatment. Both studies found 1% of the cases involved sexual maltreatment.

In addition to data from agencies such as APS that work with older individuals, two large-scale nationally representative studies, the National Elder Mistreatment Study (Acierno, Hernandez-Tejada, Muzzy, & Steve, 2009) and the National Social Life, Health, and Aging Project (Laumann, Leitsch, & Waite, 2008) have examined rates of maltreatment in community samples. With respect to maltreatment experienced in the 12 months prior to participating in the study, 4.5% to 9% of participants reported emotional/verbal mistreatment; 3.5% to 5.2% financial exploitation; 1.6% sexual mistreatment; and 0.2% to 4.6%, physical mistreatment. In both national-level and community studies, there is a wide range of reported maltreatment rates between studies. What might account for these differences?

Consider the cases presented in Box 9.1. Each one represents one or more of the types of maltreatment just discussed. What are the differing dynamics in each of these cases? Do you think that the predictors and correlates of each type of maltreatment may be different? If so, what are the different factors operating in each case? Are there also likely to be differences in the possible consequences of each of the forms of maltreatment? How might prevention and intervention efforts differ depending on the situation?

Box 9.1   Cases of Maltreatment of Older Adults

Cynthia, a 93-year-old woman with diabetes, has lived in the same home for 60 years. Recently, her granddaughter Carol and her boyfriend Kyle moved in with her to provide caregiving assistance in exchange for rent-free housing. Carol convinced Cynthia to add her to her checking account to help her pay bills. Carol is also trying to convince Cynthia to sign over the deed to the house in order to allow Carol to make house payments and generally "run things more smoothly." Neither Carol nor

(Continued)

(Continued)

her boyfriend has worked since moving in with Cynthia. Recently, Carol became physically abusive when she was intoxicated and pushed Cynthia down a short flight of stairs. Cynthia will not contact the authorities because she is embarrassed by the situation. She does not want to have her granddaughter arrested. A teller at Cynthia's bank noticed the irregular account activity and made a report to APS (Teaster et al., 2006, p. 8).

Agnes, 85 years old, lost her husband last year. Because of her own problems with arthritis and congestive heart failure, Agnes moved in with her 55-year-old daughter, Emily. Sometimes Emily feels as if she's at the end of her rope, caring for her mother, worrying about her college-age son and about her husband, who is about to be forced into early retirement. Emily has caught herself calling her mother names and accusing her mother of ruining her life. Recently, she lost her temper and slapped her mother. In addition to feeling frightened and isolated, Agnes feels trapped and worthless (American Psychological Association, 2003).

Tilly's 80-year-old husband Ian has dementia and Tilly cares for him at home. To ensure he doesn't wander off while she goes shopping, Tilly ties him to a chair and locks him in the bedroom. When she comes home and finds he has urinated in the chair, she is so incensed by the extra work she now has to do she beats him with her walking stick and threatens him. "You're a grown man. You should know better by now" (Age Concerns, 2009, p. 2).

Due to declining health, Taruna moved in with her daughter and son-in-law about 2 years ago. Lately Taruna appears to be very depressed. When [asked] what is wrong she replies that her daughter is often too busy to make her lunch, or take her shopping for new clothes or personal items. Quite often the daughter and son-in-law go out for dinner not leaving Taruna anything to eat. Taruna is embarrassed and hurt that her daughter is treating her like this but doesn't want to make a fuss (Age Concerns, 2009, p. 2).

Another major problem facing researchers in maltreatment of older adults involves identifying the dynamics and type of maltreatment. In child maltreatment, a dependent child is maltreated by a parent and in intimate partner violence (IPV), partners either maltreat each other or one partner is the primary victim of maltreatment. In the case of maltreatment of older adults, however, there is a wider range of possibilities for types of abusive relationships. For example, (1) *IPV of older adults* can occur in which long-standing IPV situations continue into old age; (2) maltreatment of older adults can be the result of *caretaker stress,* in which a family member (e.g., an independent adult child) who is caring for an impaired older adult becomes frustrated at the individual and become abusive; or (3) a well-functioning older person can be taken advantage of by an adult family member who is dependent on the person; in other words, an otherwise healthy older person is maltreated by a *dependent adult child.* Each of these types of maltreatment is discussed in the following sections.

Older Adult Intimate Partner Violence

Although maltreatment by intimate partners occurs less frequently in older populations than in younger ones, it is a significant and overlooked problem (Desmarais & Reeves, 2007). Similar to younger victims of IPV, older individuals experience emotional/psychological maltreatment, physical maltreatment, and sexual maltreatment by their spouses/partners (Fisher & Regan, 2006; Jasinski & Dietz, 2003). Such maltreatment is more frequently a matter of "domestic violence grown old" than one of caregiver stress or health issues from which the caretaker suffers (e.g., aggression related to depression or dementia) (Klein, Tobin, Salomon, & Dubois, 2008). According to the NEAIS data, maltreatment by spouses is more likely to go unreported than reported; only 19% of the cases reported to APS—as compared to 30.3% of unreported cases—are committed by spouses (NCEA, 1998). The unreported cases are incidents of abuse/neglect that sentinels were aware of but that were never reported to Adult Protective Services. The report describes the incidents as ones that "are less obvious and that would not be reported to an official agency" (p. 5-1). For example, certain forms of emotional abuse are less obvious than physical abuse and are less likely to be reported to APS. The NEAIS defined sentinels as "specially trained individuals in a variety of community agencies having frequent contact with the elderly" (p. 3). Sentinel agencies included police departments, hospitals, home health care agencies, and financial institutions.

In a study of 50 states, 30% of the perpetrators in approximately 100,000 cases of substantiated abuse of older adults were reported to be spouses or intimate partners (Teaster, 2000). Mostly due to methodological differences, rates of IPV of older adults vary widely between studies, ranging from 11.3% (Teaster et al., 2006) to 62.4% (Klein et al., 2008), but it is generally agreed that the numbers are underestimates because many cases are not reported to authorities or disclosed to researchers.

Although a substantial percentage of perpetrators against older adults are intimate partners, this type of maltreatment is the least researched. Straka and Montminy (2006) argue that older victims of IPV have been invisible or forgotten in the research, which tends to focus on IPV among younger, more at-risk victims. Moreover, even though rates of IPV against older adults are substantial, relatively little effort has been made to protect these older victims, at least in part because neither the IPV nor the elder abuse systems are specifically designed to address this form of maltreatment. IPV programs are designed with young couples in mind, and programs for older individuals are designed around the notion that caretaking relatives are maltreating the older individual. Therefore, even though older victims of IPV should conceivably have two systems to turn to for help or to investigate their plights, they often fall through the cracks (Brandl & Cook-Daniels, 2002).

Desmarais and Reeves (2007) point out that despite research indicating that women are just as likely as men to maltreat their partners, maltreatment of older males by their older female partners is rarely considered. Thus, they call for gender inclusiveness in both research and intervention efforts. Further, it appears that no research to date has specifically investigated IPV among older same-sex couples.

Maltreatment of Older Adults by Caregiving Relatives—Caregiver Stress Hypothesis

In contrast to maltreatment of older individuals by their intimate partners, the maltreatment of older individuals by adult relatives who are entrusted with their care is the most researched and widely recognized type of maltreatment of older adults. Statistics compiled by the APS, as seen in the NEAIS, indicate that frail, confused women over the age of 80 are the most likely group to experience maltreatment, primarily at the hands of family members (NCEA, 1998). According to work by Steinmetz (1988), these older individuals reside in the homes of their middle-aged children, who must adjust their lifestyles to accommodate to this new responsibility. Steinmetz (2005) noted that, "the stress, frustration, and feelings of burden experienced by caregivers who are caring for dependent elders can result in abusive and neglectful treatment" (p. 192). In support of this statement, it has been shown that the more stressful the caregiving is *perceived* to be by middle-aged adults, the more likely they are to resort to using abusive behaviors against the older adult (Steinmetz, 1988). Numerous studies have found caregiver perceptions of burden associated with multiple forms of maltreatment of older individuals (Compton, Flanagan, & Greg, 1997; Grafstrom, Nordberg, & Winblad, 1993; Lee & Kolomer, 2005; Pot, van Dyck, & Jonker, 1996; VandeWeerd & Paveza, 2005).

Maltreatment of Older Adults by an Adult Dependent Child—Adult Dependent Child Hypothesis

Proponents of the view that maltreatment of older adults is primarily committed by adult dependent children relying on their aging parents for help rather than by adult caregivers taking care of older parents point to the fact that the majority of case control studies on this issue have found that older victims of maltreatment do *not* differ from nonvictims on their health status and level of dependency (e.g., Bristowe & Collins, 1989; Godkin, Wolf, & Pillemer, 1989; Homer & Gilleard, 1990; Phillips, 1983; Pillemer 1985, 1986, 2005; Pillemer & Finkelhor, 1989; Pillemer & Suitor, 1992). Results from the National Elder Mistreatment Study revealed that older adults with greater caretaking needs were *not* at higher risk for physical or sexual maltreatment (Acierno et al., 2009). In fact, some studies have found older maltreatment victims to be *less* impaired than nonmaltreated older adults (Bristowe & Collins, 1989; Pillemer, 1985; Wolf & Pillemer, 1989). In addition, although women tend to be the primary caretakers of older adults, men are more likely than women to perpetrate maltreatment (NCEA, 1998), which points toward a weakness in the caretaker stress hypothesis.

Pillemer (2005) argued that the popular assumption that older adults are maltreated by their middle-aged, stronger caregivers stems from media attention and the attention of public officials. Indeed, we seem to be swayed morally by the notion that frail older adults should be protected from their caregiving relatives. As shown in a later section, the majority of intervention programs for maltreated older adults seem to be designed to reduce the stress of caregivers. But, as Pillemer (2005) argued, the more rigorous studies of maltreatment of older adults clearly show that we need to look at the characteristics of the perpetrator, not the characteristics of the victim, if we are to more fully understand such maltreatment.

Research on characteristics of the perpetrators shows that typically they are the ones who are dependent (e.g., Greenberg, McKibben, & Raymond, 1990; Wolfe, Strugnell, & Godkin, 1982). In a series of studies, Pillemer found that in comparison to nonvictimized older adults, older adults who were maltreated were more likely to have their adult children dependent on them in several areas, including housing, household repair, financial assistance, transportation, and cooking and cleaning (Pillemer, 1985, 1986; Pillemer & Finkelhor, 1989). More recently, in maltreatment cases involving an older woman victimized by a family member, the dwelling where the maltreatment took place was in the victim's name 81% of the time (Klein et al., 2008).

Special Issue: Stalking of Older Adults

Little research has examined the stalking of older adults by current or former intimate partners or family members. Results from the 2006 National Crime Victimization Survey's Supplemental Victim Survey on stalking revealed that 10.4 per 1,000 individuals between the ages of 50 and 64 and 3.6 per 1,000 individuals aged 65 or older were stalked (Baum, Catalano, Rand, & Rose, 2009); however, the specific relationship of older victims with their stalkers was not reported. Although the risk of stalking decreases with age (Tjaden & Thoennes, 1998; Basile, Swahn, Chen, & Saltzman, 2006), it remains important to accurately assess the prevalence among older adults, examine the nature of stalking, and develop effective methods of prevention and intervention.

Predictors and Correlates

Following is a summary of the findings of the predictors and correlates of the maltreatment of older adults at most levels of the ecological model (see also Table 9.2).

Macrosystem

Societal Views About Older Adults. Negative stereotypes about older adults may contribute to maltreatment. Ageism has been defined as "a process of systematic stereotyping of and discrimination against people because they are old . . . Old people are categorized as senile, rigid in thought and manner, old-fashioned in morality and skills" (Butler, 1975, as cited in Cohen, 2001). The media contributes to these

Table 9.2 Predictors and Correlates of the Maltreatment of Older Adults

Level of the Ecological Model	Specific Predictor	Studies
Macrosystem	Low income	Buri, Daly, Hartz, & Jogerst (2006); NCEA (1998)
Exosystem	Living in disadvantaged area	Payne & Gainey (2009)
Microsystem	Frailty of victim	Acierno, Hernandez-Tejada, Muzzy, & Steve (2009); Greenberg, McKibben, & Raymond (1990); Laumann, Leitsch, & Waite (2008); NCEA (1998)
	Female victim	NCEA (1998); Teaster et al. (2006)
	Older age of victim	NCEA (1998); Teaster et al. (2006)
	White/Caucasian victim	NCEA (1998); Teaster et al. (2006)
	Cohabitation with perpetrator	Jackson & Hafemeister (2011)
	Victim widowed or divorced	Jackson & Hafemeister (2011)
	Victim still driving	Jackson & Hafemeister (2011)
	Victim experienced family violence during childhood	Jackson & Hafemeister (2011)
	Physically/psychologically aggressive toward perpetrators	Jackson & Hafemeister (2011)
	Perception of relationship with perpetrator as poor	Jackson & Hafemeister (2011)
	Do not consider perpetrators as their caretakers	Jackson & Hafemeister (2011)
	Victim's mental health problems	Jackson & Hafemeister (2011)
Individual/ Developmental	Male	NCEA (1998)
	Under 60 years of age	NCEA (1998); Teaster et al. (2006)
	Adult child of victim	Klein, Tobin, Salomon, & Dubois (2008); Lifespan of Greater Rochester (2011); NCEA (1998); Teaster et al. (2006)
	Subjected to maltreatment as children	Fulmer et al. (2005); Steinmetz (1978)
	Alcohol/drug problems	Acierno et al. (2009); Klein et al. (2008)

Level of the Ecological Model	Specific Predictor	Studies
	Chronic psychological problems	Acierno et al. (2009); Bristowe & Collins (1989); Greenberg et al. (1990)
	Criminal histories; previous arrests	Acierno et al. (2009); Klein et al. (2008); Pillemer & Finkelhor (1989); Pillemer & Wolf (1986)
	Unemployed	Klein et al. (2008)
	Family member with emotional problems	Godkin, Wolf, & Pillemer (1989)
	Interpersonal difficulties	Godkin et al. (1989)

stereotypes by depicting older adults as harmless, frail, mentally incompetent, cranky, laughable, and unproductive (London, 2003). One study revealed that over 77% of participants aged 60 or older had experienced one or more incidents of ageism (e.g., being told "you're too old for that," patronized or "talked down to," ignored or not taken seriously) (Palmore, 2001). Such negative perceptions may lead family members to rationalize maltreatment of aging relatives (Anti-Ageism Taskforce, 2006). For example, they may perceive older adults as a drain on "the system" and a burden to society and therefore feel justified in draining the older person's assets (Anti-Ageism Taskforce, 2006). Family members may rely on negative stereotypes of aging individuals as being mentally unfit to make important decisions in order to coerce the individual into signing over power of attorney to a family member (Anti-Ageism Taskforce, 2006). Aysan Sev'er (2009) argues that general attitudes toward older adults are a risk factor for maltreatment that is rarely discussed in the literature. What role might ageism play in the perpetration of physical maltreatment, sexual maltreatment, and neglect of older adults by family members? What role might ageism play in the effectiveness of intervention and prevention efforts?

Financial Status of the Older Adult. Maltreatment reported by APS in the NEAIS was most likely to have been perpetrated against older individuals earning under $15,000 per year (NCEA, 1998). Specifically, in 91.5% of neglect cases, 75% of emotional/psychological maltreatment cases, 75.5% of physical maltreatment cases, 77.6% of financial exploitation cases, and 100% of abandonment cases, the victims made under $15,000. Other research has also found that older adults who report having a low income, not having enough money, and being on Medicare were at greater risk of neglect and abuse (Buri, Daly, Hartz, & Jogerst, 2006).

Exosystem

Only a small amount of research has examined the role of exosystem-level factors in maltreatment of older adults. One study examined 751 APS reports in

Virginia and found that reports of maltreatment of older adults come primarily from disadvantaged areas (Payne & Gainey, 2009). Results also suggested that clients from disadvantaged areas are more likely to refuse services. Why would older adults in disadvantaged areas more likely come to the attention of APS? What are the implications of these results for intervention and prevention?

Microsystem

Frailty of the Victim. Researchers who assert that maltreatment of older adults is committed primarily by overstressed caretaking relatives tend to focus on the characteristics of the victim that predispose them to be at risk of maltreatment. For example, in a Wisconsin sample of 204 cases of abused older adults, 51% of the victims were frail, 12% had Alzheimer's, and 20% were homebound (Greenberg, McKibben, & Raymond, 1990). In comparison to the Wisconsin older population in general (in which 20% shared a household with someone other than a spouse), 73% of the abused older adults lived with an adult child (75% however, lived in the older person's home, not the child's home). In these cases, the frailty and incapacities of the older person were viewed as factors that put them at risk for maltreatment by their caregiver relatives.

The NEAIS also provides evidence that frailty in older people may put them at risk for maltreatment (NCEA, 1998). According to APS reports, the majority of older victims of maltreatment were unable (47.9%) or somewhat unable (28.7%) to care for themselves and sometimes confused (27.9%) or very confused and disoriented (31.6%). However, these statistics stand in stark contrast to those characterizing cases reported by sentinels: only 18.8% were unable to care for themselves, 33.1% were somewhat able to, 7.5% were very confused and disoriented, and 37.9% were somewhat confused. Thus, the cases that were not necessarily reported to APS were ones where the older adults showed higher functioning.

Some research indicates that frailty is associated with some types of maltreatment but not others. For example, the National Elder Maltreatment Study found that poor health was *not* a significant risk factor for physical, emotional, sexual, or financial maltreatment by a family member, but it was for neglect (Acierno et al., 2009). Laumann et al. (2008) assessed physical vulnerability as a combination of ability to engage in activities of daily living, mobility, and sensory function. They found that such vulnerability increased the odds of verbal but not financial maltreatment. Why do you think these two studies found contradictory results? How can researchers best determine the extent to which poor health makes older adults vulnerable to various forms of maltreatment?

Gender, Age, and Race of the Victim. According to both APS and sentinel reports of the NEAIS, older women were more likely to be victimized than older men, even after accounting for older women's overrepresentation in the population (NCEA, 1998). This was the case for every type of maltreatment reported to APS except for abandonment, in which men were more likely to be victimized. Teaster et al.'s (2006) survey of state APS agencies also found that older maltreatment victims are predominantly female.

According to APS findings in the NEAIS, the majority of reported maltreatment incidents were perpetrated against the oldest of the senior group—those who were aged 80 or older—and the reports continually decreased as the age of the victim decreased (NCEA, 1998). This pattern held true for maltreatment of older adults overall, and for neglect, emotional maltreatment, physical maltreatment, and financial exploitation (sexual maltreatment and abandonment occurred too infrequently for rates by age to be estimated). A different picture emerged for cases reported by sentinels: those who were aged 60 to 70 were the most likely to suffer from physical maltreatment, emotional maltreatment, neglect, and self-neglect. Those aged 71 to 80 were the most likely to suffer from abandonment, and those over age 80 were the most likely to be neglected. Similarly, Teaster et al. (2006) found that the largest percent of victimized older adults (42.8%) were 80 years of age or older. Results from the National Elder Mistreatment Study indicated that individuals aged 71 years or older were at *less* risk for physical and emotional maltreatment than were individuals between 60 and 70 years of age (Acierno et al., 2009). Because of these conflicting results, we cannot conclude with certainty that the oldest old are more at risk for maltreatment.

Regarding race, the NEAIS found that the majority of the victims were White (84%), followed by Black (8.3%), Hispanic (5.1%), Asian (2.1%), and Native American (0.4%) (NCEA, 1998). White older adults were overrepresented in every category of maltreatment, with the exception of abandonment, in which a slight majority of victims (57.3%) were Black. A recent study of APS cases involving victims 60 years old or older found a slightly different distribution of races (Teaster et al., 2006). Of substantiated cases, 77.1% were Caucasian, 21.2% were African American, and the remaining were American Indian/Alaskan Native, Asian, or Native Hawaiian/Pacific Islander. The National Elder Maltreatment Study found that minority older adults were at greater risk for potential neglect but not for physical mistreatment, sexual mistreatment, or current financial exploitation by a family member (Acierno et al., 2009).

Other Victim Characteristics. One study examined a number of risk factors for maltreatment of older individuals in comparison to their younger counterparts (Jackson & Hafemeister, 2011). Results revealed that older victims of physical maltreatment were more likely to be victims of the other forms of maltreatment, cohabit with their perpetrators, be widowed or divorced, still be driving, have experienced family violence during childhood, and be physically or psychologically aggressive toward their perpetrators. They were also more likely to perceive the quality of the relationship with the perpetrator as poor, to have been victimized by their perpetrators over a long period of time, and to be less likely to consider the perpetrators as their caretakers. Additionally, older physical maltreatment victims were more likely to have some mental health problems but not cognitive deficits.

Individual/Developmental

Researchers tend to concentrate on characteristics of the perpetrator (i.e., on individual/ developmental level factors) that predict the maltreatment of older adults when they assume that it is the dependency of the perpetrator on the older adult, not the other way around, that is the primary contributing factor. These predictors seem to mirror the most powerful predictors found for child and spousal maltreatment. For example, the perpetrators may have been subject to maltreatment themselves when they were children (Fulmer et al., 2005), often by the older parent they are now abusing (e.g., Steinmetz, 1978). Perpetrators are also likely to have problems with drugs and alcohol (Acierno et al., 2009; Klein et al., 2008), and may also have chronic psychological problems (Acierno et al., 2009, Bristowe & Collins, 1989; Greenberg, McKibben, & Raymond, 1990). Furthermore, they are more likely to have mental and emotional problems, be hospitalized for those problems, be violent and possibly arrested in other situations, have criminal histories (Acierno et al., 2009; Klein et al., 2008; Pillemer & Finkelhor, 1989; Pillemer & Wolf, 1986), and be unemployed (Klein et al., 2008). Finally, in comparison to families not character- ized by maltreatment of older adults, those experiencing such maltreatment are more likely to have a family member with emotional and interpersonal difficulties and to be more socially isolated (Godkin, Wolf, & Pillemer, 1989).

Other studies also provide data on individual/developmental level characteristics of the perpetrators. According to both APS and sentinel reports in the NEAIS, the majority of perpetrators were men (53% and 63.1% respectively) (NCEA, 1998). According to APS reports in the NEAIS, men were more likely to commit every type of maltreatment except neglect (NCEA, 1998). In contrast, more recent APS data show that just over half (52.7%) of perpetrators are women (Teaster et al., 2006).

With regard to age, the NEAIS found that the majority of perpetrators were under the age of 60 (66% according to APS reports and 60.7% according to sentinel reports), and individuals under 60 committed the majority of all types of maltreat- ment (NCEA, 1998). Similarly, Teaster et al. (2006) found that 75.1% of perpetra- tors were under the age of 60, with the largest percent (25.6%) between 40 and 49 years of age. Results across studies indicates that the most common perpetrator is an adult child (Klein et al., 2008; Lifespan of Greater Rochester, 2011; NCEA, 1998; Teaster et al., 2006).

Special Issue: Maltreatment of Caretakers

Although not a well-researched area, several studies have shown that older adults can be abusive toward their caretakers, usually their spouses or children. For instance, between 29% and 33% of older adults are physically aggressive toward their caretakers (Coyne, Reichman, & Berbig, 1993; Phillips, Torres de Ardon, & Briones, 2000; Shugarman, Fries, Wolf, & Morris, 2003), and 16% of older adults may be *severely* violent toward their caretakers (Paveza et al., 1992). In addition, 34% to 51% of older adults have been shown to be verbally aggressive toward their caretakers, 18% to 34% physically aggressive, and 7% sexually abusive (Hamel et al., 1990; Shugarman et al., 2003; Steinmetz, 1988). When comparing these statistics to those of caretaker maltreatment toward older adults, one wonders which problem is more severe. Hamel et al. (1990) reported that maltreatment of caretakers appeared to be a function of long-standing interaction patterns between the older adults and the caretaker. This result was confirmed by Phillips et al. (2000), who found that many caretakers did not view the behaviors as abusive; rather, the behaviors were seen as normal and merely the way the older person had behaved for years. In addition, four variables seemed to predict caretaker maltreatment: younger age of the victim, greater difference between the caretaker's past and present images of the older adult, a perception of a power imbalance in favor of the older adult, and greater interpersonal conflict (Phillips et al., 2000).

Consequences

Psychological/Medical Outcomes

A number of psychosocial and physical consequences of maltreatment of older adults have been identified. Physically maltreated older adults are at an increased risk for injuries, and neglected older adults are at an increased risk for malnutrition and dehydration. One study that followed older residents of New Haven, Connecticut, for 13 years (Lachs, Williams, O'Brien, Pillemer, & Charlson, 1998) found that those who were maltreated at any time during the follow-up period had a poorer survival rate (9%) than those who were self-neglecting (17%) and those who were never maltreated (40%). In addition, older victims of maltreatment were significantly more distressed than non-victims; however, victims who had more social support, a higher sense of mastery, more feelings of self-efficacy, and active reaction patterns were less distressed than their counterparts (Comijs, Penninx, Knipscheer, & van Tilburg, 1999).

A clinical study of community-dwelling women 60 years of age or older found that those who had been maltreated reported significantly more health conditions than those who had not been maltreated (Fisher & Regan, 2006). Psychological maltreatment alone or in conjunction with other types of maltreatment was associated with more physical problems (e.g., digestive problems, chronic pain) and mental health issues (e.g., depression/anxiety). Similarly, Mouton, Rodabough, Rovi, Bryski, and Katerndahl (2010) found that, in a sample of women between 50 and 79 years old, exposure to physical maltreatment, verbal maltreatment, or both was associated with a decrease in overall mental health. In addition, depression, suicidal ideation, shame, and guilt are all possible consequences of maltreatment, although it is unclear whether the maltreatment or the symptoms came first (Anetzberger, 1998; Pillemer & Finkelhor, 1988; Reis & Nahmiash, 1997). Finally, maltreatment of older adults is associated with higher mortality (Dong, 2005; Lachs & Pillemer, 1998).

Homicide of Older Adults

Death resulting directly from maltreatment is a potential outcome of maltreatment of older adults. An example of this outcome is presented in Box 9.2. As you read this case, consider what types of abusive behaviors the daughter may have perpetrated against her father in the past. Also consider which of the three dynamics of maltreatment of older adults this case represents: is it a case of IPV, maltreatment perpetrated by a caregiving child, or maltreatment perpetrated by an adult dependent child? How common do you think such a scenario may be? How often do you think maltreatment of older adults results in the death of the victimized individual?

Box 9.2	The Murder of Handy Morrow

Handy Morrow was an 85-year-old man who lived in Detroit with his daughter Edna. Handy liked to tape record religious sermons from the radio; however, one day while he tried to record a sermon, his daughter was playing her television set too loudly. Handy asked Edna to turn her television down, but she refused. After the verbal conflict that followed, Handy went down into the cellar and turned off the electricity to Edna's room. Edna became so enraged by Handy's act that she started yelling at him. The entire argument to this point, and the incidents that follow, were all recorded on Handy's tape recorder. While Edna was yelling at Handy, "thwacks" could be heard in the background, and Handy was heard groaning. Edna then yelled, "Shut your face! I don't want to hear you! I don't want to see you!" Apparently, the "thwacks" that were heard were blows from a tire iron that Edna used to beat her father. Handy was found four days later by his grandson. By that time, Handy was covered in his own waste and hideously bruised, with a broken arm. In addition, he had not been fed or given anything to drink since the incident with Edna. Handy died 24 days later.

SOURCE: Bachman, 1993

The rates and dynamics of homicide against older adults are difficult to ascertain, probably because so few older adults are murdered. Therefore, subdividing the murders that were perpetrated against older adults into the types of offender-victim relationships results in unreliable numbers. Nonetheless, a few national and state studies have been undertaken to determine who kills older adults and why. According to statistics from the Uniform Crime Report (UCR), between 1992 and 1997, 1,000 murders were committed against older adults. During that time period, the average population of older adults was 31.3 million; therefore, the murder rate for older adults was 3.2 per 100,000 (Klaus, 2000). People known to the victim committed half of these murders, with relatives and intimates committing 25% of all murders against older adults in those years. In addition, older victims of murder were twice as likely to have been killed by a relative or intimate than younger victims. According to the UCR, murder rates among older adults have remained stable since 1998 (Klaus, 2005).

One source of data on the identity of a relative who kills an older adult comes from the Bureau of Justice Statistics report on age and intimate partner homicide. According to the FBI's Supplementary Homicide Reports, between the years 1993 and 1999, the rate of intimate partner homicide against females ages 65 and over was between 0.5 and 0.7 per 1,000 females, and for males, it was between 0.1 and 0.2 per 1,000 males (Rennison, 2001). Using the National Incident-Based Reporting System data for the period 2000 to 2005, Krienert and Walsh (2010) found that among homicide victims, 41.5% of the women and 13.9% of the men aged 60 or older were killed by a spouse.

Karch and Nunn (2011) analyzed data from the National Violent Death Reporting System between 2003 and 2007 pertaining to homicides of older adults by a caregiver.

Victims 80 years of age or older were more likely to be female whereas those between 50 and 79 were slightly (51.7%) more likely to be male. The largest category of victim-suspect relationship was husband followed by son and then daughter. In fewer instances, the perpetrators were wives (especially for victims between 50 and 79), brothers, sisters, and daughters-in-law.

Prevention and Intervention

To start this chapter on maltreatment of older adults, we introduced the case of a 70-year-old woman who was being physically maltreated by her 37-year-old son. During that incident, the woman called the police, and this was the third time she had called police in the previous few years. The first time happened two years prior—during that incident her son had thrown things around the house, spit in her face, and threatened to kill her. When a judge questioned her about the incident, she stated that she was deeply hurt by what he had done, especially because he was the one who used to protect her from her husband's maltreatment when he was alive. Even though she was hurt, she stated she needed him around the house because he did all of the heavy work for her, including shoveling and yard work. Her son received 18 months probation because of this incident (Doege, 2002a).

While still on probation, her son acted out in a drunken rage again—he smashed her bedroom mirror, destroyed a television set, and grabbed his mother's arm so tightly he ripped off a piece of her skin. This time, her son served only 140 days in prison, partly because of the pleas that she gave for his freedom. In the incident that introduced this chapter, which occurred nine months after he was released from prison, he was charged with aggravated battery and obstructing an officer. The mother stopped cooperating with prosecutors, and the son was then charged with six counts of intimidation of a witness (Doege, 2002a).

Researchers in the field of maltreatment of older adults point to numerous reasons why older adults are sometimes unwilling to take the necessary steps to free themselves from maltreatment. There exist a number of internal and external barriers that older adults experience when maltreated (Beaulaurier, Seff, Newman, & Dunlop, 2005; Beaulaurier, Seff, Newman, & Dunlop, 2007). Internal barriers are those that involve victims' reactions to the maltreatment as well as the internalization of the behavior. Such barriers include powerlessness (i.e., accepting the perpetrator's total control) and self-blame (i.e., feeling they are responsible and deserve the maltreatment). Many victims feel compelled to protect the family. For example, they may want to make sure that the perpetrator does not harm others in the family or they may want to protect the perpetrator. There is also a reluctance to turn in a loved one, which seems to be more pronounced when the perpetrator is a child rather than a spouse (Vinton, 1991). Feeling hopeless can prevent victims from seeking help because they may believe there is no help available for someone their age or for a victim who is not badly injured (Beaulaurier et al., 2005). There may also be a belief, which is particularly strong among some older adults due to generational norms, that it is inappropriate to share the secrets of the abusive behavior with strangers or even friends (Beaulaurier et al., 2005; Vinton, 2002).

External barriers involve older victims' reactions to individuals or systems external to themselves and the perpetrators (Beaulaurier et al., 2007). One external barrier is the victims' fear that their families would not be supportive of their efforts to end the maltreatment. This fear has some basis in reality as research indicates that families are often unsupportive (Fugate, Landis, Riordan, Naureckas, & Engel, 2005; Lutenbacher, Cohen, & Mitzel, 2003). Other external barriers include fear of unsupportive clergy responses (e.g., not being referred to services, offering little help while maintaining the status quo), fear of negative criminal justice responses (e.g., concern that the police will ridicule the victim), perceptions of poor community responses (e.g., believing that there is no help available for older victims), and fear of being placed in a nursing home. There are also concerns for older victims similar to the ones that the 70-year-old woman in the above story voiced: If their perpetrators were removed from the home, then there is the possibility that the older adult would be isolated and no one would be there to help with transportation, finances, or chores (Doege, 2002a). Perpetrators often isolate their victim and tell them that no one will believe or help them, or they threaten them in some way (e.g., to not give them money or deport them) (Beaulaurier et al., 2007). The victim's belief in what the perpetrator says or threatens to do presents a strong barrier to seeking help from either formal or informal resources.

State and Federal Policies on Maltreatment of Older Adults

By 1991, all states had statutes addressing abuse of older adults in their laws and/or had amended their existing APS laws to bring older adults under APS protection. Currently, every state has an intervention agency—usually the APS serves in that capacity—that handles cases of abuse of older adults; however, there is little if any uniformity in the laws across the states regarding definitions of, and provisions for, abuse of older adults. In many cases of abuse of older adults, domestic violence laws (for cases of IPV involving an older person) or guardianship laws (for cases in which a frail older person needs to be removed from an abusive home) can be relied on (Griffin, 1999b; Jones, 1994; Williams & Griffin, 1996).

Forty-seven states have mandatory reporting laws, such that professionals who care for older adults must report suspected cases of abuse; failure to do so usually can result in some kind of misdemeanor. Colorado, New Jersey, and South Dakota have voluntary reporting. Of those states with mandatory reporting, 18 states not only require mandatory reporting from professionals, but also from *anyone* who suspects abuse of an elder.

Having mandated reporting laws in place, however, does not ensure that all suspected cases are reported. Even though many older adults go to the doctor on a regular basis, some research has found that in states in which physicians are mandated to report abuse of older adults, fewer than 10% of referrals to APS are made by health care professionals (Lachs, 2003). A review of the literature on knowledge, detection, and reporting of elder abuse by health and social care professionals, revealed that only about half of the detected cases were reported (Cooper, Selwood, & Livingston, 2009). Some researchers surmise that the reluctance to report by physicians results from a conflict between doctor-patient confidentiality and the law (American Psychological Association, 2004a; Rodriquez, Wallas, Woolf, & Manglione, 2006; West, Bledsoe, Jenkins, & Nora, 2002). Physicians may also be afraid that reporting will result in escalation of the maltreatment (West et al., 2002). Furthermore, an older patient is an adult who has certain rights, such as the right to self-determination. If an older adult understands that she or he is being abused but wishes to remain in that situation, a physician may believe that there is little that can be done, or that removal from the situation into a nursing home is the most appropriate action (e.g., Gottlich, 1994; Macolini, 1995). Research indicates that simply implementing mandatory reporting and educating professionals about abuse of older adults does not ensure that all cases of abuse are reported, investigated, or substantiated (Rodriquez et al., 2006; Jogerst, Daly, Dawson, Brinig, & Schmuch, 2003). Considering these results, what can be done to increase reporting of abuse of older adults by mandated reporters?

Some progress with addressing abuse of older adults has been made at the federal level. The Elder Justice Act of 2009 was enacted in 2010 as part of the Patient Protection and Affordable Care Act. It authorized over $777 million over four years and established an Elder Abuse Coordinating Council to make recommendations to the Secretary of Health and Human Services on the coordination of activities of federal, state, local, and private agencies and entities relating to maltreatment of older adults. It also established an Advisory Board on Elder Abuse, Neglect, and Exploitation composed of experts in the field of maltreatment of older adults who provide a strategic plan for the field of elder justice. The act authorizes funding in a number of areas, including funding for improvement of APS's response to abuse of older adults, development of Elder Abuse, Neglect, and Exploitation Forensic Centers, and improvement of the Department of Health and Human Service's data collection and dissemination of research results (Elder Justice Coalition, 2012).

Some states have implemented their own policies regarding abuse of older adults. For example, in 1988 Illinois passed the Elder Abuse and Neglect Act, which resulted in the establishment of the Elder Abuse and Neglect Program that was developed to respond to reports of abuse and to work with victims in resolving the situation (State of Illinois, 2009). Further, close to half of all states maintain an abuse registry or a database of alleged perpetrators (Teaster et al., 2006). Several states that do not maintain a registry or database place reports about perpetrators in substantiated cases in other state crime databases (Teaster et al., 2006).

Criminal Justice System Responses to Maltreatment of Older Adults

Abuse of older adults was originally conceptualized as more of a social and medical problem than as a criminal problem (Payne, 2002); however, during the early 1990s, abuse and neglect of older adults were increasingly criminalized. As part of this process, police were expected to detect cases of abuse and judges were expected to make judgments concerning those cases, despite the fact that neither group received adequate guidance or training in the handling of such cases. Although criminal sentences for perpetrators against older adults increased on the basis of the assumption that this criminal justice response would have a deterrent effect, there has been little research supporting the deterrent rationale (Payne, 2002).

State laws are the primary source of sanctions, remedies, and protections related to maltreatment of older adults (Center for Elders and the Courts, 2012). The first statutes designed to protect older adults from maltreatment were modeled after the child maltreatment statutes. As is true of the legal response to child maltreatment, maltreatment of older adults can be addressed in either civil or criminal courts (Heisler & Quinn, 1995). In the criminal justice system, older victims of maltreatment, like victims of child maltreatment, are not asked to "press charges" against their perpetrator; that is the decision of the prosecuting attorney. Moreover, just as the judicial system may make decisions concerning the best placement of an abused child, many state laws pertaining to maltreatment of older adults provide for the imposition of a guardianship over victims of maltreatment who are not deemed competent to protect themselves from, for example, "undue influence" (such as when a family member or other caregiver is draining their financial resources). In addition, in cases of both child maltreatment and maltreatment of older adults, the criminal justice system cannot intervene unless criminal behavior has occurred or is occurring (Heisler & Quinn, 1995). Finally, as is the case with child maltreatment and IPV, not all cases of maltreatment of older adults are reported to APS.

Many crimes committed against older adults are "traditional" crimes such as assault, domestic violence, and theft (Nerenberg, 2008). Some states have created new laws that hold perpetrators of maltreatment of older adults liable (Berson, 2010); other states have created special offenses (Nerenberg, 2008). For example, Delaware passed a bill in 2010 that creates a new criminal offense—crime against the vulnerable or infirm—which imposes enhanced penalties for 61 offenses, including reckless endangering, assault, terroristic threatening, unlawful sexual contact, fraud, rape, robbery, burglary, identity theft and forgery (State of Delaware, 2010). However, criminal cases involving older adults are few and tend to involve serious and life-threatening incidents, and prosecution is uncommon (Heisler, 2003).

There are no national data on the processing of reports of maltreatment of older adults through the civil or criminal justice systems. Although a few localized studies provide some evidence concerning the nature of such maltreatment cases, they typically do not give a breakdown of the processing of familial versus extrafamilial maltreatment cases. In one of the few studies, a survey of officers in four Alabama police precincts in 1991 and 1992 revealed that the percentage of officers who reported observing maltreatment of older adults ranged from 32.7% for exploitation to 43.2% for neglect. The main predictors of whether observed cases were reported included the race of the officers (Black officers were less likely to report), greater percentage of contacts with older adults, the belief that maltreatment was not minor, and knowledge of the punishments for failure to report. In general, officers reported dissatisfaction with the Alabama system of APS; however, familiarity with the law, confidence in the ability to detect and report maltreatment, and knowledge of punishments for failure to report raised satisfaction slightly (Daniels, Baumhover, Formby, & Clark-Daniels, 1999).

At the federal level, a significant disparity exists between efforts to deal with child maltreatment versus maltreatment of older adults in the commitment of financial resources: Of the federal funding available for victims of maltreatment as of 2001, 93.3% went to child maltreatment, 6.7% to IPV, and only 0.08% to maltreatment of older adults (Hamilton, 2001). The federal government increased its attention toward maltreatment of older adults through the Elder Justice Act of 2009, although federal criminal law that specifically addresses abuse of older adults remains limited. The Older Americans Act, which was reauthorized in 2006, authorizes funding for the National Center on Elder Abuse, which works with numerous organizations to promote and support elder abuse awareness, initiatives, multidisciplinary responses to maltreatment of older adults, and professional training and education (Administration on Aging, 2012). The Enhanced Training and Services to End Violence and Abuse of Women in Later Life Program is a section under the Violence Against Women Act of 2005 and is administered by the Office on Violence Against Women. This program provides funding for training and services to address maltreatment, including stalking, of victims 50 years old or older (U.S. Department of Justice, 2012). Connolly (2010) makes a number of recommendations for improving the criminal justice system's response to maltreatment of older adults. These include

- enhancing research and evaluation;
- enhancing forensics related to maltreatment of older adults;
- promoting victim advocacy;
- building an infrastructure to support prosecutions;
- establishing a central library or clearinghouse of materials on maltreatment of older adults;
- enhancing training of prosecutors, judges, court personnel, and other professionals;
- promoting coordination between criminal justice personnel (e.g., prosecutors, police) and other professionals (e.g., APS, geriatricians, domestic violence experts, forensic pathologists);
- reforming and enacting laws pertaining to maltreatment of older adults; and
- raising awareness and improving advocacy.

The American Bar Association recommends that special units be developed to improve case processing involving abused older adults, in addition to having specially trained prosecutors (Berson, 2010). Box 9.3 provides cases that involved effective intervention by both APS and the criminal justice system.

Box 9.3   Cases of Maltreatment of Older Adults in the APS System

In Connecticut, a 95-year-old widow was admitted to the hospital in a semicomatose state, suffering from dehydration and malnutrition. A physician observed her son fondling his mother inappropriately, punching her, and verbally abusing her. An investigation disclosed serious neglect and possible sexual abuse by the son. Adult Protective Services (APS) secured a restraining order against the son, became temporary conservator of the woman, and placed her in a long-term care facility.

In Iowa, after an 83-year-old woman moved in with her son following surgery, he obtained a voluntary guardianship and power of attorney (POA), and appropriated more than $150,000 worth of her resources. APS was able to substantiate an elder

(Continued)

(Continued)

abuse report on the son, finding that he used undue influence to get his mother, while confused, to sign the voluntary guardianship and POA. A civil suit against the son restored the woman's resources.

In Kansas, a mentally ill young woman physically and verbally abused her 90-year-old grandmother and 68-year-old mother. This woman was very volatile and threatening, sometimes hit her mother, brought strange men who stole things into the home, and forged checks on her mother's account. The police had been called several times, but each time the woman was able to convince them that nothing was going on, and then she would retaliate against the two women. An APS worker got her court-ordered into the state psychiatric hospital. When she was later released, APS obtained a restraining order to keep her away from the two older women, and set up a plan in which she could avoid criminal prosecution only if she had no contact with the two women and continued to participate in mental health treatment. The worker also found alternative housing for the two women so that the daughter would not know where they lived.

SOURCE: Hamilton, 2001

Multidisciplinary Approaches to Prevention and Intervention

Because maltreatment cases involving older adults are diverse and complex, many communities have established multidisciplinary teams (MDTs) composed of professionals who "learn what services, approaches, and resource are available from other agencies and disciplines; share information and expertise; identify and respond to systemic problems; and ensure offender accountability" (Nerenberg, 2006, p. 15). Examples of professionals who typically participate in MDTs are law enforcement personnel, mental health practitioners, physicians, lawyers, domestic violence advocates, and financial institutions (Nerenberg, 2006). More recently, specialized teams have been created that address specific issues (Nerenberg, 2006; Twomey et al., 2010). One common type is a Financial Abuse Specialist Team that meets soon after a financial abuse report has been made so immediate action can be taken to secure assets and prevent further abuse (Nerenberg, 2006; Malks, Buckmaster, & Cunningham, 2003). Another example is Elder Fatality Review Teams that, similar to Child Fatality Review Teams, assess injuries and causes of death, examine events that occurred immediately prior to the death, identify problems with the system, and assist in prosecution (Nerenberg, 2006). A third type of specialized MDT is the Elder Abuse Forensic Center. Team members make home visits with APS and other professionals in order to conduct psychological and/or medical evaluations and assist in gathering evidence for prosecution (Schneider, Mosqueda, Falk, & Huba, 2010). A fourth type of team is medically oriented (Teaster, Nerenberg, & Stansbury, 2003) and provides medical assessment, chart reviews and consultations, and often includes experts in geriatrics, forensics, and emergency medicine (Nerenberg, 2008).

Prevention Intervention for Maltreatment by Stressed Caregivers

Advocates argue that in order for maltreatment of older adults to be dealt with effectively, we must educate the public about the problem, increase the availability of respite care, increase the supports available for families caring for older adults, and encourage counseling and treatment for the problems that contribute to maltreatment of older adults (American Psychological Association, 2003). The available interventions focus mostly on the type of maltreatment in which the stressed adult caregiver maltreats the frail older adult. As mentioned previously, this is the most widely known type of maltreatment, and consequently, it receives the most intervention efforts, even if it is not the only, or even the most prevalent form of maltreatment of older adults. A variety of interventions are available for stressed caregivers. These interventions are typically based on the family systems approach that assumes that the family unit needs assistance, not just the individual caretaker. Interventions include caregiver education and training programs, long-term planning and case management, telephone support, support groups, respite programs, support services (e.g., home delivered meals, attendant care), counseling, and legal and financial planning (Nerenberg, 2008).

In a study of intervention strategies for the maltreatment of older adults, one of the approaches that professionals (e.g., nurses, social workers, physical therapists) rated as the most successful in changing the perpetrator was the provision of assistance to caregivers, including support groups, respite, family counseling, and counseling to reduce stress, anxiety, and depression (Nahmiash & Reis, 2000). An education and anger management intervention program for people who maltreat older adults proved successful in reducing the amount of strain, depression, and anxiety experienced by the perpetrator (Campbell Reay & Browne, 2002). In addition, physically aggressive caretakers reported declines in their use of physical aggression, although their average rate of using physically aggressive tactics was still quite high. These declines in psychological and behavioral problems were maintained at follow-up.

Interventions with Perpetrators of IPV Against Older Adults

A few batterer treatment programs have adapted techniques for older male perpetrators of IPV. Such programs provide group and individual counseling that focus on helping the perpetrators control violent impulses, improve communication skills, take responsibility for their actions, and change their attitudes about violence against women. Increasingly, programs that serve batterers of all ages are including older perpetrators (Nerenberg, 2008). Older perpetrators, however, often have needs that may not be well addressed by existing programs. For example, aggression and agitation can result from depression and dementia (Desmarais & Reeves, 2007). Thus, programs that address depression and dementia are, in some cases, more appropriate for reducing or eliminating aggressive and violent behaviors than batterer treatment programs (Desmarais & Reeves, 2007), and domestic violence workers need to be educated about the special needs of older perpetrators. In addition, officials dealing with cases involving maltreated older adults (e.g., APS workers) should become familiar with domestic violence services (Harris, 1996). Maltreatment of older adults by their intimate partners presents complex challenges for both the domestic violence and elder maltreatment systems. Both fields recognize the need for an integrated approach to IPV of older adults (Hightower, Smith, & Hightower, 2001; Vinton, 2003).

Prevention/Intervention for Older Victims of Maltreatment

Because maltreatment of older adults takes many forms and has numerous detrimental effects on victims, a variety of interventions have been developed. For example, victims may live in shelters or long-term residential facilities (Reingold, 2006) or receive community-based case management (Brownell & Wolden, 2002). One organization provides a mobile outreach van, staffed by a nurse, social worker, and law student that visits senior centers, malls, and communities where large numbers of older adults live (Reingold, 2006). Older adults are provided with information, education, referrals, and, if needed, immediate intervention. Very few of these types of interventions have been evaluated for their effectiveness.

Examples of interventions aimed at empowering victims include psychoeducational support groups (Brownell & Heiser, 2006) and self-help clinics for court-related issues such as obtaining orders of protection (Nerenberg, 2008). Currently, there exist a number of intervention programs to prevent financial maltreatment. These types of programs, which may be run by social service agencies, assist the elder in writing checks for their monthly expenses and in preparing budgets to help them manage their expenses. They also offer the older adults a safe place to hold their valuables and to cash checks (Baron & Welty, 1996). Some public agencies, private nonprofit agencies, and for-profit businesses provide daily money management programs that help older adults pay bills, write checks, and make bank deposits (Nerenberg, 2006, 2008). Fraud prevention programs are also available in some areas (Nerenberg, 2008).

How effective are these interventions? Ploeg, Fear, Hutchinson, MacMillan, and Bolan (2009) conducted a review of 10 studies that assessed effectiveness of various interventions. They found that none of the interventions had an effect on case resolution, social and psychological client outcomes, or relocation of the victim. In fact, one study found an increase of recurrence of maltreatment six months (but not 12 months) after intervention implementation. Why might these programs produce such disappointing results?

Interventions Specific to Older Victims of Partner Violence

"Few, if any, services or programs are designed to specifically address intimate partner abuse among elders" (Desmarais & Reeves, 2007, p. 386). Such services and programs, however, are slowly increasing in number as awareness of the problem increases. Among domestic violence programs, there has been an increasing recognition of the importance of accommodating the needs of older victims (Straka & Montminy, 2006). One study of women who used domestic violence services found that compared to younger women, women 65 years old and older were more likely to have special needs or disabilities such as hearing impairments, a need for accessibility, developmental disabilities, immobility, special dietary needs, and assistance administering medications (Lundy & Grossman, 2009).

Domestic violence shelters are increasingly an option for older female victims of IPV. For example, the Weinberg Center for Elder Abuse Prevention "is the nation's first comprehensive regional elder abuse shelter, serving elders who are 60 years old or older" (Hebrew Home, 2010). Based within a long-term care facility, the center provides older adults with services such as emergency shelter, psychological counseling, and legal advocacy. Although not limited to older victims of IPV, the Weinberg Center offers a safe place for older victims where they can receive appropriate services. Slowly, emergency shelters for older victims have been opening, such as Martha's House in Portland, Maine, and the Maricopa Elder Emergency Housing Program in Phoenix, Arizona. One shelter in East Greenwich, Rhode Island, opened in 2009 and is run by the Saint Elizabeth Community and modeled on the Weinberg Center.

Despite the availability of shelters, very few victimized older adults use them. In part, this may be because victims are not aware that shelters are an option. In general, victims lack awareness of the resources that are available to them in their communities (Hightower et al., 2001; Klein et al., 2008), and even when victims are aware that shelters are an option, some are reluctant to use them (Lachs, 2003). One group of advocates in Wisconsin teamed up with shelters for female victims of IPV to provide shelter services to older women victims of IPV. The Older Abused Women's Program was established by the Milwaukee's Women's Center in 1992 (Doege, 2002b). Analysis of potential clientele revealed that the more youthful of older women physically maltreated by their spouses or adult children were the least likely to accept services for maltreatment. By teaming up with the domestic violence advocates, members of this combined group hoped to find ways to help these women help themselves (Raymond, 2002). In addition to this project, advocates in Florida, a state that has a high percentage of older adults in its population, report that most domestic violence shelters in the state have either housed older women, participated in joint activities with older groups, and/or targeted older women for special programming (Vinton, 2002).

When older victims do turn to domestic violence shelters, they may encounter a number of problems that make it difficult, and in some cases impossible, for them to reside there (Older Women's League, 1994; Wolf, 2000). For example, shelters are often noisy and have high activity levels that can make older victims uncomfortable. Because of physical and mental conditions, the women may have difficulty completing their required work assignments. Many shelters are not wheelchair accessible so women with limited mobility may not be able to access a particular shelter. Most shelter staff have not been educated about the needs of older adults, and shelters are not typically equipped to help women with certain health-related needs such as assistance with bathing or dispensing of medicines. Victims may have difficulty getting to medical appointments and services because the shelter cannot provide transportation (Straka & Montminy, 2006). Thus, some victimized older women do not have the option of escaping to a shelter for protection.

Although the use of domestic violence shelters is a viable alternative for many victimized older women, there seem to be no similar efforts to aid victimized older men. Further, to our knowledge, no research has examined how victimized older lesbian women are received at shelters. Do you think that victimized older men and lesbians would encounter some of the same challenges that younger males and lesbians experience when seeking shelter assistance?

Maltreatment of People with Disabilities

Scope of the Problem

Child Maltreatment

Estimates of prevalence rates for maltreatment of children with disabilities vary by source. Information on cases of child maltreatment reported to CPS confirms that the proportion of children with disabilities reported for child maltreatment exceeds the proportion of children with disabilities in the population. According to the U.S. Department of Health and Human Services (USDHHS), 16% of all maltreated children in 2010 had a disability, which includes 3.9% who had a behavior problem, 3.2% who were emotionally disturbed, and 5.2% who had some other medical condition (USDHHS, 2011). This percentage is far greater than the proportion of children with disabilities in the population, which is 0.7% for children under the age of four and 5.1% for children between 5 and 15 years (Erickson, Lee, & von Schrader, 2011). Moreover, a longitudinal analysis of cases from the National Child Abuse and Neglect Data System revealed that a disability was a risk factor for re-reporting and substantiation of abuse over a two-year period (Fluke, Schusterman, Hollinshead, & Yuan, 2008). Finally, one recent review of the literature indicates that children with disabilities are more than three times as likely to be sexually abused as their nondisabled peers (Skarbek, Hahn, & Parrish, 2009).

Many researchers emphasize the lack of adequate data on violence involving children with disabilities and suggest that prevalence rates are probably higher than reported (Sullivan, 2006b, 2009). Several studies indicate that the prevalence rate of maltreatment in children with disabilities may be as high as 30%. For example, research at the Boys Town National Research Hospital indicated that 31% of school-aged children with disabilities compared to 9% of children without disabilities were maltreated (Fried, 2001). Of 49 consecutive outpatient cases seen at the Abuse Referral Clinic for Children with Disabilities in Philadelphia, 31% of children with disabilities were experiencing or were likely to experience maltreatment (Giardino, Hudson, & Marsh, 2003). Similarly, a Nebraska population-based epidemiological study of all public and parochial school children, plus all children ages 0 to 5 in special needs and early intervention programs, revealed a maltreatment prevalence rate of 31% for children with disabilities compared to 9% for children without disabilities (Sullivan & Knutson, 2000b). Across all disability types, neglect was the most common form of maltreatment, followed by physical, then emotional, and finally sexual maltreatment.

Studies of maltreatment of children with disabilities have often grouped together various forms of disability, although some of them focus on particular disabilities or differentiate between types of disability. In an Illinois study of children with "chronic conditions" (chronic physical illness, mental retardation/developmental delay, and behavioral/emotional problems), 11.7% of children had been maltreated; moreover, children with emotional/behavioral problems had been maltreated at almost twice the rate as children without chronic conditions (Jaudes & Mackey-Bilaver, 2008). With regard to intellectual disabilities, a prospective, longitudinal study of 332 low income families recruited from urban pediatric primary care clinics showed that over time, lower mental development scores predicted likelihood of a CPS report (Dubowitz et al., 2011). Among 156 autistic children in a national sample, 18.5% of the children sustained physical maltreatment, while 16.6% sustained sexual maltreatment, but with no indication of who perpetrated the maltreatment (Mandell, Walrath, Manteuffel, Sgro, & Pinto-Martin, 2005).

The type of maltreatment experienced by children with disabilities may vary in relation to the type or the level of their disability. Research suggests that there are specific risk factors that pertain to child maltreatment in families with children with disabilities, although research is still needed to better understand and define these exact predictors (Sullivan, 2009). In one New York State study, complications during pregnancy or childbirth were associated with later physical maltreatment of the child; low IQ in the child was associated with neglect; and a handicapping condition in the child was associated with sexual maltreatment (Brown, Cohen, Johnson, & Salinger, 1998).

Partner Maltreatment

There is evidence from the 2005 Behavioral Risk Factor Surveillance System, a national telephone survey developed by the Centers for Disease Control and Prevention, that women with disabilities experience all major forms of maltreatment at approximately twice the rate of other groups (Smith, 2008). Women with disabilities were 2.05 times as likely to be physically maltreated and 2.38 times as likely to experience sexual maltreatment as women without disabilities. In a North Carolina study, women with disabilities had more than four times the odds of experiencing sexual assault in the past year than women without disabilities (Martin et al., 2006). What are your speculations as to why women with disabilities are disproportionately subjected to sexual maltreatment? Why might the rates of sexual maltreatment of women with disabilities vary somewhat across regions within the United States?

Although in many studies maltreated women with different types of disability are combined together for analysis, Anderson and Leigh (2011) conducted an in-depth study of 100 deaf college women and their experiences of IPV as reported using the Conflict Tactics Scales (CTS; see Chapter 5). With regard to victimization experienced during the previous year, 91% of the young deaf women reported at least one instance of psychological aggression, 61% reported sexual coercion, and 52% physical assaults (e.g., slaps, punches, kicks, burns) that led to injuries in nearly half these cases. When these results were compared with reports from hearing college women, the rates in the deaf sample are approximately twice as high. These women also reported on their own perpetration of IPV, and the level of this aggression was in general almost as high as the violence perpetrated against them.

Given what you know about situational couple violence, does this finding surprise you? Why might you have expected that violence against the deaf women might have been much greater than violence perpetrated by them?

Other studies also show very high levels of IPV against women with disabilities. In a survey study of 305 women with disabilities in a health awareness program, 90% of the women reported that they had experienced maltreatment at some point in their life; 68% had experienced the maltreatment within the last year (Curry et al., 2011). Nearly half of the women with disabilities who had been maltreated never disclosed the maltreatment to anyone. What barriers might have impeded their reporting of the maltreatment? Could it have been a lack of certainty as to whether what they were experiencing was maltreatment? Fear that the maltreatment would get worse if they reported it? Shame or embarrassment? Fear that disclosure would lead to a whole new set of problems? According to Curry et al. (2011), all of these factors contributed to the women's reluctance to disclose their maltreatment.

Although one can find occasional acknowledgments in the literature that men with disabilities are also at risk for IPV (e.g., Cramer & Plummer, 2010; Hines, Brown, & Dunning, 2007; Nixon, 2009), there has been much less research on maltreated men with disabilities than maltreated women with disabilities. In one of the few studies providing some prevalence information regarding maltreatment of men with disabilities, Hines, Brown, and Dunning (2007) reported that out of 95 male callers to a domestic violence help line who reported their occupation, 17.9% indicated that they were disabled. Powers and Oschwald (n.d.) reviewed several studies indicating that men with disabilities are maltreated at about the same level as women with disabilities. In one study of 275 men with physical and cognitive disabilities, about 65% of the men reported having been physically maltreated and 24% sexually maltreated at least once in their lifetime (Powers, McNeff, Curry, Saxton, & Elliott, 2004, cited in Powers & Oschwald, n.d.). Why has there been so much less research concerning IPV against men with disabilities? Do you think it is likely that men and women with disabilities experience maltreatment, including IPV, at approximately equal rates?

Maltreatment of Older Adults

Although there is less research on the role of disability in elder maltreatment than in the maltreatment of women and children, research in this area is growing as the U.S. population continues to age. As noted in the section on the maltreatment of older adults in this chapter, there is only limited support for the assumption that elder maltreatment results from the development of mental and physical problems and disabilities that make older people more burdensome and a greater source of stress for family caretakers; however, research suggests that dementia does increase risk of maltreatment (Hansberry, Chen, & Grobien, 2005). According to some estimates, around 50% of older adults with dementia who are cared for by a family member suffer some form of maltreatment in the home (Cooney, Howard, & Lawlor, 2006; VandeWeerd & Paveza, 2005; Wiglesworth et al., 2010). Wiglesworth and her colleagues (2010) found that older people with dementia were at greatest risk for maltreatment by a caregiver if they themselves exhibited psychological or physical aggression. They also found that caregivers were more likely to maltreat older family members with dementia if they suffered from high anxiety, depressive symptoms, social isolation, and poor emotional well being, and perceived the older adult as a burden. Not all caregivers are family members; however, being a caregiving spouse, having a long-term involvement in caregiving, and living with the individual with dementia are all factors that have been associated with maltreatment. In addition, caregivers who had been maltreated by their older relative with dementia were more likely than caregivers who had not been maltreated to use abusive behaviors themselves. This finding of reciprocal violence between older adults with dementia and their caretakers has been found in other studies (e.g., Wiglesworth et al., 2010).

Predictors and Correlates

Although disability is itself a risk factor for maltreatment, individuals with disabilities live within contexts that can exacerbate the likelihood that they will be maltreated. As discussed below, risk factors for the maltreatment of individuals with disabilities have been identified at every ecological level.

Macrosystem

Macrosystem risk factors identified for maltreatment of people with disabilities include societal views devaluing the disabled, race/poverty, architectural barriers to escape, and lack of accessibility to and in shelters (Fried, 2001; National Coalition Against Domestic Violence, 1996; Saxton et al., 2001). Dramatic evidence for the role of social values in the maltreatment of children with disabilities comes from a study involving infanticide scenarios in which a hypothetical infant who was either severely disabled or not disabled was killed by his father. College students taking the role of jurors in a mock trial of the father reported feeling significantly less empathy for the infant victim and gave significantly shorter sentences to the father if they were told that the infant was severely disabled (Bottoms et al., 2011). What are your views on this? Would you feel less sorry for a murdered child if you knew he or she was severely disabled? Would it affect your recommendations concerning the prosecution and sentencing of the father if the child were severely disabled?

Children and adults with physical disabilities are often negatively stereotyped because they do not live up to popular social images and the cultural valuing of independent, self-sufficient, attractive, and well-functioning people (e.g., Brodwin, Orange, & Chen, 2004; Brodwin & Siu, 2007). These negative stereotypes lead to various forms of bullying of children with disabilities. A study using the National Survey of Children's Health (NSCH) data found that children with special health-care needs were 1.5 to 2 times as likely to be a victim of bullying as children without special needs (Van Cleave & Davis, 2006). Moreover, special education students are beaten at higher levels in schools than are nondisabled children (Human Rights Watch and American Civil Liberties Union Joint Report, 2008). Does it seem likely to you that these broader social values contribute to the likelihood of maltreatment of individuals with disabilities in their homes and other caregiver settings?

Traditionally, architectural barriers, restraint, and seclusion have served to keep children and adults with disabilities in positions of greater dependence and isolation than is required by their disability. Recent research and media reports addressing the use of restraint and seclusion on children with disabilities as a "last resort" treatment have indicated that these procedures are dangerous and lacking in efficacy, and have often escalated to maltreatment (Sullivan, 2009). Why might caregivers use these treatments anyway? What might be done to reduce the likelihood of such "last resort" treatments?

Since the Americans with Disabilities Act of 1990, the problem of buildings being inaccessible to people with disabilities has gradually improved. Recent research in some states has shown a great increase in the ability of shelters to make provisions for the physically disabled; for example, in a North Carolina study of community programs for domestic violence victims, 94% to 95% reported that they were either somewhat able or very able to provide effective services to people with disabilities, and described networking and increased communication with organizations dedicated to serving people with disabilities (Chang et al., 2003). In the Boys Town National Research Hospital study (Fried, 2001), both race and poverty were risk factors for maltreatment of children with disabilities. Specifically, African American and Native American children with disabilities were at increased risk for maltreatment compared to children with disabilities from other ethnic groups. This study also revealed that 14% of the maltreated children with mental retardation had family incomes below the poverty line, compared to less than 1% of their nonmaltreated peers. Moreover, women with disabilities are more likely than women without disabilities to have low incomes and be unemployed (Crossmaker, 1991), problems that can be created and exacerbated by perpetrators creating a barrier to their attainment of education (Brodwin & Siu, 2007). How do the risk factors in this study compare with what you have learned about risk factors for other forms of family violence?

Exosystem

The general values and prejudices of a macrosystem can be reflected to varying degrees in the customs and practices within particular exosystems within particular regions and states. A study of 50 state-level child welfare administrators revealed that fewer than half of the state agencies even identify developmental disabilities in child maltreatment reports, and many of these agencies did not include this information in planning services to help the families (Shannon & Agorastou, 2006); thus, many families of children with disabilities that could have been eligible for stress-reducing services did not receive them.

At a more localized community level, exosystem risk factors identified as contributing to the maltreatment of family members with disabilities include social isolation, a lack of social support, and external stresses (e.g., poverty, unemployment) on the family. For example, women with disabilities are more likely than nondisabled women to be socially isolated, which increases their vulnerability to repeat victimization (Crossmaker, 1991; Nosek, Hughes, Taylor, & Taylor, 2006). Social isolation, lack of knowledge about community resources, and inadequate care by community organizations all appear to be risk factors for maltreatment of aging individuals with disabilities (Ansello & O'Neill, 2010).

Microsystem

Microsystem-level predictors of the maltreatment of people with disabilities include characteristics of the families in which they live and characteristics of the victims that may make them more vulnerable to maltreatment. The microsystems of maltreated children and adults with disabilities are often filled with stress and violence. In his study of families of children with disabilities reported for maltreatment, P. Sullivan (2006) identified a number of microsystem differences; compared to the families without a family violence history, those with such a history were described as having more financial problems, marital problems, and parental physical or psychological problems or disability. In one study of families of children with disabilities who had been referred for either short-term hospitalization or respite care, a significant positive correlation was found between parenting stress and child maltreatment potential (Aniol, Mullins, Page, Boyd, & Chaney, 2004).

People with disabilities may have a number of characteristics—some of which may themselves be the results of maltreatment—that put them at risk for maltreatment; these risk factors include gender and personal and behavioral characteristics. For example, there is considerable evidence that among children with disabilities, boys are more likely to be maltreated than girls (e.g., Hershkowitz, Lamb, & Horowitz, 2007). Moreover, boys are found in all of maltreatment categories except emotional maltreatment at rates significantly higher than would be expected based on the frequencies of maltreatment in samples of children without disabilities (Herschkowitz et al., 2007). This higher level of risk was especially true for sexual maltreatment, where twice as many boys were victims of sexual maltreatment as would be expected. Nevertheless, even among children with disabilities, girls were more frequently victims of substantiated sexual maltreatment.

Helton and Cross (2011) found that among children with disabilities, the greater the impairment in the child's functioning, the greater the risk for physical maltreatment; conversely, children with better daily living skills were less at risk for severe assault than all other children with disabilities. Extent of disability also appears to influence the judgments of child maltreatment professionals regarding the seriousness of child maltreatment. Manders and Stoneman (2009) found that CPS caseworkers showed some empathy for abusive parents if the maltreated child was disabled, particularly if the disability was emotional/behavioral; the workers were also more likely to indicate that there should be further investigation of the case if the child had emotional/behavioral problems rather than cerebral palsy. What do you make of these findings? In what ways might outcomes for the child vary depending on the level of the CPS worker's empathy with the parent? Is the empathy a good thing or a bad thing or could it be either, depending on the circumstances? Why might the CPS workers be more likely to recommend further investigation if the purported victim had emotional and behavioral problems rather than cerebral palsy? Is this practice likely to lead to more underreporting or overreporting of maltreatment of children with disabilities?

Although emotional and behavioral problems are considered to be forms of disability, such problems can accompany other forms of disability (e.g., physical, intellectual) and act as predictors of maltreatment. For example, depression was found to be a predictor of IPV against women with disabilities in a Texas study of women attending clinics (Nosek et al., 2006). Dependence on the perpetrator for daily living assistance has also been shown to be a risk factor for IPV against female partners (Nosek, 1996).

Because of social stereotypes, victims as well as perpetrators can come to believe that maltreatment of people with disabilities is acceptable. Moreover, negative stereotypes can result in a person with a disability suffering from low self-esteem and self-confidence and may contribute to a greater vulnerability to maltreatment (Brodwin, Orange, & Chen, 2004; Brodwin & Sui, 2007). As one woman explained, "I wasn't able to say 'knock it off' to my family who was doing my personal care. I thought it was normal to be tossed around in my chair. To have a comb dragged through my hair so it comes out. To be left on a toilet for an hour . . ." (Saxton et al., 2001, p. 403).

As was true in the Helton and Cross (2011) study of children with disabilities, there is evidence that the more severe the dementia of an aging adult, the greater the likelihood of maltreatment (Wiglesworth et al., 2010). Among the characteristics of aging individuals with disabilities that make them vulnerable to maltreatment are the following: physical dependence, emotional dependence, limited financial resources, loss of a sense of control over their own bodies, learned compliance, poor social judgment, use of psychotropic medications, and self-abusive behaviors (Ansello & O'Neill, 2010). Moreover, the greater the aggressiveness of the aging individual with dementia, the greater the likelihood that their caregivers will maltreat them (Wiglesworth et al., 2010). When you consider these correlates of maltreatment, do they affect your views concerning the causes and effects of maltreatment of older adults?

Individual/Developmental

One of the characteristics of parents that puts them at risk of maltreating their children with disabilities is their disciplinary practices, which may or may not be influenced by the nature of the child's disabilities. When mothers of deaf and normally hearing children were presented a series of slides showing children engaging in age appropriate, dangerous, or destructive activities, and asked which of a set of disciplinary acts (e.g., ignoring, spanking, hitting with objects) they would use if attempting to alter the children's behavior, the mothers of the hearing impaired children were more likely than the other mothers to indicate that they would use physical discipline and escalate the discipline if the behavior did not stop (Knutson, Johnson, & Sullivan, 2004). In one of the scenarios, the child was tearing pages from a book. What would you do if you were the parent in this situation? Do you think your response to this destructive behavior would vary depending on whether the child was deaf or not? Might you be angrier at the deaf child? Why or why not?

Among the predictors of maltreatment of a woman with a disability by her partner is the perpetrator's use of drugs (Curry et al., 2009). One sample of maltreated women with disabilities described their partners as men who had hurt other people, abused drugs and alcohol, and were subject to jealous outbursts and fits of rage (Curry et al., 2009). Individual/developmental factors predictive of maltreatment of aging individuals with dementia living at home include a number of characteristics of caregivers, including anxiety, depression, and social isolation

(Wiglesworth et al., 2010). What kinds of intervention might reduce risk to women and aging family members in these circumstances?

Special Issue: Are Parents with
Disabilities at Risk for Maltreating Their Children?

All 50 states and the District of Columbia have mandatory reporting laws for child maltreatment and statutes indicating the grounds for terminating parental rights in cases of child maltreatment. Despite a lack of evidence associating parental disability with child maltreatment, 37 states have statutes allowing termination of parental rights based on disability-related issues (Lightfoot, Hill, & LaLiberte, 2010). What do you think of the practice of including parental disability as a potential factor in deciding whether parents can retain custody of children referred because of potential maltreatment? Is bias against people with disabilities likely to be the principal determinant of such provisions? Why might such provisions vary across states?

Prevention/Intervention

Box 9.4 describes a boy with cerebral palsy with evidence of frequent bruises. If you worked with a social service agency and this case was brought to your attention, would you think he may be experiencing abuse? What questions would you ask his mother? His teacher? If you determine that he is being abused, what role do you think his disabilities play in his abuse? How should this case be handled?

Box 9.4   Maltreatment of a Boy with Cerebral Palsy

Your office received a report of alleged physical maltreatment of a 5-year-old boy in your county. William has cerebral palsy, uses a wheelchair, and his head, legs and arms often make jerky, uncontrolled movements. After talking with his teacher, you find out that William recently came to school with bruises and swelling around his ears and a concussion. Similar injuries have been noted in his school files once before. Williams's mother explains the injuries by saying that he frequently hurts himself in play (Manders & Stoneham, 2009).

In recent years, there has been a gradual increase in the recognition that maltreatment prevention and intervention programs that directly target people with special needs and their families are essential. In regard to the maltreatment of children with disabilities, much of the prevention/intervention effort focuses on educating teachers and health personnel to recognize and report maltreatment of children with disabilities when it is suspected (e.g., Cosmos, 2011; Gargiulo & Kilgo, 2005) and on interagency collaboration (Baladerian, 2009). The "say no, go tell" programs do not work well with children with disabilities, but there has been a growth in self-defense programs designed to protect them (Baladerian, 2009). Given that "say no, go tell" programs are not effective, what problems do you envision in teaching self-defense to children with disabilities? Might such programs work better for children with some disabilities than others?

Despite the relative lack of intervention and prevention programs specifically targeting children with disabilities, there has been some effort to investigate the utility of several programs to determine whether they can reduce the potential for child maltreatment of such children. For example, Aniol, Mullins, Page, Boyd, and Chaney (2004) examined the extent to which a respite program for parents of children with disabilities reduced their potential for child maltreatment; unfortunately, their findings indicated that neither a respite program nor a short-term hospitalization program reduced child maltreatment potential in the parents. Is this apparent failure of these intervention programs to reduce risk a surprise to you? What other forms of intervention might be tested?

One type of intervention/prevention program for adults with disabilities focuses on safety training for those adults—for example, the Safer and Stronger audio computer-assisted self-interview program designed to increase awareness of interpersonal violence in women with disabilities, including deafness (Oschwald et al., 2009). A similar program has been developed for men with disabilities (Oschwald & Powers, 2011). Preliminary evidence from an assessment of the program for women with disabilities indicates that women with disabilities who engaged in the Safer and Stronger program found it useful (Oschwald et al., 2009). For example, more than 85% of the participants reported a preference for using the program rather than discussing violence with family, friends, or professionals, and indicated a belief that the program would be helpful for other women with disabilities. Again, the emphasis is on training of community and health workers in recognizing and reporting symptoms of maltreatment in adults with disabilities, as well as the importance of interagency collaboration (Powers, Hughes, Lund, & Wambach, 2009). Perhaps such initiatives will reduce the frequency of stories such as the following from a quadriplegic woman:

> Looking back on my experiences of abuse, during the battering relationship in 1990, I did not perceive a shelter as an option because of my need for physical accessibility and attendant care. Back in 1990, basic community services, even restaurants, were generally not accessible to me because that was just after the passage of the Americans with Disabilities Act. During the battering relationship, if I had had information on safety planning, education, and domestic violence, and had an accessible shelter available, I would have been better able to protect myself, to get out of the relationship before I was severely beaten and before the hospital and the police had to become involved to get me out. (Wisseman, 2000, para. 8)

Useful information for agencies developing programs to prevent or intervene effectively in cases of maltreatment of women with disabilities can be found at the Center for Research on Women with Disabilities (Nosek, 1999), which surveyed programs delivering maltreatment-related services nationwide. The study found that the average number of women with a physical, mental, or sensory disability served during the past year was 20; however, the number of female clients with disabilities varied broadly across programs, ranging from 0 to 12,000. Of women with disabilities receiving services, the most common type of disability was mental illness, and the least common was a visual or hearing impairment. On average, 10% of the women served by each program had a physical impairment, 7% were mentally retarded or otherwise developmentally disabled, 21% were mentally ill, and 5% had a visual or hearing impairment. For nearly half of the programs, fewer than 1% of the clients served within the past year had any physical impairment.

The most common service provided was accessible shelter or referral to an accessible safe house or hotel room (83%) (Nosek, 1999). Although a substantial percentage of the responding agencies provided some assistance to women with disabilities, less than 25% of the services responded to the survey and it is likely that there were fewer accommodations to the needs of clients with disabilities in the nonrespondents. Overall, women with disabilities continue to be underserved in domestic violence and sexual assault programs (Powers, Hughes, Lund, & Wambach, 2009).

Summary

As this chapter has shown, the maltreatment of older adults is a complex, multidimensional problem that is plagued by definitional issues. Several types of elder maltreatment have been identified, including physical maltreatment, neglect, sexual maltreatment, abandonment, psychological maltreatment, and financial exploitation. The issues of physical maltreatment and neglect seem to be the most researched. In addition, three dynamics of elder maltreatment have been found: spousal elder maltreatment, elder maltreatment by a stressed adult caregiver, and elder maltreatment by an adult dependent child. Although researchers argue about which dynamic is the most prevalent, there is evidence that each of these types exist. However, the majority of the intervention and prevention programs are aimed at the dynamic in which the older adult is maltreated by a stressed adult caregiver. There are some resources for older female victims of IPV, but few resources are currently available for either male victims or older adults being victimized by adult dependent children.

Research into the predictors of elder maltreatment show that variables such as low income, isolation, family patterns of maltreatment, substance abuse, psychopathology, and victim frailty may all play roles in the various forms of elder maltreatment. Furthermore, the victims seem to suffer greatly—they can become psychologically distressed and physically injured by the maltreatment. In addition, they have a shorter life expectancy than those older adults who are not maltreated, and may even be killed as a direct result of the maltreatment. Because of these sometimes tragic consequences of elder maltreatment, prevention and intervention programs are needed that address all the possible types of elder maltreatment. However, instituting such programs will not guarantee that the older adult victims will use them, as many do not reach out for help. Therefore, campaigns also need to be established that educate the public to issues concerning the maltreatment of older adults and the ways in which they can seek help for it.

This chapter also reviewed the scant literature on maltreatment of family members who have disabilities. Few would argue that aggression against a child or adult family member with a disability is not abusive. However, the extent to which children and adults with disabilities are at increased risk of family violence is subject to debate, and more research is needed to settle this issue. Children with disabilities certainly seem to be at heightened risk for maltreatment; however, studies are inconsistent as to whether women and older people with disabilities are at greater risk. Furthermore, there is little research as to whether adult men with disabilities are at greater risk for maltreatment, an important research question considering that adult men are more likely to become disabled as a result of an accident than are adult women. Prevention and intervention programs targeting individuals with disabilities are currently being developed, but there is little evidence so far to indicate that they are achieving a goal of lowering the rates of maltreatment of individuals with disabilities.

Discussion Questions

1. How is adult neglect different from child neglect? How does one determine whether an adult is being neglected?

2. Why do you think IPV among older adults is not as widely recognized as other forms of elder maltreatment? Why do you think IPV among older adults is not usually considered in domestic violence cases?

3. Many victims of elder maltreatment do not cooperate with authorities out of fear that their caretaker, who is the perpetrator, will leave. After an assault charge has been addressed, should it be the government's job to find the older adult another caretaker in order to protect him or her?

4. What are some reasons why physicians do not report cases of elder maltreatment? In your opinion, are these reasons ethical?

5. Why do you think many intervention programs for elder maltreatment have not been evaluated?

6. What are some specific risk factors that predict whether or not a child with disabilities will be maltreated? Why is maltreatment so common in children with mental and/or physical disabilities?

7. Why do you think women with disabilities are more likely to be subjected to sexual maltreatment?

8. What are some reasons why nearly half of the women with disabilities who have been maltreated have never disclosed the maltreatment to anyone?

9. What are some reasons why there is so much less research on the maltreatment of men with disabilities? Do you believe that men and women with disabilities may experience the same frequency and types of maltreatment?

10. Research indicates that CPS agents sometimes feel empathy for abusive parents when the child is disabled. Do you consider this a good or bad thing? Would these feelings of empathy lead to more underreporting or overreporting of maltreatment of children with disabilities?

10

Maltreatment of Siblings and Parents by Children and Adolescents

As we got older, it got worse. I would have knives pulled on me. Then I would turn around and pull a gun on... my sister or younger brother. I became very violent, especially toward my sister (Wiehe, 1997, p. 30). *[My brother] took my pet frog and stabbed it to death in front of me while I begged him not to. Then he just laughed!* (p. 54). *My brother threatened to kill me if I told our parents about him molesting me. I was 3 or 4 years of age at the time; he was about 18. He showed me the butcher block we kept in the cellar with the ax and blood. He said he'd kill me there if I told* (p. 67).

Adolescent male held knife to parent to get ride to local shopping center.... Argument about adolescent female's threat to run away from home; adolescent kicks and pushes parent.... Adolescent male argues with stepmother about being away from home too much; adolescent throws dog at stepmother (Evans & Warren-Sohlberg, 1988, pp. 207–208).

These quotes are from studies assessing what we deem "hidden forms of family violence." The first set of quotes is from a qualitative study on sibling abuse (Wiehe, 1997). Typically, the general public does not view aggression between siblings as "abuse" but as "normal sibling rivalry." Do you think the opening quotes describe nonabusive interactions? Does it make a difference who the perpetrator is? Would you consider any of the examples mere "sibling rivalry"? Does the sibling have to be older than his/her victim for the act to be considered abusive?

This last question also pertains to the second set of quotes, which are police reports from a study of "parent abuse" episodes reported to the police in a Northwestern city (Evans & Warren-Sohlberg, 1988). However, is it meaningful to say that a child is abusing his/her parents when the parents are the ones in a position of authority and power? Would you consider any of the examples given abusive? Who is ultimately at fault in these situations?

Maltreatment of Siblings

Scope of the Problem

Consider the three cases described in Box 10.1. Would you consider these three scenarios to be abusive? If so, what types of abusive behaviors are occurring? What actions, if any, would you take if you found out that these interactions were occurring in your neighbor's family? Should they be referred to the authorities? Should they get counseling? Does the fact that perpetrators and victims are siblings affect your judgments at all?

Box 10.1   Three Cases of Possible Abuse

1. I would usually be playing by myself somewhere. He would barge in mad or drunk or both and he'd want me to either get something for him or cook for him. When I would say "No," he'd get extremely angry and start hitting me, cursing at me, kicking me, pushing me around in a total frenzy of violence. It started out by slapping, pushing, cursing. The older [I] got, the more severe it became. I have suffered from a broken nose and collarbone, countless bruises and scratches. I still have a BB in my leg where he shot at me with a BB gun. He kicked me with steel-toed boots on my upper arm, and it was red and purple for weeks. I thought he had broken it. (Wiehe, 1997, pp. 17–18)

2. [When I was] about age 3, [he] started fondling me, which progressed to full sexual intercourse over the next years, starting when I was about 9 or 10 and continuing to age 15, when I ran away and became a hooker. (Wiehe, 1997, p. 64)

3. I was being constantly told how ugly, dumb, unwanted I was. Already about 2 years of age I was told, "No one wants you around. I wish you were dead...your real parents didn't want you either so they dumped you with us." I grew up feeling if my own family doesn't like me, who will? I believed everything...that I was ugly, dumb, homely, stupid, fat—even though I always was average in weight. I felt no one would ever love me. When you're little, you believe everything you're told— it can last a lifetime. (Wiehe, 1997, p. 44)

Sibling abuse is considered the most underresearched and underrecognized form of family violence. Do you think the causes, effects, and correlates of maltreatment are necessarily different if the perpetrator is a sibling rather than a parent? Because there are implicit norms that siblings fight and tease each other and that such experiences are character-building, the public at large usually does not recognize that behaviors between siblings can cross the line from simple sibling rivalry to sibling abuse. As one mother stated, "They fight all the time. Anything can be a problem . . . it's just constant, but I understand that this is normal. I talk to other people, their kids are the same way" (Steinmetz, 1997, p. 43). However, there is little evidence to support the claim that because the perpetrator is a peer or sibling of the victim, the abuse is less serious than other forms of abuse (Finkelhor, 2008).

Moreover, abuse in these relationships may have severe and long-lasting conse-quences for several reasons: sibling relationships are among the longest lasting and most influential relationships in one's life (Cafarro & Conn-Cafarro, 2005; Hoffman & Edwards, 2004); children spend more of their time growing up with their siblings than almost anyone else; these relationships involve intense and ongo-ing contact, and the abuse in these relationships is often perpetrated by another child who—because she or he is a child—is impulsive and unrestrained in their aggression (Finkelhor, 2008).

Physical Maltreatment

Although underresearched, physical violence between siblings appears to be the most prevalent form of family violence. In the 1975 National Family Violence Survey (NFVS), 800 out of every 1,000 children committed an act of violence against their siblings in the previous year; thus, on a national level, 50.4 million children were violent with their siblings (Straus & Gelles, 1990a). Many of these acts were incidents of minor violence, such as slapping and pushing; however, 530 out of every 1,000 (53%) children committed an act of severe violence (e.g., kick-ing, punching, biting, choking, attacks with a knife or gun). Although initially surprised by the amount of violence children perpetrated, Straus and Gelles argued that the results should have been expected considering that children tend to imitate and exaggerate their parents' behaviors and that there are implicit norms that per-mit violence between siblings. After all, "kids will be kids" and "it's just normal sibling rivalry."

Additional analyses of the NFVS provided prevalence rates for different types of violence perpetrated on siblings; specifically, 74% of children pushed or shoved a sibling, 42% kicked, bit, or punched a sibling, and 16% beat up a sibling. The find-ing that 530 out of 1,000 youngsters were severely violent against their siblings means that there were 19 million sibling attacks nationwide that would be consid-ered assault by legal definitions. Moreover, it was estimated that 109,000 children used a knife or gun on a sibling in that year and that 1.5 million children had used a knife or gun on a sibling at least once in their lifetime (Straus & Gelles, 1990). In addition, the statistics are likely to be underestimates for several reasons: Parents do not know about every fight their children have; most fights are probably forgotten because they are considered normal and commonplace; and the survey staff inter-viewed only parents from two-parent homes.

These data also give an idea of the ages and genders of children aggressing against siblings. Violence steadily declined as the children got older; 90% of 3- and 4-year-olds versus 64% of 15- to 17-year-olds committed an act of violence that year—an important decrease. Nevertheless, nearly two thirds of late adolescents had commit-ted an average of 19 acts of violence against their siblings in the previous year. Moreover, although there seemed to be more boys who were violent against siblings than girls (83% versus 74%), it is noteworthy that nearly 75% of girls were violent. At the youngest ages, girls and boys were nearly equal in the amount of violence perpetrated, and the difference between the sexes steadily increased with age. Severe violence was more prevalent in all-boy families (67%), followed by mixed-sex fami-lies (52%), and all-girl families (40%) (Straus, Gelles, & Steinmetz, 1980).

Table 10.1 Studies on the Prevalence of Violence in Sibling Relationships

Study	Sample	Measure of Physical Maltreatment	Rates of Maltreatment
Straus & Gelles (1990a), 1975 National Family Violence Survey	Population-based sample of two-parent families of children ages 3 to 17, N = 733	Parent-report on the Conflict Tactics Scales; severe violence is any act of violence that has a high likelihood of causing an injury (e.g., punching, kicking, beating up)	80% of children committed at least one act of violence in previous year 53% committed at least one act of severe violence
Roscoe, Goodwin, & Kennedy (1987)	School sample of 16 to 17 year olds, N = 305	Self- and parent-report on the Conflict Tactics Scales	91% of sample used violence in previous year according to both parent- and self-report
Goodwin & Roscoe (1990)	School sample of 16 to 19 year olds, N = 272	Self-report scale based on the Conflict Tactics Scales	64–65% of participants reported at least one act of violence against sibling in previous year
Langhinrichsen-Rohling & Neidig (1995)	Economically disadvantaged 18-year-olds, N = 474	Self-report on the Conflict Tactics Scales	70% reported lifetime sibling violence
Duncan (1999)	School sample of 13 to 14 year olds, N = 375	Peer Relations Questionnaire (Rigby & Slee, 1993)	24.4% self-reported pushing around or hitting 11.2% self-reported inflicting a serious injury 22% self-reported victimization from pushing around or hitting 8.1% self-reported sustaining a serious injury
Simonelli, Mullis, Elliott, & Pierce (2002)	College sample of 18 to 27 year olds, N = 120	Measure of sibling aggression devised for the study	79% reported lifetime sibling aggression victimization

Study	Sample	Measure of Physical Maltreatment	Rates of Maltreatment
Kettrey & Emery (2006)	College sample of 20-year-olds on average, N = 200	Asked about sibling with whom they had the most disagreements; self-report on the Conflict Tactics Scales	83% self-reported any physical aggression perpetration in previous year 70% self-reported any severe physical aggression perpetration in previous year
Rees-Weber (2008)	College sample with an average age of 18.8 years, N = 134	Self-report on the Conflict Tactics Scales	86.3% reported any lifetime perpetration of physical aggression
Button & Gealt (2010), 2007 Delaware Secondary School Student Survey	12 to 18 year olds, N = 8,047	Measure of sibling aggression designed for the study	42.5% reported victimization from sibling aggression within previous 30 days
Hardy, Beers, Burgess, & Taylor (2010)	College sample with an average age of 19.6 years, N = 506	Self-report on the Conflict Tactics Scales	77.2% self-reported any lifetime sibling violence perpetration 18.9% self-reported any lifetime serious violence perpetration 29.5% self-reported any lifetime serious violence victimization
Mackey, Fromuth, & Kelly (2010)	College sample of 18 to 21 year olds, N = 144	Self-report on the Conflict Tactics Scales	82% self-reported any sibling violence perpetration when they were 13 years old 53% self-reported any serious sibling violence perpetration when they were 13 years old 83% self-reported any sibling violence victimization when they were 13 years old 56% self-reported any serious sibling violence victimization when they were 13 years old

Although not as extensive, more recent studies show similar findings. A summary of these studies can be found in Table 10.1. For example, over 40% of 8th and 11th graders report violent victimization by a sibling within the previous month (Button & Gealt, 2010), 20% of middle school students report that they are regularly hit or pushed around by a sibling (Duncan, 1999), and 3% to 6% of children report severe physical abuse, such as using objects or weapons to inflict pain (Button & Gealt, 2010; Goodwin & Roscoe, 1990; Lewit & Baker, 1996).

Although some of these incidents can certainly be deemed "sibling rivalry," there is no reason to believe that all cases of violence between siblings are "normal," especially when 1.5 million children have actually wielded a knife or gun against their siblings. In the first study to specifically address the problem of sibling abuse, Vernon Wiehe (1997) gathered qualitative data on the experiences of 150 people who reported abuse by their siblings. The opening quotes to this chapter were from his study. Here are some more of their voices:

> Once my sister was ironing. She was a teenager. I was between 4 and 5. I was curious as to what she was doing. I put my hands flat up on the ironing board and she immediately put the hot iron down on my hand. She laughed and told me to get lost. (p. 21)

> I was deliberately shot in the face with a BB gun by my brother . . . I lost an eye as a result. (p. 21)

> My brother discovered that hitting in the solar plexus caused one to black out. So he would hit me and watch me pass out. (p. 22)

> My brother made several serious attempts to drown me . . . and later laughed about it. (p. 24)

Do you think that any of these cases are simply "sibling rivalry"? If not, what should be done with the perpetrator of these acts? There are cases in which the physically abusive behavior of siblings turns into siblicide—that is, one sibling kills another, as discussed in Box 10.2. Obviously, these acts of murder cannot be dismissed as "normal sibling rivalry." What should be done with the perpetrators of siblicide?

Box 10.2   Siblicide

In accordance with other researchers in the area (e.g., Gebo, 2002), we use the term "siblicide" rather than "fratricide" to refer to children who murder their siblings. We feel that "fratricide" has too much of a connotation of brothers murdering brothers, and, as statistics show, this situation is not always the case. According to the most recent statistics released in the Uniform Crime Reports from the FBI (2010b), there were 88 brothers and 19 sisters murdered in 2010. This represents 5.9% of murders committed within the family and over 0.8% of all murders that year. However, we do not know the age of the perpetrator or victim of the siblicide (i.e., child, adolescent, or adult), and there could be important variations in the characteristics of siblicide depending on the age of the siblings.

Generally, siblicide is more common among adults than among juveniles, and children under 12 usually do not kill their siblings (e.g., Gebo, 2002; Russell, Shackelford, Weekes-Shackelford, & Michalski, 2007; Underwood & Patch, 1999). In fact, among all sibling victims of homicide between the years 1976 and 1994, 78% were adults killed by their adult siblings, and only 9% were juveniles killing their juvenile siblings (Gebo, 2002). In juvenile relationships, older siblings generally are the perpetrators of homicide against their younger siblings (Daly, Wilson, Salmon, Hiraiwa-Hasegawa, & Hasegawa, 2001; Gebo, 2002), whereas the opposite is true in adult relationships: Younger siblings kill their older siblings (Gebo, 2002). Furthermore, there is generally less than a five-year age differential between the perpetrators and victims of siblicide (Gebo, 2002). Siblicide is also more common among males than among females. The most common type of siblicide is brothers killing brothers, followed by brothers killing sisters, sisters killing brothers, and finally sisters killing sisters (Daly et al., 2001; Gebo, 2002; Russell et al., 2007; Underwood & Patch, 1999).

Sexual Maltreatment

Although some people argue that sexual abuse between siblings may merely be acts of sexual curiosity, most acknowledge that sibling sexual abuse can happen, and some studies have addressed this issue. For example, Finkelhor (1980) found that among college students, 15% of females and 10% of males reported some type of sexual experience with a sibling. Two additional studies revealed that a substantial percentage of juveniles in treatment for sexual abuse had committed sexually abusive acts against a sibling: Johnson (1988) found that 46% of 47 sexually abusive boys victimized a sibling, and Pierce and Pierce (1987) found that of the 59 sexual offenses committed by 37 adolescents, 40% were against sisters and 20% were against brothers. In fact, some argue that sibling incest may be as much as five times more common than parent/child incest (e.g., Finkelhor, 1980; Smith & Israel, 1987).

In the cases of sibling sexual abuse in Wiehe's (1997) qualitative study, the majority of the perpetrators were boys who were three to ten years older than their victims, and the majority of the victims were their sisters (79%). There was usually more than just one incident. When the abuse continued, the types of abuse often became more serious and differentiated, as in the scenario presented in Box 10.1. Most of the abusive situations occurred when the parents were out of the house and had left the older sibling in charge.

Sibling incest may be one of the more severe and frequent types of sexual abuse. Although most quantitative studies involve small samples, their findings indicate that 46% to 89% of sibling incest cases involved penile penetration, and the majority of offenders committed more than 16 acts of abuse, significantly greater than father/daughter incest, stepfather/stepdaughter incest, or any other type of sexual abuse (Adler & Schutz, 1995; Cyr, Wright, McDuff, & Perron, 2002; O'Brien, 1991). Furthermore, many abusive situations occur over a four- to nine-year time span (Cole, 1982; Finkelhor, 1980; Laviola, 1992; Russell, 1986), and physical force is used in more cases of sibling incest than in father/daughter incest (Rudd & Herzberger, 1999).

For such reasons, many researchers (e.g., Jones, 2002) have argued that the current definition of sexual abuse in the literature—i.e., that there must be a five-year age discrepancy between the perpetrator and victim for sexual behavior to be considered abusive—provides serious underestimates of the extent of intrafamilial sexual abuse.

Psychological Maltreatment

Another form of sibling abuse—psychological maltreatment—may be the most excused type. After all, we were all teased at some point in time, often by our siblings, so children must learn how to handle that, right? But the kind of "teasing" that many of Wiehe's (1997) respondents experienced—the name-calling, ridicule, degradation, fear arousal, destruction of personal possessions, and torture or destruction of a pet—went far beyond simple "teasing," and the effects can last a lifetime. Consider the following examples provided by Wiehe:

> My brothers and a cousin tied me to a stake and were prepping the ground around me to set it on fire. They were stopped and built a dummy of me instead and burnt that. (p. 46)

> If my brothers found out I cared about something—for example, toys—they were taken and destroyed in front of me. (p. 52)

> My second oldest brother shot my little dog that I loved dearly. It loved me—only me. I cried by its grave for several days. Twenty years passed before I could care for another dog. (p. 54)

If you had a sibling who did any of these things to you, what would your reactions be? Could you simply ignore the experiences? Would you consider them abuse? Why or why not? Overall, somewhere between 30% and 80% of children experience some form of emotional abuse from a sibling, including belittling, teasing, making fun, intimidating and threatening, scorning, provoking, destroying possessions, and torturing and killing of pets (Button & Gealt, 2010; Duncan, 1999; Goodwin & Roscoe, 1990; Kiselica & Morrill-Richards, 2007).

Predictors and Correlates

The best and most consistent predictor of any type of sibling abuse is the presence of another type. That is, if children are physically or sexually abused by a sibling, they are likely to be emotionally abused by that same sibling—and if they are being sexually abused by a sibling, they are probably also experiencing physical abuse from the sibling (Johnson, 1988; Wiehe, 1997). Moreover, children abused by their siblings typically come from families characterized by parental physical, emotional, and/or sexual abuse of the children, and violence between the parents (Button & Gealt, 2010; Hoffman, Kiecolt, & Edwards, 2005; Kiselica & Morrill-Richards, 2007; Wiehe, 1997). In addition to this microsystem-level predictor of all types of sibling abuse, predictors of physical and sexual sibling abuse have been found at the microsystem and individual/developmental levels of the ecological model. Following is a summary of the scant literature to date.

Physical Maltreatment

Microsystem. Some characteristics of the victim have been associated with sibling physical abuse. For example, they may be withdrawn and lack assertiveness; however, it is difficult to say whether these characteristics are predictors or results of the abuse (Wiehe, 1997). Female children may be more at risk for sibling physical abuse victimization than male children (Button & Gealt, 2010), as are younger children (Finkelhor, 2008) and step-siblings (Khan & Cooke, 2008). The most extensively studied microsystem-level predictors of sibling physical abuse are characteristics of the family. Physically abusive siblings are often reproducing parental behaviors; because the parents maltreat each other, they tend to ignore and/or minimize their children's violence (Wiehe, 1997). Not surprisingly, families in which children physically abuse each other appear to be characterized by chaos, disorganization, and such problems as parental drug and alcohol abuse, parental mental illness, and/or marital difficulties (Wiehe, 1997). The parents may not only be violent but also lack warmth and positive affect. The balance of care in these families and the attention given to the children is often inappropriate. For example, the perpetrating child is often asked to take care of his or her younger sibling when the older child is still not mature enough or capable of being a caretaker (Green, 1984; Wiehe, 1997).

Individual/Developmental. Perpetrators of sibling physical abuse are frequently impulsive and quick-tempered children who often feel powerless or inferior for some reason. Usually they are older children who have a problem with a new child coming into the family. Their feelings of inferiority or powerlessness may stem in part from the lack of attention they perceive from their parents, and they may act aggressively to express hostility toward their parents, gain attention, or master their victimization status by becoming a perpetrator (Green, 1984; Wiehe, 1997). Or their feelings of inferiority and powerlessness may stem from a learning disability, some type of organic dysfunction, or some other physical or psychological impairment (Green, 1984).

Sexual Maltreatment

Microsystem. Families characterized by sibling incest have been described as distant and inaccessible (Smith & Israel, 1987) and dysfunctional in child-rearing practices and rules (Laviola, 1992). There is often marital discord, parental rejection and/or physical abuse of the perpetrator, a negative and argumentative family atmosphere, and an all-around dissatisfaction with family relations (Adler & Schutz, 1995; Rudd & Herzberger, 1999; Worling, 1995). Many of these families are large (Cyr et al., 2002; Finkelhor, 1980; Rudd & Herzberger, 1999; Russell, 1986). Sometimes either the father is not present or there is a general problem with alcoholism or mental illness in the family (Cyr et al., 2002; Meiselman, 1978; Rudd & Herzberger, 1999). Indeed, in one study nearly 34% of sibling incest cases came from single-parent homes and 26% from reconstructed families (O'Brien, 1991). Moreover, a substantial minority of sibling incest offenders may have observed sexual activity between their parents or between their parent and another adult

(Smith & Israel, 1987). On the other hand, a minority of these families may be characterized by rigid, puritanical sex values where sexual expression in the children is discouraged (O'Brien, 1991). Victimization seems to transmit through families characterized by sibling incest, as many mothers had been either sexually or physically abused themselves (Adler & Schutz, 1995). In 22% of the families in one study (O'Brien, 1991), there was another type of incestuous behavior occurring, such as father/daughter incest (Smith & Israel, 1987).

Individual/Developmental. Often, sibling perpetrators have themselves been sexually abused; clinical samples of sibling sexual abusers reveal that 23% to 67% reported a history of sexual abuse (Becker, Kaplan, Cunningham-Rathner, & Kavoussi, 1986; O'Brien, 1991; Smith & Israel, 1987). In addition, as many as 92% of sibling incest offenders may have also suffered physical abuse in their families (Adler & Schutz, 1995). Sibling incest perpetrators may also suffer from a variety of psychological problems: In one study (Adler & Schutz, 1995), 75% of the offenders had sought mental health intervention on a previous occasion for problems such as conduct disorders, attention deficit disorder, drug abuse, adjustment disorder, social phobia, dysthymia, post-traumatic stress disorder (PTSD), depression, and learning disabilities (Adler & Schutz, 1995; Becker et al., 1986). Many incest perpetrators have also had other types of sexual disorders (e.g., exhibitionism, voyeurism) that were not directed toward a sibling, and they may have been arrested for a nonsexual crime (Becker et al., 1986; O'Brien, 1991).

Consequences

Although few empirical studies have been conducted on the consequences of sibling abuse, some research shows that a large percentage of sibling abuse survivors experience some type of clinically significant psychological distress (e.g., Cyr et al., 2002). As with other types of abuse, the frequency, duration, and intensity of sibling abuse moderate the consequences, as does the parents' reaction to the abuse. Many of the victims described by Wiehe (1997) came from homes in which abuse was endemic. The parents did not always intervene in the sibling abuse and even acted in ways that further victimized the child. For example, many parents denied the suffering of the victim and minimized or ignored any evidence of abuse or its consequences. Often, the parents would blame the victims, saying they must have done something to deserve it. More commonly, they would punish both the victim and perpetrator, usually physically. Other common, but unfortunate, reactions to sibling violence are indifference because the parents have their own problems to worry about or, even worse, joining in on the abuse (Wiehe, 1997).

Wiehe (1997) reported that the parents of the victims in his study were more aware of sibling physical and emotional abuse than of sexual abuse. For several reasons, victims did not always tell their parents a sibling was sexually abusing them. First, they may have been too developmentally immature to understand what was happening to them. Often, they were threatened with retaliation if they told, or the perpetrators, especially if they noticed an autonomic pleasure reaction from the victims, would tell them that they "wanted it," and then the victims would blame themselves for the abuse. In addition, the overall climate of the home may have made it impossible to talk about the abuse. Either sex was never discussed, or the victims realized that telling would affect no change. Even if the victim was able to tell the parents about the sexual abuse, the parents would often deny what was happening. As reported in Chapter 3, the closer the perpetrator is to the mother, the less likely she is to believe the victim; in fact, mothers are least likely to believe the child if the sexual abuser is a brother (Cyr et al., 2002). Consider the effects that disclosure had on this victim:

> When I tried to tell my father about it, he called my mother and brother into the room, told them my accusations and asked him if it was true. Naturally, he said I was lying and my mother stood there supporting him. Nothing happened except that I got beaten later by my mother for daring to say anything and for "lying." My brother then knew that from then on, there was nothing he couldn't do to me. He was immune from punishment. Never again did I say a word since to do so would have only meant more abuse from the both of them. (Wiehe, 1997, p. 102)

The consequences of experiencing sibling abuse in such atmospheres are usually devastating to the victims, who often live in constant fear of further abuse. They learn not to cry for help because it often leads only to further abuse (Wiehe, 1997). As children, they may be more likely to use tobacco, alcohol, marijuana, and other substances, and to engage in aggressive and delinquent behavior (Button & Gealt, 2010). Victims of chronic sibling violence (5 or more episodes per year) display elevated trauma symptoms, particularly younger children (Finkelhor, 2008).

Even as adults, victims of sibling physical, emotional, and sexual abuse experience problems in a wide variety of areas (Russell, 1986; Wiehe, 1997). They tend to suffer from poor self-esteem and feelings of absolute worthlessness and have problems in their relationships with members of the opposite sex (Laviola, 1992; Russell, 1986; Wiehe, 1997). The experience of sibling abuse has been shown to predict the use and experience of relationship violence during adulthood (e.g., Russell, 1986; Simonelli, Mullis, Elliott, & Pierce, 2002). If a female is abused by her brother, she may have distrustful, suspicious, fearful, and even hateful feelings toward men, and many do not marry because of these feelings (Russell, 1986; Wiehe, 1997). If they do get involved in relationships, they often replay the victim role because they think it is normal. Some report that if they are married, they want to have only one child to save their own child from the experiences they had (Wiehe, 1997). Adult victims may still experience extreme anger toward their perpetrators, anger that they sometimes take out on inappropriate targets (Wiehe, 1997). Drug and alcohol problems, depression and suicidal ideation, anxiety, eating disorders, and post-traumatic stress symptoms are frequently cited as problems for sibling abuse survivors (Rudd & Herzberger, 1999; Wiehe, 1997), as are insecurity, perceived incompetence, and issues with self-esteem (Hoffman & Edwards, 2004). Many have sexual problems as adults (Laviola, 1992; Wiehe, 1997)—either becoming promiscuous (Rudd & Herzberger, 1999) or withdrawing from and avoiding sexual activity even in marriage, possibly because of flashbacks of the sexual abuse during sex (Wiehe, 1997). Sibling sexual abuse victims may experience recurrent failures in the workplace and social settings, and thus have a general dissatisfaction with life (Abrahams & Hoey, 1994), and they may suffer from shame, fear, humiliation, anger, and guilt (Kiselica & Morrill-Richards, 2007).

Prevention and Intervention

Currently, there is a dearth of formal programs for preventing or intervening in sibling abuse, probably because it has received so little recognition as a problem. Incest is always illegal, whether committed by an adult or a child, but siblings who sexually abuse a sibling may do so for the duration of their childhoods. Although the responsibility for preventing and intervening in sibling abuse should lie with the parents, are there steps that can be taken when those parents choose to ignore, minimize, or even join in on the abuse? If the parents are too wrapped up in their own problems to deal with what is happening between their children, what can be done to stop or prevent sibling abuse?

One step is to bring these behaviors to public attention. Then, if a teacher sees signs of maltreatment in a child, he or she will not excuse the abusive behaviors simply because they came from a sibling and not a parent. Child Protective Services (CPS) must then take these reports seriously and intervene, if only for the reason that in families where sibling abuse is occurring, there are often other types of abuse as well. Intervention services should then focus on the family as a whole to try to help them figure out why one child is abusing the other and what other types of abuse are going on in the family. Importantly, the therapists in these situations need to ask about whether there is any form of sibling abuse, and then take those reports seriously. The child victim will also need therapy to deal with the abuse experienced, but these steps will not be taken if the public and professionals are not educated about this type of abuse.

Maltreatment of Parents

Scope of the Problem

The maltreatment of young or middle-aged adults by their teenage or younger children has been the least researched type of family violence. One reason may be people's reluctance to stretch the term "abused" to refer to parents whose own children are aggressive toward them. If the normal parent-child relationship is one in which a parent has power over the child, is it possible for the child to assume power and abuse the parent? If so, whose fault is it? If the parents are responsible for the child's behavior and the child aggresses toward the parent, can the parent conceivably be "abused" by the very child whose behavior they are responsible for?

Regardless of whether "parent abuse" is the most appropriate term, there is considerable evidence that parents can be the victims of their children's aggression. Harbin and Madden (1979) are credited with first bringing this issue to light, while Cottrell (2001) is credited with defining this form of abuse as an act committed by a child to intentionally cause physical, psychological, or financial pain to the parent. Presumed rates differ depending on the nature of the study. For example, some researchers use population-based studies to understand the prevalence and nature of parent maltreatment (e.g., Straus & Gelles, 1990a), while others use criminal populations to gather this information (e.g., Walsh & Krienert, 2007, 2009). However, both of these types of studies are flawed because parent maltreatment is the most likely form of family violence to be hidden by the victims; parents are likely to deny the abuse or mitigate its severity in an effort to protect their children (Kethineni, 2004). Therefore, many of our estimates are underestimates of the true extent of this problem, even more so than the other types of maltreatment discussed in this book.

The 1975 NFVS, although dated, provides the most comprehensive information on a population-based sample to date. The rate of child-to-parent violence in this survey was very similar to the rate of interparental violence (Straus & Gelles, 1990a). Specifically, according to the parents, 180 of every 1,000 children aged 3 to 17 committed a violent act toward them in the previous year, and 90 of every 1,000 children aged 3 to 17 committed a severely violent act (i.e., an act with a high likelihood of causing an injury). Teenagers aged 15 to 17 are especially likely, in comparison to younger children, to inflict an injury on their parents. The NFVS showed that, in the survey year, 100 per 1,000 teenagers perpetrated a violent act, and 35 per 1,000 teenagers a severely violent act, against their parents. When the rates are projected to the U.S. population as a whole, 9.7 million parents were victims of violence from their children, and 4.8 million were victims of severe violence (Straus & Gelles, 1990a).

In another analysis of the 1975 NFVS, using only families with children aged 10 to 17, 9% of parents were victimized by at least one act of violence from their adolescents in the preceding year, projecting into 2.5 million parents nationwide (Cornell & Gelles, 1982). Further, 3% of parents were kicked, punched, beaten up, and/or had a knife or gun used on them by their adolescents that year, which equaled 900,000 parents nationwide. These numbers from the NFVS are considered to be underestimates of the true rate of child and adolescent violence toward parents because (1) the NFVS did not include families headed by single or divorced parents, and some studies show that the maltreatment of parents is more common in these types of families (e.g., Evans & Warren-Sohlberg, 1988; Livingston, 1986), and (2) most likely, the families with the most severe violence problems were not included (Ulman & Straus, 2003). However, other surveys of high school boys show similar rates of the maltreatment of parents as the NFVS: Between 7% and 11% reported using violence against their parents within the previous one to three years (Brezina, 1999; Peek, Fischer, & Kidwell, 1985). Higher rates of maltreatment were found in one survey of 18-year-old, low-income youth: Over the course of a lifetime, 32% of boys and 29.5% of girls reported hitting a parent (Langhinrichsen-Rohling & Neidig, 1995).

More recently, analyses of the National Incident Based Reporting System (NIBRS) data provided information regarding the percentage of criminal cases that involved child-to-parent violence during the years 1995 to 2005 (Walsh & Krienert, 2009). The NIBRS dataset is collected by the FBI and is much more comprehensive than the Uniform Crime Reports (UCR) dataset. It contains more information about the crime incident than the UCR, but at the same time, it has not yet been deployed nationally. For the data in this analysis, the number of sites reporting increased from 9 states comprising 481 counties (4% of the population) in 1995 to 27 states comprising 5,617 agencies in 2005; therefore, the generalizability of these analyses are difficult to ascertain. Nonetheless, Walsh and Krienert (2009) found that there were 108,231 child-to-parent violence cases during that 1995 to 2005 time period. However, they did not provide any information as to the percent of crimes this represents.

An analysis of official police reports of adolescent-to-parent violence in a Washington city between 1984 and 1987 (Evans & Warren-Sohlberg, 1988) provides useful information about disputes that can lead to an adolescent striking a parent. The 73 cases of violence by adolescents toward parents investigated by police during the three years of the study comprised approximately 5.2% of all family violence cases. In 80% of the cases, the adolescents instigated the argument with their parents; 34% of the cases were typically over aspects of the home life (e.g., responsibilities around the house, privileges, problems with siblings), 22% of the cases involved money issues (e.g., allowances and spending patterns), and 19% of the cases concerned alcohol use by the adolescent. Seven cases (9.6%) confined solely to adolescent daughter/mother disputes, involved arguments concerning sexuality.

A final study of a convenience sample of 34 families experiencing adolescent-to-mother violence found that the violence started when the child was somewhere between the ages of 8 and 16 years, with the most violent time occurring when the child was between the ages of 12 and 16 (McKenna, O'Connor, & Verco, 2010). In at least one case, the child was violent on a daily basis, and in most families, the child's violence was not confined to just one adult—she or he would be violent against another parent or adult in the household and/or siblings as well. Violent children also used a variety of psychologically abusive behaviors as well (McKenna et al., 2010), which are important to outline because some researchers suggest that violence is preceded by these psychologically abusive behaviors, which progress over time in intensity and frequency until they escalate into violence (Eckstein, 2004). Such psychologically abusive behaviors include aggressive demands of money or goods; bullying; verbally intimidating a parent (usually the mother); threats to hurt family members or pets, damage property, steal, run away, or harm themselves; manipulation; locking the family out of the house; refusing to communicate for long periods of time; lying; behaving erratically with sudden outbursts of anger; stealing money or possessions from family members; breaking or destroying household property; abusing pets; breaking or destroying others' possessions; and running up debts with the expectation that the parents would pay. About one third of these children also harmed themselves through cutting, burning, overdosing, and attempting suicide (McKenna et al., 2010).

Predictors and Correlates

Macrosystem

Two macrosystem-level variables have been investigated as possible contributors to the maltreatment of parents—namely attitudes toward aggression and ethnicity. Adolescents who assault their parents are more likely than nonassaultive adolescents to approve of delinquency and violence and believe that they will not be formally punished for their aggressive behavior (Agnew & Huguley, 1989). Furthermore, although most adolescents who assault their parents tend to be White

(Agnew & Huguley, 1989; Charles, 1986; Walsh & Krienert, 2007, 2009), analyses of criminal datasets show that minority adolescents, relative to their distribution in the population, are overrepresented in cases of parent abuse (Evans & Warren-Sohlberg, 1988; Walsh & Krienert, 2007, 2009).

Microsystem

Characteristics of the Victim. The most well-studied characteristic of victimized parents is the parent's gender. Studies consistently show that mothers are much more likely to be victimized by nonlethal aggression than fathers (Cornell & Gelles, 1982; Livingston, 1986; McKenna et al., 2010; Ulman & Straus, 2003; Walsh & Krienert, 2008; Walsh & Krienert, 2007). Among cases in the NIBRS dataset from 2002, 64% of adolescent male violence and over 81.5% of adolescent female violence was directed toward mothers; overall, 70.5% of the victims were mothers (Walsh & Krienert, 2007). In addition, *female* adolescents were more likely than male adolescents to injure their mothers (Walsh & Krienert, 2007). When *fathers* are victimized, it is usually by their older male children (Cornell & Gelles, 1982; Walsh & Krienert, 2007). One possible reason why mothers are victimized more often than fathers is that fathers typically spend less time with children and use less corporal punishment on children than mothers (Ulman & Straus, 2003).

Relationships with Peers. A few studies have examined the association of parent abuse with peer influences (Gallagher, 2004; Howard & Rottem, 2008). For example, adolescents who assault their parents are more likely than nonassaultive adolescents to have friends who assaulted their parents (Agnew & Huguley, 1989); studies also show that parent abuse is associated with belonging to a delinquent peer group (Kratcoski, 1985).

Family Dynamics. Several family-level variables are possible contributors to parent abuse. For example, low family integration (Kratcoski, 1985), weak attachments between parents and children (Agnew & Huguley, 1989), marital conflict, parental minimization of children's hitting (Charles, 1986), unstable family life, and inadequate parenting (Gallagher, 2004; Howard & Rottem, 2008) have all been shown to contribute to children hitting their parents. Single mothers seem especially prone to being hit by their children (Pelletier & Coutu, 1992). For example, in cases reported to police, 46% involved single-mother households, in contrast to 17% of households headed by single mothers nationwide at that time (Evans & Warren-Sohlberg, 1988). It has also been shown that approximately 25% of single mothers with teenagers are hit (Livingston, 1986).

Other Types of Family Violence. The most consistent finding is that children who assault their parents were victimized by violence from the very parents they are now aggressing against (Browne & Hamilton, 1998; Evans & Warren-Sohlberg, 1988; Herbert, 1987; Langhinrichsen-Rohling & Neidig, 1995). In fact, the frequency of parent abuse is strongly related to the frequency of other violence in the home (Herbert, 1987). The more frequently children witness or experience violence from their parents, the more likely they are to hit their parents (Gallagher, 2004; Herbert, 1987). Indeed, four fifths of one sample of children who had hit their parents had recently been victims of their parents' violence, and extrafamilial exposure to violence did not add to the children's tendencies to abuse their parents (Browne & Hamilton, 1998).

Several different types of family violence have been implicated as contributors to children and adolescents hitting their parents. In one study, 29% of physically abused, 24% of emotionally abused, and 29% of sexually abused children were violent toward their parents (Browne & Hamilton, 1998). Both corporal punishment (Brezina, 1999; Larzelere, 1986; Mahoney & Donnelly, 2000; Ulman & Straus, 2003) and more severe physical abuse of children (Hotaling, Straus, & Lincoln, 1990; Kratcoski, 1985; Mahoney & Donnelly, 2000; Meredith, Abbott, & Adams, 1986; Ulman & Straus, 2003) have been shown to predict children's aggression against their parents, as has sibling violence (Kratcoski, 1985). Interparental violence also predicts children's violence toward parents (Gallagher, 2004; Hotaling et al., 1990; Kratcoski, 1985; Langhinrichsen-Rohling & Neidig, 1995; Meredith et al., 1986), particularly in families in which the mother is the sole aggressor toward the father or both parents are violent toward each other (Ulman & Straus, 2003). Although being the victim of violence by parents is more strongly related to children hitting their parents than witnessing interparental violence (Ulman & Straus, 2003), parent abuse was most likely when both types of parental violence were present (Straus & Hotaling, 1980). Thus, there seems to be a cumulative effect of both parent-to-child and interparental violence on the child's violence toward the parent (Ulman & Straus, 2003).

Consider these results now in regard to the issue of labeling adolescent aggression toward a parent as "abusive." If the parents somehow contributed to their own victimization by using violence and teaching their children the appropriateness of violence, should they still be called "victims of parent abuse"? Why or why not?

Individual/Developmental

Gender. Although the NFVS showed no significant gender differences in the use of aggression toward parents (Ulman & Straus, 2003), most studies show that boys are more likely to use violence than girls (e.g., Charles, 1986; Cornell & Gelles, 1982; Evans & Warren-Sohlberg, 1988; Walsh & Krienert, 2007, 2009). Interestingly, two studies showed that girls inflicted more injuries (Charles, 1986; Walsh & Krienert, 2007), particularly against mothers (Walsh & Krienert, 2007), possibly because they tend to use an object during their aggressive incidents (Charles, 1986).

Age. Analyses of the 1975 NFVS showed that young children have the highest rates of hitting parents: 33% of three- to five-year-olds hit their parents in the previous year, compared to 10% of children ages 14 to 17 (Ulman & Straus, 2003). These results were explained by the fact that as children age, they have more control over their behavior and experience less corporal punishment from their parents; therefore, they are less likely to aggress. The majority of acts that the young children used would usually not be considered "abusive" by certain standards because they do not cause any harm or injury to the parents.

Nonetheless, the majority of children who commit more severe, concerning and injurious violence toward their parents seem to be teenagers (Harbin & Madden, 1979; Straus & Gelles, 1990a; Walsh & Krienert, 2007, 2009), although there are accounts of ten-year-olds injuring their parents (Harbin & Madden, 1979). Of child-to-parent violence cases reported to the police in the NIBRS dataset from 1995 to 2005, 15.2% were committed by children 13 and under, 47.5% by children ages 14 to 16, and 37.3% by children ages 17 to 21 (Walsh & Krienert, 2009). Finally, there is evidence that for boys, severe aggression against parents increases with age (e.g., Agnew & Huguley, 1989; Cornell & Gelles, 1982), whereas daughters' severe aggression decreases with age (Agnew & Huguley, 1989). In fact, boys are significantly older when they assault their parents than girls are (Kethineni, 2004; Walsh & Krienert, 2007), which may reflect their later onset of developmental maturity.

Other Personality and Behavioral Predictors. Other individual/developmental variables predictive of aggression against parents include adolescent psychosocial problems. A substantial percentage of adolescents who assault their parents have prior police records and/or contact with a social service agency (Evans & Warren-Sohlberg, 1988), are delinquent at school (Cornell & Gelles, 1982), and have a history of substance abuse (Gallagher, 2004; Howard & Rottem, 2008; Pelletier & Coutu, 1992; Schiff & Cavaiola, 1993). However, a minority of adolescents arrested for assaulting their parents were drinking or using drugs at the time of the arrest (Walsh & Krienert, 2007, 2009). Moreover, an inflated sense of entitlement; health, behavioral, or learning difficulties; and previous trauma as a result of abuse or bullying have also been implicated in children's violence toward parents (Gallagher, 2004; Howard & Rottem, 2008).

Consequences

Several physical and psychological consequences have been shown to result from child-to-parent violence. For example, in the 2002 NIBRS dataset, 43.1% of fathers sustained a minor injury and 2.9% sustained a major injury, whereas 39.5% of mothers sustained a minor injury and 1.1% sustained a major injury (Walsh & Krienert, 2007). In depth interviews with 34 parents show other potential consequences (McKenna et al., 2010). For example, nearly half said they were fearful for their own safety and over a third said they were fearful for the safety of other children in the household. More than two thirds said they were very stressed and anxious; about half said they were depressed, angry, and/or frustrated; and over one third said they were sad and/or unable to cope. About a quarter of the parents felt shame, guilt, or self-blame; and almost one third felt isolated and alone in their struggles (McKenna et al., 2010).

Parents also reported that their children's violence affected their health, and financial and social well-being. About half reported health problems, including high blood pressure, stress, and migraines, and that any preexisting health problems had been exacerbated by their child's violence. About a quarter reported that the violence had drained their financial resources because they were unable to work due to the stress or injuries incurred, and/or the child had destroyed valuable possessions and property. About two thirds reported significant relationship problems with their partners, friends, and/or extended family members because of the child's violence (McKenna et al., 2010).

Finally, affected parents reported that the child's violence had a negative impact on other family members. For example, siblings feared for their safety and were distressed or depressed. These siblings also did not like the violent child and sometimes resented the fact that the violent child became the focus of the parents' energies, leaving the nonviolent siblings to feel neglected (McKenna et al., 2010).

The most well-researched consequence of parent abuse is also the gravest possible consequence, the death of the parent. Between 1995 and 2005, of the 108,310 cases of violence by children toward parents, 79 (0.07%) of them were parricides (Walsh & Krienert, 2008). Consider the case in Box 10.3. What factors do you think prompted Terry to kill the parents who supposedly cared for him? Consider that Terry's father attempted to stab Terry once and pulled a gun on him once. How culpable do you think Terry is for his actions considering the situation he was in?

Box 10.3   Kids Who Kill Parents

Terry Adams and his two older sisters had long been physically and emotionally abused by their parents, both alcoholics....Once [Terry's sisters] were gone, Terry became the sole target of the abuse. At the age of 16, he decided there was no alternative but to leave...and make it on his own. Terry had to go through his parents' bedroom to get out of the house. While he was attempting to escape this way during the early morning hours, Mr. Adams woke up and confronted his son. Terry told his dad that he was tired of the way he was living, that he was old enough to make it on his own, and that he knew what he was doing...Maybe he could not leave home legally, Terry told his dad, but he didn't care: He was leaving anyway. Mr. Adams slugged his son, knocking him down. When the youth got back up, his father pushed him over, and he fell into a closet where several guns were kept—including a .22 caliber rifle. Terry grabbed the rifle and fired at his father. He remembered his father screaming, "Oh my God!" Terry's mother, who was in bed when her husband was shot, woke up when the gun went off. Terry could not remember actually shooting his parents, particularly his mother. All he could remember was her face "when she sat up in bed...the agony within the terror....The rest of it is more or less, sort of hazed out for me. I remember waking up completely. Standing there looking at two dead bodies. Two people. What have I done now, you know. Like it was a dream."...Court records showed that four petitions alleging neglect, abuse, and physical abuse in the Adams home had been filed and investigated by the state social services agency. Three of the petitions named Terry as the victim and had been filed in the two years preceding the homicides. The latest referral was made when Terry was 15....Ten months after the state agency terminated supervision, Mr. and Mrs. Adams were dead.

SOURCE: Heide, 1995, pp. xiii–xiv

Adolescent Parricide

The most recent statistics from the FBI's Uniform Crime Reports (2010) show that in 2010, 107 mothers and 135 fathers were killed by their children, which represents 1.9% of all homicides and 13.4% of all family homicides. Neither the age of the offender nor the age of the victim was recorded in these data, so it is impossible to know how many of these parents were victims of elder abuse versus how many were victims of parent abuse. However, one extensive study of homicide data between the years 1976 and 1999 may provide a clearer picture (Heide & Petee, 2007). Throughout this period, 5,781 parents were killed; 36.5% of the fathers and 25% of the mothers who were killed were killed by adolescents 19 years of age and under.

Who Kills and How? In Heide and Petee's (2007) analysis, sons were responsible for approximately 87% of patricides and 84% of matricides, which is proportional to the gender distribution of homicide offenders in general. In the majority of cases, the child who killed his parent was a White, non-Hispanic male. The proportion of Black youth who killed their parents (27.8%) exceeded their representation in the population (12% to 13%) at that time but was less than their representation as homicide offenders in general (51%) (Heide & Petee, 2007). In an earlier analysis of FBI data, Heide (1995) found that guns are typically the weapon of choice for adolescent parricide offenders: 82% of the fathers, 75% of the stepfathers, 65% of the mothers, and 56% of the stepmothers were killed with a gun.

Who Was Killed? Parents who were murdered were typically White, non-Hispanic (Heide & Petee, 2007). Prior analyses showed that murdered stepparents were typically younger than murdered biological parents, and murdered male parents were on average younger than murdered female parents. Moreover, mothers were significantly more likely to be White than fathers were (Heide, 1995).

Why Did the Adolescents Kill? Heide (1995) identified three types of adolescent parricide offenders: (1) the severely abused child; (2) the severely mentally ill child; and (3) the dangerously antisocial child. The *severely abused child* is the most frequently encountered adolescent parricide offender: Over 90% of adolescent parricide offenders were abused by their parents, could no longer tolerate the abuse, and thus perceived the homicide as an act of desperation. *Severely mentally ill children* are psychotic individuals with disorganized personalities; they tend to have distorted perceptions and disjointed communication skills. When more than one family member is killed and there is extreme violence or dismemberment of the bodies, most likely the child was severely mentally ill. *Dangerously antisocial children* have a sociopathic personality but do not experience the delusions or hallucinations that might affect severely mentally ill children. However, they do display irrational behavior, poor judgment, and shallow emotions. They do not learn from experience, nor do they experience anxiety or guilt over their violations of the rights of others. In many cases, these typologies are not mutually exclusive—any given adolescent parricide offender could fall into one, two, or all three of these categories (Heide, 1995).

For the most part, adolescent parricide offenders tend to suffer from severe maltreatment and have few alternatives to remove themselves from the maltreatment. They typically suffer both abuse and neglect, and often experience injuries and threats of serious injury or death. The family is typically characterized by severe spousal abuse and alcoholism/heavy drinking, both of which predate the child abuse. Many children who experience this type of home environment do not kill their parents; however, typically, adolescent parricide offenders had made unsuccessful attempts to get help and, around the time of the homicide, had been increasingly considering either suicide or flight as a means of escape. The homicide was usually a reaction to a perceived or real imminent threat from their parents. Generally, adolescent parricide offenders do not have an extensive delinquent history, if any. However, a gun is usually easily accessible in the house. During the homicide, parricide offenders typically report a dissociative state, and the parent's death is usually seen as a relief for both the adolescent and other family members (Heide, 1995).

There seem to be important differences between homes in which the mother was killed by a son and those in which the father was killed by a son. In homes where matricide occurred, the mother was typically psychologically and sexually abusive of her son. The fathers were passive and pacified their wives, while being physically and emotionally distant and nonsupportive of their sons (Cormier, Angliker, Gagne, & Markus, 1978). In homes in which patricide occurred, the fathers were usually severely physically abusive, especially of the mothers, who were typically weak, helpless, and passive. The sons watched this abuse and were often called on by their mothers to protect them (Cormier et al., 1978). When daughters killed their parents, it was usually the case that the parents were abusive (Cormier et al., 1978).

What Do We Do with the Offenders? Reactions of the judicial system to the adolescent parricide offender are becoming more compassionate, and the battered child defense has been successfully used in trials of parricide offenders. With proper intervention, many adolescent parricide offenders can function normally within society and be productive. Treatment is usually consonant with that of the severely abused child—for example, the offenders must understand the family dynamics that led them to murder (Heide, 1995). Experts stress that adolescent parricide offenders should not go to prison because good therapy is usually not available there (Heide, 1995). However, they should be institutionalized for a few years, until they are able to obtain therapy and gain self-control (Duncan & Duncan, 1971; Russell, 1984).

Prevention and Intervention

Although it is unknown how frequently parents seek help when their children are violent and abusive toward them, at least one study provides some indication as to what parents experience when they try to seek help. This was an interview study of 34 parents whose children were violent toward them, and overall, these parents reported that when they sought help, they were typically not believed or they were blamed for the violent behavior of their children (McKenna et al., 2010).

In short, there are very few, if any, services available to children who are violent toward their parents and their parent-victims. Moreover, there is a general ignorance of this problem among the general public and professionals alike. Only a minority of people in this study said that the friends or professionals from whom they sought help were very helpful, with professionals being even less helpful than friends or family members. The most helpful assistance identified by these parents included people who provided emotional support, people who actually listened to and believed them, and parent support groups. The parents also discussed services that would be helpful if the professionals who headed them were properly trained in these issues: family counseling, parenting courses, peer parental support groups, respite programs, and support for children with mental health issues. Parents also identified the need to disseminate information about the realities of child-to-parent violence to professionals and the public alike so that appropriate prevention and intervention services can be developed (McKenna et al., 2010).

Summary

This chapter reviewed the scant literature on two hidden forms of family violence, specifically violence against siblings and parents by children and adolescents. Although some argue that sibling abuse is merely sibling rivalry, many of the statistics and case examples argue otherwise; that is, many boys and girls are the victims of behaviors that could be labeled physical, sexual, and/or emotional abuse at the hands of their siblings. Furthermore, because sibling abuse is not always recognized as a form of maltreatment, these children often have few resources to help them: Their parents do not always believe they are victimized, sometimes parental behaviors further victimize them, and even when they become adults they cannot always tell their stories without ridicule because of disbelief that siblings can abuse each other. The second hidden form of maltreatment discussed, parent abuse, may not be considered abuse primarily because the children may be behaving similarly to their parents, and often their violent behavior is a reaction to the severe abuse they receive from their parents. Can children abuse their parents, then? Is there ever a situation in which innocent parents are subject to extreme violence from their children?

Discussion Questions

1. Why are acts such as hitting, kicking, punching, and slapping considered abuse when a boyfriend does this to a girlfriend, but not when a sibling does it to another sibling?

2. Why do you suppose sibling violence decreases with age?

3. Are you surprised by the gender differences in sibling abuse? Why or why not?

4. Do you believe the child's gender has an effect on the impact of sibling abuse? Why or why not?

5. What are your thoughts on the prevalence of college students who reported having some type of sexual experience with a sibling? Are you surprised?

6. Do you believe parents should be held legally accountable for sibling maltreatment? Is refraining from getting help abusive? What should parents do when they find their child has been abused by a sibling? What resources should be made available for parents? Are current resources adequate?

7. How can children 'abuse' their parents who are the power figures or the one with the power and control in the relationship?

8. Why is parental maltreatment more common in single-parent or divorced families? How does this alter a parent's power or authority?

9. Parental maltreatment is one of the least reported types of maltreatment. Why is it so underreported? What would be a parent's mindset? How would this mindset compare or differ from a victim who has undergone spousal maltreatment?

10. Mothers are much more likely to be maltreated by their children (by nonlethal means) than fathers. Why is this so? What would make them the more likely target?

11. Why/how would corporal punishment of children increase their tendency to maltreat their parents? What else leads to a greater tendency to maltreat one's parents? What could lower the risk of parental maltreatment?

12. What are the consequences of parental maltreatment for the victimized parents? What are the consequences for the maltreating children? What could lessen these consequences?

PART V

Cultural Issues in Family Violence

11

Ecological Contexts of Family Violence

Four-year-old Marchella Pierce died in September 2010 weighing only eighteen pounds. For her short life, she knew nothing but poverty and hardship—she called "home" a decrepit house in Brooklyn and suffered daily at the hands of her substance-abusing mother, who often drugged and bound the little girl to her bed. Four individuals were arrested in connection with Marchella's death; two of those arrested were Marchella's mother, Carlotta Brett-Pierce (aged 31), for murder, and Marchella's grandmother, Loretta Brett (age 56) for manslaughter. Notably for the criminal justice system, Damon Adams (age 37) a Children's Services caseworker and his supervisor, Chereece Bell (age 34) were charged with criminally negligent homicide. Charles J. Hynes, the Brooklyn district attorney, considered the case of Marchella Pierce's horrible death as "evidence of alleged systemic failures" in New York City's child welfare agency. According to prosecutors, caseworkers ignored the family and bleak state of Marchella Pierce. Marchella's great-aunt Levonnia Parnell, commented, "That's not a child that asked to be here. No child deserves what she got. She got a nightmare" (Kleinfield, 2011, p. A1).

Kendra was living with Roberto, her 34-year-old boyfriend, and her two young daughters, Diana and Rhiannon. At the time, Kendra was unemployed and pregnant with her third child. Roberto, a construction worker, was having immense trouble finding consistent employment. Because of the difficult economic circumstances, the family could not afford to pay their bills or debts, or buy necessary household items or sufficient groceries. One month prior to the current incident, both Kendra and Roberto had been incarcerated for possession of illicit substances, public intoxication, and committing acts of domestic violence. On this occasion, while drunk, Kendra's comments to Roberto concerning an alleged infidelity escalated into a physical altercation. When questioned, Kendra reported that her husband had repeatedly slapped her, pushed her, and hit her on numerous instances in the past. Furthermore, Roberto often threatened to abandon Kendra and take Diana and Rhiannon as a means of control (Donohue et al., 2010, p. 108).

In considering the role of cultural context in family violence, we focus on "culture-as-meaning"—for example, notions within a social group as to what it means to be abusive and attitudes as to the role of government in family affairs. Although the United States is a diversified, multicultural society, certain forms of violence and certain sets of hierarchical relationships have been considered by large segments of society as not just justifiable but morally correct. Moreover, in some ways, the traditional valuing of freedom from government control has helped to maintain violence in the home.

Most Americans know it is against the law to abuse children and the elderly. Many also know that wives can take out restraining orders against husbands to protect themselves from abuse. It is probably less well known that it is possible for husbands to seek similar legal protections if they fear abuse from their wives. Yet, despite all the recent violence prevention legislation, the United States has a long tradition of tolerating violence within the home and by its own institutions. We begin this chapter by briefly placing America's culture of violence into an historical framework. We then provide an overview of the research literature concerning tolerance of violence and abuse in the majority culture. Finally, we identify selected norms within the macrosystem that are an important part of the cultural context of family violence.

The Contemporary Context

In the United States today, homicide (generally as a result of maltreatment), accounts for over one in five injury-related deaths in infants under one year of age (Child Trends Data Bank, 2010). Homicide, typically through beatings or suffocation, has also been identified as the fourth leading cause of death of children ages 1 to 4. It is committed largely by family members—typically mothers in the first few months, and often fathers or stepfathers in later months (Child Trends Data Bank, 2010). Moreover, these rates are likely to be underestimates. According to one analysis, from 1985 through 1996, the total number of homicides due to abuse in children younger than 11 years was more likely to be 9,467 rather than the 2,973 reported (Herman-Giddens et al., 1999).

Similar to estimates of other forms of family violence, estimates of child fatalities from abuse vary based on reporting agency, but in all cases the numbers are distressingly high. The U.S. Department of Health and Human Services (USDHHS, 2011) reported that there were an estimated 1,560 child maltreatment fatalities in 2010, for an estimated rate of 2.07 children per 100,000. In addition, about 40.8% of these victims suffered from multiple types of child maltreatment, 32.6% from neglect exclusively, and 22.9% from physical abuse. Approximately four fifths of child fatalities (79.2%) were perpetrated by one or more parents, of which 29.2% were caused by the mother acting alone and 21.9% by both parents (USDHHS, 2011).

The rates of child maltreatment deaths in the United States are among the highest in the industrialized world, with over 25 children dying every week from maltreatment. This rate is either the highest or third highest rate (following Mexico and Portugal) of child maltreatment deaths of the 30 industrialized member nations of the Organization of Economic Cooperation and Development (UNICEF, 2003). The main conclusion of this UNICEF study was that the

> challenge of ending child abuse . . . is . . . breaking the link between adults' problems and children's pain. It ought not to be part of family culture, or of our societies' culture, for the psychological, social, or economic stresses of adults to be vented on children, or for problems and frustrations to be so easily translated into abuse of the defenseless. The task is therefore one of creating a culture of nonviolence towards children. (UNICEF, 2003, p. 22)

According to Michael Petit, president of Every Child Matters, the child maltreatment death rate in America is three times that of Canada and eleven times that of Italy. Seventy-five percent of these deaths occur when the child is younger than four, while almost half occur before the child reaches his or her first birthday (Petit, 2011).

Women are more likely to be murdered by intimates than by any other assailant. Homicide by an intimate partner is the seventh leading cause of premature death for women in general in the United States and is the leading cause of death for African American women between the ages of 15 and 45 years (Greenfeld et al., 1998). According to Bureau of Justice Statistics (Catalano, Smith, Snyder, & Rand, 2009), in 2007, 24% of female homicide victims were murdered by a spouse or ex-spouse and an additional 21% were the victims of a boyfriend or girlfriend. Other information from the Bureau of Justice Statistics (Catalano, Smith, Snyder, & Rand, 2009) indicated that between 1993 and 2007, the rate of murder by a spouse declined 41% for women and 54% for men; rates of murder by a boyfriend or girlfriend also declined during this time. On the other hand, the percentage of women homicide victims who were killed by an intimate partner increased from 40% in 1993 to 45% in 2007, while the percentage of male homicide victims killed by an intimate partner declined slightly from 6% in 1993 to 5% in 2007. Moreover, women are twice as likely as men to be killed by intimate partners and constitute 70% of the victims, a rate that has remained almost unchanged since 1993.

It appears that in approximately 70% to 80% of all intimate partner homicides, regardless of which partner was killed, the woman was involved in a physically violent relationship in which either or both partners were physically aggressive (e.g., Greenfeld et al., 1998). Although homicide is only one index of violence, it is noteworthy that the United States has the highest female homicide rate of 25 high-income nations. Although the United States contains only 32% of the female population living within these 25 nations, it accounts for 70% of all female homicides and 84% of all female firearm homicides. Approximately 4,000 women are murdered in the United States each year—at a rate that is five times that of all the other high-income countries combined. A woman in the United States is eight times more likely than a woman in England and Wales, three times more likely than a woman in Canada, and five times more likely than a woman in Germany to be murdered (Hemenway, Shinoda-Tagawa, & Miller, 2002).

These high rates of violence against women are consistent with the relatively high rate of violent crime overall in the United States (Felson, 2002). Accordingly, violence against men is also an epidemic in the United States. The majority of this violence is perpetrated by other men—most typically unrelated men, but violence by female partners also occurs. In fact, the majority of victims of both male and female violence in this country are male (Felson, 2002). Between 1976 and 2000, over 500,000 males and females over the age of 12 had been murdered—the majority by somebody they knew, and about 11% by an intimate. As perpetrators of murder, women were more likely to kill somebody as a result of an argument or by poison (Fox & Zawitz, 2002). In addition, American men may be more at risk of sustaining violence from their wives than men in other countries (Kumagai & Straus, 1983).

Finally, every year, there may be at least two million older Americans who are maltreated by family members. According to the National Elder Abuse Incidence Study of 1996, two thirds of the perpetrators of elder abuse were adult children or spouses. These maltreated elders tend to die earlier than nonabused elders, even in the absence of chronic conditions or life-threatening disease (American Psychological Association, 2003). A more recent study (Acierno et al., 2010) of a nationally representative sample of nearly 6,000 community-living elders yielded prevalence rates of 4.6% for emotional abuse, 1.6% for physical abuse, 0.6% for sexual abuse, 5.1% for potential neglect, and 5.2% for current financial abuse by a family member.

In previous chapters, you have learned a great deal about the predictors and correlates of various forms of family violence. The purpose of this chapter is to situate family violence within the broader culture of violence characteristic of the United States. People do not harm family members just when they are angry or drunk, or just because they observed and/or experienced violence in childhood. Often they cause harm because they live in a culture that tolerates violence and provides rationales for various forms of aggression. Not all members of a society subscribe to all the cultural beliefs and values that may predominate in their society, but if we are to understand why so many people in the United States abuse and neglect their family members, we need to consider major perspectives on violence and punishment both within families and in the culture as a whole.

Perspectives on Corporal Punishment and Child Physical Abuse

Since 2001, more than 20,000 children in the United States are estimated to have been killed in their homes at the hands of family members—nearly four times the number of American soldiers killed in Iraq and Afghanistan. In 2009 alone, close to 2,500 children died as a result of maltreatment (Petit, 2011). Before proceeding, read the items in Box 11.1, and indicate the extent to which you agree with each statement.

Box 11.1	Attitudes Toward Corporal Punishment

Read each statement below and indicate the extent to which you agree with it by choosing a number from 1 (strongly disagree) to 7 (strongly agree).

   (a) Punishing a child physically when he/she deserves it will make him/her a responsible and mature adult.

(Continued)

(Continued)

    (b) Giving mischievous children a quick slap is the best way to quickly end trouble.

    (c) An adult should beat a child with a strap or stick for being expelled.

    (d) A parent hitting a child when he/she does something bad on purpose teaches the child a good lesson.

    (e) Young children who refuse to obey should be whipped.

    (f) Children should be spanked for temper tantrums.

    (g) A child's habitual disobedience should be punished physically.

SOURCE: Anderson, Benjamin, Wood, & Bonacci, 2006

A major issue in the American macrosystem is the extent to which spanking should be considered a form of abuse. Some investigators have argued that spanking is primordial violence, teaching generation after generation that violence is socially legitimate, despite its harmful effects (Straus, 2005b). Whether the label of abuse is applied to spanking or not, various professional groups and international human rights organizations have argued that spanking is not a disciplinary tactic that promotes the well-being of the child and that it violates the innate human rights of the child (e.g., Walker, Brooks, & Wrightsman, 1999).

Nevertheless, in the United States, there is strong cultural support for physically punishing children. According to a 2008 nationally representative survey, 77% of men and 65% of women between the ages of 18 and 65 agreed with the idea that sometimes a child needs a "good hard spanking" (Child Trends Data Bank, 2009). Studies with less representative samples have also shown considerable support for corporal punishment. For example, in one college sample (Flynn, 1998), a majority of the participants considered physical punishment to be appropriate for three- and four-year-olds who took something that did not belong to them, misbehaved in public, and talked back to or hit one of their parents; indeed, nearly 90% of the college students considered spanking to be appropriate discipline for a toddler in at least one of those hypothetical situations. Although support for corporal punishment of older children was less strong, 60% viewed physical punishment as appropriate for 7- or 8-year-olds who stole or talked back (Flynn, 1998). What are your views concerning how such forms of misbehavior should be handled?

In a recent study of more than 600 students from a midwestern college, 87% of the respondents held that parents should be allowed to spank their children, and 52% said the government should not interfere with parents whipping children for bad behavior (Lambert, Jenkins, & Ventura, 2009). How would you interpret these findings? Is it possible that some of the students are not supportive of corporal punishment but nevertheless believed that the government should not be circumscribing parental rights to rear their children as they see fit? What are your views on the role of governments vis a vis parental child-rearing practices?

Despite evidence of strong support for corporal punishment in this country, there is also some evidence that this support has shown modest declines over the years, especially since the 1980s when surveys emerged measuring the public's attitudes toward corporal punishment (Straus & Mathur, 1996). Moreover, there is evidence that support for corporal punishment varies across demographic groups. For example, support for corporal punishment has been shown to be stronger in men than in women and in Republicans than in Democrats. Support for corporal punishment has also declined more markedly in women than in men (Child Trends Data Bank, 2009).

Although support for corporal punishment may be declining in this country, the Americans' perspectives on corporal punishment show much greater tolerance than is found in many other countries where corporal punishment of children is illegal and is viewed as a violation of the United Nations Convention on the Rights of the Child (e.g., Pollard, 2003). A report to the United Nations General Assembly in October 2006 from the Secretary General's Study of Violence against Children urged all member states of the United Nations to ban all forms of violence against children, including corporal punishment (Committee on the Rights of the Child, 2006). However, in one of the few efforts in the United States to legislate against corporal punishment, a Massachusetts state legislator introduced a bill to ban spanking in the home in 2007, and it was quickly defeated (Cope, 2010).

There is also a tendency to differ between the lay public and relevant professionals and among relevant professional groups (e.g., social service workers, criminal justice workers) regarding levels of tolerance of violence against children, and readiness to label violence as abusive. When asked to judge the seriousness of vignettes dealing with psychological abuse (publicly ridiculing a child), neglect (leaving a child outside in a car at a shopping center for several hours in the cold of winter), and physical abuse (slapping a child in the face with an open hand, knocking him down, and splitting his lip), lay respondents and juvenile detectives judged the situations as more abusive than did Child Protective Services (CPS) workers (Kean & Dukes, 1991).

Review your responses to the survey questions in Box 11.1. How do your views compare to the ones you have read about in this section? If you responded with any number other than 1 for any of the items, does that mean you are showing some tolerance for child abuse? Would you interpret scores other than 1 as reflecting some reasoning or process other than tolerance for aggression?

Perspectives on Child Sexual Abuse

In 1982, a judge in Wisconsin sentenced a man to 90 days in a work-release program following his trial on the charge of sexually assaulting the five-year-old daughter of the woman with whom he was living. The explanation provided by the judge for his lenient sentence was, "I am satisfied we have an unusually sexually promiscuous young lady. And [the defendant] did not know enough to refuse. No way do I believe he initiated sexual contact" (Nyhan, 1982, in Finkelhor & Redfield, 1984, p. 108). Do you think a five-year-old child can be sexually promiscuous? Should a child ever be held responsible for an adult's behavior? What kinds of cultural values might have contributed to the judge's analysis of this case? This case occurred in 1982; do you think a judge today would have a similar interpretation?

Research subsequent to that judicial decision has revealed a number of variables that influence the extent to which people view specific types of child sexual abuse as serious and/or abusive. Consider the following vignette:

Helen, age 8, has been very moody over the past 6 months and her parents were concerned about her. They sent Helen to see a psychotherapist, whom she has been seeing once a week on a regular basis. This week she told her therapist that she was abused one time by her father a few weeks ago. The incident occurred when she was home alone with her father one night when her mother had to work late. Her dad came into her bedroom to tuck her in bed and say goodnight. This was their typical routine. On this night, her dad pulled the sheets off of her and put his hands on her underwear. He knelt beside her bed and rubbed her vagina through her underwear. Helen told her therapist that "he was doing something to my private parts for a very long time." When the therapist asked Helen to guess how long her father was hurting her, Helen replied "About 10 minutes." After a while he stopped rubbing, tucked her in bed, and said goodnight. He also told her not to tell anyone about this. Helen told her therapist that this was the first time anything like this had happened. (Bornstein, Kaplan, & Perry, 2007, p. 380)

Please indicate the extent to which you view the events described in this scenario as (a) traumatic, (b) a serious form of abuse, (c) a generally occurring event, and (d) a problem that is likely to recur within the particular relationship described. Use a 7-point scale (e.g., from 1, not at all, to 7, extremely) to indicate your judgments. Now, read the scenario again, only this time substitute the name Rick for the name Helen, and change the pronouns to be consistent with a male victim. Does that change or affect your judgments of how traumatic and serious the father's sexual behavior is, the chance of such behavior occurring in society, and the likelihood of it recurring in this particular relationship? Why or why not? What if we replace the word "father" with "mother" in the scenario, making the mother the perpetrator of the behavior with her daughter? Her son? What would your rating scale responses be if the perpetrator was a male or female babysitter? When Bornstein, Kaplan, and Perry (2007) presented the different versions of this scenario to 199 participants (both university students and nonstudent adults), they found that the sexual behavior was viewed as more traumatic and more serious when perpetrated by a parent than by a babysitter, and seen as least traumatic when it was done by a female adult to a male victim. Girls were viewed as more likely to be victims than boys, and abuse by a father was seen as a more common occurrence than abuse by a babysitter. Recurrence was judged to be more likely for heterosexual than homosexual abuse when the perpetrator was a male. What do you think of these findings? Are any of them surprising?

Several other studies have also examined the extent to which characteristics of some sort of sexual predation by an adult influence the extent to which the predatory behavior is seen as abusive. For example, if children are portrayed as acting passively in response to sexual abuse, the situation is rated as less abusive, even when the child is very young (e.g., age 0 to 6) (Mellott, Wagner, & Broussard, 1997). What is your view? If an adult seeks sexual pleasure by fondling the genitals of a 2-year-old, 5-year-old, or 12-year-old, is the behavior any less abusive if the child does not resist strongly? And does it matter how old the child is? Some researchers have found that older victims (e.g., 13- or 15-year-olds) of child sexual abuse are blamed more for their abuse than younger victims (e.g., 6- or 7-year-olds) (Back & Lips, 1998; Maynard & Wiederman, 1997). Is this judgment appropriate?

Although the evidence is mixed, both the gender of the child and the gender of the perpetrator sometimes influence people's judgments about whether a particular sexual behavior is abusive. In one study, students rated scenarios where the abuser was of a different sex from the child as less abusive than same-sex scenarios (Maynard & Wiederman, 1997). When the victim was described as a 15-year-old, less blame was attributed to the perpetrator than when an adult of either sex was described as molesting a 7-year-old; the least blame was attributed to an adult involved with an opposite-sex adolescent. When the perpetrator was described as a man, the harmful effects were assumed to be worse if the victim was a boy than a girl (Mellott et al., 1997). Do you agree with the judgments of these students? Why or why not?

Other characteristics influencing the extent to which individuals judge sexual aggression against children as abusive include the amount of parenting experience—the greater the experience, the more serious the abuse is judged to be (Portwood, 1998). Moreover, greater valuing of children is associated with lower tolerance for sexual maltreatment (Ferrari, 2002), and there is some evidence that the greater one's degree of conformity to traditional sex roles, the more one blames sexually abused children for their own abuse (Ford, Schindler, & Medway, 2001).

Although some ethnic groups (e.g., Latinos) appear to be less tolerant of child sexual abuse than other groups (Fontes, Cruz, & Tabachnick, 2001), overall, Americans seem somewhat reluctant to put full blame on perpetrators of sexual abuse—or even to call their behavior abusive—except in the most egregious circumstances or when the perpetrator is the same sex as the victim. According to Daro (2002),

> It is not uncommon for individuals to identify extenuating circumstances when things that are labeled "abuse" reflect behaviors or attitudes commonplace among their peers or understandable given their social context. This type of definitional manipulation recently led a U.S. Catholic Cardinal to distinguish between a priest who repeatedly abuses young boys versus a priest who, under the possible influence of alcohol, returns the sexual affections of a 16-year-old girl. (p. 1132)

This tendency to apportion degrees of blame in relation to sexually abusive behaviors makes it difficult to develop a coherent and effective public policy response (Daro, 2002).

Internationally, child sexual abuse is much more widespread than experts once thought. In such countries as Australia, Costa Rica, Israel, Jordan, Spain, Tanzania, and overwhelmingly in South Africa, child sexual abuse is considered a "serious problem" (Pereda, Guilera, Forns, and Gomez-Benito, 2009) According to Pereda et al. (2009), 7.9% of males and 19.7% of females in 22 countries (including the ones previously noted) were victims of some type of sexual abuse prior to age eighteen. Thus, the United States is not unique in the extent to which its children experience this type of abuse. Does it surprise you to learn that child sexual abuse occurs relatively frequently in countries with such different cultures? Why or why not?

Perspectives on Neglect

Consider the first case at the beginning of this chapter. Is Marchella a neglected child? What if she had been injured just as often as she was, but there was no physical evidence of it? Marchella's parents hit each other. Does that affect the extent to which you view Marchella as being maltreated? Do you think assault charges should be filed? Against whom? Should anything else be done?

Research addressing cultural values and judgments related to child neglect has indicated that community samples interpret some scenarios more seriously than social workers and child welfare workers, such as the statement, "There is trash in the child's home, and some corners of rooms have piles of junk or trash" (Dubowitz, Klockner, Starr, & Black, 1998; Rose & Meezan, 1995). Do you have any speculations as to the causes of such differences? What should be the criteria for judging signs of neglect as serious enough to justify reporting a family to CPS? In one community sample, 25% of the respondents did not consider regularly sending a child to school in dirty clothes as a form of child maltreatment (Price et al., 2001). Do you agree?

Concerning child neglect, McSherry (2007) worries that society makes "a mole-hill out of a mountain" in both the United States and the United Kingdom. In her view, despite the fact that child neglect is a serious form of child maltreatment, it appears to be the most common form of maltreatment and can have long-term serious consequences for children. The definitions of neglect continue to vary across states, and there is no general consensus as to the definition of neglect; child protection agencies give higher priority to abuse than to neglect cases. McSherry (2007) believes that earlier recognition and greater prioritization of neglect is crucial.

Dubowitz (2007) concurs with the importance of addressing the "neglect of neglect," and links the failure to attend adequately to neglect in part to issues related to responsibility for the neglect—does it lie with parents or with the kinds of social, economic, and political forces associated with economic and other forms of inequality? For example, both McSherry (2007) and Dubowitz (2007) ask whether it should be considered a form of neglect if parents delegate to an elementary school age child (e.g., 8 or 10 years old) responsibility for baby-sitting a somewhat younger sibling. What do you think? Are there any circumstances that might affect how neglectful you would consider such a circumstance? Does it matter whether the family has one or two parents in residence? Whether the parent(s) must work two jobs to feed and clothe the children and keep a roof over their heads? Whether they are immigrants from another country with different cultural views on sibling responsibility?

Perspectives on the Abuse of Female Partners

Consider the following scenario (adapted from Feld & Felson, 2008):

A young man, John, gets very angry at his wife, Beth, for no good reason. John swears at Beth in front of a group of Beth's friends and hits her hard enough to bruise her arm.

What do you think would be an appropriate response for Beth in this situation? Indicate the extent to which you agree or disagree (strongly agree, somewhat agree, somewhat disagree, or strongly disagree) with each of the following statements:

1. Beth should hit John back.

2. It would be wrong for Beth to hit John back.

3. Beth would be justified to hit John back.

4. If you were Beth in this situation, you would hit John back.

Using an experimental design, Feld and Felson (2008) administered several different versions of this scenario to a representative sample of American adults to assess views on retaliation. They found considerable variation in the acceptability of retaliation, depending on the genders and relationships involved. Specifically, the respondents indicated that it is more acceptable to retaliate within nonmarital than within marital relationships and more acceptable for females than for males to retaliate. Overall, men showed greater acceptance of retaliation than women did, except when men were retaliating against women.

Earlier research from the 1980s indicated considerable support by men for men using violence against a female partner who offended them in some way. For example, in a sample of male college students in the 1980s, 75% indicated they would be likely to hit a wife if she had sex with another man, and nearly 40% said there was some likelihood they would hit a wife if she refused to have sex or told friends that her partner was sexually pathetic (Briere, 1987). Overall, more than 79% of these men identified at least one circumstance under which they would be likely to hit a wife. Among both college students and adults, 30% or more of each group said that battered women had at least some responsibility for their own battering (Aubrey & Ewing, 1989). Not surprisingly, women were found to be less tolerant of a husband hitting his wife than men are (Locke & Richman, 1999). These findings are somewhat different from those of Feld and Felson (2008), who found that male respondents were no more supportive than female respondents of a man retaliating against a woman. Do you think there has been a cultural change in attitudes toward hitting a woman or might methodological differences explain the apparent difference in findings?

Perspectives on Marital Rape

Consider the statements in Box 11.2 made by undergraduate students when they were asked for their opinions of "marital rape." Their opinions were gathered in the 1980s. Do you think such views could still be found today? What is *your* view—should sexual assault of a wife be just as serious a crime as the sexual assault of a stranger? Should there be any extenuating circumstances making it acceptable for a husband to physically force his wife to have sex?

Box 11.2	Is Rape Something That Can Happen in Marriage?

"No. When you get married you are supposedly in love and you shouldn't even think of lovemaking as rape under any circumstances."

"[No.] Sexual relations are a part of marriage and both members realize this before they make a commitment."

(Continued)

(Continued)

"[No.] If the wife did not want to have sex…after many months the husband may go crazy. [Rape] would be an alternative to seeking sexual pleasure with someone else."

"[No.] If she doesn't want to have sex for a long amount of time and has no reason for it—let the old man go for it."

SOURCE: Finkelhor & Yllo, 1983, p. 128

One approach to the cultural context of marital rape is to consider the relevant laws. In the United States, rape was traditionally considered to be intercourse forced by a man on a woman who was not his wife (Russell, 1990). Until 1977, when the first marital rape law was passed, husbands could batter their wives to gain sexual access with no legal recriminations. Only gradually, through strong efforts of the feminist community, have sexual assault laws changed, but not without considerable resistance. In Maine, during the legislative battle to remove the marital rape exemption, one legislator argued, "Any woman who claims she has been raped by her spouse has not been properly bedded" (National Center for Victims of Crime, 2003, para. 2).

Marital rape is now considered a crime in all 50 states and the District of Columbia; nevertheless, in many states, marital rape is still a lesser offense than other forms of rape. In West Virginia, spousal sexual assault is defined as "unconsented sexual penetration or sexual intrusion of the perpetrator's spouse involving forcible compulsion or deadly weapon or infliction of serious bodily injury" (National Center for Victims of Crime, 2003, para. 2)—an offense that is a felony, punishable by imprisonment for two to ten years. If the same acts are committed against a person not married to the perpetrator, the sentence is 10 to 35 years. In California, a person who commits nonspousal rape by means of force, violence, duress, menace, or fear of immediate and unlawful bodily injury may not be sentenced to probation or a suspended sentence—a prohibition that does not apply to individuals who use the same means to commit spousal rape. In Kansas, sexual battery consists of "the intentional touching of the person of another who is 16 or more years of age, who is not the spouse of the offender and who does not consent thereto, with the intent to arouse or satisfy the sexual desires of the offender or another" (National Center for Victims of Crime, 2003, para. 9). In Ohio, the offense of sexual battery does not apply to a spouse, and the offense of rape by the use of a drug or intoxicant impairing the victim's ability to resist applies only to a spouse living apart from the victim.

Despite differences among state laws, there is widespread recognition that marital rape occurs. In a national survey, 73% of the respondents agreed that husbands sometimes use force, such as hitting, holding down, or using a weapon to make their wives have sex, and a majority agreed that if a husband forces his wife to have sex because he thinks she is leading him on or because she continually refuses sexual relations, he has raped her (Basile, 2002). Minority participants were less likely than White respondents to think that wife rape occurs. Moreover, the older the respondents, the less likely they were to believe that marital rape can occur or that the behaviors described in the marital rape scenarios were really examples of rape.

To what extent do survey respondents have views consistent with laws characterizing marital rape as a lesser offense than nonmarital rape? College students made the strongest rape-supportive attributions (e.g., not labeling the sexual assault as rape, not viewing it as violent, not viewing it as a violation of the woman's rights) when judging a rape that occurred within the context of marriage (Ewoldt, Monson, & Langhinrichsen-Rohling, 2000). However, the students were considerably less tolerant of a rape when the marriage was dissolving than when it was intact. In general (and not surprisingly), women's attitudes are less rape-supportive than men's (Ewoldt et al., 2000). Judgments are also less supportive of marital rape when the husband is described as having previously engaged in physical violence against his wife (Langhinrichsen-Rohling & Monson, 1998).

Perspectives on the Abuse of Male Partners

Consider the second scenario at the beginning of this chapter. Would you agree that the husband is guilty of wife abuse if he has committed the acts she describes? How about the wife? Is she guilty of husband abuse? If so, in what way?

There is, within the United States macrosystem and within some minority cultures, considerable tolerance for women's aggression against men. In general, intimate aggression is seen as more serious when performed by a man against a woman than by a woman against a man (Bethke & DeJoy, 1993). A series of four surveys with nationally representative samples (Straus, Kaufman Kantor, & Moore, 1997) provided provocative data concerning approval of violence by women toward men. In 1968, approximately equal percentages of respondents (~20%; 26.4% of men and 18.4% of women) said they could imagine circumstances where they would approve of a husband slapping his wife in the face or a wife slapping her husband in the face. In subsequent decades, approval rates for slapping a wife declined—to 13% in 1985, 12% in 1992, and 10% in 1994. By contrast, rates of approval for a wife slapping a husband remained stable over time at a little over 20%. Interestingly, as recently as 1994, the percentage of men who approved of a wife slapping a husband (31%) was nearly twice that of women who approved of the same behavior (16%). On the other hand, among college students from the United States, Latin America, and Asia, *women* showed significantly higher tolerance than men for a wife killing or mutilating her husband if he frequently abuses her—an approval rating that was significantly higher in the participants born in the United States than in Asian or Latin American participants (Gabler, Stern, & Miserandino, 1998).

It appears that one reason there is greater tolerance for physical violence by wives than by husbands is the assumption that women's violence is less likely to cause harm. Other relevant assumptions are that men are better able to escape an abusive situation if they want to and are more at fault if they get hit by their wives (Lehmann & Santilli, 1996). Yet the rate of IPV against men is likely underestimated due to the male victims' reluctance to admit IPV. Forty percent of men say that the reason they do not report to authorities is because the IPV is a private or personal matter, compared to 22% of women (Catalano, 2007). Perhaps the most pervasive and enduring cultural belief affecting views on domestic violence is the feminist view that for reasons of power and control, men are generally the aggressors and women are generally the victims. Straus (2009) has noted that despite the fact that over the previous 30 years, more than 200 studies have shown that women commit violence against their partners at about the same rate as men and for many of the same reasons, neither the general public nor practitioners have acknowledged this fact. In previous chapters, you have read much of the evidence concerning violence by women. Why do you think the view persists that for the most part it is only men who are abusive in relationships? What are some of the likely consequences of this belief—for female aggressors, male victims, and the cultural response to domestic violence?

Perspectives on Elder Maltreatment

Before reading this section, consider the case in Box 11.3. Have you just read a case of elder abuse? If yes, who is the perpetrator, and who is the victim? What, if any, would be the appropriate response of a social service agency to this situation? (Note: Mr. Smith is too incapacitated to leave his home or to be left alone. Mrs. Smith feels that after so many years of caring for her husband in the face of his abuse, she cannot now abandon him.)

Box 11.3   Mr. and Mrs. Smith

Mrs. Smith, age 65 years, is the primary caregiver to her 75-year-old husband, who has been treated for manic depression for 20 years and was diagnosed a year ago as being in the early stages of Alzheimer's disease. Mrs. Smith reports to her caregivers support group that her husband's condition has been getting worse. In a recent incident, Mrs. Smith was babysitting her 9-year-old grandson when Mr. Smith became increasingly agitated, blocked the TV that Mrs. Smith and her grandson were watching, screamed profanities at her, called her names, lunged at her, and threatened her. She reported that she jumped up, pushed him back, sent her grandson out of the room, and gradually led Mr. Smith to their bedroom where she ordered him to stay. In a subsequent visit with a support group counselor, Mrs. Smith and her son revealed that Mr. Smith was a "mean alcoholic" who had been physically and emotionally abusive to his wife and son for many years and was becoming physically aggressive again.

SOURCE: Bergeron, 2001

In general, cultural values in the United States provide fewer rationalizations for physical aggression against the elderly than for physical aggression in parent-child and spousal relationships. Nevertheless, there is some tolerance under some circumstances for particular forms of elder maltreatment. For example, although college students judge physical abuse of an elder as significantly more abusive than psychological abuse, financial abuse, and medical neglect, they tend to view abusive behaviors (e.g., tranquilizing an elderly mother to avoid embarrassment when there are guests in the home) as more justifiable when the elderly parent is agitated or senile. Indeed, students have rated the abusiveness of an agitated, unstable parent as higher than the abusiveness of the caretaker who sedated her (Mills, Vermette, & Malley-Morrison, 1998). Both college students and adult community members labeled physical aggression against the elderly as abusive and as having harmful results, but considered the physical aggression to be more abusive and more harmful when the perpetrator was middle-aged than when elderly—again implying some tolerance of *spousal* violence, independent of age (Childs, Hayslip, Radika, & Reinberg, 2000).

In general, it seems that the majority culture and experts in the field of elder abuse do not substantially differ in the behaviors they consider abusive (e.g., forcing an elder to do something he or she does not want to do) (Hudson, Armachain, Beasley, & Carlson, 1998); however, although most of the community members in the Hudson et al. study said that even one incident of slapping or hitting was sufficient to warrant the label of abuse, the experts tended to reserve the term "abuse" for acts "of sufficient frequency and/or intensity" (p. 100). This finding presents an interesting contrast to the research on views on child abuse, where experts tend to see hitting and slapping of children as more abusive than community members do.

Finally, within the area of elder neglect, as in the case of child neglect, there has been a major effort to achieve a uniform definition of the concept. Might there be disadvantages as well as advantages to a universalistic definition? Lee and Eaton (2009) and Lee, Gibson, and Chaisson (2011) suggest that efforts to conform to a single general definition may interfere with providing culturally appropriate services to various immigrant populations. When Lee et al. (2011) asked a sample of aging Korean immigrants living in the United States how they defined elder neglect, there were several common themes in the responses:

(a) "[Neglect is] being indifferent and leaving [parents] alone. There's nothing as awful as indifference . . . every bad thing happens because of indifference. You cannot be indifferent to your parents if you are concerned about them";

(b) "It is not having any concern [about the elderly parents]. Children are not concerned about their parents; they don't visit, greet regularly, support, and so on. All of these [examples] are a kind of abuse"; and

(c) "[An example of neglect is] exclusion of the elder from family activities or events because adult children believe that parents are too old. People show avoidance when they see older parents and do not let them be involved in any activities. Having them attend in any way will be desirable. I wish young people cared more about what the elders think, as they will get older too" (p. 129).

What do you think about these examples? Do they show a great deal of cultural specificity to you? Or do you think that these forms of elder neglect may be found in many different groups within the United States today?

The Broader Ecological Context

Norms concerning the treatment of children, intimate partners, and elderly parents are embedded within a broader cultural framework. Although many characteristics of the American macrosystem play a role in family violence, there are four in particular that warrant special consideration: (1) protection of the right to own firearms; (2) media violence and pornography; (3) legalized capital punishment; and (4) tolerance for poverty and economic inequality. Table 11.1 summarizes information concerning each of these contextual factors.

Firearms

Personal ownership of guns appears to be more widespread in this country than in any other developed nation, with approximately 47% of U.S. households owning a gun and 34% of all Americans personally owning a gun, the highest rates in nearly two decades (Saad, 2011). Household ownership of guns ranges from a low of 36% in the East to a high of 54% in the South (Saad, 2011). Furthermore, an estimated 200 million firearms are in private American hands (Reuters, 2007). In 2011, although a majority of Americans supported measures to keep guns away from criminals (e.g., by requiring a background check and a five-day waiting period before a handgun can be purchased), more than 74% opposed limiting gun ownership to the police and other authorized persons, a record high since Gallup first began asking that question in 1959 (Jones, 2011). Moreover, for the first time since 1997, more Americans (53%) opposed rather than supported (43%) a ban on semiautomatic guns or rifles, and for the first time since 1990, a minority of Americans (44%) favored stricter gun laws (up until 2007, a majority of Americans had been in favor of stricter gun laws), which seemed to be tied to the finding that the majority of Americans (60%) wanted the government to enforce current laws rather than pass new laws. In general, the people most likely to support bans on handguns were: women, people between the ages of 18 and 29 years, non-college-educated, Easterners, Democrats, and those who have no guns in the household. On the other hand, men, people between the ages of 30 and 49 years, college-educated, Southerners, Republicans, and those who live in households with guns were least likely to support bans on handguns (Jones, 2011).

The resistance to increased gun control laws in the United States is important because of the significant role that guns play in violence within the home. According to a report from the Centers for Disease Control and Prevention (1997):

> The United States is unequaled in its rate of firearm injuries and fatalities. An international comparison of 26 industrialized countries found that the firearm death rate for U.S. children under 15 was 12 times higher than the rates for the other 25 countries combined. (para. 2)

Firearms are also involved in a substantial percentage of domestic violence homicides (see discussion in Chapter 5), as well as in crippling injuries. In the year 2000, 95% of female firearm homicide victims were murdered by a male—usually an intimate partner (Violence Policy Center, 2000). Other research has indicated

Table 11.1 Ecological Contexts of American Violence

	Study	Description of Samples	Major Findings
Firearms	Centers for Disease Control and Prevention (1997)	An international comparison of 26 industrialized countries	Firearm death rate for U.S. children under 15 was 12 times higher than for the other 25 industrialized countries combined
	Reuters (2007)	Gun registration expert estimates; household surveys; proxy indicators	United States has 90 guns for every 100 persons; is most heavily armed society in the world More than half of the new weapons manufactured annually around the world are bought in United States
	Saad (2011)	National population-based sample of 1,005 adults aged 18 and older living in United States; telephone interviews conducted October 6–9, 2011 (Gallup poll)	Approximately 47% of U.S. households own a gun 34% of all Americans personally own a gun, the highest rate in nearly two decades Household gun ownership ranged from a low of 36% in the East to a high of 54% in the South
	Jones (2011)	National population-based sample of 1,005 adults aged 18 and older living in United States; telephone interviews conducted October 6–9, 2011 (Gallup poll)	More than 74% opposed limiting gun ownership to the police and other authorized persons More Americans (53%) opposed rather than supported (43%) a ban on semiautomatic guns or rifles 44% favored stricter gun laws 60% wanted the government to enforce current laws rather than pass new laws
	Violence Policy Center (2011)	FBI Homicide Report data	93% of female firearm homicide victims (in single victim/single offender situation) were murdered by a male they knew; 63% of these victims were murdered by an intimate partner 296 women were shot and killed by husband or intimate partner during an argument

(Continued)

Table 11.1 (Continued)

	Study	Description of Samples	Major Findings
	Cooper & Smith (2011)	FBI Supplementary Homicide Reports	From 1980–2008, over two thirds of victims murdered by a spouse or ex-spouse were killed by guns
			In 2008, 53% of all female intimate partner homicide victims were killed with a gun
Media Violence and Pornography	Bergen (1996)	A study of wife rape victims	One third reported their partners viewed pornography, which was correlated with the most sadistic rapes
	Federman (1998), National Television Violence Study	Random selection of TV programs, 23 channels, over 3 years	40% of violent acts are committed by attractive role model characters, but 75% of violence results in no punishment
			In 71% of violent scenes, there is no remorse, criticism, or penalty for violence
			More than half of scenes show violence that would be lethal or incapacitating in real life
			Less than 20% show long-term consequences of violence
	Zolondek, Abel, Northey, & Jordan (2001)	A sample of 485 juvenile sex offenders	Over 30% reported viewing child pornography
	Wilson et al. (2002)	Database from National Television Violence Study	Estimated 60% of television programs and 70% of television series geared toward children contain violence
			TV violence is glamorized and sanitized
	Stahl & Fritz (2002)	A study of over 200 private school students grades 7–10	21% had visited a pornographic website at least once for over three minutes
			33% had visited a pornographic website more than four times over three months

Study	Description of Samples	Major Findings
Huesmann, Moise-Titus, Podolski, & Eron (2003)	Longitudinal study of people between the ages of 6 and 10, who grew up in the 1970s and 1980s and were interviewed about 15 years later; study contained follow-up archival (N = 450) and interview data (N = 329)	Men who viewed violence as children were significantly more likely to have pushed, grabbed, or shoved their spouses Women who viewed violence as children were four times more likely to have thrown something at their spouses, and had punched, beaten, or choked another adult
Kanuga & Rosenfeld (2004)	Kaiser Family Foundation survey; a random sample telephone survey of 1,209 young people ages 15–24	70% of adolescents ages 15–17 were exposed to unwanted pornographic websites
Shope (2004)	271 women participating in a battered women's program	Sexual abuse increased significantly when the batterers used pornography
Christakis & Zimmerman (2007)	Children in a nationally representative sample collected in 1997 and reassessed in 2002	Viewing violent TV programs during preschool years was positively associated with later antisocial behavior in boys
Wolak, Mitchell, & Finkelhor (2007)	Telephone survey of nationally representative sample of 1,500 youth Internet users	42% of young Internet users reported exposure to online pornography in the past year, of which 66% was unwanted exposure
American Academy of Child and Adolescent Psychiatry (2011)	Review of literature of children's exposure to television violence	Children may become immune to violence, accept violence as a way to solve problems, or imitate TV violence Children who see shows that depict violence as realistic, frequent, or unpunished are more likely to imitate what they see Extensive viewing increases aggressiveness Children with emotional, behavioral, learning, or impulse control problems are more easily influenced by TV violence

(Continued)

Table 11.1 (Continued)

	Study	Description of Samples	Major Findings
Capital Punishment, Incarceration, and Arrests	Hartney (2006)	Cross-cultural analysis of available reports	United States incarcerates largest number of people in world; has greater than 4% of world population but more than 23% of world's incarcerated population; imprisons the most women in the world
	Amnesty International (2010)	International databases	In the United States, more than 1,000 people have been executed since 1993; during this period over 40 countries (including South Africa) have passed legislation to abolish the death penalty
	Newport (2011)	National population-based sample of 1,005 adults aged 18 and older living in United States; telephone interviews conducted October 6–9, 2011 (Gallup poll)	61% of Americans support the death penalty for individuals convicted of murder, which reflects a 19% drop over the past 17 years 40% of Americans said the death penalty is not imposed often enough 25% said it is used too often, the highest such percentage that Gallup has measured since 2001 27% said that it is imposed about the right amount
Social and Economic Inequality	Gelles (1992)	An analysis of the 1985 National Family Violence Survey, a representative sample of 6,002 families	Violence toward children was 4% higher, severe violence 46% higher, and very severe violence 100% higher in impoverished families than in families living above the poverty line
	Drake & Pandey (1996)	A 1992 study of Missouri child abuse and neglect cases	High poverty neighborhoods reported the highest incidents of child maltreatment

Study	Description of Samples	Major Findings
McCloskey (1996)	Interviews with 365 battered and nonbattered women	Income inequality favoring women contributed to wife abuse, whereas income equality favoring Whites contributed to intimate partner violence in Black communities
Miles-Doan (1998)	A study of family violence cases in a high crime county in Florida	Highest rate of family violence occurred in neighborhoods with the lowest levels of economic resources
Smeeding, Rainwater, & Burtless (2000)	A cross-national analysis of poverty in 18 developed nations	U.S. poverty rate of 17.8% was substantially higher compared to the other 17 countries
Fajnzylber, Lederman, & Loayza (2001)	A cross-national analysis of available reports	Income inequality was associated with violent crime, including homicide
ChildStats (2004)	Key national well-being indicators of the United States	On average, 20% of children in the United States live below poverty level, but those living in extreme poverty has increased. 11.6 million children lived below the poverty level in 2002
Berger (2004)	Data from the National Longitudinal Survey of Youth, specifically 17,871 complete observations of children between birth and 9 years old, who were observed in 1986, 1988, 1992, 1994, 1996 & 1998	Low income was positively correlated with frequent spanking and overall child maltreatment
Land (2010)	Child and Youth Well-Being Index Project, indicators of well-being	Approximately 21% of children lived below the poverty line in 2010

that when there are one or more guns in the home, the risk of suicide among women increases nearly five times and the risk of homicide more than triples—due largely to homicides at the hands of a spouse, intimate acquaintance, or close relative (Violence Policy Center, 2000).

Despite this rise in resistance to gun control in the United States, some legislation has been passed to reduce the role of firearms in domestic homicide. In 1994, Congress passed the Protective Order Gun Ban, which prohibits gun possession by a person against whom there is a restraining or protective order for domestic violence, and in 1996, it passed the Domestic Violence Misdemeanor Gun Ban, which prohibits anyone convicted of a misdemeanor crime of domestic violence or child abuse from purchasing or possessing a gun. Individual states are making strides toward more gun control as well. For instance, in 2009, California enacted a new law providing additional requirements for the sale of common handgun ammunition. The law went into effect in February of 2011 and stipulates that sales of handgun ammunition must occur in person and ammunition dealers must keep records of sales for at least five years (Egelko, 2009).

Media Violence and Pornography

On average, Americans, either intentionally or unintentionally, are exposed to large doses of violence in the media and of pornography. Children are particularly susceptible to the negative effects of viewing violent acts. According to a study conducted by Wilson and his associates, approximately 60% of television programs contain violence and close to 70% of television series produced for children contain violence (Wilson et al., 2002).

Forty percent of the violent acts portrayed are committed by characters that are considered attractive role models, and 75% of the violence results in no form of punishment and/or reprimand (National Television Violence Study, 1996). On average, American children see more than 8,000 murders and more than 100,000 other violent acts (e.g., assaults, rapes) on network television by the end of elementary school (Bushman & Anderson, 2001). Moreover, the level of violence portrayed on television is not a simple reflection of reality. For example, approximately 50% of the crimes portrayed in reality-based TV programs are murders, yet only 2% of the crimes reported by the FBI are murders (Oliver, 1994, cited in Bushman & Anderson, 2001).

Outside of the media industry, there is widespread acceptance of the extensive scientific data indicating that observing violence increases violence. Six major professional societies—the American Psychological Association, American Academy of Pediatrics, American Academy of Child and Adolescent Psychiatry, American Medical Association, American Academy of Family Physicians, and American Psychiatric Association—signed a joint statement on the hazards of exposing children to media violence, noting that "at this time, well over 1,000 studies . . . point overwhelmingly to a causal connection between media violence and aggressive behavior in some children" (Joint Statement, 2000, p. 1, cited in Bushman & Anderson, 2001, p. 488).

The general availability of violence on television, in movies, on the Internet, and in video games is evidence of this country's acceptance of violence (Harrington &

Dubowitz, 1999) that can lead to violence by and against children. In a comprehensive review of media violence and children's behavior, Wood, Wong, and Chachere (1991) concluded that viewing violent media *causes* children to behave aggressively. If children learn to view the use of violence as acceptable, how are they going to behave when they become adults and their children and/or intimate partners upset or frustrate them? Some evidence (American Academy of Child and Adolescent Psychiatry, 2011) suggests that children who view programs in which violence is depicted realistically, frequently, or as unpunished are more likely to imitate, become immune to, or accept violence as a problem-solving mechanism. Furthermore, children who exhibit emotional, behavioral, learning, or impulse control problems are more vulnerable to being influenced by violent content. These harmful effects may surface directly or appear later in life, even when the children's environment shows no tendency toward violence.

Other studies have demonstrated specific links between viewing television violence in childhood and later aggression, including partner maltreatment. For example, a longitudinal study of the relationship between TV violence viewing at ages six to ten and adult aggressive behavior approximately 15 years later showed that men who were high TV violence viewers as children were significantly more likely to have pushed, grabbed, or shoved their spouses than men who had watched less violent TV as children (Huesmann, Moise-Titus, Podolski, & Eron, 2003). Similarly, women who were high TV violence viewers as children were more likely to have thrown something at their spouses, and had punched, beaten, or choked another adult four times more than the rate of other women.

Pornography is another multibillion-dollar industry in the United States that may influence tolerance of family aggression. In addition, the explosion of the Internet business has made pornography readily available to children of all ages. In 2007, according to Wolak, Mitchell, and Finkelhor, 42% of youth Internet users had been exposed to online pornography in the past year. Of this 42%, the majority (66%) reported only unwanted exposure. A Kaiser Family Foundation survey revealed that 70% of adolescents aged 15 to 17 years had unintentionally been exposed to pornographic websites (Kanuga & Rosenfeld, 2004). Moreover, the Internet has been used for trafficking in child pornography, engaging children in inappropriate sexual interactions, and attempting to recruit them for abusive purposes (Kanuga & Rosenfeld, 2004). A study of over 200 private school students from grades 7 through 10 revealed that 21% had visited a pornographic website at least once for over three minutes, and 33% had visited such sites more than four times (Stahl & Fritz, 2002). Several students said they had been invited to participate in sexual activity as a result of their online communications.

Although studies of the association between exposure to media pornography and later maltreatment are rare, there is some research linking exposure to pornography with various forms of maltreatment of women and children. In a sample of juvenile sex offenders, over 30% of the victimizers reported viewing child pornography (Zolondek, Abel, Northey, & Jordan, 2001). In a study of victims of wife rape, one third of the victimized women reported that their partners viewed pornography, and the partner's use of pornography was associated with the most sadistic rapes (Bergen, 1998). Reports from women in a battered women's shelter revealed that the likelihood of sexual abuse as part of the violent relationship significantly increased when the batterers used pornography (Shope, 2004).

Capital Punishment

The United Nations, the European Union, Amnesty International, the Organization of American States, and other groups have all passed resolutions against capital punishment, which has declined in recent years in most parts of the world. The United States is the only democracy where the death penalty is still frequently put into practice (Harries, 1995). Between 1976 (when the Supreme Court reinstated capital punishment after a nine-year hiatus) and March 2012, approximately 1,289 people were put to death in this country for capital crimes, with 1,058 occurring in the South, 150 in the Midwest, 77 in the West, and 4 in the Northeast (Death Penalty Information Center, 2012). Overall, 56% of those executed were White, 34% were Black, 8% were Latino, and 2% were of other races/ethnicities. Currently, despite substantial evidence that capital punishment is not an effective deterrent to crime (Barak, 2003; Milburn & Conrad, 1996), the death penalty is supported by statute in 34 states. Executions take place primarily in the South (especially Texas and Virginia, where 590 of the 1,289 executions have taken place) and disproportionately involve Black men (Death Penalty Information Center, 2012). Moreover, several studies show that the death penalty is much more likely in cases involving White victims (Pierce & Radelet, 2005, 2011; Unah & Boger, 2001), with those who killed Whites three to four times as likely to be executed as those who killed either Blacks or Latinos (Pierce & Radelet, 2005; Unah & Boger, 2001).

Nearly 400 juveniles (youth under the age of 18) have also been executed in the United States, including 22 in the period 1973 to 2003, which is a violation of international law (Child Welfare League of America, 2002). Nearly two thirds of these recent executions of minors occurred in Texas, which during that period put to death more juveniles than the rest of the world combined. In all other nations, the practice of executing juveniles is not accepted (Streib, 2003), and in 2005, the U.S. Supreme Court followed suit by striking down the death penalty for juveniles in this country (Death Penalty Information Center, 2012).

When asked whether they support capital punishment, a majority of people in the United States indicate their approval, a fact that has been used by the Supreme Court as evidence that the death penalty is consistent with community standards. The 2011 edition of Gallup's annual Crime Survey found that 61% of Americans support the death penalty for individuals convicted of murder, which reflects a 19% point drop over the past 17 years. In fact, support for the death penalty reached its peak from the mid-1980s through the mid-1990s, with an all-time high of 80% favoring the death penalty in 1994 (Newport, 2011). When delving deeper into the issue, 40% of Americans said that the death penalty is not imposed often enough. That is the lowest percentage since May 2001 when Gallup first asked this question. On the other hand, 25% said it is used too often, the highest such percentage that Gallup has measured since 2001, and 27% said that it is imposed about the right amount. However, many respondents who indicated support of a sentence of life in prison without the possibility of parole instead of the death penalty also indicated that there were individual circumstances in which they would favor the death penalty (e.g., Timothy McVeigh Oklahoma City bombing case) (Newport, 2011).

Thus, although support for the death penalty has been declining in recent years, the majority of Americans still approve of it as a form of punishment for murder. What does this tolerance of capital punishment have to do with family violence?

- Many violent prisoners, and particularly many prisoners on death row, have themselves been victims of family violence (American Academy of Child and Adolescent Psychiatry, 2000).
- Support for the use of corporal punishment of children in homes and schools is highest in the same states that show the greatest support for the death penalty (Cohen, 1996).
- Many death penalty supporters grew up in homes where corporal punishment was accepted as necessary; they internalized childhood messages concerning punishment and retribution, and unconsciously seek outlets for their suppressed anger (Milburn & Conrad, 1996).
- Tolerance for the death penalty, in violation of international laws and trends, is part of a social and cultural context in which punishment, retribution, and violence are legitimized and sanctioned as appropriate responses to undesired behavior.

Social and Economic Inequality

Although the United States is in many ways one of the wealthiest nations in the world, it also has a persistently high number of individuals and families living in poverty. Our discussions in previous chapters have made it clear that poverty is a major risk factor for child abuse and other forms of family violence. Child poverty is not equally distributed around the world, and it is remarkably prevalent in the United States despite the relative wealth of the country. In 2008, approximately 13% of all children in 34 member countries of the Organisation for Economic Co-operation and Development (OECD) lived in poverty; rates by country ranged from less than 8% in the Nordic countries to over 20% in Chile, Israel, Mexico, Turkey, and the United States (OECD, 2011). The evidence is overwhelming that poverty is associated with a broad range of social problems, including various forms of violence. These problems include higher birth rates in unwed mothers, teen pregnancy, crime and delinquency, drug-related problems, child maltreatment, and higher rates of infant mortality (Drake & Pandey, 1996). One analysis of data from the 1985 National Family Violence Survey revealed that overall violence toward children was 4% higher, severe violence was 46% higher, and very severe violence was 100% higher in poor families than in families living above the poverty line (Gelles, 1992, as cited in Burgess, Leone, & Kleinbaum, 2000). A 1992 study of Missouri child abuse and neglect cases revealed that high poverty neighborhoods had the highest number of reported and substantiated incidents of child maltreatment (Drake & Pandey, 1996), while data from the National Longitudinal Survey of Youth revealed that low income is associated with both frequent spanking and overall child maltreatment (Berger, 2004). In a study of family violence cases in a very high crime county in Florida, the highest rates of family violence were found in neighborhoods with the lowest levels of economic resources (Miles-Doan, 1998). There are also numerous studies demonstrating a link between poverty and intimate partner violence (Rank, 2001), and although there is less research on the link between poverty and elder abuse, there is some evidence that poverty is a risk factor for elder maltreatment (Lachs, Williams, O'Brien, Hurst, & Horwitz, 1997).

Throughout its history, both the citizenry and the power structure in the United States have varied enormously in their willingness to address social problems such as family violence and poverty (Pleck, 1989). Cancian, Slack, and Yang (2010) examined data collected for the Child Support Demonstration Evaluation (CSDE) and the TANF Integrated Data Project, to assess the effects of providing small increments in child support to an experimental group of mothers receiving welfare benefits. They found that over a two-year period, the mothers receiving even a small amount of additional child support were less likely to be reported to the child welfare system for child maltreatment than a control group of mothers who received no such supplement. Because they used an experimental design to examine income as a predictor of child maltreatment, Cancian et al. concluded that they demonstrated that low income is a cause of child maltreatment. Nonetheless, it may not be poverty *per se* that is the causal agent of maltreatment as much as related factors such as social and/ or economic inequality. Income inequality (the juxtaposition of extreme poverty with extreme wealth) is associated with both interpersonal and collective violence (Mercy, Krug, Dahlberg, & Zwi, 2003). Income inequality—a gap between rich and poor that has increased steadily in the United States in recent decades—was one of the targets of the Occupy Movement that captured attention in the United States in 2011 and 2012. It was also identified as a problem by President Obama. How big a problem is it? Based on the World Fact Book produced by the CIA in 2009, Fisher (2011) points out that on the Gini index (a measure of statistical dispersion) for income inequality, the United States has one of the highest levels of income inequality in the world—worse not only in comparison to Western Europe, but also in comparison to most of West Africa and North Africa; indeed the level of income inequality in the United States is similar to that in Rwanda, Uganda, and Ecuador.

There is also evidence that income inequality favoring women rather than overall poverty contributes to violence against female intimate partners (McCloskey, 1996) and that income inequality favoring Whites over Blacks may contribute to intimate partner violence in the Black community (Aborampah, 1989). In a cross-national analysis that included the United States, previous findings were confirmed that income inequality is associated with violent crime, including homicide (Fajnzylber, Lederman, & Loayza, 2001). Given that immigrants and people of color are disproportionately represented at poverty levels and the primary victims of social inequality, it should be no surprise that rates of family violence sometimes are higher in those communities than in the majority community, although differential reporting practices may also play a role in these figures (Malley-Morrison & Hines, 2004).

Summary

In this chapter, you have learned that in the United States, (a) homicide, generally as a result of maltreatment, accounts for over one in five injury-related deaths in infants under a year of age; (b) the rates of child maltreatment are among the highest in the industrialized world; (c) homicide by an intimate partner is a leading cause of premature death in women; and (d) every year at least two million older Americans are maltreated by family members. Given what you have read about the causes and correlates of family violence in previous chapters, what connections do you see between that violence and the observations that the United States is: (a) the most heavily armed society in the world; (b) a society in which violence is glorified and easily accessed in the public media; (c) a country that incarcerates the largest number of people in the world; (d) a country with strong support and use of the death penalty; and (e) a country with a substantially higher poverty rate than 18 other developed nations? Are there connections between family violence and norms supporting violence under particular circumstances that are also pervasive in the United States? In the final two chapters, we give further consideration to the role of cultural context in contributing to—or protecting from—violence in families, with particular attention to race/ethnicity and religious cultures. As you read these chapters, consider how your own background has contributed to your views on such issues as corporal punishment, punishment of marital infidelity, and the legitimacy of violence as a response to presumed transgressions by family members.

Discussion Questions

1. Why might the United States have one of the highest child maltreatment death rates within the 30 industrialized member nations of the Organisation for Economic Co-operation and Development? What policies could countries with lower death rates have that might account for their lower death rates? Might any of these policies be feasible for implementation within the United States?

2. UNICEF states that child abuse may be stopped by "breaking the link between adults' problems and children's pain." What are your thoughts on this statement? If you agree, how do we break this link?

3. Reflect on the violence statistics of the United States that you read. Had you previously realized the prevalence of violence within the country? What had your thoughts been regarding the juxtaposition of the U.S. violence rates with those of other nations? How does this new cross-national information align with your previous perception of violence prevalence within the United States?

4. What are your views on spanking? What are you opinions with respect to the views offered by experts and international human rights groups? If you are against spanking, how would you respond to someone who says, "Of course I will spank my child. I was spanked and I turned out fine."? If you are in favor of spanking, how would you respond to the experts' arguments against spanking and the empirical evidence indicating that spanking is a predictor of later aggression and psychological problems?

5. What cultural factors exist that may be responsible for the American refusal to place full blame on heterosexual perpetrators of sexual abuse? What cultural factors exist that may be responsible for the greater American readiness to place full blame on

homosexual perpetrators of sexual abuse? Does the sex, or sexual preference, of the perpetrator matter when assessing and assigning blame in cases of sexual abuse? Why or why not?

6. The statements in Box 11.2 were made by undergraduate students. Do you think an older population would have responded in a similar manner? What about a younger population? A more or less educated population? Do you believe that marital rape exists or do you support the views in Box 11.2? Why?

7. One reason that IPV against men is more acceptable than IPV against women is the assumption that abused men have a greater ability to escape a relationship than abused women. Can you detect faulty reasoning in this assumption? How so? Children and finances are sometimes shared "assets" within a relationship, married or otherwise. How might the existence of shared assets affect an abused man's ability to escape an abusive relationship?

8. Have you noticed the prevalence of violence in your own viewing of movies, television, music videos, video games, and Internet use? Reflect on your experiences. Has this ubiquitous violence affected your view of violence in everyday life? Do you view violence as a "normal" part of life or something that happens on rare occasions? Is violence something that occurs among strangers or within our interpersonal relationships?

12

Racial/Ethnic Issues in Family Violence

Jose is a 3.5 year old Latino male who is not potty trained. According to his mother, Jose is too lazy to come inside or stop playing to go to the bathroom and goes whenever and wherever he wants to. Jose has a stuttering problem, can only form 2–3 word sentences, and has difficulty communicating his wants and needs. He constantly looks down and avoids engaging in eye-to-eye contact. Jose's mother reports that she has extreme difficulty controlling her son, stating that he is very active and always getting into trouble. Jose appears withdrawn, nervous, and timid. Mom is constantly yelling at and criticizing Jose. While Jose was putting on his coat, Mom yelled, "That's not the right way, dummy!" although Jose managed to get his coat on fine (Child Welfare Pre-Service Trainer Guide, 2011).

Although bruises and scratches may not be visible, can we still consider Jose's situation to be a case of child maltreatment? If so, what factors may have contributed to the mother's maltreatment of Jose? Are cultural values concerning child maltreatment and appropriate parenting consistent across cultures? In what ways may they be different and why?

In the previous chapter, we explored various macrosystem values in the United States that may contribute to family violence. In this chapter, we focus on different racial/ethnic minority communities to investigate how cultural identities may serve alternatively as either protective factors or risk factors against maltreatment. We provide a brief discussion of various racial/ethnic minority groups in this country, the heterogeneity between and within these groups, the conceptions of family violence within the groups, the prevalence and predictors of family violence, and explore possible protective factors against maltreatment within these minorities. We also consider outcomes of the various forms of family violence, and prevention and intervention efforts tailored toward racial/ethnic minority groups in order to better serve everyone's needs.

Race and Ethnicity in the United States

According to the 2010 U.S. Census, there were over 308 million people in the United States; of this population, 72.4% were White, 16.3% Latino, 12.6% African American, 4.8% Asian, and 0.9% Native American (U.S. Bureau of the Census, 2011). As of 2011, there are 74.5 million children who live in America; of this number, 41.2 million (55.3%) are White, 16.8 million (22.5%) Latino, 11.3 million (15.1%) African American, 3.5 million (4.7%) Asian/Pacific Islander, and 951,000 (1.3%) Native American (Children's Defense Fund [CDF], 2011).

Many of the racial/ethnic minorities in this country have higher levels of poverty and other associated risks than the majority White community, which could put them at higher risk for various types of family violence. For example, when compared to White children in the United States, African American children are at an increased risk of being born at low birth weight and with decreased or no prenatal care. African American babies, relative to White babies, are much more likely to be placed in foster homes, to lack family stability, to have unmet medical needs, and to die before their first birthdays (CDF, 2011).

In addition, in America today, Black and Latino children are at an increased risk of living at or below the poverty line. For children under age five, 41.9% of Blacks and 35% of Latinos are classified as poor (as compared to about 15% of White children). Extreme poverty, defined as living at half the poverty level or below, is experienced by more than one in six Black children and one in seven Latino children (whereas one in twenty White children live in extreme poverty) (CDF, 2011).

As mentioned in previous chapters, despite the high correlation of poverty with family violence and other social ills, it may not be poverty per se that is the causal agent of family violence as much as related factors such as social and/or economic inequality. Income inequality (the juxtaposition of extreme poverty with extreme wealth) is associated with both interpersonal and collective violence (Mercy, Krug, Dahlberg, & Zwi, 2003). There is also evidence that rather than overall poverty, income inequality favoring women over men contributes to intimate partner violence (IPV) against women (McCloskey, 1996) and that income inequality favoring Whites over Blacks may contribute to IPV in the Black community (Aborampah, 1989). In a cross-national analysis that included the United States, previous findings confirmed that income inequality is associated with violent crime, including homicide (Fajnzylber, Lederman, & Loayza, 2001). Given that immigrants and people of color are disproportionately represented at poverty levels and the primary victims of social inequality, it should be no surprise that rates of family violence sometimes are higher in those communities than in the majority community, although differential reporting practices may also play a role in these figures (Malley-Morrison & Hines, 2004).

Child Maltreatment

Perspectives on Corporal Punishment, Child Abuse, and Neglect

Although the majority of families in the United States view corporal punishment as appropriate and necessary, such support may vary somewhat across racial/ethnic groups. For example, within many Black communities, spanking and other forms of physical punishment are considered "appropriate discipline" rather than abuse (e.g., Giovannoni & Becerra, 1979; Alvy, 1987). However, race/ethnicity is often confounded with income, and low-income parents generally approve of spanking more than middle-income parents do (e.g., Heffer & Kelly, 1987).

Another major racial/ethnic group in this country, Latinos appear, in some cases, to have *more* stringent definitions of child abuse than do other cultural groups (Malley-Morrison & Hines, 2004). For example, in a study of Whites, Latinos, and Chinese Americans, the Latinos and Whites judged beating a 12-year-old girl with a cane and burning a mark into her arm for stealing, and beating a child for not doing homework as more serious abuse than did the Chinese (Hong & Hong, 1991).

Concerning issues related to sexual abuse, many Native Americans view sexuality in a somewhat different light than the mainstream American public—either defining themselves as more sexually "free" or engaging in sexual activities at a younger age with older partners. For example, out of a sample of 52 Native American women, 76% reported sexual contact before the age of 18 with someone who was 5 or more years older (Lehavot, Walters, & Simoni, 2010).

Child neglect has long been a matter of controversy in American society. The tendency of mothers to rate neglect as more serious or abusive than Child Protective Services (CPS) workers has been found in several racial/ethnic groups. In a study comparing White, Latino, and Black mothers with CPS workers, the mothers rated all the categories of child neglect (e.g., physical neglect, emotional neglect, and lack of supervision) as more serious than the CPS workers did (Rose & Meezan, 1995). Moreover, Rose (1999) found that there may be important differences in judgments of neglect between racial/ethnic groups as well: Black and Latino mothers rated the types of neglect as more serious than did the White mothers. Another cross-cultural study showed that Chinese respondents judged leaving a 9-year-old boy alone to feed and take care of himself at night, and refusing to take a withdrawn 8-year-old girl to a counselor, as significantly less serious than Latinos judged these actions (Hong & Hong, 1991). What kinds of experiential or cultural factors might account for such differences?

Rates of Child Maltreatment in Racial/Ethnic Minority Families

As discussed in Chapters 2 through 4, child maltreatment is a major problem in America today. Child maltreatment occurs in all racial/ethnic groups, although some research suggests that certain racial/ethnic groups may be at higher risk of maltreatment than others. Table 12.1 summarizes studies providing estimates of child maltreatment rates in African American, Latino, Asian American, and Native American families.

A number of studies have compared rates of maltreatment between Whites and other racial/ethnic minority groups. For example, findings from the National Child Abuse and Neglect Data System (NCANDS) indicate racial/ethnic differences in child victimization rates. According to NCANDS data collected in 2010, 21.9% of the reported cases were African American, 21.4% were Latino, and 44.8% were White (U.S. Department of Health and Human Services [USDHHS], 2011). Thus, African American children were overrepresented in child maltreatment cases with respect to

Table 12.1   Prevalence of Child Maltreatment within Major Racial/Ethnic Minority Groups

Study	Description of Sample and Measure	Type of Maltreatment Assessed	Rates of Maltreatment
African American			
National Child Abuse and Neglect Data System (NCANDS); U.S. Department of Health and Human Services (2010)	National child maltreatment reports to Child Protective Services (CPS)	General maltreatment and child abuse fatalities	• 21.9% of reported maltreatment cases were Black children • 28.1% of child abuse fatalities were Black children
Fields, Malebranche, & Feist-Price (2008)	Volunteer convenience sample of Black men who have had sex with men from 3 cities; self-report	Sexual	• 32% of the men reported child sexual abuse
Freisthler, Bruce, & Needell (2007)	Purposive sample from 91 neighborhoods, Northern California; child maltreatment reports	General maltreatment	• 1 in 32 Black children had substantiated child maltreatment reports • Black children were three times more likely than Latino children and five times more likely than White children to have experienced a substantiated report of child maltreatment
Amodeo, Griffin, Fassler, Clay, & Ellis (2006)	Volunteer community sample of Black and White women, Boston area; self-report	Sexual	• 34.1% of the Black women reported child sexual abuse
Crouch, Hanson, Saunders, Kilpatrick, & Resnick (2000)	National probability sample of adolescents (ages 12–17); telephone self-report interview; National Survey of Adolescents	Abusive punishment	• Prevalence of physically abusive punishment did not vary by racial/ethnic group within the lower income • Within upper income group, African American youth reported significantly higher rates (16.8%) of physically abusive punishment compared to White (6.1%) and Latino (5.9%) youth

Study	Description of Sample and Measure	Type of Maltreatment Assessed	Rates of Maltreatment
Latino			
NCANDS; U.S. Department of Health and Human Services (2010)	National child maltreatment reports to CPS	General maltreatment; child abuse fatalities	• 21.4% of child maltreatment reports were Latino children • 16.6% of child abuse fatalities were Latino children
Alzate & Rosenthal (2009)	National Study of Child and Adolescent Well-Being (NSCAW) CPS sample (N=5,501) of children in the United States who were referred for investigation of child maltreatment in 1999 and 2000; child maltreatment reports	Sexual and physical abuse; neglect	• 12% of the Latino cases of child maltreatment were for sexual abuse versus 11% for the non-Latino cases • 32% of the Latino cases of child maltreatment were for physical abuse versus 26% for the non-Latino cases • 56% of the Latino cases of child maltreatment were for neglect versus 63% of the non-Latino cases
Newcomb, Munoz, & Carmona (2009)	Convenience sample of 223 Latino and White American 16–19-year-old high school students; self-report	Sexual	• Latinos (44%) were significantly more likely to experience CSA compared to Whites (27%)
Freisthler et al. (2007)	Purposive sample from 91 neighborhoods, Northern California; child maltreatment reports	General maltreatment	• 1in 91 Latino children had substantiated child abuse reports • Latino children were 1.8 times more likely than White children to have a substantiated report of child maltreatment
Crouch et al. (2000)	National probability sample of adolescents (ages 12–17); telephone self-report interview; National Survey of Adolescents	Abusive punishment	• Prevalence of physically abusive punishment did not vary by racial/ethnic group within the lower income • Within upper income group, African American youth reported significantly higher rates (16.8%) of physically abusive punishment compared to White (6.1%) and Latino (5.9%) youth

(Continued)

Table 12.1 (Continued)

Study	Description of Sample and Measure	Type of Maltreatment Assessed	Rates of Maltreatment
Asian American			
NCANDS; U.S. Department of Health and Human Services (2010)	National child maltreatment reports to CPS	General maltreatment; child abuse fatalities	• 0.9% of child maltreatment reports were Asian American children • 0.9% of child abuse fatalities were Asian American children
Maker (2005)	Female university students from Midwest and California; self-report	Physical	• 73% of South Asian/Middle Eastern students reported child maltreatment • 65% of the East Asian students reported child maltreatment
Native American			
NCANDS; U.S. Department of Health and Human Services (2010)	National child maltreatment reports to CPS	General maltreatment; child abuse fatalities	• 1.1% of child maltreatment cases were Native American • 0.8% of child abuse fatality cases were Native American
Duran et al. (2004)	234 American Indian women, age 18–45, outpatients Indian Health Services Hospital, Albuquerque, NM; self-report	Sexual and physical maltreatment; neglect	• 44.4% reported child sexual abuse • 41.5% reported child physical abuse • 62.8% of participants experienced physical and/or emotional neglect as children
Hobfoll et al. (2002)	160 adult Native American women recruited from comm unity centers for AIDS prevention study; Childhood Trauma Questionnaire	Sexual and physical/emotional maltreatment	• 42% of sample experienced child sexual abuse • 56% of sample experienced physical and/or emotional maltreatment

their representation in the population as a whole, whereas White children were underrepresented. Rates of victimization were 14.6/1,000 children for African American, 11.0/1,000 for Native American, 8.8/1,000 for Latino, 7.8/1,0000 for White, and 1.9/1,000 for Asian children. Thus, African American and Native American children were at the highest risk for child maltreatment. In another study using a national sample, Alzate and Rosenthal (2009) reported that compared to non-Latino boys, Latino boys had a higher likelihood of physical maltreatment. Other research has indicated that Latino children in general are more likely than White children to have experienced a substantiated report of child maltreatment (Church, Gross, & Baldwin, 2005; Freisthler, Gruenewald, Remer, Lery, & Needell, 2007), although not all studies (e.g., Fluke, Yuan, Hedderson, & Curtis, 2003; Hill, 2007)—including the NCANDS study on official child maltreatment reports—support this conclusion.

Although race/ethnicity may predict child maltreatment rates, there appears to be an influence of socioeconomic status as well. For example, in an analysis of census and child welfare reporting information from Missouri, Drake, Lee, and Jonson-Reid (2009) found an interaction between race and poverty in the reporting of child maltreatment. Specifically, Black children were reported for maltreatment much more often than White children at the least extreme poverty levels, but the opposite was true at the most severe levels of poverty. The relationship between poverty and child maltreatment reporting actually was somewhat stronger in regard to White than Black families.

Relative to other racial/ethnic minorities, child maltreatment has been studied less in Native Americans and Asian Americans; however, there is some evidence regarding child maltreatment rates in these groups. The NCANDS data show that Native Americans experience the second highest rates of reported child maltreatment, while Asian Americans experience the lowest (USDHHS, 2011). With respect to Asian Americans, other analyses confirm that reported rates of child maltreatment are lower than other racial/ethnic groups in the United States (Pelczarski & Kemp, 2006; Zhai & Gao, 2009). In localized studies focusing on Native Americans (e.g., Duran et al., 2004; Hobfoll et al. 2002), high rates of child maltreatment have also been found, which is consistent with NCANDS data. For example, Duran et al. (2004) found that 76.5% of their 234 Native American female participants (ages 18 to 45) reported experiencing at least one type of child maltreatment, and 81.3% of participants reporting emotional maltreatment had also been physically and/or sexually maltreated as a child. Furthermore, 27.8% had experienced both physical and sexual abuse, and 82.5% of the women who experienced severe maltreatment as a child were subjected to at least three forms of maltreatment. Somewhat lower rates were found in a study on health promotion on reservations in Montana, where 56% of women reported some type of childhood physical and/or emotional maltreatment (Hobfoll et al., 2002).

Assessing levels of child neglect in racial/ethnic minority families is complicated by the fact that not all races/ethnicities are equally likely to be investigated for neglect. In the CPS probability sample of the National Survey of Child and Adolescent Well-Being, Alzate and Rosenthal (2009) found a lower percentage of neglect investigations for Latino children (56%) than for non-Latino children (63%), and that Latino boys experienced a lower percentage of neglect investigations than did Latina girls (51% of investigations involved boys, while 66% involved girls). Does Alzate's and Rosenthal's finding in this nationally representative sample mean that there is a lower incidence of child neglect in the Latino population? Does it mean that Latina girls are neglected more than Latino boys? What other explanations might account for these findings?

Although an issue that is difficult to discuss and often underreported, child sexual abuse in U.S. culture is not a rare phenomenon (see Chapter 3); it has also been identified in all racial/ethnic minority groups considered in this chapter. Most likely to be victimized by child sexual abuse, regardless of ethnicity, are girls (Alzate & Rosenthal, 2009). Specifically, the odds of sexual abuse for girls, regardless of ethnicity, are nearly four times higher than the rates for boys (Alzate & Rosenthal, 2009). However, there is some evidence that Latina girls are more at risk for child sexual abuse than White girls (Newcomb, Munoz, & Camona, 2009). Specifically, in one study, Latino children were significantly more likely to experience sexual abuse (44%) compared to Whites (27%), and female Latinas (54%) had the highest prevalence overall (Newcomb et al., 2009). Sexual abuse is also a topic of concern in the Native American population. For example, among 160 unmarried Native American women between the ages of 16 and 29, 42% reported having been victims of childhood sexual abuse (Hobfoll et al., 2002). Similarly, Duran et al. (2004) found that Native American women reported multiple kinds and occurrences of child sexual abuse, with 44.4% of the women reporting at least one past experience of sexual abuse.

At least two important considerations limit the ability to draw strong conclusions concerning the prevalence of child maltreatment in racial/ethnic minority groups. First, ethnic lumping continues to complicate efforts to compare racial/ethnic groups (Miller & Cross, 2006). Ethnic lumping involves collapsing diverse ethnic groups (e.g., Mexican Americans, Cubans, Puerto Ricans) into categories (e.g., Latinos) for purposes of group comparisons with little regard for the diversity within those heterogeneous groups (Malley-Morrison & Hines, 2007). Second, there has been a dearth of research investigating different forms of child maltreatment among and between racial/ethnic groups (Behl, Crouch, May, Valente & Conyngham, 2001; Miller & Cross, 2006). Behl and colleagues (2001) conducted a content analysis assessing the extent to which race/ethnicity has been considered in child maltreatment research. Selecting articles published in three major child maltreatment journals during a 20 year period (1977 to 1998), they found that fewer than 7% of the studies focused on race or ethnicity. In addition, from 1995 to 1998, only 24.5% of the articles used race/ethnicity in their data analysis. In a follow-up to Behl et al.'s study, Miller and Cross (2006) reported that although there was increased attention to race/ethnicity in studies published between 1999 and 2002, the percentage of studies analyzing the role of race/ethnicity in child maltreatment continued to be relatively low.

Intimate Partner Violence

Perspectives on Intimate Partner Violence

In our review of literature on perspectives on IPV, we were unable to find any studies examining minority group perspectives on the maltreatment of male partners; thus, we focus this section on the few studies of racial/ethnic differences in perspectives on maltreatment of female partners. Findings concerning racial/ethnic differences in rates of approval of the maltreatment of female partners are fairly limited and indicate that gender plays a more important role in judgments than ethnicity, and that across racial/ethnic groups, women are more opposed to violence against women than men. Studies comparing tolerance of the maltreatment of female partners in Blacks versus Whites generally reveal no racial/ethnic difference or indicate that White men are more tolerant of the maltreatment of female partners than Black men. For example, according to national survey data from 1968, 1992, and 1994, Blacks were less likely to approve of a husband slapping his wife than Whites were, and from 1968 to 1994, the percentage of respondents approving of a husband slapping his wife decreased for Blacks but not for Whites (Straus, Kaufman Kantor, & Moore, 1997). In a study of judgments concerning the abusiveness of various forms of husband's psychological aggression against wives (e.g., treating her as an inferior, not being willing to talk about things that are important to her), African American participants tended to view these behaviors as more abusive than did White participants (Follingstad, Helff, Binford, Runge, & White, 2004). Similarly, in a study from Norfolk, Virginia, of tolerance for IPV, Whites scored higher in tolerance than non-Whites (Button, 2008).

By contrast, Latinos appear to be somewhat more tolerant of aggression against female partners than members of other racial/ethnic groups—in part because of cultural values of *machismo* (Malley-Morrison & Hines, 2004). For example, in one study, although White women found "pulling hair," "biting," "constraint against will," "slapping," "throwing objects," and "pushing, shoving, or grabbing" to be abusive, Mexican American women did not. Moreover, White women judged acts such as burning with a cigarette, throwing things, slapping, and constraining against one's will as more serious than did Mexican American women (Torres, 1991). Similarly, Asian Americans appear to be less likely than Whites to define a husband's shoving his wife or smacking her in the face as domestic violence (Family Violence Prevention Fund, 1993). What are the possible implications of these definitional differences when Latina or Asian women are faced with a situation that many White women would label "abusive"? Does it seem that perhaps Latinas and Asians may be less likely to see themselves as victims and less likely to seek help when assaulted by their male partners? Why might that be?

In addition, it appears that Asian Americans may be more tolerant of the maltreatment of female partners than both Whites *and* Latinos (Gabler, Stern, & Miserandino, 1998). In many Asian languages, there is not even a term for "domestic violence" (Lemberg, 2002). Perspectives on the extent to which there are particular circumstances justifying the maltreatment of female partners also vary among the many different Asian American communities. For example, about half of a sample of Chinese Americans thought that hitting a spouse was justifiable in cases of defense of self or a child (Yick & Agbayani-Siewert, 1997). Moreover, the older Chinese American respondents showed tolerance of IPV perpetrated in response to a wife's extramarital affair. By contrast, a sample of Filipino American students tended to view physical violence as unjustifiable under any circumstances, although Filipino men were more likely than Filipino women to tolerate physical violence if the woman was flirting or unfaithful (Agbayani-Siewert & Flanagan, 2001). Among respondents with Chinese, Vietnamese, Cambodian, and Korean heritages (Yoshioka, DiNoia, & Ullah, 2001), the two groups with Southeast Asian origins (Cambodians and

Vietnamese) were more likely than the Chinese and Koreans to endorse male privilege (e.g., "A husband is entitled to have sex with his wife whenever he wants it.") and less likely to endorse alternatives to living with violence (e.g., "Wife beating is grounds for divorce."). Of all groups, the Korean Americans were the least likely to view violence as justified in particular situations (e.g., when the wife has sex with another man). Thus, Asian communities differ not only in cultural aspects such as language and religion, but also in their attitudes toward the maltreatment of female partners. Consequently, all studies in which Asians with different heritages are combined in a single "Asian American" sample must be viewed with caution (Yoshioka et al., 2001). These examples also show the danger of "ethnic lumping" in general. That is, there could also be important variations in tolerance for IPV within the categories of Latino, Black, Native American, Asian, and White.

Native Americans seem to have a somewhat different view of IPV than found in the U.S. macrosystem, viewing it not as a gender issue but as a human or family issue (Malley-Morrison & Hines, 2004). This view probably stems from traditions in many Native American communities of relative gender equality, traditions that had their origins prior to European contact. Currently, community leaders recognize that both men and women in these communities use violence against their partners; in their view, to eliminate family violence (or violence in general), both types of aggression must be addressed. Moreover, the common practice in the majority judicial system of blaming the man for the conflict and ignoring the woman's role is considered inappropriate and ineffective (Durst, 1991).

Rates of Intimate Partner Violence in Racial/Ethnic Minority Communities

Table 12.2 provides a summary of some of the key studies of rates of IPV in the major racial/ethnic minority communities in the United States. Because some of these studies report findings from just one racial/ethnic group and because of differences in sampling and other methodological issues, it is important not to overinterpret the differences shown across races/ethnicities when the rates come from different studies. On the other hand, several studies provide some comparative information. For example, according to the National Crime Victimization Survey (NCVS) (Rennison, 2001; see Chapter 5), there are no differences in IPV victimization between Latinos and non-Latinos, regardless of gender. However, there were differences among other racial/ethnic groups. Specifically, the NCVS showed higher rates of IPV against Black women than against White women or "other races," whereas rates of IPV against men were lower and more similar across groups (Rennison & Planty, 2003). Similarly, in the 1995 National Study of Couples (Caetano, Cunradi, Clark, & Schafer, 2000) which used the Conflict Tactics Scales (Straus, Hamby, Boney-McCoy, & Sugarman, 1996; see Chapter 5), rates of IPV were highest among Blacks: The prevalence of IPV against women was 11.5% among White couples, 17% among Latinas, and 23% among Blacks, and for IPV against men, rates were 15% among Whites, 21% among Latinos, and 30% among Blacks. The National Violence Against Women Survey (NVAWS) (Tjaden & Thoennes, 2000a) provides rates of IPV across all major racial/ethnic minority groups discussed in this country. Overall, they

Table 12.2 Prevalence of Intimate Partner Violence within Major Racial/Ethnic Minority Groups

Study	Description of Sample and Measure	Type of Maltreatment Assessed	Rates of Maltreatment
African American			
Rennison & Planty (2003)	National Crime Victimization Survey (NCVS), 1993–1999; representative national crime survey; Self-report over prior year	Physical IPV	*IPV against women*: • 10.7% of Blacks • 7.8% of Whites • 4.5% of other races *IPV against men*: • 1.9% of Blacks • 1.3% of Whites • 0.8% of other races
Tjaden & Thoenes (2000a)	National Violence Against Women (NVAW) survey with telephone interviews of a nationally representative sample of 8,000 women and 8,000 men; self-report over lifetime	Physical IPV	• Among African American women (n = 780): 26.3% reported physical IPV victimization • Among African American men (n = 659): 10.8% reported physical IPV victimization
Caetano, Cunradi, Clark, & Schafer (2000)	1995 National Couples Study; 1,635 couples; 555 White, 358 Black, 527 Latino; nationally representative of 48 contiguous states; oversampling of Blacks and Latinos; Conflict Tactics Scales	Physical IPV	*IPV against women*: • 17% of Latinas • 23% of Blacks • 11.5% of Whites *IPV against men*: • 21% of Latinos • 30% of Blacks • 15% of Whites
Latino			
Gonzalez-Guarda, Peragallo, Urrutia, Vasquez, & Mitrani (2008)	Convenience samples of Latina women from South Florida; self-report survey	General maltreatment	• 51.3% reported at least one form of IPV from their partners • 30.0% reported physical and/or sexual IPV • 27.5% reported more than one type of IPV victimization

(Continued)

Table 12.2 (Continued)

Study	Description of Sample and Measure	Type of Maltreatment Assessed	Rates of Maltreatment
Rennison (2001)	National Crime Victimization Survey (NCVS), 1993–1999; representative national crime survey; self-report over prior year	Physical IPV	• No difference in IPV victimization rates between Latinos and non-Latinos, regardless of gender (approx. 8/1,000 women and 1.5/1,000 men)
Tjaden & Thoenes (2000a)	National Violence Against Women (NVAW) survey with telephone interviews of a nationally representative sample of 8,000 women and 8,000 men; self-report over lifetime	Physical IPV	• Among Latina women (n = 628): 21.2% reported physical IPV victimization • Among Latino men (n = 581): 6.5% reported physical IPV victimization
Caetano, Cunradi, Clark, & Schafer (2000)	1995 National Study of Couples; 1,635 couples; 555 White, 358 Black, 527 Latino; nationally representative of 48 contiguous states; oversampling of Blacks and Latinos; Conflict Tactics Scales	Physical IPV	*IPV against women:* • 17% of Latinas • 23% of Blacks • 11.5% of Whites *IPV against men:* • 21% of Latinos • 30% of Blacks • 15% of Whites
Asian American			
Chang, Shen, & Takeuchi (2009)	1,470 Asian Americans interviewed for the National Latino and Asian American Study; representative national survey; Conflict Tactics Scales	Minor and severe physical IPV victimization	*Minor IPV victimization:* • 10.2% of women • 12.0% of men *Severe IPV victimization:* • 1.5% of women • 2.6% of men *Minor IPV among women:* • 3.2% of Vietnamese • 6.4% of Filipino • 5.6% of Chinese *Minor IPV among men:* • 1.8% of Vietnamese • 4.9% of Filipino • 6.5% of Chinese

Study	Description of Sample and Measure	Type of Maltreatment Assessed	Rates of Maltreatment
			Severe IPV among women: • 1.4% of Vietnamese • 1.0% of Filipino • 0.4% of Chinese *Severe IPV among men*: • 0.04% of Vietnamese • 1.3% of Filipino • 1.1% of Chinese
Leung & Cheung (2008)	Convenience sample of 1,577 Asian respondents in the greater Houston, TX area; 610 were Chinese, 517 Vietnamese, 154 Indian, 123 Korean, 101 Filipino, and 72 Japanese; Conflict Tactics Scales	Physical IPV	*Overall IPV (both men and women combined) by ethnicity*: • 22.4% for Vietnamese • 21.8% for Filipino • 19.5% for Indians • 19.5% for Koreans • 9.7% for Japanese • 9.7% for Chinese *IPV victimization by gender*: • Men: 17.6% • Women: 15.3%
Tjaden & Thoenes (2000a)	National Violence Against Women (NVAW) survey with telephone interviews of a nationally representative sample of 8,000 women and 8,000 men; self-report over lifetime	Physical IPV	• Among Asian American women (n = 133): 12.8% reported physical IPV victimization • Among Asian American men (n = 165): no precise estimates were available
Native American			
Evans-Campbell, Lindhorst, Huang, & Walters (2006)	Representative sample of urban Native Americans in New York City; self-report survey	General maltreatment	• 40% reported a history of IPV
Tjaden & Thoenes (2000a)	National Violence Against Women (NVAW) survey with telephone interviews of a nationally representative sample of 8,000 women and 8,000 men; self-report over lifetime	Physical IPV	• Among Native American women (n = 88): 30.7% reported physical IPV victimization • Among Native American men (n = 105): 11.4% reported physical IPV victimization

found the highest rates of IPV against both women and men among Native Americans, followed by African Americans, Latinos, and finally Asian Americans.

Two studies among Asian Americans vividly display the problem of ethnic lumping. Although the population-based studies cited above show that Asian Americans as a group have the lowest rates of IPV, we see marked differences across various Asian subgroups. For example, Chang, Shen, and Takeuchi (2009) found that minor IPV victimization was reported by 10.2% of the Asian American women and 12.0% of the men; severe IPV victimization was reported by 1.5% of the women and 2.6% of the men. Among the women, rates of minor IPV were highest for the Filipina group (6.4%), followed by the Chinese (5.6%), and then the Vietnamese (3.2%). For the men, the rates were highest among the Chinese men (6.5%), followed by the Filipino (4.9%), and then the Vietnamese (1.8%). For severe IPV, 1.4% of the Vietnamese women, 1.0% of the Filipino women, and 0.4% of the Chinese women reported victimization, whereas 1.3% of the Filipino men, 1.1% of the Chinese men, and 0.04% of the Vietnamese men reported victimization.

Similarly, Leung and Cheung (2008) found higher rates of IPV victimization among women than men: 15.3% of the women and 17.6% of the men reported IPV by their partners. However, the reported rates of IPV victimization by Asian subgroup differed from the Chang et al. (2009) study. Specifically, across genders, Vietnamese (22.4%) and Filipinos (21.8%) were more likely to have been IPV victims, whereas Chinese (9.7%) and Japanese (9.7%) were less likely to have been IPV victims; the rates for Koreans (19.5%) and Indians (19.5%) were between these two extremes.

Why do you think these two studies found differing rates of IPV by Asian subgroup, even though both studies used the Conflict Tactics Scales? Note that in both studies, the men reported more IPV by their partners than the women did. Is such a difference consistent with the findings you read in the relevant chapters for IPV in the United States overall? How would you explain the higher level of perpetration by women than by men?

Maltreatment of Older Adults

Perspectives on the Maltreatment of Older Adults in Racial/Ethnic Minority Families

The research on attitudes toward the maltreatment of older adults has been done within a single racial/ethnic minority community or has compared views among different racial/ethnic communities. For example, in judging hypothetical examples of the maltreatment of older adults, Native Americans gave higher ratings of severity than did White Americans (Hudson & Carlson, 1999). Furthermore, Native Americans were more likely than Whites to agree strongly that physically or verbally forcing elders to do something they did not want to do was abusive. Members of two different Native American tribes generally agreed that the maltreatment of older adults could be demonstrated in physical, psychological, social, or financial ways, and that maltreatment could have negative effects on older adults in any or all of those ways. Moreover, some

Native American respondents stated that "elder abuse" is "being disrespectful of or not honoring the elderly and their place in history"; "to treat an elder as less than human"; and "injuries to an elder's body, heart, mind, or spirit" (Hudson, Armachain, Beasley, & Carlson, 1998). On the other hand, there were behaviors that the majority culture tended to view as abusive but many Native Americans did not—specifically in regards to financial issues. Some evidence suggests that when aging Native Americans give their money to other family members seeking financial help, social service agencies in the majority culture may view them as financially exploited and therefore abused, whereas the elder Native American does not share this view (e.g., Brown, 1998).

"You must don't hit your momma!" This injunction has been identified as a major theme in the Black community. According to Griffin (1999a), physical abuse of elderly mothers is typically not committed. Research shows that Blacks are about as intolerant of the maltreatment of older individuals as Whites, and in many cases even more intolerant. For example, among older Black, White, and Korean American women recruited from churches and social service agencies, 73% of the Blacks rated an entire set of 13 elder mistreatment scenarios as abusive, as compared with 50% of Korean Americans and 67% of Whites (Moon & Williams, 1993). Interviews with Black, Korean American, and White older adults reveal that Blacks are less tolerant than Whites of verbal and financial abuse but not of hitting (Moon & Benton, 2000). In focus groups composed of older Whites, Blacks, Puerto Ricans, and Japanese Americans, Black older adults were distinguished by emphases on (1) love as the central responsibility of the family; (2) withholding love through ignoring older adults or subjecting them to harsh or profane language as the worst thing family members could do to them; and (3) the importance of context in determining whether an act is abusive (Anetzberger, Korbin, & Tomita, 1996). Black caregivers stressed the role of the oldest daughter in caring for elderly relatives and insisted that when certain behaviors such as yelling at or ignoring a demanding elderly relative were performed under stress, they might be understandable, but they were not respectable or acceptable. When asked to provide their own examples of extreme elder abuse, a sample of African Americans focused on various forms of physical mistreatment, neglect, and abandonment (Tauriac & Scruggs, 2006). Do these findings surprise you? Why or why not? What advantages can you see in asking people to indicate what they think is seriously abusive, moderately abusive, and mildly abusive in family relationships rather than providing them with scenarios and asking them to judge the abusiveness of the various forms of mistreatment portrayed in the scenarios?

Although the popular image of the treatment of older adults in Asian countries emphasizes honor and respect, these outward expressions may mask tolerance of aggression toward the elderly (e.g., Koyano, 1989; Malley-Morrison, You, & Mills, 2000). When asked to judge scenarios portraying situations of elder maltreatment (e.g., a daughter-in-law drugging her mother-in-law when guests visited to avoid being embarrassed by her), fewer Korean American than White or Black women viewed the hypothetical situations as abusive (Moon & Williams, 1993). Compared to White and Black older adults, Korean American older adults were the most tolerant of elder abuse, the most likely to blame the victims for elder abuse, and the most negative toward outside help when elder abuse was taking place (Moon & Benton, 2000).

As was true in regard to the maltreatment of female intimate partners, Asian American groups appear to differ among themselves in judgments concerning the kinds of behavior that constitute the maltreatment of older adults. For example, compared to Japanese Americans, Taiwanese Americans in one study (Moon, Tomita, & Jung-Kamei, 2001) were more likely to disapprove of a caregiver who ties a physically or mentally impaired adult in bed and more likely to disapprove of yelling at elderly parents. Financial exploitation was most tolerated by Korean Americans, who also were most likely to blame elderly victims for their own abuse. Taiwanese Americans were the least tolerant of leaving bedridden elderly parents alone occasionally for a few hours.

There appear to be very few studies addressing Latino perspectives on the maltreatment of older family members. In a study of Japanese, Puerto Rican, and White responses regarding various types of elder abuse, Puerto Rican elders and adult caregivers indicated that psychological neglect, such as excluding from activities, not communicating, and isolating, were the worst types of elder abuse (Anetzberger et al., 1996). The results of these studies appear to illustrate the power of the Latino concept of *respeto* (respect) for the elderly. On the other hand, Nerenberg (1999) found that whereas the majority's definition of elder abuse includes financial exploitation, this is not typically true of Latinos. That is, as shown for Native Americans, elderly Latinos feel it is their duty to their family to share their resources if necessary, even if it means that they must sacrifice their own needs for food, medication, or other necessities. In one of the few studies comparing racial/ethnic groups on their level of tolerance for elder abuse as portrayed in a scenario, Fitzpatrick and Hamill (2011) found no significant differences in tolerance among the Latinos, Whites, or "others." Box 12.1 provides the scenario. Are you surprised by the lack of differences in tolerance for the abuse portrayed in the scenario?

Box 12.1   Elder Abuse Scenario from Fitzpatrick and Hamill (2011)

Karen, a 73 year-old woman, recently became a widow because her husband died. She then moved into her daughter's home. She has always enjoyed a close and loving relationship with her daughter. Since moving in, Karen has been diagnosed with Alzheimer's disease. Now she often cries, screams, yells, and throws things at her daughter. One time, she embarrassed her daughter and her guests at the dinner table by yelling at everyone there. Since then, whenever her daughter invites guests to their home, she gives Karen tranquilizers, telling her that the doctor ordered the medication because it is good for her, even though he didn't. Her daughter does not tell her mother that they are tranquilizers.

Rates of the Maltreatment of Older Adults in Racial/Ethnic Minority Families

Table 12.3 provides a summary of studies providing rates of the maltreatment of older adults in the major racial/ethnic minority groups in the United States. The amount of research available on this topic appears to be quite limited, although there have been a few national studies as well as some more localized studies with

Table 12.3   Prevalence of the Maltreatment of Older Adults Within the Major Racial/Ethnic Minority Groups

Study	Description of Sample and Measure	Type of Maltreatment Assessed	Rates of Maltreatment
Non-White			
Acierno et al. (2010)	The National Elder Mistreatment Study, 2008; stratified random-digit-dialing in an area probability sample in 48 contiguous states; telephone interviews	1-year prevalence of physical, sexual, emotional, or financial mistreatment or potential neglect	• No significant differences in actual elder mistreatment between Whites and non-Whites when other factors controlled for • Rates not provided
Laumann, Leitsch, and Waite (2008)	National Social Life, Health and Aging Project; Population-based, nationally representative study asking older adults about recent experiences of maltreatment	Verbal, financial, physical	• Odds of verbal maltreatment were lower for Latinos than for Whites • Odds of financial maltreatment were higher for African Americans and lower for Latinos than for Whites • Rates by ethnicity not provided
African American			
Tatara & Kuzmeskus (1997)	Nationwide elder abuse reports from 1996	Domestic elder abuse	• 18.7% of domestic elder abuse victims were African American
Latino			
Tatara & Kuzmeskus (1997)	Nationwide elder abuse reports from 1996	Domestic elder abuse	• 10% of domestic elder abuse victims were Latino
Asian American			
Tatara & Kuzmeskus (1997)	Nationwide elder abuse reports from 1996	Domestic elder abuse	• Less than 1% of domestic elder abuse victims were Asian/Pacific Islanders
Native American			
Tatara & Kuzmeskus (1997)	Nationwide elder abuse reports from 1996	Domestic elder abuse	• Less than 1% of domestic elder abuse victims were Native American

convenience samples. Overall, the results are mixed: Some show racial/ethnic differences in reports of elder maltreatment, while others do not. For example, analyses of the National Elder Mistreatment study revealed no racial/ethnic differences in mistreatment based on comparisons of Whites and non-Whites (Acierno et al., 2010), whereas in a different nationally representative sample of community-dwelling older

Americans, Laumann, Leitsch, and Waite (2008) found that older African Americans reported more financial maltreatment but not more verbal maltreatment, and Latinos reported less verbal and financial maltreatment.

An analysis of self-reports of maltreatment using the Conflict Tactics Scales with older Americans in the state of New York indicated that 65.5% of the victims were White, 26.3% were African American, 7.6% were Latino, 1.9% were Native American/Aleut Eskimo, and 1.6% were Asian/Pacific Islander. The overall ethnic distribution of the sample was 75.5% White, 19% African American, 6% Latino, 0.8% American Indian/Aleut/Eskimo, and 1.2% Asian/Pacific Islander. Thus, based on their overall proportions in the sample, African Americans, Latino, and Native Americans were somewhat overrepresented in the self-reports of elder abuse, and Whites and Asian/Pacific Islanders were somewhat underrepresented.

Predictors and Correlates

Research on risk factors for family violence come at all levels of the ecological model, although the research in ethnic/racial minority communities is not as thorough as it is in the majority U.S. culture. Nonetheless, when reading the risk factors for the various types of family violence, think about what you learned from previous chapters. Are there any risk factors that seem to cut across all races and ethnicities in this country? What risk factors may be unique to a given racial/ethnic minority community or to minority groups in general in this country?

Macrosystem

There appear to be two interrelated macrosystem predictors of violence in racial/ethnic minority families in the United States today: (a) a punitive value system that has led this country to imprison more of our citizens than any other country in the world (Hartney, 2006); and (b) racism in our society.

In the mid-1970s, only 2% of the country's population ever spent any time in prison (Wildeman & Western, 2010). Today, the country imprisons approximately seven times more people than the western European average, and only a few of the former Soviet Republics and South Africa approach the U.S. rate. Related to high levels of incarceration in the United States is the continued legality of capital punishment on a federal level and in most states. Although use of capital punishment—declared by Amnesty International to be the ultimate Human Rights violation—has generally been declining around the world, it continues to occur in the United States. These issues take on added importance for our current discussion because likelihood of incarceration varies disproportionately by race/ethnicity (National Council on Crime and Delinquency, 2007; Wildeman & Western, 2010), as does the imposition of death sentences. There is evidence, for example, that individuals who kill Whites are more than 3 to 4 times as likely as individuals who kill Blacks and Latinos to be sentenced to death (Pierce & Radelet, 2005). Incarceration, like capital punishment, affects not just the immediate victims but families and neighborhoods as well. According to Wildeman and Western (2010):

One of every four African American children born in 1990 had a father go to prison. For children of high school dropouts, the share was one-half. For whites, by contrast, only seven of every one hundred children born in 1990 whose fathers were high school dropouts experienced paternal imprisonment. (p. 162)

Wildeman and Western attribute the large increase in incarceration both to economic factors—particularly decrease in employment for young Black youth—and an increasingly punitive mindset in the United States. From earlier chapters, you learned that poverty and single-parent families are risk factors for family violence. Both of these factors are found disproportionately in families of color.

Clashes between cultural values may also increase the likelihood of family violence. Consider the cases in Box 12.2. What cultural values may be coming into play in each of these cases? What variables are consistent with predictors of family violence across racial/ethnic groups?

Box 12.2   Three Cases of Intimate Partner Homicide

- Prosecutors allege Dae Kwon Yun, 54, was distraught after his garment-manufacturing business failed and his wife filed for divorce. He allegedly locked himself, daughter Ashley, 11, and son Alexander, 10, in his SUV and set it afire. Yun stumbled out. The children died. Yun, still hospitalized with burns, has been charged with murder (para. 10).

- Bong Joo Lee, 40, shot and killed his 5-year-old daughter, Iris, then killed himself, says Sgt. Bill Megenney of the Fontana, Calif., police. Lee had been unemployed and owed a $200,000 gambling debt, Megenney says (para. 11).

- Sang In Kim, 55, fatally shot his wife, Young Ok, 50, and their son, Matthew, 8, and wounded their 16-year-old daughter before killing himself. Police haven't disclosed a motive (para. 12).

SOURCE: Kasindorf, 2006

Risk Factors for Child Maltreatment

Table 12.4 provides a summary of risk factors for child maltreatment at each of the levels of the ecological model. At the macrosystem level, certain belief systems have been identified as risk factors for child maltreatment, particularly in the Asian American and Latino American cultures. These include Confucian principles in child-rearing practices, an emphasis on filial piety in children, indigenous healing practices, fatalism and acceptance of suffering, and beliefs supportive of physical punishment among Asian Americans (Larsen, Kim-Goh, & Nguyen, 2008; Zhai & Gao, 2009), and rigid gender roles and a focus on respect, obedience, and loyalty among Latino Americans (Alzate & Rosenthal, 2009). The pressure on young girls to be more mature can also lead to neglect in young Latina females (Alzate & Rosenthal, 2009). Poverty, unemployment, and underemployment have been identified as risk factors for child maltreatment in general and sexual abuse in particular in the Latino and

Table 12.4 Risk Factors for Child Maltreatment at Each Level of the Ecological Model

Level of Ecological Model	Type(s) of Maltreatment	Risk Factor	Racial/Ethnic Group(s)	Studies
Macrosystem	Physical	Confucian principles in child rearing practices	Asian Americans	Larsen, Kim-Goh, & Nguyen (2008)
	Physical	Emphasis on filial piety of children	Asian Americans	Larsen, Kim-Goh, & Nguyen (2008)
	Physical	Indigenous healing practices	Asian Americans	Larsen, Kim-Goh, & Nguyen (2008)
	Physical	Fatalism and the acceptance of suffering	Asian Americans	Larsen, Kim-Goh, & Nguyen (2008)
	Physical	Beliefs in physical punishment	Asian Americans	Zhai & Gao (2009)
	Physical	Cultural focus on respect, obedience, and loyalty	Latino Americans	Alzate & Rosenthal (2009)
	Physical	Rigid gender roles	Latino Americans	Alzate & Rosenthal (2009)
	General maltreatment; sexual	Poverty; un- or under-employed	Latino & African Americans	Church, Gross, & Baldwin (2005); Freisthler, Bruce, & Needell (2007); McDaniel & Slack (2005)
	General maltreatment; sexual	Lower parental education	Native, African, and Asian Americans	Dubowitz, Kim, Black, Weisbart, Semiatin, & Magder (2011); Kalra (2006); Lehavot, Walters, & Simoni (2010)

Level of Ecological Model	Type(s) of Maltreatment	Risk Factor	Racial/Ethnic Group(s)	Studies
Exosystem	Physical	Family acculturative stress	Asian Americans	Larsen, Kim-Goh, & Nguyen (2008)
	Psychological; physical	Mothers' perceptions of more negative neighborhood processes	Latino Americans	Guterman, Lee, Taylor, & Rathouz (2009)
Microsystem	General maltreatment	Female-headed household	Latino Americans	Church et al. (2005); Freisthler et al. (2007)
	General maltreatment	Families with a greater number of life events	African Americans	Li, Godinet, & Amsberger (2011)
	General maltreatment	Moving to a new home	African Americans	McDaniel & Slack (2005)
	General maltreatment	A new baby in the household	African Americans	McDaniel & Slack (2005)
	General maltreatment	More children in the family	African Americans	Dubowitz et al. (2011)
	Physical	Male children	African Americans	MacKenzie, Nicklas, Brooks-Gunn, & Waldfogel (2011)
	Physical	First-born children	African Americans	MacKenzie et al. (2011)
	Physical	Children with a difficult temperament	African Americans	MacKenzie et al. (2011)
	General maltreatment	Children suspended or expelled from school	African Americans	McDaniel & Slack (2005)

(Continued)

Table 12.4 (Continued)

Level of Ecological Model	Type(s) of Maltreatment	Risk Factor	Racial/Ethnic Group(s)	Studies
	General maltreatment	Child's low performance on standardized developmental assessments	African Americans	Dubowitz et al. (2011)
	Physical	Low levels of warmth within couple's relationship	African and Latino Americans	Moore & Florsheim (2008)
	General maltreatment; physical	Violence or psychological aggression between parents	Latino and Asian Americans	Chang et al. (2008); Moore & Florsheim (2008)
Individual/ Development	Physical	Younger parents or adolescent parents	African and Latino Americans	Moore & Florsheim (2008)
	Spanking	Paternal parenting stress	Latino Americans	Lee, Guterman, & Lee (2008)
	General maltreatment	A history of childhood maltreatment (e.g., experiencing physical abuse or neglect, sexual abuse, or witnessing IPV between parents)	African and Native Americans	Li et al. (2011); Libby, Orton, Beals, Buchwald, & Manson (2008)
	General maltreatment; physical	Parental mental illness	African and Asian Americans	Chang, Rhee & Berthold (2008); Dubowitz et al. (2011); Mapp (2006)
	General maltreatment	Parental drug use	African and Asian Americans	Chang, Rhee, & Berthold (2008); Dubowitz et al. (2011)
	General maltreatment	Being arrested	African Americans	McDaniel & Slack (2005)

African American communities (Church, Gross, & Baldwin, 2005; Freisthler, Bruce, & Needell, 2007; McDaniel & Slack, 2005), as has lower parental education in the Native and Asian American communities (Dubowitz et al., 2011; Kalra, 2006; Lehavot et al., 2010). Financial hardships can lead to stress and physical violence, or even to a lack of resources causing neglect (Freisthler et al., 2007).

Exosystem risk factors include stresses from acculturation and conflicting cultural views, which lead to heightened likelihood of physical child maltreatment in Asian Americans (Larsen, Kim-Goh, & Nguyen, 2008). Maternal perceptions of negative neighborhood processes are also associated with a higher likelihood of both physical and psychological child maltreatment in Latino American families (Guterman, Lee, Taylor, & Rathouz, 2009).

Microsystem risk factors tend to form three clusters: family-level risks, child-level risks, and couple-level risks. At the family level, child maltreatment in general is found more often in female-headed households in the Latino American community (Church et al., 2005; Freisthler et al., 2007), whereas sexual maltreatment occurs at a higher rate among African American families that have a single parent or one biological and one stepparent (Rao, DiClemente, & Ponton, 1992). Overall, African American families that experience a greater number of life events have higher rates of maltreatment (Li, Godinet, & Arnsberger, 2011). Such life events can include moving to a new home or the birth of a new child (McDaniel & Slack, 2005). Relatedly, the more children there are in African American families, the greater the likelihood of child maltreatment (Dubowitz et al., 2011). Also among African Americans, male children are at greater risk for physical maltreatment (MacKenzie et al., 2011), whereas female children are at greater risk for sexual maltreatment (King, 2004). First-born children in African American families are also at greater risk for physical maltreatment, and several characteristics of African American children put them at risk for physical punishment and maltreatment in general. These include having a difficult temperament (MacKenzie, Nicklas, Brooks-Gunn, & Waldfogel, 2011), being suspended or expelled from school (McDaniel & Slack, 2005), and low performance on standardized developmental assessments (Dubowitz et al., 2011). At the couple-level of the microsystem, lower levels of interparental warmth is associated with the physical maltreatment of children in both African American and Latino American families (Moore & Florsheim, 2008), and violence or psychological aggression between parents is associated with both physical maltreatment and child maltreatment in general in both Asian American and Latino American families (Chang, Siyon, & Megan Berthold, 2008; Moore & Florsheim, 2008).

Finally, there are several individual/developmental factors that increase the risk of parents maltreating their children. In both the African American and Latino American communities, younger parents and adolescent parents are at greater risk for physically harming their children (Moore & Florsheim, 2008), which is perhaps related to the parenting stress, a risk factor for Latino fathers (Lee, Guterman, & Lee, 2008). African American and Native American parents who have a history of maltreatment in their families of origin—whether it is a history of experiencing or witnessing violence or sexual abuse—are at heightened risk for maltreating their own children (Li et al., 2011; Libby, Orton, Beals,

Buchwald, & Manson, 2008). Among African American and Asian American parents, mental illness (Chang et al., 2008; Dubowitz et al., 2011; Mapp, 2006) and drug use (Chang et al., 2008; Dubowitz et al., 2011) predict their perpetration of child maltreatment, as does a history of arrest among African American parents (McDaniel & Slack, 2005).

Risk Factors for Intimate Partner Violence

Table 12.5 summarizes risk factors for IPV at all levels of the ecological model in the various racial/ethnic minority communities. Several cultural values, the experience of racism, and poverty all contribute to IPV at the macrosystem level. For example, cultural values such as honor, secretiveness, marital devotion, priority of the family, traditional gender roles, cultural taboos about speaking of sex and rape, and tolerance to violence place individuals from Asian, Latino, and Native American communities at risk for IPV (Ahrens, Rios-Mandel, Isas, & del Carmen Lopez, 2010; Cheung, Leung, & Tsui, 2009; Oetzel & Duran, 2004; Rizo & Macy, 2011; Weidel, Provencio-Vasquez, Watson, & Gonzalez-Guarda, 2008; Weil & Lee, 2004). Many minority group members also show an increased likelihood to not report IPV when it occurs, because the idea that reporting violence to an outside authority goes against these cultural values (Aheren et al., 2010; Cheung et al., 2009; Rizo & Macy, 2011; Wahab & Olson, 2004; Weil & Lee, 2004). Also on a macrosystem level, in Native and Latino Americans, oppression (such as racism) has been linked to increased risk of men perpetrating IPV (Rizo & Macy, 2011; Wahab & Olson, 2004). As with child maltreatment, poverty is a macrosystem risk factor for IPV in all the racial/ethnic minority families discussed in this chapter. Poverty, low education, unemployment, and financial dependence all increase chances of IPV in relationships (Duran et al., 2009; Goodman, Dutton, Vankos, & Weinfurt, 2005; Malcoe, Duran, & Montgomery, 2004; Oetzel & Duran., 2004; Rizo & Macy, 2011; Sanderson, Coker, Roberts, Tortolero, & Reininger, 2004; Taft, Bryantdavis, Woodward, Tillman, & Torres, 2009; Weidel et al., 2008; Weil & Lee, 2004; Wenzel, Tucker, Elliott, Marshall, & Williamson, 2004) perhaps because they act as stressors for the family (Weil & Lee, 2004).

Among the exosystem factors contributing to IPV in the Asian and Latino American communities are inaccessibility, underutilization, and lack of knowledge concerning social services (Rizo & Macy, 2011; Weidel et al., 2008; Weil & Lee, 2004). Social isolation and poor social support also contribute to IPV in Latino and African American communities (Goodman et al., 2005; Rizo & Macy, 2011; Taft et al., 2009; Wenzel et al., 2004), as does violence in the neighborhood for African Americans (Goodman et al., 2005; Taft et al., 2009; Wenzel et al., 2004).

At the microsystem level, there are various couple- and victim-level predictors of IPV. Although at the macrosystem level, living in poverty increases the chances of IPV, Latina women who earn greater incomes than their partners (regardless of income level) showed increased risk of being victimized (Weidel et al., 2008). Similarly, the more acculturated a Latina is in comparison to her male partner, the greater risk she has for being victimized (Weidel et al., 2008). For African American women and men, using and abusing drugs puts them at risk for IPV victimization (Hien & Ruglass, 2009). At the individual/developmental level,

Table 12.5 Risk Factors for Intimate Partner Violence at Each Level of the Ecological Model

Level of Ecological Model	Risk Factor	Gender(s) of Perpetrator	Racial/Ethnic Group(s)	Studies
Macrosystem	Familism or priority of family over individual	Male	Asian and Latino Americans	Ahrens, Rios-Mandel, Isas, & del Carmen Lopez (2010); Weil & Lee (2004)
	Secretiveness	Female	Asian Americans	Cheung, Leung, & Tsui (2009)
	Lack of enforcement against domestic violence in country of origin	Male	Latino Americans	Rizo & Macy (2011)
	Tolerance of violence	Male & female	Asian Americans	Cheung et al. (2009); Weil & Lee (2004)
	Patriarchal norms, traditional gender roles	Male	Latino and Native Americans	Oetzel & Duran (2004); Rizo & Macy (2011); Weidel et al. (2008)
	Racial/ethnic discrimination and institutional oppression	Male	Latino and Native Americans	Rizo & Macy (2011); Wahab & Olson (2004)
	Poverty, low SES, financial dependence, unemployment	Male	African, Latino, Asian, and Native Americans	Duran et al. (2009); Goodman et al. (2005); Malcoe, Duran, & Montgomery (2004); Oetzel & Duran (2004); Rizo & Macy (2011); Sanderson, Coker, Roberts, Tortolero, & Reininger (2004); Taft, Bryantdavis, Woodward, Tillman, & Torres (2009); Weidel, Provencio-Vasquez, Watson, & Gonzalez-Guarda (2008); Weil & Lee (2004); Wenzel, Tucker, Elliott, Marshall, & Williamson (2004)
	Low education	Male	African Americans	Goodman et al (2005); Taft et al. (2009); Wenzel et al. (2004)
	Stress	Male	Asian Americans	Weil & Lee (2004)

(Continued)

Table 12.5 (Continued)

Level of Ecological Model	Risk Factor	Gender(s) of Perpetrator	Racial/Ethnic Group(s)	Studies
Exosystem	Inaccessibility/lack of knowledge of social services	Male	Asian and Latino Americans	Rizo & Macy (2011); Weil & Lee (2004)
	Poor social support/social isolation	Male	Latino and African Americans	Goodman et al. (2005); Rizo & Macy (2011); Taft et al. (2009); Wenzel et al. (2004)
	Neighborhood violence	Male	African Americans	Goodman et al. (2005); Taft et al. (2009); Wenzel et al. (2004)
Microsystem	Women who earn more money than their partners are at higher risk for being IPV victims	Male	Latino Americans	Weidel et al. (2008)
	A more acculturated woman who is highly integrated into American society with a less acculturated man who upholds traditional Latino cultural beliefs	Male	Latino Americans	Weidel et al. (2008)
	IPV victim's substance misuse and abuse	Male & female	African Americans	Hien & Ruglass (2009)

Level of Ecological Model	Risk Factor	Gender(s) of Perpetrator	Racial/Ethnic Group(s)	Studies
Individual/ Developmental	U.S. born	Male	Asian Americans	Chang, Shen, & Takeuchi (2009)
	Younger age	Male	Asian Americans	Chang et al. (2009)
	Alcohol and/or substance abuse	Male and female	Latino, Asian, and African Americans	Caetano et al. (2000); Chang et al. (2009); Gonzalez-Guarda, Peragallo, Urrutia, Vasquez, & Mitrani (2008); Hien & Ruglass (2009); Sanderson et al. (2004); Weidel et al. (2008)
	Family history of alcoholism	Male	Native Americans	Duran et al. (2009)
	History of childhood trauma, physical abuse, and/or sexual abuse	Male and female	African Americans	Hien & Ruglass (2009); Ramos et al. (2004); Wenzel et al. (2004)
	Recent experience of physical violence/fight	Male and female	African and Latino Americans	Sanderson et al. (2004); Wenzel et al. (2004)
	Carrying a weapon	Male	Latino Americans	Sanderson et al. (2004)
	Early age at first intercourse	Male	Latino Americans	Sanderson et al. (2004)
	Psychological distress	Male and female	African Americans	Wenzel et al. (2004)

various demographics, characteristics, and histories of the perpetrator predict their use of IPV. U.S.-born Asian American men are at greater risk for perpetrating IPV than their non-U.S.-born counterparts, as are younger Asian American men (Chang et al., 2009). Alcohol and substance abuse predicts Latino, Asian, and African American men's and women's use of IPV (Caetano et al., 2000; Chang et al., 2009; Gonzalez-Guarda et al., 2008; Hien & Ruglass, 2009; Sanderson et al., 2004; Weidel et al., 2008), whereas a family history of alcoholism predicts Native American men's use of IPV (Duran et al., 2009). Another type of family history—that of childhood trauma, physical abuse, and/or sexual abuse—predicts African American men's and women's use of IPV (Hien & Ruglass, 2009; Ramos, Carlson, & McNutt, 2004; Wenzel et al., 2004). Adult revictimization also predicts men's and women's use of IPV among African and Latino Americans (Sanderson et al., 2004; Wenzel et al., 2004), as does psychological distress (Wenzel et al., 2004).

Risk Factors for the Maltreatment of Older Adults

Table 12.6 provides a brief summary of research on risk factors for the maltreatment of older adults in the various racial/ethnic minority communities discussed in this chapter. Financial reasons appear to be a prime macrosystem factor for the maltreatment of older adults. Financial strain on a family can cause stress that is then taken out on elders, especially in African American and Native America homes (Maxwell & Maxwell, 1992; Tauriac & Scruggs, 2006). Older individuals also have an increased likelihood of being exploited for their economic resources. This may be linked to cultural values (such as with Native Americans) or may be associated with psychological disorders, such as Alzheimer's disease (Brown, 1989; Parra-Cardona, Meyer, Schiamberg, & Post, 2007). Older individuals also may experience a lack of social and health services, or disrespectful treatment from these providers. These interactions—or lack thereof—are the primary exosystem factor that creates a sense of isolation and neglect in elderly victims (Beyene, Becker, & Mayen, 2002; Blanchard & Lurie, 2004; Tauriac et al., 2006).

In addition, microsystem risk factors for the maltreatment of older adults in families include an overburdened family system among African Americans (Tauriac et al., 2006). Similarly, larger families in the Asian American communities put older adults at risk for neglect (Lee, Gibson, & Chaisson, 2011). Various characteristics of older adults also put them at risk for being maltreated. These include their older age (Tauriac et al., 2006) and chronic health conditions that result in mental impairment (Lachs & Pillemer, 2006). When older individuals are dependent on their families for their physical, economic, and emotional needs, it can cause stress that leads to maltreatment, especially in families that are already strained or overburdened (Montoya, 1997; Tauriac et al., 2006). At the individual/developmental level, African American caregivers who abuse drugs are at greater risk of maltreating their older family members (Tauriac et al., 2006). Moreover, in the Asian American community, older adults are most likely to feel lonely and experience neglect from family caregivers who are too busy (Brown, 1989; Dong, Simon, Gorbien, Percak, & Golden, 2007; Passmore & Cummins, 2004).

Table 12.6 Risk Factors for the Maltreatment of Older Adults at Each Level of the Ecological Model

Level of Ecological Model	Risk Factors	Racial/Ethnic Groups	Studies
Macrosystem	Financial strain/poverty	African and Native Americans	Maxwell & Maxwell (1992); Tauriac & Scruggs (2006)
	Cultural privilege and duty to share with their families (risk for financial exploitation)	Native Americans	Brown (1989)
Exosystem	Sense of isolation (limited interactions with systems outside nuclear family)	Latino Americans	Beyene et al. (2002)
Microsystem	Overburdened family system	African Americans	Tauriac et al. (2006)
	Large families (risk for neglect)	Asian Americans	Lee, Gibson, & Chaisson (2011)
	Old age	African Americans	Tauriac et al. (2006)
	Physical, economic, emotional dependence of the victim on the caregiver	Latino Americans	Montoya (1997)
	Chronic health conditions that result in mental impairment	Latino Americans	Lachs & Pillemer (2006)
Individual/ Developmental	Drug abuse	African Americans	Tauriac et al. (2006)
	Caregiver is too busy (risk for neglect)	Asian Americans	Lee et al. (2011)

Protective Factors Against Family Violence

There are also a range of protective factors, some of which are directly related to race/ethnicity, operating to reduce the likelihood of the different forms of family violence. Again, think about which of these factors may be unique to each community or to minority groups in general, and think about which ones seem to cut across all races and ethnicities in this country.

Protective Factors Against Child Maltreatment

Table 12.7 summarizes research identifying protective factors in relation to child maltreatment in different racial/ethnic groups. At the macrosystem level, familism

Table 12.7   Protective Factors Against Child Maltreatment

Level of Ecological Model	Type of Maltreatment	Protective Factors	Racial/ Ethnic Groups	Studies
Macrosystem	General maltreatment	Societal emphasis on family harmony and reputation	Asian Americans	Zhai & Gao (2009)
	General maltreatment	Familism	Latino Americans	Elliott & Urquiza (2006)
	Sexual	Conservative cultural norms discouraging sexual activity at an early age	Asian Americans	Chen et al. (2004)
	Sexual	Loss of face	Asian Americans	Hall, Teten, DeGarmo, Sue, & Stephens (2005)
Exosystem	General maltreatment	High levels of social support	African Americans	Champion, Shain, & Piper (2004); Li, Godinet, & Amsberger (2011)
Microsystem	General maltreatment	Mothers who attained 12 or more years of education	African Americans	Li et al. (2011)
	General maltreatment	Married parents	African Americans	Lee, Guterman, & Lee (2008); Li et al. (2011)
	Physical	Parental warmth	African Americans	Haskett, Allaire, Kreig, & Hart (2008)
	Physical	Parental sensitivity to child pro- and anti-social behaviors	African Americans	Haskett et al. (2008)
Individual/ Developmental	Sexual	Men with a greater number of sexual experiences were at lower risk of perpetrating child sexual abuse	Asian Americans	Hall et al. (2005)

has been found to be an important protective factor for Asian Americans and Latinos. Familism emphasizes placing value on family (including extended family), and the importance of family obligations, obedience, and loyalty. The promotion of family harmony and the ideal of the intact family unit can reduce the likelihood of child maltreatment (Elliot & Urquiza, 2006; Zhai & Gao, 2009). Note that this value also serves as a risk factor as well for child maltreatment (Table 12.4). In what ways does the importance of family put some at risk for child maltreatment at the same time that it protects others? Other macrosystem protective factors for Asian Americans include the emphasis on social support, social advocacy, and promoting conservative social norms that discourage sexual activity at an early age (Chen, Dunne, & Han, 2004; Singh, Hays, Chung, & Watson, 2010). Viewing the preservation of social identity (to prevent "loss of face") as an ideal is a highly protective factor against child sexual abuse perpetration in Asian American men. This factor has no such impact on White men, which demonstrates that it is dependent on culture (Hall, Teten, DeGarmo, Sue, & Stephens, 2005).

For African Americans, protective factors at the exosystem level include social support and the availability of personal and structural resources (Champion, Shain, & Piper, 2004; Li, Godinet, & Amsberger, 2011). It appears that social support moderates the risk of levels of stress and maternal depression, thus decreasing the likelihood of child maltreatment (Li et al., 2011); however, there is some variation among racial/ethnic groups in preferred type of support. According to Freisthler et al. (2007), Latino families tend to rely more heavily on informal support networks for resources, whereas White families rely on greater access to economic and formal resources for support. To what extent do these different forms of support reflect broader cultural values? Do you think that for members of any racial/ethnic group, seeking support in culturally synchronic ways may strengthen the role of these protective factors in reducing child maltreatment? What are the implications for clinicians of evidence that somewhat different forms of support play a protective role in different racial/ethnic groups?

At the microsystem level, studies of the role of education and marital status as protective factors have provided somewhat diverse results. Findings from a largely African American and highly impoverished sample from the Longitudinal Studies of Child Abuse and Neglect revealed that a two-parent household and maternal education at least through high school protected children against a maltreatment report (Li et al., 2011). Opposite results were found in the Fragile Families and Child Wellbeing Study, which contained a predominantly racial/ethnic minority sample from 20 large American cities (Lee, Guterman, & Lee, 2008). Specifically, among African American fathers, cohabiting with—rather than being married to—the child's mother was associated with lower levels of physical aggression and spanking, a pattern not found in White or Latino fathers. For Latino fathers, those with higher levels of education (compared to the reference group of less than a high school degree) were more likely to have spanked their child in the past month.

Among the more psychological microsystem factors that have been investigated, parental warmth and parental sensitivity to children's needs have been shown to contribute to child well-being (Haskett, Allaire, Kreig, & Hart, 2008). In a study containing predominantly African American parents and children, Haskett and associates (2008) found that parental sensitivity was associated with lower levels of parental aggression. In addition, parental sensitivity seemed to have a buffering effect, reducing the negative effects of aggressive discipline on child outcomes.

Finally, in regard to individual/developmental protective factors, Asian American men who have more sexual experiences are at lower risk of sexually abusing their children (Hall et al., 2005). Hall and colleagues (2005) believe that because consensual relationships are available, men with more sexual experiences are less motivated to be sexually abusive. Can you think of other reasons why men with more sexual experiences would be less likely to sexually abuse their children?

Protective Factors Against Intimate Partner Violence

Similar to child maltreatment, a number of protective factors have been identified with regard to IPV in racial/ethnic minority communities (see Table 12.8). At the macrosystem level, strong ethnic identity, spiritual coping, and being immersed in traditions are all protective factors for Native Americans (Oetzal & Duran, 2004). One Texas study of dating violence victimization in a sample of Latino high school students revealed that girls who were less acculturated to U.S. values and placed greater importance on their ethnicity showed a reduced likelihood of being victimized (Sanderson et al., 2004). In addition, being born outside the United States was a protective factor. Why do you think this might be so? Why would the more acculturated Latina girls, born in the United States have an increased likelihood of experiencing IPV from their partners, and what factors might be associated with being born outside the United States and being less acculturated that could help protect girls from IPV?

At the exosystem level, increases in social support are important because they buffer against ongoing IPV as well as aid individuals to end abusive relationships (Gout, 2010; Wenzel et al., 2004). Social support systems are likely to be most effective when they are not only culturally specific services, but also when they are tailored to the individual's needs (Cheung et al., 2009; Evans-Campbell, Lindhorst, Huang, & Walters, 2006) and when they consider the role of historical trauma (Evans-Campbell, 2008). Incorporating traditional practices in a therapeutic setting seems to help buffer Native Americans from IPV (Saylors & Daliparthy, 2006). Finally, at the microsystem level, it appears that less frequent drinking on the part of both partners decreases the risk of IPV occurring in that relationship (Caetano et al., 2000). Given what you learned in previous chapters regarding the relationship between IPV and alcohol abuse, why do you think less frequent drinking among both partners serves as a protective factor?

Protective Factors Against the Maltreatment of Older Adults

In regard to protective factors against the maltreatment of older adults in racial/ethnic minority communities, a similar trend appears as with child maltreatment and IPV (see Table 12.9). At the macrosystem level, emphasizing ideals such as strong ties to family and respect for others, culture, and tradition all reduce risks of the maltreatment of older adults in Latino American communities (Montoya, 1997). When Latino families are in an exosystem environment that fosters individuals to embrace

Table 12.8 Protective Factors Against Intimate Partner Violence

Level of Ecological Model	Protective Factors	Gender(s) of Perpetrators	Racial/ Ethnic Groups	Studies
Macrosystem	Strong ethnic identity, and immersion in traditions	Male	Latino Americans	Oetzel & Duran (2004); Sanderson, Coker, Roberts, Tortolero, & Reininger (2004)
Exosystem	Increased social support	Male and female	African and Native Americans	Gout (2010); Wenzel, Tucker, Elliott, Marshall, & Williamson (2004)
	Presence of instrumental support	Male	Native Americans	Gout (2010)
	Availability of therapy	Male and female	African Americans	Wenzel et al. (2004)
	Incorporating traditional practices in a community therapeutic setting	Male	Native Americans	Saylors & Daliparthy (2006)
Microsystem	Less frequent drinking in both partners	Male	Latino Americans	Caetano et al. (2000)

personal, familial, and cultural strengths, there is a lower likelihood of maltreatment against the older adults (Parra-Cardona, Meyer, Schiamberg, & Post, 2007). Similarly, tribal resilience among Native Americans protects them from the maltreatment of their older members (Carson, 1995). Education of the caregivers of the older adults in the Latino community serves to protect families from experiencing the maltreatment of their older members as well (Parra-Cardona et al., 2007). Finally, at the microsystem level, extended family networks and the flexibility of family roles among African Americans (Tauriac & Scruggs, 2006) and family resiliency among Native Americans (Carson, 1995) protects families against elder maltreatment.

Outcomes of Family Violence in Racial/Ethnic Minority Groups

Outcomes of Child Maltreatment

As is true of child maltreatment in the majority culture, there is evidence that child maltreatment in racial/ethnic minority groups can have long-lasting negative psychological and physical health consequences. For example, victims of child sexual abuse

Table 12.9   Protective Factors Against the Maltreatment of Older Adults

Level of Ecological Model	Protective Factors	Racial/ Ethnic Groups	Studies
Macrosystem	Incorporating individual *personalismo*, *la familia*, *communidad*, the Church, and other cultural strengths of the community	Latino Americans	Montoya (1997)
	Filial piety, ties to traditional Asian attitudes, such as veneration of elders	Asian Americans	Chen (1979)
Exosystem	Presence of nurturing, therapeutic environments that enable families to embrace personal, familial, and cultural strengths	Latino Americans	Parra-Cardona, Meyer, Schiamberg, & Post (2007)
	Tribal resiliency	Native Americans	Carson (1995)
	Educating caregivers of older adults	Latino Americans	Parra-Cardona et al. (2007)
Microsystem	Extended family networks and flexibility of family roles	African Americans	Tauriac & Scruggs (2006)
	Family resiliency	Native Americans	Carson (1995)

suffer myriad consequences as a result of their difficult experiences. As mentioned in Chapter 3, perpetrators of this type of maltreatment often coax and manipulate children into defenseless subordination. Thus, regardless of gender or racial/ethnic group, victims report greater psychological distress than non-abused peers (Newcomb, Munoz, & Carmona, 2009).

All forms of maltreatment, however, can have devastating consequences for racial/ ethnic minority children. For example, in a sample of Native American women at a health clinic, there was a strong relationship between maltreatment in childhood and lifetime prevalence of six forms of psychological disorders (Duran et al., 2004). The lifetime prevalence of mental disorders was generally highest among women who were both sexually and physically abused as children, and the most common disorders were alcohol and/or drug dependence, mood disorders (including major depression), anxiety, and post traumatic stress disorder (PTSD). The lifetime prevalence of any mental disorder among the women who had experienced all four forms of maltreatment (child sexual abuse, physical abuse, emotional abuse, and neglect) was 94.4% (Duran et al., 2004).

Similarly, among a different sample of Native American women, child maltreatment was significantly related to greater emotional distress, sexual risk behaviors, anger, and depression. Moreover, Native American women reporting greater physical and emotional maltreatment had a significantly higher number of STDs (5.14 times more likely than non-maltreated women) (Hobfoll et al., 2002). Additionally, Yuan, Koss, Polacca, and Goldman (2006) found that among Asian American men and women, multiple types of childhood maltreatment contributed to increased risk of assault later in life—by family members, acquaintances, or strangers. Why do you think child maltreatment is associated with these specific outcomes later in life? Do you think that the short- and long-term psychological outcomes for racial/ethnic minority victims of child maltreatment may be worse or the same as for victims in the majority community? What cultural factors in each of these communities may buffer or exacerbate any symptoms?

Probably the most extreme outcome of child maltreatment is death, the risk of which is greatest during the first few days of a child's life. Herman-Giddens, Smith, Mittal, Carlson, and Butts (2003) reviewed all death cases of infants under four days of age in North Carolina from 1985 through 2000. They found that 34 newborns were killed or discarded by their parents, which projects to 2.1 per 100,000 newborns per year; Black newborns were overrepresented (52.9%) as cases in comparison to their representation in the overall population of newborns (28%). Overall in this country in 2010, there were 1,227 child fatalities due to maltreatment (USDHHS, 2011). Of these, 535 (43.6%) were White, 345 (28.1%) were African American, 204 (16.6%) were Latino, 11 (0.9%) were Asian American, 10 (0.8%) were Native Americans, 54 (4.4%) were of two or more races, and 68 (5.5%) were of unknown ethnicity. Rates per 100,000 were 3.91 for African Americans, 1.94 for Native Americans, 1.89 for Latinos, 1.68 for Whites, 0.60 for Asian Americans, and 3.65 for children of two or more races. To what extent are these proportions and rates consistent with other proportions and rates you have learned about in this chapter? Which groups seem to be at greater risk for child maltreatment fatalities? Which groups are at lower risk? Why?

Outcomes of Intimate Partner Violence

As is true for victims of child maltreatment, members of racial/ethnic minority groups who have been subjected to IPV can suffer long-term psychological and physical health problems or indeed die from their maltreatment. Several studies have addressed outcomes of IPV in all the racial/ethnic minority communities discussed in this chapter. For example, Native American women who had experienced IPV are five times more likely to have PTSD and 2.5 times more likely to have a mood disorder than Native American women who had not experienced IPV (Duran et al., 2009). Similarly, among New York City Native Americans, there were much higher rates of depression in women who had experienced IPV than those who had not (Evans-Campbell, Lindhorst, Huang, & Walters, 2006). Physical injuries have been found as well among Native American women: In a study of women recruited in a tribally operated clinic, 40.1% reported lifetime partner-perpetrated injuries and 31.1% specifically reported injuries to their neck, head, or face (Malcoe, Duran, & Montgomery, 2004).

Similar patterns have been found with African, Asian, and Latino American women who have experienced IPV. For example, among African American female emergency department patients who had been victimized by their partners within the last year, depression and suicidality were significantly correlated with psychological, physical, and sexual IPV (Houry, Kemball, Rhodes, & Kaslow, 2006). In a sample of low income African American and Latina women in Chicago, the experience of intimate terrorism (see Chapter 5) was associated with seeking medical treatment for injuries, and with poor health and psychological distress (Leone, Johnson, Cohan, & Lloyd, 2004). Finally, in a sample of African American, Asian American, Latino and European American college students that also included male IPV victims, the level of partner and coercive violence was significantly and positively correlated with mental illness symptoms, in all groups except Asian men (Prospero & Kim, 2009). How do these outcomes compare with what you learned about the outcomes of IPV in the majority community? Why do you think there is so little research on outcomes of IPV against men in the various racial/ethnic minority communities?

Outcomes of Maltreatment of Older Adults

There appear to be very few published studies on the outcomes of the maltreatment of older adults in racial/ethnic minority communities. In an analysis of outcomes of maltreatment from the National Elder Mistreatment Study, Cisler, Begle, Amstadter, and Acierno (2011) identified the following outcomes and indicated that there were no racial/ethnic group differences in these outcomes: needing help with activities of daily living, poor physical health, and emotional symptoms with functional impairment. In the only study we found that focused on one of the racial/ethnic minority communities in this chapter, qualitative responses to an open-ended interview revealed that older immigrant Koreans associated neglect with a variety of psychological and emotional difficulties, including feelings of being unappreciated, sadness that children do not meet their obligations, and loneliness (Lee, Gibson, & Chaisson, 2011).

Prevention and Intervention

With the knowledge that family violence does in fact occur on a daily basis to a substantial part of the population, steps need to be taken to help victims and to prevent innocents from being harmed. While we would like to consider current efforts to be widely used and effective, research shows that might not be the case. The research, as discussed below, reveals gaps in the current intervention and prevention policies and services. Taking an opportunity to distinguish between what is effective and what is ineffective is vital for the improvement of our current systems and the development of future ones.

Considerations for Interventions

Child Maltreatment

When considering proper intervention for child maltreatment, one needs to consider whether racial biases enter into the decision to report and investigate child maltreatment cases, and the decision to refer victims and their families to treatment. Moreover, we need to consider whether the providers of those treatment programs are culturally competent to deliver their services to the range of potential clients. It is not quite clear how policies within each state's social service agencies influence which children get the needed care (Kolko, Seleyo, & Brown, 1999), but among the factors that have been identified by the U.S. Department of Health and Human Services (2001) are that non-White or non-Latino children were more likely to receive services than their White or Latino counterparts; however, it is unclear why.

As described previously in this chapter, African American children tend to be overrepresented in child maltreatment cases, and this overrepresentation does not seem to be due to racial biases in child maltreatment reports (Drake, Lee, & Jonson-Reid, 2009). Nonetheless, racial identity is a strong predictor for placement into foster care, with African American children having 44% higher odds of being placed into foster care than White children. In addition, African American children with emotional problems and with a substantiated sexual abuse case, who are between the ages of four and eleven, had higher odds of being in foster care services in comparison to their White counterparts (Knott & Donovan, 2010). Thus, although racial biases do not seem to influence reporting of maltreatment among African American families, such biases may enter into decisions to place African American children into foster care.

The decision to investigate a child physical abuse report may be subject to biases for the Latino community. Evidence suggests that a higher percentage of physical abuse investigations are conducted for Latino children than for non-Latino children. For example, relative to non-Latino boys who experience 29% of physical abuse investigations, Latino boys experience 43% of physical abuse investigations (Alzate & Rosenthal, 2009). Higher proportions of investigations may introduce biases that make child physical abuse rates *appear* disproportionately more prevalent in the Latino population than they actually are. Thus, the researchers comment that racial/ethnic differences need to be better observed in the child welfare system, which can then lead to improved cultural competency in that system.

As mentioned previously, among Native American women, experiences of child maltreatment has a strong relationship with multiple mental disorders in Native American women later in life (Duran et al., 2004). With the high risk of such outcomes, Duran and colleagues (2004) suggest that increased funds and other resources be placed on prevention and treatment programs, especially for Native American female victims. Issues such as racism, sexism, and religious intolerance are all externalized and internalized attitudes and behaviors that continue to victimize Native American families (Duran et al., 2004), and would need to be considered in such programming.

When reviewing childhood sexual abuse cases, Walsh and Krienert (2007) found that not all children received examinations equally. Girls, younger children, children who were injured, and those with suspected penetration were more likely to receive exams. In addition, White children were more likely to receive exams compared to children of other races and ethnicities. More research should examine the reasoning processes and the community structures that enhance or deter the receipt of an exam, and education should be targeted toward referring sexual abuse victims for exams based on elements of the case, not the racial/ethnic identity of the victim.

Intimate Partner Violence

Female IPV victims face many challenges and barriers that can prevent their successful use of both the social service and criminal justice systems. Such barriers need to be considered as we look to improve these systems to make them more culturally competent. Some barriers cut across both the minority and majority communities and include: (1) fear of retaliation by their perpetrator (or someone else seeking vengeance on his or her behalf); (2) victim-blaming attitudes among criminal justice personnel; (3) resistance within the criminal justice system to treating domestic assaults as seriously as other assaults of equal impact; (4) poverty and all its associated factors (e.g., transportation problems, inability to take time off from work); (5) fear of abandonment by one's religious or ethnic community; and (6) general distrust of the criminal justice system (Hart, 1993). However, barriers against the use of the criminal justice system and other social services do vary by racial/ethnic group as well.

Overall, minority women—and African American women in particular—are less likely to seek help for IPV victimization, whether that help comes in the form of police reporting, family services, or social services (Kaukinen, 2004). These findings are consistent with research that points to racial/ethnic differences in response to trauma. African American women tend to engage in withdrawal behaviors as a consequence of their violent victimization rather than reaching out to others for assistance. Even elderly African American women are less likely to seek personal emotional support (Grossman & Lundy, 2003). These studies highlight a need for victim-based strategies that consider these withdrawal behaviors among African American victims.

Latino minorities show a somewhat similar pattern of help-seeking behaviors. Latina IPV victims seek help at lower rates that White IPV victims (Grossman & Lundy, 2003). One reason may be that Latinas may fear legal ramifications to themselves or their family members, such as deportation if they are not legal citizens (Parra-Cardona et al., 2007). There are also possible language and cultural barriers, especially if knowledge of available support systems is limited. Parra-Cardona et al. (2007) suggest therapy practices that not only address the specific issues that have led to the IPV, but also those practices that remain cognizant of the ways in which provision of services may be perceived differently. Understanding the distrust that Latina victims have toward institutions is important for overcoming such barriers.

Shim and Hwang (2005) found similar barriers among female Asian IPV victims. However, these barriers were not simply limited to language, resources, or lack of knowledge. Cultural standards—particularly among female Korean IPV victims— were also key reasons for women choosing not to call for police assistance. Korean cultural standards dictate that the wife should obey the husband no matter the costs, so when a husband abuses his wife, the community views the abuse as just. The community is quicker to blame the wife for committing some injustice (such as an affair) than they are to place any blame on the husband. The fear of community rejection, paired with the loss of resources that would come from the husband being arrested, was a major reason for female Korean IPV victims to not seek police assistance (Shim & Hwang, 2005).

When comparing these racial/ethnic minority groups to White female victims of IPV, we see that White women are more likely to engage in higher levels of help-seeking behaviors that include reporting incidents to police, seeking assistance from friends and family, and requesting help from psychiatrists and social service agencies (Kaukinen, 2004). However, do these same help-seeking tendencies occur in male victims of IPV? In general, men are less likely to seek help than women for IPV victimization (Cheung, Leung, & Tsui, 2009). Men are also disadvantaged in IPV investigations, whether they are the victim or offender, as they are often treated less favorably than women by the law enforcement system, which leads to a lower likelihood of reporting victimization to the authorities. When men do report IPV, the police are less likely to lay charges against female perpetrators than they are for the same acts by male perpetrators (Brown, 2004). In addition, there are fewer resources that are specifically available for male victims (Cheung et al., 2009).

Although same-sex couples are not often addressed in literature, research with Native Americans shows that sexual minorities within this community have disproportionately high levels of IPV (Lehavot, Walters, & Simoni, 2010). Specifically, 78% of sexual minority women had been physically assaulted and 85% had been sexually assaulted. These results suggest an urgent need for agencies that specialize in the effects of IPV among victims who are both racial/ethnic and sexual minorities, as well as ways to increase police assistance.

Special considerations also need to be addressed among Native American female IPV victims in general. As mentioned previously, Native American women have the highest rates of IPV among all racial/ethnic groups in the United States (see Table 12.2). Traditional models of research have proven to be poorly suited for facilitating change in this community. Holkup, Tripp-Reimer, Salois, and Weinert (2004) suggest using an approach that has the whole community join together as full and equal partners of the research process to develop intervention strategies. Such research has a strong potential for addressing the health disparities of female IPV victims by creating interventions that are tailored to cultural standards and expectations. Their suggested model focuses on family conferencing with culturally competent team members to address issues in the family that lead to IPV and how these issues can be resolved.

Although there is evidence that members of racial/ethnic minorities in this country are less likely to seek help, there are mixed results regarding whether they are referred for help at differing rates. For example, in one sample, even though Latina women were at greater risk than African American women for sexual abuse by husbands or ex-husbands, they were less likely to be referred to a domestic violence service program by police or other legal services (Grossman & Lundy, 2003). On the other hand, in a Seattle sample, not only were Latina women *more* likely to receive aid from a crisis intervention program, but Asian women were as well (Kernic & Bonomi, 2007). This study showed that female victims of physical IPV who were Asian or Latina may have been more likely to have crisis intervention activated due to fewer resources or due to a greater proportion of non-English speakers among these groups. However, activation of this program first requires a recommendation by police officers who arrive on scene to a report of violence.

Within the criminal justice system, one attempt to lessen levels of IPV was the implementation of mandatory or preferred arrest policies in almost all states. However, evidence regarding the effectiveness of arrest as a deterrent is weak. Studies in Milwaukee (Sherman et al., 1992), Dade County, Florida (Pate & Hamilton, 1992), and Colorado Springs (Berk, Campbell, Klap, & Western, 1992), suggest that arrest may affect different groups of men differently. For example, it appears that arrest reduces subsequent violence in employed men, but not unemployed men, and in White men, but not in Black men (Sherman et al., 1992). Arresting the perpetrator may have other negative consequences as well. In those situations where separation of the offender and victim does not occur after the offender is free from jail, the result may be an increase in the severity of IPV. For those individuals who expect that type of backlash, arrest policies create fear and distrust toward law enforcement, which can deter the victim from calling the police in the future (Shim & Hwang, 2005). Women of various races report "a desire for police to be more responsive, treat victims with dignity, listen to them, and send appropriate messages to victims and to batterers" (Wolf, Ly, Hobart, & Kernic, 2003).

Maltreatment of Older Adults

Although it is unclear whether certain racial/ethnic groups are at greater or lesser risk for the maltreatment of older individuals (see Table 12.3), in those cases where older adults are maltreated by their family members, special considerations for intervention based on race and ethnicity must be considered. In one study of female victims of elder maltreatment, White elderly women were more likely to self-refer to social service programs than minority women were (Grossman & Lundy, 2003). Thus, similar help-seeking behaviors may be occurring among minority victims of elder maltreatment as we observed among minority victims of IPV. Grossman and Lundy (2003) note that we must be aware and acknowledge the needs of elderly victims. "Abused elders come from different groups and have varying needs based on race and ethnicity, which may be best met by a variety of systems" (p. 1450). An understanding of the context of this violence and the response of service systems is vital to provide direction and create protection services for this population (Grossman & Lundy, 2003).

Considerations for Preventative Measures

Child Maltreatment

There are various risk factors for childhood maltreatment. As was shown in Table 12.4 one macrosystem factor that cuts across racial/ethnic groups is poverty. Drake, Lee, and Jonson-Reid (2009) state that poverty is the most important factor in the prediction of child maltreatment, and because African American children are more likely to be residing in impoverished neighborhoods than White children, they are at higher risk for child maltreatment. White children who are raised in these same areas may also have these same high rates, so it may not be race/ethnicity that is a factor, but poverty itself (Drake et al., 2009). Thus, prevention of child maltreatment may be an issue of preventing poverty.

On the other hand, when looking at female juvenile delinquents, Chauhan and Repucci (2009) found that neighborhood disadvantage was not associated with self-reported antisocial behaviors. "It is encouraging that high levels of neighborhood disadvantage do not automatically equate to high levels of other adverse experiences such as maternal risk or parental abuse" (Chauhan & Repucci, 2009). However, if all these girls were already high risk, it is possible that the sampling was just not representative. Chauhan and Repucci (2009) express the concern that efforts must continue to be directed at both the individual and community level when designing interventions and preventions for child maltreatment.

Although it is arguable whether preventing poverty will lead to prevention of child maltreatment within the various racial/ethnic minority groups (particularly those that are more economically disadvantaged), drug abuse prevention as a means to prevent child maltreatment is even more controversial. Whiteford and Vitucci (1997) argue that low-income women of color are particularly victimized by the prosecutors of the war on drugs in this country. They report that women who are Black, have limited resources, use illegal drugs while pregnant, and give birth in public hospitals are the group most likely to be targeted for criminal prosecution. Indeed, approximately 70% of the women prosecuted for drug use while pregnant are women of color. Whiteford and Vitucci (1997) interpret these research findings as showing that laws jailing pregnant women for their addictions are concerned less with protecting the unborn than with punishing women for being poor, pregnant, and addicted. Do you agree? Do you think that lowering rates of drug abuse in this country will lead to lower rates of child maltreatment, particularly in those communities that are disproportionately affected by drug abuse? Would incarcerating pregnant women who are abusing drugs lower rates of drug abuse and consequently child maltreatment?

In a California study of how drug-exposed infants were processed in the social service and juvenile justice systems (Sagatun-Edwards, Saylor, & Shifflett, 1995), there was an overrepresentation of Black and Latino cases and an underrepresentation of White and Asian cases as compared to their relative distributions in the urban county covered by the court. During the process of the court hearings, a total of 52 infants (~20%) were ultimately returned home. Although racial/ethnic minority cases were disproportionately represented and rated as higher risk than White cases in the initial hearing, when controlling for other risk factors, it was mothers' compliance with court orders and attendance at hearings that significantly predicted whether the child could be reunified with the mother (Sagatun-Edwards & Saylor, 2000).

Intimate Partner Violence

Preventative measures for IPV must first begin with an analysis of risk and protective factors to understand who is at highest risk for IPV. A variety of risk factors have been consistently reported across races/ethnicities: substance abuse by the perpetrator (Caetano et al., 2000; Chang et al., 2009; Gonzalez-Guarda et al., 2008; Hien & Ruglass, 2009; Sanderson et al., 2004; Weidel et al., 2008), the perpetrator's exposure to and experience of violence in the childhood home (Hien & Ruglass, 2009; Ramos et al., 2004; Wenzel et al., 2004), poor social support and social isolation (Goodman et al., 2005; Rizo & Macy, 2011; Taft et al., 2009; Wenzel et al., 2004), and low income and low education levels (Duran et al., 2009; Goodman et al., 2005; Malcoe et al., 2004; Oetzel & Duran, 2004; Rizo & Macy, 2011; Sanderson et al., 2004; Taft et al., 2009; Weidel et al., 2008; Weil & Lee, 2004; Wenzel et al., 2004). Thus, targeting these risk factors can ultimately prevent IPV across racial/ethnic groups, with some studies arguing that the best preventative measure against IPV may be in how we aid these individuals when they are children (Henning, Jones, & Holdford, 2003). Contextual factors must still be taken into account, and prevention strategies must be tailored with consideration of preventing future risks (McIntyre & Widom, 2011). Other factors have been more inconsistent in the prediction of IPV among racial/ethnic minorities. Marital status is one such factor. Some studies found that there was an increased risk of IPV for married individuals (Cardona et al., 2007; Grossman & Lundy, 2003; Kernic & Bonomi, 2007), whereas others show that being separated, divorced, or cohabitating is the greater risk (Yuan et al., 2006). Immigrant status is also another inconsistent factor, as some research has shown a correlation between being an immigrant and a decrease in the likelihood of being an IPV victim (Cuevas & Sabina, 2010), whereas others have found that being an immigrant is associated with an increased risk of being victimized (Cardona et al., 2007). Thus, more research is necessary before we target such variables in any prevention efforts.

One victim-level factor that seems to be highly predictive of IPV is the experience of previous maltreatment (Acierno et al., 2010; Cuevas & Sabina, 2010; Henning, Jones, & Holdford, 2003; Lehavot, Walters, & Simoni, 2010; Yuan et al., 2006). Revictimization (the existence of previous maltreatment of the same type) and polyvictimization (the existence of previous maltreatments of different types; see Chapter 4) point to the presence of victim characteristics that in some way increase risk. Targeting those mechanisms that place victims at risk for future revictimization may prove beneficial in the prevention of IPV. From a service-level perspective, we currently see that sexual abuse services and domestic violence services are often kept separated. However, with research pointing to previous victimization as predicting future IPV, a combining of services may be more beneficial to increasing help-seeking behaviors because such a combination would not make individuals choose one service over another (Cuevas & Sabina, 2010) and could prevent future revictimization.

It is important to note that because the majority of the research in this area has been cross-sectional, we cannot definitively state that these characteristics are causal factors of IPV. It is possible that some of these risk factors are consequences of IPV or that some third variable contributes to both the IPV and the risk factor. For example, relationship dissatisfaction may be a result of IPV, and not the cause of the IPV itself (Henning, Jones, & Holdford, 2003). This could explain why some research has been inconsistent on whether factors such as marital status and immigrant status increase or decrease the likelihood of IPV. Future research should look further into these characteristics to see if they are truly causal of IPV. But, is this even possible without crossing ethical lines?

In addition to determining risk factors, having an understanding of the potential broad range of experiences of victimization can help efforts to prevent it from occurring, especially for those minority groups where victimization most occurs. Cuevas and Sabina (2010) recommend including a range of victimization types when assessing IPV in order to create a comprehensive and complete profile of victimization. As part of this profile and in ways that are culturally sensitive, service providers must address the fear and shame that comes with being maltreated in order to increase help-seeking (Cuevas & Sabina, 2010). Yuan et al. (2006) emphasize the need to "target prevention materials and resources and community services, including domestic shelters, to specific groups" (p. 1585). They also express the need for initiatives that are directed toward the possible perpetrators of IPV. For example, when working with Native American populations, they emphasize a need to focus on gender-role definitions, the negative effects of colonialism, and traditions that discourage male violence (Yuan et al., 2006).

Maltreatment of Older Adults

While the maltreatment of older adults that is physical and/or sexual in nature shares many of the same risk factors as those discussed above for IPV, the emotional maltreatment and neglect of older adults has additional risk factors, including the older adult's dependency on others, caregivers with high amounts of stress, caregiver alcohol and substance abuse, the victim's diagnosis of a psychological illness, and low income (Cardona et al., 2007) (see Table 12.6 for more information). Prevention strategies that focus on these factors need to be created for the protection of older adults across races and ethnicities, especially for those who may require care for psychological reasons.

Summary

In comparison to the majority culture, racial/ethnic minorities in the United States experience poverty, racism, discrimination, and social inequality to a greater degree, which are risk factors for family violence. The various racial/ethnic minorities often differ among themselves and from the White majority on their views of various forms of family violence, although there are some inconsistencies among the findings. Identifying racial/ethnic similarities and differences in perspectives on and experience of family violence is complicated by the common practice of ethnic lumping—that is, creating racial/ethnic groups composed of participants with very different cultural values and experiences. For example, analyses have shown that different groups of Asian Americans can differ markedly from each other in both their perspectives and prevalence of IPV.

A number of studies have reported differences in child maltreatment rates, with some studies showing higher rates in Black and Latino samples and lower rates in Asian samples, but not all the findings fit these patterns and race/ethnicity is often confounded with poverty. Child sexual abuse appears to be disproportionately high among Latino and Native American girls. Native American and Black communities seem to suffer disproportionate rates of IPV, while Asian Americans are at lower risk in comparison to their representation in the population. Although there is little research on the maltreatment of older individuals, there currently appear to be few differences in prevalence across racial/ethnic groups, with a low tolerance of such behaviors in general.

There are a number of macrosystem risk factors for family violence in the United States that may raise risk levels in racial/ethnic minority families, including a punitive value system and racism. More specific risk factors for child maltreatment in minority families include poverty, certain cultural beliefs such as traditional gender roles, various forms of stress, other types of maltreatment and dysfunction in the home, and parental mental illness and substance abuse. Risk factors for IPV include cultural values such as traditional gender roles, poverty, poor social support and social isolation, substance abuse, and a childhood history of maltreatment. Risk factors for the maltreatment of older adults include financial strains, inadequate access to social services, stresses on the family system and caregiver in particular, impairment of the older adult, and substance abuse of the caregiver. Protective factors include familism, emphasis on social support, availability of social support, and a strong ethnic identity.

Outcomes of maltreatment in racial/ethnic minority families mirror those that we observed in the majority culture, and range from physical injuries and psychological problems to death. There are many barriers to help-seeking in racial/ethnic minority families, and there is mixed evidence regarding whether our criminal justice and social service systems provide equitable treatment across the various racial/ethnic groups. Both intervention and prevention measures should take into account evidence regarding outcomes, risk factors, and protective factors across and within racial/ethnic groups. Ultimately, increased cultural sensitivity and competence would aid in the prevention and intervention of family violence in all communities in the United States.

Discussion Questions

1. Considering the many cultural differences in people's ideas about what constitutes child maltreatment, is it right to impose Western standards on them? Should agencies such as CPS and APS consider such differences when conducting investigations and making decisions about what actions to take (e.g., removing a child from the home)? Should there be some degree of leniency by APS and the criminal justice system?

2. Why is it important to consider race and ethnicity in studies of family violence? When research finds higher rates of maltreatment in the families or relationships of ethnic minorities, to what extent can factors other than race/ethnicity explain these higher rates?

3. Why has there been a lack of focus on the role of race/ethnicity in family violence research? How might such a focus contribute to negative biases against racial and ethnic minorities?

4. Why are the rates of child sexual abuse higher among Latina girls than White girls? How do you think the rates of child sexual abuse among African American, Asian American, and Native American girls compare to those of Latina and White girls? If you expect a difference, why? If not, why not?

5. Considering that research has found racial/ethnic differences in tolerance for various forms of IPV, what are the implications for prevention of and intervention with individuals from varying racial and ethnic backgrounds? Should prevention programs target specific racial/ethnic groups? In what ways might it be beneficial for victims and perpetrators to be in treatment groups with individuals of the same race and/or ethnicity? Might there be any disadvantages?

6. Some research finds high rates of child maltreatment, IPV, and stalking among Native Americans in the United States. What might account for this? To what extent might their history of oppression contribute to these rates?

7. Why are there racial/ethnic differences in perspectives on abuse of older family members? To what extent would promoting more respectful attitudes toward older adults lead to a reduction in their abuse by family members? How difficult would it be to change people's thoughts and opinions about aging and the value of older adults to society?

8. Why might older African Americans, Latinos, and Native Americans have higher rates of self-reported maltreatment than older Whites and Asians? To what extent might culture, experiences of oppression, and socioeconomic status play a role?

9. To what extent do different cultural values protect family members from abuse and neglect, and to what extent do they contribute to maltreatment? How can such values be utilized in preventing and intervening with various forms of maltreatment that occurs in families of different ethnic and racial backgrounds?

10. Among Native Americans, racism and removal from their ancestral lands has been linked to increased IPV perpetration. What is the connection? How might these factors be causally related?

11. If our society as a whole emphasized familism (i.e., emphasizing family values, obligations, obedience, and loyalty) more strongly, would there be a significant reduction in maltreatment in families? Why or why not?

12. How important is it that treatment programs for both perpetrators and victims of family violence be culturally sensitive? What are some ways that service providers should tailor their interventions for individuals of different races, ethnicities, religions, ages, sexual orientations, genders, socioeconomic statuses, to name a few?

13. How can CPS agencies determine if bias plays a role in child maltreatment investigations, receipt of services, and child placement decisions involving minority families? How can those agencies eliminate such bias?

14. What needs to be done to increase the willingness of racial/ethnic minorities to seek help for family violence issues from social services and the criminal justice system? What changes must social services and the criminal justice system make to be more acceptable sources of assistance? Can all barriers be overcome?

13

Religious Influences on Family Violence

> "[C]onsider Kristy, a 7-year old Caucasian girl who was a victim of sexual abuse by her father, a deacon within a Baptist church. In attempting to intimidate her into silence about the abuse, her father told her that she would 'go to Hell and God would hate her' if she ever told anyone of the abuse. Kristy was removed from the abusive situation, referred for psychotherapy, and placed in foster care, but came to view God as angry and frightening" (Walker, Reese, Hughes, & Troskie, 2010, p. 174).

> "Even after she reached out for help the final straw was when her husband accused her of being immodest and wrenched their infant daughter from her arms as she breastfed. Karen hesitated, due to fears of how she would make it on her own and what she perceived as a shanda [shame] for having failed to achieve Shalom Bayit" (Rathner, 2008, p. 19).

> "A few years back, while in the states, I received a chilling phone call from a scared sister; voice shaking and tears falling she said, 'Suhaib, my husband . . . my husband beat me! He beat me in front of our apartment in front of non-Muslims!' I later found out that she went to the hospital with a fractured skull" (Musaji, 2009, para. 2).

> "Our pastor asked my wife and me, 'When do you plan to start spanking your son? He's not a baby any more, you know. Don't you think he's ready for his first spanking?' We were stunned. We didn't know how to answer. We had decided before we were married that we would not raise our children the way we were raised, that we would not spank. Now, my wife and I don't feel comfortable at church. Every time the pastor greets us, we imagine he is silently asking, 'Well, have you started spanking yet?'" (Riak, 2002, p. 1).

An important component of the cultural context in which most Americans are reared is religion. In this chapter, we consider the complex role played by religious affiliation, religiosity, spirituality, and religious conservatism in family violence.

Religion in the United States

"What is your religion, if any?" When a national sample of Americans was asked this question, 79.8% provided some affiliation—listing one of the twelve main religious traditions found in the United States (American Religious Identification Survey, 2008). Religious membership at the beginning of the 21st century was approximately 51.3% Protestant, 24% Catholic, 16% unaffiliated, 2% unidentified Christian, 1.7% Jewish and less than 1% for each of the other religious affiliations (e.g., Buddhism, Hinduism, Islam) (PEW Research Center, 2007). It is also important to note that Muslims, Hindus, Buddhists, Protestants, Catholics, and Jews can belong to a number of different religious communities within the broad umbrella of their religion. For example, the PEW Research Center (2007) identifies 17 major Protestant denominations, most of which include several distinct traditions and affiliations.

Necessary Distinctions

In this chapter, *religion* refers to religious affiliation—that is, membership in a particular religious community. *Religiosity* refers to the behavioral, motivational, and cognitive aspects of individual participation in a religious community, and can be differentiated into two types: intrinsic and extrinsic. *Extrinsic religiosity* refers to religious behavior motivated by external and often self-serving reinforcers. *Intrinsic religiosity* refers to religious behavior motivated by feelings of personal conviction (Allport & Ross, 1967). Del Rio and White (2012) argue that it is important to distinguish spirituality from religiosity. In their view, spirituality is "an attitude toward life, making sense of life, relating to others, and seeking unity with the transcendent" (p. 1). From this perspective, spirituality is closely akin to intrinsic religiosity, although individuals can be spiritual without belonging to a religious community. As we show, some organized religions have been criticized, particularly by women's rights advocates, for supporting—or at least not adequately resisting—subjugation of women and children in ways that may result in their abuse. By contrast, spirituality and religiosity, particularly intrinsic religiosity, can sometimes serve as protective factors reducing the likelihood of abuse or reducing its negative effects.

Other important constructs in debates over the role of religion in family violence are religious conservatism and religious fundamentalism. Ellison and Sherkat (1993) suggested that the ideological orientations of the conservative Protestant denominations (the "religious right") include a belief in biblical literalism, a view of human nature as sinful and prone to egoism, and a heightened sensitivity to issues of sin and punishment. Conservative Protestants include two main groups—fundamentalists, who believe in the literalness and infallibility of the Bible, and evangelicals, who may see the Bible more metaphorically (Ellison, Burr, & McCall, 2003). According to some experts, there are four major types of Protestantism: 1) liberals (Congregationalists, Episcopalians, Methodists); 2) moderates (Presbyterians, Disciples of Christ); 3) conservatives (American Lutherans, American Baptists); and 4) fundamentalists (Southern Baptists, Missouri Synod Lutherans) (Glock & Stark, 1965). Other researchers have classified Protestant denominations in somewhat different ways, but Lutherans and Southern Baptists are typically seen as conservative and/or fundamentalist.

Moreover, the other major religions also have religious communities varying from somewhat liberal to conservative and fundamentalist (Hertel & Hughes, 1987).

Fundamentalists of any major religion are likely to believe that their holy texts are inerrant (i.e., infallible) and literally true. However, fundamentalists are selective in the texts they proclaim as establishing the laws of conduct. When feminists and others are critical of the negative role of religion in family violence, it is often the religious culture of the fundamentalist branches of different religions that are the primary concern.

Religions as Cultural Systems

All religious sects and denominations encapsulate a set of cultural values. Even within Christianity, Judaism, and Islam, there are enormous differences in cultural values across different religious subcommunities. To understand family violence is to recognize religious groups as cultural groups, in which cultural identity becomes part of people's worldviews and influences their cognitions, with family violence conceptualized in ways that are consistent with cultural norms (Foss & Warnke, 2003). Each community has, for instance, its own subjective meanings for the concept of punishment—who should be punished, by whom, and how. It has been argued that in the New England Protestant tradition, which still has a powerful influence on American culture, there is no room for the authoritarian, but fuzzy and forgiving orientation of Roman Catholicism (Melossi, 2001). From the Puritanical Protestant perspective, anyone perceived to be disobeying a law must be punished. Although Catholic traditions are also paternalistic, the authoritarianism is softer, with more room for indulgences and absolution.

Each religious community also has its own subjective meanings for the roles of "husband," "wife," and "children." Each has scripture with descriptions of family roles and relationships—descriptions that often become prescriptions, especially with the modern global movement toward religious fundamentalism (e.g., Herriot, 2009). According to fundamentalist interpretations of the scriptures of all the major religions, a woman's place is in the home, where her duties include raising her husband's children, serving as his helpmate, and respecting his authority in all earthly matters. In the face of feminist and human rights efforts to achieve gender equality, such tenets can lead to frustration and conflict in families, which in turn can lead to violence and maltreatment.

Consider the excerpts from several major holy books provided in Box 13.1. How do you interpret them? What are their implications for relationships between husbands and wives, parents and children? Do they seem to provide a rationale for men's dominance over women and parental beating of children? Do they lend themselves to interpretations providing justification for violence within family relationships?

Box 13.1	Excerpts from Holy Books on Family Relationships

The Bible, The Old and New Testaments

- To the woman he said, "I will greatly multiply your pain in childbearing; in pain, you shall bring forth children, yet your desire shall be for your husband, and he shall rule over you" (Genesis 3:16).

- If anyone sets his heart on being a bishop he desire a noble task...He must manage his own family well and see that his children obey him with proper respect. If anyone does not know how to manage his own family, how can he take care of God's church? (Timothy 3:1–5).
- Discipline your son while there is still hope; do not set your heart on his destruction (Proverbs 19:18).
- He who spares the rod hates his son (Proverbs 13:24).
- "I took this woman (in marriage) and slept with her and did not find proof of virginity in her," then the girl's father and mother shall take the proof of her virginity to the elders of the town, at the town gate...if, on the other hand, the accusation is true and no proof of the girl's virginity is found, then they shall bring her out to the door of her father's house and the men of her town shall stone her to death...She has committed an outrage in Israel by playing the prostitute in her father's house; you shall rid yourselves of this wickedness (Deuteronomy 22:14–21).
- To the woman he said: "I will intensify the pangs of your childbearing, in pain shall you bring forth children. Yet your urge shall be for your husband, and he shall be your master"; and "for man did not originally spring from woman, but woman was made out of man; and man was not created for woman's sake, but woman for the sake of man" (I Corinthians 11:8–9).

The Qur'an and Other Islamic Holy Writings

- Men are the protectors and maintainers of women, because God has given the one more (strength) than the other, and because they support them from their means. Therefore the righteous women are devoutly obedient, and guard in (the husband's) absence what God would have them guard. As to those women on whose part ye fear disloyalty and ill-conduct, admonish them (first), (Next), refuse to share their beds, (And last) beat them (lightly); but if they return to obedience, seek not against them Means (of annoyance): For God is Most High, great (above you all) (Ayah 34 of Surah 4).
- In inheritance, the son inherits as much as two daughters (Quran 4:11).

Hindu Texts

- A virtuous woman should serve her husband like a god (Manu 5:147–164).
- A wife, a son, and a slave, these three are declared to have no property; the wealth which they earn is (acquired) for him to whom they belong (Manu 8:416).
- In childhood a female must be subject to her father, in youth to her husband, when her lord is dead to her sons; a woman must never be independent (Manu 5:148).

Obviously, these passages do not provide all the relevant messages in the holy writings of the religions represented in the box. Each religion also has scripture with very different messages from these. Moreover, within every major religion there are controversies over the interpretations of these and other texts (e.g., Hassouneh-Phillips, 2003).

Even among members of the faithful who consider their sacred texts to be the direct word of God, there are debates over how particular words should be translated and the extent to which particular interpretations of texts are correct (Bartkowski, 1996).

In general, feminists and proponents of international human rights have argued that writings from all the major religious texts have been used—and misused—within patriarchal systems to maintain the power and authority of men, and to keep women and children in subordinate positions, by force if necessary (e.g., Dutcher-Walls, 1999). Organized religions are viewed as upholding coercion by men—for example, in promulgating the notion that men are "entitled" to sex with their wives, whether their wives want to engage in sex or not (Basile, 1999). From this perspective, the problem is not so much with the religions per se as in the misuse of their texts for political purposes, specifically for maintaining male dominance. One psychiatrist described the case of an abused woman whose husband used the family's conservative Christian faith not only to justify his abuse, but also to disrupt his wife's relationship with the therapist trying to help her with her anxiety and depression. This husband declared that the therapist "was a liberal and a feminist sent by Satan to tempt the patient to repudiate her marital and maternal obligations" (Stotland, 2000, p. 696). Moreover, the husband threatened, the wife would go to Hell if she stayed in therapy.

It is probably not coincidental that the feminist movement, the international human rights movement, and the new conservatism (which is closely tied to religious conservatism) have acted as competing forces over the past few decades. As women around the globe have fought to gain greater educational, employment, and political opportunities, and as their struggles have become incorporated into the human rights movement, political forces directed at maintaining the status quo have united with fundamentalist religious leaders striving to maintain a hierarchical social structure with clearly delineated gender roles and power resting firmly in the hands of men (e.g., Gül & Gül, 2000).

Any adequate consideration of the role of religion in family violence must recognize that within the world's major religions and spiritual orientations there are countless sects and denominations, and the belief systems held by different sects within a broader religious grouping may vary widely. Indeed, it is possible that the highly conservative or fundamentalist factions of different religions have more in common with each other than with the more liberal denominations within the same religion. Given the international religious fundamentalist surge, and its pressuring of women into subservient roles, much of the research on the role of religion in family violence has involved comparisons of fundamentalists with other religious groups.

Consider now the excerpts in Box 13.2. These excerpts have quite different messages from those in Box 13.1, and are emphasized by the more liberal congregational cultures preferring to focus on messages of mutual respect in the Bible (Alsdurf & Alsdurf, 1988), the Qur'an (Hendricks, 1998; Rahim, 2000), and Hindu religious texts (Rahim, 2000). These passages are often cited by reformists arguing that despite the traditional mistreatment of women and children within presumably religious homes and communities, it is possible to seek equal human rights and still stay within a religious fold (e.g., Hendricks, 1998; Rahim, 2000).

Box 13.2   Different Messages from Holy Books

The Bible, The New Testament

- Husbands love your wives, just as Christ loved the church and gave himself up for her to make her holy … In this same way husbands ought to love their wives as their own bodies. He who loves his wife loves himself. After all, no one ever hated his own body, but he feeds and cares for it, just as Christ does the church (Paul, Ephesians 5:25–28).
- Fathers, do not exasperate (scold or punish too harshly) your children; instead, bring them up in the training and instruction of the Lord (Paul, Ephesians 6:4).

The Qur'an

- And among His signs is that He created for you mates from among yourselves that you may live in tranquility with them, and He has put love and mercy between you; verily, in that are signs for people who reflect (30:21).
- None honours women except he who is honourable, and none despises them except he who is despicable (Hadith).
- Whosoever has a daughter and he does not bury her alive, does not insult her, and does not favor his son over her, God will enter him into Paradise (Ibn Hanbal, No. 1957). Whosoever supports two daughters till they mature, he and I will come in the day of judgment as this (and he pointed with his two fingers held together).

Prophet Muhammad

- The best of you is the best to his family, and I am the best among you to my family. The most perfect believers are the best in conduct and best of you are those who are best to their wives (Ibn-Hanbal, No. 7396).

Hindu Sacred Texts

- Where women are honored, there the gods are pleased … Where the female relations live in grief, the family soon wholly perishes; but that family where they are not unhappy ever prospers (Laws of Manu, as cited in Radhakrishnan & Moore, 1989, pp. 189–190).
- He only is a perfect man who consists (of three persons united): his wife, himself, and his offspring (Laws of Manu, as cited in Radhakrishnan & Moore, 1989, p. 190).
- The wife and husband, being the equal halves of one substance, are equal in every aspect; therefore, both should join and take equal parts in all work, religious and secular (The Vedas, as cited in Polisi, 2003).

If religious people simply adopted the values expressed in Box 13.2, would that reduce family violence? Or is increased secularization the only effective response to violence in families? Does the increasing political power of the religious right, both in the United States and abroad, endanger women and threaten to enshrine corporal punishment of children even as European countries ban it from homes and schools? Can women fight for their rights for freedom from violence and still be at ease with their religions?

Controversies over the Interpretation of Texts

A good example of controversies between conservative practitioners of a religion and more liberal practitioners can be found in the debate concerning how children should be reared. There is ample evidence that childrearing practices of conservative Protestants are influenced by a particular set of theologically related beliefs and values. One important question is whether these Protestants interpret the Bible correctly. For example, many conservative Protestants argue that the Bible says, "Spare the rod and spoil the child," but it has been widely pointed out that this statement does not come directly from the Bible. Also, nowhere does the Bible say that if parents do not hit their children with a rod, the children will be spoiled, and numerous authors have noted that "the rod" refers to a shepherd's staff, which is used to guide, not hit, sheep (think of "Thy rod and thy staff they comfort me") (e.g., Carey, 1994; Deley, 1988). Consider also this quotation from Proverb 29:15, "The rod from correction imparts wisdom, but a child left to himself disgraces his mother." Does this scripture warn parents to discipline their children early (Benedict, 2000), or could such an assumption be another case of misinterpretation of the Bible?

Controversies concerning the meaning of texts in the "inerrant" Bible abound, even among conservative Protestants (Bartkowski, 1996). Ross Campbell (1989), a popular conservative evangelical parenting specialist urges Christian parents to rear their children with unconditional love rather than corporal punishment, and admonishes conservative Christian parents to avoid the "punishment trap." In stark contrast to Dobson (1987), another author of child-rearing manuals for conservative Protestants, Campbell argues that the frequent use of corporal punishment (1) diminishes beneficial guilt in the child and inhibits the development of conscience; (2) degrades, dehumanizes, and humiliates the child; (3) teaches the child to be aggressive and punitive; (4) can be physically damaging; and (5) equates morally correct action with avoiding parental detection of infractions (Campbell, 1989). In a recent study of Christians of various denominations who regularly attended religious services, extrinsic religiosity was positively associated with increased physical maltreatment potential (Rodriguez & Henderson, 2010). Those Christians who considered the Bible as literally true were also more socially conformist, and hence, showed greater maltreatment potential.

Among Muslims, the Qur'an is considered to be the highest religious authority regarding wife beating. According to Ammar (2007), there are four ways to interpret the Qur'anic verse 34 of Al Nisa, which is the chapter on wife beating:

> The first is an interpretation that sees wife beating as permissible if a wife does not obey her husband (Al-Samharani, 1989, pp. 155–163). The second interpretation understands Islam as permitting wife beating but with conditions of consideration for her safety (Abu Shaqah, 1994; Al-banna, 1997). The third interpretation regards Qur'anic Verse 34 of Al Nisa chapter to be addressing exceptions when wife beating is allowed because it is generally unacceptable (Sisters in Islam, 1991 as cited in Ammar, 2007). The fourth and last

interpretation uses linguistic rules to show that Verse 34 of Al Nisa chapter has been misinterpreted and does not even refer to beating when using the Arabic word *idribu-hunna* (Suliman, 2001). (Al Nisa, verse 34, p. 518 as cited in Ammar, 2007)

All of these interpretations are based on different readings of other parts of the Qu'ran, and Islamic women in the United States are treated very differently depending on the interpretation. Thus, the ability to work effectively with Muslim families where the wives are beaten can be helped by understanding the extent to which particular passages from the Qu'ran are used to justify the beating.

Within the Jewish community, it is often the Torah ideal of *Shalom Bayit* ("peace in the home") that keeps battered Jewish wives from leaving their abusive partners—who often say their battering is justified by their wives failure to provide *Shalom Bayit*. In one case:

> Saul threw clocks, telephones, and food at Fran; forced her to have sex against her will; kept her up all night talking incessantly; twisted her arm to keep her awake (even though she had to work the next day while he slept late); never listened to her opinions; and badgered her endlessly until she would concur with his view. Fran feared that if she spoke to others about her abuse, she would be disbelieved and told to make *Shalom Bayit*. (Grodner & Sweifach, 2004)

Within the Jewish community today, there are many organizations known as *Shalom Bayit* that work to assist women in abusive relationships, arguing that the Torah provides no justification for abuse of wives. It is clear that whether the text is Catholic, Protestant, Islamic, or Jewish, these holy books are subject to a variety of interpretations and thereby a range of justifications for mistreatment of wives and other family members.

Religious Affiliation and Religious Conservatism as Risk Factors for Family Violence

Child Maltreatment

If you were asked to identify "religion-related" cases of child maltreatment, what kinds of maltreatment would come to mind? Sexual abuse by priests? Ritualistic abuse? Withholding of medical care? All of these and others were identified by a sample of over 2,000 mental health professionals from across the United States (Bottoms, Shaver, Goodman, & Qin, 1995). Among the examples given were withholding medical care, abuse perpetrated by persons with religious authority, and attempts to rid a child of evil. One clinician reported, "The aunt truly believed she could beat the devil out of the children" (Bottoms et al., 1995, p. 93). In most of these abuse cases, the perpetrators were Protestant.

Corporal Punishment and Child Physical Maltreatment

Much of the limited research on cultural values concerning child-rearing and child discipline within different religions has focused on the values and beliefs of conservative Protestants as compared with other groups. Conservative Protestants have a distinct set of cultural values supportive of corporal punishment encapsulated in many of their child-rearing manuals. An analysis of best-selling conservative and mainstream Protestant child-rearing manuals revealed that the mainstream Protestant manuals emphasized democratic parent-child relationships and open communication between parents and children, while conservative Protestant manuals emphasized obedience and submission (Bartkowski & Ellison, 1995). Whereas mainstream manuals emphasized the parental use of reasoning tactics, the conservative manuals emphasized corporal punishment. In particular, the conservative manuals recommended that parents use a rod to administer physical punishment to children whenever children show willful defiance to parental authority. One fundamentalist Southern Baptist guidebook warns parents that they must gain firm control over their manipulative young children before they are outsmarted (Benedict, 2000). According to the handbook, children who receive early corporal punishment grow up with necessary social skills and are well-adjusted in emotional temperament, as compared to insufficiently disciplined children. Many towns that have a majority population who espouse evangelical Protestant religious beliefs are also more likely to use corporal punishment in their school systems (Dupper & Montgomery, 2008). This is seen in nine of the 21 states where corporal punishment in schools remains legal.

It is somewhat difficult to obtain a clear picture of differences between religious groups, in both endorsement and use of corporal punishment and in frequency of child abuse reports for several reasons: (1) different investigators have classified religions differently and grouped them together in divergent ways; (2) lumping together different Protestant denominations in order to compare Protestants and Catholics, as has been done in some studies, ignores the wide range of values characterizing the different Protestant denominations; (3) measures of constructs such as religiosity and religious conservatism have varied considerably across studies; and (4) variables such as geography, ethnicity, and social class tend to be confounded with affiliation.

Despite these limitations, some important findings have emerged. National survey data support the propositions that there are differences between religions in support of corporal punishment, and the endorsement of particular religious beliefs (e.g., that the Bible is the literal word of God) is positively associated with convictions concerning corporal punishment. For example, the first wave of the National Survey of Families and Households (NSFH) revealed that Jewish parents were significantly less likely than Protestant or Catholic parents to use corporal punishment, and Protestant parents were more likely than parents with no religious affiliation to use that form of punishment (Xu, Tung, & Dunaway, 2000). According to the 1990 National Longitudinal Study of Youth (Giles-Sims, Straus, & Sugarman, 1995), Catholics had the lowest use of spanking of all the groups studied. In a more localized study of couples in a Southwestern city (Gershoff, Miller, & Holden, 1999), conservative Protestant parents spanked their children more often than mainline Protestant, Roman Catholic, and unaffiliated parents. Moreover, 29% of the conservative Protestant parents said they spanked their children three or more times a week, as compared to only 3% of Roman Catholic and none of the unaffiliated parents. Whereas the conservative Protestants emphasized the instrumental benefits of spanking, the mainline Protestants and Roman Catholics anticipated more negative effects of spanking. Mainline Protestant and unaffiliated parents were more likely to indicate that they would try to reason with their children about misbehavior than conservative Protestants. The national General Social Survey of 1988 had similar findings: Conservative Protestants were significantly more supportive of corporal punishment than members of other religious groups (Ellison & Sherkat, 1993). What are your views on the child-rearing advice of conservative Protestants? If punishing a child with a rod is advised in a child-rearing manual, can it still be abusive? If people believe that "a good beating" is not just condoned, but demanded, by their religious texts, what arguments might nevertheless justify labeling the beating as abusive?

Two smaller religious denominations of particular interest to researchers are Quakers (because of their advocacy of nonviolence) and Mormons (because of their strict patriarchal traditions). A survey of nearly 300 Quakers revealed that 75% of mothers and 69% of fathers reported violence toward their children (Brutz & Ingoldsby, 1984). As compared to national norms, Quaker mothers and fathers reported more kicking, biting, and punching of their children, all of which are typically considered to be abusive in mainstream society. Interestingly, Quaker parents reported less slapping and hitting with objects, which may be the most normative forms of corporal punishment among Protestants in general. In contrast to the national sample, where some fathers reported beating their children and threatening or using guns or knives on their children, no Quaker fathers reported these forms of violence against their children. Thus, even though Quakers advocate nonviolence, it does not necessarily mean that they do not physically punish their children; they may just use different forms of physical punishment than the majority culture. In a study of Mormons, rates of severe child physical maltreatment were slightly lower in a Utah sample (80% Mormon) than the rates in the United States as a whole (9.3% versus 10.7%) (Rollins & Oheneba-Sakyi, 1990). Thus, rates of child maltreatment in Mormons appear to be the same or slightly less than nationwide rates, even though the patriarchal structure of their religion would lead some to theorize that they would be more likely to physically punish their children.

Despite considerable differences among congregational communities within religions, there has been very little research comparing the smaller Christian and non-Christian denominations and sects on their values and practices. In a rare comparative study in a convenience sample of nearly 500 people, Malley-Morrison and Hines (2003) found that Christians, as a group, reported having experienced significantly more corporal punishment than Jews, Hindus, and atheists/agnostics. When comparisons were made among principle denominational groupings, they found that Presbyterians tended to be somewhat less tolerant of corporal punishment than both conservative Protestants and Catholics. Jews had experienced less corporal punishment as children, and were also somewhat less tolerant of it, than conservative Protestants. Conservative Jews were more tolerant of corporal punishment than Reformed Jews. Finally, the agnostic/atheist groups had experienced less corporal punishment than the Catholics, but were more supportive of parental use of corporal punishment than Buddhists, Reformed Jews, and conservative Jews.

Although denominational differences have been found, the espousal of particular religious beliefs may be a more important predictor of aggression in families than simple religious affiliation. In the NSFH survey, the degree of endorsement of items such as, "I regard myself as a religious fundamentalist," was significantly positively correlated with parents' likelihood of using corporal punishment (Xu et al., 2000). In another analysis of the NSFH data, Ellison and Bradshaw (2009) did not find differences in views on corporal punishment based on denominational affiliation, but did find that conservative Protestant beliefs (e.g., belief in Hell) were strongly predictive of support for corporal punishment. There is also evidence that some of the more external aspects of religion (e.g., attendance at services) may be a stronger predictor of risk for corporal punishment than religious affiliation. For example, in a study of college students with some expressed interest in religion, Dyslin and Thomsen (2005) found no evidence of an association between religious affiliation and risk of perpetrating child maltreatment, but did find a significant positive correlation between extrinsic religiosity and risk of child maltreatment.

An analysis of parents' reported use of physical punishment to discipline preschool and elementary school-aged children showed that parents who believed that the Bible is the inerrant word of God that provides answers to all human problems used corporal punishment more frequently than parents with less conservative theological views (Ellison, Bartkowski, & Segal, 1996). Moreover, the extent to which parents view their role as sanctified (having spiritual significance) also contributes to their use of corporal punishment and the impact of this punishment. For example, Murray-Swank, Mahoney, and Kenneth (2006) found that sanctification of the parental role was associated with less use of corporal punishment in mothers with liberal biblical beliefs but with greater use of corporal punishment with conservative religious views. In another recent study, parents who had a more literal interpretation of the Bible scored higher on abuse potential (Rodriguez & Henderson, 2010). Moreover, parents who considered religion as more instrumental, serving a means to an end, had an increased risk to engage in physical maltreatment toward their children (Rodriguez & Henderson, 2010). Analyses of the national General Social Survey of 1988 revealed that endorsements of the items, "Human nature is fundamentally perverse and corrupt," and, "Those who violate God's rules must be punished," were the strongest predictors of tolerance of corporal punishment (Ellison & Sherkat, 1993). In a reexamination of relationships between religious beliefs and attitudes toward corporal punishment, using data from the 1998 National Opinion Research Center General Social Survey (GSS), Ellison and Bradshaw (2009) showed that conservative Protestant beliefs, especially hierarchical images of God and belief in Hell, but not denominational affiliation, were associated with support for corporal punishment.

Other studies confirm the finding that a conservative worldview may contribute more to approval of corporal punishment than religion or religiosity. A 1995 national Gallup Poll revealed that parents who were more conservative in their social ideologies had more positive attitudes toward physical discipline (Jackson et al., 1999). Similarly, an analysis of the 1998 GSS data showed that respondents identifying themselves as politically conservative were more supportive of corporal punishment than self-identified liberals and moderates (Ellison & Bradshaw, 2009). In a random sample from Oklahoma City, even after accounting for socioeconomic and demographic variables, belief in the literalness of the Bible accounted for a large share of the differences between religious groups in the degree of advocacy of corporal punishment (Grasmick, Bursik, & Kimpel, 1991). Similarly, among Protestants from five central and southern states, both men and women who believed in a literal interpretation of the Bible showed greater endorsement of statements such as, "Children should always be spanked when they misbehave," and, "Parents spoil their children by picking them up and comforting them when they cry" (Wiehe, 1990, pp. 178–179). Furthermore, conservative Christian beliefs may shift the victim's view of abuse, increasing the likelihood of accepting sufferings as redemptive (Gilligan, 2009).

Independent of the issue of whether corporal punishment is abusive, some studies have specifically addressed physical child abuse as a problem that may vary by religion. In the first National Family Violence Survey, the rate of child physical maltreatment was lowest among Jews and highest in families where one or both parents had a "minority religious affiliation" (Straus, Gelles, & Steinmetz, 1980). The lower rates of family violence among Jews may be related to their generally higher levels of income, education, and employment. Conversely, members of minority religions may experience more discrimination, stress, and isolation from mainstream society, characteristics that may lead to greater violence within their homes (Straus et al., 1980).

Table 13.1 provides a summary of major studies of the relationship between religion and corporal punishment.

Psychological Maltreatment

Consider a parent saying to a child, "God will punish you for your misbehavior." Is this statement a form of psychological maltreatment? What is the likely effect of such a statement on the child? Do you think regular threats of this sort are more or less abusive than corporal punishment? Why? In one study, such a statement was reported by 10% of Methodists, Presbyterians, and Lutherans; 20% of Catholics; and 25% of Baptists and Fundamentalists (Nelsen & Kroliczak, 1984). Consider also the views of a woman who described "religious abuse" as well as sexual abuse by her brother during childhood. She holds that the sexual abuse by her brother, combined with sexist attitudes toward women within her family and community, and her father's appeal to religious dogma to support his denigration of women, all had serious negative psychological effects on her: "It was like the messages I got all the time, you know, 'God says you're second best.' . . . your dad saying, 'God's right, you are [second best].' And then my brothers taking on the same thing. I had all these things, like, 'oh my god, where do I fit in?'" (Smith, 1997, p. 423). Would you agree with her characterization of her family's behavior as "religious abuse"?

Child Sexual Maltreatment

There is little research with representative samples to provide reliable estimates of the prevalence of intrafamilial sexual abuse in different religious groups. Of nearly 1,000 women living in the San Francisco area (Bolen, 1998), the following percentages of women reported having experienced childhood sexual abuse: approximately 43% of Protestants, 37% of Jews, 37% of Catholics, and 30% of those with other affiliations; there were no significant differences in prevalence, and no breakdown

Table 13.1 Religion and Corporal Punishment

Study	Description of Sample	Major Findings
Straus, Gelles, & Steinmetz (1980), National Family Violence Survey	Representative sample of 2,143 American families	• The rate of child physical maltreatment was lowest among Jews, and highest in families where one or both parents had a "minority religious affiliation"
Brutz & Ingoldsby (1984)	Sample of 288 Quakers	• A survey of nearly 300 Quakers revealed that 75% of mothers and 69% of fathers reported violence toward their children • Quaker mothers and fathers reported more kicking, biting, and punching of their children but less slapping and hitting with objects when compared to national norms • Although Quakers advocate nonviolence, they may use different forms of physical punishment than the majority culture
Rollins & Oheneba-Sakyi (1990)	Random sample of 1,471 Utah residential units	• In a study of Mormons, rates of severe child physical maltreatment were slightly lower in a Utah sample (80% Mormon) than the rates in the United States as a whole (9.3% versus 10.7%)
Wiehe (1990)	Protestant sample of 881 people from five central and southern states	• Both men and women who believed in a literal interpretation of the Bible showed greater endorsement of statements that support spanking and condemn comforting their children
Giles-Sims, Straus, & Sugarman (1995), National Longitudinal Study of Youth 1990	National sample of up to 7,725 women between the ages of 14 and 21 when originally recruited in 1979	• Catholic parents spanked their children the least out of all the groups that were studied
Ellison, Bartkowski, & Segal (1996), National Survey of Families and Households (NSFH) of 1987–88	National sample of 4,076 parents of toddlers and preschoolers (ages 1–4) and older children (ages 5–11); contains oversamples of Blacks, Puerto Ricans, Mexican Americans, single-parent families, families with stepchildren, cohabiting couples, and recently married persons	• Parents who believed the Bible is the literal word of God and provides answers to all human problems used corporal punishment more frequently than parents with less conservative theological views

Study	Description of Sample	Major Findings
Gershoff, Miller, & Holden (1999)	A localized sample of 132 parents of 3-year-old children in a southwestern city	• Conservative Protestant parents spanked their children more often than mainline Protestants, Roman Catholics, and unaffiliated parents • 29% of conservative Protestant parents reported spanking their children three or more times a week, compared to 3% of Roman Catholics and none of unaffiliated parents
Xu, Tung, & Dunaway (2000), National Survey of Families and Households of 1988	A national sample of 13,017 respondents from 9,643 households	• Protestant parents were more likely than non-religious parents to use corporal punishment
Malley-Morrison & Hines (2003)	A convenience sample of nearly 500 people	• Christians reported having experienced significantly more corporal punishment than Jews, Hindus, and atheists/agnostics • Conservative Protestants and Catholics were more tolerant of corporal punishment
Dyslin & Thomsen (2005)	436 college students identified with one of four religious groups (conservative Protestant, mainline Protestant, Catholic, or unaffiliated)	• No relationship found between religious affiliation and risk of perpetrating child maltreatment • No evidence that child physical maltreatment risk was related to religious interest or participation, intrinsic religiosity, or orthodoxy • However, extrinsic religiosity was significantly positively correlated with risk of child maltreatment
Ellison & Bradshaw (2009), National Opinion Research Center General Social Survey of 1998	A national sample of 2,832 English-speaking persons 18 years or older living in non-institutional arrangements	• Conservative Protestant beliefs, not denominational affiliation, were associated with support for corporal punishment
Rodriguez & Henderson (2010)	A sample of 207 Christians of various denominations who regularly attended religious services	• Conservative parents who believed in a more literal interpretation of the Bible scored higher on abuse potential

was given for intrafamilial versus extrafamilial abuse. A survey of nearly 3,000 professional women from across the United States presented a somewhat different picture: approximately 39% of women with agnostic/atheistic parents, 32% with families
of some religion other than conservative Christianity, and 18% from conservative
Christian families reported some form of childhood sexual abuse (either intra- or
extra-familial) (Elliott, 1994). More specifically, women raised in conservative
Christian homes where there was little emphasis on incorporating religious values
into family life (i.e., low intrinsic religiosity) reported significantly higher rates of
sexual abuse than women raised in Christian homes with higher integration of religious values (i.e., high intrinsic religiosity) or women raised in non-conservative
Christian homes. Elliott speculated that conservative Christians, who do not integrate their professed beliefs into their lifestyles, may use those doctrines primarily to
justify their own controlling tactics with family members and intimidate their victims
into silence.

Although incest is prohibited by both Hebrew and Christian scripture, it is
clear that it occurs in many homes (see Chapter 3)—including conservative
Protestant homes. In one study of 35 women who had been sexually abused in
childhood in their conservative Protestant homes (Gil, 1988), the mean age of the
girls when the incest began was just under six years, with a range from 2 to
16 years; 37% of the women had been preschoolers when the sexual abuse
started. The abusers were fathers in 66% of the cases and stepfathers in 34% of
the cases. The natural fathers were evenly distributed across the denominational
categories (including Presbyterians, Methodists, Lutherans, Baptists, and
Fundamentalists who espoused conservative Christian values); however, 82% of
the abusive stepfathers were Fundamentalists. The natural fathers were more
likely to perpetrate the more serious forms of sexual abuse (e.g., involving penetration) than the stepfathers. In a recent survey of 380 Orthodox Jewish married
women (Yehuda, Rosenbaum, Labinsky, & Schmeidler, 2007), 26% reported that
they had endured at least one incident of sexual abuse, with 30% of the sample
indicating that they had been abused by a family member, and 16% reporting that
they had experienced the abuse by age 13.

Box 13.3   Three Cases of Childhood Sexual Abuse

Joan's father was an alcoholic who had left home for six years, joined Alcoholics
Anonymous, and returned to the family within the previous year. Joan's mother had
turned to religion for support in dealing with her husband's infidelity and abandonment of the family. Joan, a teenager, abused drugs and alcohol and was sexually
abused by her father when she was seven. Her mother became very angry when
Joan entered a rehab program, and showed more concern about appearances than
about her daughter's substance or sexual abuse (Schmidt, 1995).

Sarah, a 40-year-old Jewish woman, grew up in a religiously observant kosher
home with parents who had fled Eastern Europe during World War II and had lost
many relatives in the concentration camps. Her father was psychologically abusive

to his wife, and physically abusive to Sarah's brothers. Because of the Holocaust, he isolated his family from Jews and non-Jews alike, and preached that his family should never trust a non-Jew. When Sarah was 4 or 5 years old, she was sexually molested by one of her brothers. She was able to prevent further sexual abuse by telling her mother that her brother had hit her, but he was psychologically abusive toward her throughout her childhood, and physically attacked her when she was 13. The mother walked in on this attack, but left the room without saying anything (Featherman, 1995).

Lacey, a Seventh Day Adventist was repeatedly raped by her older brother in her pre-adolescent years. Her sister reported being sexually assaulted by the same brother as well as by their father. Both women were completely ostracized by other family members, who said neither of the men could have been capable of such behavior. Lacey's husband was an administrator of one of the Adventist institutions, and Lacey did not want to damage his career by reporting on her brother's abuse, but became very concerned when her brother was appointed to a position in a boarding academy for youth in South America (Taylor & Fontes, 1995).

Although our current knowledge of prevalence rates of child sexual abuse within families as a function of religious affiliation is incomplete, there is some agreement that the effects of sexual molestation may vary depending on the family's religious beliefs. Box 13.3 presents the stories of three women sexually abused in childhood—an Anglo-Saxon Protestant, a Jew, and a Seventh Day Adventist. What is your view of the role of religion in each woman's experience? In what ways, if any, did the particular religious culture in which each woman was raised contribute either to the abuse itself or to the girl's response to the abuse? What aspects of the abusive situations seem independent of the particular religious heritage of each woman?

Child Neglect

A major form of religion-related child maltreatment identified by a national sample of mental health professionals is the withholding of medical care for religious reasons (Bottoms et al., 1995). Approximately 10% of neglect cases identified by professionals involved this form of neglect. Most of the parents in these cases were classified as "fundamentalist" (e.g., Mormon, Pentecostal, and Seventh Day Adventist). Among fundamentalists, a number of different religious beliefs lead to resistance against certain forms of medical care. For example, Jehovah's Witnesses believe that the Bible prohibits blood transfusions and therefore any procedures necessitating a transfusion (Flowers, 1984). Christian Scientists believe that sickness and pain are errors of the mortal mind, all diseases are mental conditions, and healing the sick must involve driving out misperceptions rather than using procedures like medications, which only relieve suffering temporarily but do not cure the problem. The principal exception to the Christian Science system is the use of medical care in childbirth and to set broken bones.

Box 13.4	Two Cases of Faith-Based Abuse

"Timothy and Rebecca Wyland of Oregon City, Ore., were convicted in June of felony criminal mistreatment for allowing their infant daughter to develop a baseball-sized growth above her eye that threatened her vision. The parents belong to Followers of Christ Church, which prays for healing instead of seeking medical attention." (Gallegos, 2011, p. 1)

"When Kay Burdette's 17-year-old son became sick with flu-like symptoms, the faithful mother chose the same prescription she has used for years: prayer. This time, though, her son Jesse did not recover and Burdette was charged with manslaughter. Pale, coughing and weighing only 130 pounds at the end, Jesse died in his mother's bed the night of March 19, 2008. His mom called a friend from their charismatic, non-denominational church, then her daughter. She never called 911 nor sought medical assistance. 'Because of my religious beliefs I trust in God to forgive my sins and for physical healing,' she told investigators." (Reeves, 2011, p. 1)

There is some evidence that at least 10 children a year die from religion-based child medical neglect, although the incidence of religion-related child fatalities and suffering is probably much higher (Gallegos, 2011). Although more than half the American states have granted some form of immunity to parents who harm their children by refusing medical care, laws are changing in many states. For example, in 1999, members of the Oregon Medical Association helped overturn five of Oregon's nine statutes providing religious protections for parents. In the first case described in Box 13.4, the parents of the infant daughter with the untreated growth were sentenced to 90 days in jail and three years' probation because they tried to use faith healing to treat the abnormal growth above her eye (Gallegos, 2011). What is your view of this case? Was the judgment of the court fair? In the second case in Box 13.4, the mother, who cleaned houses for a living, was charged with manslaughter but allowed to plead guilty to a misdemeanor (criminally negligent homicide). The district attorney in the case indicated that given that her son had died, he wondered how much more Burdett could be punished. Although she could have been sentenced to a year in jail and a $6,000 fine, the judge gave her a 6-month suspended sentence (Reeves, 2011). What is your view of this case? Was the judgment of the court fair? It is possible that the second case might have been treated differently if the faith-related negligence had not taken place in the Bible belt? Should this cultural variable affect the judgment of the case? If you disagree with the judges' decisions in these cases, what might have been better decisions and why?

Consider the case of *In re Sampson,* in which the court was asked to intervene on behalf of a 15-year-old boy with a serious facial deformity resulting from a medical condition called neurofibromatosis. Because of this condition, the boy was extremely emotionally withdrawn, would not attend school, and was virtually illiterate. Although his condition was not life-threatening, his physicians indicated that they could improve his appearance surgically. Because the procedure would involve considerable medical risk, they were unwilling to undertake the procedure without authorization to provide blood transfusions if necessary. The mother, a Jehovah's Witness, refused to agree to the surgery if there was a chance that it would require a transfusion (Knepper, 1995). Is the mother's refusal in this case to allow her son to have the corrective surgery a type of neglect, some other form of maltreatment, or appropriate parenting within the context of her religion? If you were the judge considering the physicians' argument that surgery would benefit the boy, what would your conclusion be? In this case, the court decided the boy was a neglected minor, and ordered his mother to permit the surgery and to consent to a transfusion if the doctors decided it was necessary during the course of treatment. Do you concur with this decision? Why or why not?

The debate over parental failure to obtain medical care for their children for religious reasons has generally been one of balancing the children's medical needs with parental rights to rear children in accordance with their religious beliefs. The issue becomes more complex when we consider childhood immunizations, which involve not just the well-being of the individual child but the well-being of the community. If fundamentalist families objecting to immunizations are concentrated in fairly large communities, any refusal to allow immunizations has the potential for creating a rather serious public health risk for the whole community (Ross & Aspinwall, 1997). The American Academy of Pediatrics has taken the position that, "Constitutional guarantees of freedom of religion do not permit children to be harmed through religious practices, nor do they allow religion to be a valid legal defense when an individual harms or neglects a child" (Ross & Aspinwall, 1997, pp. 202–203). Do you agree? If so, what steps should be taken to ensure that all children in the United States get needed medical care?

Because of the strong concern with religious freedom in the United States, the criminal justice system has faced numerous barriers and social ambivalence in addressing cases of religion-related child maltreatment. On the one hand, the Supreme Court ruled in 1944 that "the right to practice religion freely does not include liberty to expose the community or child to communicable disease or the latter to ill health or death" (Sinal, Cabinum-Foeller, & Socolar, 2008, p. 705). On the other hand, in 1974, the U.S. Department of Health, Education, and Welfare mandated that in cases of child abuse and neglect, states receiving federal child abuse prevention and treatment grants had to provide religious exemptions. The majority of states established such exemptions within 10 years and most of them retained these exemptions even after the federal government removed them from the federal mandate in 1983. In a review of 50 court-mediated disputes between physicians and families refusing medical treatment for their children, Ridgway (2004) found that in 90% of the cases involving religion-based objections, the courts ruled in favor of the physicians and medical care for the children. Are these findings encouraging to you? Do you believe that the best way to contest any negative contribution of religious organizations to family violence and neglect is through the courts? Are there better alternatives?

Outcomes of Religion-Related Child Maltreatment

Research on outcomes of religion-based child maltreatment has typically focused on mortality and psychological effects. One nationwide study of child fatalities between 1975 and 1995 (Asser & Swan, 1998) revealed 140 cases where children died because parents withheld medical care for conditions whose survival rates with medical care would have exceeded 90%; in an additional 18 cases, survival rates with medical care would have exceeded 50%. These children had a wide range of treatable medical conditions at the time of their deaths—for example, dehydration, diabetes, burns, measles, meningitis, pneumonia, and appendicitis. When one 2-year-old choked on a bite of banana, her parents frantically called members of their religious circle for prayer during the hour she still showed signs of life. The father of a 5-month-old son reported that after four days of fever, his son started having apneic (cessation of breathing) spells. During each spell, the father "rebuked the spirit of death" and his son perked up and began to breathe again. The next day he died from bacterial meningitis (Asser & Swan, 1998). A teenage girl asked teachers for help getting medical care refused by her parents for fainting spells. She ran away from home, but was returned to the custody of her father by law enforcement officials. She died three days later from a ruptured appendix. Of a total of 172 religion-based child mortality cases, the breakdown by religion was as follows: 23—Church of the First Born, 12—End Time Ministries, 64—Faith Assemblies, 16—Faith Tabernacles, 28—Christian Science, and 29—other denominations or unaffiliated (Asser & Swan, 1998).

Among the cases of religion-based child maltreatment reported by mental health professionals (Bottoms et al., 1995), one third of the victims who had been abused, ostensibly to rid them of evil, admitted in adulthood that they had considered suicide. Dissociative disorders were also fairly high in both the ridding-evil group and the medical neglect group. A boy from a Jehovah's Witness family that had engaged in punitive efforts to rid him of evil spirits was dissociative, could not concentrate, and was doing poorly in school. Reports from professionals also reveal that victims of multiple forms of religion-based family maltreatment have significantly more depression, insomnia, somatic problems, fearfulness and phobias, substance abuse, social withdrawal, and inappropriate aggressiveness than victims experiencing sexual abuse only (Goodman, Bottoms, Redlich, Shaver, & Diviak, 1998). Children who are also victims of religion-related maltreatment display more hostility, psychoticism, phobic and paranoid ideation, and somatization than victims whose maltreatment was not religion-related (Bottoms, Nielson, Murray, & Filipas, 2003).

One woman explains the impact of her experiences of abuse: "I was raped by my uncle when I was 12 and my husband has beaten me for years. For my whole life, when I have gone to a doctor, to my priest, or to a friend to have my wounds patched up, or for a shoulder to cry on, they dwell on my bruises, my cuts, my broken bones . . . but it's not my body that I really wish could get fixed. The abuse in my life has taken away my trust in people and in life. . . . It's taken away my faith in God, my faith in goodness winning out in the end, and maybe worst of all, it's taken away my trust in myself" (DeKeseredy & Schwartz, 2001, p. 29). One related study found that reports of childhood experiences of physical discipline were associated with the rejection of family belief systems (Webb & Otto Whitmer, 2003), and another showed a decline in personal religiousness after childhood maltreatment (Walker, Reid, O'Neill, & Brown, 2009).

Maltreatment of Intimate Partners

Table 13.2 summarizes information from reports on IPV in relation to religious affiliation. As is true of the research on child maltreatment and religion, there is a dearth of national population-based studies providing comparative prevalence rates for intimate partner maltreatment across different religions. More typical are small studies comparing intimate partner violence (IPV) rates in samples of adults from particular religious communities with national IPV rates, and studies providing rates for different religious groups within a relatively circumscribed population. Although two nationwide studies have been conducted on religious affiliation and IPV, both have significant methodological shortcomings. For example, among battered women nationwide who responded to a survey published in *Woman's Day* magazine, 39% of their batterers were Protestant, 31% were Catholic, 15% were other religions, and 5% reported no religion (Bowker, 1988). In this sample, the Protestants and unaffiliated respondents seem underrepresented in relation to their proportions in the population. In a study with a similar methodology, public service announcements published in local newspapers throughout the United States advertised that spouses who were physically abused were being sought for a study (Horton, Wilkins, & Wright, 1988). Among the nearly 500 people who responded, 58% were Protestant, 20% were Catholic, 1% were Jewish, 10% were another religion, and 11% indicated no religious affiliation. In this case, it is the Jewish, Catholic, and no religious affiliation respondents who appear underrepresented in relation to their proportions in the population. However, the samples in both of these studies are self-selected and non-population-based, so generalization is not possible.

In a somewhat more representative community sample (Makepeace, 1997), individuals identifying with Christian denominations (Protestant, Catholic, Mormon) had "moderate" courtship violence rates (no percentage provided), whereas the rates were relatively high (nearly 29%) among respondents reporting no religion and exceedingly low for Jewish respondents (less than 6%). Within particular Christian denominations, some of the early clinical data suggest that IPV may be a bit higher among Catholics than Protestants. For example, in one study, non-battering men who had religious affiliations tended to be Protestant, whereas the batterers were typically Catholic (Star, 1978). Another study found that certain aspects of Fundamentalist Protestant Christianity, such as male dominance of the family, can be used to reinforce an abuser's behavior and the victim's submission (Foss & Warnke, 2003).

In one recent study of 1,476 religious Christian women from a southwest metropolitan region, Wang, Horne, Levitt, and Kleges (2009) found that slightly over half of the women reported having experienced at least one form of domestic maltreatment (physical or emotional aggression, threats of aggression, sexual assault, or stalking) from an intimate partner. Although they found no significant differences between women from conservative affiliations versus women from liberal and moderate affiliations in rates of self-reported domestic violence, they did find greater likelihood of victimization in women from congregations unsupportive of divorce in cases of IPV.

In a San Antonio, Texas study of a low-income, predominantly Hispanic sample recruited from a health clinic, Katerndahl and Obregon (2007) found that incompatibility in religious beliefs was a predictor of husband-to-wife violence. In particular, as compared with their husbands, abused wives had higher levels of personal forgiveness and sense of being judged by their religious community or God, and lower levels of perceived benefits from their religious community and sense of closeness to God.

The results of this study, similar to the results of the Wang et al. (2009) study, add support to the view that it is important to consider not just religious affiliation as a predictor of IPV, but also the values and beliefs of the particular faith communities with which the couples associate.

As was true of child maltreatment, spousal maltreatment can be found among Quakers, known for their anti-violence attitudes. In one sample of Quakers, 86% of the wives and 77% of the husbands reported using at least one act of verbal/ psychological spousal aggression in the previous year (Brutz & Allen, 1986). Rates of *physical* aggression were much lower—0.5% for women and 0.2% for men. For both men and women, the frequency of both verbal/psychological and physical aggression were negatively associated with their level of religious participation; however, Quaker wives showed higher levels of physical violence than Quaker husbands at both the high and low levels of religious involvement. In the case of the wives, the greater their involvement in peace activism, the lower their violence against their husbands. By contrast, in the case of the husbands, the greater their involvement in peace activism, the higher their level of both verbal/psychological and physical aggression against their wives. Why do you think this pattern occurs?

A study of nearly 1,500 Utah households (80% Mormon) revealed that Utah rates of IPV per 1,000 households were slightly higher than the national average—a rate that contrasts with their child maltreatment rates, which were slightly below the national average (Rollins & Oheneba-Sakyi, 1990). In the Utah sample, the average rate of severe husband-to-wife violence was 3.4% (compared with 3% in the national sample), and the average rate of severe wife-to-husband violence was 5.3% (compared with 4.4% in the national sample). Among the religiously orthodox Mormons, the rates of husband-to-wife severe physical violence were substantially lower than the rates for the less orthodox. Thus, as was the case with child maltreatment, it seems that members of a congregation who espouse particular tenets of a religion and participate in the external aspects of the religion, but do not integrate the values deeply into their lives, are more likely to use aggression in the family. Rates of severe wife-to-husband physical violence did not vary in relation to orthodoxy.

As is true in relation to child maltreatment, only a few non-representative studies provide some evidence concerning the prevalence of IPV in religions other than Christianity. Estimates of IPV in American Jewish families range from 15% to 30%, depending on the nature of the study and sample, and the year in which the study was conducted (Horsburgh, 1995). Some authors have argued that the maltreatment of wives may be especially acute in Orthodox communities, particularly among the Hasidim (Horsburgh, 1995). One study found evidence that sexual maltreatment of Jewish wives occurred at a rate slightly higher than shown in the national statistics for sexual maltreatment, with more ultra-Orthodox wives than modern-Orthodox wives reporting sexual maltreatment (Yehuda et al., 2007); moreover, the ultra-orthodox wives were significantly more likely to report forced sex by their husbands than were the modern-orthodox wives. Another study indicated that the rate of IPV in Jewish communities is at least equal to national statistics indicating that one in four women are physically maltreated, but that their rates are likely to be higher if nonphysical forms of maltreatment are included (Rathner, 2008).

Table 13.2   Religion and Intimate Partner Violence

Study	Description of Sample	Major Findings
Brutz & Allen (1986)	290 Quaker spouses	• 86% of the Quaker wives and 77% of husbands reported using at least one act of verbal/psychological spousal aggression in the previous year • Rates of physical aggression were much lower—0.5% for women and 0.2% for men
Makepeace (1987)	2,338 students from seven colleges	• Individuals identifying with Christian denominations (Protestant, Catholic, Mormon) had "moderate" courtship violence rates • The rates were relatively high (nearly 29%) among respondents reporting no religion • The rates were exceedingly low for Jewish respondents (less than 6%)
Rollins & Oheneba-Sakyi (1990)	1,500 Utah households (80% Mormon)	• Utah rates of IPV per 1,000 households were slightly higher than the national average • Average rate of extreme husband-to-wife violence was 3.4% (compared with 3% in the national sample), and the average rate of severe wife-to-husband violence was 5.3% (compared with 4.4% nationally) • Rates of severe husband-to-wife physical violence were substantially lower among the orthodox Mormons than among the less orthodox Mormons • Rates of severe wife-to-husband physical violence did not vary in relation to orthodoxy
Memon (1997)	Estimate of the North American Council for Muslim Women, based on reports from Muslim leaders, social workers, and activists	• About 10% of the Muslim women in the United States are physically or sexually maltreated by their Muslim husbands
Kulwicki & Miller (1999)	162 women and 40 men in 202 Arab American homes	• 17% of the women and 43% of the men approved of a man slapping his wife if she insults him in public • 59% of both the men and women approved his slapping if she hit him first

(Continued)

Table 13.2 (Continued)

Study	Description of Sample	Major Findings
Yehuda, Rosenbaum, Labinsky, & Schmeidler (2007)	380 Orthodox Jewish married women responding to survey advertised on Jewish sites	• Sexual maltreatment of Jewish wives occurred at a rate slightly higher than the national averages for sexual maltreatment • More ultra-Orthodox wives than modern-Orthodox wives reported sexual maltreatment
Katerndahl & Obregon (2007)	Low-income, predominantly Hispanic sample recruited from a health clinic in San Antonio, Texas	• Incompatibility in religious beliefs was a predictor of husband-to-wife violence
Wang, Horne, Levitt, & Kleges (2009)	1,476 religious Christian women from a southwest metropolitan region	• Slightly over half of the Christian women reported having experienced at least one form of domestic maltreatment (physical or emotional aggression, threats of aggression, sexual assault, or stalking) from an intimate partner • There existed a greater likelihood of IPV victimization in women from congregations unsupportive of divorce

Despite pervasive American stereotypes about the maltreatment of Islamic women, rates of maltreatment of female partners appear to be relatively low among American Muslim women—perhaps because of underreporting. An estimate of the North American Council for Muslim Women, based on reports from Muslim leaders, social workers, and activists, is that approximately 10% of the Muslim women in this country are physically or sexually maltreated by their Muslim husbands (Memon, 1997). If verbal and emotional maltreatment are included in the estimates, it is expected that this figure "would rise considerably" (Alkhateeb & Abugideiri, 2007, p. 3). Moreover, interviews conducted by nine domestic violence organizations found that of 1,962 Muslim women served annually, more than half experienced various types of maltreatment, including emotional, verbal, financial, and spiritual maltreatment (Alkhateeb, 2009). In a study of 162 women and 40 men in 202 Arab American homes, 17% of the women and 43% of the men approved of a man slapping his wife if she insults him in public, and 59% of both the men and women approved his slapping if she hit him first (Kulwicki & Miller, 1999).

Some Muslim American women may have an experience that is relatively unique as compared to other American women (other than Mormons) and which they sometimes consider abusive, specifically their husband's "misuse of polygamy"

(Hassouneh-Phillips, 2001b). In one sample of 17 Muslim American women, more than 50% had some experience with polygamy; of these nine women, seven had been victims of physical and emotional maltreatment, and the remaining two were victims solely of emotional maltreatment. Although the majority of these women did not think of polygamy in general as abusive, they considered it abusive for their husbands to distort or stray from Islamic principles in order to pursue additional wives for their own pleasure. One woman said, "I divorced him when he tried to marry my sister who was my ward. And she was 13. And he told me that this would be really good because my sister liked him. She was a child and he had all the flash and dazzle. But when he asked about marrying her . . . I knew then that I would never allow him to marry my sister—to touch my sister" (Hassouneh-Phillips, 2001b, p. 742).

Just as the concept of *Shalom Bayit* can bind battered Jewish women to their abusers and perpetuate maltreatment, Muslim women also face intense family and religious pressures for their silence. In fact, many immigrant Muslim women fail to acknowledge themselves as victims because in their home country, it may be legal or acceptable for men to physically punish or even kill their wives for dishonoring the family (Kirtz, 2008). This fear of reporting maltreatment when combined with the perpetrator's threat of having the women deported suggests an underreporting of IPV in Muslim communities.

According to Islamic principles, marriage is a matter of entering into a contract, and wives have a right to a divorce if their husbands do not live up to the contract—for example, through being abusive (Hassouneh-Phillips, 2001a). One Muslim American woman explained,

> I was kicked, and he could go on for hours, kicking me and calling me bad names. Finally, we got kicked out of that apartment complex, and then I got an Islamic separation. . . . Then he says, "Oh, I am going to be good. I am not going to hit you. I am not going to do anything." All the things he said, "You can go to the sisters meetings. I'm going to stop smoking. I'm going to put it all in a contract," because we had an Islamic divorce. . . . And he wrote it. He promised me he is not going to punch me or hit me or kick me. . . . He must keep the promises made in the first marriage contract. And one, I am allowed to work with women and/or children. Two, I am allowed to go to the sisters meetings and their other activities. . . . Three, I can have my own business. . . . Four, he will quit smoking. . . . Five, he will go to anger management classes and the program for batterers. . . . Six, he will not hit me, will not curse me, he will not accuse me of bad things, will not threaten to kill me, will not kick me, spit on me, urinate on me, or do anything to insult me or harm me, and seven if he does not keep and follow these conditions, I am not responsible to give him his rights, and I have the right to divorce if I request it. (Hassouneh-Phillips, 2001a, pp. 937–938)

This woman's story tells a lot about her marriage and her husband's behavior toward her. What kinds of maltreatment can you identify? In what ways, if any, does this woman's experience seem related to her religion? Does her religion serve as either a positive or negative role in her situation? What, if any, universal features does her case have?

Positive Roles of Religion and Religiosity

Affection in Conservative Protestant Child-Rearing

Some efforts have been made to identify the potentially positive aspects of conservative Protestant child-rearing techniques. National survey data have indicated that when dealing with their children, conservative Protestants spank more but yell less (Bartkowski & Wilcox, 2000). Moreover, conservative Protestants report hugging and praising their children more than other parents, and within conservative Protestant parents, conservative theological values are significantly positively correlated with the amount of hugging and praising provided to the children (Wilcox, 1998). What do you think might be the overall effect on children of a pattern of child-rearing where physical discipline is swift and often harsh, but the children are rarely yelled at and often receive praise and hugs for desired behavior?

Protective Role of Religion and Religiosity

The majority of the relevant literature, perhaps because much of it is written from a feminist or human rights perspective, focuses on the negative role of religion in family violence, especially particular religious affiliations and the espousal of particular fundamentalist values. However, there are also important findings on the protective role that religion can play in human life. In general, both religiosity and spirituality have been identified as protective factors against a broad range of personal ills, many of which are risk factors for violence in families. For example, personal religiosity among adolescents is a protective factor against substance abuse (Bahr & Hoffmann, 2008; Resnick, 1997). Moreover, a mother's religiosity is negatively associated with the onset age for adolescent drinking—the more religious the mother, the less likely her adolescent was to start drinking across a two year time span. Among adults, religiosity appears to be a protective factor in regard to mental health (Strawbridge, Shema, & Cohen, 2001). Among both adolescents and adults, religiosity has shown an inhibitory effect on engagement in delinquent and criminal activities (Benda & Toombs, 2000), and on engagement in risky sexual activities (Kendall-Tackett, 2003).

Not only may religiosity sometimes operate to reduce engaging in negative behaviors associated with maltreatment in the family, it may also contribute to the development of other characteristics that mediate against the use of interpersonal violence. For example, religiosity in parents is associated with prosocial attributes in their adolescent children (Lindner Gunnoe, Hetherington, & Reiss, 1999). There are also findings directly supportive of a protective role for religiosity in regard to family conflict, violence, and maltreatment. Religious beliefs directly related to perceived sacred qualities in a marriage and beliefs that God is manifested in marriage have been associated with overall marital adjustment, less marital conflict, and less verbal aggression in marriage (Mahoney et al., 1999). Moreover, the reciprocal of a risk factor can be a protective factor; thus, whereas religious conservatism is a risk factor for family violence, a more moderate religious philosophy can serve as a protective factor.

Based on an extensive review of the literature pertaining to religion and corporal punishment or child maltreatment, Socolar, Cabinum-Foeller, and Sinal (2008) conclude both that "conservative/fundamentalist Protestants spank and physically abuse their children more than other Christian groups" (p. 709) and that religiosity and church attendance can sometimes serve as a protective factor against family violence. Research concerning a protective role for religiosity in relation to family violence has tended to provide two types of support: (1) evidence that religiosity is an inhibitory factor that reduces the likelihood of adult family members aggressing against each other or their children, and (2) evidence that religiosity in victims of family violence serves as a protective factor reducing some of the negative effects associated with victimization. Both sets of findings are important reminders that the role of religion in relation to child maltreatment is complex.

Religiosity as a Factor Reducing Spousal Maltreatment

We have already shown that there is some evidence that spousal maltreatment is lower when there is greater rather than lesser integration of religious values into the family life (Elliott, 1994). A related question is whether frequency of attendance at religious services reduces the likelihood of marital aggression. Ellison, Trinitapoli, Anderson, and Johnson (2007) found a negative correlation between the frequency with which religious services were attended (a measure of extrinsic religiosity) and likelihood of IPV. However, African American women were nearly twice as likely to experience IPV as compared with non-Hispanic White women with similar levels of religious attendance and comparable demographic characteristics. For men, religious attendance greatly reduces the likelihood of perpetrating IPV, and this protective function of religion is particularly strong in African American men.

It also appears that within homes in which violence has taken place, religiosity can have an ameliorating effect on some of the aggression. In a nationally based sample of battered women (the *Woman's Day* sample; Bowker, 1988), the women's reports revealed that husbands who attended church relatively frequently were less likely to drink alcohol before assaulting their wives, were less likely to use weapons in their assaults, and showed less involvement in a male subculture of violence (Bowker, 1988). In another national sample of abused women (Horton et al., 1988), higher levels of religiosity appeared to increase the chances that abused wives could achieve an abuse-free, happy future, even when they remained in their marriage. In their study of abused Christian women, Wang et al. (2009) found that more than 70% of the women who had terminated an abusive relationship reported that their faith gave them the strength to do so.

Religiosity Protecting Against Negative Effects of Maltreatment

In a review of 34 studies of the role of spirituality and religiosity in the outcomes of different forms of child maltreatment, Walker, Reid, O'Neill and Brown (2009) found some evidence that religiosity/spirituality can moderate the development of symptoms of psychopathology following child maltreatment. Religion can also serve as a protective factor by providing social support for victims of abuse. In a sample of women who reported a history of child sexual abuse, some indicated that their spirituality created a sense of community, stability, hope, and other positive changes (Baker, 2007).

For sexually abused adolescents, being religious or spiritual appears to be a protective factor against negative psychological outcomes in females, but not males (Chandy, Blum, & Resnick, 1996). Moreover, among sexually abused adolescent girls, religiosity may be a protective factor against purging as a psychiatric response to abuse (Perkins & Luster, 1999). It is possible that sexually abused girls who are highly religious may be more likely to view themselves and their bodies in a more positive light than girls who are less religious. Their participation in religious activities and strong belief in the importance of God appear to act as buffer against the risk factors associated with purging.

There is additional information concerning the role of spirituality in individuals sexually abused as children. For example, in one qualitative study, 14 female child sexual abuse survivors reported that their spirituality helped them heal by helping them forgive the offender, welcome good people into their lives, and understand that the abuse was not their fault (Houg, 2008). As one of these survivors said,

> I think that, well, I know, that what got me through my hardest times was having faith. And having faith that things would turn out better, and believing and trusting that. And I know that that is why my life is as good as it is right now. My life is so wonderful right now. I am very recovered and I owe most of that to faith. (Houg, 2008, p. 127)

Although the abuse led them to turn away from religious institutions, many began to view God as someone more personal, as a superior being who saved them from the effects of abuse. Similarly, Knapik, Martsolf, and Draucker (2008) noted that spiritual transformation guided both male and female survivors of sexual abuse in their struggle to cope with their experience, and their movement toward insights and strengths as a result of their abuse. What are your views on the findings of such studies on a positive role of religion in the outcomes experienced by survivors of abuse? What limitations do you see to the studies? What are their implications for leaders of religious communities who learn about abuse to one or more of their members?

In a study of the role of religiosity in psychological outcomes among maltreated and non-maltreated children, Kim, McCullough, and Cicchetti (2009) found that maltreated children demonstrated significantly more externalizing symptoms (e.g., aggression) than nonmaltreated children; however, she also found that the relationship between religiosity, maltreatment, and symptoms varied by gender. Specifically, religiosity served as a protective factor for maltreated girls; that is, maltreated girls who emphasized the importance of faith had lower levels of internalizing symptoms (e.g., withdrawal, anxiety, depression, somatic complaints) than maltreated girls for whom faith was less important. However, neither spirituality nor church attendance appeared to play a protective role for boys. What are the implications of such findings for counselors working with families in which corporal punishment and child maltreatment are occurring? Should the response to such families vary depending on whether they are conservative Protestant or not? If the parents are very affectionate with their children but believe that severe physical punishment is God's will, should the response to the family be different from what it would be if the parents seem perpetually angry and abusive? Should the counselors be investigating levels of religiosity in the children as well as the parents in making judgments about the potential outcomes of the maltreatment?

In some cases, religiosity appears to help both adult and child survivors of maltreatment cope better with their abusive experiences. In a community sample of formerly abused women from around the United States, approximately 25% said that their religious beliefs gave them "hope," "strength," and "courage" (Horton et al., 1988). These positive emotions may help interrupt the intergenerational transmission of aggression. In one sample of high school students from public schools on the East Coast and in the South, a measure of religiosity that included both intrinsic and extrinsic components was inversely related to the use of violence in abused adolescents (Benda & Corwyn, 2002). Religious settings can also provide young victims the opportunities within an accessible community to experience social support, receive positive messages, and obtain peaceful resolution of problems (Herrenkohl, Tajima, Whitney, & Huang, 2005).

The Response of Religious Institutions to the Maltreatment of Spouses

A substantial portion of battered women turn to religious leaders to try to find relief from their suffering. Although the situation seems to be improving, there is some evidence that clergy members may justify, discount, or deny that IPV occurs in their congregations, further alienating women who are victims of IPV (Foss & Warnke, 2003). Overall, the victims' criticisms of the clerical responses revealed five major themes: (1) making the victims feel trapped within a dangerous relationship; (2) showing a lack of understanding and validation of the women's experience and minimizing the abuse; (3) providing no alternatives or practical suggestions; (4) blaming the victims for their victimization or making them feel responsible for the abuse; and (5) leaving them feeling helpless with no way to escape. By contrast, the victims who reported positive experiences with their clergy commented that their advisors provided "validation" and "approval." Clergy who agreed that safety, even if it meant separation or divorce, was necessary or at least acceptable received the highest praise. Also appreciated within this sample of women were a few clergy who recommended, and in some cases even helped pay for, outside counseling or an educational opportunity.

Historically, across religions, a typical response of clergy has been to tell women to stay with their husbands, keep the family together, and try harder not to anger their husbands. Box 13.5 provides several of these women's stories. What similarities and differences do you see in these stories? What do you think may be the sources underlying the clerics' efforts to preserve the marriages of these women from diverse religious backgrounds?

Box 13.5	Religious Counsel for Battered Women

"My husband was verbally abusive and very controlling. We were very involved in our church, so I had long been indoctrinated into believing that getting a divorce is a sin. I was told by the people at my church that the reason I was unhappy in my marriage was that I didn't submit enough to my husband." (Shore, 2010, para. 3)

"I would never in my wildest nightmares have dreamed that my husband would ever abuse me but he did. My husband is a Christian, but his rage at things is unreal. I took our two-month-old son and fled after the fourth time he struck me, but I had received counsel that it was my duty to stay and suffer for Jesus' sake." (Alsdurf & Alsdurf, 1988, p. 221)

"I have seen it presented that if you suffer at the hands of your husband that you will receive *ajars* [rewards] from Allah for doing so, so do not help him reform, do not get counseling, do not try to seek a better way. Just accept his abuse and *Allah* will bless you for it ... you know, accept the oppression because when you die you will go to heaven." (Hassouneh-Phillips, 2003, p. 688)

One woman, beaten for years, was 60 years old when she left her husband and entered a shelter. The rabbi called her and convinced her to return home. When she again entered the shelter after another beating, the rabbi convinced her to give the husband a second chance. The third time she sought refuge (she suffered from a broken rib), the rabbi again advised her to come home. He told her that her husband wanted to repent by taking her to visit the Holy Land. (Horsburgh, 1995)

"I talked with a group of priests who told me that they had no one in their church who needed "this kind" of help. They told me that women who were beaten could stop it if they really wanted to. They said such women do not honor their husbands and should expect some punishment." (Zambrano, 1985, p. 213)

Personal accounts of the response of religious authorities to women's experience of maltreatment often indicate that the message to battered wives is that suffering is good, that it helps ensure a place in heaven. Tracy (2011) provides numerous examples of the failure of evangelical Christian pastors to address—and even to recognize—IPV among their practitioners. Pyles (2007), in a study of community response to IPV in Wyoming, found that in some cases churches proved to be a major source of support for many survivors of IPV, but in other cases, churches contributed to the problems faced by battered woman. As one staff member at a local domestic violence shelter said,

> If the pastor is taking the scripture wrong and saying, you know, that the man is the head of the house and he's the ruler and all that kind of stuff, that could even give the men the lord-of-the-house feeling to where they are in control of their women. (Pyles, 2007, p. 286)

Another worker at a domestic violence shelter commented,

> I think being abused is very minimized in a family because fathers are under stress; they're heads of the households, and if you were doing what you were supposed to

be doing, you obviously wouldn't be getting beaten . . . Religion is a big thing. And I think it's instilled in them that if they pray . . . to be more patient and . . . to live through this, then [they'll] . . . be a better Catholic and they're going to . . . , you know, go straight to Heaven. (Pyles, 2007, p. 286).

In regard to Muslim Americans, Hendricks commented,

A number of Muslim leaders, religious counselors, and even parents . . . counsel abused women with these two notions (determinism and endurance). Their suffering at the hands of tyrannical husbands is a result of the decrees of Allah and therefore have to be born with the patience expected of pious and obedient women. To add insult to injury they are often told that their decreed misfortune is a result of their laxity in executing the tenets of the Shariah. The question I have to ask is simple: How much more perversion are we as the ummah of Allah and his prophet Muhammad (SAW) expected to tolerate? (1998, para. 11)

Although there is little information in the literature about the response of clergy to sexual maltreatment in marriage, some research has indicated that more conservative clergymen, similar to many other members of society, tend to blame the victims when women are raped. In a scenario study with Protestant clergymen (Sheldon & Parent, 2002), the more sexist the clergymen were, the more unfavorable their attitudes toward rape victims. Moreover, the more fundamentalist their religious values, the more sexist their attitudes and the more they blamed the victim. Even in response to the marital rape scenario, over 20% of the clergymen assigned some responsibility for the rape to the wife. One clergyman, in explaining his views, said that the wife "said 'no' but didn't resist as the Bible refers to resisting, as crying out" (p. 242).

Nevertheless, religious leaders have made several strides to combat IPV in their communities. Because so many family members turn to their clergy for help in dealing with issues of family violence, many religious organizations have responded with declarations and position statements designed to improve the response of their clergy to victims of violence in families. For example, Grodner and Sweifach (2004) describe a value-sensitive approach to IPV within the Orthodox Jewish home, and Kaufman (2010) describes progress within the broader Jewish community, noting the growing number of books that are helping to empower abused Jewish women to seek help and the growing number of programs designed to assist them. In addition, the General Assembly commissioners of the Presbyterian Church, following two years of work of a domestic violence task force, issued a statement identifying three goals: (1) protect victims from further abuse; (2) stop the abuser's violence and hold the abuser accountable; and (3) restore the family relationship, if possible, or mourn the loss of the relationship (Silverstein, 2001). The Islamic Society of North America (2004) issued the following statement:

As Muslims we understand that violence and coercion used, as a tool of control in the home, is oppression and not accepted in Islam. Marriage in the Islamic context is a means of tranquility, protection, peace and comfort. Abuse of any kind is in conflict to the principles of marriage. Any justification of abuse is in opposition to what Allah (SWT) has revealed and the example of Prophet Muhammad. (pp. 1–2)

In addition, many programs have been developed to providing training, consciousness-raising, and insight to religious leaders from many communities (Friedrich, 1988; Hoffman-Mason & Bingham, 1988). In one recent report, the clerical council known as the Majilis Ash'Shura of Philadelphia and the Delaware Valley adopted a tough policy of publicly shunning Muslims who abuse their spouses (Holmes, 2005). Much effort by Islamic advocacy organizations has been aimed at increasing awareness of family violence and pushing the taboo subject into the public eye.

Summary

Family violence appears to occur in all major religions, although it is found in some congregational cultures more than others. Child and spousal maltreatment seem to be associated most strongly with fundamentalist religious values across religions. Many victims of family violence turn to their religious authorities for help, but may be dissatisfied with the response they receive. In some cases, the experience of family violence turns individuals away from their religion. In other cases, victims find their religion a source of solace. Efforts are being made to help clergy become more responsive to family violence. As you reflect on what you have read in earlier chapters, consider how the predictors, correlates, and outcomes of the various forms of family violence may either vary by or be consistent across religions. Do you think, for example, that being sexually abused by a parent has the same causes and/or consequences in a Catholic family as in a Methodist or Muslim family? Are the effects of battering likely to be the same for a wife who turns to a fundamentalist Christian or Muslim clergyman as for an unaffiliated wife who turns to her local shelter? How about abused men? If they belong to a conservative and patriarchal religious community, might being abused by their wives have a different effect on them than in would on men belonging to more liberal congregations?

Discussion Questions

1. Do religious beliefs and interpretations of holy books seem to provide justifications for mistreating family members? If abusers assert that their holy books justify their behavior, what arguments can be directed at those assertions?

2. Can a person be a devout member of his or her religion and refrain from mistreating family members or would he or she be violating religious tenets by not being punitive?

3. If you were asked to identify "religion-related" cases of child maltreatment, what kinds of maltreatment would come to mind?

4. Why do you think different religious groups differ in their uses of and opinions concerning corporal punishment?

5. Can spanking, hitting, or kicking be labeled abusive if parents believe they are just doing what their religion tells them to do?

6. Should parents be penalized if they choose not to seek medical attention for their children for religious reasons? Does your opinion change if the parents choose not to immunize their children for either religious or non-religious reasons?

7. Do you believe it is right for officials to intervene in cases involving religious maltreatment of children? Should the parents be sentenced to jail time? Why or why not?

8. Why do you think sexual maltreatment of Jewish wives occurs at high rates while child physical maltreatment is lowest among Jews?

9. Would you consider polygamy to be a form of intimate partner abuse? Why or why not?

10. Why are African American women nearly twice as likely to experience IPV as non-Hispanic White women with similar levels of religious attendance and comparable demographic characteristics?

11. Why do you think being religious or spiritual appears to be a protective factor against negative psychological outcomes in women, but not men?

12. What should be done about religious leaders who justify, discount, or deny that IPV occurs in their congregations?

13. What response do you think abused men seeking help would get from a conservative religious community as compared to a more liberal religious community?

References

Abbey, A. (2002). Alcohol-related sexual assault: A common problem among college students. *Journal of Studies on Alcohol, 14,* 118–127.

Abbey, A., McAuslan, P., & Ross, L. T. (1998). Sexual assault perpetration by college men: The role of alcohol, misperception of sexual intent, and sexual beliefs and experiences. *Journal of Social and Clinical Psychology, 17,* 167–195.

Abbey, A., McAuslan, P., Zawacki, T., Clinton, A. M., & Buck, P. O. (2001). Attitudinal, experiential, and situational predictors of sexual assault perpetration. *Journal of Interpersonal Violence, 16*(8), 784–807.

Abbey, A., Ross, L. T., McDuffie, D., & McAuslan, P. (1996). Alcohol and dating risk factors for sexual assault among college women. *Psychology of Women Quarterly, 20,* 147–169.

Abel, G. G., & Rouleau, J. L. (1990). The nature and extent of sexual assault. In W. L. Marshall, D. R. Laws, & H. E. Barbaree (Eds.), *Handbook of sexual assault: Issues, theories, and treatment of the offender* (pp. 9–21). New York, NY: Plenum.

Aber, J. L., Allen, J. P., Carlson, V., & Cicchetti, D. (1989). The effects of maltreatment on development during early childhood: Recent studies and their theoretical, clinical, and policy implications. In D. Cicchetti & V. Carlson (Eds.), *Child maltreatment: Theory and research on the causes and consequences of child abuse and neglect* (pp. 579–619). New York, NY: Cambridge University Press.

Aborampah, O. M. (1989). Black male-female relationships: Some observations. *Journal of Black Studies, 19,* 320–342.

Abraham, S. (1997). *Revenge: A dish best served cold: A personal story* [Electronic Version]. Retrieved December 8, 2003, from http://www.menweb.org/scottrev.htm.

Abrahams, J., & Hoey, H. (1994). Sibling incest in a clergy family: A case study. *Child Abuse and Neglect, 18,* 1029–1035.

Acierno, R., Hernandez, M., Amstadter, A., Resnick, H., Steve, K., Muzzy, W., & Kilpatrick, D. G. (2010). Prevalence and correlates of emotional, physical, sexual, and financial abuse and potential neglect in the United States: The National Elder Mistreatment Study. *American Journal of Public Health, 100*(2), 292–297.

Acierno, R., Hernandez-Tejada, M., Muzzy, W., & Steve, K. (2009). *The National Elder Mistreatment Study.* Washington, DC: National Institute of Justice.

Acierno, R., Resnick, H. S., Kilpatrick, D. G., Saunders, B. E., & Best, C. L. (1999). Risk factors for rape, physical assault, and posttraumatic stress disorder in women: Examination of differential multivariate relationships. *Journal of Anxiety Disorders, 13,* 541–563.

Adams, C. (1993). I just raped my wife! What are you going to do about it, pastor? In E. Buchwald, P. Fletcher & M. Roth (Eds.), *Transforming a rape culture* (pp. 57–86). Minneapolis, MN: Milkweed.

Adams-Curtis, L. E., & Forbes, G. B. (2004). College women's experiences of sexual coercion: A review of cultural, perpetrator, victim, and situational variables. *Trauma, Violence, and Abuse, 5*(2), 91–122.

Adler, N. A., & Schutz, J. (1995). Sibling incest offenders. *Child Abuse and Neglect, 19,* 811–819.

Administration on Aging. (2012). *National Center on Elder Abuse (Title II).* Accessed February 8, 2012, from http://www.aoa.gov/AoA_programs/Elder_Rights/NCEA/index.aspx.

Agbayani-Siewert, P., & Flanagan, A. Y. (2001). Filipino American dating violence: Definitions, contextual justifications, and experiences of dating violence. *Journal of Human Behavior in the Social Environment, 3,* 115–133.

Age Concern. (2009). *Examples of Elder Abuse and Neglect.* Retrieved August 6, 2012, from http://www.agewell.org.nz/pdf/elder_abuse_stories.pdf.

Agnew, R., & Huguley, S. (1989). Adolescent violence towards parents. *Journal of Marriage and the Family, 51,* 699–711.

Aguilar, R. J., & Nightingale, N. N. (1994). The impact of specific battering experiences on the self-esteem of abused women. *Journal of Family Violence, 9,* 35–45.

Ahrens, C., Rios-Mandel, L., Isas, L., & del Carmen Lopez, M. (2010). Talking about interpersonal violence: Cultural influences on Latinas' identification and disclosure of sexual assault and intimate partner violence. *Psychological Trauma: Theory, Research, Practice, and Policy, 2*(4), 284–295.

Alaggia, R., & Krishenbaum, S. (2005). Speaking the unspeakable: Exploring the impact of family dynamics on child sexual abuse disclosures. *Families in Society, 86*(2), 227–234.

Aldarondo, E., & Straus, M. A. (1994). Screening for physical violence in couple therapy: Methodological, practical, and ethical considerations. *Family Process, 33,* 425–439.

Alexander, P. C., & Lupfer, S. L. (1987). Family characteristics and long-term consequences associated with sexual abuse. *Archives of Sexual Behavior, 16,* 235–245.

Alexy, E. M., Burgess, A. W., Baker, T., & Smoyak, S. A. (2005). Perceptions of cyberstalking among college students. *Brief Treatment and Crisis Intervention, 5,* 279–289.

Alkhateeb, M. (2009). DV organizations serving Muslim women: Preliminary results of a 2009 quantitative survey. *Peaceful Families Project.* Retrieved from http://www.peacefulfamilies .org/DVOrgsSurvey.pdf.

Alkhateeb, M. B., & Abugideiri, S. E. (2007). *Change from within: Diverse perspectives on domestic violence in Muslim communities.* Great Falls, VA: Peaceful Families Project.

Alkhateeb S. (n.d.). *Ending domestic violence in Muslim families* [Electronic Version]. Retrieved July 2003 from http://www.themodernreligion.com/index2.html.

Allegretto, S. A., & Arthur, M. M. (2001). An empirical analysis of homosexual/heterosexual male earnings differentials: Unmarried and unequal? *Industrial and Labor Relations Review, 54*(3), 631–646.

Allen, C., & Leventhal, B. (1999). History, culture, and identity: What makes GLBT battering different. In B. Leventhal & S. Lundy (Eds.), *Same-sex domestic violence: Strategies for change* (pp. 73–81). Thousand Oaks, CA: Sage.

Allen, D. M., & Tarnowski, K. G. (1989). Depressive characteristics of physically abused children. *Journal of Abnormal Child Psychology, 17,* 1–11.

Allen, R. J., & Miller, J. (1995). The expert as educator: Enhancing the rationality of verdicts in child abuse prosecutions. *Psychology, Public Policy and Law, 1,* 323–328.

Allport, G. W., & Ross, J. M. (1967). Personal religious orientation and prejudice. *Journal of Personality and Social Psychology, 5,* 432–443.

Alsdurf, P., & Alsdurf, J. M. (1988). Wife abuse and scripture. In A. L. Horton & J. A. Williamson (Eds.), *Abuse and religion: When praying isn't enough* (pp. 221–227). Lexington, MA: Lexington Books.

Altemeier, W., O'Connor, S., Vietze, P., Sandler, H., & Sherrod, K. (1982). Antecedents of child abuse. *Journal of Pediatrics, 100,* 823–829.

Alvy, K. T. (1987). *Black parenting.* New York, NY: Irvington.

Alzate, M., & Rosenthal, J. (2009). Gender and ethnic differences for Hispanic children referred to child protective services. *Children and Youth Services Review, 31,* 1–7.

Amanda. (2006). The meaning of power. *Ballastexistenz.* Retrieved from https://ballastexistenz .wordpress.com/2006/03/28/the-meaning-of-power/.

Amar, A. F. (2006). College women's experience of stalking: Mental health symptoms and changes in routines. *Archives of Psychiatric Nursing, 20*(3), 108–116.

American Academy of Child and Adolescent Psychiatry. (2000). *Policy statement: Juvenile death sentences* [Electronic Version]. Retrieved March 2004 from http://www.aacap.org/ publications/policy/pS42.htm.

American Academy of Child and Adolescent Psychiatry. (2011). *Facts for families: Children and TV violence.* Washington, DC: Author.

American Academy of Family Physicians. (2004). *Violence* (position paper). [Electronic Version]. Retrieved July 26, 2003, from http://www.aafp.org/x7132.xml.

American Bar Association Commission on Domestic Violence. (2008, July). *Domestic violence civil protection orders by state: Overview of CPO protections for LGBT victims of domestic violence* [Electronic Version]. Retrieved from http://www.americanbar.org/content/dam/ aba/publishing/cdv_enewsletter/LGBTCoversheet_CPO_chart.authcheckdam.pdf.

American Civil Liberties Union. (1999). *ACLU fact sheet: Overview of lesbian and gay parenting, adoption and foster care* [Electronic Version]. Retrieved September 2003 from http:// www.aclu.org/LesbianGayRights/LesbianGayRights.cfm?ID=9212&c=104.

American College Health Association. (2004). *National college health assessment: Reference group executive summary Spring 2004.* Baltimore, MD: Author.

American Professional Society on the Abuse of Children. (1995). *Guidelines for the psychosocial evaluation of suspected psychological maltreatment in children and adolescents.* Chicago, IL: Author.

American Psychological Association. (2003). *Elder abuse and neglect: In search of solutions* [Electronic Version]. Retrieved August 6, 2012, from http://www.apa.org/pi/aging/ resources/guides/elder-abuse.aspx.

American Psychological Association. (2004a). Guidelines for psychological practice with older adults. *American Psychologist, 59,* 236–260.

American Psychological Association. (2004b). *Sexual orientation, parents, and children* [Electronic Version]. Retrieved February 11, 2012, from http://www.apa.org/about/gover nance/council/policy/parenting.aspx.

American Religious Identification Survey. (2008). *ARIS 2008 Summary Report.* Hartford, CT: Institute for the Study of Secularism in Society & Culture.

Ammar, N. H. (2007). Wife battery in Islam: A comprehensive understanding of interpretations. *Violence Against Women 13*(5), 516–526.

Ammerman, R., Putnam, F., Altaye, M., Chen, L., Holleb, L., Stevens, J., . . . Van Ginkel, J. B. (2009). Changes in depressive symptoms in first time mothers in home visitation. *Child Abuse and Neglect, 33,* 127–138.

Ammerman, R. T. (1991). The role of the child in physical abuse: A reappraisal. *Violence and Victims, 6,* 87–101.

Amnesty International. (2010). *Amnesty International Report 2010.* Retrieved from http:// report2010.amnesty.org/.

Amodeo, M., Griffin, M., Fassler, I., Clay, C., & Ellis, M. (2006). Childhood sexual abuse among Black women and White women from two-parent families. *Child Maltreatment, 11*(3), 237–246.

Anderson, C. A., Benjamin, A. J., Wood, P. K., & Bonacci, A. M. (2006). Development and testing of the Velicer attitudes toward violence scale: Evidence for a four-factor model. *Aggressive Behavior, 32,* 122–136.

Anderson, J., Martin, J., Mullen, P. E., Romans, S., & Herbison, P. (1993). Prevalence of child-hood sexual abuse in a community sample of women. *Journal of the American Academy of Child and Adolescent Psychiatry, 32,* 911–919.

Anderson, K. M. (2010). *Enhancing resilience in survivors of family violence.* New York, NY: Springer.

Anderson, L. A., & Whiston, S. C. (2005). Sexual assault education programs: A meta-analytic examination of their effectiveness. *Psychology of Women Quarterly, 29,* 374–388.

Anderson, M. L., & Leigh, I. W. (2011). Intimate partner violence against deaf female college students. *Violence Against Women, 17*(7), 822–834.

Anderson, P. B. (1998a). Variations in college women's self reported heterosexual aggression. *Sexual Abuse: A Journal of Research and Treatment, 10*(4), 283–292.

Anderson, P. B. (1998b). Women's motives for sexual initiation and aggression. In P. B. Anderson & C. Struckman-Johnson (Eds.), *Sexually aggressive women: Current perspectives and controversies* (pp. 79–93). New York, NY: Guilford Press.

Anderson, P. B., & Aymami, R. (1993). Reports of female initiation of sexual contact: Male and female differences. *Archives of Sexual Behavior, 22,* 335–344.

Anetzberger, G. J. (1987). *Etiology of elder abuse by adult offspring.* Springfield, IL: Charles C. Thomas.

Anetzberger, G. J. (1998). Psychological abuse and neglect: A cross-cultural concern to older Americans. In A. Foundation (Ed.), *Understanding and combating elder abuse in minority communities* (pp. 141–151). Long Beach, CA: Archstone Foundation.

Anetzberger, G. J., Korbin, J. E., & Tomita, S. K. (1996). Defining elder mistreatment in four ethnic groups across two generations. *Journal of Cross-Cultural Gerontology, 11,* 187–212.

Aniol, K., Mullins, L. L., Page, M. C., Boyd, M. L., & Chaney, J. M. (2004). The relationship between respite care and child abuse potential in parents of children with developmental disabilities: A preliminary report. *Journal of Developmental and Physical Disabilities, 16,* 273–285.

Ansello, E. F., & O'Neill, P. (2010). Abuse, neglect, and exploitation: Considerations in aging with lifelong disabilities. *Journal of Elder Abuse & Neglect, 22,* 105–130.

Anti-Ageism Taskforce at the International Longevity Center. (2006). *Ageism in America.* Available at http://www.mailman.columbia.edu/academic-departments/centers/international-longevity-center/publications.

Appel, A. E., & Holden, G. W. (1998). The occurrence of spouse and physical child abuse: A review and appraisal. *Journal of Family Psychology, 12,* 578–599.

Archer, J. (2000). Sex differences in aggression between heterosexual couples: A meta-analytic review. *Psychological Bulletin, 126,* 651–680.

Arias, I. (1999). Women's responses to physical and psychological abuse. In X. B. Arriaga & S. Oskamp (Eds.), *Violence in intimate relationships* (pp. 139–162). Thousand Oaks, CA: Sage.

Arias, I., & Pape, K. T. (1999). Psychological abuse: Implications for adjustment and commitment to leave violent partners, Article for miniseries on psychological abuse. *Violence and Victims, 14,* 55–67.

Armesto, J. (2002). Developmental and contextual factors that influence gay fathers' parental competence: A review of the literature. *Psychology of Men & Masculinity, 3*(2), 67–78.

Aroon, P. J. (2010, December 15). *International Violence Against Women Act approved by Senate Foreign Relations Committee.* Retrieved from http://hillary.foreignpolicy.com/posts/2010/12/15/international_violence_against_women_act_approved_by_senate_foreign_relations_commi.

Asherah, K. L. (2003). *The myth of mutual abuse* [Electronic Version]. Retrieved May 7, 2004, from http://www.nwnetwork.org/articles/4.html.

Asser, S. M., & Swan, R. (1998). Child fatalities from religion-motivated medical neglect. *Pediatrics, 101,* 625–629.

Associated Press. (1998). *No bail for father charged with murdering his daughter* [Electronic Version]. Retrieved February 23, 2004, from http://www.cnn.com/US/9812/01/missing .gir1.02/.

Astin, B., Lawrence, K. J., & Foy, D. W. (1993). Posttraumatic stress disorder among battered women: Risk and resiliency factors. *Violence and Victims, 8,* 17–28.

Astor, R. A. (1994). Children's moral reasoning about family and peer violence: The role of provocation and retribution. *Child Development, 65,* 1054–1067.

Aubrey, M., & Ewing, C. P. (1989). Student and voter subjects: Differences in attitudes towards battered women. *Journal of Interpersonal Violence, 4,* 289–297.

Augoustinos, M. (1987). Developmental effects of child abuse: Recent findings. *Child Abuse and Neglect, 11,* 15–27.

Aulivola, M. (2004). Outing domestic violence: Affording appropriate protections to gay and lesbian victims. *Family Court Review, 42*(1), 162–177.

Austin, J., & Dankwort, J. (1997). *A review of standards for batterer intervention programs* [Electronic Version]. Retrieved August 6, 2012, from http://www.vawnet.org/applied -research-papers/print-document.php?doc_id=393.

Avakame, E. F., & Fyfe, J. J. (2001). Differential police treatment of male-on-female spousal violence: Additional evidence on the leniency thesis. *Violence Against Women, 7,* 22–45.

Ayoub, C., Willett, J. B., & Robinson, D. S. (1992). Families at risk of child maltreatment: Entry-level characteristics and growth in family functioning during treatment. *Child Abuse and Neglect, 16,* 495–511.

Azar, S. T., Ferraro, M. H., & Breton, S. J. (1998). Intrafamilial child maltreatment. In T. H. Ollendick & M. Hersen (Eds.), *Handbook of child psychopathology* (pp. 483–504). New York, NY: Plenum.

Azar, S. T., & Siegel, B. R. (1990). Behavioral treatment of child abuse: A developmental perspective. *Behavior Modification, 14,* 279–300.

Babcock, J. C., Green, C. E., & Robie, C. (2004). Does batterers' treatment work? A meta-analytic review of domestic violence treatment outcome research. *Clinical Psychology Review, 23,* 1023–1053.

Babcock, R. J. H. (2000). Psychology of stalking. In P. Infield & G. Platford (Eds.), *The law of harassment and stalking* (pp. 1–8). London, UK: Butterworths.

Bachman, R. (1993). The double edged sword of violent victimization against the elderly: Patterns of family and stranger perpetration. *Journal of Elder Abuse & Neglect, 5,* 59–76.

Back, S., & Lips, H. M. (1998). Child sexual abuse: Victim age, victim gender, and observer gender as factors contributing to attributions of responsibility. *Child Abuse and Neglect, 22,* 1239–1252.

Badgett, M. V. L. (1995). The wage effects of sexual orientation discrimination. *Industrial and Labor Relations Review, 48,* 426–739.

Baer, J. S., Stacy, A., & Larimer, M. (1991). Biases in the perception of drinking norms among college students. *Journal of Studies on Alcohol, 52*(6), 580–586.

Bahr, S. J., & Hoffman, J. P. (2008). Religiosity, peers, and adolescent drug use. *Journal of Drug Issues, 38*(3), 3743–3769.

Baker, D. J. (2002). *Civil protection order: How is this piece of paper going to protect me?* School of Law Enforcement Supervision, Session XX. Criminal Justice Institute. Retrieved from http://www.cji.edu/papers/BakerDelores.pdf.

Baker, S. R. (2007). Resilience as process among women over 50 who report a history of childhood sexual abuse (Doctoral dissertation). University of Toronto, Toronto, Canada.

Baladerian, N. J. (2009). *Child abuse and neglect of children with disabilities* [Electronic Version]. Retrieved from http://www.disabled-world.com/disability/awareness/child-abuse -disabilities.php.

Baldry, A. C. (2003). "Stick and stones hurt my bones but his glance and words hurt more": The impact of physiological abuse and physical violence by current and former partners on battered women in Italy. *International Journal of Forensic Mental Health*, 2(1), 47–57.

Balos, B., & Trotsky, I. (1988). Enforcement of the domestic abuse act in Minnesota: A preliminary study. *Law and Inequality, 6*, 83–125.

Balsam, K., & Szymanski, D. M. (2005). Relationship quality and domestic violence in women's same-sex relationships: The role of minority stress. *Psychology of Women Quarterly, 29*, 258–269.

Baltes, P. B., Reese, H. W., & Nesselroade, J. R. (1977). *Life-span developmental psychology: Introduction to research methods.* Monterey, CA: Brooks/Cole.

Banyard, V. L., Moynihan, M. M., & Plante, E. G. (2007). Sexual violence prevention through bystander education: An experimental evaluation. *Journal of Community Psychology, 35*(4), 463–481.

Banyard, V. L., Plante, E. G., & Moynihan, M. M. (2004). Bystander education: Bringing a broader community perspective to sexual violence prevention. *Journal of Community Psychology, 32*(1), 61–79.

Banyard, V. L., Ward, S., Cohn, E. S., Plante, E. G., Moorhead, C., & Walsh, W. (2007). Unwanted sexual contact on campus: A comparison of women's and men's experiences. *Violence and Victims, 22*(1), 52–70.

Barak, G. (2003). *Violence and nonviolence: Pathways to understanding.* Thousand Oaks, CA: Sage.

Bard, L., Carter, D., Cerce, D., Knight, R., Rosenberg, R., & Schneider, B. (1983). *A descriptive study of rapists and child molesters: Developmental, clinical and criminal characteristics.* Bridgewater, MA: Mimeo.

Barling, J., O'Leary, K. D., Jouriles, E. N., Vivian, D., & MacEwen, K. E. (1987). Factor similarity of the Conflict Tactics Scales across samples, spouses, and sites: Issues and implications. *Journal of Family Violence, 2,* 37–54.

Barnett, D., Ganiban, J., & Cicchetti, D. (1999). Maltreatment, negative expressivity, and the development of type D attachments from 12 to 24 months of age. *Monographs of the Society for Research in Child Development, 64,* 97–118.

Barnett, O. W. (2000). Why battered women do not leave, Part 1: External inhibiting factors within society. *Trauma, Violence & Abuse, 1*(4), 343–372.

Barnett, O. W. (2001). Why battered women do not leave, Part 2: External inhibiting factors—social support and internal inhibiting factors. *Trauma, Violence, & Abuse, 2*(1), 3–35.

Baron, S., & Welty, A. (1996). Elder abuse. *Journal of Gerontological Social Work, 25,* 33–57.

Barr, R. G., Barr, M., Fujiwara, T., Conway, J., Catherine, N., & Brant, R. (2009). Do educational materials change knowledge and behaviour about crying and shaken baby syndrome? A randomized control trial. *Canadian Medical Association Journal, 180*(7), 727–733.

Barron, D. J. (2010, April 27). *Whether the criminal provisions of the Violence Against Women Act apply to otherwise covered conduct when the offender and victim are the same sex, Memorandum opinion for the Acting Deputy Attorney General.* [White Paper]. New York, NY: Center for HIV Law and Policy.

Barth, R. P., Landsverk, J., Chamberlain, P., Reid, J. B., Rolls, J. A., Hurlburt, M. S., . . . Kohl, P. L. (2005). Parent-training programs in child welfare services: Planning for a more evidence-based approach to serving biological parents. *Research on Social Work Practice, 15*(5), 353–371.

Bartholomew, K., Regan, K. V., White, M. A., & Oram, D. (2008). Patterns of abuse in male same-sex relationships. *Violence and Victims, 23*(5), 617–636.

Bartkowski, J. (1996). Beyond biblical literalism and inerrancy: Conservative Protestants and the hermeneutic interpretation of scripture. *Sociology of Religion, 57,* 259–272.

Bartkowski, J. P., & Ellison, C. G. (1995). Divergent models of childrearing in popular manuals: Conservative Protestants vs. the mainstream experts. *Sociology of Religion, 56,* 21–34.

Bartkowski, J. P., & Wilcox, W. B. (2000). Conservative Protestant child discipline: The case of parental yelling. *Social Forces, 79,* 265–290.

Basile, K. (1999). Rape by acquiescence: The ways in which women "give in" to unwanted sex with their husbands. *Violence Against Women, 5,* 1036–1058.

Basile, K. C. (2002a). Attitudes toward wife rape: Effects of social background and victim status. *Violence and Victims, 17,* 341–354.

Basile, K. C. (2002b). Prevalence of wife rape and other intimate partner sexual coercion in a nationally representative sample of women. *Violence and Victims, 17*(5), 511–524.

Basile, K. C., & Hall, J. E. (2011). Intimate partner violence perpetration by court-ordered men: Distinctions and intersections among physical violence, sexual violence, psychological abuse, and stalking. *Journal of Interpersonal Violence, 26*(2), 230–253.

Basile, K. C., Swahn, M. H., Chen, J., & Saltzman, L. E. (2006). Stalking in the United States: Recent national prevalence estimates. *American Journal of Preventative Medicine 31*(2), 172–175.

Bassuk, E., Dawson, R., & Huntington, N. (2006). Intimate partner violence in extremely poor women: Longitudinal patterns and risk markers. *Journal of Family Violence, 21*(6), 387–399.

Bath, H. I., & Haapala, D. A. (1993). Intensive family preservation services with abused and neglected children: An examination of group differences. *Child Abuse and Neglect, 17,* 213–225.

Baum, K., Catalano, S., Rand, M., & Rose, K. (2009). *Stalking victimization in the United States.* [Special report]. Washington, DC: Bureau of Justice Statistics. Available at http://www.ovw.usdoj.gov/docs/stalking-victimization.pdf.

Baumann, B., & Kolko, D. J. (2005). *Improving the cultural relevancy of an evidence-based intervention for physically abusive families.* Center for Minority Health. Pittsburgh, PA: University of Pittsburgh.

Baumle, A. K., Compton, D., & Poston Jr., D. L. (2009). *Same-sex partners: The demography of sexual orientation.* Albany, NY: State University of New York Press.

Baumle, A. K., & Poston, D. L. (2011). The economic cost of homosexuality: Multilevel analyses. *Social Forces, 89,* 1005–1032.

Baumrind, D. (1997). Necessary distinctions. *Psychological Inquiry, 8,* 176–182.

Beaulaurier, R. L., Seff, L. R., Newman, F. L., & Dunlop, B. (2005). Internal barriers to help seeking for middle-aged and older women who experience intimate partner violence. *Journal of Elder Abuse & Neglect, 17*(3), 53–74.

Beaulaurier, R. L., Seff, L. R., Newman, F. L., & Dunlop, B. (2007). External barriers to help seeking for older women who experience intimate partner violence. *Journal of Family Violence, 22,* 747–755.

Becker, J., Kaplan, M., Cunningham-Rathner, B., & Kavoussi, R. (1986). Characteristics of adolescent incest sexual perpetrators. *Journal of Family Violence, 1,* 85–97.

Beckett, C. (2003). *Child protection: An introduction.* Thousand Oaks, CA: Sage.

Beeghly, M., & Cicchetti, D. (1994). Child maltreatment, attachment, and the self system: Emergence of an internal state lexicon in toddlers at high social risk. *Development and Psychopathology, 6,* 5–30.

Begle, A. M., Dumas, J. E., & Hanson, R. F. (2010). Predicting child abuse potential: An empirical investigation of two theoretical   frameworks. *Journal of Clinical Child & Adolescent Psychology, 39*(2), 208–219.

Behl, L. E., Crouch, J. L., May, P. F., Valente, L. A., & Conyngham, H. A. (2001). Ethnicity in child maltreatment research: A content analysis. *Child Maltreatment, 6*(2), 143–147.

Belknap, J., & Melton, H. (2005). *Are heterosexual men also victims of intimate partner abuse?* [Electronic Version]. *VAWnet.* Retrieved August 6, 2012, from http://www.ncdsv.org/images/VAWnet_AreHeterosexualMenAlsoVictimsIPV_3–2005.pdf.

Belsky, J. (1993). Etiology of child maltreatment: A developmental-ecological approach. *Psychological Bulletin, 114,* 413–434.

Belsky, J., & Vondra, J. (1989). Lessons from child abuse: The determinants of parenting. In D. Cicchetti & V. Carlson (Eds.), *Child maltreatment: Theory and research on the causes and consequences of child abuse and neglect* (pp. 153–202). New York, NY: Cambridge University Press.

Benda, B. B., & Corwyn, R. B. (2002). The effect of abuse in childhood and in adolescence on violence among adolescents. *Youth & Society, 33,* 339–365.

Benda, B. B., & Toombs, N. J. (2000). Religiosity and violence: Are they related after considering the strongest predictors? *Journal of Criminal Justice, 28,* 483–496.

Benedict, M. (2000). *The importance of disciplining children early* [Electronic Version]. Retrieved December 2011 from http://www.christian-parents.net/Children/C107_Early_Discipline.htm.

Bennice, J. A., & Resick, P. A. (2003). Marital rape: History, research, and practice. *Trauma, Violence, & Abuse, 4,* 228–246.

Berg, N., & Lien, D. (2002). Measuring the effect of sexual orientation on income: Evidence of discrimination? *Contemporary Economic Policy, 20,* 394–414.

Bergen, R., & Bukovec, P. (2006). Men and intimate partner rape: Characteristics of men who sexually abuse their partner. *Journal of Interpersonal Violence, 21*(10), 1375–1384.

Bergen, R. K. (1996). *Wife rape: Understanding the response of survivors and service providers.* Thousand Oaks, CA: Sage.

Bergen, R. K. (1998). The reality of wife rape: Women's experiences of sexual violence in marriage. In R. K. Bergen (Ed.), *Issues in intimate violence* (pp. 237–250). Thousand Oaks, CA: Sage.

Berger, L. M. (2004). Income, family structure, and child maltreatment risk. *Children and Youth Services Review, 26,* 725–748.

Berger, L. M. (2005). Income, family characteristics, and physical violence toward children. *Child Abuse and Neglect, 29,* 107–133.

Bergeron, L. R. (2001). An elder abuse case study: Caregiver stress or domestic violence? You decide. *Journal of Gerontological Social Work, 34,* 47–63.

Berk, R. A., Campbell, A., Klap, R., & Western, B. (1992). The deterrent effect of arrest: A Bayesian analysis of four field experiments. *American Sociological Review, 57,* 698–708.

Berk, R. A., Newton, P. J., & Berk, S. F. (1986). What a difference a day makes: An empirical study of the impact of shelters for battered women. *Journal of Marriage and the Family, 48,* 481–490.

Berliner, L., & Elliott, D. M. (2002). Sexual abuse of children. In J. E. Myers, L. Berliner, J. Briere, C. T. Hendrix, C. Jenny, & T. A. Reid (Eds.), *The APSAC handbook on child maltreatment* (2nd ed., pp. 55–78). Thousand Oaks, CA: Sage.

Bernard-Bonnin, A. C., Hebert, M., Daignault, I. V., & Allard-Dansereau, C. (2008). Disclosure of sexual abuse and personal and familial factors as predictors of post-traumatic stress disorder symptoms in school-aged girls. *Pediatrics and Child Health, 13,* 479–486.

Bernat, J. A., Calhoun, K. S., & Stolp, S. (1998). Sexually aggressive men's response to a date rape analogue: Alcohol as a disinhibiting cue. *Journal of Sex Research, 35,* 341–348.

Bernstein, M., & Kostelac, C. (2002). Lavender and blue: Attitudes about homosexuality and behavior towards lesbians and gay men among police officers. *Journal of Contemporary Criminal Justice, 18,* 302–328.

Berrick, J., & Barth, R. (1992). Child sexual abuse prevention: Research review and recommendations. *Social Work Research and Abstracts, 28,* 6–15.

Berrick, J. D., & Gilbert, N. (1991). *With the best of intentions: The child sexual abuse prevention movement.* New York, NY: Guilford.

Berson, S. B. (2010). Prosecuting elder abuse cases. *National Institute of Justice Journal, 265,*1.

Besharov, D. J. (2005). Overreporting and underreporting child abuse and neglect are twin problems. In D. R. Loseke, R. J. Gelles, & M. M. Cavanaugh (Eds.), *Currently controversies on family violence* (2nd ed., pp. 285–298). Thousand Oaks, CA: Sage.

Besinger, B. A., Garland, A. F., Litrownik, A. J., & Landsverk, J. A. (1999). Caregiver substance abuse among maltreated children placed in out-of-home care. *Child Welfare, 78,* 221–239.

Bethke, T., & DeJoy, D. (1993). An experimental study of factors influencing the acceptability of dating violence. *Journal of Interpersonal Violence, 8,* 36–51.

Beyene, Y., Becker, G., & Mayen, N. (2002). Perception of aging and sense of well-being among Latino elderly. *Journal of Cross-Cultural Gerontology, 17,* 155–172.

Bickel, B. (2000). *The Kayla McLean murder* [Electronic Version]. Retrieved February 23, 2004, from http://crime.about.com/library/weekly/aa043000a.htm.

Bigner, J. J. (1999). Raising our sons: Gay men as fathers. *Journal of Gay & Lesbian Social Services, 10,* 61–68.

Bigner, J. J., & Jacobsen, R. B. (1989). The value of children to gay and heterosexual fathers. *Journal of Homosexuality, 18,* 163–172.

Bigner, J. J., & Jacobsen, R. B. (1992). Adult responses to child behavior and attitudes toward fathering: Gay and non-gay fathers. *Journal of Homosexuality, 23,* 99–112.

Binggeli, N. J., Hart, S. N., & Brassard, M. R. (2000). *Psychological maltreatment: A study guide.* Thousand Oaks, CA: Sage.

Binggeli, N. J., Hart, S. N., & Brassard, M. R. (2001). *Psychological maltreatment of children.* Thousand Oaks, CA: Sage.

Bishop, S. J., & Leadbeater, B. J. (1999). Maternal social support patterns and child maltreatment: Comparison of maltreating and nonmaltreating mothers. *American Journal of Orthopsychiatry, 69,* 172–181.

Bjerregaard, B. (2000). An empirical study of stalking victimization. *Violence and Victims, 15,* 389–406.

Bjerregaard, B. (2002). An empirical study of stalking victimization. In K. E. Davis, I. H. Frieze, & R. D. Maiuro (Eds.), *Stalking: Perspectives on victims on perpetrators* (pp. 112–137). New York, NY: Springer.

Blaauw, E., Winkel, F. W., Arensman, E., Sheridan, L., & Freeve, A. (2002). The toll of stalking: The relationship between features of stalking and psychopathology of victims. *Journal of Interpersonal Violence, 17*(1), 50–63.

Black, D., Hoda, R., Makar, S., Sanders, G., & Taylor, L. (2003). The earnings effects of sexual orientation. *Industrial and Labor Relation Review, 56,* 449–469.

Black, M. C., Basile, K. C., Breiding, M. J., Smith, S. G., Walters, M. L., Merrick, M. T., . . . Stevens, M. R. (2011). *The National Intimate Partner and Sexual Violence Survey: 2010 summary report.* Atlanta, GA: National Center for Injury Prevention and Control, Centers for Disease Control and Prevention.

Black, M. C., & Breiding, M. J. (2008). Adverse health conditions and health risk behaviors associated with intimate partner violence—United States, 2005. *Morbidity and Mortality Weekly Report, 57*(5), 113–117.

Black, M. M., & Krishnakumar, A. (1999). Predicting height and weight longitudinal growth curves using ecological factors among children with and without early grown deficits. *Journal of Nutrition, 129,* 539S–543S.

Blanchard, J., & Lurie, N. (2004). R-E-S-P-E-C-T: Patient reports of disrespect in the healthcare setting and its impact on care. *Journal of Family Practice, 53,* 721–730.

Blanchfield, L. (2011, April 15). *The U.N. Convention on the Elimination of All Forms of Discrimination Against Women (CEDAW): Issues in the U.S. Ratification Debate* [Electronic Version]. Retrieved from http://assets.opencrs.com/rpts/R40750_20110415.pdf.

Blandford, J. M. (2003). The nexus of sexual orientation and gender in the determination of earnings. *Industrial and labor relations review, 56*(4), 622–642.

Block, C. R., & Chrisakos, A. (1995). Intimate partner homicide in Chicago over 29 years. *Crime and Delinquency, 41,* 496.

Block, R. W. (2003). Child fatalities. In J. E. B. Myers, L. Berliner, J. Briere, C. T. Hendrix, C. Jenny, & T. A. Reid (Eds.), *The APSAC handbook on child maltreatment* (2nd ed., pp. 293–301). Thousand Oaks, CA: Sage.

Bolen, R. M. (1998). Predicting risk to be sexually abused: A comparison of logistic regression to event history analysis. *Child Maltreatment, 3,* 157–170.

Bolen, R. M. (2005). Attachment and family violence: Complexities in knowing. *Child Abuse and Neglect, 29,* 845–852.

Bonanno, G. A., & Mancini, A. D. (2008). The human capacity to thrive in the face of potential trauma. *Pediatrics, 121,* 369–375.

Boney-McCoy, S., & Finkelhor, D. (1995). Psychosocial sequelae of violent victimization in a national youth sample. *Journal of Consulting and Clinical Psychology, 63,* 726–736.

Bonner, B. L., Crow, S. M., & Logue, M. B. (1999). Fatal child neglect. In H. Dubowitz (Ed.), *Neglected children: Research, practice, and policy* (pp. 156–173). Thousand Oaks, CA: Sage.

Bonnier, C., Nassagne, M. C., & Evrard, P. (1995). Outcome and prognosis of whiplash shaken infant syndrome: Late consequences after a symptom-free interval. *Developmental Medicine and Child Neurology, 37,* 943–956.

Booth, A., & Dabbs, J. M. (1993). Testosterone and men's marriages. *Social Forces, 72,* 463–477.

Bornstein, B. H., Kaplan, D. L., & Perry, A. R. (2007). Child abuse in the eyes of the beholder: Lay perceptions of child sexual and physical abuse. *Child Abuse and Neglect, 31,* 375–391.

Bornstein, D. R., Fawcett, J., Sullivan, M., Senturia, K. D., & Shiu-Thornton, S. (2006). Understanding the experiences of lesbian, bisexual, and trans survivors of domestic violence: A qualitative study. *Journal of Homosexuality, 51,* 159–181.

Boswell, A. A., & Spade, J. Z. (1996). Fraternities and collegiate rape culture: Why are some fraternities more dangerous places for women? *Gender & Society, 10,* 133–147.

Bottoms, B. L., Kalder, A. K., Stevenson, M. C., Oudekerk, B. A., Wiley, T. R., & Perona, A. R. (2011). Gender differences in jurors' perceptions of infanticide involving disabled and non-disabled infant victims. *Child Abuse and Neglect, 35,* 127–141.

Bottoms, B. L., Nielson, M., Murray, R., & Filipas, H. (2003). Religion-related child physical abuse: Characteristics and psychological outcomes. *Journal of Aggression, Maltreatment, and Trauma, 8*(1/2), 87–114.

Bottoms, B. L., Shaver, P. R., Goodman, G. S., & Qin, J. (1995). In the name of God: A profile of religion-related child abuse. *The Society for the Psychological Study of Social Issues, 51,* 85–111.

Botuck, S., Berretty, P., Cho, S., Tax, C. A., Archer, M., & Bennett Catteneo, L. (2009, June). *Understanding intimate partner stalking: Implications for offering victim services.* Final Report. U.S. Department of Justice. Document number 227220. Washington, DC: Government Printing Office.

Bowker, L. H. (1983, June). Marital rape. A distinct syndrome? *Social Casework, 64*(6), 347–352.

Bowker, L. H. (1988). Religious victims and their religious leaders: Services delivered to one thousand battered women by the clergy. In A. L. Horton & J. A. Williamson (Eds.), *Abuse and Religion: When praying isn't enough* (pp. 229–234). Lexington, MA: Lexington Books.

Bowker, L. H., Arbitell, M., & McFerron, J. R. (1988). On the relationship between wife beating and child abuse. In K. Yllo & M. Bograd (Eds.), *Feminist perspectives on wife abuse* (pp. 158–174). Newbury Park, CA: Sage.

Bowker, L. H., & Maurer, L. (1985). The importance of sheltering in the lives of battered women. *Response to the Victimization of Women & Children, 8*(1), 2–8.

Bowlby, J. (1969/1982). *Attachment and loss: Attachment.* New York, NY: Basic Books.

Bowlby, J. (1973). *Attachment and loss: Separation* (Vol. 2). London, UK: The Hogarth Press.

Brachfield, S., Goldberg, S., & Sloman, J. (1980). Parent-infant interaction in free play at 8 and 12 months: Effects of prematurity and immaturity. *Infant Behavior in Development, 3,* 289–305.

Brandl, B., & Cook-Daniels, L. (2002). *Domestic abuse in later life* [Electronic Version]. Retrieved August 6, 2012, from http://www.vawnet.org/applied-research-papers/print -document.php?doc_id=376.

Brassard, M. R., & Donovan, K. L. (2006). Defining psychological maltreatment. In M. M. Feerick, J. F. Knutson, P. K. Trickett, & S. M. Flanzer (Eds.), *Child abuse and neglect: Definitions, classifications, and a framework for research* (pp. 151–197). Baltimore, MD: Paul H. Brookes.

Brassard, M. R., Hart, S. N., & Hardy, D. B. (2000). Psychological and emotional abuse of children. In R. T. Ammerman & M. Hersen (Eds.), *Case studies in family violence* (2nd ed., pp. 293–319). New York, NY: Kluwer.

Brecklin, L. R., & Forde, D. R. (2001). A meta-analysis of rape education programs. *Violence and Victims, 16,* 303–321.

Brewster, M. P. (2002). Trauma symptoms of former intimate partner stalking victims. *Women and Criminal Justice, 13*(2/3), 141–161.

Brewster, M. P. (2003). Power and control dynamics in prestalking and stalking situations. *Journal of Family Violence, 18*(4), 207–217.

Brezina, T. (1999). Teenage violence toward parents as an adaptation to family strain: Evidence from a national survey of male adolescents. *Youth & Society, 30,* 416–444.

Brieding, M. J., Black, M. C., & Ryan, G. W. (2008). Prevalence and risk factors of intimate partner violence in eighteen U.S. states/territories, 2005. *American Journal of Preventive Medicine, 34*(2), 112–118.

Briere, J. (1987). Predicting self-reported likelihood of battering: Attitudes and childhood experiences. *Journal of Research in Personality, 21,* 61–69.

Briere, J., & Gil, E. (1998). Self-mutilation in clinical and general population samples: Prevalence, correlates, and functions. *American Journal of Orthopsychiatry, 68,* 609–620.

Briere, J., & Jordan, C. (2004). Violence against women: Outcome complexity and implications for assessment and treatment. *Journal of Interpersonal Violence, 19*(11), 1252–1276.

Briere, J., & Jordan, C. E. (2009). The relationship between childhood maltreatment, moderating variables, and adult psychological difficulties in women: An overview. *Trauma, Violence, and Abuse: A Review Journal, 10,* 375–388.

Briere, J., & Runtz, M. (1987). Post-sexual abuse trauma: Data and implications for clinical practice. *Journal of Interpersonal Violence, 8,* 367–379.

Briere, J., & Runtz, M. (1988). Multivariate correlates of childhood psychological and physical maltreatment among university women. *Child Abuse and Neglect, 12,* 331–341.

Briere, J., & Runtz, M. (1989). University males' sexual interest in children: Predicting potential indices of pedophilia in a nonforensic sample. *Child Abuse and Neglect, 13,* 65–75.

Briere, J., & Runtz, M. (1990). Differential adult symptomology associated with three types of child abuse histories. *Child Abuse and Neglect, 14,* 357–364.

Briere, J., Woo, R., McRae, B., Foltz, J., & Sitzman, R. (1997). Lifetime victimization history, demographics, and clinical status in female psychiatric emergency room patients. *Journal of Nervous and Mental Disease, 185,* 95–101.

Bristowe, E., & Collins, J. (1989). Family mediated abuse of noninstitutionalized frail elderly men and women in British Columbia. *Journal of Elder Abuse & Neglect, 1,* 45–64.

Brodsky, B. S., Mann, J. J., Stanley, B., Tin, A., Oquendo, M., Birmaher, B., . . . Brent, D. (2008). Familial transmission of suicidal behavior: Factors mediating the relationship between childhood abuse and offspring suicide attempts. *Journal of Clinical Psychiatry, 69,* 584–596.

Brodwin, M. G., Orange, L. M., & Chen, R. K. (2004). Societal attitudes toward sexuality regarding people who have disabilities. *Directions in Rehabilitation Counseling, 15*(4), 45–52.

Brodwin, M. G., & Siu, F. W. (2007). Domestic violence against women who have disabilities: What educators need to know. *Education, 127,* 548–551.

Bronfenbrenner, U. (1979). *The ecology of human development: Experiments by nature and design.* Cambridge, MA: Harvard University Press.

Brown, A. S. (1989). A survey on elder abuse at one Native American tribe. *Journal of Elder Abuse & Neglect, 1,* 17–37.

Brown, A. S. (1998). *Perceptions and attitudes toward mistreatment and reporting: A multicultural study* (an analysis of the Native American data). A report submitted to The National Indian Council on Aging and The National Center on Elder Abuse. Washington, DC: Government Printing Office.

Brown, E. J., & Kolko, D. J. (1999). Child victims' attributions about being physically abused: An examination of factors associated with symptom severity. *Journal of Abnormal Child Psychology, 27,* 311–322.

Brown, G. A. (2004). Gender as a factor in the response of the law-enforcement system to violence against partners. *Sexuality and Culture, 8*(3–4), 1–139.

Brown, G. R., & Anderson, B. (1991). Psychiatric morbidity in adult inpatients with childhood histories of sexual and physical abuse. *American Journal of Psychiatry, 148,* 55–61.

Brown, J., Cohen, P., Johnson, J. G., & Salzinger, S. (1998). A longitudinal analysis of risk factors for child maltreatment: Findings of a 17-year prospective study of officially recorded and self-reported child abuse and neglect. *Child Abuse and Neglect, 22,* 1065–1078.

Brown, J., Cohen, P., Johnson, J. G., & Smailes, E. M. (1999). Childhood abuse and neglect: Specificity of effects on adolescents and young adult depression and suicidality. *Journal of the American Academy of Child and Adolescent Psychiatry, 38,* 1490–1496.

Brown, M. J., & Groscup, J. (2009). Perceptions of same-sex domestic violence among crisis center staff. *Journal of Family Violence, 24,* 87–93.

Brown, S. E. (1984). Social class, child maltreatment, and delinquent behavior. *Criminology, 22,* 259–278.

Brown v. Board of Education of Topeka. (1954). (347 U.S. 483, 74 S.Ct. 686).

Browne, A. (1987). *When battered women kill*. New York, NY: Macmillan Free Press.

Browne, A., & Finkelhor, D. (1986). Impact of child sexual abuse: A review of the research. *Psychological Bulletin, 18,* 66–77.

Browne, K., & Herbert, M. (1997). *Preventing family violence*. New York: John Wiley.

Browne, K. D., & Hamilton, C. (1998). Physical violence between young adults and their parents: Associated with a history of child maltreatment. *Journal of Family Violence, 13,* 59–79.

Brownell, P., & Heiser, D. (2006). Psycho-educational support groups for older women victims of family mistreatment: A pilot study. *Journal of Gerontological Social Work, 46,* 145–160.

Brownell, P., & Wolden, A. (2002). Elder abuse intervention strategies: Social service or criminal justice? *Journal of Gerontological Social Work, 40*(1–2), 83–100.

Brubaker, M. D., Garrett, M. T., & Dew, B. J. (2009). Examining the relationship between internalized heterosexism cause substance abuse among lesbian, gay, and bisexual individuals: A critical review. *Journal of LGBT Issues in Counseling, 3*(1), 62–89.

Brutz, J. L., & Allen, C. M. (1986). Religious commitment, peace activism, and marital violence in Quaker families. *Journal of Marriage and the Family, 48,* 491–502.

Brutz, J. L., & Ingoldsby, B. B. (1984). Conflict resolution in Quaker families. *Journal of Marriage and the Family, 46,* 21–26.

Bryant-Davis, T. (2010). Cultural considerations of trauma: Physical, mental and social correlates of intimate partner violence exposure. *Psychological Trauma: Theory, Research, Practice, and Policy, 2*(4), 263–265.

Budd, T., & Mattinson, J. (2000). *Stalking: Findings from the 1998 British Crime Survey*. London, UK: Home Office.

Bufkin, J., & Eschholz, S. (2000). Images of sex and rape: A content analysis of popular film. *Violence Against Women, 6,* 1317–1344.

Buhi, E. R., Clayton, H., & Surrency, H. (2008). Stalking victimization among college women and subsequent help-seeking behaviors. *Journal of American College Health, 57*(4), 419–425.

Bulman, P. (2010). Elder abuse emerges from the shadows of public consciousness. *National Institute of Justice Journal, 265,* 4–9.

Burgess, A. W., Baker, T., Greening, D., Hartman, C., Burgess, A. G., Douglas, J. E., . . . Halloran, R. (1997). Stalking behaviors within domestic violence. *Journal of Family Violence, 12*(4), 389–403.

Burgess, A. W., Harner, H., Baker, T., Hartman, C., & Lole, C. (2001). Batterer stalking patterns. *Journal of Family Violence, 16,* 309–321.

Burgess, E. S., & Wurtele, S. K. (1998). Enhancing parent-child communication about sexual abuse: A pilot study. *Child Abuse and Neglect, 22,* 1167–1175.

Burgess, R. L., & Conger, R. D. (1978). Family interactions in abusive, neglectful, and normal families. *Child Development, 49,* 1163–1173.

Burgess, R. L., Leone, J. M., & Kleinbaum, S. M. (2000). Social and ecological issues in violence toward children. In R. T. Ammerman & M. Hersen (Eds.), *Case studies in family violence* (2nd ed., pp. 15–38). New York, NY: Plenum.

Buri, H., Daly, J. M., Hartz, A. J., & Jogerst, G. J. (2006). Factors associated with self-reported elder mistreatment in Iowa's frailest elders. *Research on Aging, 28*(5), 562–581.

Burke, P. J., Stets, J. E., & Pirog-Good, M. A. (1988). Gender identity, self-esteem, and physical and sexual abuse in dating relationships. *Social Psychology Quarterly, 51*(3), 272–285.

Burke, T. W., Jordan, M. L., & Owen, S. S. (2002). Cross-national comparison of gay and lesbian domestic violence. *Journal of Contemporary Criminal Justice, 18,* 231–257.

Burns, K., Chethik, L., Burns, W. J., & Clark, R. (1991). Dyadic disturbances in cocaine-abusing mothers and their infants. *Journal of Clinical Psychology, 47,* 316–319.

Busch, A., & Rosenberg, M. (2004). Comparing women and men arrested for domestic violence: A preliminary report. *Journal of Family Violence, 19,* 49–58.

Bushman, B. J., & Anderson, C. J. (2001). Media violence and the American public: Scientific facts versus media misinformation. *American Psychologist, 56,* 477–489.

Buttell, F. P., & Carney, M. M. (2002). Psychological and demographic predictors of attrition among batterers court ordered into treatment. *Social Work Research, 26*(1), 31–42.

Button, D. (2008). Social disadvantage and family violence: Neighborhood effects on attitudes about intimate partner violence and corporal punishment. *American Journal of Criminal Justice, 33*(1), 130–147.

Button, D. M., & Gealt, R. (2010). High risk behaviors among victims of sibling violence. *Journal of Family Violence, 25,* 131–140.

Buzawa, E., Austin, T. L., & Buzawa, C. G. (1995). Responding to crimes of violence against women: Gender differences versus organizational imperatives. *Crime and Delinquency, 41,* 443–466.

Buzawa, E., Buzawa, C., & Stark, E. (2011). *Responding to domestic violence: The integration of criminal justice and human services.* Thousand Oaks, CA: Sage.

Buzawa, E. S., Austin, T. L., Bannon, J., & Jackson, J. (1992). Role of victim preference in determining police response to victims of domestic violence. In E. S. Buzawa & C. G. Buzawa (Eds.), *Domestic violence: The changing criminal justice response.* Westport, CT: Auburn House.

Buzawa, E. S., & Buzawa, C. G. (2003). *Domestic violence: The criminal justice response.* Thousand Oaks, CA: Sage.

Buzawa, E. S., Hotaling, G., Klein, A., & Byrne, J. (1999). *Response to domestic violence in a pro-active court setting: Final report.* Washington, DC: National Institute of Justice.

Byrne, C. A., Kilpatrick, D. G., Howley, S. S., & Beatty, D. (1999). Female victims of partner versus nonpartner violence: Experiences with the criminal justice system. *Criminal Justice and Behavior, 26,* 275–292.

Cabral, A., & Coffey, D. (1999). Creating courtroom accessibility. In B. Leventhal & S. Lundy (Eds.), *Same-sex domestic violence: Strategies for change* (pp. 57–69). Thousand Oaks, CA: Sage.

Caesar, P. L. (1988). Exposure to violence in the families-of-origin among wife-abusers and maritally nonviolent men. *Violence and Victims, 3,* 49–63.

Caetano, R., & Cunradi, C. (2003). Intimate partner violence and depression among Whites, Blacks, and Hispanics. *Annals of Epidemiology, 13,* 661–665.

Caetano, R., Cunradi, C., Clark, C. L., & Schaefer, J. (2000). Intimate partner violence and drinking patterns among White, Black, and Hispanic couples in the U.S. *Journal of Substance Abuse, 11*(2), 123–138.

Caetano, R., Vaeth, R. A. C., & Ramisetty-Mikler, S. (2008). Intimate partner violence victim and perpetrator characteristics among couples in the United States. *Journal of Family Violence, 23*(6), 507–518.

Cafaro Schneider, D., Mosqueda, L., Falk, E., & Huba, G. J. (2010). Elder abuse forensic centers. *Journal of Elder Abuse & Neglect, 22,* 255–274.

Cafarro, J. V., & Conn-Cafarro, A. (2005). Treating sibling abuse families. *Aggression and Violent Behavior, 10,* 604–623.

Cahill, L. T., Kaminer, R. K., & Johnson, P. G. (1999). Developmental, cognitive, and behavioral sequalae of child abuse. *Child and Adolescent Psychiatric Clinics of North America, 8,* 827–843.

Cahn, N. (1992). Prosecuting domestic violence crimes. In E. S. Buzawa & C. G. Buzawa (Eds.), *Domestic violence: The changing criminal justice response* (pp. 95–112). Westwood, CT: Auburn House.

Caldwell, M. F. (2002). What we do not know about juvenile sexual reoffense risk. *Child Maltreatment, 7,* 291–302.

Caliso, J. A., & Milner, J. S. (1992). Childhood history of abuse and child abuse screening. *Child Abuse and Neglect, 16,* 647–659.

Camacho, C. M., & Alarid, L. F. (2008). The significance of the victim advocate for domestic violence victims in municipal court. *Violence and Victims, 23*(3), 288–300.

Cameron, P. (2003). Domestic violence among homosexual partners. *Psychological Reports, 93,* 410–416.

Campbell, J., & Soeken, K. L. (1999). Forced sex and intimate partner violence: Effects on women's risk and women's health. *Violence Against Women, 5*(9), 1017–1035.

Campbell, J. C., & Alford, P. (1989). The dark consequences of marital rape. *American Journal of Nursing, 89,* 946–949.

Campbell, R. (1989). *How to really love your child.* Wheaton, IL: Victor Books.

Campbell, R. (2008). The psychological impact of rape victims' experiences with the legal, medical, and mental health systems. *American Psychologist, 63,* 702–717.

Campbell, R. (2009). Rape survivors' experiences with the legal and medical system. *Violence Against Women, 12,* 30–45.

Campbell Reay, A. M., & Browne, K. D. (2002). The effectiveness of psychological interventions with individuals who physically abuse or neglect their elderly dependents. *Journal of Interpersonal Violence, 17,* 416–431.

Cancian, M., Slack, K. S., & Yang, M. Y. (2010). *The Effect of Family Income on Risk of Child Maltreatment.* Retrieved from http://www.irp.wisc.edu.

Candib, L. M. (1999). Incest and other harms to daughters across cultures. *Women's Studies International Forum, 22,* 185–201.

Cantos, A. L., Neale, J. M., & O'Leary, K. D. (1997). Assessment of coping strategies of child abusing mothers. *Child Abuse and Neglect, 21,* 631–636.

Cappell, C., & Heiner, R. B. (1990). The intergenerational transmission of family aggression. *Journal of Family Violence, 5,* 135–151.

Carbone-Lopez, K., Kruttschnitt, C., & MacMillan, R. (2006). Patterns of intimate partner violence and their associations with physical health, psychological distress, and substance use. *Public Health Reports, 121,* 382–392.

Carey, G., & Goldman, D. (1997). Genetics of antisocial behavior. In D. Stoff, J. Brelling, & J. Demiser (Eds.), *Handbook of Antisocial Personality* (pp. 243–254). New York, NY: Wiley.

Carey, T. A. (1994). Spare the rod and spoil the child. Is this a sensible justification for the use of punishment in child rearing? *Child Abuse and Neglect, 18,* 1005–1010.

Carney, M., & Buttell, F. (2005). Exploring the relevance of attachment theory as a dependent variable in the treatment of women mandated into treatment for domestic violence offenses. *Journal of Offender Rehabilitation, 41,* 33–62.

Carney, M., Buttell, F., & Dutton, D. G. (2007). Women who perpetrate intimate partner violence: A review of the literature with recommendations for treatment. *Aggression and Violent Behavior, 12,* 108–115.

Carney, M. M., & Buttell, F. P. (2004). A multidimensional evaluation of a treatment program for female batterers: A pilot study. *Research on Social Work Practice, 14*(4), 249–258.

Carson, D. K. (1995). American Indian elder abuse: Risk and protective factors among the oldest Americans. *Journal of Elder Abuse & Neglect, 7*(1), 17–39.

Carter, P. (2001). *HHS reports new child abuse and neglect statistics* [Electronic Version]. Retrieved August 6, 2012, from http://archive.hhs.gov/news/press/2001pres/20010402.html.

Carter, V., & Myers, M. R. (2007). Exploring the risks of substantiated physical neglect related to poverty and parental characteristics: A national sample. *Children and Youth Services Review, 29*(1), 110–121.

Cascardi, M., Langhinrichsen, J., & Vivian, D. (1992). Marital aggression: Impact, injury, and health correlates for husbands and wives. *Archives of Internal Medicine, 152,* 1178–1184.

Cascardi, M., O'Leary, K. D., Lawrence, E. E., & Schlee, K. A. (1995). Characteristics of women physically abused by their spouses and who seek treatment regarding marital conflict. *Journal of Consulting and Clinical Psychology, 63,* 616–623.

Casey, E. A., Beadnell, B., & Lindhorst, T. P. (2009). Predictors of sexually coercive behavior in a nationally representative sample of adolescent males. *Journal of Interpersonal Violence, 24*(7), 1129–1147.

Catalano, S. (2007). *Intimate partner violence in the United States* [Electronic Version]. Retrieved October 1, 2007, from http://bjs.ojp.usdoj.gov/index.cfm?ty=pbdetail&iid=1000.

Catalano, S., Smith, E., Snyder, H., & Rand, M. (2009). *Female victims of violence.* Washington, DC: The Bureau of Justice Statistics.

Cavanaugh, M., & Gelles, R. J. (2005). The utility of male domestic violence offender typologies: New directions for research, policy and practice. *Journal of Interpersonal Violence, 20*(2), 155–166.

Cazenave, N. A., & Zahn, M. A. (1992). Women, murder, and male domination: Police reports of domestic homicide in Chicago and Philadelphia. In E. C. Viano (Ed.), *Intimate violence: Interdisciplinary perspectives* (pp. 83–96). Washington, DC: Hemisphere.

CBSNews. (2010, May 5). *George Huguely's story of Yeardley Love's death* [Electronic Version]. Retrieved from http://www.cbsnews.com/stories/2010/05/05/earlyshow/main6462429.shtml?tag=mncol;lst;1.

Center for Domestic Violence Prevention. (2003). [Electronic Version]. Retrieved August 6, 2012, from http://www.raisingvoices.org/cedovip.php.

Center for Effective Discipline. (2010). *U.S.: Corporal punishment and paddling statistics by state and race.* Retrieved June 30, 2011, from http://www.stophitting.com/index.php?page=statesbanning.

Center for Elders and the Courts. (2012). *Elder abuse and neglect basics: Elder abuse laws.* National Center for State Courts. Available at http://www.eldersandcourts.org.

Center for Research on Women with Disabilities. (1999). *National study of women with physical disabilities* [Electronic Version]. Retrieved May 4, 2004, from http://www.bcm.edu/ crowd/national_study/national_study.html.

Centers for Disease Control and Prevention. (1997). Rates of homicide, suicide, and firearm-related death among children—26 industrialized countries [Electronic Version]. *Morbidity and Mortality Weekly Report.* Retrieved May 20, 2004, from http://www. cdc.gov/mmwr/preview/mmwrhtml/00046149.htm.

Centers for Disease Control and Prevention. (2002). Variations in homicide risk during infancy-United States, 1989–1998 [Electronic Version]. *Morbidity and Mortality Weekly Report.* Retrieved May 20, 2004, from http://www.cdc.gov/mmwr/preview/mmwrhtml/mm5109a3.htm.

Cercone, J. J., Beach, S. R. H., & Arias, I. (2005). Gender symmetry in dating intimate partner violence: Does similar behavior imply similar constructs? *Violence and Victims, 20*(2), 207–218.

Chaffin, M., Silovsky, J. F., Funderburk, B., Valle, L., Brestan, E. V., Balachova, T., . . . Bonner, B. L. (2004). Parent-child interaction therapy with physically abusive parents: Efficacy for reducing future abuse reports. *Journal of Consulting and Clinical Psychology, 72,* 500–510.

Champion, J., Shain, R., & Piper, J. (2004). Minority adolescent women with sexually transmitted diseases and a history of sexual or physical abuse. *Issues in Mental Health Nursing, 25,* 293–316.

Chan, K. L., Straus, M. A., Brownridge, D. A., Tiwari, A., & Leung, W. C. (2008). Prevalence of dating partner violence and suicidal ideation among male and female university students worldwide. *Journal of Midwifery and Women's Health, 53*(6), 529–537.

Chance, T. (2003, July). *Our children are dying: Understanding and improving national maltreatment fatality data.* Paper presented at the 8th International Family Violence Research Conference, Portsmouth, NH.

Chandy, J. M., Blum, R. W., & Resnick, M. D. (1996). Gender-specific outcomes for sexually abused adolescents. *Child Abuse and Neglect, 20,* 1219–1231.

Chang, D., Shen, B., & Takeuchi, D. (2009). Prevalence and demographic correlates of intimate partner violence in Asian Americans. *International Journal of Law and Psychiatry, 32,* 167–175.

Chang, J., Rhee, S., & Berthold, S. M. (2008). Child abuse and neglect in Cambodian refugee families: Characteristics and implications for practice. *Child Welfare, 87*(1), 141–160.

Chang, J., Siyon, R., & Megan Berthold, S. (2008). Child abuse and neglect in Cambodian refugee families: Characteristics and implications for practice. *Child Welfare, 87*(1), 141–161.

Chang, J. C., Martin, S. L., Moracco, K. E., Dulli, L., Scandlin, D., Loucks-Sorrel, M. B., . . . Bou-Saada, I. (2003). Helping women with disabilities and domestic violence: Strategies, limitations, and challenges of domestic violence programs and services. *Journal of Women's Health, 12*(7), 699–708.

Charles, A. V. (1986). Physically abused parents. *Journal of Family Violence, 1,* 343–355.

Chauhan, P., & Repucci, N. D. (2009). The impact of neighborhood disadvantage and exposure to violence on self-report of antisocial behavior among girls in the juvenile justice system. *Journal of Youth Adolescence, 38,* 401–416.

Chen, J., Dunne, M. P., & Han, P. (2004). Child sexual abuse in China: A study of adolescents in four provinces. *Child Abuse and Neglect, 28*(11), 1171–1186.

Chen, P. N. (1979). A study of Chinese American elderly residing in hotel rooms. *Social Casework, 60*(2), 89–95.

Cheung, M., Leung, P., & Tsui, V. (2009). Asian male domestic violence victims: Services exclusive for men. *Journal of Family Violence, 24,* 447–462.

Child Trends Data Bank. (2009). *Attitudes toward spanking* [Electronic Version]. Retrieved from www.childtrendsdatabank.org/?q=node/187.

Child Trends Data Bank. (2010). *Infant homicide* [Electronic Version]. Retrieved from www .childtrendsdatabank.org/alphalist?q=node/79.

Child Welfare Information Gateway. (2010). *Infant Safe Haven laws: Summary of state laws.* Washington, DC: U.S. Department of Health and Human Services, Administration for Children and Families.

Child Welfare League of America. (n.d.). *Promoting Safe and Stable Families (PSSF) Program* [Electronic Version]. Retrieved October 2003 from http://www.cwla.org/advocacy/pssf.htm.

Child Welfare League of America. (2001). *Alcohol, and other drugs abuse: A critical child welfare issue.* [Electronic Version]. Retrieved January 2004 from http://www.chhs.ca.gov/ initiatives/CAChildWelfareCouncil/Documents/ChildWelfareLeague.pdf.

Child Welfare League of America. (2002). *Juvenile offenders and the death penalty: Is justice served?* [Electronic Version]. Retrieved January 2004 from http://www.cwla.org/programs/ juvenilejustice/juveniledeathpenalty.pdf.

Child Welfare Pre-Service Trainer Guide. (2011). *Effects of abuse and neglect on child development.* Retrieved from http://centerforchildwelfare.fmhi.usf.edu/kb/PreServiceCurriculum/ Core%20108_SP_PG_030111.pdf.

Children's Defense Fund. (2011).*The State of America's Children.* Retrieved from www .childrensdefense.org.

Childs, H. W., Hayslip, B., Jr., Radika, L. M., & Reinberg, J. A. (2000). Young and middle-aged adults' perceptions of elder abuse. *Gerontologist, 40*, 75–85.

ChildStats. (2004). *America's children in brief: Key national indicators of well-being, 2004* [Electronic Version]. Retrieved August 16, 2004, from http://childstats.gov/americaschildren/pdf/ac04brief.pdf.

Christakis, D. A., & Zimmerman, F. J. (2007). Violent television viewing during preschool is associated with antisocial behavior during school age. *Pediatrics, 120*(5), 993–999.

Christian, C. W., Block, R., & Committee on Child Abuse and Neglect. (2009). Abusive head trauma in infants and children. *Pediatrics, 123*, 1409–1411.

Christian, S. (2004). *Substance-exposed newborns: New federal law raises some old issues.* Washington, DC: National Conference of State Legislatures.

Chu, J. A., & Dill, D. L. (1990). Dissociative symptoms in relation to childhood physical and sexual abuse. *American Journal of Psychiatry, 147*, 887–892.

Church, W., Gross, E., & Baldwin, J. (2005). Maybe ignorance is not always bliss: The disparate treatment of Hispanics within the child welfare system. *Children and Youth Services Review, 27*, 1279–1292.

Cisler, J. M., Begle, A. M., Amstadter, A. B., & Acierno, R. (2012). Mistreatment and self-reported emotional symptoms: Results from the national elder mistreatment study. *Journal of Elder Abuse & Neglect, 24*(3), 216–230.

Clain, S. H., & Leppel, K. (2001). An investigation into sexual orientation discrimination as an explanation for wage differences. *Applied Economics, 33*(1), 37–47.

Clements-Nolle, K., Marx, R., Guzman, R., & Katz, M. (2001). HIV prevalence, risk behaviors, health care use, and mental health status of transgender persons: Implications for public health intervention. *American Journal of Public Health, 91*, 915–921.

Cohen, D. (1996). Law, social policy, and violence: The impact of regional cultures. Law, social policy, and violence. *Journal of Personality and Social Psychology, 70*, 961–978.

Cohen, E. S. (2001). The complex nature of ageism: What is it? Who does it? Who perceives it? *Gerontologist, 41*(5), 576–577.

Cohen, J. A., Deblinger, E., Mannarino, A. P., & Steer, R. A. (2004). A multisite, randomized controlled trial for children with sexual abuse-related PTSD symptoms. *Journal of the American Academy of Child and Adolescent Psychiatry, 43*, 393–402.

Cohen, J. A., & Mannarino, A. P. (1997). A treatment study for sexually abused preschool children: Outcome during a one-year follow-up. *Journal of the American Academy of Child and Adolescent Psychiatry, 36*, 1228–1235.

Cohen, J. A., & Mannarino, A. P. (2000). Incest. In R. T. Ammerman & M. Hersen (Eds.), *Case studies in family violence* (2nd ed., pp. 209–230). New York, NY: Kluwer.

Cohen, J. A., Mannarino, A. P., & Deblinger, E. (2006). *Treating trauma and traumatic grief in children and adolescents.* New York, NY: Guilford.

Cohen, J. A., Mannarino, A. P., & Knudsen, K. (2004). Treating childhood traumatic grief: A pilot study. *Journal of the American Academy of Child and Adolescent Psychiatry, 43*(10), 1225–1233.

Cohen, J. A., Mannarino, A. P., & Knudsen, K. (2005). Treating sexually abused children: One year follow-up of a randomized control trial. *Child Abuse and Neglect, 29*, 135–145.

Cohen, J. A., Perel, J. M., DeBellis, M. D., Friedman, M. J., & Putnam, F. W. (2002). Treating traumatized children: Clinical implications of the psychobiology of posttraumatic stress disorder. *Trauma, Violence, & Abuse, 3*, 91–108.

Cohen, L. J., Gans, S. W., McGeoch, P. G., Poznnsky, O., Itskovich, Y., Murphy, S., . . . Galynker, I. I. (2002). Impulsive personality traits in male pedophiles versus healthy controls: Is pedophilia an impulsive-aggressive disorder? *Comprehensive Psychiatry, 43*, 127–134.

Cohen, P., Brown, J., & Smailes, E. M. (2001). Child abuse and neglect and the development of mental disorders in the general population. *Development and Psychopathology, 13,* 981–999.

Cohn, A. H., & Daro, D. (1987). Is treatment too late: What ten years of evaluative research tells us. *Child Abuse and Neglect, 11,* 433–442.

Coker, A., Smith, P., McKeown, R., & King, M. (2000). Frequency and correlates of intimate partner violence by type: Physical, sexual, and psychological battering. *American Journal of Public Health, 90*(4), 553–559.

Coker, A. L., Davis, K. E., Arias, I., Desai, S., Sanderson, M., Brandt, H. M., . . . Smith, P. H. (2002). Physical and mental health effects of intimate partner violence for men and women. *American Journal of Preventive Medicine, 23*(4), 260–268.

Coker, A. L., Weston, R., Creson, D. L., Justice, B., & Blakeney, P. (2005). PTSD symptoms among men and women survivors of intimate partner violence: The role of risk and protective factors. *Violence and Victims, 20,* 625–643.

Cole, E. (1982). Sibling incest: The myth of benign sibling incest. *Women and Therapy, 1,* 79–89.

Collins, J. J., & Messerschmidt, P. M. (1993). Epidemiology of alcohol-related violence. *Alcohol Health and Research World, 17,* 93–101.

Comijs, H. C., Penninx, B. W., Knipscheer, K. P., & van Tilburg, W. (1999). Psychological distress in victims of elder mistreatment: The effects of social support and coping. *Journal of Gerontology: Series B: Psychological Sciences and Social Sciences, 54B,* 240–245.

Committee on the Rights of the Child. (2006). *Convention on the Rights of the Child.* United Nations, 42nd session. New York, NY: Office of the United Nations High Commissioner for Human Rights.

Compton, S. A., Flanagan, P., & Gregg, W. (1997). Elder abuse in people with dementia in Northern Ireland: Prevalence and predictors in cases referred to a psychiatry of old age service. *International Journal of Geriatric Psychiatry, 12,* 632–635.

Comstock, G. D. (1991). The police as perpetrators of anti-gay/lesbian violence. In G. D. Comstock (Ed.), *Violence against lesbians and gay men* (pp. 152–162, Appendix C). New York, NY: Columbia University Press.

Connolly, C., Huzurbazar, S., & Routh-McGee, T. (2000). Multiple parties in domestic violence situations and arrest. *Journal of Criminal Justice, 28,* 181–188.

Connolly, M.-T. (2010). Where elder abuse and the justice system collide: Police power, *parens patriae,* and 12 recommendations. *Journal of Elder Abuse & Neglect, 22,* 37–93.

Coohey, C. (1995). Neglectful mothers, their mothers, and partners: The significance of mutual aid. *Child Abuse and Neglect, 19,* 885–895.

Coohey, C. (2000). The role of friends, in-laws, and other kin in father-perpetrated child abuse. *Child Welfare, 79,* 373–402.

Coohey, C., & Braun, N. (1997). Toward an integrated framework for understanding child physical abuse. *Child Abuse and Neglect, 21,* 1081–1094.

Cook, P. W. (2009). *Abused men: The hidden side of domestic violence* (2nd ed.). Wesport, CT: Praeger.

Cooney, C., Howard, R., & Lawlor, B. (2006). Abuse of vulnerable people with dementia by their carers: Can we identify those most at risk? *International Journal of Geriatric Psychiatry, 41*(21), 564–571.

Cooper, A., & Smith, E. (2011). *Homicide trends in the United States, 1980–2008.* Bureau of Justice Statistics. Retrieved from http://www.bjs.ojp.usdoj.gov.

Cooper, C., Selwood, A., & Livingston, G. (2009). Knowledge, detection, and reporting of abuse by health and social care professionals: A systematic review. *American Journal of Geriatric Psychiatry, 17*(10), 826–838.

Cope, K. (2010). The age of discipline: The relevance of age to the reasonableness of corporal punishment. *Law and Contemporary Problems, 73,* 167–188.

Copenhaver, S., & Grauerholz, E. (1991). Sexual victimization among sorority women: Exploring the links between sexual violence and institutional practices. *Sex Roles, 24*(1–2), 31–41.

Corliss, H. L., Cochran, S. D., & Mays, V. M. (2002). Reports of parental maltreatment during childhood in a United States population based survey of homosexual, bisexual and heterosexual adults. *Child Abuse and Neglect, 26,* 1165–1178.

Cormier, B. M., Angliker, C. C. J., Gagne, P. W., & Markus, B. (1978). Adolescents who kill a member of the family. In J. M. Eekelaar & S. N. Katz (Eds.), *Family violence: An international and interdisciplinary study* (pp. 466–478). Toronto, CA: Butterworth.

Cornell, C. P., & Gelles, R. J. (1982). Adolescent to parent violence. *Urban and Social Change Review, 15,* 8–14.

Cosmos, C. (2011). *Abuse of children with disabilities* [Electronic Version]. Retrieved from http://www.cec.sped.org/AM/Template.cfm?Section=Home&CAT=none&TEMPLATE=/CM/ContentDisplay.cfm&CONTENTID=1298.

Cottrell, B. (2001). *Parent abuse: The abuse of parents by their teenage children.* Retrieved December 20, 2011, from http://www.canadiancrc.com/PDFs/Parent_Abuse-Abuse_of_Parents_by_Their_Teenage_Children_2001.pdf.

Coyne, A. C., Reichman, W. E., & Berbig, L. J. (1993). The relationship between dementia and elder abuse. *American Journal of Psychiatry, 150,* 643–646.

Craft, S. M., & Serovich, J. M. (2005). Family-of-origin factors and partner violence in the intimate relationships of gay men who are HIV positive. *Journal of Interpersonal Violence, 20*(7), 777–791.

Craig, M. E., Kalichman, S., & Follingstad, D. R. (1989). Verbal coercive sexual behavior among college students. *Archives of Sexual Behavior, 18,* 421–434.

Craig Shea, M. E. (1998). When the tables are turned: Verbal sexual coercion among college women. In P. B. Anderson & C. Struckman-Johnson (Eds.), *Sexually aggressive women: Current perspectives and controversies* (pp. 94–104). New York, NY: Guilford Press.

Cramer, E. P., & Plummer, S. (2010). Social work practice with abused persons with disabilities. In L. L. Lockhart & F. S. Danis (Eds.), *Domestic violence: Intersectionality and culturally competent practice.* New York, NY: Columbia University Press.

Crittenden, P. M. (1992). Children's strategies for coping with adverse home environments: An interpretation using attachment theory. *Child Abuse and Neglect, 16,* 329–343.

Crittenden, P. M. (1999). Child neglect: Causes and contributors. In H. Dubowitz (Ed.), *Neglected children: Research, practice, and policy* (pp. 47–68). Thousand Oaks, CA: Sage.

Crittenden, P. M., Claussen, A. H., & Sugarman, D. B. (1994). Physical and psychological maltreatment in middle childhood and adolescence. *Development and Psychopathology, 6,* 145–164.

Cross, T. P., Walsh, W. A., Simone, M., & Jones, L. M. (2003). Prosecution of child abuse: A meta-analysis of rates of criminal justice decisions. *Trauma, Violence & Abuse, 4,* 323–340.

Crossmaker, M. (1991). Behind locked doors: Institutional sexual abuse. *Sexuality and Disability, 9,* 201–218.

Crouch, J., Hanson, R., Saunders, B., Kilpatrick, D., & Resnick, H. (2000). Income, race/ethnicity, and exposure to violence in youth: Results from the National Survey of Adolescents. *Journal of Community Psychology, 28*(6), 625–641.

Crouch, J. L. (2000). Income, race/ethnicity, and exposure to violence in youth: Results from the National Survey of Adolescents. *Journal of Community Psychology, 28,* 625–641.

Crouch, J. L., Risser, H. J., Skowronski, J. J., Milner, J. S., Farc, M. M., & Irwin, L. M. (2010). Does accessibility of positive and negative schema vary by child physical abuse risk? *Child Abuse and Neglect: The International Journal, 34,* 886–895.

Cruz, J. M., & Firestone, J. M. (1998). Exploring violence and abuse in gay male relationships. *Violence and Victims, 13,* 159–173.

Cuevas, C., & Sabina, C. (2010). *Final report: Sexual assault among Latinas (SALAS) study.* Boston, MA: Northeastern University; Middletown, PA: Penn State Harrisburg.

Cullen, B. J., Smith, P. H., Funk, J. B., & Haaf, R. A. (2000). A matched cohort comparison of a criminal justice system's response to child sexual abuse: A profile of perpetrators. *Child Abuse and Neglect, 24,* 569–577.

Culp, R. E., Little, V., Letts, D., & Lawrence, H. (1991). Maltreated children's self-concept: Effects of a comprehensive treatment program. *American Journal of Orthopsychiatry, 61,* 114–121.

Cunradi, C. B., Caetano, R., Clark, C., & Schafer, J. (2000). Neighborhood poverty as a predictor of intimate partner violence among White, Black, and Hispanic couples in the United States. *Annals of Epidemiology, 10,* 297–308.

Cupach, W. R., & Spitzberg, B. H. (2004). *The dark side of relationship pursuit: From attraction to obsession and stalking.* Mahwah, NJ: Erlbaum.

Curry, M. A., Renker, P., Hughes, R. B., Robinson-Whelen, S., Oschwald, M. M., Swank, P., . . . Powers, L.E. (2009). Development of measures of abuse among women with disabilities and the characteristics of their perpetrators. *Violence Against Women, 15*(9), 1001–1025.

Curry, M. A., Renker, P., Robinson-Whelen, S., Hughes, R. B., Swank, P., Oschwald, M. M., & Powers, L. E. (2011). Facilitators and barriers to disclosing abuse among women with disabilities. *Violence and Victims, 26*(4), 430–444.

Curtis, P. A., & McCullough, C. (1993). The impact of alcohol and other drugs on the child welfare system. *Child Welfare, 72,* 533–542.

Cuskey, W. R., & Wathey, B. (1982). *Female addiction.* Lexington, MA: Lexington Books.

Cyr, M., Wright, J., McDuff, P., & Perron, A. (2002). Intrafamilial sexual abuse: Brother-sister incest does not differ from father-daughter and stepfather-stepdaughter incest. *Child Abuse and Neglect, 26,* 957–973.

D'Augelli, A. R. (1992). Lesbian and gay male undergraduates' experiences of harassment and fear on campus. *Journal of Interpersonal Violence, 7,* 383–395.

D'Augelli, A. R., & Grossman, A. H. (2001). Disclosure of sexual orientation, victimization, and mental health among lesbian, gay, and bisexual older adults. *Journal of Interpersonal Violence, 16,* 1008–1027.

D'Augelli, A. R., Grossman, A. H., & Starks, M. T. (2008). Families of lesbian, gay, and bisexual youth: What do parents and siblings know and how do they react? *Journal of GLBT Family Studies, 4,* 95–115.

Dadds, M., Smith, M., Weber, Y., & Robinson, A. (1991). An exploration of family and individual profiles following father-daughter incest. *Child Abuse and Neglect, 15,* 575–586.

Dallam, S. J., Gleaves, D. H., Cepeda-Benito, A., Silberg, J. L., Kraemer, H. C., & Spiegel, D. (2001). The effects of child sexual abuse: Comment on Rind, Tromovitch, and Bauserman (1998). *Psychological Bulletin, 127,* 715–733.

Daly, M., Wilson, M., Salmon, C. A., Hiraiwa-Hasegawa, M., & Hasegawa, T. (2001). Siblicide and seniority. *Homicide Studies, 5,* 30–45.

Daniels, R. S., Baumhover, L. A., Formby, W. A., & Clark-Daniels, C. L. (1999). Police discretion and elder mistreatment: A nested model of observation, reporting, and satisfaction. *Journal of Criminal Justice, 27,* 209–225.

Daro, D. (1991). Prevention programs. In C. Hollin & K. Howells (Eds.), *Clinical approaches to sex offenders and their victims* (pp. 285–306). New York, NY: John Wiley.

Daro, D. (1994). Prevention of child sexual abuse. *The Future of Children, 4*(2), 198–223.

Daro, D. (2002). Public perception of child abuse: Who is to blame? *Child Abuse and Neglect, 26,* 1131–1133.

Daro, D., & Cohn, A. (1988). Child maltreatment evaluation efforts: What have we learned? In G. Hotaling, D. Finkelhor, J. Kirkpatrick & M. A. Straus (Eds.), *Coping with family violence: Research and policy perspectives* (pp. 275–287). Newbury Park, CA: Sage.

Daro, D., & Connelly, A. C. (2002). Child abuse prevention: Accomplishments and challenges. In J. E. B. Myers, L. Berliner, J. Briere, C. T. Hendrix, C. Jenny & T. A. Reid (Eds.), *The APSAC handbook on child maltreatment* (2nd ed., pp. 431–448). Thousand Oaks, CA: Sage.

Daro, D., Edelson, J. L., & Pinderhughes, H. (2004). Finding common ground in the study of child maltreatment, youth violence, and adult domestic violence. *Journal of Interpersonal Violence, 19,* 282–298.

Daro, D., & Gelles, R. J. (1992). Public attitudes and behaviors with respect to child abuse prevention. *Journal of Interpersonal Violence, 7*(4), 517–531.

Daro, D., & Harding, K. (1999). Healthy Families America: Using research to enhance practice. *Future of Children, 9,* 152–176.

Davidson, H. (1988). Failure to report child abuse: Legal penalties and emerging issues. In A. Maney & S. Wells (Eds.), *Professional responsibility in protecting children* (pp. 93–103). New York, NY: Praeger.

Davidson, H. (1997). The legal aspects of corporal punishment in the home: When does physical discipline cross the line to become child abuse? *Children's Legal Rights Journal, 17,* 18–29.

Davis, K. C., Stoner, S. A., Norris, J., George, W. H., & Masters, N. T. (2009). Women's awareness of and discomfort with sexual assault cues: Effects of alcohol consumption and relationship type. *Violence Against Women, 15*(9), 1106–1125.

Davis, K. E., Ace, A., & Andra, M. (2000). Stalking perpetrators and psychological maltreatment of partners: Anger-jealousy, attachment insecurity, need for control, and breakup context. *Violence and Victims, 15,* 407–425.

Davis, R. C., & Smith, B. E. (1995). Domestic violence reforms: Empty promises of fulfilled expectations. *Crime and Delinquency, 41,* 541–552.

Davis, R. C., Smith, B. E., & Nickles, L. (1998). Prosecuting domestic violence cases with reluctant victims: Assessing two novel approaches in Milwaukee. In *Legal interventions in family violence: Research findings and policy implications* (pp. 71–72). Washington, DC: National Institute of Justice and the American Bar Association.

Davis, R. C., Taylor, B. G., & Maxwell, C. D. (1998). Does batterer treatment reduce violence? A randomized experiment in Brooklyn. *Justice Quarterly, 18,* 171–201.

Day, N. L., & Richardson, G. A. (1994). Comparative teratogenicity of alcohol and other drugs. *Alcohol Health and Research World, 18,* 42–48.

Death Penalty Information Center. (2012). *Number of executions by state and region since 1976* [Electronic Version]. Retrieved April 9, 2012, from http://www.deathpenaltyinfo.org/number-executions-state-and-region-1976.

Deblinger, E., Lippmann, J., & Steer, R. A. (1999). Two-year follow-up study of cognitive behavioral therapy for sexually abused children suffering posttraumatic stress symptoms. *Child Abuse and Neglect, 23,* 1371–1378.

Deblinger, E., Mannarino, A. P., Cohen, J. A., & Steer, R. A. (2006). A follow-up study of a multisite, randomized, controlled trial for children with sexual abuse-related PTSD symptoms. *Journal of the American Academy of Child and Adolescent Psychiatry, 45,* 1474–1484.

Deblinger, E., McLeer, S. V., Atkins, M. S., Ralphe, D., & Foa, E. (1989). Post-traumatic stress in sexually abused, physically abuse, and non-abused children. *Child Abuse and Neglect, 13,* 403–408.

Deblinger, E., McLeer, S. V., & Henry, D. E. (1990). Cognitive behavioral treatment for sexually abused children suffering post-traumatic stress: Preliminary findings. *Journal of the American Academy of Child and Adolescent Psychiatry, 29,* 747–752.

Dehon, C., & Weems, C. F. (2010). Emotional development in the context of conflict: The indirect effects of interparental violence on children. *Journal of Child and Family Studies, 19,* 287–297.

DeJong, A. R. (1998). Impact of child sexual abuse medical examinations on the dependency and criminal systems. *Child Abuse and Neglect, 22,* 645–652.

DeKeseredy, W. S., & Schwartz, M. D. (2001). Definitional issues. In C. M. Renzetti, J. L. Edleson, & R. K. Bergen (Eds.), *Sourcebook on violence against women* (pp. 23–34). Thousand Oaks, CA: Sage.

Del Rio, C. M., & White, L. J. (2012). Separating spirituality from religiosity: A hylomorphic attitudinal perspective. *Psychology of Religion and Spirituality, 4*(2), 123–142.

Deley, W. W. (1988). Physical punishment of children: Sweden and the U.S.A. *Journal of Comparative Family Studies, 19,* 419–431.

Dell'Anno, M. (2012, February 6). Chief Deputy City Attorney of the San Diego Domestic Violence Unit. [Personal communication].

DeLozier, P. P. (1982). Attachment theory and child abuse. In M. Parkes & J. Stevenson-Hindle (Eds.), *The place of attachment in human behavior* (pp. 95–117). New York, NY: Basic Books.

DePanfilis, D. (1999). Intervening with families when children are neglected. In H. Dubowitz (Ed.), *Neglected children: Research, practice, and policy* (pp. 211–236). Thousand Oaks, CA: Sage.

DePanfilis, D. (2011). Child protection system. In J. E. B. Myers (Ed.), *The APSAC handbook on child maltreatment* (3rd ed., pp. 39–52). Thousand Oaks, CA: Sage.

Derlega, V. J., Winstead, B. A., Pearson, M. R., Janda, L. J., Dutton, L. B., Ferrer, R., . . . Greene, K. (2011). Unwanted pursuit in same-sex relationships: Effects of attachment styles, investment model variables, and sexual minority stressors. *Partner Abuse, 2*(3), 300–322.

DeShaney v. Winnebago County Department of Social Services. (1989). (489 U.S. 189, No. 87–154).

Desmarais, S. L., & Reeves, K. A. (2007). Gray, black, and blue: The state of research and intervention for intimate partner abuse among elders. *Behavioral Sciences and the Law, 25,* 377–391.

Dias, M., Smith, K., deGuehery, K., Mazur, P., Li, V., & Shaffer, M. (2005). Preventing abusive head trauma among infants and young children: A hospital-based parent education program. *Pediatrics, 115,* e470–e477.

DiLalla, L. F., & Gottesman, I. I. (1991). Biological and genetic contributors to violence: Widom's untold tale. *Psychological Bulletin, 109,* 125–129.

DiPlacido, J. (1998). Minority stress among lesbians, gay men, and bisexuals: A consequence of heterosexism, homophobia, and stigmatization. In G. Herek (Ed.), *Stigma and sexual orientation: Understanding prejudice against lesbians, gay men, and bisexuals* (pp. 138–159). Thousand Oaks, CA: Sage.

Dobash, R. E., & Dobash, R. P. (1988). Research as social action: The struggle for battered women. In K. Yllo & M. Bograd (Eds.), *Feminist perspectives on wife abuse* (pp. 51–74). Newbury Park, CA: Sage.

Dobash, R. P., Dobash, R. E., Wilson, M., & Daly, M. (1992). The myth of sexual symmetry in marital violence. *Social Problems, 39,* 71–91.

Dobson, J. C. (1987). *Parenting isn't for cowards.* Waco, TX: Word Books.

Dodge, K. A., Bates, J. E., & Pettit, G. S. (1990). Mechanisms in the cycle of violence. *Science, 250,* 1678–1683.

Dodge, K. A., Pettit, G. S., & Bates, J. E. (1994). Socialization mediators of the relation between socioeconomic status and child conduct problems. *Child Development, 65,* 649–665.

Doege, D. (2002a). *Battered, torn, but not broken: For many older women, love hurts* [Electronic Version]. Retrieved December 5, 2003, from http://www.jsonline.com/lifestyle/people/ju102/56906.asp.

Doege, D. (2002b). *Women find solace, strength to leave in support group* [Electronic Version]. Retrieved December 5, 2003, from http://www.jsonline.com/lifestyle/people/ ju102/56895.asp.

Dolz, L., Cerezo, M. A., & Milner, J. S. (1997). Mother-child interactional patterns in high- and low-risk mothers. *Child Abuse and Neglect, 21,* 1149–1158.

Domestic Abuse Helpline for Men and Women (2011). Available at www.dahmw.org.

Dong, M., Anda, R. F., Felitti, V. J., Dube, S. R., Williamson, D. F., Thompson, T. J., . . . Giles, W. H. (2004). The interrelatedness of multiple forms of childhood abuse, neglect, and household dysfunction. *Child Abuse and Neglect, 28,* 771–784.

Dong, X. (2005). Medical implications of elder abuse and neglect. *Clinics in Geriatric Medicine, 21*(2), 293–313.

Dong, X., Simon, M. A., Gorbien, M., Percak, J., & Golden, R. (2007). Loneliness in older Chinese adults: A risk factor for elder mistreatment. *Journal of American Geriatric Society, 55*(11), 1831–1835.

Donnelly, D. A., Cook, K. J., & Wilson, L. (1999). Provision and exclusion: The dual face of services to battered women in three Deep South states. *Violence Against Women, 5,* 710–741.

Donohue, B. C., Romero, V., Herdzik, K., Lapota, H., Abdel Al, R., Allen, D. N., . . . Van Hasselt, V. B. (2010). Concurrent treatment of substance abuse, child neglect, bipolar disorder, post-traumatic stress disorder, and domestic violence: A case examination involving family behavior therapy. *Clinical Case Studies, 9*(2), 106–124.

Dopke, C. A., & Milner, J. S. (2000). Impact of child compliance on stress appraisals, attributions, and disciplinary choices in mothers at high and low risk for child physical abuse. *Child Abuse and Neglect, 24,* 493–504.

Douglas, E. M., & Hines, D. A. (2011). The helpseeking experiences of men who sustain intimate partner violence: An overlooked population and implications for practice. *Journal of Family Violence, online first*. Retrieved from http://www.ncbi.nlm.nih.gov/pubmed/21935262.

Douglas, H. (1991). Assessing violent couples. *Families in Society, 72,* 525–535.

Doumas, D. M., Pearson, C. L., Elgin, J. E., & McKinley, L. L. (2008). Adult attachment as a risk factor for intimate partner violence: The "mispairing" of partners' attachment styles. *Journal of Interpersonal Violence, 23,* 616–634.

Dowd, L., Leisring, P. A., & Rosenbaum, A. (2005). Partner aggressive women: Characteristics and treatment attrition. *Violence and Victims, 20*(2), 219–233.

Downs, W. R., & Miller, B. A. (1998). Relationships between experiences of parental violence during childhood and women's psychiatric symptomatology. *Journal of Interpersonal Violence, 13,* 438–455.

Drake, B., Lee, S. M., & Jonson-Reid, M. (2009). Race and child maltreatment reporting: Are Blacks overrepresented? *Children and Youth Services Review, 31*(3), 309–316.

Drake, B., & Pandey, S. (1996). Understanding the relationship between neighborhood poverty and specific types of child maltreatment. *Child Abuse and Neglect, 20,* 1003–1018.

Dubowitz, H. (Ed.). (1999). *Neglected children: Research, practice, and policy.* Thousand Oaks, CA: Sage.

Dubowitz, H. (2007). Understanding and addressing the "neglect of neglect": Digging into the molehill. *Child Abuse and Neglect, 31,* 603–606.

Dubowitz, H., Black, M. M., Cox, C. E., Kerr, M. A., Litrownik, A. J., Radhakrishna, A., . . . Runyan, D. K. (2001). Father involvement and children's functioning at age 6: A multi-site study. *Child Maltreatment, 6,* 300–309.

Dubowitz, H., Kim, J., Black, M. M., Weisbart, C., Semiatin, J., & Magder, L. S. (2011). Identifying children at high risk for a child maltreatment report. *Child Abuse and Neglect, 35,* 96–104.

Dubowitz, H., Klockner, A., Starr, R. H., & Black, M. M. (1998). Community and professional definitions of child neglect. *Child Maltreatment, 3,* 235–243.

Duke, A., & Davidson, M. M. (2009). Same-sex intimate partner violence: Lesbian, gay and bisexual affirmative outreach and advocacy. *Journal of Aggression, Maltreatment & Trauma, 18,* 795–816.

Duminy, F. J., & Hudson, D. A. (1993). Assault inflicted by hot water. *Burns, 19,* 426–428.

DuMont, K., Mitchell-Herzfeld, S., Greene, R., Lee, E., Lowenfels, A., Rodriguez, M., . . . Dorabawila, V. (2008). Healthy Families New York (HFNY) randomized trial: Effects on early child abuse and neglect. *Child Abuse and Neglect, 32,* 295–315.

Duncan, D. F. (1990). Prevalence of sexual assault victimization among heterosexual and gay/lesbian university students. *Psychological Reports, 66,* 65–66.

Duncan, J. W., & Duncan, G. M. (1971). Murder in the family. *American Journal of Psychiatry, 127,* 74–78.

Duncan, L. E., & Williams, L. M. (1998). Gender role socialization and male-on-male vs. female-on-male child sexual abuse. *Sex Roles, 39,* 765–785.

Duncan, R. D. (1999). Peer and sibling aggression: An investigation of intra- and extra-familial bullying. *Journal of Interpersonal Violence, 14*(8), 871–886.

Dunford, F. W., Huizinga, D., & Elliott, D. (1989). The role of arrest in domestic assault: The Omaha Police Experiment. *Criminology 28,* 183–206.

Dunham, K., & Senn, C. Y. (2000). Minimizing negative experiences: Women's disclosure of partner abuse. *Journal of Interpersonal Violence, 15,* 251–261.

Dupont-Morales, M. A. (1998). The female stalker. In L. J. Moriarty & R. A. Jerin (Eds.), *Current Issues in Victimology Research* (pp. 223–238). Durham, NC: Carolina Academic Press.

Dupont-Morales, M. A. (1999). De-gendering predatory violence: The female stalker. *Humanity and Society 23,* 366–379.

Dupper, D. R., & Montgomery-Dingus, A. E. (2008). Corporal punishment in U.S. public schools: A continuing challenge for school social workers. *Children and Schools, 30*(4), 243–250.

Duran, B., Malcoe, L. H., Sanders, M., Waitzkin, H., Skipper, B., & Yager, J. (2004). Child maltreatment prevalence and mental disorders outcomes among American Indian women in primary care. *Child Abuse & Neglect, 28*(2), 131–145.

Duran, B., Oetzel, J., Parker, T., Malcoe, L. H., Lucero, J., & Jiang, Y. (2009). Intimate partner violence and alcohol, drug, and mental disorders among American Indian women in primary care. *American Indian Alaskan Native Mental Health Research, 16*(2), 11–27.

DuRant, R., Champion, H., Wolfson, M., Omli, M., McCoy, T., D'Agostino, R. B., . . . Mitra, A. (2007). Date fighting experiences among college students: Are they associated with other health-risk behaviors? *Journal of American College Health, 55*(5), 291–296.

Durst, D. (1991). Conjugal violence: Changing attitudes in two northern Native communities. *Community Mental Health Journal, 27,* 359–373.

Dutcher-Walls, P. (1999). Sociological directions in feminist biblical studies. *Social Compass, 46,* 441–453.

Dutton, D. G. (1985). An ecologically nested theory of male violence toward intimates. *International Journal of Women's Studies, 8,* 404–413.

Dutton, D. G. (1995). Male abusiveness in intimate relationships. *Clinical Psychology Review, 15,* 567–581.

Dutton, D. G. (2005). Domestic abuse assessment in child custody disputes: Beware the domestic violence research paradigm. *Journal of Child Custody, 2,* 23–42.

Dutton, D. G. (2007). *The abusive personality: Violence and control in intimate relationships* (2nd ed.). New York, NY: Guilford.

Dutton, D. G., & Corvo, K. (2006). Transforming a flawed policy: A call to revive psychology and science in domestic violence research and practice. *Aggression and Violent Behavior, 11,* 457–483.

Dutton, D. G., Saunders, K., Starzomski, A. J., & Bartholomew, K. (1994). Intimacy anger and insecure attachment as precursors of abuse in intimate relationships. *Journal of Applied Social Psychology, 24*(15), 1367–1386.

Dutton, D. G., & Strachan, C. E. (1987). Motivational needs for power and spouse-specific assertiveness in assaultive and nonassaultive men. *Violence and Victims, 2,* 145–156.

Dutton, L. B., & Winstead, B. A. (2006). Predicting unwanted pursuit: Attachment, relationship satisfaction, relationship alternatives, and breakup distress. *Journal of Social and Personal Relationships, 23*(4), 565–586.

Dutton, M. A. (1996). *Critique of the "battered woman syndrome" model* [Electronic Version]. Retrieved March 22, 2004, from http://www.vaw.umn.edu/documents/ vawnet/bws/bws.html.

Dye, M. L., & Davis, K. E. (2003). Stalking and psychological abuse: Common factors and relationship-specific characteristics. *Violence and Victims, 18*(2), 163–180.

Dyselin, C. W., & Thomsen, C. J. (2005). Religiosity and risk of perpetrating child physical abuse: An empirical investigation. *Journal of Psychology & Theology, 33,* 291–298.

Eaton, L., Kaufman, M., Fuhrel, A., Cain, D., Cherry, C., Pope, H., . . . Kalichman, S. E. (2008). Examining factors co-existing with interpersonal violence in lesbian relationships. *Journal of Family Violence, 23,* 697–705.

Eckenrode, J., Laird, M., & Doris, J. (1993). School performance and disciplinary problems among abused and neglected children. *Developmental Psychology, 29,* 53–62.

Eckstein, N. J. (2004). Emergent issues in families experiencing adolescent-to-parent abuse. *Western Journal of Communications, 68*(4), 365–388.

Egeland, B., & Erickson, M. F. (1987). Psychologically unavailable caregiving. In M. Brassard, B. Germain, & S. Hart (Eds.), *Psychological maltreatment of children and youth* (pp. 110–120). Elmsford, NY: Pergamon.

Egeland, B., & Sroufe, L. A. (1981). Developmental sequelae of maltreatment in infancy. In B. Rizley & D. Cicchetti (Eds.), *New directions for child development: Developmental perspectives in child maltreatment* (pp. 77–92). San Francisco, CA: Jossey-Bass.

Egeland, B., Sroufe, L. A., & Erickson, M. F. (1983). Developmental consequences of different patterns of maltreatment. *Child Abuse and Neglect, 7,* 456–469.

Egelko, B. (2009, October 13). *Schwarzenegger signs ammo-regulation bill* [Electronic Version]. Retrieved from http://www.sfgate.com/cgi-bin/article.cgi?f=/c/a/2009/10/12/BA551A4M82.DTL.

Ehrensaft, M. K., Cohen, P., Brown, J., Smailes, E., Chen, H., & Johnson, J. G. (2003). Intergenerational transmission of partner violence: A 20-year prospective study. *Journal of Consulting and Clinical Psychology, 71*(4), 741–753.

Ehrensaft, M. K., Moffitt, T. E., & Caspi, A. (2004). Clinically abusive relationships in an unselected birth cohort: Men's and women's participation and developmental antecedents. *Journal of Abnormal Psychology, 113*(2), 258–271.

Ehrensaft, M. K., Moffitt, T. E., & Caspi, A. (2006). Is domestic violence followed by an increased risk of psychiatric disorders among women but not among men? A longitudinal cohort study. *American Journal of Psychiatry, 163*(5), 885–892.

Eigenberg, H., McGuffee, K., Berry, P., & Hall, W. (2003). Protective order legislation: Trends in state statutes. *Journal of Criminal Justice, 31,* 411–422.

Elder Abuse and Neglect Act and Related Laws. (2009). Springfield, IL: Department on Aging. Available at http://www.state.il.us/aging/1news_pubs/publications/ea-act_book.pdf.

Elder Justice Coalition. (n.d.). *Elder Justice Act Summary*. Available at http://www.elderjusti cecoalition.com/docs/EJA-Summary-772010.pdf.

Elliott, D., Browne, K., & Kilcoyne, J. (1995). Child sexual abuse prevention: What offenders tell us. *Child Abuse and Neglect, 19, 579–584*.

Elliott, D. M. (1994). Impaired object relations in professional women molested as children. *Psychotherapy, 21, 79–86*.

Elliott, D. M., & Briere, J. (1992). Sexual abuse trauma among professional women: Validating the Trauma Symptom Checklist-40 (TSC-40). *Child Abuse and Neglect, 16, 391–398*.

Elliott, D. M., & Briere, J. (1994). Forensic sexual abuse evaluations of older children: Disclosures and symptomatology. *Behavioral Sciences and the Law, 12, 261–277*.

Elliott, K., & Urquiza, A. (2006). Ethnicity, culture and child maltreatment. *Journal of Social Issues, 62(4), 787–809*.

Elliott, M. (1993). *Female sexual abuse of children: The ultimate taboo*. New York, NY: John Wiley.

Elliott, P. (1996). Shattering illusions: Same-sex domestic violence. In C. M. Renzetti & C. H. Miley (Eds.), *Violence in gay and lesbian domestic partnerships* (pp. 107–116). New York, NY: Harrington Park Press.

Ellison, C. G., Bartkowski, J. P., & Segal, M. L. (1996). Conservative Protestantism and the parental use of corporal punishment. *Social Forces, 74, 1003–1028*.

Ellison, C. G., & Bradshaw, M. (2009). Religious beliefs, sociopolitical ideology, and attitudes toward corporal punishment. *Journal of Family Issues, 30(3), 320–340*.

Ellison, C. G., Burr, J. A., & McCall, P. L. (2003). The enduring puzzle of Southern homicide: Is regional religious culture the missing piece? *Homicide Studies, 7, 326–352*.

Ellison, C. G., & Sherkat, D. E. (1993). Conservative Protestantism and support for corporal punishment. *American Sociological Review, 58, 131–144*.

Ellison, C. G., Trinitapoli, J. A., Anderson, K. L., & Johnson, B. R. (2007). Race/ethnicity, religious involvement, and domestic violence. *Violence Against Women, 13(11), 1094–1112*.

Ellsberg, E., Jansen, H., Heise, L., Watts, C. H., & Garcia-Moreno, C. (2008). Intimate partner violence and women's physical and mental health in the WHO multi-country study on women's health and domestic violence: An observational study. *The Lancelet, 371*, 1165–1172.

Emery, R. E. (1989). Family violence. *American Psychologist, 44, 321–328*.

Emery, R. E., & Laumann-Billings, L. (1998). An overview of the nature, causes and consequences of abusive family relationships: Toward differentiating maltreatment and violence. *American Psychologist, 53, 121–135*.

Englander, E. K. (1997). *Understanding violence*. Mahwah, NJ: Lawrence Erlbaum.

English, D., Upadhyaya, M., Litrownik, A. J., Marshall, J., Runyan, D., Graham, J., . . . Dubowitz, H. (2005). Maltreatment's wake: The relationship of maltreatment dimensions to child outcome. *Child Abuse and Neglect, 29(5), 597–619*.

Ensign, C., & Jones, P. (2007). Gender-inclusive work with victims and their children in a co-ed shelter. In J. Hamel & T. Nicholls (Eds.), *Family interventions in domestic violence: A handbook of gender-inclusive theory and treatment* (pp. 561–578). New York: Springer.

Epstein, D. (1999). Effective intervention in domestic violence cases: Rethinking the roles of prosecutors, judges, and the court system. *Yale Journal of Law and Feminism, 11, 3–50*.

Erickson, M. F., & Egeland, B. (2011). Child neglect. In J. E. B. Myers (Ed.), *The APSAC handbook on child maltreatment* (3rd ed., pp. 103–124). Thousand Oaks, CA: Sage.

Erickson, M. F., Egeland, B., & Pianta, R. C. (1989). The effects of maltreatment on the development of young children. In D. Cicchetti & V. Carlson (Eds.), *Child maltreatment: Theory and research on the causes and consequences of child abuse and neglect* (pp. 647–684). New York, NY: Cambridge University Press.

Erickson, W., Lee, C., & von Schrader, S. (2011). *Disability statistics from the 2009 American Community Survey (ACS)*. Ithaca, NY: Cornell University Rehabilitation Research and Training Center on Disability Demographics and Statistics (StatsRRTC).

Eron, L. D. (1997). The development of antisocial behavior from a learning perspective. In D. M. Stoff, J. Breiling, & J. D. Maser (Eds.), *Handbook of antisocial behavior* (pp. 140–147). New York, NY: John Wiley.

European Network of Ombudsmen for Children. (2001). *The European Network of Ombudsmen for Children (ENOC) seeks an end to all corporal punishment of children in Europe.* Statement released both at the European Seminar on Ending all Physical Punishment of Children and at the European Congress on Child Abuse and Neglect, Barcelona, Spain, October 19, 2001.

Evans-Campbell, T. (2008). Historical trauma in American Indian/Native Alaska communities. *Journal of Interpersonal Violence, 23*(3), 316–338.

Evans-Campbell, T., Lindhorst, T., Huang, B., & Walters, K. (2006). Interpersonal violence in the lives of urban American Indian and Alaska Native women: Implications for health, mental health, and help-seeking. *American Journal of Public Health, 96*(8), 1416–1422.

Evans, E. D., & Warren-Sohlberg, L. (1988). A pattern analysis of adolescent abusive behavior toward parents. *Journal of Adolescent Research, 3,* 201–216.

Ewoldt, C. A., Monson, C. M., & Langhinrichsen-Rohling, J. (2000). Attributions about rape in a continuum of dissolving marital relationships. *Journal of Interpersonal Violence, 15*(11), 1175–1182.

Ezzell, C. E., Swenson, C. C., & Brondino, M. J. (2000). The relationship of social support to physically abused children's adjustment. *Child Abuse and Neglect, 24,* 641–651.

Fagan, J., & Browne, A. (1994). Violence between spouses and intimates: Physical aggression between women and men in intimate relationships. In A. J. Reiss & J. A. Roth (Eds.), *Understanding and preventing violence* (Vol. 3, pp. 115–292). Washington, DC: National Research Council, National Academy of Sciences.

Fajnzylber, P., Lederman, D., & Loayza, N. (2001). *Inequality and violent crime* [Electronic Version]. Retrieved August 21, 2001, from http://poverty.worldbank.org/library/topic/3362/12830/.

Fals-Stewart, W. (2003). The occurrence of partner physical aggression on days of alcohol consumption: A longitudinal diary study. *Journal of Consulting and Clinical Psychology, 71,* 41–52.

Family Equality Council. (2012, Feb. 12). *Second-parent adoption laws.* Retrieved from http://www.familyequality.org/get_informed/equality_maps/second-parent_adoption_laws/.

Family Violence Prevention Fund. (1993). *Men beating women: Ending domestic violence— A qualitative and quantitative study of public attitudes on violence against women.* San Francisco, CA: Author.

Famularo, R., Fenton, T., & Kinscherff, R. T. (1992). Medical and developmental histories of maltreated children. *Clinical Pediatrics, 31,* 536–541.

Fantuzzo, J. W., delGaudio, W. A., Atkins, M., Meyers, R., & Noone, M. (1998). A contextually relevant assessment of the impact of child maltreatment on the social competencies of low-income urban children. *Journal of the American Academy of Child and Adolescent Psychiatry, 37,* 1201–1208.

Farc, M. M., Crouch, J. L., Skowronski, J. J., & Milner, J. S. (2008). Hostility ratings by parents at risk for child physical abuse: Impact of chronic and temporary schema activation. *Child Abuse and Neglect, 32,* 177–193.

Fargo, J. D. (2009). Pathways to adult sexual revictimization: Direct and indirect behavioral risk factors across the lifespan. *Journal of Interpersonal Violence, 24,* 1771–1791.

Farrell, W. (1993). *The myth of male power.* New York, NY: Berkley Books.

Fathers for Life. (2006). *Allen Wells—Battered husband—divorce—suicide.* Retrieved December 13, 2011, from http://fathersforlife.org/suicides/Allen_Wells/key_page.htm.

Featherman, J. M. (1995). Jews and sexual child abuse. In L. A. Fontes (Ed.), *Sexual abuse in nine North American cultures: Treatment and prevention* (pp. 128–155). Thousand Oaks, CA: Sage.

Feder, L., & Forde, D. R. (2000). *A test of the efficacy of court-mandated counseling for domestic violence offenders: The Broward experiment.* Washington, DC: National Institute of Justice.

Feder, L., & Wilson, D. (2005). A meta-analytic review of court-mandated batterer intervention programs. *Journal of Experimental Criminology, 1*(2), 239–262.

Federal Bureau of Investigation. (2010a). *Crime in the United States—2009.* Washington, DC: U.S. Department of Justice.

Federal Bureau of Investigation. (2010b). *Crime in the United States, 2010.* Retrieved November 26, 2011, from http://www.fbi.gov/about-us/cjis/ucr/crime-in-the-u.s/2010/crime-in-the-u.s.-2010/tables/10shrtb110.xls.

Federal Bureau of Investigation. (2010c). *Uniform Crime Reports: Hate Crime Statistics* [Electronic Version]. Retrieved February 12, 2012, from http://www.fbi.gov/about-us/cjis/ucr/hate-crime/2010/narratives/hate-crime-2010-victims.

Federman, J. (Ed.). (1998). *National television violence study executive summary* (Vol. 3). Santa Barbara: University of California. Retrieved from http://www.saybrook.edu/sites/default/files/faculty/NTVVSexecsum.pdf.

Feiring, C., & Taska, L. (2005). The persistence of shame following sexual abuse: A longitudinal look at risk and recovery. *Child Maltreatment, 10,* 337–349.

Feiring, C., Taska, L., & Lewis, M. (1999). Age and gender differences in children's and adolescent's adaptation to sexual abuse. *Child Abuse and Neglect, 23,* 115–128.

Feld, S., & Felson, R. (2008). Gender norms and retaliatory violence against spouses and acquaintances. *Journal of Family Issues, 29*(5), 692–703.

Feld, S. L., & Straus, M. A. (1989). Escalation and desistance of wife abuse in marriage. *Criminology, 27*(1), 141–161.

Feldman, R. S., Salzinger, S., Rosario, M., Hammer, M., Alvarado, L., & Caraballo, L. (1989). *Parent and teacher ratings of abused and non-abused children's behavior.* New York, NY: American Academy of Child Psychiatry.

Felson, R. B. (2002). *Violence and gender reexamined.* Washington, DC: American Psychological Association.

Felson, R. B., & Messner, S. F. (2000). The control motive in intimate partner violence. *Social Psychology Quarterly, 63,* 86–94.

Ferrari, A. M. (2002). The impact of culture upon child rearing practices and definitions of maltreatment. *Child Abuse and Neglect, 26,* 793–813.

Ferraro, K. J. (2003). The words change, but the melody lingers: The persistence of the battered woman syndrome in criminal cases involving battered women. *Violence Against Women, 9,* 110–129.

Ferraro, K. J., & Johnson, J. M. (1983). How women experience battering: The process of victimization. *Social Problems, 30,* 325–339.

Fiebert, M. S., & Gonzalez, D. M. (1997). College women who initiate assaults on their male partners and the reasons offered for such behavior. *Psychological Reports, 80,* 583–590.

Fiebert, M. S., & Tucci, L. M. (1998). Sexual coercion: Males victimized by females. *Journal of Men's Studies, 6,* 127–133.

Fields, S. D., Malebranche, D., & Feist-Price, S. (2008). Childhood sexual abuse in black men who have sex with men: Results from three qualitative studies. *Cultural Diversity and Ethnic Minority Psychology 14,* 385–390.

Finkelhor, D. (1979). *Sexually victimized children*. New York, NY: Free Press.

Finkelhor, D. (1980). Sex among siblings: A survey of prevalence, variety, and effects. *Archives of Sexual Behavior, 9,* 171–193.

Finkelhor, D. (1984). *Child sexual abuse: New theory and research*. New York, NY: Free Press.

Finkelhor, D. (1993). Epidemiological factors in the clinical identification of child sexual abuse. *Child Abuse and Neglect, 17,* 67–70.

Finkelhor, D. (1994). Current information on the scope and nature of child sexual abuse. *Future of Children, 4,* 31–53.

Finkelhor, D. (2005). The main problem is underreporting child abuse and neglect. In D. R. Loseke, R. J. Gelles, & M. M. Cavanaugh (Eds.), *Current controversies on family violence* (2nd ed., pp. 299–310). Thousand Oaks, CA: Sage.

Finkelhor, D. (2008). *Childhood victimization: Violence, crime, and abuse in the lives of young people*. New York, NY: Oxford University Press.

Finkelhor, D., Hotaling, G. T., Lewis, J. A., & Smith, C. (1990). Sexual abuse in a national survey of adult men and women: Prevalence, characteristics, and risk factors. *Child Abuse and Neglect, 14,* 19–28.

Finkelhor, D., Jones, L., & Shattuck, A. (2011). *Updated trends in child maltreatment, 2010* [Electronic Version]. Retrieved from http://www.unh.edu/ccrc/pdf/CV203_Updated%20 trends%202010%20FINAL_12-19-11.pdf.

Finkelhor, D., Ormrod, R., & Turner, H. A. (2009). Lifetime assessment of polyvictimization in a national sample of children and youth. *Child Abuse and Neglect, 33,* 403–411.

Finkelhor, D., & Redfield, D. (1984). How the public defines sexual abuse. In D. Finkelhor (Ed.), *Child sexual abuse: New theory and research*. New York, NY: Free Press.

Finkelhor, D., & Strapko, N. (1992). Sexual abuse prevention education: A review of evaluation studies. In D. J. Willis, E. Holden, & M. Rosenberg (Eds.), *Prevention of child maltreatment: Developmental and ecological perspectives* (pp. 150–167). New York, NY: John Wiley.

Finkelhor, D., Turner, H. A., Ormrod, R., & Hamby, S. L. (2009). Violence, abuse, and crime exposure in a national sample of children and youth. *Pediatrics, 124,* 1411–1423.

Finkelhor, D., & Yllo, K. (1983). Rape in marriage: A sociological view. In D. Finkelhor, R. J. Gelles, G. T. Hotaling, & M. A. Straus (Eds.), *The dark side of families* (pp. 119–130). Beverly Hills, CA: Sage.

Finkelhor, D., & Yllo, K. (1985). *License to rape: Sexual abuse of wives*. New York, NY: Holt, Rinehart & Winston.

Finney, A. (2006). *Domestic violence, sexual assault and stalking: Findings from the 2004/05 British crime survey*. London, UK: Research Development and Statistics Directorate, Home Office.

Fisher, B. S., Cullen, F. T., & Turner, M. G. (2000). *The sexual victimization of college women*. Washington, DC: National Institute of Justice and Bureau of Justice Statistics.

Fisher, B. S., Cullen, F. T., & Turner, M. G. (2002). Being pursued: Stalking victimization in a national study of college women. *Criminology and Public Policy, 1*(2), 257–308.

Fisher, B. S., Daigle, L. E., Cullen, F. T., & Turner, M. G. (2003). Reporting sexual victimization to the police and others: Results from a national-level study of college women. *Criminal Justice and Behavior, 30*(1), 6–38.

Fisher, B. S., & Regan, S. L. (2006). The extent and frequency of abuse in the lives of older women and their relationship with health outcomes. *Gerontologist, 46*(2), 200–209.

Fisher, M. (2011). Map: U.S. ranks near bottom on income inequality. *The Atlantic*. Retrieved from http://www.theatlantic.com/international/archive/2011/09/map-us-ranks-near-bottom -on-income-inequality/245315/.

Fitzgerald, M. M., Schneider, R. A., Salstrom, S., Zinzow, H. M., Jackson, J., & Fossel, R. V. (2008). Child sexual abuse, early family risk, and childhood parentification: Pathways to current psychosocial adjustment. *Journal of Family Psychology, 22,* 320–324.

Fitzpatrick, M. J., & Hamill, S. B. (2011). Elder abuse: Factors related to perceptions of severity and likelihood of reporting. *Journal of Elder Abuse & Neglect, 23*(1), 1–16.

Fitzpatrick, M. K., Salgado, D. M., Suvak, M. K., King, L. A., & King, D. W. (2004). Associations of gender and gender-role ideology with behavioral and attitudinal features of intimate partner aggression. *Psychology of Men & Masculinity, 5*(2), 91–102.

Flanzer, J. R. (2005). Alcohol and other drugs are key causal agents of violence. In D. R. Loseke, R. J. Gelles, & M. M. Cavanaugh (Eds.), *Current controversies on family violence* (2nd ed.). Thousand Oaks, CA: Sage.

Fleck-Henderson, A. (2000). Domestic violence in the child protection system: Seeing double. *Children and Youth Services Review, 22,* 333–354.

Fleming, J., Mullen, P., & Bammer, G. (1997). A study of potential risk factors for sexual abuse in childhood. *Child Abuse and Neglect, 21,* 49–58.

Fleming, J. M. (1997). Prevalence of childhood sexual abuse in a community sample of Australian women. *Medical Journal of Australia, 166,* 65–68.

Flicker, S. M., Cerulli, C., Zhao, X., Tang, W., Watts, A., Xia, Y., . . . Talbot, N. L. (2011). Concomitant forms of abuse and help-seeking behavior among white, African American, and Latina women who experience intimate partner violence. *Violence Against Women, 17*(8), 1067–1085.

Flisher, A. J., Kramer, R. A., Hoven, C. W., Greenwald, S., Alegria, M., Bird, H. R., . . . Moore, R. E. (1997). Psychosocial characteristics of physically abused children and adolescents. *Journal of the American Academy of Child and Adolescent Psychiatry, 36,* 123–131.

Flores, S. A., & Hartlaub, M. G. (1998). Reducing rape-myth acceptance in male college students: A meta-analysis of intervention studies. *Journal of College Student Development, 39,* 438–448.

Flowers, R. B. (1984). Withholding medical care for religious reasons. *Journal of Religion and Health, 23,* 268–282.

Fluke, J. D., Schusterman, G. R., Hollinshead, D. M., & Yuan, Y. Y. T. (2008). Longitudinal analysis of repeated child abuse reporting and victimization: Multistate analysis of associated factors. *Child Maltreatment, 13*(1), 76–88.

Fluke, J. D., Yuan, Y. T., Hedderson, J., & Curtis, P. A. (2003). Disproportionate representation of race and ethnicity in child maltreatment: Investigation and victimization. *Children and Youth Services Review, 25*(5/6), 359–373.

Flynn, C. P. (1998). To spank or not to spank: The effect of situation and age of child on support for corporal punishment. *Journal of Family Violence, 13,* 21–37.

Follingstad, D., Helff, C., Binford, R., Runge, M., & White, J. (2004). Lay persons' versus psychologists' judgments of psychologically aggressive actions by a husband and wife. *Journal of Interpersonal Violence, 19*(8), 916–942.

Follingstad, D. R., Bradley, R. G., Laughlin, J. E., & Burke, L. K. (1999). Risk factors and correlates of dating violence: The relevance of examining frequency and severity levels in a college sample. *Violence and Victims, 14*(4), 365–380.

Follingstad, D. R., Brennan, A. F., Hause, E. S., Polek, D. S., & Rutledge, L. L. (1991). Factors moderating physical and psychological symptoms of battered women. *Journal of Family Violence, 6,* 81–95.

Follingstad, D. R., Rutledge, L. L., Berg, B. J., Hause, E. S., & Polek, D. S. (1990). The role of emotional abuse in physically abusive relationships. *Journal of Family Violence, 5,* 107–120.

Follingstad, D. R., Wright, S., Lloyd, S., & Sebastian, J. A. (1991). Sex differences in motivations and effects in dating violence. *Family Relations, 40,* 51–57.

Fontes, L. A., Cruz, M., & Tabachnick, J. (2001). Views of child sexual abuse in two cultural communities: An exploratory study among African Americans and Latinos. *Child Maltreatment, 6,* 103–117.

Forbes, G. B., & Adams-Curtis, L. E. (2001). Experiences with sexual coercion in college males and females: Role of family conflict, sexist attitudes, acceptance of rape myths, self-esteem, and the big-five personality factors. *Journal of Interpersonal Violence, 16,* 865–889.

Forbes, G. B., Adams-Curtis, L. E., & White, K. B. (2004). First- and second-generation measures of sexism, rape myths and related beliefs, and hostility in college students' experiences with dating aggression and sexual coercion. *Violence Against Women, 10,* 236–261.

Ford, D. A. (1983). Wife battery and criminal justice: A study of victim decision-making. *Family Relations, 32*(463–475).

Ford, H. H., Schindler, C. B., & Medway, F. J. (2001). School professionals' attributions of blame for child sexual abuse. *Journal of School Psychology, 39,* 25–44.

Foss, L. L., & Warnke, M. A. (2003). Fundamentalist Protestant Christian women: Recognizing cultural and gender influences on domestic violence. *Counseling & Values, 48*(1), 14.

Fossos, N., Kaysen, D., Neighbors, C., Lindgren, K. P., & Hove, M. C. (2011). Coping motives as a mediator of the relationship between sexual coercion and problem drinking in college students. *Addictive Behaviors, 36,* 1001–1007.

Foubert, J. D. (2000). The longitudinal effects of a rape-prevention program on fraternity men's attitudes, behavioral intent, and behavior. *Journal of American College Health, 48,* 158–163.

Foubert, J. D., & Marriott, K. A. (1997). Effects of a sexual assault peer education program on men's beliefs in rape myths. *Sex Roles, 36,* 259–268.

Fox, J. A., & Zawitz, M. W. (2002). *Homicide trends in the United States* [Electronic Version]. Retrieved August 16, 2004, from http://www.ojp.usdoj.gov/bjs/homicide/ homtrnd.htm.

Fraser, B. (1986). A glance at the past, a gaze at the present, a glimpse at the future: A critical analysis of the development of child abuse reporting statutes. *Journal of Juvenile Law, 10,* 641–686.

Fraser, C., Olsen, E., Lee, K., Southworth, C., & Tucker, S. (2010). The new age of stalking: Technological implications for stalking. *Juvenile and Family Court Journal, 61*(4), 39–55.

Fray-Witzer, E. (1999). Twice abused: Same-sex domestic violence and the law. In B. Leventhal & S. Lundy (Eds.), *Same-sex domestic violence: Strategies for change* (pp. 19–42). Thousand Oaks, CA: Sage.

Freisthler, B., Bruce, E., & Needell, B. (2007). Understanding the geospatial relationship of neighborhood characteristics and rates of maltreatment for black, Hispanic, and white children. *Social Work, 52*(1), 7–16.

Freisthler, B., Gruenewald, P. J., Ring, L., & LaScala, E. A. (2008). An ecological assessment of the population and environmental correlates of childhood accident, assault, and child abuse injuries. *Alcoholism: Clinical and Experimental Research, 32,* 1969–1975.

Freisthler, B., Gruenewald, P. J., Remer, L. G., Lery, B., & Needell, B. (2007). Exploring the spatial dynamics of alcohol outlets and Child Protective Services referrals, substantiations, and foster care entries. *Child Maltreatment, 12,* 114–124.

Freyd, J. J. (2002). Memory and dimensions of trauma: Terror may be "all-too-well-remembered" and betrayal buried. In J. R. Conte (Ed.), *Critical issues in child sexual abuse: Historical, legal, and psychological perspectives* (pp. 139–173). Thousand Oaks, CA: Sage.

Fried, S. (2001). *Cognitive, economic, and ethnic diversity among maltreated children with disabilities abusing children.* Paper presented at the 13th National Conference on Child Abuse and Neglect. Retrieved December 2003 from http:// nccanch.acf.hhs.gov/profess/conferences/cbconference/resourcebook/140.cfm.

Friedrich, J. (1988). A model program for training religious leaders to work with abuse. In A. L. Horton & J. A. Williamson (Eds.), *Abuse and religion: When praying isn't enough* (pp. 181–187). Lexington, MA: Lexington Books.

Friedrich, W. N. (2001). *Psychological assessment of sexually abused children and their families*. Thousand Oaks, CA: Sage.

Frieze, I. H. (1983). Investigating the causes and consequences of marital rape. *Signs, 8,* 532–553.

Frodi, A. M., & Lamb, M. E. (1980). Child abusers' responses to infants' smiles and cries. *Child Development, 51,* 238–241.

Frye, V., Manganello, J., Campbell, J., Walton-Moss, B., & Wilt, S. (2006). The distribution of and factors associated with intimate terrorism and situational couple violence among a population-based sample of urban women in the United States. *Journal of Interpersonal Violence, 21*(10), 1286–1313.

Fugate, M., Landis, L., Riordan, K., Naureckas, S., & Engel, B. (2005). Barriers to domestic violence help seeking. *Violence Against Women, 11*(3), 290–310.

Fulmer, T., Paveza, G., VandeWeerd, C., Fairchild, S., Guadagno, L., Bolton-Blatt, M., . . . Norman, R. (2005). Dyadic vulnerability and risk profiling for elder neglect. *Gerontologist, 45*(4), 525–534.

Fyfe, J. J., Klinger, D. A., & Flavin, J. (1997). Differential police treatment of male-on-female spousal violence. *Criminology, 35,* 455–473.

Gabler, M., Stern, S., & Miserandino, M. (1998). Latin American, Asian, and American cultural differences in perception of spousal abuse. *Psychological Reports, 83,* 587–592.

Gallagher, E. (2004). Youth who victimise their parents. *Australian and New Zealand Journal of Family Therapy, 25*(2), 94–105.

Gallegos, A. (2011, Sept.19). Miracle vs. medicine: When faith puts care at risk. *Amednews, 11,* pp. 1–6.

Ganzarain, R. (1992). Narcissistic and borderline personality disorders in cases of incest. *Group Analysis, 25,* 491–494.

Garbarino, J., & Collins, C. C. (1999). Child neglect: The family with a hole in the middle. In H. Dubowitz (Ed.), *Neglected children: Research, practice, and policy* (pp. 1–23). Thousand Oaks, CA: Sage.

Garbarino, J., & Kostelny, K. (1992). Child maltreatment as a community problem. *Child Abuse and Neglect, 16,* 455–464.

Garbarino, J., & Sherman, D. (1980). High-risk neighborhoods and high-risk families: The human ecology of child maltreatment. *Child Development, 51,* 188–198.

Gargiulo, R. M., & Kilgo, J. L. (2005). *Young children with special needs*. Clifton Park, NY: Thomson.

Garner, J., Fagan, J. A., & Maxwell, C. (1995). Published findings from the spouse assault replication program: A critical review. *Journal of Quantitative Criminology, 11*(1), 3–28.

Garner, J., & Maxwell, C. (2000). What are the lessons of the police arrest studies? In S. Ward & D. Finkelhor (Eds.), *Program evaluation and family violence research* (pp. 83–114). New York, NY: Routledge.

Garner, J., & Maxwell, C. (2008). *The crime control effects of prosecuting intimate partner violence in Hamilton County, Ohio: Reproducing and extending the analyses of Wooldredge and Thistlewaite*. Department of Justice. Document number 222907. Washington, DC: Government Printing Office.

Gates, G. J., & Cooke, A. M. (2011). *Census Snapshot: 2010* [Electronic Version]. Retrieved February 12, 2012, from http://williamsinstitute.law.ucla.edu.

Gaudin, J. M. (1993). Effective interventions with neglectful families. *Criminal Justice & Behavior, 20,* 66–89.

Gaudin, J. M. (1999). Child neglect: Short-term and long-term outcomes. In H. Dubowitz (Ed.), *Neglected children: Research, practice, and policy* (pp. 89–108). Thousand Oaks, CA: Sage.

Gaudin, J. M., Polansky, N. A., Kilpatrick, A. C., & Shilton, P. (1996). Family functioning in neglectful families. *Child Abuse and Neglect, 20,* 363–377.

Gay Men's Domestic Violence Project. (2011). [Electronic Version]. Retrieved December 3, 2011, from http://gmdvp.org/about-us/services/.

Gebo, E. (2002). A contextual exploration of siblicide. *Violence and Victims, 17,* 157–168.

Geeraert, L., Van den Noorgate, W., Grietens, H., & Onghena, P. (2004). The effects of early prevention programs for families with young children at risk for physical child abuse and neglect: A meta-analysis. *Child Maltreatment, 9*(3), 277–291.

Gelles, R. J. (1974). *The violent home: A study of physical aggression between husbands and wives.* Beverly Hills, CA: Sage.

Gelles, R. J. (1992). Poverty and violence toward children. *American Behavioral Scientist, 35,* 258–274.

Gelles, R. J. (1999). Male offenders: Our understanding from the data. In M. Harway & J. M. O'Neil (Eds.), *What causes men's violence against women?* (pp. 36–48). Thousand Oaks, CA: Sage.

Gelles, R. J. (2000). Controversies in family preservation programs. *Journal of Aggression, Maltreatment, and Trauma, 3,* 239–252.

Gelles, R. J. (2005). Protecting children is more important than preserving families. In D. R. Loseke, R. J. Gelles, & M. M. Cavanaugh (Eds.), *Current controversies on family violence* (2nd ed., pp. 329–340). Thousand Oaks, CA: Sage.

Gelles, R. J., & Cavanaugh, M. M. (2005). Association is not causation: Alcohol and other drugs do not cause violence. In D. R. Loseke, R. J. Gelles, & M. M. Cavanaugh (Eds.), *Current controversies on family violence* (2nd ed.). Thousand Oaks, CA: Sage.

Gelles, R. J., & Straus, M. A. (1988). *Intimate violence: The causes and consequences of abuse in the American family.* New York, NY: Simon & Schuster.

Gelles, R. J., & Straus, M. A. (1990). The medical and psychological costs of family violence. In M. A. Straus & R. J. Gelles (Eds.), *Physical violence in American families: Risk factors and adaptations to violence in 8,145 families* (pp. 425–430). New Brunswick, NJ: Transaction.

George, D., Phillips, M., Doty, L., Umhau, J., & Rawlings, R. (2006). A model linking biology, behavior and psychiatric diagnoses in perpetrators of domestic violence. *Medical Hypotheses, 67,* 345–353.

George, W. H., Cue, K. L., Lopez, P. A., Crowe, L. C., & Norris, J. (1995). Self-reported alcohol expectancies and postdrinking sexual inferences about women. *Journal of Applied Social Psychology, 25,* 164–186.

Gershater-Molko, R. M., Lutzker, J. R., & Welsh, D. (2003). Project SafeCare: Improving health, safety, and parenting skills in families reported for, and at-risk for child maltreatment. *Journal of Family Violence, 18,* 377–386.

Gershoff, E. T. (2002). Corporal punishment by parents and associated child behaviors and experiences: A meta-analytic and theoretical review. *Psychological Bulletin, 128,* 539–579.

Gershoff, E. T. (2008). *Report on physical punishment in the United States: What research tells us about its effects on children.* Columbus, OH: Center for Effective Discipline.

Gershoff, E. T., Miller, P. C., & Holden, G. W. (1999). Parenting influences from the pulpit: Religious affiliation as a determinant of parental corporal punishment. *Journal of Family Psychology, 13,* 307–320.

Gesson, L. (2004, June 25). *Domestic violence against people with disabilities: The untold story* [Electronic Version]. Retrieved from http://www.unitedspinal.org/publications/action/2004/06/25/domestic-violence-against-people-with-disabilities-the-untold-story/.

Gewirtz, A. H., & Edelson, J. L. (2007). Young children's exposure to intimate partner violence: Towards a developmental risk and resilience framework for research and intervention. *Journal of Family Violence, 22,* 151–163.

Ghetti, S., Alexander, K. W., & Goodman, G. S. (2002). Legal involvement in child sexual abuse cases: Consequences and interventions. *International Journal of Law and Psychiatry, 25,* 235–251.

Giardino, A. P., Hudson, K. M., & Marsh, J. (2003). Providing medical evaluations for possible child maltreatment to children with special health care needs. *Child Abuse and Neglect, 27,* 1179–1186.

Gidycz, C. A., Orchowski, L., King, C., & Rich, C. L. (2008). Sexual victimization and health-risk behaviors: A prospective analysis of college women. *Journal of Interpersonal Violence, 23*(6), 744–763.

Gil, E. (2006). *Helping abused and traumatized children.* New York, NY: Guilford.

Gil, V. E. (1988). In thy father's house: Self-report findings of sexually abused daughters from conservative Christian homes. *Journal of Psychology and Theology, 16,* 144–152.

Giles-Sims, J. (1983). *Wife battering: A systems theory approach.* New York, NY: Guilford Press.

Giles-Sims, J. (1998). The aftermath of partner violence. In J. L. Jasinski & L. M. Williams (Eds.), *Partner violence: A comprehensive review of 20 years of research* (pp. 44–72). Thousand Oaks, CA: Sage.

Giles-Sims, J., Straus, M. A., & Sugarman, D. B. (1995). Child, maternal, and family characteristics associated with spanking. *Family Relations, 44*(2), 170–178.

Gillham, B., Tanner, G., Cheyne, B., Freeman, I., Rooney, M., & Lambie, A. (1998). Unemployment rates, single parent density, and indices of child poverty: Their relationship in different categories of child abuse and neglect. *Child Abuse and Neglect, 22,* 79–90.

Gilligan, P. (2009). Considering religion and beliefs in child protection and safeguarding work: Is any consensus emerging? *Child Abuse Review, 18,* 94–110.

Giordano, P. C., Millhollin, T. J., Cernkovich, S. A., Pugh, M. D., & Rudolph, J. L. (1999). Delinquency, identity, and women's involvement in relationship violence. *Criminology, 37,* 17–37.

Giorgio, G. (2002). Speaking silence: Definitional dialogues in abusive lesbian relationships. *Violence Against Women, 8*(10), 1233–1259.

Giovannoni, J., & Billingsley, A. (1970). Child neglect among the poor: A study of parental adequacy in families of three ethnic groups. *Child Welfare, 49,* 196–204.

Giovannoni, J. M., & Becerra, R. M. (1979). *Defining child abuse.* New York, NY: Free Press.

Girshick, L. B. (2002a). No sugar, no spice: Reflections on research on woman-to-woman sexual violence. *Violence Against Women, 8,* 1500–1520.

Girshick, L. B. (2002b). *Woman-to-woman sexual violence: Does she call it rape?* Boston, MA: Northeastern University Press.

Gladue, B. A., Boechler, M., & McCaul, K. D. (1989). Hormonal response to competition in human males. *Aggressive Behavior, 15,* 409–422.

Glass, N., Rollins, C., & Bloom, T. (2009). Expanding our vision: Using a human rights framework to strengthen our service response to female victims of male intimate partner violence. In D. J. Whitaker & J. R. Lutzker (Eds.), *Preventing partner violence: Research and evidence-based intervention strategies* (pp. 193–217). Washington, DC: American Psychological Association.

Gleason, W. J. (1993). Mental disorders in battered women: An empirical study. *Violence and Victims, 8,* 53–68.

Glenn, N., & Marquardt, E. (2001). *Hooking up, hanging out, and hoping for Mr. Right: College women on dating and mating today.* New York, NY: Institute for American Values.

Globus-Goldberg, N. (2001). *An emotional abuse survivor's story* [Electronic Version]. Retrieved November 13, 2012, from http://www.springtideresources.org/resource/emotional-abuse-survivors-story-nancy.

Glock, C. Y., & Stark, R. (1965). *Religion and society in tension.* Chicago, IL: Rand McNally.

Godbout, N., Dutton, D. G., Lussier, Y., & Sabourin, S. (2009). Early exposure to violence, domestic violence, attachment representations, and marital adjustment. *Personal Relationships, 16,* 365–384.

Goddard, A. B., & Hardy, T. (1999). Assessing the lesbian victim. In B. Leventhal & S. Lundy (Eds.), *Same-sex domestic violence: Strategies for change* (pp. 193–200). Thousand Oaks, CA: Sage.

Godkin, M. A., Wolf, R. S., & Pillemer, K. A. (1989). A case-comparison analysis of elder abuse and neglect. *International Journal of Aging and Human Development, 28,* 207–225.

Gold, E. R. (1986). Long-term effects of sexual victimization in childhood: An attributional approach. *Journal of Consulting and Clinical Psychology, 54,* 471–475.

Goldberg, R. T., Pachas, W. N., & Keith, D. (1999). Relationship between traumatic events in childhood and chronic pain. *Disability and Rehabilitation: An International Multidisciplinary Journal, 21,* 23–30.

Goldblatt, H. (2003). Strategies of coping among adolescents experiencing interparental violence. *Journal of Interpersonal Violence, 18*(5), 532–552.

Goldenson, J., Geffner, R., Foster, S., & Clipson, C. (2007). Female domestic violence offenders: Their attachment security, trauma symptoms, and personality organization. *Violence and Victims, 22*(5), 532–545.

Golding, J. M., Alexander, M. C., & Stewart, T. L. (1999). On the social psychology of hearsay evidence. *Psychology, Public Policy, and Law, 5,* 473–484.

Goldman, J., & Salus, M. K. (2003). *A coordinated response to child abuse and neglect: The foundation for practice.* Washington, DC: U.S. Department of Health and Human Services.

Goldstein, S. E., Chesir-Teran, D., & McFaul, A. (2008). Profiles and correlates of relationship aggression in young adults' romantic relationships. *Journal of Youth and Adolescence, 37,* 251–265.

Gomby, D. (2005). Home visitation in 2005: Outcomes for children and parents. *Investing in Kids Working Paper No. 7.* Retrieved from http://legis.wisconsin.gov/lc/committees/study/2008/SFAM08/files/GombyHVoutcomes2005.pdf.

Gómez, A. M. (2011). Testing the cycle of violence hypothesis: Child abuse and adolescent dating violence as predictors of intimate partner violence in young adulthood. *Youth & Society, 43,* 171–192.

Gondolf, E. W. (1988). The effect of batterer counseling on shelter outcome. *Journal of Interpersonal Violence, 3,* 275–289.

Gondolf, E. W. (1995). *Discharge criteria for batterer programs* [Electronic Version]. Retrieved November 13, 2003, from http://www.mincava.umn.edu/papers/gondolf/discharg.htm.

Gondolf, E. W., & Fisher, E. R. (1988). *Battered women as survivors: An alternative to treating learned helplessness.* Lexington, MA: Lexington Books.

Gondolf, E. W., & Foster, R. A. (1991). Preprogram attrition in batterer programs. *Journal of Family Violence, 6,* 337–349.

Gonzales, J. (2012, Feb. 6). Victim Advocate, San Diego Domestic Violence Unit. [Personal communication].

Gonzalez-Guarda, R. M., Peragallo, N., Urrutia, M. T., Vasquez, E. P. (2008). HIV risk, substance abuse and intimate partner violence among Hispanic females and their partners. *Journal of the Association of Nurses in AIDS Care, 19*(4), 252–266.

Goodlin, W., & Dunn, C. S. (2010). Three patterns of domestic violence in households: Single victimization, repeat victimization, and co-occurring victimization. *Journal of Family Violence, 25,* 107–122.

Goodman, G. S., Bottoms, B. L., Redlich, A., Shaver, P. R., & Diviak, K. (1998). Correlates of multiple forms of victimization in religion-related child abuse cases. *Journal of Aggression, Maltreatment, and Trauma, 2*, 273–295.

Goodman, G. S., Quas, J. A., Bulkley, J., & Shapiro, C. (1999). Innovations for child witnesses: A national survey. *Psychology, Public Policy and the Law, 5*, 255–281.

Goodman, L., Dutton, M. A., Vankos, N., & Weinfurt, K. (2005). Women's resources and use of strategies as risk and protective factors for reabuse over time. *Violence Against Women, 11*(3). 311–336.

Goodwin, M., & Roscoe, B. (1990). Sibling violence and agonistic interactions among middle adolescents. *Adolescence, 25*, 451–475.

Gormley, B., & Lopez, F. G. (2010). Psychological abuse perpetration in college dating relationships: Contributions of gender, stress, and adult attachment orientations. *Journal of Interpersonal Violence, 25*(2), 204–218.

Gosselin, D. K. (2000). *Heavy hands: An introduction to the crimes of domestic violence.* Upper Saddle River, NJ: Prentice-Hall.

Gottesman, I. I., Goldsmith, H. H., & Carey, G. (1997). A developmental and genetic perspective on aggression. In N. L. Segal, G. E. Weisfield, & C. C. Weisfield (Eds.), *Uniting psychology and biology: Integrative perspectives on human development* (pp. 107–130). Washington, DC: American Psychological Association.

Gottlich, V. (1994). Beyond granny bashing: Elder abuse in the 1990s. *Clearinghouse Review, 28*, 371–381.

Gout, N. D. (2010). *Protective factors against intimate partner violence among American Indian and Alaska Native mothers* (Doctoral dissertation). Boston, MA: Boston University.

Gover, A. R., Kaukinen, C., & Fox, K. A. (2008). The relationship between violence in the family of origin and dating violence among college students. *Journal of Interpersonal Violence, 23*, 1667–1693.

Gowan, J. (1993). *Effects of neglect on the early development of children: Final report.* Washington, DC: National Clearinghouse on Child Abuse and Neglect, National Center on Child Abuse and Neglect, Administration for Children and Families.

Grafstrom, M., Nordberg, A., & Winblad, B. (1993). Abuse is in the eye of the beholder. *Scandinavian Journal of Social Medicine, 21*, 247–255.

Graham-Bermann, S. A., Gruber, G., Girz, L., & Howell, K. H. (2009). Ecological factors discriminating among profiles of resiliency and psychopathology in children exposed to intimate partner violence. *Child Abuse and Neglect, 33*(9), 648–660.

Graham-Bermann, S. A., & Hughes, H. M. (2003). Intervention for children exposed to interparental violence (IPV): Assessment of needs and research priorities. *Clinical Child and Family Psychology Review, 6*(3), 189–204.

Graham-Bermann, S. A., & Seng, J. S. (2005). Violence exposure and traumatic stress symptoms as additional predictors of health problems in high-risk children. *Journal of Pediatrics, 146*, 349–354.

Graham-Kevan, N., & Archer, J. (2005). Investigating three explanations of women's relationship aggression. *Psychology of Women Quarterly, 29*, 270–277.

Grasmick, H. G., Bursik, R. J., Jr., & Kimpel, M. (1991). Protestant fundamentalism and attitudes toward corporal punishment of children. *Violence and Victims, 6*, 283–298.

Graves, K. N., Sechrist, S. M., White, J. W., & Paradise, M. J. (2005). Intimate partner violence perpetrated by college women with the context of a history of being victimized. *Psychology of Women Quarterly, 29*, 278–289.

Green, A. H. (1984). Child abuse by siblings. *Child Abuse and Neglect, 8*, 311–317.

Greenbaum, J., Dubowitz, H., Lutzker, J. R., Johnson, K. D., Orn, K., Kenniston, J., . . . Moeser, M. (2008). *Practice guidelines: Challenges in the evaluation of child neglect.* Elmhurst, IL: American Professional Society on the Abuse of Children.

Greenberg, J. R., McKibben, M., & Raymond, J. A. (1990). Dependent adult children and elder abuse. *Journal of Elder Abuse & Neglect, 2,* 73–86.

Greenfeld, L. A. (1996). *Child victimizers: Violent offenders and their victims.* Washington, DC: U.S. Department of Justice.

Greenfeld, L. A., Rand, M. R., Craven, D., Klaus, P. A., Perkins, C. A., Ringel, C., . . . Fox, J. A. (1998). *Violence by intimates: Analysis of data on crimes by current or former spouses, boyfriends, and girlfriends* [Electronic Version]. Retrieved August 16, 2004, from http://www.ojp.usdoj .gov/bjs/pub/pdf/vi.pdf.

Greenwood, G. L., Relf, M. V., Huang, B., Pollack, L. M., Canchola, J. A., & Catania, J. A. (2002). Battering victimization among a probability-based sample of men who have sex with men. *American Journal of Public Health, 92,* 1964–1969.

Griffin, L. W. (1999a). Elder mistreatment in the African American community: You just don't hit your mama!!! In T. Tatara (Ed.), *Understanding elder abuse in minority communities* (pp. 13–26). Philadelphia, PA: Brunner/Mazel.

Griffin, L. W. (1999b). Understanding elder abuse. In R. L. Hampton (Ed.), *Family violence: Prevention and treatment* (pp. 260–287). Thousand Oaks, CA: Sage.

Grodner, E., & Sweifach, J. (2004). Domestic violence in the Orthodox Jewish home: A value-sensitive approach to recovery. *Affilia, 19*(3), 305–316.

Groenen, A., & Vervaeke, G. (2009). Violent stalkers: Detecting risk factors by the police. *European Journal of Criminal Policy Research, 15,* 279–291.

Gross, A. M., Winslett, A., Roberts, M., & Gohm, C. L. (2006). An examination of sexual violence against college women. *Violence Against Women, 12*(3), 288–300.

Grossman, S. F., & Lundy, M. (2003). Use of domestic violence services across race and ethnicity by women aged 55 and older: The Illinois experience. *Violence Against Women, 9*(12), 1442–1452.

Groth, A. N., Hobson, W., & Gary, R. (1982). Child molester: Clinical observations. In J. Conte & D. Shore (Eds.), *Social work and child sexual abuse* (pp. 129–144). New York, NY: Hayworth Press.

Gruskin, E. P., Hart, S., Gordon, N., & Ackerson, L. (2001). Patterns of cigarette smoking and alcohol use among lesbians and bisexual women enrolled in a large health maintenance organization. *American Journal of Public Health, 91,* 976–979.

Grych, J., & Kinsfogel, K. M. (2010). Exploring the role of attachment style in the relation between family aggression and abuse in adolescent dating relationships. *Journal of Aggression, Maltreatment, and Trauma, 19*(6), 624–640.

Gül, S. S., & Gül, H. (2000). The question of women in Islamic revivalism in Turkey: A review of the Islamic press. *Current Sociology, 4,* 1–26.

Guterman, N., Lee, S., Taylor, C., & Rathouz, P. (2009). Parental perceptions of neighborhood processes, stress, personal control, and risk for physical child abuse and neglect. *Child Abuse and Neglect, 33,* 897–906.

Hale-Carlsson, G., Hutton, B., Fuhrman, J., Morse, D., McNutt, L., & Clifford, A. (1996). Physical violence and injuries in intimate relationships—New York, Behavioral Risk Factor Surveillance System, 1994. *Morbidity and Mortality Weekly Report, 45,* 765–767.

Hall, G. C. N., Teten, A. L., DeGarmo, D. S., Sue, S., & Stephens, K. A. (2005). Ethnicity, culture, and sexual aggression: Risk and protective factors. *Journal of Consulting and Clinical Psychology, 73,* 830–840.

Hamberger, L. K., & Arnold, J. (1990). The impact of mandatory arrest on domestic violence perpetrator counseling services. *Family Violence and Sexual Assault Bulletin, 6,* 11–12.

Hamberger, L. K., & Guse, C. E. (2002). Men's and women's use of intimate partner violence in clinical samples. *Violence Against Women, 8*(11), 1301–1331.

Hamberger, L. K., & Hastings, J. E. (1991). Personality correlates of men who batter and non-violent men: Some continuities and discontinuities. *Journal of Family Violence, 6,* 131–147.

Hamburg, D. (1992). *Today's children: Creating a future for a generation in crisis*. New York, NY: Times Books.

Hamby, S. L. (1998). Partner violence: Prevention and intervention. In J. L. Jasinski & L. M. Williams (Eds.), *Partner violence: A comprehensive review of 20 years of research* (pp. 210–258). Thousand Oaks, CA: Sage.

Hamel, M., Gold, D. P., Andres, D., Reis, M., Dastoor, D., Grauer, H., . . . Bergman, H. (1990). Predictors and consequences of aggressive behavior by community-based dementia patients. *Gerontologist, 30,* 206–211.

Hamilton, A. R. (2001, June 14). Testimony provided for the National Association of Adult Protective Services Administrators. *United States Senate Hearings on Saving our Seniors: Preventing Elder Abuse, Neglect and Exploitation.* Washington, DC: Government Printing Office.

Hammer, R. (2003). Militarism and family terrorism: A critical feminist perspective. *The Review of Education, Pedagogy, and Cultural Studies, 25,* 231–256.

Hammock, G., & O'Hearn, R. E. (2002). Psychological aggression in dating relationships: Predictive models for males and females. *Violence and Victims, 17*(5), 525–540.

Hansberry, M. R., Chen, E., & Gorbien, M. J. (2005). Dementia and elder abuse. *Clinics in Geriatric Medicine, 21,* 315–332.

Hanson, K. A., & Gidycz, C. A. (1993). Evaluation of a sexual assault prevention program. *Journal of Consulting and Clinical Psychology, 61,* 1046.

Hanson, R. F., Resnick, H. S., Saunders, B. E., Kilpatrick, D. G., & Best, C. L. (1999). Factors related to the reporting of childhood rape. *Child Abuse and Neglect, 23,* 559–569.

Hanson, R. K., Gordon, A., Harris, A. J. R., Marques, J. K., Murphy, W., Quinsey, V. L., . . . Seto, M. C. (2002). First report of the Collaborative Outcome Project on the effectiveness of psychological treatment for sex offenders. *Sexual Abuse: A Journal of Research and Treatment, 14,* 169–194.

Hanson, R. K., & Morton-Bourgon, K. (2005). The characteristics of persistent sexual offenders: A meta-analysis of recidivism studies. *Journal of Consulting and Clinical Psychology, 73,* 1154–1163.

Hanson, R. K., & Slater, S. (1988). Sexual victimization in the history of sexual abusers: A review. *Annals of Sex Research, 1,* 485–499.

Harbin, H., & Madden, D. (1979). Battered parents: A new syndrome. *American Journal of Psychiatry, 136,* 1288–1291.

Hardesty, J. L., Oswald, R. F., Khaw, L., & Fonseca, C. (2011). Lesbian, bisexual mothers and intimate partner violence: Help seeking in the context of social and legal vulnerability. *Violence Against Women, 17*(1), 28–46.

Hardy, M., Beers, B., Burgess, C., & Taylor, A. (2010). Personal experience and perceived acceptability of sibling aggression. *Journal of Family Violence, 25,* 65–71.

Harkins, L., & Beech, A. R. (2007). A review of the factors that can influence the effectiveness of sexual offender treatment: Risk, need, responsivity, and process issues. *Aggression and Violent Behavior, 12,* 615–627.

Harmon, R. B., Rosner, R., & Owens, H. (1995). Obsessional harassment and erotomania in a criminal court population. *Journal of Forensic Sciences, 40*(1), 188–196.

Harmon, R. B., Rosner, R., & Owens, H. (1998). Sex and violence in a forensic population of obsessional harassers. *Psychology, Public Policy, and the Law, 4*(1/2), 236–249.

Harper, J. (1991). Children's play: The differential effects of intrafamilial physical and sexual abuse. *Child Abuse and Neglect, 15,* 89–98.

Harries, K. (1995). The last walk: A geography of execution in the United States, 1786–1985. *Political Geography, 14,* 473–495.

Harrington, D., & Dubowitz, H. (1999). Preventing child maltreatment. In R. L. Hampton (Ed.), *Family violence: Prevention and treatment* (2nd ed., pp. 122–147). Thousand Oaks, CA: Sage.

Harrington, N. T., & Leitenberg, H. (1994). Relationship between alcohol consumption and victim behaviors immediately preceding sexual aggression by an acquaintance. *Violence and Victims, 9,* 315–324.

Harris, S. B. (1996). For better or for worse: Spouse abuse grown old. *Journal of Elder Abuse & Neglect, 8,* 1–33.

Harris, W. W., Lieberman, A. F., & Marans, S. (2007). In the best interests of society. *Journal of Child Psychology and Psychiatry, 48*(3–4), 392–411.

Hart, B. (1986). Lesbian battering: An examination. In K. Lobel (Ed.), *Naming the violence: Speaking out about lesbian battering* (pp. 173–189). Seattle, WA: Seal Press.

Hart, B. (1993). Battered women and the criminal justice system. *American Behavioral Scientist, 36,* 624–628.

Hart, S. N., Binggeli, N. J., & Brassard, M. R. (1998). Evidence of the effects of psychological maltreatment. *Journal of Emotional Abuse, 1*(1), 27–58.

Hart, S. N., Brassard, M. R., Binggeli, N. J., & Davidson, H. A. (2002). Psychological maltreatment. In J. E. B. Myers, L. Berliner, C. T. Briere, C. J. Hendrix, & T. A. Reid (Eds.), *The APSAC handbook on child maltreatment* (2nd ed., pp. 79–103). Thousand Oaks, CA: Sage.

Hart, S. N., Brassard, M. R., Davidson, H. A., Rivelis, E., Diaz, V., & Binggeli, N. J. (2011). Psychological maltreatment. In J. E. B. Myers (Ed.), *The APSAC handbook on child maltreatment* (3rd ed., pp. 125–144). Thousand Oaks, CA: Sage.

Hartney, C. (2006). *Youth under 18 in the adult criminal justice system.* Fact Sheet. National Council on Crime and Delinquency. Retrieved from www.nccdglobal.org/sites/default/files/publication_pdf/factsheet-youth-in-adult-system.pdf

Haskett, M., Allaire, J., Kreig, S., & Hart, K. (2008). Protective and vulnerability factors for physically abused children: Effects of ethnicity and parenting context. *Child Abuse and Neglect, 32,* 567–576.

Hassouneh, D., & Glass, N. (2008). The influence of gender role stereotyping on women's experiences of female same-sex intimate partner violence. *Violence Against Women, 14*(3), 310–325.

Hassouneh-Phillips, D. (2001a). "Marriage is half of faith and the rest is fear of Allah": Marriage and spousal abuse among American Muslims. *Violence Against Women, 7,* 927–946.

Hassouneh-Phillips, D. (2001b). Polygamy and wife abuse: A qualitative study of Muslim women in America. *Health Care for Women International, 22,* 735–748.

Hassouneh-Phillips, D. (2003). Strength and vulnerability: Spirituality in abused American Muslim women's lives. *Issues in Mental Health Nursing, 24,* 681–694.

Haugaard, J. J., & Seri, L. G. (2003). Stalking and other forms of intrusive contact after the dissolution of adolescent dating or romantic relationships. *Violence and Victims, 18*(3), 279–297.

Hawley, T. L., Halle, T. G., Drasin, R. E., & Thomas, N. G. (1995). Children of addicted mothers: Effects of the crack epidemic on the caregiving environment and the development of preschoolers. *American Journal of Orthopsychiatry, 65,* 364–379.

Hayes, A. M., Webb, C., Grasso, D., Cummings, J. A., Vahlsing, J., & Helie, K. (2009). *Processes that inhibit and facilitate change in trauma-focused cognitive behavioral therapy for youth exposed to interpersonal trauma.* Unpublished manuscript.

Hazzard, A. (1990). Prevention of child sexual abuse. In R. Ammerman & M. Hersen (Eds.), *Treatment of family violence* (pp. 354–384). New York, NY: Wiley.

Healey, K., Smith, C., & O'Sullivan, C. (1998). *Batterer intervention: Program approaches and criminal justice strategies* [Electronic Version]. Retrieved May 7, 2004, from http://www .ncjrs.org/pdf files/168638.pdf.

Hebrew Home at Riverdale. (2010). Retrieved from http://www.hebrewhome.org/abuse recovery.asp.

Heffer, R. W., & Kelley, M. L. (1987). Mothers' acceptance of behavioral interventions for children: The influence of parental race and income. *Behavior Therapy, 2,* 153–163.

Heide, K. M. (1995). *Why kids kill parents: Child abuse and adolescent homicide.* Thousand Oaks, CA: Sage.

Heide, K. M., & Petee, T. A. (2007). Parricide: An empirical analysis of 24 years of U.S. data. *Journal of Interpersonal Violence, 22*(11), 1382–1399.

Heinlein, G., & Beaupre, B. (2002). *Shelters must detail help for men* [Electronic Version]. Retrieved September 29, 2002, from http://www.noexcuse4abuse.org/ news/detroit_shelter .html.

Heintz, A. J., & Melendez, R. M. (2006). Intimate partner violence and HIV/STD risk among lesbian, gay, bisexual, and transgender individuals. *Journal of Interpersonal Violence, 21*(2), 193–208.

Heisler, C. J. (2003). Elder abuse and the criminal justice system: New awareness, new responses. *American Society of Aging, 24*(2), 52–58.

Heisler, C. J., & Quinn, M. J. (1995). A legal perspective. *Journal of Elder Abuse & Neglect, 7,* 23–40.

Helfrich, C. A., & Simpson, E. K. (2006). Improving services for lesbian clients: What do domestic violence agencies need to do? *Health Care for Women International, 27,* 344–361.

Helton, J. J., & Cross, T. P. (2011). The relationship of child functioning to parental physical assault: Linear and curvilinear models. *Child Maltreatment, 16,* 126–136.

Hemenway, D., Shinoda-Tagawa, T., & Miller, M. (2002). Firearm availability and female homicide victimization rates among 25 populous high-income countries. *Journal of the American Medical Women's Association, 57,* 100–104.

Hemenway, D., Solnick, S., & Carter, J. (1994). Child-rearing violence. *Child Abuse and Neglect, 18,* 1011–1020.

Hendricks, S. S. (1998). *A study in the understanding of authority and abuse of power in Muslim marriages.* Presented at the Women's Conference of the 2nd International Islamic Unity Conference. Washington, D.C.

Henman, M. (1996). Domestic violence: Do men under report? *Forensic Update, 47,* 3–8.

Henning, K., & Feder, L. (2004). A comparison of men and women arrested for domestic violence: Who presents the greater threat? *Journal of Family Violence, 19*(2), 69–80.

Henning, K., Jones, A., & Holdford, R. (2003). Treatment needs of women arrested for domestic violence: A comparison with male offenders. *Journal of Interpersonal Violence, 18*(8), 839–856.

Henning, K., & Klesges, L. M. (2003). Prevalence and characteristics of psychological abuse reported by court-involved battered women. *Journal of Interpersonal Violence, 18*(8), 857–871.

Henning, K., & Renauer, B. (2005). Prosecution of women arrested for intimate partner abuse. *Violence and Victims, 20*(3), 171–189.

Heppner, M. J., Humphrey, C. F., Hillenbrand-Gunn, T. L., & Debord, K. A. (1995). The differential effects of rape prevention programming on attitudes, behavior, and knowledge. *Journal of Counseling Psychology, 42,* 508–518.

Heppner, M. J., Neville, H. A., Smith, K., Kivlighan, D. M., & Gershuny, B. S. (1999). Examining immediate and long-term efficacy of rape prevention programming with racially diverse college men. *Journal of Counseling Psychology, 46,* 16–26.

Herbert, M. (1987). *Conduct disorders of childhood and adolescence.* Chichester, UK: Wiley.

Herek, G. (2004). Beyond homophobia: Thinking about sexual prejudice and stigma in the twenty-first century. *Sexuality Research and Social Policy, 1*(2), 6–24.

Herek, G. M. (1989). Hate crimes against lesbians and gay men: Issues for research and policy. *American Psychologist, 44,* 948–955.

Herek, G. M., Gillis, J. R., Cogan, J. C., & Glunt, E. K. (1997). Hate crime victimization among lesbian, gay, and bisexual adults: Prevalence, psychological correlates, and methodological issues. *Journal of Interpersonal Violence, 12,* 195–215.

Herkov, M. J., Gynther, M. D., Thomas, S., & Myers, W. C. (1996). MMPI differences among adolescent inpatients, rapists, sodomists, and sexual abusers. *Journal of Personality Assessment, 66,* 81–90.

Herman-Giddens, M., Brown, G., Verbiest, S., Carlson, P., Hooten, E., Howell, E., . . . Butts, J. D. (1999). Underascertainment of child abuse mortality in the United States. *Journal of the American Medical Association, 282,* 463–467.

Herman-Giddens, M. E., Smith, J. B., Mittal, M., Carlson, M., & Butts, J. D. (2003). Newborns killed or left to die by a parent: A population-based study. *Journal of the American Medical Association, 289,* 1425–1429.

Hermans, E. J., Ramsey, N. F., & van Honk, J. (2008). Exogenous testosterone enhances responsiveness to social threat in the neural circuitry of social aggression in humans. *Biological Psychiatry, 63,* 263–270.

Hermin, J. (1981). *Father-daughter incest.* Cambridge, MA: Harvard University Press.

Herrenkohl, E. C., Herrenkohl, R. C., Egolf, B. P., & Russo, M. J. (1998). The relationship between early maltreatment and teenage parenthood. *Journal of Adolescence, 21,* 291–303.

Herrenkohl, E. C., Herrenkohl, R. C., Rupert, L. J., Egolf, B. P., & Lutz, J. G. (1995). Risk factors for behavioral dysfunction: The relative impact of maltreatment, SES, physical health problems, cognitive ability, and quality of parent-child interaction. *Child Abuse and Neglect, 19,* 191–203.

Herrenkohl, E. C., Herrenkohl, R. C., & Toedter, L. J. (1983). Perspectives on the intergenerational transmission of abuse. In D. Finkelhor, R. J. Gelles, G. T. Hotaling, & M. A. Straus (Eds.), *The dark side of families: Current family violence research* (pp. 305–316). Newbury Park, CA: Sage.

Herrenkohl, R. C., Egolf, B. P., & Herrenkohl, E. C. (1997). Preschool age antecedents of adolescent assaultive behavior: Results from a longitudinal study. *American Journal of Orthopsychiatry, 67,* 422–432.

Herrenkohl, R. C., Herrenkohl, E. C., Egolf, B. P., & Wu, P. (1991). The developmental consequences of child abuse: The Lehigh Longitudinal Study. In R. H. Starr & D. A. Wolfe (Eds.), *The effects of child abuse and neglect* (pp. 57–81). New York, NY: Guilford.

Herrenkohl, T. I., Tajima, E. A., Whitney, S. D., & Huang, B. (2005). Protection against antisocial behavior in children exposed to physically abusive discipline. *Journal of Adolescent Health, 36,* 457–465.

Herriot, P. (2009). *Religious fundamentalism: Global, local and personal.* New York, NY: Rutledge.

Hershkowitz, I., Lamb, M. E., & Horowitz, D. (2007). Victimization of children with disabilities. *American Journal of Orthopsychiatry, 77,* 629–635.

Hertel, B. R., & Hughes, M. (1987). Religious affiliation, attendance, and support for "pro-family" issues in the United States. *Social Forces, 65,* 858–882.

Hetherton, J. (1999). The idealization of women: Its role in the minimization of child sexual abuse by females. *Child Abuse and Neglect, 23,* 161–174.

Hettrich, E. L., & O'Leary, K. D. (2007). Females' reasons for their physical aggression in dating relationships. *Journal of Interpersonal Violence, 22*(9), 1131–1143.

Heyman, R. E., & Smith Slep, A. M. (2006). Creating and field-testing diagnostic criteria for partner and child maltreatment. *Journal of Family Psychology, 20*(3), 397–408.

Hien D., & Ruglass L. (2009). Interpersonal partner violence and women in the United States: An overview of prevalence rates, psychiatric correlates and consequences and barriers to help seeking. *International Journal of Law and Psychiatry, 32*(1), 48–55.

Higgins, D. J., & McCabe, M. P. (2000). Multi-type maltreatment and the long-term adjustment of adults. *Child Abuse Review, 9,* 6–18.

Hightower, J., Smith, M. J., & Hightower, H. (2001). *Silent and invisible: A report on abuse and violence in the lives of older women in British Columbia and Yukon.* Vancouver, BC: BC Society of Transition Houses.

Hill, R. B. (2007). *An analysis of racial/ethnic disproportionality and disparity at the national, state, and county levels.* Casey-CSSP Alliance for Racial Equity in Child Welfare. Retrieved from http://www.aecf.org/~/media/Pubs/Topics/Child%20Welfare%20Permanence/Other/AnAnalysisofRacialEthnicDisproportionalityand/Bob%20Hill%20report%20natl%20state%20racial%20disparity%202007.pdf.

Himelein, M. J. (1995). Risk factors for sexual victimization in dating: A longitudinal study of college women. *Psychology of Women Quarterly, 19,* 31–48.

Hines, D. A. (2001, August). *Effects of emotional abuse against men in intimate relationships.* Paper presented at the 109th Annual Convention of the American Psychological Association. San Francisco, CA.

Hines, D. A. (2007a). Post-traumatic stress symptoms among men who sustain partner violence: A multi-national study of university students. *Psychology of Men & Masculinity, 8,* 225–239.

Hines, D. A. (2007b). Predictors of sexual coercion against women and men: A multilevel, multinational study of university students. *Archives of Sexual Behavior, 36,* 403–422.

Hines, D. A. (2008). Borderline personality and intimate partner aggression: An international multi-site, cross-gender analysis. *Psychology of Women Quarterly, 32,* 290–302.

Hines, D. A. (2009). *Can male victims of domestic violence get the help they need?* Paper presented at the From Ideology to Inclusion Conference: New Directions in Domestic Violence Research and Intervention. Los Angeles, CA.

Hines, D. A., Armstrong, J. L., Palm Reed, K. M., & Cameron, A. Y. (in press). Gender differences in sexual assault victimization among college students. *Violence and Victims.*

Hines, D. A., Brown, J., & Dunning, E. (2007). Characteristics of callers to the Domestic Abuse Helpline for Men. *Journal of Family Violence, 22,* 63–72.

Hines, D. A., & Douglas, E. M. (2009). Women's use of intimate partner violence against men: Prevalence, implications, and consequences. *Journal of Aggression, Maltreatment, and Trauma, 18,* 572–586.

Hines, D. A., & Douglas, E. M. (2010a). A closer look at men who sustain intimate terrorism by women. *Partner Abuse, 1*(3), 286–313.

Hines, D. A., & Douglas, E. M. (2010b). Intimate terrorism by women towards men: Does it exist? *Journal of Aggression, Conflict, and Peace Research, 2*(3), 36–56.

Hines, D. A., & Douglas, E. M. (2011a). The reported availability of U.S. domestic violence services to victims who vary by age, sexual orientation, and gender. *Partner Abuse, 2*(1), 3–30.

Hines, D. A., & Douglas, E. M. (2011b). Symptoms of post-traumatic stress disorder in men who sustain intimate partner violence: A study of helpseeking and community samples. *Psychology of Men & Masculinity, 12*(2), 112–127.

Hines, D. A., & Douglas, E. M. (2011c). Understanding the use of violence among men who sustain intimate terrorism. *Partner Abuse, 2*(3), 259–283.

Hines, D. A., & Malley-Morrison, K. (2001a). *Effects of emotional abuse against men in intimate relationships.* Paper presented at the American Psychological Association's Annual Convention, San Francisco, CA.

Hines, D. A., & Malley-Morrison, K. (2001b). Psychological effects of partner abuse against men: A neglected research area. *Psychology of Men & Masculinity, 2,* 75–85.

Hines, D. A., & Malley-Morrison, K. (2003, July). *Abusive childhood experiences: Effects in late adolescent boys.* Paper presented at the 8th International Family Violence Research Conference, Portsmouth, NH.

Hines, D. A., & Palm Reed, K. M. (2011). *A formative evaluation of a campus bystander program for sexual assault and dating violence prevention.* Paper presented at the Ending Domestic & Sexual Violence: Innovations in Practice & Research Conference, Portsmouth, NH.

Hines, D. A., & Saudino, K. J. (2002). Intergenerational transmission of intimate partner violence: A behavioral genetic perspective. *Trauma, Violence & Abuse, 3,* 210–225.

Hines, D. A., & Saudino, K. J. (2003). Gender differences in psychological, physical, and sexual aggression among college students using the Revised Conflict Tactics Scales. *Violence and Victims, 18,* 197–218.

Hines, D. A., & Saudino, K. J. (2004). Genetic and environmental influences on intimate partner aggression: A preliminary study. *Violence and Victims, 19,* 79–97.

Hines, D. A., & Saudino, K. J. (2008). Personality and intimate partner aggression in dating relationships: The role of the "big five." *Aggressive Behavior, 34,* 593–604.

Hines, D. A., & Straus, M. A. (2007). Binge drinking and violence against dating partners: The mediating effect of antisocial traits and behaviors in a multinational perspective. *Aggressive Behavior, 33,* 441–457.

Hirschel, D., & Buzawa, E. (2002). Understanding the context of dual arrest with directions for future research. *Violence Against Women, 8*(12), 1449–1473.

Hirschel, D., Buzawa, E., Pattavina, A., & Faggiani, D. (2007). Domestic violence and mandatory arrest laws: To what extent do they influence police arrest decisions? *Journal of Criminal Law and Criminology, 98*(1), 255–298.

Hirschel, J. D., & Hutchinson, I. W. (1992). Female spousal abuse and the police response: The Charlotte, North Carolina, experiment. *Journal of Criminal Law and Criminology, 83,* 73–119.

Hoagwood, K., & Stewart, J. M. (1989). Sexually abused children's perceptions of family functioning. *Child and Adolescent Social Work, 6,* 139–149.

Hobfoll, S., Bansal, A., Schurg, R., Young, S., Pierce, C., Hobfoll, I., . . . Johnson, R. (2002). The impact of perceived child physical and sexual abuse history on Native American women's psychological well-being and AIDS risk. *Journal of Counseling and Clinical Psychology, 70*(1), 252–257.

Hodges, K. M. (2000). Trouble in paradise: Barriers to addressing domestic violence in lesbian relationships. *Law and Sexuality, 9,* 311–331.

Hoffman, K. L., & Edwards, J. N. (2004). An integrated theoretical model of sibling violence and abuse. *Journal of Family Violence, 19*(3), 185–200.

Hoffman, K. L., Kiecolt, J., & Edwards, J. N. (2005). Physical violence between siblings: A theoretical and empirical analysis. *Journal of Family Issues, 26,* 1103–1130.

Hoffman-Mason, C., & Bingham, R. P. (1988). Developing a sensitivity for culture and ethnicity in family violence. In A. L. Horton & J. A. Williamson (Eds.), *Abuse and religion: When praying isn't enough* (pp. 138–143). Lexington, MA: Lexington Books.

Holden, E. W., & Nabors, L. (1999). The prevention of child neglect. In H. Dubowitz (Ed.), *Neglected children: Research, practice, and policy* (pp. 174–190). Thousand Oaks, CA: Sage.

Holkup, P. A., Tripp-Reimer, T., Salois, E. M., & Weinert, C. (2004). Community-based participatory research: An approach to intervention research with a Native American community. *Advanced Nursing Science, 27*(3), 162–175.

Holmes, K. E. (2005, June 17). Muslims strike at spouse abuse [Electronic Version]. *The Philadelphia Inquirer.* Retrieved December 2011 from http://articles.philly.com/2005–06–17/news/25438189_1_american-muslims-spouse-abuse-amina-wadud.

Holmes, W. C., & Slap, G. B. (1998). Sexual abuse of boys: Definition, prevalence, correlates, sequelae, and management. *Journal of the American Medical Association, 280,* 1855–1862.

Holt, V. L., Kernic, M. A., Lumley, T., Wolf, M. E., & Rivara, F. P. (2002). Civil protection orders and risk of subsequent police-reported violence. *Journal of the American Medical Association, 288*(5), 589–594.

Holt, V. L., Kernic, M. A., Wolf, M. E., & Rivara, F. P. (2003). Do protection orders affect the likelihood of future partner violence and injury? *American Journal of Preventive Medicine, 24*(1), 16–21.

Holtzworth-Munroe, A., Smutzler, N., & Sandin, E. (1997). A brief review of the literature on husband violence. *Aggression and Violent Behavior, 2,* 179–213.

Holtzworth-Munroe, A., & Stewart, G. L. (1994). Typologies of male batterers: Three subtypes and the differences among them. *Psychological Bulletin, 116,* 476–497.

Homer, A. C., & Gilleard, C. (1990). Abuse of elderly people by their carers. *British Medical Journal, 301,* 1359–1362.

Hong, G. K., & Hong, L. K. (1991). Comparative perspectives in child abuse and neglect: Chinese versus Hispanics and Whites. *Child Welfare, 70,* 463–475.

Horsburgh, B. (1995). Lifting the veil of secrecy: Domestic violence in the Jewish community. *Harvard Women's Law Journal, 18,* 171–209.

Horton, A. L., Wilkins, M. M., & Wright, W. (1988). Women who ended abuse: What religious leaders and religion did for these victims. In A. L. Horton & J. A. Williamson (Eds.), *Abuse and religion: When praying isn't enough* (pp. 235–246). Lexington, MA: Lexington Books.

Horwitz, A. V., Widom, C., McLaughlin, J., & White, H. R. (2001). The impact of childhood abuse and neglect on adult mental health: A prospective study. *Journal of Health and Social Behavior, 42,* 184–201.

Hotaling, G. T., Straus, M. A., & Lincoln, A. J. (1990). Intrafamily violence and crime and violence outside the family. In M. A. Straus & R. J. Gelles (Eds.), *Physical violence in American families: Risk factors and adaptations to violence in 8,145 families* (pp. 431–472). New Brunswick, NJ: Transaction.

Hotaling, G. T., & Sugarman, D. B. (1986). An analysis of risk markers in husband to wife violence: The current state of knowledge. *Violence and Victims, 1,* 101–124.

Hotte, J. P., & Rafman, S. (1992). The specific effects of incest on prepubertal girls from dysfunctional families. *Child Abuse and Neglect, 16,* 273–283.

Houg, B. L. (2008). *The role of spirituality in the ongoing recovery process of female sexual abuse survivors* (Doctoral dissertation). University of Minnesota, Twin Cities, Minnesota.

Houry, D., Kemball, R., Rhodes, K. V., & Kaslow, N. J. (2006). Intimate partner violence and mental health symptoms in African American female ED patients. *American Journal of Emergency Medicine, 24*(4), 444–450.

Houston, E., & McKirnan, D. J. (2007). Intimate partner abuse among gay and bisexual men: Risk correlates and health outcomes. *Journal of Urban Health: Bulletin of the New York Academy of Medicine, 84*(5), 681–690.

Howard, C. J. (2011). Neurobiological correlates of partner abusive men: Equifinality in perpetrators of intimate partner violence. *Psychological Trauma: Theory, Research, Practice, and Policy, 4*(3), 330–337.

Howard, D. E., Griffin, M. A., & Boekeloo, B. O. (2008). Prevalence and psychological correlates of alcohol-related sexual assault among university students. *Adolescence, 43*(172), 734–750.

Howard, J., & Rottem, N. (2008). *It all starts at home: Male adolescent violence to mothers. A research report.* Inner South Community Health Services, Inc. and Child Abuse Research. Melbourne, AU: Monash University.

Hubbard, G. B. (1989). Mothers' perceptions of incest: Sustained disruption and turmoil. *Archives of Psychiatric Nursing, 3,* 34–40.

Hucker, S., Langevin, R., Dickey, R., Handy, L., Chambers, J., Wright, S., . . . Wortzman, G. (1988). Cerebral damage and dysfunction in sexually aggressive men. *Annals of Sex Research, 1,* 33–47.

Hucker, S., Langevin, R., Wortzman, G., Bain, J., Handy, L., Chambers, J., . . . Wright, S. (1986). Neuropsychological impairment in pedophiles. *Canadian Journal of Behavioral Science, 18,* 440–448.

Hudson, M. F., Armachain, W. D., Beasley, C. M., & Carlson, J. R. (1998). Elder abuse: Two Native American views. *Gerontologist, 38*(5), 538–548.

Hudson, M. F., & Carlson, J. R. (1999). Elder abuse: Its meaning to Caucasians, African Americans, and Native Americans. In T. Tatara (Ed.), *Understanding elder abuse in minority populations* (pp. 187–204). Philadelphia, PA: Brunner/Mazel.

Huesmann, L. R., Moise-Titus, J., Podolski, C. L., & Eron, L. D. (2003). Longitudinal relations between children's exposure to TV violence and their aggressive and violent behavior in young adulthood: 1977–1992. *Developmental Psychology, 39,* 201–221.

Human Rights Watch & American Civil Liberties Union Joint Report. (2008). *A violent education: Corporal punishment of children in US public schools.* Available from hrw.org/reports/2008/us0808/us0808webwcover.pdf.

Humphrey, J. A., & White, J. W. (2000). Women's vulnerability to sexual assault from adolescence to young adulthood. *Journal of Adolescent Health, 27,* 419–424.

Humphries Lynch, S. (1997). Elder abuse: What to look for, how to intervene. *American Journal of Nursing, 97,* 27–32.

Hutchings, B., & Mednick, S. A. (1977). Criminality in adoptees and their adoptive and biological parents: A pilot study. In S. A. Mednick & K. O. Christiansen (Eds.), *Biosocial bases of criminal behavior* (pp. 127–141). New York, NY: Gardner Press.

In re Gault (387 U.S. 1). (1967). United States Supreme Court decision. Washington, DC: Government Printing Office.

Ingraham v. Wright (430 U.S. 651, 51 L.Ed.2d 71). (1977). United States Supreme Court decision. Washington, DC: Government Printing Office.

Iovanni, L., & Miller, S. L. (2001). Criminal justice system responses to domestic violence: Law enforcement and the courts. In C. M. Renzetti, R. K. Bergen, & J. L. Edleson (Eds.), *Sourcebook on violence against women* (pp. 303–328). Thousand Oaks, CA: Sage.

Islamic Society of North America. (2004). *The Islamic response to domestic violence* [Electronic Version]. Retrieved July 2004 from http://www.isna.net/dv/islamicresponse.asp.

Island, D., & Letellier, P. (1991). *Men who beat the men who love them.* New York, NY: Harrington Park Press.

Jackson, S., Thompson, R. A., Christiansen, E. H., Colman, R. A., Wyatt, J., & Buckendahl, C. W. (1999). Predicting abuse-prone parental attitudes and discipline practices in a nationally representative sample. *Child Abuse and Neglect, 23,* 15–29.

Jackson, S. L., & Hafemeister, T. L. (2011). Risk factors associated with elder abuse: The importance of differentiating by type of elder maltreatment. *Violence and Victims, 26*(6), 738–757.

Jacobson, N. S., Gottman, J. M., Gortner, E., Berns, S., & Shortt, J. W. (1996). Psychological factors in the longitudinal course of battering: When do the couples split up? When does the abuse decrease? *Violence and Victims, 11,* 371–392.

Jaffe, P. G., Crooks, C. V., & Wolfe, D. A. (2003). Legal and policy responses to children exposed to domestic violence: The need to evaluate intended and unintended consequences. *Clinical Child and Family Psychology Review, 6,* 205–213.

Jakupcak, M. (2003). Masculine gender role stress and men's fear of emotions as predictors of self-reported aggression and violence. *Violence and Victims, 18,* 533–541.

Jakupcak, M., Lisak, D., & Roemer, L. (2002). The role of masculine ideology and masculine gender role stress in men's perpetration of relationship violence. *Psychology of Men & Masculinity, 3,* 97–106.

Jasinski, J. L., & Dietz, T. L. (2003). Domestic violence and stalking among older adults: An assessment of risk markers. *Journal of Elder Abuse & Neglect, 15*(1), 3–18.

Jaudes, P. K., Ekwo, E., & Voorhis, J. V. (1995). Association of drug abuse and child abuse. *Child Abuse and Neglect, 19,* 1065–1075.

Jaudes, P. K., & Mackey-Bilaver, L. (2008). Do chronic conditions increase young children's risk of being maltreated? *Child Abuse and Neglect, 32,* 671–681.

Jehu, D. (1988). *Beyond sexual abuse: Therapy with women who were childhood victims.* Chichester, UK: Wiley.

Jennings, K. T. (1993). Female child molesters: A review of the literature. In M. Elliott (Ed.), *Female sexual abuse of children: The ultimate taboo* (pp. 241–257). New York, NY: John Wiley.

Jogerst, G. J., Daly, J. M., Dawson, J. D., Brinig, M. F., & Schmuch, G. A. (2003). Required elder abuse education for Iowa mandatory reporters. *Journal of Elder Abuse & Neglect, 15*(1), 59–73.

Johnson, C. F. (2002). Physical abuse: Accidental versus intentional trauma in children. In J. E. B. Myers, L. Berliner, J. Briere, C. T. Hendrix, C. Jenny, & T. A. Reid (Eds.), *The APSAC handbook on child maltreatment* (2nd ed., pp. 249–268). Thousand Oaks, CA: Sage.

Johnson, J. G., Cohen, P., Brown, J., Smailes, E. M., & Bernstein, D. P. (1999). Childhood maltreatment increases risk for personality disorders during early adulthood. *Archives of General Psychiatry, 56,* 600–606.

Johnson, J. G., Cohen, P., & Smailes, E. M. (2001). Childhood verbal abuse and risk for personality disorders during adolescence and early adulthood. *Comprehensive Psychiatry, 42,* 16–23.

Johnson, J. G., Smailes, E. M., Cohen, P., Brown, J., & Bernstein, D. P. (2000). Associations between four types of childhood neglect and personality disorder symptoms during adolescence and early adulthood: Findings of a community-based longitudinal study. *Journal of Personality Disorders, 14,* 171–187.

Johnson, K. (2009). *State-based home visiting: Strengthening programs through state leadership.* New York, NY: National Center for Children in Poverty, Columbia University.

Johnson, M. A., Stone, S., Lou, C., Ling, J., Claassen, J., & Austin, M. J. (2008). Assessing parent education programs for families involved with child welfare services: Evidence and implications. *Journal of Evidence-Based Social Work, 5*(1–2), 191–236.

Johnson, M. P. (1995). Patriarchal terrorism and common couple violence: Two forms of violence against women. *Journal of Marriage and the Family, 57,* 283–294.

Johnson, M. P. (2001). Conflict and control: Symmetry and asymmetry in domestic violence. In A. Booth & A. C. Crouter (Eds.), *Couples in conflict* (pp. 95–104). Hillsdale, NJ: Erlbaum.

Johnson, M. P. (2006). Conflict and control: Gender symmetry and asymmetry in domestic violence. *Violence Against Women, 12*(11), 1003–1018.

Johnson, M. P. (2008). *A typology of domestic violence: Intimate terrorism, violent resistance, and situational couple violence.* Lebanon, NH: Northeastern University Press.

Johnson, M. P., & Ferraro, K. J. (2000). Research on domestic violence in the 1990s: Making distinctions. *Journal of Marriage and the Family, 62,* 948–963.

Johnson, M. P., & Leone, J. M. (2005). The differential effects of intimate terrorism and situational couple violence: Findings from the National Violence Against Women Survey. *Journal of Family Issues, 26*(3), 322–349.

Johnson, T. C. (1988). Child perpetrators: Children who molest other children: Preliminary findings. *Child Abuse and Neglect, 12,* 219–229.

Johnson, T. J., Wendel, J., & Hamilton, S. (1998). Social anxiety, alcohol expectancies and drinking-game participation. *Addictive Behaviors, 23,* 65–79.

Jones, D. P. H. (2002). Is sexual abuse perpetrated by a brother different from that committed by a parent? [Editorial]. *Child Abuse and Neglect, 26,* 955–956.

Jones, J. M. (2011). *Record-low 26% in U.S. favor handgun ban: Support for stricter gun laws in general is lowest Gallup has measured* [Electronic Version]. Retrieved April 9, 2012, from http://www.gallup.com/poll/150341/Record-Low-Favor-Handgun-Ban.aspx.

Jones, J. S. (1994). Elder abuse and neglect: Responding to a national problem. *Annals of Emergency Medicine, 23,* 845–848.

Jones, L., & Finkelhor, D. (2009). *Updated trends in child maltreatment, 2007.* Durham, NH: University of New Hampshire, Crimes Against Children Research Center.

Jordan, C. E., Logan, TK, Walker, R., & Nigoff, A. (2003). Stalking: An examination of the criminal justice response. *Journal of Interpersonal Violence, 18*(2), 148–165.

Jordan, C. E., Wilcox, P., & Pritchard, A. J. (2007). Stalking acknowledgement and reporting among college women experiencing intrusive behaviors: Implications for the emergence of a "classic stalking case." *Journal of Criminal Justice, 35,* 556–569.

Joseph, R. (1999). The neurology of traumatic dissociative amnesia: Commentary and literature review. *Child Abuse and Neglect, 23,* 715–727.

Kahn, F. I., Welch, T. L., & Zillmer, E. A. (1993). MMPI-2 profiles of battered women in transition. *Journal of Personality Assessment, 60,* 100–111.

Kalichman, S. C., Benotsch, E., Rompa, D., Gore-Felton, C., Austin, J., Luke, W., . . . Simpson, D. (2001). Unwanted sexual experiences and sexual risks in gay and bisexual men: Associations among revictimization, substance use, and psychiatric symptoms. *Journal of Sex Research, 38,* 1–9.

Kalmuss, D. (1984). The intergenerational transmission of marital aggression. *Journal of Marriage and the Family, 46,* 11–19.

Kalof, L. (1993). Rape supportive attitudes and sexual victimization experiences of sorority and nonsorority women. *Sex Roles, 29,* 767–780.

Kalra, P. (2006). *The prevalence, characteristics, and predictors of child sexual abuse and adult sexual assault among Latina, East Asian, South Asian, and Middle Eastern women.* (Doctoral Dissertation). University of Denver. Retrieved from http://gradworks.umi.com/32/31/3231095.html.

Kamphius, J. H., Emmelkamp, P. M. G., & de Vries, V. (2004). Informant personality descriptions of postintimate stalkers using the five factor profile. *Journal of Personality Assessment, 82*(2), 169–178.

Kanin, E. J. (1985). Date rapists: Differential sexual socialization and relative deprivation. *Archives of Sexual Behavior, 14,* 219–231.

Kansler, Z. (2011, February). Same sex domestic abuse and orders of protection [Electronic Version]. *Albany Government Law Review.* Retrieved February 19, 2012, from http://aglr.wordpress.com/2011/02/06/same-sex-domestic-abuse-and-orders-of-protection/.

Kantor, G. K., & Little, L. (2003). Defining the boundaries of child neglect: When does domestic violence equate with parental failure to protect? *Journal of Interpersonal Violence, 18,* 338–355.

Kanuga, M., & Rosenfeld, W. D. (2004). Adolescent sexuality and the Internet: The good, the bad, and the URL. *Journal of Pediatric and Adolescent Gynecology, 17,* 117–124.

Kaplan, S., Pelcovitz, D., Salzinger, S., Mandel, F. S., & Weiner, M. (1998). Adolescent physical abuse: Risk for adolescent psychiatric disorders. *American Journal of Psychiatry, 155,* 949–959.

Karch, D., & Nunn, K. C. (2011). Characteristics of elderly and other vulnerable adult victims of homicide by a caregiver: National violent death reporting system. *Journal of Interpersonal Violence, 26*(1), 137–157.

Karjane, H. K., Fisher, B. S., & Cullen, F. T. (2002). *Campus sexual assault: How America's institutions of higher education respond.* Newton, MA: Education Development Center.

Kashani, J. H., & Allan, W. D. (1998). *The impact of family violence on children and adolescents.* Thousand Oaks, CA: Sage.

Kashani, J. H., Daniel, A. E., Dandoy, A. C., & Holcomb, W. R. (1992). Family violence: Impact on children. *Journal of the American Academy of Child and Adolescent Psychiatry, 31,* 181–189.

Kasian, M., & Painter, S. L. (1992). Frequency and severity of psychological abuse in a dating population. *Journal of Interpersonal Violence, 7,* 350–364.

Kasindorf, M. (2006, May 17). L.A. confronts Asian family abuse. *USA Today.* Retrieved from www.usatoday.com/news/nation/2006–05–17-koreatown_x.htm.

Katerndahl, D. A., & Obregon, M. L. (2007). An exploration of the spiritual and psychosocial variables associated with husband-to-wife abuse and its effect on women in abusive relationships. *International Journal of Psychiatry in Medicine, 37*(2), 113–126.

Katz, J. (1994). *Mentors in Violence Prevention (MVP) Trainer's Guide.* Boston, MA: Northeastern University.

Katz, J., Kuffel, S. W., & Coblentz, A. (2002). Are there gender differences in sustaining dating violence? An examination of frequency, severity, and relationship satisfaction. *Journal of Family Violence, 17,* 247–271.

Kaufman, C. G. (2010). Domestic violence and the Jewish community: The literature expands. *Nashim: A Journal of Jewish Women's Studies and Gender issues, 20,* 172–175.

Kaufman, J., & Cicchetti, D. (1989). Effects of maltreatment on school-age children's socio-emotional development: Assessments in day-camp setting. *Developmental Psychology, 25,* 516–524.

Kaufman, J., & Zigler, E. (1987). Do abused children become abusive parents? *American Journal of Orthopsychiatry, 57,* 186–192.

Kaufman, J. G., & Widom, C. S. (1999). Childhood victimization, running away, and delinquency. *Journal of Research in Crime and Delinquency, 36,* 347–370.

Kaufman Kantor, G., & Asdigian, N. L. (1996). When women are under the influence: Does drinking or drug use by women provoke beatings by men? In M. Galanter (Ed.), *Recent developments in alcoholism.* New York, NY: Plenum.

Kaufman Kantor, G., & Straus, M. A. (1990). The "drunken bum" theory of wife beating. In M. A. Straus & R. J. Gelles (Eds.), *Physical violence in American families: Risk factors and adaptations to violence in 8,145 families* (pp. 203–226). New Brunswick, NJ: Transaction.

Kaukinen, C. (2004). The help-seeking strategies of female violent-crime victims: The direct and conditional effects of race and the victim-offender relationship. *Journal of Interpersonal Violence, 19*(9), 967–990.

Kaukinen, C., & DeMaris, A. (2009). Sexual assault and current mental health: The role of help-seeking and police responses. *Violence Against Women, 15,* 1331–1357.

Kaura, S. A., & Lohman, B. J. (2007). Dating violence victimization, relationship satisfaction, mental health problems, and acceptability of violence: A comparison of men and women. *Journal of Family Violence, 22,* 367–381.

Kaysen, D., Neighbors, C., Martell, J., Fossos, N., & Larimer, M. E. (2006). Incapacitated rape and alcohol use: A prospective analysis. *Addictive Behaviors, 31,* 1820–1832.

Kazak, A. E. (1989). Families of chronically ill children: A systems and social-ecological model of adaptation and challenge. *Journal of Consulting and Clinical Psychology, 57,* 25–30.

Kazdin, A. E. (2010). *Parenting expert warns against physical punishment* [Electronic Version]. Retrieved from http://www.apa.org/news/press/releases/2010/05/corporal-punishment.aspx.

Kean, R. B., & Dukes, R. L. (1991). Effects of witness characteristics on the perception and reportage of child abuse. *Child Abuse and Neglect, 15,* 423–435.

Keiley, M. K., Howe, T. R., Dodge, K. A., Bates, J. E., & Pettit, G. E. (2001). The timing of child physical maltreatment: A cross-domain growth analysis of impact on adolescent externalizing and internalizing problems. *Development and Psychopathology, 13,* 891–912.

Keilitz, S. L., Davis, D., Efkeman, H. S., Flango, C., & Hannaford, P. L. (1998). *Civil protection orders: Victims' views on effectiveness.* National Institute of Justice research preview publication. Retrieved May 2004, from U.S. Department of Justice: http://www.ncjrs.org/pdffiles/fs000191.pdf.

Kelleher, K., Chaffin, M., Hollenberg, J., & Fischer, E. (1994). Alcohol and drug disorders among physically abusive and neglectful parents in a community-based sample. *American Journal of Public Health, 84,* 1586–1590.

Kelley, S. J. (1992). Parenting stress and child maltreatment in drug-exposed children. *Child Abuse and Neglect, 16,* 317–328.

Kelley, S. J. (2002). Child maltreatment in the context of substance abuse. In J. E. B. Myers, L. Berliner, J. Briere, C. T. Hendrix, C. Jenny, & T. A. Reid (Eds.), *The APSAC handbook on child maltreatment* (2nd ed., pp. 105–117). Thousand Oaks, CA: Sage.

Kellogg, N. D., & Menard, S. W. (2003). Violence among family members of children and adolescents evaluated for sexual abuse. *Child Abuse and Neglect, 27*(1), 1367–1376.

Kelly, C. E., & Warshafsky, L. (1987). *Partner abuse in gay male and lesbian couples.* Paper presented at the Third National Conference for Family Violence Research, Durham, NH.

Kelly, J. B., & Johnson, M. P. (2008). Differentiation among types of intimate partner violence: Research update and implications for interventions. *Family Court Review, 46*(3), 476–499.

Kelly, R. J., Wood, J. J., Gonzalez, L. S., MacDonald, V., & Waterman, J. (2002). Effects of mother-son incest and positive perceptions of sexual abuse experiences on the psychosocial adjustment of clinic-referred men. *Child Abuse and Neglect, 26,* 425–441.

Kelly, V. (2004). Psychological abuse of women: A review of the literature. *The Family Journal, 12*(4), 383–388.

Kemp, A., Rawlings, E. I., & Green, B. L. (1991). Post-traumatic stress disorder in battered women: A shelter sample. *Journal of Traumatic Stress, 4,* 137–149.

Kempe, C. H., Silverman, F. N., Steele, B. F., Droegemueller, W., & Silver, H. K. (1962). The battered-child syndrome. *Journal of the American Medical Association, 181,* 17–24.

Kendall-Tackett, K., Williams, L. M., & Finkelhor, D. (1993). Impact of sexual abuse on children: A review and synthesis of recent empirical studies. *Psychological Bulletin, 113,* 164–180.

Kendall-Tackett, K. A. (2003). *Treating the lifetime health effects of childhood abuse.* New York, NY: Civic Research Institute.

Kenny, M. C., Capri, V., Thakkar-Kolar, R. R., Ryan, E., & Runyon, M. K. (2008). Child sexual abuse: From prevention to self-protection. *Child Abuse Review, 17,* 36–54.

Kent, A., & Waller, G. (2000). Childhood emotional abuse and eating psychopathology. *Clinical Psychology Review, 20,* 887–903.

Kernic, M. A., & Bonomi, A. E. (2007). Female victims of domestic violence: Which victims do police refer to crisis intervention?. *Violence and Victims, 22*(4), 463–473.

Kessler, R. C., Molnar, B. E., Feurer, I. D., & Appelbaum, M. (2001). Patterns and mental health predictors of domestic violence in the United States: Results from the National Comorbidity Survey. *International Journal of Law and Psychiatry, 24*(4), 487–508.

Kethineni, S. (2004). Youth-on-parent violence in a central Illinois county. *Youth Violence and Juvenile Justice, 2*(4), 374–394.

Kettrey, H. H., & Emery, B. C. (2006). The discourse of sibling violence. *Journal of Family Violence, 21,* 407–416.

Khan, R., & Cooke, D. J. (2008). Risk factors for severe inter-sibling violence: A preliminary study of a youth forensic sample. *Journal of Interpersonal Violence, 23,* 1513–1530.

Kienlen, K. K., Birmingham, D. L., Solberg, K. B., O'Regan, J. T., & Meloy, J. R. (1997). A comparative study of psychotic and nonpsychotic stalking. *Journal of the American Academy of Psychiatry and Law, 25,* 317–334.

Kilmer, J. R., Larimer, M. E., Parks, G. A., Dimeff, L. A., & Marlatt, G. A. (1999). Liability management or risk management? Evaluation of a Greek system alcohol policy. *Psychology of Addictive Behaviors, 13*(4), 269–278.

Kilpatrick, D. G., Acierno, R., Resnick, H. S., Saunders, B. E., & Best, C. L. (1997). A 2-year longitudinal analysis of the relationship between violent assault and substance use in women. *Journal of Consulting and Clinical Psychology, 65,* 834–847.

Kilpatrick, D. G., Ruggiero, K. J., Acierno, R., Saunders, B. E., Resnick, H. S., & Best, C. L. (2003). Violence and risk of PTSD, major depression, substance abuse/dependence, and comorbidity: Results from the National Survey of Adolescents. *Journal of Consulting and Clinical Psychology, 71*(4), 692–700.

Kim, H., & Kim, H. (2005). Incestuous experience among adolescents: Prevalence, family problems, perceived family dynamics, and psychological characteristics. *Public Health Nursing, 22*(6), 472–482.

Kim, J., McCullough, M. E., & Cicchetti, D. (2009). Parents' and children's religiosity and child behavioral adjustment among maltreated and nonmaltreated children. *Journal of Child and Family Studies, 18*(5), 594–605.

King, N., Tonge, B. J., Mullen, P. E., Myerson, N., Heyne, D., Rollings, S., . . . Ollendick, T. H. (2000). Sexually abused children and post-traumatic stress disorder. *Counseling Psychology Quarterly, 13,* 365–375.

Kingsnorth, R. F., Macintosh, R. C., Berdahl, T., Blades, C., & Rossi, S. (2001). Domestic violence: The role of interracial/ethnic dyads in criminal court processing. *Journal of Contemporary Criminal Justice, 17,* 123–141.

Kirtz, J. (2008, January 31). Abuse of U.S. Muslim women is greater than reported, advocacy groups say. *Fox News.* Retrieved from www.foxnews.com/story/0,2933,327187,00.html

Kiselica, M. S., & Morrill-Richards, M. (2007). Sibling maltreatment: The forgotten abuse. *Journal of Counseling and Development, 85,* 148–161.

Klaus, P. (2000). *Crimes against persons age 65 or older, 1992–97* [Electronic Version]. Retrieved January 2004 from http://www.ojp.usdoj.gov/bjs/pub/ pdf/cpa6597.pdf.

Klaus, P. (2005). *Crimes against persons age 65 or older, 1993–2002* [Electronic Version]. Available at http://www.bjs.gov/content/pub/pdf/cpa6502.pdf.

Klawitter, M. M., & Flatt, V. (1998). The effects of state and local antidiscrimination policies on earnings for gays and lesbians. *Journal of Policy Analysis and Management, 17*(4), 658–686.

Klein, A., Salomon, A., Huntington, N., Dubois, J., & Lang, D. (2009). *A statewide study of stalking and its criminal justice response.* U.S. Department of Justice. Document number 228354. Washington, DC: Government Printing Office.

Klein, A., Tobin, T., Salomon, A., & Dubois, J. (2008). *A statewide profile of abuse of older women and the criminal justice response.* Summary by the U.S. Department of Justice. Available at https://www.ncjrs.gov/pdffiles1/nij/grants/222460.pdf.

Kleinfield, N. R. (2011, May 9). A bleak life, cut short at 4, harrowing from the start. *The New York Times.* (New York edition ed., pp. A1).

Klimes-Dougan, B., & Kistner, J. (1990). Physically abused preschoolers' response to peers' distress. *Developmental Psychology, 26,* 599–602.

Klinesmith, J., Kasser, T., & McAndrew, F. (2006). Guns, testosterone, and aggression: An experimental test of a mediational hypothesis. *Association for Psychological Science, 17*(7), 568–571.

Klitzman, R. L., Greenberg, J. D., Pollack, L. M., & Dolezal, C. (2002). MDMA ("ecstasy") use, and its association with high risk behaviors, mental health, and other factors among gay/bisexual men in New York City. *Drug and Alcohol Dependence, 66,* 115–125.

Knapik, G. P., Martsolf, D. S., & Draucker, C. B. (2008). Being delivered: Spirituality in survivors of sexual violence. *Issues in Mental Health Nursing, 29,* 335–350.

Knauer, N. (2001). Same sex domestic violence: Claiming a domestic sphere while risking negative stereotypes. In K. D. Lemon (Ed.), *Domestic violence law* (pp. 203–212). St. Paul, MN: West Group.

Knepper, K. (1995). Withholding medical treatment from infants: When is it child neglect? *University of Louisville Journal of Family Law, 33,* 1–54.

Knott, T., & Donovan, K. (2010). Disproportionate representation of African-American children in foster care: Secondary analysis of the National Child Abuse and Neglect Data System, 2005. *Children and Youth Services Review, 32,* 679–684.

Knox, M. (2010). On hitting children: A review of corporal punishment in the United States. *Journal of Pediatric Health Care, 24,* 103–107.

Knudsen, D. D. (1988). Child sexual abuse and pornography: Is there a relationship? *Journal of Family Violence, 3,* 253–267.

Knutson, J. F., Johnson, C. R., & Sullivan, P. M. (2004). Disciplinary choices of mothers of deaf children and mothers of normally hearing children. *Child Abuse and Neglect, 28,* 925–937.

Kolko, D. J. (1996). Individual cognitive behavioral treatment and family therapy for physically abused children and their offending parents: A comparison of clinical outcomes. *Child Maltreatment, 1,* 322–342.

Kolko, D. J. (2002). Child physical abuse. In J. E. B. Myers, L. Berliner, J. Briere, C. T. Hendrix, C. Jenny, & T. A. Reid (Eds.), *The APSAC handbook on child maltreatment* (2nd ed., pp. 21–54). Thousand Oaks, CA: Sage.

Kolko, D. J., Moser, J., & Hughes, J. (1989). Classroom training in sexual victimization awareness and prevention skills: An extension of the Red Flag/Green Flag people program. *Journal of Family Violence, 4*(1), 25–45.

Kolko, D. J., Seleyo, J., & Brown, E. J. (1999). The treatment histories and service involvement of physically and sexually abusive families: Description, correspondence, and clinical correlates. *Child Abuse and Neglect, 23,* 459–476.

Korbin, J. E. (1980). The cultural context of child abuse and neglect. *Child Abuse and Neglect, 4,* 3–13.

Korbin, J. E., Coulton, C. J., Chard, S., Platt-Houston, C., & Su, M. (1998). Impoverishment and child maltreatment in African American and European American neighborhoods. *Development and Psychopathology, 10,* 215–233.

Kosciw, J. G., Greytak, E. A., Diaz, E. M., & Bartkiewicz, M. J. (2010). *The 2009 School Climate Survey: The experiences of lesbian, gay, bisexual, and transgender youth in our nation's schools.* New York, NY: Gay, Lesbian, and Straight Education Network.

Koss, M. P. (1988). Hidden rape: Sexual aggression and victimization in a national sample of students in higher education. In A. W. Burgess (Ed.), *Rape and sexual assault II* (pp. 3–25). New York, NY: Garland.

Koss, M. P., & Dinero, T. E. (1989). Discriminant analysis of risk factors for sexual victimization among a national sample of college women. *Journal of Consulting and Clinical Psychology, 57*(2), 242–250.

Koss, M. P., Figueredo, A. J., & Prince, R. J. (2002). Cognitive meditation of rape's mental, physical and social health impact: Tests of four models in cross-sectional data. *Journal of Consulting and Clinical Psychology, 70,* 926–941.

Koss, M. P., & Gaines, J. A. (1993). The prediction of sexual aggression by alcohol use, athletic participation, and fraternity affiliation. *Journal of Interpersonal Violence, 8,* 94–108.

Koss, M. P., Gidycz, C. A., & Wisniewski, N. (1987). The scope of rape: Incidence and prevalence of sexual aggression and victimization in a national sample of higher education students. *Journal of Consulting and Clinical Psychology, 55,* 162–170.

Koss, M. P., Leonard, K. E., Beezley, D. A., & Oros, C. J. (1985). Nonstranger sexual aggression: A discriminant analysis of the psychological characteristics of undetected offenders. *Sex Roles, 12,* 981–992.

Kosson, D. S., Kelly, J. C., & White, J. W. (1997). Psychopathy-related traits predict self-reported sexual aggression among college men. *Journal of Interpersonal Violence, 12,* 241–254.

Kotch, J. B., Lewis, T., Hussey, J., English, D., Thompson, R., Litrownik, A. J., . . . Dubowitz, H. (2008). Importance of early neglect for childhood aggression. *Pediatrics, 121*(4), 725–731.

Koyano, W. (1989). Japanese attitudes toward the elderly: A review of research findings. *Journal of Cross-Cultural Psychology, 4,* 335–345.

Kratcoski, P. C. (1985). Youth violence directed toward significant others. *Journal of Adolescence, 8,* 145–157.

Krebs, C., Breiding, M. J., Browne, A., & Warner, T. (2011). The association between different types of intimate partner violence experienced by women. *Journal of Family Violence, 26,* 487–500.

Krebs, C. P., Lindquist, C. H., Warner, T. D., Fisher, B. S., & Martin, S. L. (2007). *The Campus Sexual Assault Study.* Washington, DC: U. S. Department of Justice.

Krienert, J. L., & Fleisher, M. S. (2005). "It ain't happening here": Working to understand prison rape. *Criminologist, 30,* 2–6.

Krienert, J. L., & Walsh, J. A. (2010). Eldercide: A gendered examination of elderly homicide in the United States. *Homicide Studies 14*(1), 52–71.

Krob, M. J., Johnson, A., & Jordan, M. H. (1986). Burned and battered adults. *Journal of Burn Care and Rehabilitation, 7,* 529–531.

Krug, R. S. (1989). Adult male reports of childhood sexual abuse by mothers: Case descriptions, motivations, and long-term consequences. *Child Abuse and Neglect, 13,* 111–119.

Kubik, E. K., & Hecker, J. E. (2005). Cognitive distortions about sex and sexual offending: A comparison of sex offending girls, delinquent girls, and girls from the community. *Journal of Child Sexual Abuse, 14,* 43–69.

Kuehnle, K., & Sullivan, A. (2001). Patterns of anti-gay violence: An analysis of incident characteristics and victim reporting. *Journal of Interpersonal Violence, 16,* 928–943.

Kuehnle, K., & Sullivan, A. (2003). Gay and lesbian victimization: Reporting factors in domestic violence and bias incidents. *Criminal Justice and Behavior, 30,* 85–96.

Kulwicki, A., & Miller, J. (1999). Domestic violence in the Arab American population: Transformation environmental conditions through community education. *Issues in Mental Health Nursing, 20*(3), 199–215.

Kumagai, F., & Straus, M. A. (1983). Conflict resolution tactics in Japan, India, and the USA. *Journal of Comparative Family Studies, 14,* 377–392.

Kurtz, P. D., Gaudin, J. M., Howing, P. T., & Wodarski, J. S. (1993). The consequences of physical abuse and neglect on the school age child: Mediating factors. *Children and Youth Services Review, 15*(2), 85–104.

Lachs, M., & Pillemer, K. (1998). The morality of elder mistreatment. *Journal of the American Medical Association, 280*(5), 428–432.

Lachs, M. S. (2003). Elder justice: Medical forensic issues concerning abuse and neglect (draft report): Medical forensic roundtable discussion. Detection and diagnosis: What are the forensic markers for identifying physical and psychological signs of elder abuse and neglect? [Electronic Version]. Retrieved March 22, 2002, from http://www.ojp.usdoj.gov/nij/elderjust/elder_05.html.

Lachs, M. S., & Pillemer, K. A. (2006). Abuse and neglect of elderly persons. *The New England Journal of Medicine, 332*(7), 437–443.

Lachs, M. S., Williams, C., O'Brien, S., Hurst, L., & Horwitz, R. (1997). Risk factors for reported elder abuse and neglect: A nine-year observational cohort study. *Gerontologist, 37,* 469–474.

Lachs, M. S., Williams, C. S., O'Brien, S., Pillemer, K. A., & Charlson, M. E. (1998). The mortality of elder mistreatment. *Journal of the American Medical Association, 280,* 428–432.

Lackie, L., & deMan, A. F. (1997). Correlates of sexual aggression among male university students. *Sex Roles, 37,* 451–457.

Lambert, E., Jenkins, M., & Ventura, L. (2009). The influence of gender, race, age, academic level, and political affiliation on corporal punishment attitudes. *Professional Issues in Criminal Justice, 4*(3&4), 51–67.

Land, K. C. (2010). Child and youth well-being index. *Foundation for Child Development.* Retrieved from http://fcd-us.org/sites/default/files/FINAL%202010%20CWI%20Annual%20Release.pdf.

Landolt, M. A., & Dutton, D. G. (1997). Power and personality: An analysis of gay male intimate abuse. *Sex Roles, 37,* 335–359.

Lang, R. A., Langevin, R., Van Santen, V., Billingsley, D., & Wright, P. (1990). Marital relations in incest offenders. *Journal of Sex and Marital Therapy, 16,* 214–229.

Langeland, W., & Hartgers, C. (1998). Child sexual and physical abuse and alcoholism: A review. *Journal of Studies on Alcohol, 59,* 336–348.

Langevin, R., Handy, L., Hook, H., Day, D., & Russon, A. (1983). Are incestuous fathers pedophilic and aggressive? In R. Langevin (Ed.), *Erotic preference, gender identity, and aggression.* New York, NY: Erlbaum.

Langevin, R., Wortzman, G., Dickey, R., Wright, P., & Handy, L. (1988). Neuropsychological impairment in incest offenders. *Annals of Sex Research, 1,* 401–415.

Langhinrichsen-Rohling, J. (2005). Top ten greatest "hits": Important findings and future directions for interpersonal violence research. *Journal of Interpersonal Violence, 20,* 108–118.

Langhinrichsen-Rohling, J., & Monson, C. M. (1998). Marital rape: Is the crime taken seriously without co-occurring physical abuse? *Journal of Family Violence, 13,* 433–443.

Langhinrichsen-Rohling, J., Monson, C. M., Meyer, K. A., Caster, J., & Sanders, A. (1998). The associations among family-of-origin violence and young adults' current depressed, hopeless, suicidal, and life-threatening behavior. *Journal of Family Violence, 13,* 243–261.

Langhinrichsen-Rohling, J., & Neidig, P. H. (1995). Violent backgrounds of economically disadvantaged youth: Risk factors for perpetrating violence? *Journal of Family Violence, 10,* 379–397.

Langhinrichsen-Rohling, J., Palarea, R. W., Cohen, J., & Rohling, M. (2000). Breaking up is hard to do: Unwanted pursuit behaviors following the dissolution of a romantic relationship. *Violence and Victims, 15,* 73–90.

Lanktree, C., Briere, J., & Zaidi, L. (1991). Incidence and impact of sexual abuse in a child outpatient sample: The role of direct inquiry. *Child Abuse and Neglect, 15,* 447–453.

Larimer, M. E., Lydum, A. R., Anderson, B. K., & Turner, A. P. (1999). Male and female recipients of unwanted sexual contact in a college student sample: Prevalence rates, alcohol use, and depression symptoms. *Sex Roles, 40,* 295–308.

Laroche, D. (2005). *Aspects of the context and consequences of domestic violence—Situational couple violence and intimate terrorism in Canada in 1999*. Quebec, CA: Institut de la statistique du Quebec.

Laroche, D. (2008). *Context and consequences of domestic violence against men and women in Canada in 2004*. Quebec, CA: Institut de la statistique du Quebec.

LaRose, L., & Wolfe, D. (1987). Psychological characteristics of parents who abuse or neglect their children. In B. Lahey & A. E. Kazdin (Eds.), *Advances in clinical child psychology* (Vol. 10, pp. 55–97). New York, NY: Plenum.

Larsen, S., Kim-Goh, M., & Nguyen, T. (2008). Asian American immigrant families and child abuse: Cultural considerations. *Journal of Systemic Therapies, 27*(1), 16–29.

Larson, C. S., Terman, D. L., Gomby, D., Quinn, L. S., & Behrman, R. E. (1994). Sexual abuse of children: Recommendations and analysis. *Future of Children, 4*(2), 4–30.

Larzelere, R. (1986). Moderate spanking: Model or deterrent of children's aggression in the family? *Journal of the Family Violence, 1*, 27–36.

Larzelere, R. E., & Kuhn, B. R. (2007). *Comparing child outcomes of physical punishment and alternative disciplinary tactics: A meta-analysis* [Electronic Version]. Retrieved from http://humansciences.okstate.edu/facultystaff/Larzelere/mappvalsum.pdf.

Laumann, E. O., Leitsch, S. A., & Waite, L. J. (2008). Elder mistreatment in the United States: Prevalence estimates from a nationally representative study. *Journals of Gerontology, 63B*(4), 248–254.

Laviola, M. (1992). Effects of older brother-younger sister incest: A study of the dynamics in 17 cases. *Child Abuse and Neglect, 16*, 409–421.

Lawrence and Garner v. Texas (539 U.S. 558, 123 S. Ct. 2472, 156 L. Ed. 2d 508). (2003). United States Supreme Court decision. Washington, DC: Government Printing Office.

Lawrenz, F., Lembo, R., & Schade, S. (1988). Time series analysis of the effect of a domestic violence directive on the number of arrests per day. *Journal of Criminal Justice, 16*, 493–498.

Lawyer, S., Resnick, H. S., Bakanic, V., Burkett, T., & Kilpatrick, D. G. (2010). Forcible, drug-facilitated, and incapacitated rape and sexual assault among undergraduate women. *Journal of American College Health, 58*(5), 453–460.

Lee, H. Y., & Eaton, C. K. (2009). Financial abuse in elderly Korean immigrants: Mixed analysis of the role of culture on perception and help-seeking intention. *Journal of Gerontologic Social Work, 52*(5), 463–488.

Lee, H. Y., Gibson, P., & Chaisson, R. (2011). Elderly Korean immigrants' socially and culturally constructed definitions of elder neglect. *Journal of Aging Studies, 25*, 126–134.

Lee, M., & Kolomer, S. (2005). Caregiver burden, dementia, and elder abuse in South Korea. *Journal of Elder Abuse & Neglect, 17*, 61–74.

Lee, S., Guterman, N., & Lee, Y. (2008). Risk factors for paternal physical child abuse. *Child Abuse and Neglect, 32*, 846–858.

Lehavot, K., Walters, K., & Simoni, J. (2010). Abuse, mastery, and health among lesbian, bisexual, and two-spirit American Indian and Alaska native women. *Psychology of Violence, 1*, 53–67.

Lehmann, M., & Santilli, N. R. (1996). Sex differences in perception of spousal abuse. *Journal of Social Behavior & Personality, 11*, 229–239.

LeJeune, C., & Follette, V. (1994). Taking responsibility: Sex differences in reporting dating violence. *Journal of Interpersonal Violence, 9*(1), 133–140.

Lemberg, J. (2002, July 21). Spouse abuse in South Asian marriages may be high [Electronic Version]. *Women's News*. Retrieved March 12, 2004, from http://www.womensenews.org/article.cfm/dyn/aid/979/context/archive.

Leonard, K. E. (2005). Alcohol and intimate partner violence: When can we say that heavy drinking is a contributing cause of violence? *Addiction, 100*(4), 422–425.

Leonard, K. E. (2011, March 31). Director of the Research Institute on Additions, University at Buffalo, The State University of New York. [Personal communication.]

Leone, J. M., Johnson, M. P., Cohan, C., & Lloyd, S. E. (2004). Consequences of male partner violence for low-income minority women. *Journal of Marriage and Family, 66*(2), 472–490.

Lesnik-Oberstein, M., Koers, A. J., & Cohen, L. (1995). Parental hostility and its sources in psychologically abusive mothers: A test of the three-factory theory. *Child Abuse and Neglect, 19,* 33–49.

Lesserman, J., Li, Z., Drossman, D., Toomey, T. C., Nachman, G., & Glogau, L. (1997). Impact of sexual and physical abuse dimensions on health status: Development of an abuse severity measure. *Psychosomatic Medicine, 59,* 152–160.

Letellier, P. (1994). Gay and bisexual male domestic violence victimization: Challenges to feminist theory and responses to violence. *Violence and Victims, 9,* 95–106.

Letellier, P. (1996). Twin epidemics: Domestic violence and HIV infection among gay and bisexual men. *Journal of Lesbian and Gay Social Services, 4,* 69–81.

Letellier, P. (1999). Rape. In B. Leventhal & S. E. Lundy (Eds.), *Same-sex domestic violence.* Thousand Oaks, CA: Sage.

Leung, P., & Cheung, M. (2008). A prevalence study on partner abuse in six Asian American ethnic groups in the USA. *International Social Work, 51*(5), 635–649.

Leventhal, B. (1990). Confronting lesbian battering. In P. Elliot (Ed.), *Confronting lesbian battering* (pp. 16–18). St. Paul, MN: Minnesota Coalition for Battered Women.

Levesque, R. J. (2001). *Culture and family violence: Fostering change through human rights law.* Washington, DC: American Psychological Association.

Levinson, D. (1989). *Family violence in a cross-cultural perspective.* Newbury Park, CA: Sage.

Lewis, D. O., Lovely, R., Yeager, C., & Femina, D. (1989). Toward a theory of the genesis of violence: A follow-up study of delinquents. *Journal of the American Academy of Child and Adolescent Psychiatry, 28,* 431–436.

Lewis, D. O., Shanok, S. S., & Balla, D. A. (1979). Parental criminality and medical histories of delinquent children. *American Journal of Psychiatry, 136,* 288–292.

Lewit, E. M., & Baker, L. S. (1996). Children as victims of violence. *Future of Children, 6*(3), 147–156.

Li, F., Godinet, M. T., & Arnsberger, P. (2011). Protective factors among families with children at risk of maltreatment: Follow up to early school years. *Children and Youth Services Review, 33,* 139–148.

Libby, A., Orton, H., Beals, J., Buchwald, D., & Manson, S. (2008). Childhood abuse and later parenting outcomes in two American Indian tribes. *Child Abuse and Neglect, 32,* 195–211.

Lie, G. Y., & Gentlewarrier, S. (1991). Intimate violence in lesbian relationships. Discussion of survey findings and practice implications. *Journal of Social Service Research, 15,* 41–59.

Lie, G. Y., Schilit, R., Bush, J., Montagne, M., & Reyes, L. (1991). Lesbians in currently aggressive relationships: How frequently do they report aggressive past relationships? *Violence and Victims, 6,* 121–135.

Lieberman, A. F., & Knorr, K. (2007). The impact of trauma: A developmental framework for infancy and early childhood. *Psychiatric Annals, 37*(6), 416–422.

Lifespan of Greater Rochester (2011). *Under the radar: New York State Elder Abuse Prevalence Study.* New York, NY: Weil Cornell Medical Center, New York City Department for the Aging. Available at http://www.ocfs.state.ny.us/main/reports/Under%20the%20Radar%2005%2012%2011%20final%20report.pdf.

Lightfoot, E., Hill, K., & LaLiberte, T. (2010). The inclusion of disability as a condition for termination of parental rights. *Child Abuse and Neglect, 34*(12), 927–934.

Lilith, R. (2001). Reconsidering the abuse that dare not speak its name: A criticism of recent legal scholarship regarding same-gender domestic violence. *Michigan Journal of Gender and Law, 7,* 181–219.

Lindner Gunnoe, M., Hetherington, E. M., & Reiss, D. (1999). Parental religiosity, parenting style, and adolescent social responsibility. *Journal of Early Adolescence, 19,* 199–225.

Lindsey, D., Martin, S., & Doh, J. (2002). The failure of intensive casework services to reduce foster care placements: An examination of family preservation studies. *Child & Youth Services Review, 24,* 743–775.

Lipschitz, D. S., Winegar, R. K., Nicolaou, A. L., Hartnick, E., Wolfson, M., & Southwick, S. M. (1999). Perceived abuse and neglect as risk factors for suicidal behavior in adolescent inpatients. *Journal of Nervous and Mental Disease, 187,* 32–39.

Lipsky, S., Field, C. A., Caetano, R., & Larkin, G. L. (2005). Posttraumatic stress disorder symptomatology and comorbid depressive symptoms among abused women referred from emergency department care. *Violence and Victims, 20,* 645–659.

Lisak, D., Hopper, J., & Song, P. (1996). Factors in the cycle of violence: Gender rigidity and emotional constriction. *Journal of Traumatic Stress, 7,* 507–523.

Lisak, D., & Ivan, C. (1995). Deficits in intimacy and empathy in sexually aggressive men. *Journal of Interpersonal Violence, 10,* 296–308.

Lisak, D., & Miller, P. M. (2002). Repeat rape and multiple offending among undetected rapists. *Violence and Victims, 17*(1), 73–84.

Lisak, D., & Roth, S. (1988). Motivational factors in nonincarcerated sexually aggressive men. *Journal of Personality and Social Psychology, 55,* 795–802.

Lisak, D., & Roth, S. (1990). Motives and psychodynamics of self-reported, unincarcerated rapists. *American Journal of Orthopsychiatry, 60,* 268–280.

Livingston, L. R. (1986). Children's violence to single mothers. *Journal of Sociology and Social Welfare, 13,* 920–933.

Locke, L. M., & Richman, C. L. (1999). Attitudes toward domestic violence: Race and gender issues. *Sex Roles, 40,* 227–247.

Lockhart, L. L., White, B. W., Causby, V., & Isaac, A. (1994). Letting out the secret: Violence in lesbian relationships. *Journal of Interpersonal Violence, 9,* 469–492.

Loeber, R., & Strouthamer-Loeber, M. (1986). Family factors as correlates and predictors of juvenile conduct problems and delinquency. In M. Tonry & N. Morris (Eds.), *Crime and justice: An annual review of the research* (Vol. 7). Chicago, IL: University of Chicago Press.

Lofquist, D. (2011, September). Same-sex couple households, *American Community Survey Briefs.* U.S. Department of Commerce.

Loftus, E., & Ketcham, K. (1994). *The myth of repressed memory: False memories and allegations of sexual abuse.* New York, NY: St. Martin's Griffin.

Logan, TK, Cole, J., & Shannon, L. (2007). A mixed-methods examination of sexual coercion and degradation among women in violent relationships who do and do not report forced sex. *Violence and Victims, 22*(1), 71–94.

Logan, TK, Cole, J., Shannon, L., & Walker, R. (2006). *Partner stalking: How women respond, cope, and survive.* New York, NY: Springer.

Logan, TK, Leukefeld, C., & Walker, B. (2000). Stalking as a variant of intimate violence: Implications from a young adult sample. *Violence and Victims, 15,* 91–111.

Logan, TK, Nigoff, A., Walker, R., & Jordan, C. (2002). Stalker profiles with and without protective orders: Reoffending or criminal justice processing. *Violence and Victims, 17,* 541–553.

Logan, TK, & Walker, R. (2009). Partner stalking: Psychological dominance or "business as usual." *Trauma, Violence, and Abuse, 10*(3), 247–270.

Logan, TK, & Walker, R. (2010). Toward a deeper understanding of the harms caused by partner stalking. *Violence and Victims, 25*(4), 440–455.

Lohrmann-O'Rourke, S., & Zirkel, P. A. (1998). The case law on aversive interventions for students with disabilities. *Exceptional Children, 65,* 101–123.

Lombardi, E. (2001). Enhancing transgender health care. *American Journal of Public Health, 91,* 869–872.

Lombardi, E. L., & van Servellen, G. (2000). Building culturally sensitive substance use prevention and treatment programs for transgendered populations. *Journal of Substance Abuse Treatment, 19,* 291–296.

London, K., Bruck, M., Ceci, S. J., & Shuman, D. W. (2005). Disclosure of child sexual abuse: What does the research tell us about the ways that children tell? *Psychology, Public Policy, and Law, 11,* 194–226.

London, K., Bruck, M., Wright, D., & Ceci, S. J. (2008). Review of the contemporary literature on how children report sexual abuse to others: Findings, methodological issues, and implications for forensic interviewers. *Memory, Special Issue: New Insights into Trauma and Memory, 16,* 29–47.

London, M. (2003). Crafting support services for older women. *Victimization of the Elderly and Disabled, 6,* 5–6.

Longdon, C. (1993). A survivor's and therapist's viewpoint. In M. Elliott (Ed.), *Female sexual abuse of children: The ultimate taboo* (pp. 50–60). New York, NY: John Wiley.

Loseke, D. R. (1992). *The battered woman and shelters: The social construction of wife abuse.* Albany, NY: State University of New York Press.

Loseke, D. R., & Kurz, D. (2005). Men's violence toward women is the serious social problem. In D. R. Loseke, R. J. Gelles, & M. M. Cavanaugh (Eds.), *Current controversies on family violence* (2nd ed., pp. 79–96). Thousand Oaks, CA: Sage.

Lundy, M., & Grossman, S. F. (2009). Domestic violence service users: A comparison of older and younger women victims. *Journal of Family Violence, 24,* 14.

Lung, C. T., & Daro, D. (1996). *Current trends in child abuse reporting and fatalities: The results of the 1995 annual fifty-state survey.* Chicago, IL: National Committee to Prevent Child Abuse.

Luntz, B., & Widom, C. S. (1994). Antisocial personality disorder in abused and neglected children grown up. *Journal of Psychiatry, 151,* 670–674.

Lutenbacher, M., Cohen, A., & Mitzel, J. (2003). Do we really help? Perspectives of abused women. *Public Health Nursing, 20*(1), 56–64.

MacKenzie, M. J., Nicklas, E., Brooks-Gunn, J., & Waldfogel, J. (2011). Who spanks infants and toddlers? Evidence from the fragile families and child well-being study. *Children and Youth Services Review, 33*(2), 284–290.

Mackey, A. L., Fromuth, M. E., & Kelly, D. B. (2010). The association of sibling relationship and abuse with later psychological adjustment. *Journal of Interpersonal Violence, 25,* 955–968.

MacMillan, H., MacMillan, J., Offord, D., Griffith, L., & MacMillan, A. (1994). Primary prevention of child sexual abuse: A critical review. Part II. *Journal of Child Psychology and Psychiatry, 35,* 857–876.

Macolini, R. M. (1995). Elder abuse policy: Consideration in research and legislation. *Behavioral Sciences and the Law, 13,* 349–363.

Madonna, P. G., VanScoyk, S., & Jones, D. P. (1991). Family interactions with incest and non-incest families. *American Journal of Psychiatry, 148,* 46–49.

Magen, R. (1999). In the best interest of battered women: Reconceptualizing allegations of failure to protect. *Child Maltreatment, 4,* 127–135.

Mahoney, A., & Donnelly, W. O. (2000). *Adolescent-to-parent physical aggression in clinic-referred families: Prevalence and co-occurrence with parent-to-adolescent physical aggression*. Durham, NH: Family Research Laboratory, University of New Hampshire.

Mahoney, A., Donnelly, W. O., Boxer, P., & Lewis, T. (2003). Marital and severe parent-to-adolescent physical aggression in clinic-referred families: Mother and adolescent reports on co-occurrence and links to child behavior problems. *Journal of Family Psychology, 17,* 3–19.

Mahoney, A., Pargament, K. I., Jewell, T., Swank, A. B., Scott, E., Emery, E., . . . Rye, M. (1999). Marriage and the spiritual realm: The role of proximal and distal religious constructs in marital functioning. *Journal of Family Psychology, 13,* 1–18.

Main, M., & George, C. (1985). Responses of abused and disadvantaged toddlers to distress in agemates: A study in the day care setting. *Developmental Psychology, 21,* 407–412.

Maiuro, R. D., & Eberle, J. A. (2008). State standards for domestic violence perpetrator treatment: Current status, trends, and recommendations. *Violence and Victims, 23*(2), 133–155.

Makepeace, J. (1981). Courtship violence among college students. *Family Relations, 30,* 97–100.

Makepeace, J. (1987). Social factor and victim-offender differences in courtship violence. *Family Relations, 36,* 87–91.

Makepeace, J. (1997). Courtship violence as a process: A developmental theory. In A. P. Cardarelli (Ed.), *Violence between intimate partners: Patterns, causes, and effects* (pp. 29–47). Boston, MA: Allyn & Bacon.

Makepeace, J. M. (1986). Gender differences in courtship violence victimization. *Family Relations, 35,* 383–388.

Maker, A. H. (2005). Child physical abuse: Prevalence, characteristics, predictors, and beliefs about parent-child violence in South Asian, Middle Eastern, East Asian, and Latina women in the United States. *Journal of Interpersonal Violence, 20*(11), 1406–1428.

Malamuth, N. M., Linz, D., Heavey, C. L., Barnes, G., & Aker, M. (1995). Using the confluence model of sexual aggression to predict men's conflict with women: A 10-year follow-up study. *Journal of Personality and Social Psychology, 69,* 353–369.

Malcoe, L., Duran, B., & Montgomery, J. (2004). Socioeconomic disparities in intimate partner violence against Native American women: A cross-sectional study. *BMC Medicine, 2*(20), 1–14.

Malecha, A., McFarlane, J., Gist, J., Watson, K., Batten, E., Hall, I., . . . Smith, S. (2003). Applying for and dropping a protection order: A study with 150 women. *Criminal Justice Policy Review, 14,* 486–504.

Malinosky-Rummell, R., Ellis, J. T., Warner, J. E., Ujcich, K., Carr, R. E., & Hansen, D. J. (1991, November). *Individualized behavioral intervention for physically abusive and neglectful families: An evaluation of the family interaction skills project*. Paper presented at the 25th Annual Convention of the Association for the Advancement of Behavior Therapy. New York, New York.

Malinosky-Rummell, R., & Hansen, D. J. (1993). Long-term consequences of childhood physical abuse. *Psychological Bulletin, 114,* 68–79.

Malks, B., Buckmaster, J., & Cunningham, L. (2003). Combating elder financial abuse: A multidisciplinary approach to a growing problem. *Journal of Elder Abuse & Neglect, 15,* 55–70.

Malley-Morrison, K., & Hines, D. A. (2003, July). *Religion, corporal punishment, and attitudes toward aggression*. Paper presented at the 8th International Family Violence Research Conference. Portsmouth, NH.

Malley-Morrison, K., & Hines, D. A. (2004). *Family violence in a cultural perspective: Defining, understanding, and combating abuse*. Thousand Oaks, CA: Sage.

Malley-Morrison, K., & Hines, D. A. (2007). Attending to the role of race/ethnicity in family violence research. *Journal of Interpersonal Violence, 22*(8), 943–972.

Malley-Morrison, K., You, H. S., & Mills, R. B. (2000). Young adult attachment styles and perceptions of elder abuse: A cross-cultural study. *Journal of Cross-Cultural Gerontology, 15,* 163–184.

Mallon, G. P. (1998). *We don't exactly get the welcome wagon: The experiences of gay and lesbian adolescents in child welfare systems.* New York, NY: Columbia University Press.

Malloy, L. C., Lyon, T. D., & Quas, J. A. (2007). Filial dependency and recantation of child sexual abuse allegations. *Journal of the American Academy of Child and Adolescent Psychiatry, 46,* 162–170.

Malone, J., Tyree, A., & O'Leary, K. D. (1989). Generalization and containment: Different effects of past aggression for wives and husbands. *Journal of Marriage and the Family, 51,* 687–697.

Manchikanti Gomez, A. (2011). Testing the cycle of violence hypothesis: Child abuse and adolescent dating violence as predictors of intimate partner violence in young adulthood. *Youth & Society, 43,* 171–192.

Mandell, D. S., Walrath, C. M., Manteuffel, B., Sgro, G., & Pinto-Martin, J. A. (2005). The prevalence and correlates of abuse among children with autism served in comprehensive community-based mental health settings. *Child Abuse & Neglect, 29,* 1359–1372.

Manders, J. E., & Stoneman, Z. (2009). Children with disabilities in the child protective service program: An analog study of investigation and case management. *Child Abuse & Neglect, 33,* 229–237.

Manly, J. T., Kim, J. E., Rogosch, F. A., & Cicchetti, D. (2001). Dimensions of child maltreatment and children's adjustment: Contributions of developmental timing and subtype. *Development and Psychopathology, 13,* 759–782.

Mann, C. R. (1996). *When women kill.* New York, NY: State University of New York Press.

Mannarino, A. P., & Cohen, J. A. (1996). A follow-up study on factors that medicate the development of psychological symptomatology in sexually abused girls. *Child Maltreatment, 1,* 246–260.

Mannarino, A. P., Cohen, J. A., & Berman, S. P. (1994). The relationship between pre-abuse factors and psychological symptomatology in sexually abused girls. *Child Abuse and Neglect, 18,* 63–71.

Mapp, S. (2006). The effects of sexual abuse as a child on the risk of mothers physically abusing their children: A path analysis using systems theory. *Child Abuse and Neglect, 30,* 1293–1310.

Margolies, L., Becker, M., & Jackson-Brewer, K. (1987). Internalized homophobia: Identifying and treating the oppressor within. In Boston Lesbian Collective (Ed.), *Lesbian psychologies: Explorations and challenges* (pp. 229–241). Urbana, IL: University of Illinois Press.

Margolies, L., & Leeder, E. (1995). Violence at the door: Treatment of lesbian batterers. *Violence Against Women, 1,* 139–157.

Marrujo, B., & Kreger, M. (1996). Definition of roles in abusive lesbian relationships. In C. M. Renzetti & C. H. Miley (Eds.), *Violence in gay and lesbian domestic partnerships* (pp. 22–33). New York, NY: Harrington Park Press/Haworth Press.

Marshall, L. L. (1996). Psychological abuse of women: Six distinct clusters. *Journal of Family Violence, 11,* 379–409.

Marshall, L. L., & Rose, P. (1990). Premarital violence: The impact of origin violence, stress, and reciprocity. *Violence and Victims, 5,* 51–64.

Marshall, P. D., & Norgard, K. E. (1983). *Child abuse and neglect: Sharing responsibility.* New York, NY: Wiley.

Martin, E. K., Taft, C. T., & Resick, P. A. (2007). Review of martial rape. *Aggression and Violent Behavior, 12*(3), 329–347.

Martin, M. E. (1997). Police promise: Community policing and domestic violence victim satisfaction. *Policing, 20,* 519–529.

Martin, S., Ray, N., Sotres-Alvarez, D., Kupper, L. L., Moracco, K. E., Dickens, P., . . . Gizlice, Z. (2006). Physical and sexual assault of women with disabilities. *Violence Against Women, 12*(9), 823–837.

Martino, S. C., Collins, R. L., & Ellickson, P. L. (2005). Cross-lagged relationships between substance use and intimate partner violence among a sample of young adult women. *Journal of Studies on Alcohol, 66*(1), 139–148.

Martone, M., Jaudes, P. K., & Cavins, M. K. (1996). Criminal prosecution of child sexual abuse cases. *Child Abuse and Neglect, 20,* 457–464.

Matthews, J. K. (1993). Working with female sexual abusers. In M. Elliott (Ed.), *Female sexual abuse of children: The ultimate taboo* (pp. 61–78). New York, NY: John Wiley.

Maxwell, C., Garner, J., & Fagan, J. A. (2002). *The effects of arrest on intimate partner violence: New evidence from the spouse assault replication program.* Washington, DC: National Institutes of Justice.

Maxwell, E. K., & Maxwell, R. J. (1992). Insults to the body civil: Mistreatment of elderly in two Plains Indian tribes. *Journal of Cross-Cultural Gerontology, 7*(11), 3–23.

May, P. A., & Gossage, P. (2001). Estimating the prevalence of fetal alcohol syndrome: A summary. *Alcohol Research & Health, 25,* 159–167.

Maynard, C., & Wiederman, M. (1997). Undergraduate students' perceptions of child sexual abuse: Effects of age, sex, and gender-role attitudes. *Child Abuse and Neglect, 21,* 833–844.

McAlpin, J. P. (2003). *N.J. draws fire over starvation case: Caseworkers fired; horrific abuse brings 2nd probe of agency* [Electronic Version]. Retrieved November 17, 2003, from http://www.boston.com/news/nation/articles/2003/10/28/.

McAuslan, P., Abbey, A., & Zawacki, T. (1998, June). *Acceptance of pressure and threats to obtain sex and sexual assault.* Paper presented at the Society for the Psychological Study of Social Issues (SPSSI) Convention. Ann Arbor, MI.

McClain, P. W., Sacks, J. J., Froehlke, R. G., & Ewigman, B. G. (1993). Estimates of fatal child abuse and neglect, United States, 1979 through 1988. *Pediatrics, 91,* 338–343.

McClennen, J. C. (2005). Domestic violence between same-gender partners: Recent findings and future research. *Journal of Interpersonal Violence, 20,* 149–154.

McClennen, J. C., Summers, A. B., & Daley, J. G. (2002). The lesbian partner abuse scale. *Research on Social Work Practice, 12,* 277–292.

McClennen, J. C., Summers, A. B., & Vaughan, C. (2002). Gay men's domestic violence: Dynamics, help-seeking behaviors, and correlates. *Journal of Gay & Lesbian Social Services, 14,* 23–49.

McCloskey, K. A., & Raphael, D. N. (2005). Adult perpetrator gender asymmetries in child sexual assault victim selection: Results from the 2000 National Incident-Based Reporting System. *Journal of Child Sexual Abuse, 14,* 1–24.

McCloskey, L. A. (1996). Socioeconomic and coercive power within the family. *Gender and Society, 10,* 449–463.

McCord, J. (1983). A forty-year perspective on effects of child abuse and neglect. *Child Abuse and Neglect, 7,* 265–270.

McCurdy, K. (2005). The influence of stress and support on maternal attitudes. *Child Abuse and Neglect, 29,* 251–268.

McDaniel, M., & Slack, K. (2005). Major life events and the risk of a child maltreatment investigation. *Children and Youth Services Review, 27*(2), 171–195.

McDonald, R., Jouriles, E. N., Briggs-Gowan, M. J., Rosenfield, D., & Carter, A. S. (2007). Violence toward a family member, angry adult conflict, and child adjustment difficulties: Relations in families with 1- to 3-year-old children. *Journal of Family Psychology, 21*(2), 176–184.

McDonald, R., Jouriles, E. N., Ramisetty-Mikler, S., Caetano, R., & Green, C. E. (2006). Estimating the number of American children living in partner-violent families. *Journal of Family Psychology, 20,* 137–142.

McDonald, R., Jouriles, E. N., Tart, C. D., & Minze, L. C. (2009). Children's adjustment problems in families characterized by men's severe violence toward women: Does other family violence matter? *Child Abuse and Neglect, 33,* 94–101.

McFarlane, J. (2007). Pregnancy following partner rape. *Trauma, Violence, and Abuse, 8*(2), 127–134.

McFarlane, J. & Malecha, A. (2005, October). *Sexual assault among intimates: Frequency, consequences and treatment.* Final Report. U.S. Department of Justice. Document number 211678. Washington, DC: Government Printing Office.

McFarlane, J., Malecha, A., Gist, J., Watson, K., Batten, E., & Hall, I. (2004). Protection orders and intimate partner violence: An 18-month study of 150 Black, Hispanic, and White women. *American Journal of Public Health, 94,* 613–618.

McFayden, R. G., & Kitson, W. J. H. (1996). Language comprehension and expression among adolescents who have experienced childhood physical abuse. *Journal of Child Psychology and Psychiatry and Allied Disciplines, 37,* 551–562.

McGough, L. S. (1997). Stretching the blanket: Legal reforms affecting child witnesses. *Learning and Individual Differences, 9,* 317–340.

McGrath, R. J., Cumming, G. F., & Burchard, B. L. (2003). *Current practices and trends in sexual abuser management: Safer society 2002 nationwide survey.* Brandon, VT: Safer Society Press.

McGregor, B. A., Carver, C. S., Antoni, M. H., Weiss, S., Yount, S., & Ironson, G. (2001). Internalized homophobia and distress among lesbian women who have been treated for breast cancer. *Psychology of Women Quarterly, 25,* 1–9.

McIntyre, J. K., & Widom, C. S. (2011). Childhood victimization and crime victimization. *Journal of Interpersonal Violence, 26*(4), 640–663.

McKay, M., Stoewe, J., McCadam, K., & Gonzales, J. (1998). Increasing access to child mental health services for urban children and their care givers. *Health and Social Work, 23,* 9–15.

McKenna, M., O'Connor, R., & Verco, J. (2010). *Exposing the dark side of parenting: A report of parents' experiences of child and adolescent family violence.* South Australia, AU: The Regional Alliance Addressing Child and Adolescent Violence in the Home.

McLaughlin, T. L., Heath, A. C., Bucholz, K. K., Madden, P. A., Bierut, L. J., Slutske, W. S., . . . Martin, N. G. (2000). Childhood sexual abuse and pathogenic parenting in the childhood recollections of adult twin pairs. *Psychological Medicine, 30,* 1293–1302.

McNamara, J. R., Ertl, M. A., Marsh, S., & Walker, S. (1997). Short-term response to counseling and case management intervention in a domestic violence shelter. *Psychological Reports, 81,* 1243–1251.

McNamara, J. R., Tamanini, K., & Pelletier-Walker, S. (2008). The impact of short-term counseling at a domestic violence shelter. *Research on Social Work Practice, 18*(2), 132–136.

McNeely, R. L., Cook, P. W., & Torres, J. B. (2001). Is domestic violence a gender issue, or a human issue? *Journal of Human Behavior in the Social Environment, 4,* 227–251.

McSherry, D. (2007). Understanding and addressing the "neglect of neglect": Why are we making a mole-hill out of a mountain? *Child Abuse and Neglect, 31,* 607–614.

Mechanic, M. B., Weaver, T. L., & Resick, P. A. (2008). Risk factors for physical injury among help-seeking battered women: An exploration of multiple abuse dimensions. *Violence Against Women, 14*(10), 1148–1165.

Medeiros, R. A., & Straus, M. A. (2006). Risk factors for physical violence between dating partners: Implications for gender-inclusive prevention and treatment of family violence. In J. Hamel & T. Nicholls (Eds.), *Family interventions in domestic violence: A handbook of gender-inclusive theory and treatment* (pp. 59–85). New York, NY: Springer.

Mehta, M. D. (2001). Pornography in Usenet: A study of 9,800 randomly selected images. *CyberPsychology and Behavior, 4,* 695–703.

Meiselman, K. C. (1978). *Incest: A psychological study of causes and effects with treatment recommendations.* San Francisco, CA: Jossey-Bass.

Mellott, R. N., Wagner, W. G., & Broussard, S. D. (1997). India vs. United States undergraduates' attitudes concerning child sexual abuse: The impact of survivor sex, survivor age, survivor response, respondent sex, and country of origin. *International Journal of Intercultural Relations, 21,* 305–318.

Melossi, D. (2001). The cultural embeddedness of social control: Reflections on the comparison of Italian and North-American cultures concerning punishment. *Theoretical Criminology, 5,* 403–424.

Meloy, J. R. (1998) The psychology of stalking. In J. R. Meloy (Ed.), *The psychology of stalking: Clinical and forensic perspectives* (pp. 2–23). San Diego, CA: Academic Press.

Meloy, J. R. (1999). Stalking: An old behavior, a new crime. *Psychiatric Clinics of North America, 22,* 85–99.

Meloy, J. R., Davis, B., & Lovette, J. (2001). Risk factors for violence among stalkers. *Journal of Threat Assessment, 1,* 3–16.

Melton, H. C. (2007). Stalking in the context of intimate partner abuse: In the victims' words. *Feminist Criminology, 2*(4), 347–363.

Melton, H. C., & Belknap, J. (2003). He hits, she hits: Assessing gender differences and similarities in officially reported intimate partner violence. *Criminal Justice and Behavior, 30*(3), 328–348.

Memon, K. (1993, March/April). Wife abuse in the Muslim community. *Islamic Horizons,* 24–35.

Memon, K. (1997). *Wife abuse in the Muslim community* [Electronic Version]. Retrieved July 2003 from http://www.zawaj.com/articles/abuse_ memon.html.

Mercy, J. A., Krug, E. G., Dahlberg, L. L., & Zwi, A. B. (2003). Violence and health: The United States in a global perspective. *American Journal of Public Health, 93,* 256–261.

Meredith, W. H., Abbott, D. A., & Adams, S. L. (1986). Family violence: Its relation to marital and parental satisfaction and family strengths. *Journal of Family Violence, 1,* 299–305.

Merrill, G. S. (1998). Understanding domestic violence among gay and bisexual men. In R. K. Bergen (Ed.), *Issues in intimate violence* (pp. 129–141). Thousand Oaks, CA: Sage.

Merrill, G. S., & Wolfe, V. A. (2000). Battered gay men: An exploration of abuse, help seeking, and why they stay. *Journal of Homosexuality, 39,* 1–30.

Merritt, D. H. (2009). Child abuse potential: Correlates with child maltreatment rates and structural measures of neighborhoods. *Children and Youth Services Review, 31*(8), 927–934.

Merskey, J. P., & Reynolds, A. J. (2007). Child maltreatment and violent delinquency: Disentangling main effects and subgroup effects. *Child Maltreatment, 12*(3), 246–258.

Messman-Moore, T. L., Coates, A. A., Gaffey, K. J., & Johnson, C. F. (2008). Sexuality, substance use, and susceptibility to victimization: Risk for rape and sexual coercion in a prospective study of college women. *Journal of Interpersonal Violence, 23*(12), 1730–1746.

Migliaccio, T. A. (2001). Marginalizing the battered male. *The Journal of Men's Studies, 9*(2), 205–226.

Mignon, S. I. (1998). Husband battering: A review of the debate over a controversial social phenomenon. In N. A. Jackson & G. C. Oates (Eds.), *Violence in intimate relationships: Examining sociological and psychological issues* (pp. 137–160). Boston, MA: Butterworth-Heinemann.

Mihalic, S. W., & Elliott, D. (1997). If violence is domestic, does it really count? *Journal of Family Violence, 12,* 293–311.

Milburn, M. A., & Conrad, S. D. (1996). *The politics of denial.* Cambridge, MA: MIT Press.

Miles-Doan, R. (1998). Violence between spouses and intimates: Does neighborhood context matter? *Social Forces, 77*, 623–645.

Miller, A., & Cross, T. (2006). Ethnicity in child maltreatment research. *Child Maltreatment, 11*(1), 16–26.

Miller, D. H., Greene, K., Causby, V., White, B. W., & Lockhart, L. L. (2001). Domestic violence in lesbian relationships. *Women and Therapy, 23,* 107–127.

Milletich, R. J., Kelley, M. L., Doane, A. N., & Pearson, M. R. (2010). Exposure to interparental violence and childhood physical and emotional abuse as related to physical aggression in undergraduate dating relationships. *Journal of Family Violence, 25*(7), 627–637.

Millett, L., Lanier, P., & Drake, B. (2011). Are economic trends associated with child maltreatment? Preliminary results from the recent recession using state level data. *Children and Youth Services Review, 33*(7), 1280.

Mills, L. G. (1998). Mandatory arrest and prosecution polices of domestic violence: A critical literature review and the case for more research to test victim empowerment approaches. *Criminal Justice and Behavior, 25,* 306–318.

Mills, L. G. (1999). Killing her softly: Intimate abuse and the violence of state interventions. *Harvard Law Review, 113,* 551–613.

Mills, L. G. (2000). Woman abuse and child protection: A tumultuous marriage (part 1). *Children and Youth Services Review, 22,* 199–205.

Mills, L. G. (2003). *Insult to injury: Rethinking our response to intimate abuse.* Princeton, NJ: Princeton University Press.

Mills, R. B., Vermette, V., & Malley-Morrison, K. (1998). Judgments about elder abuse and college students' relationship with grandparents. *Gerontology and Geriatrics Education, 19,* 17–30.

Milner, J. S. (1994). Assessing physical child abuse risk: The child abuse potential inventory. *Clinical Psychology Review, 14,* 547–583.

Milner, J. S. (1998). Individual and family characteristics associated with intrafamilial child physical and sexual abuse. In P. K. Trickett & C. J. Schellenbach (Eds.), *Violence against children in the family and community* (pp. 141–170). Washington, DC: American Psychological Association.

Milner, J. S. (2003). Social information processing in high-risk and physically abusive parents. *Child Abuse and Neglect, 27,* 7–20.

Mize, K. D., & Shackelford, T. K. (2008). Intimate partner homicide methods in heterosexual, gay, and lesbian relationships. *Violence and Victims, 23,* 98–114.

Moffitt, T. E., Caspi, A., Rutter, M., & Silva, P. A. (2001). *Sex differences in antisocial behaviour: Conduct disorder, delinquency and violence in the Dunedin longitudinal study.* Cambridge, UK: Cambridge University Press.

Mohandie, K., Meloy, J. R., McGowan, M., & Williams, J. (2006). The RECON typology of stalking: Reliability and validity based upon a large sample of North American stalkers. *Journal of Forensic Sciences, 51*(1), 147–155.

Mohler-Kuo, M., Dowdall, G. W., Koss, M. P., & Wechsler, H. (2004). Correlates of rape while intoxicated in a national sample of college women. *Journal of Studies on Alcohol, 65*(1), 37–45.

Molidor, C. E. (1995). Gender differences of psychological abuse in high school dating relationships. *Child and Adolescent Social Work Journal, 12,* 119–134.

Molina, O., Lawrence, S. A., Azhar-Miller, A., & Rivera, M. (2009). Divorcing abused Latina immigrant women's experiences with domestic violence support groups. *Journal of Divorce & Remarriage, 50*(7), 459–471.

Mollerstrom, W. W., Patchner, M. M., & Milner, J. S. (1992). Family functioning and child abuse potential. *Journal of Clinical Psychology, 48,* 445–454.

Molnar, B. E., Buka, S. L., Brennan, R. T., Holton, J. K., & Earls, F. (2003). A multilevel study of neighborhoods and parent-to-child physical aggression: Results from the Project on Human Development in Chicago neighborhoods. *Child Maltreatment, 8,* 84–97.

Monson, C. M., Langhinrichsen-Rohling, J., & Taft, C. T. (2009). Sexual aggression in intimate relationships. In K. D. O'Leary & E. M. Woodin (Eds.), *Psychological and physical aggression in couples: Causes and interventions* (pp. 37–57). Washington DC: American Psychological Association.

Montoya, V. (1997). Understanding and combating elder abuse in Hispanic communities. *Journal of Elder Abuse & Neglect, 9*(2), 5–17.

Moon, A., & Benton, D. (2000). Tolerance of elder abuse and attitudes toward third-party intervention among African American, Korean American, and White elderly. *Journal of Multicultural Social Work, 6,* 283–303.

Moon, A., Tomita, S. K., & Jung-Kamei, S. (2001). Elder mistreatment among four Asian American groups: An exploratory study on tolerance, victim blaming and attitudes toward third-party intervention. *Journal of Gerontological Social Work, 36,* 53–169.

Moon, A., & Williams, O. (1993). Perceptions of elder abuse and help-seeking patterns among African American, Caucasian American, and Korean American elderly women. *Gerontologist, 33,* 386–395.

Moore, D., & Florsheim, P. (2008). Interpartner conflict and child abuse risk among African American and Latino adolescent parenting couples. *Child Abuse and Neglect, 32,* 463–475.

Moretti, M. M., Obsuth, I., Odgers, C. L., & Reebye, P. (2006). Exposure to maternal vs. paternal partner violence, PTSD, and aggression in adolescent girls and boys. *Aggressive Behavior, 32*(4), 385–395.

Morrow, J. (1994). Identifying and treating battered lesbians. *San Francisco Medicine, 17,* 20–21.

Morse, B. J. (1995). Beyond the Conflict Tactics Scales: Assessing gender differences in partner violence. *Violence and Victims, 10,* 251–272.

Morton, E., Runyan, C., Moracco, K. E., & Butts, J. D. (1998). Partner homicide-suicide involving female homicide victims: A population based study in North Carolina, 1988–1992. *Violence and Victims, 13,* 91–106.

Mouilso, E. R., & Calhoun, K. S. (2011). A mediation model of the role of sociosexuality in the associations between narcissism, psychopathy, and sexual aggression. *Psychology of Violence, 2*(1), 1–12.

Mouton, C. P., Rodabough, R. J., Rovi, S. L., Bryski, R. G., & Katerndahl, D. A. (2010). Psychosocial effects of physical and verbal abuse in postmenopausal women. *Annals of Family Medicine, 8*(3), 206–213.

Mullen, P. E., Martin, J. L., Anderson, J. C., Romans, S. E., & Herbison, P. (1993). Childhood sexual abuse and mental health in adult life. *British Journal of Psychiatry, 163,* 721–732.

Mullen, P. E., Martin, J. L., Anderson, J. C., Romans, S. E., & Herbison, G. P. (1994). The effect of child sexual abuse on social, interpersonal and sexual function in adult life. *British Journal of Psychiatry, 165,* 35–47.

Mullen, P. E., Martin, J. L., Anderson, J. C., Romans, S. E., & Herbison, G. P. (1996). The longitudinal impact of the physical, emotional, and sexual abuse of children: A community study. *Child Abuse and Neglect, 20,* 7–21.

Mullen, P. E., Pathe, M., & Purcell, R. (2009). The therapeutic approach to the stalker. In P. E. Mullen, M. Pathé, & R. Purcell (Eds.), *Stalkers and their victims* (2nd ed.) (pp. 251–261). Cambridge, UK: Cambridge University Press.

Mumm, S., & Cupach, W. R. (2010). Turning points in the progression of obsessive relational intrusion of stalking. *Violence and Victims, 25*(6), 707–727.

Municipality of Anchorage (2000). *Analysis of police actions and characteristics of reported domestic violence in Anchorage, Alaska ten year study, 1989–1998.* Anchorage, AK: Author.

Murphy, C. M., & Cascardi, M. (1999). Psychological abuse in marriage and dating relationships. In R. L. Hampton (Ed.), *Family violence prevention and treatment* (2nd ed., pp. 198–226). Thousand Oaks, CA: Sage.

Murphy, C. M., & Hoover, S. A. (1999). Measuring emotional abuse in dating relationships as a multifactorial construct. *Violence and Victims, 14,* 39–53.

Murphy, C. M., & Hoover, S. A. (2001). Measuring emotional abuse in dating relationships as a multifactorial construct. In K. D. O'Leary & R. D. Maiuro (Eds.), *Psychological abuse in violent domestic relations* (pp. 29–46). New York, NY: Springer.

Murphy, C. M., O'Farrell, T. J., Fals-Stewart, W., & Feehan, M. (2001). Correlates of intimate partner violence among male alcoholic patients. *Journal of Consulting and Clinical Psychology, 69,* 528–540.

Murphy, C. M., & O'Leary, K. D. (1989). Psychological aggression predicts physical aggression in early marriage. *Journal of Consulting and Clinical Psychology, 57,* 579–582.

Murray-Swank, A., Mahoney, A., & Kenneth, I. (2006). Sanctification of parenting: Links to corporal punishment and parental warmth among biblically conservative and liberal mothers. *International Journal for the Psychology of Religion, 16*(4), 271–287.

Murty, S. A., Peek-Asa, C., Zwerling, C., Stromquist, A. M., Burmeister, L. F., & Merchant, J. A. (2003). Physical and emotional partner abuse reported by men and women in a rural community. *American Journal of Public Health, 93*(7), 1073–1075.

Musaji, S. (2009). Domestic violence and abuse in the Muslim community—resource collection. *The American Muslim.* Retrieved from http://www.theamericanmuslim.org/tam.php/features/articles/violence_and_abuse_in_the_family/0016062.

Myers, J. E. (1998). *Legal issues in child abuse and neglect practice* (2nd ed.). Thousand Oaks, CA: Sage.

Myers, J. E. B. (2002). The legal system and child protection. In J. E. B. Myers, L. Berliner, J. Briere, C. T. Hendrix, C. Jenny, & T. A. Reid (Eds.), *The APSAC handbook on child maltreatment* (2nd ed., pp. 305–328). Thousand Oaks, CA: Sage.

Myers, J. E. B. (2005). *Myers on evidence in child, domestic, and elder abuse cases.* New York, NY: Aspen.

Nahmiash, D., & Reis, M. (2000). Most successful intervention strategies for abused older adults. *Journal of Elder Abuse & Neglect, 12,* 53–70.

National Center for Victims of Crime. (2003). *Spousal rape laws: 20 years later* [Electronic Version]. Retrieved January 4, 2004, from http://www.ncvc.org/ ncvc/main.aspx?dbName=DocumentViewer&DocumentID=3270.

National Center for Victims of Crime. (2004). *Stalking. Problem-oriented guides for police.* Problem-Specific Guides Series, No. 22. U.S. Department of Justice, Office of Community Oriented Policing Services. Retrieved from http://www.cops.usdoj.gov/default.asp?Item=1073.

National Center for Victims of Crime. (2007). *The Model Stalking Code Revisited.* Available at http://www.ncvc.org/src/AGP.Net/Components/DocumentViewer/Download.aspxnz?DocumentID=45930.

National Center on Elder Abuse. (1998). *National Elder Abuse Incidence Study of 1996.* Retrieved October 1, 2002, from http://www.aoa.gov/naic/publicaitionlist.html.

National Coalition Against Domestic Violence. (1996). *Open minds, open doors: Working with women with disabilities resource manual.* Harrisburg, PA: Author.

National Coalition Against Domestic Violence. (2003). *About NCADV* [Electronic Version]. Retrieved September 16, 2003, from http://www.ncadv.org/about.htm.

National Coalition of Anti-Violence Programs. (2000). *Lesbian, gay, transgender and bisexual (LGBT) domestic violence in 1999: A report of the National Coalition of Anti-Violence Programs* [Electronic Version]. Retrieved May 7, 2004, from http://www.avp.org.

National Coalition of Anti-Violence Programs. (2001). *Lesbian, gay, bisexual and transgender domestic violence in 2000: A report of the National Coalition of Anti-Violence Programs* [Electronic Version]. Retrieved May 7, 2004, from http://www.avp.org.

National Coalition of Anti-Violence Programs. (2002). *Lesbian, gay, bisexual, and transgender domestic violence in 2002.* New York, NY: Author.

National Coalition of Anti-Violence Programs. (2003). *Lesbian, gay, bisexual and transgender domestic violence in 2002: A report of the National Coalition of Anti-Violence Programs* [Electronic Version]. Retrieved May 7, 2004, from http://www.avp.org.

National Coalition of Anti-Violence Programs. (2010). *Lesbian, gay, bisexual, transgender, queer, and HIV-affected intimate partner violence* [Electronic Version]. Retrieved August 9, 2011, from http://www.avp.org.

National Coalition of Anti-Violence Programs. (2011). *Lesbian, gay, bisexual, transgender, queer, and HIV-affected intimate partner violence* [Electronic Version]. Retrieved February 11, 2012, from http://www.avp.org.

National Council on Crime and Delinquency. (2007). *And justice for some: Differential treatment of youth of color in the justice system.* Available at: http://www.nccdglobal.org/sites/default/files/publication_pdf/justice-for-some.pdf

National Institute on Drug Abuse. (2011). *Prenatal exposure to drugs of abuse—May 2011: A research update from the National Institute on Drug Abuse.* Retrieved from http://www.drugabuse.gov/pdf/tib/prenatal.pdf.

National Television Violence Study. (1996). Available at http://209.29.148.33/english/resources/research_documents/reports/violence/upload/National-Television-Violence-Study-Year-Three-1996–97-Report-pdf.pdf.

Nayak, M. B., & Milner, J. S. (1998). Neuropsychological functioning: Comparison of mothers at high- and low-risk for child abuse. *Child Abuse and Neglect, 22,* 687–703.

Nelsen, H. M., & Kroliczak, A. (1984). Parental use of the threat "God will punish": Replication and extension. *Journal for Scientific Study of Religion, 23,* 267–277.

Nelson, B. (1984). *Making an issue of child abuse.* Chicago, IL: University of Chicago Press.

Nelson, E. C., Heath, A. C., Madden, P. A., Cooper, L., Dinwiddie, S. H., Bucholz, K. K., . . . Martin, N. G. (2002). Association between self-reported childhood sexual abuse and adverse psychosocial outcomes: Results from a twin study. *Archives of General Psychiatry, 59,* 139–145.

Nerenberg, L. (1999). *Forgotten victims of elder financial crime and abuse: A report and recommendations.* Goldman Institute on Aging for the National Center on Aging (NCEA). Retrieved from http://www.ncea.aoa.gov/ncearoot/main_site/pdf/publication/fvefca.pdf.

Nerenberg, L. (2006). Communities respond to elder abuse. *Journal of Gerontological Social Work, 46,* 5–33.

Nerenberg, L. (2008). *Elder abuse prevention: Emerging trends and promising strategies.* New York, NY: Springer.

New, M. J., Stevenson, J., & Skuse, D. (1999). Characteristics of mothers of boys who sexually abuse. *Child Maltreatment, 4,* 21–31.

Newberger, E. H. (1999). *The men they will become: The nature and nurture of male character.* Reading, MA: Perseus Books.

Newberger, E. H., & Bourne, R. (1978). The medicalization and legalization of child abuse. *American Journal of Orthopsychiatry, 48,* 593–607.

Newberger, E. H., Hampton, R. L., Marx, T. J., & White, K. M. (1986). Child abuse and pediatric social illness: An epidemiological analysis and ecological reformulation. *American Journal of Orthopsychiatry, 56,* 589–601.

Newby, J. H., Ursano, R. J., McCarroll, J. E., Martin, L. T., Norwood, A. E., & Fullerton, C. S. (2003). Spousal aggression by U.S. Army female soldiers toward employed and unemployed civilian husbands. *American Journal of Orthopsychiatry, 73,* 288–293.

Newcomb, M., Munoz, D., & Carmona, J. (2009). Child sexual abuse consequences in community samples of Latino and European American adolescents. *Child Abuse and Neglect, 33,* 533–544.

Newport, F. (2011). *In U.S., support for death penalty falls to 39-year low: Fifty-two percent say the death penalty is applied unfairly* [Electronic Version]. Retrieved April 9, 2012, from http://www.gallup.com/poll/150089/support-death-penalty-falls-year-low.aspx.

Ney, P. G., Fung, T., & Wickett, A. R. (1994). The worst combinations of child abuse and neglect. *Child Abuse and Neglect, 18,* 705–714.

Nixon, J. (2009). Defining the issue: The intersection of domestic abuse and disability. *Social Policy & Society, 8*(4), 175–485.

Noll, J. G., Shenk, C. E., & Putnam, K. T. (2009). Childhood sexual abuse and adolescent pregnancy: A meta-analytic update. *Journal of Pediatric Psychology, 34,* 366–378.

Norris, J., & Cubbins, L. A. (1992). Dating, drinking, and rape: Effects of victim's and assailant's alcohol consumption on judgments of their behavior and traits. *Psychology of Women Quarterly, 16,* 179–191.

Norris, J., Nurius, P. S., & Dimeff, L. A. (1996). Through her eyes: Factors affecting women's perception of and resistance to acquaintance sexual aggression threat. *Psychology of Women Quarterly, 20,* 123–145.

Norris, S., Huss, M., & Palarea, R. E. (2011). A pattern of violence: Analyzing the relationship between intimate partner violence and stalking. *Violence and Victims, 26*(1), 103–115.

Norton, I. M., & Schauer, J. (1997). A hospital-based domestic violence group. *Psychiatric Services, 48*(9), 1186–1190.

Norwood, R. (1988). *Letters from women who love too much: A closer look at relationship addiction and recovery.* New York, NY: Pocket Books.

Nosek, M. A. (1996). Wellness among women with physical disabilities. *Sexuality and Disability, 14,* 165–181.

Nosek, M. A., Howland, C. A., & Young, M. E. (1997). Abuse of women with disabilities: Policy implications. *Journal of Disability Policy Studies, 8,* 157–176.

Nosek, M. A., Hughes, R. B., Taylor, H. B., & Taylor, P. (2006). Disability, psychosocial, and demographic characteristics of abused women with physical disabilities. *Violence Against Women, 12*(9), 838–850.

Nosek, M. S. (1999). *National study of women with physical disabilities* [Electronic Version]. Retrieved May 4, 2004, from http://www.bcm.edu/crowd/index.cfm?pmid=1408.

O'Brien, M. J. (1991). Taking sibling incest seriously. In M. Patton (Ed.), *Family and sexual abuse: Frontline research and evaluation* (pp. 75–92). Newbury Park, CA: Sage.

O'Farrell, T. J., Fals-Stewart, W., Murphy, M., & Murphy, C. M. (2003). Partner violence before and after individually based alcoholism treatment for male alcoholic patients. *Journal of Consulting and Clinical Psychology, 71,* 92–102.

O'Farrell, T. J., & Murphy, C. M. (1995). Marital violence before and after alcoholism treatment. *Journal of Consulting and Clinical Psychology, 63,* 256–262.

O'Hearn, R. E., & Davis, K. E. (1997). Women's experience of giving and receiving emotional abuse: An attachment perspective. *Journal of Interpersonal Violence, 12,* 375–391.

O'Leary, K. D. (1988). Physical aggression between spouses: A social learning theory perspective. In V. B. Van Hasselt, R. L. Morrison, A. S. Bellack, & M. Hersen (Eds.), *Handbook of family violence* (pp. 31–56). New York, NY: Plenum.

O'Leary, K. D. (1999). Psychological abuse: A variable deserving critical attention in domestic violence. *Violence and Victims, 14,* 3–23.

O'Leary, K. D., Barling, J., Arias, I., Rosenbaum, A., Malone, J., & Tyree, A. (1989). Prevalence and stability of physical aggression. *Journal of Consulting and Clinical Psychology, 57,* 263–268.

O'Leary, K. D., Heyman, R. E., & Neidig, P. H. (1999). Treatment of wife abuse: A comparison of gender-specific and couple approaches. *Behavior Assessment, 30,* 475–505.

O'Leary, K. D., Malone, J., & Tyree, A. (1994). Physical aggression in early marriage: Prerelationship and relationship effects. *Journal of Consulting and Clinical Psychology, 62,* 594–602.

O'Leary, K. D., Woodin, E. M., & Fritz, P. T. (2006). Can we prevent the hitting? Implications for the prevention of partner violence. *Journal of Aggression, Maltreatment & Trauma, 13*(3/4), 125–181.

Oates, R. K., & Bross, D. C. (1995). What have we learned about treating child physical abuse? A literature review of the last decade. *Child Abuse and Neglect, 19,* 463–473.

Oates, R. K., Ryan, M. G., & Booth, S. M. (2000). Child physical abuse. In R. T. Ammerman & M. Hersen (Eds.), *Case studies in family violence* (2nd ed., pp. 133–156). New York, NY: Kluwer.

Oetzel, J., & Duran, B. (2004). Intimate partner violence in American Indian and/or Alaska Native communities: A social ecological framework of determinants and interventions. *American Indian & Alaska Native Mental Health Research: The Journal of the National Center, 11*(3), 49–68.

Office of the Attorney General, State of California (1999). *Report on arrest for domestic violence in California, 1998.* Sacramento, CA: Author.

Okun, L. (1986). *Woman abuse: Facts replacing myths.* Albany, NY: State University of New York Press.

Older Women's League. (1994). *Mother's Day Report.* Washington, DC: Author.

Olds, D. L., Eckenrode, J., Henderson, C. R., Kitzman, H., Powers, J., Cole, R., . . . Kuckey, D. (1997). Long-term effects of home visitation on maternal life course and child abuse and neglect. *Journal of the American Medical Association, 278,* 637–642.

Olds, D. L., Henderson, C. R., Chamberlin, R., & Tatelbaum, R. (1986). Preventing child abuse and neglect: A randomized trial of home nurse visitation. *Pediatrics, 78,* 65–78.

Olds, D. L., Robinson, J., O'Brien, R., Luckey, D., Pettitt, L. M., Henderson, C. R., . . . Talmi, A. (2002). Home visiting by paraprofessionals and by nurses: A randomized, control trial. *Pediatrics, 110*(3), 486–496.

Ondersma, S. J., Chaffin, M., Berliner, L., Cordon, I., Goodman, G. S., & Barnett, D. (2001). Sex with children is abuse: Comment on Rind, Tromovitch, and Bauserman (1998). *Psychological Bulletin, 127,* 707–714.

Orcutt, H. K., Garcia, M., & Pickett, S. M. (2005). Female-perpetrated intimate partner violence and romantic attachment style in a college student sample. *Violence and Victims, 20*(3), 287–302.

Organisation for Economic Co-operation and Development (OECD). (2011). *Growing unequal? Income distribution in OECD countries.* Retrieved from http://www.oecd.org/document/53/0,3746,en_2649_33933_41460917_1_1_1_1,00.html.

Oschwald, M., & Powers, L. (2011). *Development of a safety-planning tool for men with disabilities.* Available at http://www.rri.pdx.edu/safety_planning_tool.php.

Oschwald, M., Renker, P., Hughes, R. B., Arthur, A., Powers, L. E., & Curry, M. A. (2009). Development of an accessible audio computer-assisted self-interview (A-CASI) to screen for abuse and provide safety strategies for women with disabilities. *Journal of Interpersonal Violence, 24*(6), 1014–1035.

Osofsky, J. D. (2003). Prevalence of children's exposure to domestic violence and child maltreatment: Implications for prevention and intervention. *Clinical Child and Family Psychology Review, 6,* 161–170.

Owen, A. E., Thompson, M. P., & Kaslow, N. J. (2006). The mediating role of parenting stress in the relation between intimate partner violence and child adjustment. *Journal of Family Psychology, 20*(3), 505–513.

Pagelow, M. D. (1984). *Family violence.* New York, NY: Praeger.

Painter, K., & Farrington, D. P. (1998). Marital violence in Great Britain and its relationship to marital and non-marital rape. *International Review of Victimology, 5,* 257–276.

Palmore, E. (2001). The ageism survey: First findings. *Gerontologist, 41*(5), 572–575.

Parish, W. L., Wang, T., Laumann, E. O., Pan, S., & Luo, Y. (2004). Intimate partner violence in China: National prevalence, risk factors, and associated health problems. *International Family Planning Perspectives, 30*(4), 174–181.

Parker, H., & Parker, S. (1986). Father-daughter sexual abuse: An emerging perspective. *American Journal of Orthopsychiatry, 56,* 531–549.

Parks, K., & Fals-Stewart, W. (2004). The temporal relationship between college women's alcohol consumption and victimization experiences. *Alcoholism: Clinical and Experimental Research, 28*(4), 625–629.

Parra-Cardona, J., Meyer, M., Schiamberg, L., & Post, L. (2007). Elder abuse and neglect in Latino families: An ecological and culturally relevant theoretical framework for clinical practice. *Family Process, 46*(4), 451–470.

Passmore, S. R., & Cummins, J. J. (2004). Elder caregiving on the US/Mexican border: The impact of the changing Hispanic family on the informal caregiving system. *Journal of Mental Health & Aging, 10*(2), 131–143.

Pate, A. M., & Hamilton, E. E. (1992). Formal and informal deterrents to domestic violence: The Dade County spouse assault experiment. *American Sociological Review, 57,* 691–707.

Pathe, M. T., Mullen, P. E., & Purcell, R. (2000). Same-gender stalking. *Journal of the American Academy of Psychiatry and Law Online, 28*(2), 191–197.

Pattavina, A., Hirschel, D., Buzawa, E., & Faggiani, D. (2007). Policy, place, and perpetrators: Using NIBRS to examine arrest practices in intimate partner violence. *Justice Research and Policy, 9*(2), 31–52.

Pattavina, A., Hirschel, D., Buzawa, E., Faggiani, D., & Bentley, H. (2007). Comparison of the police response to heterosexual versus same-sex intimate partner violence. *Violence Against Women, 13*(4), 374–394.

Patterson, C. J. (2000). Family relationships of lesbians and gay men. *Marriage and Family, 62*(4), 1052–1069.

Patterson, C. J. (2003). *Lesbian and gay parenting* [Electronic Version]. Retrieved August 24, 2004, from http://www.apa.org/pi/parent.html.

Patton, C. L., Nobles, M. R., & Fox, K. A. (2010). Look who's stalking: Obsessive pursuit and attachment theory. *Journal of Criminal Justice, 38,* 282–290.

Paulozzi, L. J., Saltzman, L. A., Thompson, M. J., & Holmgreen, P. (2001). Surveillance for homicide among intimate partners: United States, 1981–1998. *CDC Surveillance Summaries, 50*(SS-3), 1–16.

Paveza, G. J., Cohen, D., Eisdorfer, C., Freels, S., Semla, T., Ashford, J. W., . . . Levy, P. (1992). Severe family violence and Alzheimer's disease: Prevalence and risk factors. *Gerontologist, 32,* 493–497.

Payne, B., & Gainey, R. (2009). Mapping elder mistreatment cases: Interactions between mistreatment, dementia, service utilization, access to services, and disadvantage. *Journal of Human Behavior in the Social Environment 19,* 1025–1041.

Payne, B. K. (2002). An integrated understanding of elder abuse and neglect. *Journal of Criminal Justice, 30,* 535–547.

Peebles, J., & Lombardi, K. (2010). *"Undetected Rapists" on campus: A troubling plague of repeat offenders: A chilling case at a friendly school—sexual assault at Texas A&M*

[Electronic Version]. Center for Public Integrity. Retrieved from http://www.publicinteg rity.org/investigations/campus_assault/articles/entry/1948/.

Peek, C. W., Fischer, J. L., & Kidwell, J. S. (1985). Teenage violence toward parents: A neglected dimension of family violence. *Journal of Marriage and the Family, 47,* 1051–1058.

Pelczarski, Y., & Kemp, S. P. (2006). Patterns of child maltreatment referrals among Asian and Pacific Islander families. *Child Welfare, 85*(1), 5–31.

Pelletier, D., & Coutu, S. (1992). Substance abuse and family violence in adolescents. *Canada's Mental Health, 40,* 6–12.

Pence, E., & Paymar, M. (1993). *Education groups for men who batter: The Duluth Model.* New York, NY: Springer.

Pennsylvania v. Ritchie (480, U.S. 39). (1987). United States Supreme Court decision. Washington, DC: Government Printing Office.

Pereda, N., Guilera, G., Forns, M., & Gomez-Benito, J. (2009, June). The prevalence of child sexual abuse in community and student samples: A meta-analysis. *Clinical Psychology Review, 29*(4), 328–338.

Perez, C. M., & Widom, C. S. (1994). Childhood victimization and long term intellectual and academic outcomes. *Child Abuse and Neglect, 18,* 617–633.

Perkins, D. F., & Luster, T. (1999). The relationship between sexual abuse and purging: Findings from community-wide surveys of female adolescents. *Child Abuse and Neglect, 23,* 371–382.

Peterman, L. M., & Dixon, C. G. (2003). Domestic violence between same-sex partners: Implications for counseling. *Journal of Counseling and Development, 81,* 40–47.

Petit, M. (2011, October 17). *America's child death shame.* Available at http://venusproject.org/americas-child-death-shame.html.

Peugh, J., & Belenko, S. (2001). Examining the substance use patterns and treatment needs of incarcerated sex offenders. *Sexual Abuse: A Journal of Research and Treatment, 13*(3), 179–195.

Pew Forum on Religion & Public Life. (2007). *U.S. Religious Landscape Survey.* Retrieved from http://religions.pewforum.org/pdf/affiliations-all-traditions.pdf.

Phillips, L. R. (1983). Abuse and neglect of the frail elderly at home: An exploration of theoretical relationships. *Journal of Advanced Nursing, 8,* 379–392.

Phillips, L. R., Torres de Ardon, E., & Briones, G. S. (2000). Abuse of female caregivers by care recipients: Another form of elder abuse. *Journal of Elder Abuse & Neglect, 12,* 123–143.

Pianta, R., Egeland, B., & Erickson, M. F. (1989). The antecedents of maltreatment: Results of the Mother-Child Interaction Research Project. In D. Cicchetti & V. Carlson (Eds.), *Child maltreatment: Theory and research on the causes and consequences of child abuse and neglect* (pp. 203–253). New York, NY: Cambridge University Press.

Pico-Alfonso, M. A., Garcia-Linares, M. I., Celda-Navarro, N., Blasco-Ros, C., Echeburua, E., & Martinez, M. (2006). The impact of physical, psychological, and sexual intimate male partner violence on women's mental health: Depressive symptoms, posttraumatic stress disorder, state anxiety, and suicide. *Journal of Women's Health, 15*(5), 599–611.

Pierce, G., & Radelet, M. (2005). The impact of legally inappropriate factors on death sentencing in California homicides, 1990–1999. *Santa Clara Law Review, 46,* 1–47.

Pierce, G., & Radelet, M. (2011). Death sentencing in East Baton Rouge Parish, 1990–2008. *Louisiana Law Review, 71,* 647–673.

Pierce, L. H., & Pierce, R. L. (1987). Incestuous victimization by juvenile sex offenders. *Journal of Family Violence, 2,* 351–364.

Pillemer, K. (1985). The dangers of dependency: New findings on domestic violence against elderly. *Social Problems, 33,* 146–158.

Pillemer, K. (1986). Risk factors in elder abuse: Results from a case-control study. In K. Pillemer & R. S. Wolf (Eds.), *Elder abuse: Conflict in the family* (pp. 236–263). Dover, MA: Auburn House.

Pillemer, K. (2005). Elder abuse is caused by the deviance and dependence of abusive caregivers. In D. R. Loseke, R. J. Gelles, & M. M. Cavanaugh (Eds.), *Current controversies on family violence* (pp. 207–220). Thousand Oaks, CA: Sage.

Pillemer, K., & Finkelhor, D. (1988). The prevalence of elder abuse: A random sample survey. *Gerontologist, 28*, 51–57.

Pillemer, K., & Finkelhor, D. (1989). Causes of elder abuse: Caregiver stress versus problem relatives. *American Journal of Orthopsychiatry, 59*, 179–187.

Pillemer, K., & Suitor, J. J. (1992). Violence and violent feelings: What causes them among family caregivers. *Journal of Gerontology, 47*, S165–S172.

Pillemer, K., & Wolf, R. (Eds.). (1986). *Elder abuse: Conflict in the family.* Dover, MA: Auburn House.

Pimlott-Kubiak, S., & Cortina, L. M. (2003). Gender, victimization, and outcomes: Reconceptualizing risk. *Journal of Consulting and Clinical Psychology, 71*(3), 528–539.

Pinder v. Johnson (54 F.3d 1169 CA 4). (1995). United States Court of Appeals for the Fourth Circuit. Richmond, Virginia.

Pinheiro, P. S. (2006). *World report on violence against children.* Geneva, Switzerland: United Nations. Available at http://www.unicef.org/violencestudy/I.%20World%20Report%20on%20Violence%20against%20Children.pdf.

Pinto, L. A., Sullivan, E. L., Rosenbaum, A., Wyngarden, N., Umhau, J. C., Miller, M. W., . . . Taft, C. T. (2010). Biological correlates of intimate partner violence perpetration. *Aggression and Violent Behavior, 15*, 387–398.

Piran, N., Lerner, P., Garfinkel, P. E., Kennedy, S. H., & Brouillette, C. (1988). Personality disorders in anorexic patients. *International Journal of Eating Disorders, 7*, 589–599.

Pleck, E. (1989). Criminal approaches to family violence, 1640–1980. In L. Ohlin & M. Tonry (Eds.), *Family violence* (pp. 19–57). Chicago, IL: University of Chicago Press.

Pleck, E. (2004). *Domestic tyranny: The making of American social policy against family violence from colonial times to the present.* Champaign, IL: University of Illinois Press.

Ploeg, J., Fear, J., Hutchison, B., MacMillan, H., & Bolan, G. (2009). A systematic review of interventions for elder abuse. *Journal of Elder Abuse & Neglect, 21*, 187–210.

Plomin, R., Chipuer, H. M., & Neiderhiser, J. M. (1994). Behavioral genetic evidence for the importance of nonshared environment. In E. M. Hetherington, D. Reiss, & R. Plomin (Eds.), *Separate social worlds of siblings: Importance of nonshared environment on development.* Hillsdale, NJ: Lawrence Erlbaum.

Plummer, C. A. (2005). Child sexual abuse prevention is appropriate and successful. In D. R. Loseke, R. J. Gelles, & M. M. Cavanaugh (Eds.), *Current controversies on family violence* (2nd ed., pp. 527–270). Thousand Oaks, CA: Sage.

Polansky, N. A. (1979). Help for the help-less. *Smith College Studies in Social Work, 49*, 169–191.

Polansky, N. A., Chalmers, M. A., Butenwieser, E., & Williams, D. P. (1981). *Damaged parents: An anatomy of child neglect.* Chicago, IL: University of Chicago Press.

Polansky, N. A., Gaudin, J. M., Ammons, P. W., & Davis, K. B. (1985). The psychological ecology of the neglectful mother. *Child Abuse and Neglect, 9*, 265–275.

Polisi, C. E. (2003). *Universal rights and cultural relativism: Hinduism and Islam deconstructed* [Electronic Version]. Retrieved December 2003 from http://www.jhubc.it/bcjournal/articles/polisi.cfm.

Pollack, S. D., Cicchetti, D., Hornung, K., & Reed, A. (2000). Recognizing emotion in faces: Development effects of child abuse and neglect. *Developmental Psychology, 36*, 679–688.

Pollard, D. A. (2003). *Banning corporal punishment: A constitutional analysis.* Pollard Printer, 448–492. Retrieved from http://www.wcl.american.edu/journal/lawrev/52/Pollard.pdf.

Pope, H. G., Hudson, J. I., Bodkin, A., & Oliva, P. (1998). Questionable validity of dissociative amnesia in trauma victims. *British Journal of Psychiatry, 172,* 210–215.

Portwood, S. G. (1998). The impact of individuals' characteristics and experiences on their definitions of child maltreatment. *Child Abuse and Neglect, 22,* 437–452.

Pot, A. M., Van Dyck, R., & Jonker, C. (1996). Verbal and physical aggression against demented elderly by informal caregivers in the Netherlands. *Social Psychiatry and Psychiatric Epidemiology, 31,* 156–162.

Potoczniak, M. J., Mourot, J. E., Crosbie-Burnett, M., & Potoczniak, D. J. (2003). Legal and psychological perspectives on sex-same domestic violence: A multisystemic approach. *Journal of Family Psychology, 17,* 252–259.

Powers, L. E., Hughes, R. B., Lund, E. M., & Wambach, M. (2009). Interpersonal violence and women with disabilities: A research update. *VAWnet: Applied Research Forum, National Online Resource Center on Domestic Violence.* Harrisburg, PA. Retrieved from http://www.vawnet.org/summary.php?doc_id=2077&find_type=web_desc_AR

Powers, L., & Oschwald, M. (n.d.). *Violence and Abuse Against People with Disabilites: Experiences, Barriers, and Prevention Strategies.* Retrieved from http://www.directcare clearinghouse.org/download/AbuseandViolenceBrief%203-7-04.pdf.

Powers, L. E., McNeff, E., Curry, M., Saxton, M., & Elliott, D. (2004). *Preliminary findings on the abuse experiences of men with disabilities.* Portland, OR: Oregon Health & Science University Center on Self-Determination.

Price, J. H., Islam, R., Gruhler, J., Dove, L., Knowles, J., & Stults, G. (2001). Public perceptions of child abuse and neglect in a midwestern urban community. *Journal of Community Health, 26,* 271–284.

Prince, J. E., & Arias, I. (1994). The role of perceived control and the desirability of control among abusive and nonabusive husbands. *American Journal of Family Therapy, 22,* 126–134.

Prospero, M., & Kim, M. (2009). Mutual partner violence: Mental health symptoms among female and male victims in four racial/ethnic groups. *Journal of Interpersonal Violence, 24*(12), 2039–2056.

Purcell, R., Pathe, M. T., & Mullen, P. E. (2001). A study of women who stalk. *American Journal of Psychiatry, 158,* 2056–2060.

Pyles, L. (2007). The complexities of the religious response to domestic violence: Implications for faith-based initiatives. *Journal of Women and Social Work 22*(3), 281–291.

Radelet, M. L., & Pierce, G. L. (2005). *Facts about the death penalty.* Retrieved from www.deathpenaltyinfo.org.

Radhakrishnan, S., & Moore, C. A. (Eds.). (1989). *A source book in Indian philosophy.* Princeton, NJ: Princeton University Press.

Radke-Yarrow, M., & Klimes-Dougan, B. (2002). Parental depression and offspring disorders: A developmental perspective. In S. H. Goodman & I. H. Gotlib (Eds.), *Children of depressed parents: Mechanisms of risk and implications for treatment* (pp. 155–173). Washington, DC: American Psychological Association.

Rahim, H. (2000). Virtue, gender and the family: Reflections on the religious texts in Islam and Hinduism. *Journal of Social Distress and the Homeless, 9,* 187–199.

Raine, A. (1993). *The psychopathology of crime: Criminal behavior as a clinical disorder.* San Diego, CA: Academic Press.

Ramos, B. M., Carlson, B. E., & McNutt, L. A. (2004). Lifetime abuse, mental health, and African American women. *Journal of Family Violence, 19,* 153–164.

Rank, M. R. (2001). The effect of poverty on America's families: Assessing our research knowledge. *Journal of Family Issues, 22*(7), 882–903.

Rao, K., DiClemente, R. J., & Ponton, L. E. (1992). Child sexual abuse of Asians compared with other populations. *Journal of the American Academy of Child and Adolescent Psychiatry, 31,* 880–886.

Rathbun, A. E. (2010). Marrying into financial abuse: A solution to protect the elderly in California. *San Diego Law Review, 47,* 227–274.

Rathner, J. L. (2008, Spring). Jewish domestic abuse: Putting a Jewish face on a common, ugly truth. *B' Nai B'rith Magazine.* Available at http://bnaibrith.org/magazines/2008SpringBBM/domestic_abuse.cfm.

Ray, K. C., Jackson, J. L., & Townsley, R. M. (1991). Family environments of victims of intrafamilial and extrafamilial child sexual abuse. *Journal of Family Violence, 6,* 365–374.

Ray, N. (2006). *Lesbian, gay, bisexual and transgender youth: An epidemic of homelessness.* New York, NY: National Gay and Lesbian Task Force Policy Institute and the National Coalition for the Homeless.

Raymond, J. (2002). Building a statewide network of services for older abused women. *Nexus, 8,* 10–11.

Rebovich, D. (1996). Prosecution response to domestic violence: Results of a survey of large jurisdictions. In E. S. Buzawa & C. G. Buzawa (Eds.), *Do arrests and restraining orders work?* Thousand Oaks, CA: Sage.

Reece, R. M. (2011). Medical evaluation of physical abuse. In J. E. B. Myers (Ed.), *The APSAC handbook on child maltreatment* (3rd ed., pp. 181–194). Thousand Oaks, CA: Sage.

Rees-Weber, M. (2008). A new experimental method assessing attitudes towards adolescent dating and sibling violence using observations of violent interactions. *Journal of Adolescence, 31,* 857–876.

Reeves, J. (2011, August 3). Alabama lab lost key evidence in praying mom's case. *Associated Press,* pp. 1–2.

Reid, J., Macchetto, P., & Foster, S. (1999). *No safe haven: Children of substance-abusing parents.* New York, NY: National Center on Addiction and Substance Abuse at Columbia University.

Reid, J. B., Kavenaugh, K., & Baldwin, D. V. (1987). Abusive parents' perceptions of child problem behavior: An example of parental bias. *Journal of Abnormal Child Psychology, 15,* 457–466.

Reid, R. J., Bonomi, A. E., Rivara, F. P., Anderson, M. L., Fishman, P. A., Carrell, D. S., . . . Thompson, R. S. (2008). Intimate partner violence among men: Prevalence, chronicity, and health effects. *American Journal of Preventive Medicine, 34*(6), 478–485.

Reingold, D. A. (2006). An elder abuse shelter program: Build it and they will come, a long term care based program to address elder abuse in the community. *Journal of Gerontological Social Work, 46,* 123–135.

Reis, M., & Nahmiash, D. (1997). Abuse of seniors: Personality, stress, and other indicators. *Journal of Mental Health and Aging, 3,* 337–356.

Relf, M. V., Huang, B., Campbell, J., & Catania, J. (2004). Gay identity, interpersonal violence, and HIV risk behaviors: An empirical test of theoretical relationships among a probability-based sample of urban men who have sex with men. *Journal of the Association of Nurses in AIDS Care, 15,* 14–26.

Rennison, C. M. (2001a). *Violent victimization and race, 1993–98.* Washington, DC: Government Printing Office.

Rennison, C. M. (2001b). *Intimate partner violence and age of victim, 1993–99* [Electronic Version]. Retrieved December 2002 from http://www.ojp. usdoj.gov/bjs/abstract/ipva99.htm.

Rennison, C. M. (2002). *Rape and sexual assault: Reporting to police and medical attention, 1992–2000* [Electronic Version]. Retrieved February 12, 2003, from http://www .ojp.usdoj .gov/bjs/abstract/rsarp00.htm.

Rennison, C. M., & Planty, M. (2003). Nonlethal intimate partner violence: Examining race, gender, and income patterns. *Violence and Victims, 18*(4), 433–443.

Rennison, C. M., & Welchans, S. (2000). *Intimate partner violence.* Retrieved from http://www.bjs.gov/index.cfm?ty=pbdetail&iid=1002.

Renzetti, C. M. (1989). Building a second closet: Third party responses to victims of lesbian partner abuse. *Family Relations, 38,* 157–163.

Renzetti, C. M. (1992). *Violent betrayal: Partner abuse in lesbian relationships.* Newbury Park, CA: Sage.

Renzetti, C. M. (1997). Violence in lesbian and gay relationships. In L. L. O'Toole & J. R. Schiffman (Eds.), *Gender violence: Interdisciplinary perspectives* (pp. 285–293). New York, NY: New York University Press.

Renzetti, C. M. (1998). Violence and abuse in lesbian relationships: Theoretical and empirical issues. In R. K. Berger (Ed.), *Issues in intimate violence* (pp. 117–127). Thousand Oaks, CA: Sage.

Reppucci, N. D., Haugaard, J. J., & Antonishak, J. (2005). Is there empirical evidence to support the effectiveness of child sexual abuse prevention programs? In D. R. Loseke, R. J. Gelles, & M. M. Cavanaugh (Eds.), *Current controversies on family violence* (2nd ed., pp. 271–283). Thousand Oaks, CA: Sage.

Resnick, M. D., Bearman, P. S., Blum, R. W., Bauman, K. E., Harris, K. M., Jones, J., . . . Udry, J. R. (1997). Protecting adolescents from harm: Findings from the National Longitudinal Study on Adolescent Health. *Journal of the American Medical Association, 278,* 823–832.

Reuters. (2007). *Guns and gun ownership in the United States.* Retrieved from http://www . reuters.com/article/2007/04/17/us-usa-crime-shootings-guns-idSN17434020070417.

Rhagavan, C., Mennerich, A., Sexton, E., & James, S. (2006). Community violence and its direct, indirect, and mediating effects on intimate partner violence. *Violence Against Women, 12*(12), 1132–1149.

Riak, J. (2002). *Where are the Christians who oppose corporal punishment? An invitation from PTAVE, December 2002* [Electronic Version]. Retrieved December 30, 2003, from http://www.nospank.net/cnp.htm.

Richards, L. (1990). Advocacy for lesbians in abusive relationships. In P. Elliot (Ed.), *Confronting lesbian battering* (pp. 93–99). St. Paul: Minnesota Coalition for Battered Women.

Ridgway, D. (2004). Court-mediated disputes between physicians and families over the medical care of children. *Archives Pediatric and Adolescent Medicine,* 891–896.

Rigby, K., & Slee, P. T. (1993). *The Peer Relations Questionnaire (PRQ).* Adelaide, AU: University of South Australia.

Rind, B., Tromovitch, P., & Bauserman, R. (1998). A meta-analytic examination of assumed properties of child sexual abuse using college samples. *Psychological Bulletin, 124,* 22–53.

Rispens, J., Aleman, A., & Goudena, P. (1997). Prevention of child sexual abuse victimization: A meta-analysis of school programs. *Child Abuse and Neglect, 2,* 975–987.

Ristock, J. L. (2002). *No more secrets: Violence in lesbian relationships.* New York, NY: Routledge.

Ristock, J. L. (2003). Exploring dynamics of abusive lesbian relationships: Preliminary analysis of a multisite, qualitative study. *American Journal of Community Psychology, 31,* 329–341.

Rizo, C. F., & Macy, R. J. (2011). Help seeking and barriers of Hispanic partner violence survivors: A systematic review of the literature. *Aggression & Violent Behavior, 16*(3), 250–264.

Roberts, A. L., Austin, B., Corliss, H., Vandermorris, A. K., & Koenen, K. C. (2010). Pervasive trauma exposure among U.S. sexual orientation minority adults and risk of posttraumatic stress disorder. *American Journal of Public Health, 100*(12), 2433–2441.

Roberts, A. L., McLaughlin, K. A., Conron, K. J., & Koenen, K. C. (2011). Adulthood stressors, history of childhood adversity, and risk of perpetration of intimate partner violence. *American Journal of Preventive Medicine, 40*(2), 128–138.

Roberts, K. A. (2005). Associated characteristics of stalking following the termination of romantic relationships. *Applied Psychology in Criminal Justice, 1*(1), 15–35.

Roberts, N., & Noller, P. (1998). The associations between adult attachment and couple violence: The role of communication problems and relationship satisfaction. In J. A. Simpson & W. S. Rholes (Eds.), *Attachment theory and close relationships* (pp. 317–350). New York, NY: Guilford.

Robertson, K., & Murachver, T. (2007). It takes two to tangle: Gender symmetry in intimate partner violence. *Basic and Applied Social Psychology, 29*(2), 109–118.

Robins, R. W., Caspi, A., & Moffitt, T. E. (2002). It's not just who you're with, it's who you are: Personality and relationship experiences across multiple relationships. *Journal of Personality, 70,* 925–964.

Rodriguez, C. M. (2006). Emotional functioning, attachment style, and attributions as predictors of child abuse potential in domestic violence victims. *Violence and Victims, 21*(2), 199–212.

Rodriguez, C. M., & Henderson, R. C. (2010). Who spares the rod? Religious orientation, social conformity and child abuse potential. *Child Abuse and Neglect, 34*(2), 84–94.

Rodriguez, C. M., & Richardson, M. J. (2007). Stress and anger as contextual factors and preexisting cognitive schemas: Predicting parental child maltreatment risk. *Child Maltreatment, 12*(4), 325–337.

Rodriguez, M. A., Wallace, S. P., Woolf, N. H., & Mangione, C. M. (2006). Mandatory reporting of elder abuse: Between a rock and a hard place. *Annals of Family Medicine, 4*(5), 403–409.

Rohrbaugh, J. B. (2005). Domestic violence in same-gender relationships. *Family Court Review, 44* (2), 287–299.

Rollins, B. C., & Oheneba-Sakyi, Y. (1990). Physical violence in Utah households. *Journal of Family Violence, 5,* 301–309.

Rooney, J., & Hanson, R. K. (2001). Predicting attrition from treatment programs for abusive men. *Journal of Family Violence, 16,* 131–149.

Rorke-Adams, L., Duhaime, A. C., Jenny, C., & Smith, W. L. (2009). Head trauma. In R. M. Reece & C. W. Christian (Eds.), *Child abuse: Medical diagnosis and management.* Elk Grove Village, IL: American Academy of Pediatrics.

Rorty, M., Yager, J., & Rossotto, E. (1994). Childhood sexual, physical, and psychological abuse in bulimia nervosa. *American Journal of Psychiatry, 151,* 1122–1126.

Roscoe, B., Goodwin, M. P., & Kennedy, D. (1987). Sibling violence and agonistic interactions experienced by early adolescents. *Journal of Family Violence, 2,* 121–137.

Rose, S., & Meezan, W. (1995). Child neglect: A study of the perceptions of mother and child welfare workers. *Children and Youth Services Review, 17,* 471–486.

Rose, S. J. (1999). Reaching consensus on child neglect: African American mothers and child welfare workers. *Children and Youth Services Review, 21,* 463–479.

Rosen, K. H. (1996). The ties that bind women to violent premarital relationships: Processes of seduction and entrapment. In D. D. Cahn & S. A. Lloyd (Eds.), *Family violence from a communication perspective* (pp. 151–176). Thousand Oaks, CA: Sage.

Rosenbaum, A., & O'Leary, K. D. (1981). Marital violence: Characteristics of abusive couples. *Journal of Consulting and Clinical Psychology, 49,* 63–71.

Rosenberg, M. S., Giberson, R. S., Rossman, B. B., & Acker, M. (2000). The child witness of family violence. In R. T. Ammerman & M. Hersen (Eds.), *Case studies in family violence* (2nd ed., pp. 259–292). New York, NY: Kluwer.

Ross, L. F., & Aspinwall, T. J. (1997). Religious exemptions to the immunization statutes: Balancing public health and religious freedom. *Journal of Law, Medicine & Ethics, 25,* 202–209.

Ross, R. R., & Allgeier, E. R. (1996). Behind the pencil/paper measure of sexual coercion: Interview-based clarification of men's interpretations of Sexual Experience Survey items. *Journal of Applied Social Psychology, 26,* 1587–1616.

Rouse, L. P. (1990). The dominance motive in abusive partners: Identifying couples at risk. *Journal of College Student Development, 31,* 330–335.

Rudd, J. M., & Herzberger, S. D. (1999). Brother-sister incest/father-daughter incest: A comparison of characteristics and consequences. *Child Abuse and Neglect, 23,* 915–928.

Ruggiero, K. J., McLeer, S. V., & Dixon, J. F. (2000). Sexual abuse characteristics associated with survivor psychopathology. *Child Abuse and Neglect, 24,* 951–964.

Runyon, M. K., & Deblinger, E. (2008). Pediatrician's role in the treatment and prevention of child sexual abuse. In M. A. Finkel & A. P. Giardino (Eds.), *Medical evaluation of child sexual abuse: A practical guide.* Elk Grove Village, IL: American Academy of Pediatrics.

Runyon, M. K., Deblinger, E., & Schroeder, C. M. (2009). Pilot evaluation of outcomes of combined parent-child cognitive-behavioral group therapy for families at-risk for child physical abuse. *Cognitive Behavioral Practice, 16,* 101–118.

Runyon, M. K., & Urquiza, A. J. (2011). Child physical abuse: Intervention for parents who engage in coercive parenting practices and their children. In J. E. B. Myers (Ed.), *The APSAC Handbook on Child Maltreatment* (3rd ed., pp. 195–212). Thousand Oaks, CA: Sage.

Rupper, D. R., & Montgomery Dingus, A. E. (2008). Corporal punishment in U.S. public schools: A continuing challenge for school social workers. *Children and Schools, 30*(4), 243–250.

Russ, B. (2003). *First report of the Governor's Commission on Child Protection: Strengthening child protection services in New Hampshire.* State of New Hampshire. Available at http://nhdcyf.info/Report%200n%20child%20protection.pdf.

Russell, D. E. (1986). *The secret trauma: Incest in the lives of girls and women.* New York, NY: Basic Books.

Russell, D. E. (1990). *Rape in marriage.* Indianapolis: Indiana University Press.

Russell, D. E. (1995). The prevalence, trauma, and sociocultural causes of incestuous abuse of females: A human rights issue. In R. J. Kleber & C. R. Figley (Eds.), *Beyond trauma: Cultural and societal dynamics. Plenum series on stress and coping* (pp. 171–186). New York, NY: Plenum.

Russell, D. H. (1984). A study of juvenile murderers of family members. *International Journal of Offender Therapy and Comparative Criminology, 28,* 177–192.

Russell, D. P., Shackelford, T. K., Weekes-Shackelford, V. A., & Michalski, R. L. (2007). A preliminary investigation of siblicide as a function of genetic relatedness. *Journal of Forensic Sciences, 52,* 738–739.

Russo, A. (1999). Lesbians organizing lesbians against battering. In B. Leventhal & S. Lundy (Eds.), *Same-sex domestic violence: Strategies for change* (pp. 83–96). Thousand Oaks, CA: Sage.

Rutter, M. (1985). Resilience in the face of adversity: Protective factors and resistance to psychiatric disorder. *British Journal of Psychiatry, 147,* 598–611.

Ryan, K. M. (1998). The relationship between courtship violence and sexual aggression in college students. *Journal of Family Violence, 13*(4), 377–394.

Saad, L. (2011). *Self-reported gun ownership in U.S. is highest since 1993: Majority of men, Republicans, and Southerners report having a gun in their households* [Electronic Version]. Retrieved April 9, 2012, from http://www.gallup.com/poll/150353/Self-Reported -Gun-Ownership-Highest-1993.aspx.

Sabina, C., & Straus, M. A. (2008). Polyvictimization by dating partners and mental health among U.S. college students. *Violence and Victims, 23*(6), 667–682.

Sackett, L. A., & Saunders, D. G. (2001). The impact of different forms of psychological abuse on battered women. In K. D. O'Leary & R. D. Maiuro (Eds.), *Psychological abuse in violent domestic relations* (pp. 197–212). New York, NY: Springer.

SAFE. (2011). Stop Abuse For Everyone. Available at http://www.safe4all.org/.

Sagatun-Edwards, I., & Saylor, C. (2000). Drug-exposed infant cases in juvenile court: Risk factors and court outcomes. *Child Abuse and Neglect, 24*, 925–937.

Sagatun-Edwards, I., Saylor, C., & Shifflett, B. (1995). Drug-exposed infants in the social welfare system and the juvenile court. *Child Abuse and Neglect, 19*, 83–91.

Salomon, A., Bassuk, S. S., & Huntington, N. (2002). The relationship between intimate partner violence and the use of addictive substances in poor and homeless single mothers. *Violence Against Women, 8*(7), 785–815.

Salter, A. C. (2003). *Predators: Pedophiles, rapists, & other sex offenders: Who they are, how they operate, and how we can protect ourselves and our children.* New York, NY: Basic Books.

Salzinger, S., Feldman, R. S., & Hammer, M. (1993). The effects of physical abuse on children's social relationships. *Child Development, 64*, 169–187.

Sampson, Z. C. (2012, Feb. 8). George Huguely trial: Virginia lacrosse player emailed Yeardley Love "I should have killed you" [Electronic Version]. *Huffington Post.* Retrieved from http://www.huffingtonpost.com/2012/02/08/george-huguely-trial-virg_n_1264031.html.

Sanday, P. R. (1996). Rape-prone versus rape-free campus cultures. *Violence Against Women, 2*, 191–208.

Sanderson, M., Coker, A., Roberts, R., Tortolero, S., & Reininger, B. (2004). Acculturation, ethnic identity, and dating violence among Latino ninth-grade students. *Preventive Medicine, 39*(2), 373–383.

Saunders, B. E., Berliner, L., & Hanson, R. F. (Eds.). (2003). *Child physical and sexual abuse: Guidelines for treatment (Final report: January 15, 2003).* Charleston, SC: National Crime Victims Research and Treatment Center.

Saunders, B. E., Kilpatrick, D. G., Hanson, R. F., Resnick, H. S., & Walker, M. E. (1999). Prevalence, case characteristics, and long-term psychological correlates of child rape among women: A national survey. *Child Maltreatment, 4*, 187–200.

Saunders, D. G. (1988). Wife abuse, husband abuse, or mutual combat? A feminist perspective on the empirical findings. In K. Yllo & M. Bograd (Eds.), *Feminist perspectives on wife abuse* (pp. 90–113). Newbury Park, CA: Sage.

Saunders, D. G. (1992). A typology of men who batter: Three types derived from cluster analysis. *American Journal of Orthopsychiatry, 62*, 264–275.

Saunders, D. G. (1994). Post-traumatic stress symptom profiles of battered women: A comparison of survivors in two settings. *Violence and Victims, 9*, 31–44.

Saunders, D. G., & Browne, A. (2000). Intimate partner homicide. In R. T. Ammerman & M. Hersen (Eds.), *Case studies in family violence* (2nd ed., pp. 415–449). New York, NY: Kluwer.

Saxton, M., Curry, M., Powers, L. E., Maley, S., Eckels, K., & Gross, J. (2001). Bring my scooter so I can leave you: A study of disabled women handling abuse by personal assistance providers. *Violence Against Women, 7*, 393–417.

Saylors, K., & Daliparthy, N. (2006). Violence against Native Women in substance abuse treatment. *American Indian & Alaska Native Mental Health Research: The Journal of the National Center, 13*(1), 32–51.

Scannapieco, M., & Connell-Carrick, K. (2002). Focus on the first years: An eco-developmental assessment of child neglect for children 0 to 3 years of age. *Child & Youth Services Review, 24*, 601–621.

Schafer, J., Caetano, R., & Clark, C. L. (1998). Rates of intimate partner violence in the United States. *American Journal of Public Health, 88*, 1702–1704.

Schiamberg, L. B., & Gans, D. (2000). Elder abuse by adult children: An applied ecological framework for understanding contextual risk factors and the intergenerational character of quality of life. *International Journal of Aging and Human Development, 50*, 329–335.

Schiff, M., & Cavaiola, A. A. (1993). Child abuse, adolescent substance abuse, and "deadly violence." *Journal of Adolescent Chemical Dependency, 2*, 131–141.

Schilit, R., Lie, G., & Montagne, M. (1990). Substance use as a correlate of violence in intimate lesbian relationships. *Journal of Homosexuality, 19*, 51–65.

Schmidt, M. (1995). Anglo Americans and sexual child abuse. In L. A. Fontes (Ed.), *Sexual abuse in nine North American cultures: Treatment and prevention* (pp. 156–175). Thousand Oaks, CA: Sage.

Schneider, D. C., Mosqueda, L., Falk, E., & Huba, G. J. (2010). Elder abuse forensic centers. *Journal of Elder Abuse & Neglect, 22*, 255–274.

Schumacher, J. A., Slep, A. M. S., & Heyman, R. E. (2001). Risk factors for child neglect. *Aggression and Violent Behavior, 6*, 231–254.

Schutter, L. S., & Brinker, R. P. (1992). Conjuring a new category of disability from prenatal cocaine exposure: Are the infants unique biological or caretaking casualties? *Topics in Early Childhood Special Education, 11*, 84–111.

Schwartz-Watts, D., & Morgan, D. W. (1998). Violent versus nonviolent stalkers. *Journal of the American Academy of Psychiatry and the Law, 26*(2), 241–245.

Sedlak, A. J., & Broadhurst, D. D. (1996). *Executive summary of the Third National Incidence Study of child abuse and neglect (NIS-3)* [Electronic Version]. Retrieved August 6, 2012, from http://www.childwelfare.gov/pubs/statsinfo/nis3.cfm.

Sedlak, A. J., Mettenburg, J., Basena, M., Petta, I., McPherson, K., Greene, A., . . . Li, S. (2010). *Fourth National Incidence Study of Child Abuse and Neglect (NIS–4) Report to Congress.* Washington, DC: U.S. Department of Health and Human Services, Administration for Children and Families.

Segal, Z. V., & Stermac, L. E. (1990). The role of cognition in sexual assault. In W. L. Marshall, D. R. Laws, & H. E. Barbaree (Eds.), *Handbook of sexual assault: Issues, theories, and treatment of the offender* (pp. 161–174). New York, NY: Plenum.

Sen, A. (1998). Universal truths: Human rights and the Westernizing illusion. *Harvard International Review, 20*(3), 40–43.

Seto, M. C., & Barbaree, H. E. (1997). Sexual aggression as antisocial behavior: A developmental model. In D. M. Stoff, J. Breiling, & J. D. Maser (Eds.), *Handbook of Antisocial Behavior.* New York, NY: John Wiley.

Sev'er, A. (2009). *More than wife abuse that has gone old: A conceptual model for violence against the aged in Canada and the U.S.* Department of Sociology, University of Toronto. Available at https://tspace.library.utoronto.ca/bitstream/1807/17675/1/morethan_wifeabuse.pdf.

Shahar, G. (2001). Maternal personality and distress as predictors of child neglect. *Journal of Research in Personality, 35*, 537–545.

Shannon, P., & Agorastou, M. (2006). Identifying children with developmental disabilities receiving child protection services: A national survey of child welfare administrators. *Families in Society: The Journal of Contemporary Social Services, 87*(3), 351–357.

Shapiro, J. P., Leifer, M., Martone, M. W., & Kassem, L. (1992). Cognitive functioning and social competence as predictors of maladjustment in sexually abused girls. *Journal of Interpersonal Violence, 7,* 156–164.

Sheldon, J. P., & Parent, S. L. (2002). Clergy's attitudes and attributions of blame toward female rape victims. *Violence Against Women, 8,* 233–256.

Shelton, A. J., Atkinson, J., Risser, J. M. H., McCurdy, S. A., Useche, B., & Padgett, P. M. (2005). The prevalence of partner violence in a group of HIV-infected men. *AIDS Care, 17*(7), 814–818.

Sheridan, L. P., Blaauw, E., & Davies, G. M. (2003). Stalking: Knowns and unknowns. *Trauma, Violence, & Abuse, 4*(2), 148–162.

Sherman, L., & Berk, R. (1984). The specific deterrent effects of arrest for domestic assault. *American Sociological Review, 49,* 261–272.

Sherman, L. W., Schmidt, J. D., Rogan, D. P., Smith, D. A., Gartin, P. R., Cohn, E. G., . . . Bacich, A. R. (1992). The variable effects of arrest on criminal careers: The Milwaukee domestic violence experiment. *Journal of Criminal Law and Criminology, 83,* 137–169.

Shields, N. M., & Hanneke, C. R. (1983). Battered wives' reactions to marital rape. In D. Finkelhor, R. J. Gelles, G. T. Hotaling, & M. A. Straus (Eds.), *The dark side of families* (pp. 132–148). Beverly Hills, CA: Sage.

Shim, W., & Hwang, M. J. (2005). Implication of an arrest in domestic violence cases: Learning from Korean social workers' experiences in the U.S. *Journal of Family Violence, 20*(5), 313–328.

Shook, N. J., Gerrity, d. A., Jurich, J., & Segrist, A. E. (2000). Courtship violence among college students: A comparison of verbally and physically abusive couples. *Journal of Family Violence, 15*(1), 1–22.

Shope, J. H. (2004). When words are not enough: The search for the effect of pornography on abused women. *Violence Against Women, 10,* 56–72.

Shore, J. (2010). *Church to abused wife: "Stay with him."* Retrieved from http://johnshore .com/2010/04/06/church-to-abused-wife-stay-with-him/.

Shugarman, L. R., Fries, B. E., Wolf, R. S., & Morris, J. N. (2003). Identifying older people at risk of abuse during routine screening practices. *Journal of the American Geriatric Society, 51*(1), 24–31.

Shurman, L. A., & Rodriguez, C. M. (2006). Cognitive-affective predictors of women's readiness to end domestic violence relationships. *Journal of Interpersonal Violence, 21*(11), 1417–1439.

Shusterman, G. R., Hollinshead, D., Fluke, J. D., & Yuan, Y. T. (2005). *Alternative responses to child maltreatment: Findings from NCANDS.* Washington, DC: U.S. Department of Health and Human Services.

Silverman, A. B., Reinherz, H. Z., & Giaconia, R. M. (1996). The long-term sequelae of child and adolescent abuse: A longitudinal community study. *Child Abuse and Neglect, 8,* 709–723.

Silverman, J. G., & Williamson, G. M. (1997). Social ecology and entitlements involved in battering by heterosexual college males: Contributions of family and peers. *Violence and Victims, 12*(2), 147–164.

Simonelli, C. J., & Ingram, K. M. (1998). Psychological distress among men experiencing physical and emotional abuse in heterosexual dating relationships. *Journal of Interpersonal Violence, 13,* 667–681.

Simonelli, C. J., Mullis, T., Elliott, A. N., & Pierce, T. W. (2002). Abuse by siblings and subsequent experiences of violence within dating relationships. *Journal of Interpersonal Violence, 17,* 103–121.

Simons, D., Wurtele, S. K., & Heil, P. (2002). Childhood victimization and lack of empathy as predictors of sexual offending against women and children. *Journal of Interpersonal Violence, 17,* 1291–1307.

Simons, L., Gwin, D., Brown, M. J., & Gross, J. (2008). Alcohol and other drug use among college students: Intimate partner violence and health-compromising behaviors. *Alcoholism Treatment Quarterly, 26*(3), 347–364.

Simons, R. L., Whitbeck, L. B., Conger, R. D., & Wu, C. (1991). Intergenerational transmission of harsh parenting. *Developmental Psychology, 27,* 159–171.

Simpson, E. K., & Helfrich, C. A. (2005). Lesbian survivors of intimate partner violence: Provider perspectives on barriers to accessing services. *Journal of Gay & Lesbian Social Services, 18*(2), 39–59.

Simpson, L. E., & Christensen, A. (2005). Spousal agreement regarding relationship aggression on the Conflict Tactics Scales-2. *Psychological Assessment, 17*(4), 423–432.

Sinal, S. H., Cabinum-Foeller, E., & Socolar, R. (2008). Religion and medical neglect. *Southern Medical Journal, 101*(7), 703–706.

Sinclair, H. C., & Frieze, I. H. (2000). Initial courtship behavior and stalking: How should we draw the line? *Violence and Victims, 15,* 23–40.

Singh, A., Hays, D., Chung, Y. B., & Watson, L. (2010). South Asian immigrant women who have survived child sexual abuse: Resilience and healing. *Violence Against Women, 16*(4), 444–458.

Sirles, E., & Franke, P. J. (1989). Factors influencing mothers' reactions to intrafamilial sexual abuse. *Child Abuse and Neglect, 13,* 131–139.

Skarbek, D., Hahn, K., & Parrish, P. (2009). Stop sexual abuse in special education: An ecological model of prevention and intervention strategies for sexual abuse in special education. *Sexuality and Disability, 27,* 155–164.

Slack, K. S., Holl, J., Altenbernd, L., McDaniel, M., & Stevens, A. B. (2003). Improving the measurement of child neglect for survey research: Issues and recommendations. *Child Maltreatment, 8,* 98–111.

Smeeding, T. A., Rainwater, L., & Burtless, G. (2000). *United States poverty in a cross-national context (Luxembourg Income Study Working Paper Series No. 244).* Syracuse, NY: Syracuse University, Maxwell School of Citizenship and Public Affairs.

Smetana, J. G., Toth, S. L., Cicchetti, D., Bruce, J., Kane, P., & Daddis, C. (1999). Maltreated and nonmaltreated preschoolers' conceptions of hypothetical and actual moral transgressions. *Developmental Psychology, 35,* 269–281.

Smith, D. L. (2008, March). Disability, gender and intimate partner violence; Relationships from the behavioral risk factor surveillance system. *Sexuality and Disability, 26*(1), 15–28.

Smith, D. W., Letourneau, E. J., Saunders, B. E., Kilpatrick, D. G., Resnick, H. S., & Best, C. L. (2000). Delay in disclosure of childhood rape: Results from a national survey. *Child Abuse and Neglect, 24,* 273–287.

Smith, H., & Israel, E. (1987). Sibling incest: A study of the dynamics of 25 cases. *Child Abuse and Neglect, 11,* 101–108.

Smith, M., & Fong, R. (2004). *Children of neglect: When no one cares.* New York, NY: Brunner-Routledge.

Smith, P. H., Moracco, K. E., & Butts, H. D. (1998). Partner homicide in context. *Homicide Studies, 2,* 400–421.

Smith, P. H., White, J. W., & Holland, L. J. (2003). A longitudinal perspective on dating violence among adolescent and college-age women. *American Journal of Public Health, 93*(7), 1104–1109.

Smith, R., & Loring, M. T. (1994). The trauma of emotionally abused men. *Psychology: A Journal of Human Behavior, 31,* 1–4.

Smith, S. K. (1997). Women's experiences of victimizing sexualization, Part II: Community and longer term personal impacts. *Issues in Mental Health Nursing, 18,* 417–432.

Smith, T. W., & Martos, L. (1999, December). *Attitudes towards and experience with guns: A state-level perspective* [Electronic Version]. Retrieved February 2004 from http://cloud9 .norc.uchicago.edu/dlib/gunst.htm.

Snyder, C. R., & Pulvers, K. M. (2001). Dr. Seuss, the coping machine, and "Oh the places you'll go." In C. R. Snyder (Ed.), *Coping with stress: Effective people and processes* (pp. 3–29). New York, NY: Oxford University Press.

Socolar, R., Cabinum-Foeller, E., & Sinal, S. H. (2008). Is religiosity associated with corporal punishment or child abuse? *Southern Medical Journal, 101*(7), 707–710.

Soler, H., Vinayak, P., & Quadagno, D. (2000). Biosocial aspects of domestic violence. *Psychoneuroendocrinology, 25,* 721–739.

Somer, E., & Szwarcberg, S. (2001). Variables in delayed disclosure of child sexual abuse. *American Journal of Orthopsychiatry, 71,* 332–341.

Sommer, R., Barnes, G. E., & Murray, R. P. (1992). Alcohol consumption, alcohol abuse, personality and female perpetrated spouse abuse. *Personality and Individual Differences, 13,* 1315–1323.

Sorenson, S. B., Upchurch, D. M., & Shen, H. (1996). Violence and injury in marital arguments: Risk patterns and gender differences. *American Journal of Public Health, 86,* 35–40.

Spaccarelli, S. (1994). Stress, appraisal, and coping in child sexual abuse: A theoretical and empirical review. *Psychological Bulletin, 116,* 1–23.

Speziale, B., & Ring, C. (2006). Intimate violence among lesbian couples: Emerging data and critical needs. *Journal of Feminist Family Therapy, 18,* 85–96.

Spitzberg, B. H. (2002). The tactical topography of stalking victimization and management. *Trauma, Violence, and Abuse, 3,* 361–288.

Spitzberg, B. H., Cupach, W. R., & Ciceraro, L. D. L. (2010). Sex differences in stalking and obsessive relational intrusion: Two meta-analyses. *Partner Abuse, 1*(3), 259–285.

Spitzberg, B. H., & Hoobler, G. (2002). Cyberstalking and the technologies of interpersonal terrorism. *New Media and Society, 4*(1), 71–92.

Spitzberg, B. H., & Rhea, J. (1999). Obsessive relational intrusion and sexual coercion victimization. *Journal of Interpersonal Violence, 14*(1), 3–20.

Spitzberg, B. H., & Veksler, A. E. (2007). The personality of pursuit: Personality attributions of unwanted pursuers and stalkers. *Violence and Victims, 22*(3), 275–289.

Stacey, W. A., Hazlewood, L. R., & Shupe, A. (1994). *The violent couple.* Westport, CT: Praeger.

Stahl, C., & Fritz, N. (2002). Internet safety: Adolescents' self-report. *Journal of Adolescent Health, 31,* 7–10.

Stalking Resource Center. (2012). *Analyzing Stalking Laws.* National Center for Victims of Crime. Available at http://www.ncvc.org/src/AGP.Net/Components/DocumentViewer/ Download.aspxnz?DocumentID=41531.

Stanley, J. K., Bartholomew, K., Taylor, T., Landolt, M. A., & Oram, D. (2006). An exploration of partner violence in male same-sex relationships. *Journal of Family Violence, 21,* 31–41.

Star, B. (1978). Comparing battered and non-battered women. *Victimology, 3,* 32–44.

Stark, E., & Flitcraft, A. (1988). Violence among intimates: An epidemiological review. In V. B. Van Hasselt, R. L. Morrison, A. S. Bellack, & M. Hersen (Eds.), *Handbook of family violence* (pp. 293–317). New York, NY: Plenum.

Stark, V. (2007). *Coercive control: How men entrap women in personal life.* New York, NY: Oxford University Press.

State of Delaware. (2010). *Governor signs bill protecting vulnerable and infirm adults from abuse.* Retrieved on February 1, 2012, from http://governor.delaware.gov/news/2010/1007 july/20100716-hb348.shtml.

State of Georgia. (2002). *Family violence intervention provider statute.* Atlanta, GA: Author.

State of Illinois. (2009). *Elder abuse and neglect act.* Retrieved on February 1, 2012, from http://www.ilga.gov/legislation/ilcs/ilcs3.asp?ActID=1452&ChapterID=31.

Stein, J. A., Golding, J. M., Siegel, J. M., Burnam, M. A., & Sorenson, S. B. (1988). Long-term psychological sequelae of child sexual abuse: The Los Angeles epidemiologic catchment area study. In G. E. Wyatt & G. J. Powell (Eds.), *Lasting effects of child sexual abuse* (pp. 135–154). Newbury Park, CA: Sage.

Steinmetz, S. (1997). *The cycle of violence: Aggressive and abusive family interaction.* New York, NY: Praeger.

Steinmetz, S. K. (1977). Wifebeating, husbandbeating—A comparison of the use of physical violence between spouses to resolve marital fights. In M. Roy (Ed.), *Battered women: A psychosociological study of domestic violence* (pp. 63–72). New York, NY: Van Nostrand Reinhold.

Steinmetz, S. K. (1978). Battered parents. *Society, 15,* 45–55.

Steinmetz, S. K. (1988). *Duty bound: Elder abuse and family care.* Newbury Park, CA: Sage.

Steinmetz, S. K. (2005). Elder abuse is caused by the perception of stress associated with providing care. In D. R. Loseke, R. J. Gelles, & M. M. Cavanaugh (Eds.), *Current controversies on family violence* (pp. 191–206). Thousand Oaks, CA: Sage.

Stephenson, R., Khosropour, C., & Sullivan, P. (2010, August). Reporting of intimate partner violence among men who have sex with men in an online survey. *Western Journal of Emergency Medicine, 11*(3), 242–246.

Stermac, L., Del Bove, G., Brazeau, P., & Bainbridge, D. (2006). Patterns in sexual assault violence as a function of victim perpetrator degree of relatedness. *Journal of Aggression, Maltreatment & Trauma, 13*(1), 41–58.

Stets, J. E. (1990). Verbal and physical aggression in marriage. *Journal of Marriage and the Family, 52,* 501–514.

Stets, J. E. (1991). Psychological aggression in dating relationships: The role of interpersonal control. *Journal of Family Violence, 6,* 97–114.

Stets, J. E., & Straus, M. A. (1990). Gender differences in reporting marital violence and its medical and psychological consequences. In M. A. Straus & R. J. Gelles (Eds.), *Physical violence in American families: Risk factors and adaptation to violence in 8,145 families* (pp. 151–166). New Brunswick, NJ: Transaction.

Stewart, A. L., & Maddren, K. (1997). Police officers' judgment of blame in family violence: The impact of gender and alcohol. *Sex Roles, 37,* 921–934.

Stith, S. M., Crossman, R. K., & Bischof, G. P. (1991). Alcoholism and marital violence: A comparative study of men in alcohol treatment programs and batterer treatment programs. *Alcoholism Treatment Quarterly, 8,* 3–20.

Stith, S. M., Green, N. M., Smith, D. B., & Ward, D. B. (2008). Marital satisfaction and marital discord as risk markers for intimate partner violence: A meta-analytic review. *Family Violence, 23,* 149–160.

Stith, S. M., Rosen, K. H., & McCollum, E. E. (2003). Effectiveness of couples treatment for spouse abuse. *Journal of Marriage and Family Therapy, 29,* 407–426.

Stoneman, J. E., & Manders, J. E. (2009). Children with disabilities in the child protective services system: An analog study of investigation and case management. *Child Abuse & Neglect, 33,* 229–237.

Stotland, N. L. (2000). Tug-of-war: Domestic abuse and the misuse of religion. *American Journal of Psychiatry, 157,* 696–702.

Stover, C., Meadows, A., & Kaufman, J. (2009). Interventions for intimate partner violence: Review and implications for evidence-based practice. *Professional Psychology: Research and Practice, 40*(3), 223–233.

Straight, E. S., Harper, F. W. K., & Arias, I. (2003). The impact of partner psychological abuse on health behaviors and health status in college women. *Journal of Interpersonal Violence, 18,* 1035–1054.

Straka, S. M., & Montminy, L. (2006). Responding to the needs of older women experiencing domestic violence. *Violence Against Women, 12*(3), 251–367.

Straus, M. A. (1980). Wife-beating: How common and why? In M. A. Straus & G. T. Hotaling (Eds.), *The social causes of husband-wife violence.* Minneapolis: University of Minnesota Press.

Straus, M. A. (1990a). Injury and frequency of assault and the "representative sample fallacy" in measuring wife beating and child abuse. In M. A. Straus & R. J. Gelles (Eds.), *Physical violence in American families: Risk factors and adaptations to violence in 8,145 families* (pp. 75–89). New Brunswick, NJ: Transaction.

Straus, M. A. (1990b). Measuring intrafamily conflict and violence: The Conflict Tactics (CT) Scales. In M. A. Straus & R. J. Gelles (Eds.), *Physical violence in American families: Risk factors and adaptations to violence in 8,145 families* (pp. 29–47). New Brunswick, NJ: Transaction.

Straus, M. A. (1990c). Social stress and marital violence in a national sample of American families. In M. A. Straus & R. J. Gelles (Eds.), *Physical violence in American families: Risk factors and adaptations to violence in 8,145 families* (pp. 181–202). New Brunswick, NJ: Transaction.

Straus, M. A. (1994). *Beating the devil out of them: Corporal punishment in American families.* New York, NY: Lexington Books.

Straus, M. A. (1995). Trends in cultural norms and rates of partner violence: An update to 1992. In S. Stith & M. A. Straus (Eds.), *Understanding partner violence: Prevalence, causes, consequences, and solutions* (pp. 30–33). Minneapolis, MN: National Council on Family Relations.

Straus, M. A. (1999). The controversy over domestic violence by women: A methodological, theoretical, and sociology of science analysis. In X. B. Arriaga & S. Oskamp (Eds.), *Violence in intimate relationships* (pp. 17–44). Thousand Oaks, CA: Sage.

Straus, M. A. (2005a). Women's violence toward men is a serious social problem. In D. R. Loseke, R. J. Gelles, & M. M. Cavanaugh (Eds.), *Current controversies on family violence* (2nd ed., pp. 55–77). Thousand Oaks, CA: Sage.

Straus, M. A. (2005b). Children should never, ever, be spanked no matter what the circumstances. In D. R. Loseke, R. J. Gelles, & M. M. Cavanaugh (Eds.), *Current controversies on family violence* (2nd ed., pp. 137–157). Thousand Oak, CA: Sage.

Straus, M. A. (2006). Future research on gender symmetry in physical assaults on partners. *Violence Against Women, 12*(11), 1086–1097.

Straus, M. A. (2008a). Dominance and symmetry in partner violence by male and female university students in 32 nations. *Child & Youth Services Review, 30,* 252–275.

Straus, M. A. (2008b). *Prevalence and effects of mutuality in physical and psychological aggression against dating partners by university students in 32 nations.* Paper presented at the International Family Aggression Society Conference. University of Central Lancashire, Lancashire, UK. Retrieved from http://pubpages.unh.edu/~mas2/ID64B-PR64%20IFAS.pdf.

Straus, M. A. (2009). Why the overwhelming evidence on partner physical violence by women has not been perceived and is often denied. *Journal of Aggression, Maltreatment, & Trauma, 18*(6), 552–571.

Straus, M. A. (2010). Prevalence, societal causes, and trends in corporal punishment by parents in world perspective. *Law and Contemporary Problems, 73*(1), 1–30.

Straus, M. A. (2011). *Research on spanking by parents: Implications for public policy.* Paper presented at the 4th National Research Conference on Child and Family Programs and Policy, Bridgewater, Massachusetts.

Straus, M. A., & Gelles, R. J. (1986). Societal change and change in family violence from 1975 to 1985 as revealed by two national surveys. *Journal of Marriage and the Family, 48,* 465–479.

Straus, M. A., & Gelles, R. J. (1988). How violent are American families? Estimates from the national family violence resurvey and other studies. In G. T. Hotaling, D. Finkelhor, J. T. Kirkpatrick, & M. A. Straus (Eds.), *Family abuse and its consequences: New directions in research* (pp. 14–36). Beverly Hills, CA: Sage.

Straus, M. A., & Gelles, R. J. (1990a). How violent are American families? Estimates from the National Family Violence Resurvey and other studies. In M. A. Straus & R. J. Gelles (Eds.), *Physical violence in American families: Risk factors and adaptations to violence in 8,145 families* (pp. 95–112). New Brunswick, NJ: Transaction.

Straus, M. A., & Gelles, R. J. (1990b). Societal change and change in family violence from 1975 to 1985 as revealed by two national surveys. In M. A. Straus & R. J. Gelles (Eds.), *Physical violence in American families: Risk factors and adaptations to violence in 8,145 families* (pp. 113–132). New Brunswick, NJ: Transaction.

Straus, M. A., Gelles, R. J., & Steinmetz, S. (1980). *Behind closed doors: Violence in the American family.* Garden City, NY: Anchor.

Straus, M. A., & Gozjolko, K. (2007). *Intimate terrorism and injury of dating partners by male and female university students in 32 nations.* Paper presented at the Stockholm Criminology Prize Symposium. Stockholm, Sweden.

Straus, M. A., Hamby, S. L., Boney-McCoy, S., & Sugarman, D. (1996). The Revised Conflict Tactics Scales (CTS-2): Development and preliminary psychometric data. *Journal of Family Issues, 17,* 283–316.

Straus, M. A., Hamby, S. L., Finkelhor, D., Moore, D. W., & Runyan, D. (1998). Identification of child maltreatment with the Parent-Child Conflict Tactics Scales: Development and psychometric data for a national sample of American parents. *Child Abuse & Neglect, 22*(4), 249–270.

Straus, M. A., & Hotaling, G. T. (Eds.). (1980). *The social causes of husband-wife violence.* Minneapolis: University of Minnesota Press.

Straus, M. A., & Kaufman Kantor, G. (2005). Definition and measurement of neglectful behavior: Some principles and guidelines. *Child Abuse and Neglect, 29*(1), 19–29.

Straus, M. A., Kaufman Kantor, G., & Moore, D. W. (1997). Change in cultural norms approving marital violence from 1968 to 1994. In G. Kaufman Kantor & J. L. Jasinski (Eds.), *Out of darkness: Contemporary perspectives on family violence* (pp. 3–16). Thousand Oaks, CA: Sage.

Straus, M. A., & Mathur, A. K. (1996). Social change and the trends in approval of corporal punishment by parents from 1968 to 1994. In D. Frehsee, W. Horn, & K-D. Bussmann (Eds.), *Family violence against children: A challenge for society* (pp. 91–105). New York: Walter de Gruyter & Co.

Straus, M. A., & Medeiros, R. A. (2002). *Gender differences in risk factors for physical violence between dating partners by university students.* Paper presented at the American Society of Criminology Conference, Chicago, IL.

Straus, M. A., & Paschall, M. J. (2009). Corporal punishment by mothers and development of children's cognitive ability: A longitudinal study of two nationally representative age cohorts. *Journal of Aggression, Maltreatment, and Trauma, 18*(5), 459–483.

Straus, M. A., & Runyan, D. K. (1997). Physical abuse. In S. B. Friedman, M. M. Fisher, S. K. Schonberg, & E. M. Alderman (Eds.), *Comprehensive adolescent health care* (2nd ed.). St. Louis, MO: Mosby-Year Book.

Straus, M. A., & Smith, C. (1990). Family patterns and child abuse. In M. A. Straus & R. J. Gelles (Eds.), *Physical violence in American families: Risk factors and adaptations to violence in 8,145 families* (pp. 245–262). New Brunswick, NJ: Transaction.

Straus, M. A., & Stewart, J. H. (1999). Corporal punishment by American parents: National data on prevalence, chronicity, severity, and duration in relation to child and family characteristics. *Clinical Child and Family Psychology Review, 2*(2), 55–70.

Straus, M. A., Sugarman, D. B., & Giles-Sims, J. (1997). Spanking by parents and subsequent antisocial behavior of children. *Archives of Pediatric Adolescent Medicine, 151,* 761–767.

Straus, M. A., & Sweet, S. (1992). Verbal/symbolic aggression in couples: Incidence rates and relationships to personal characteristics. *Journal of Marriage and the Family, 54,* 346–357.

Strawbridge, W. J., Shema, S. J., Cohen, R. D., & Kaplan, G. A. (2001). Religious attendance increases survival by improving and maintaining good health behaviors, mental health, and social relationships. *Annals of Behavioral Medicine, 23,* 68–74.

Streib, V. L. (2003). *The juvenile death penalty today: Death sentences and executions for juvenile crimes, January 1, 1973-June 30, 2003* [Electronic Version]. Retrieved March 2004. Available at https://www.ncjrs.gov/app/abstractdb/AbstractDBDetails.aspx?id=206314.

Strube, M. J. (1988). The decision to leave an abusive relationship: Empirical evidence and theoretical issues. *Psychological Bulletin, 104,* 236–250.

Struckman-Johnson, C., & Struckman-Johnson, D. (1994). Men pressured and forced into sexual experience. *Archives of Sexual Behavior, 23,* 93–114.

Struckman-Johnson, C., & Struckman-Johnson, D. (1998). The dynamics and impact of sexual coercion of men by women. In P. B. Anderson & C. Struckman-Johnson (Eds.), *Sexually aggressive women: Current perspectives and controversies* (pp. 121–143). New York, NY: Guilford Press.

Stuart, G. L., Moore, T. M., Gordon, K. C., Ramsey, S. E., & Kahler, C. W. (2006). Psychopathology in women arrested for domestic violence. *Journal of Interpersonal Violence, 21*(3), 376–389.

Sugarman, D. B., & Frankel, S. L. (1996). Patriarchal ideology and wife-assault: A meta-analytic review. *Journal of Family Violence, 11,* 13–40.

Suitor, J. J., Pillemer, K., & Straus, M. A. (1990). Marital violence in a life course perspective. In M. A. Straus & R. J. Gelles (Eds.), *Physical violence in American families: Risk factors and adaptations to violence in 8,145 families* (pp. 305–320). New Brunswick, NJ: Transaction.

Sullivan, C. M. (2006). Interventions to address intimate partner violence: The current state of the field. In J. R. Lutzker (Ed.), *Preventing violence: Research and evidence-based intervention strategies* (pp. 195–212). Washington, DC: American Psychological Association.

Sullivan, C. M., Tan, C., Basta, J., Rumptz, M., & Davidson, W. S. (1992). An advocacy intervention program for women with abusive partners: Initial evaluation. *American Journal of Community Psychology, 20,* 309–332.

Sullivan, P. (2006). Children with disabilities exposed to violence: Legal and public policy issues. In M. M. Feerick, & G. B. Silverman (Eds.), *Children exposed to violence* (pp. 213–237). Baltimore, MD: Brookes.

Sullivan, P. (2009). Violence exposure among children with disabilities. *Clinical Child and Family Psychology Review, 12*(2), 196–216.

Sullivan, P. M., & Knutson, J. F. (2000a). Maltreatment and disabilities: A population-based epidemiological study. *Child Abuse and Neglect, 24*(10), 1257–1273.

Sullivan, P. M., & Knutson, J. F. (2000b). The prevalence of disabilities and maltreatment among runaway children. *Child Abuse and Neglect, 24,* 1275–1288.

Swan, S. C., & Snow, D. L. (2003). Behavioral and psychological differences among abused women who use violence in intimate relationships. *Violence Against Women, 9,* 75–109.

Sweet, M., & Appelbaum, M. (2004). Is home visiting an effective strategy? A meta-analytic review of home visiting programs for families with young children. *Child Development, 75,* 1435–1456.

Swift, C. F., & Ryan-Finn, K. (1995). Perpetrator prevention: Stopping the development of sexually abusive behavior. In C. F. Swift (Ed.), *Sexual assault and abuse: Sociocultural context of prevention* (pp. 13–44). New York, NY: Haworth.

Szymanski, D. M., & Chung, Y. B. (2003). Internalized homophobia in lesbians. *Journal of Lesbian Studies, 7,* 115–125.

Szymanski, D. M., Chung, Y. B., & Balsam, K. F. (2001). Psychosocial correlates of internalized homophobia in lesbians. *Measurement and Evaluation in Counseling and Development, 34,* 27–38.

Taft, C., Bryantdavis, T., Woodward, H., Tillman, S., & Torres, S. (2009). Intimate partner violence against African American women: An examination of the socio-cultural context. *Aggression and Violent Behavior, 14*(1), 50–58.

Tasker, F., & Golombox, S. (1997). *Growing up in a lesbian family.* New York, NY: The Guilford Press.

Tatara, T., & Kuzmeskus, L. (1997). *Reporting of elder abuse in domestic settings.* Washington, DC: National Center on Elder Abuse.

Tauriac, J., & Scruggs, N. (2006). Elder abuse among African Americans. *Educational Gerontology, 32*(1), 37–48.

Taylor, C., & Fontes, L. A. (1995). Seventh Day Adventists and sexual child abuse. In L. A. Fontes (Ed.), *Sexual abuse in nine North American cultures: Treatment and prevention* (pp. 176–199). Thousand Oaks, CA: Sage.

Teaster, P. B. (2000). Sexual abuse of older adults. *Journal of Elder Abuse & Neglect, 12*(3/4), 1–16.

Teaster, P. B., Dugar, T. A., Mendiondo, M. S., Abner, E. L., Cecil, K. A., & Otto, J. M. (2006). *The 2004 Survey of State Adult Protective Services: Abuse of Adults 60 Years and Older.* The National Center on Elder Abuse. Available at http://www.ncea.aoa.gov/Main_Site/ pdf/2-14–06%20FINAL%2060+REPORT.pdf.

Teaster, P. B., Nerenberg, L., & Stansbury, K. L. (2003). A national look at elder abuse multi-disciplinary teams. *Journal of Elder Abuse & Neglect, 15,* 91–107.

Temple, J. R., Weston, R., Rodriguez, B. F., & Marshall, L. L. (2007). Differing effects of partner and non-partner sexual assault on women's mental health. *Violence Against Women, 13*(3), 285–297.

Testa, M., Livingston, J. A., & Leonard, K. E. (2003). Women's substance use and experiences of intimate partner violence: A longitudinal investigation among a community sample. *Addictive Behaviors, 28*(9), 1649–1664.

Testa, M., Vanzile-Tamsen, C., & Livingston, J. A. (2004). The role of victim and perpetrator intoxication on sexual assault outcomes. *Journal of Studies on Alcohol, 65*(3), 320–330.

Tewksbury, R., & Mustaine, E. E. (2001). Lifestyle factors associated with the sexual assault of men: A routine activity theory analysis. *Journal of Men's Studies, 9*(2), 153–182.

Thomas, A., & Chess, S. (1977). *Temperament and development.* New York, NY: Bruner-Mazel.

Thompson, M., Koss, M. P., Kingree, J., Goree, J., & Rice, J. (2011). A prospective mediational model of sexual aggression among college men. *Journal of Interpersonal Violence, 26*(13), 2716–2734.

Thompson, R. S., Bonomi, A. E., Anderson, M., Reid, R. J., Dimer, J. A., Carrell, D., & Rivara, F. P. (2006). Intimate partner violence: Prevalence, types, and chronicity in adult women. *American Journal of Preventive Medicine, 30*(6), 447–457.

Thurman v. City of Torrington (595 F. Supp. 1521). (1984). United States District Court D. Connecticut.

Tigert, L. M. (2001). The power of shame: Lesbian battering as a manifestation of homophobia. *Women & Therapy, 23,* 73–85.

Timmer, S., Urquiza, A. J., Zebell, N., & McGrath, J. (2005). Parent-child interaction therapy: Application to physically abusive and high-risk parent-child dyads. *Child Abuse and Neglect, 29,* 825–842.

Tjaden, P., & Thoennes, N. (1998). Stalking in America: Findings from the National Violence Against Women Survey. *National Institute of Justice Journal,* 1–20.

Tjaden, P., & Thoennes, N. (2000a). *Extent, nature, and consequences of intimate partner violence: Findings from the National Violence Against Women Survey.* Retrieved September 9, 2003, from http://www.ojp.usdoj.gov/nij/pubs-sum/181867.htm.

Tjaden, P., & Thoennes, N. (2000b). Prevalence and consequences of male-to-female and female-to-male intimate partner violence as measured by the National Violence Against Women Survey. *Violence Against Women, 6*(2), 142–161.

Tjaden, P. & Thoennes, N. (2000c). *Full report of the prevalence, incidence, and consequences of violence against women.* Department of Justice. NCJ 183781. Washington, DC: Government Printing Office.

Tjaden, P., Thoennes, N., & Allison, C. J. (1999). Comparing violence over the life span in samples of same-sex and opposite sex cohabitants. *Violence and Victims, 14,* 413–425.

Tjaden, P. G. (2009). Stalking policies and research in the United States: A twenty year retrospective. *European Journal on Criminal Policy & Research, 15*(3), 261–278.

Tolman, R. M. (1989). The development of a measure of psychological maltreatment of women by their male partners. *Violence and Victims, 4,* 159–178.

Tomoda, A., Suzuki, H., Rabi, K., Sheu, Y., Polcari, A., & Teicher, M. H. (2009). Reduced prefrontal cortical gray matter volume in young adults exposed to harsh corporal punishment. *NeuroImage, 47,* T66–T71.

Torres, S. (1991). A comparison of wife abuse between two cultures: Perceptions, attitudes, nature, and extent. *Issues in Mental Health Nursing, 12,* 113–131.

Tracy, S. R. (2011). *Calling the Evangelical church to truth: Domestic violence and the Gospel.* Retrieved from http://www.mendingthesoul.org/files/2011/12/callingevchurchtruth6-30rev.pdf.

Trickett, P. K., Mennen, F. E., Kim, K., & Sang, J. (2009). Emotional abuse in a sample of multiply maltreated, urban young adolescents: Issues of definition and identification. *Child Abuse and Neglect, 33,* 27–35.

Truman, J. L., & Mustaine, E. E. (2009). Strategies for college student stalking victims: Examining the information and recommendations available. *American Journal of Criminal Justice, 34,* 69–83.

Truman, J. L., & Rand, M. R. (2010). *Criminal Victimization, 2009.* Retrieved from http://bjs.ojp.usdoj.gov/index.cfm?ty=pbdetail&iid=2217.

Tsai, B. (2000). The trend toward specialized domestic violence courts: Improvements on an effective innovation. *Fordham Law Review, 68,* 1285–1327.

Tuel, B. D., & Russell, R. K. (1998). Self-esteem and depression in battered women: A comparison of lesbian and heterosexual survivors. *Violence Against Women, 4,* 344–362.

Turell, S. C. (2000). A descriptive analysis of same-sex relationship violence for a diverse sample. *Journal of Family Violence, 15,* 281–293.

Turner, H. A., Finkelhor, D., & Ormrod, R. K. (2006). The effect of lifetime victimization on the mental health of children and adolescents. *Social Science and Medicine, 62,* 13–27.

Turney, D. (2000). The feminizing of neglect. *Child and Family Social Work, 5,* 47–56.

Twomey, M. S., Jackson, G., Li, H., Marino, T., Melchior, L. A., Randolph, J. F., . . . Wysong, J. (2010). The successes and challenges of seven multidisciplinary teams. *Journal of Elder Abuse & Neglect, 22,* 291–305.

Tyler, K. A., Hoyt, D. R., & Whitbeck, L. B. (1998). Coercive sexual strategies. *Violence and Victims, 13*(1), 47–61.

U.S. Bureau of the Census. (2011). *Overview of Race and Hispanic Origin: 2010*. Available at http://www.census.gov/prod/cen2010/briefs/c2010br-02.pdf.

U.S. Department of Health and Human Services. (2001). *12 Years of Reporting Child Maltreatment, 2001*. Washington, DC: Administration for Children and Families, Administration on Children Youth and Families, Children's Bureau.

U.S. Department of Health and Human Services. (2002). *Evaluation of family preservation and reunification programs: Final report*. Retrieved August 18, 2011, from http://aspe.hhs.gov/hsp/evalfampres94/Final/.

U.S. Department of Health and Human Services. (2010). *Child Maltreatment 2009*. Washington, DC: Government Printing Office.

U.S. Department of Health and Human Services. (2011). *Child Maltreatment 2010*. Washington, DC: Government Printing Office.

U.S. Department of Justice. (2012). Enhanced Training and Services to End Violence and Abuse of Women Later in Life Program. *Office on Violence Against Women*. Accessed February 6, 2012, from http://www.ovw.usdoj.gov/ovwgrantprograms.htm#7.

Ulman, A., & Straus, M. A. (2003). Violence by children against mothers in relation to violence between parents and corporal punishment by parents. *Journal of Comparative Family Studies, 34*, 41–60.

Ullman, S. E. (1997). Review and critique of empirical studies of rape avoidance. *Criminal Justice and Behavior, 24*, 177–209.

Unah, I., & Boger, J. C. (2001). *Race and the death penalty in North Carolina: An empirical analysis: 1993–1997* [Electronic Version]. Retrieved April 9, 2012, from http://www.unc.edu/~jcboger/NCDeathPenaltyReport2001.pdf.

Underwood, R. C., & Patch, P. C. (1999). Siblicide: A descriptive analysis of sibling homicide. *Homicide Studies: An Interdisciplinary & International Journal, 3*, 333–348.

UNICEF. (2003). A league table of child maltreatment deaths in rich nations. *Innocenti Report Cards, 5*. Available at http://ideas.repec.org/p/ucf/inreca/inreca03-7.html.

United Nations. (1948, December 10). *Universal Declaration of Human Rights*. Available at http://www.state.gov/documents/organization/169986.pdf.

United Nations (1993). *Declaration on the Elimination of Violence Against Women*. Available at http://www.un.org/documents/ga/res/48/a48r104.htm.

Usborne, D. (2003). *Starvation horror story sparks review of foster and adoption system* [Electronic Version]. Retrieved November 17, 2003, from http://www.cyc-net.org/features/ft-horrorstory.html.

van Anders, S., Goldey, K., & Kuo, P. (2011). The steroid/peptide theory of social bonds: Integrating testosterone and peptide responses for classifying social behavioral contexts. *Psychoneuroendocrinology, 36*(9), 1265–1275.

Van Cleave, J., & Davis, M. M. (2006). Bullying and peer victimization among children with special health care needs. *Pediatrics, 118(4),* 1212–1219. Available from http://pediatrics.aappublications.org/content/118/4/e1212.full.

van Roode, T., Dickson, N., Herbison, P., & Paul, C. (2009). Child sexual abuse and persistence of risky sexual behaviors and negative sexual outcomes over adulthood: Findings from a birth cohort. *Child Abuse and Neglect, 33*, 161–172.

VandeWeerd, C., & Paveza, G. J. (2005). Verbal mistreatment in older adults: A look at persons with Alzheimer's disease and their caregivers in the state of Florida. *Journal of Elder Abuse & Neglect, 17*, 11–30.

Vasquez, D., & Falcone, R. (1997). Cross gender violence. *Annals of Emergency Medicine, 29*(3), 427–429.

Vecoli, L. (1990). The shelter's response to lesbian battering. In P. Elliot (Ed.), *Confronting lesbian battering* (pp. 73–74). St. Paul: Minnesota Coalition for Battered Women.

Veneziano, C., Veneziano, L., & LeGrand, S. (2000). The relationship between adolescent sex offender behaviors and victim characteristics with prior victimization. *Journal of Interpersonal Violence, 15,* 363–374.

Vest, J. R., Catlin, T. K., Chen, J. J., & Brownson, R. C. (2002). Multistate analysis of factors associated with intimate partner violence. *American Journal of Preventive Medicine, 22,* 156–164.

Vestal, C. (2009, April 8). Gay marriage legal in six states [Electronic Version]. *Stateline Daily News Service.* Retrieved from http://www.stateline.org/live/details/story?content Id=347390.

Vickers, L. (1996). The second closet: Domestic violence in lesbian and gay relationships: A Western Australian perspective. *Murdoch University Electronic Journal of Law, 3,* 1–27.

Vinton, L. (1991). Factors associated with refusing services among maltreated elderly. *Journal of Elder Abuse & Neglect, 3,* 89–103.

Vinton, L. (2002). *Questions and answers about older abused women* [Electronic Version]. Retrieved December 1, 2003, from http://ssw.fsu.edu/qaolderwomen/qaolderwomen.pdf.

Vinton, L. (2003). A model collaborative project toward making domestic violence centers elder ready. *Violence Against Women, 9*(12), 1504–1513.

Violence Policy Center. (2000). *Facts on firearms and domestic violence.* Retrieved from http://www.vpc.org/fact_sht/domviofs.htm.

Violence Policy Center. (2011). *Nevada ranks #1 in rate of women murdered by men for second year in a row according to VPC study released annually for domestic violence awareness month in October.* Retrieved from http://www.vpc.org/press/1109dv.htm.

Vissing, Y. M., Straus, M. A., Gelles, R. J., & Harrop, J. W. (1991). Verbal aggression by parents and psychosocial problems of children. *Child Abuse and Neglect, 15,* 223–238.

Vivian, D., & Langhinrichsen-Rohling, J. (1994). Are bi-directionally violent couples mutually victimized? A gender sensitive comparison. *Violence and Victims, 9,* 107–124.

Vogeltanz, N. D., Wilsnack, S. C., Harris, T. R., Wilsnack, R. W., Wonderlich, S. A., & Kristjanson, A. F. (1999). Prevalence and risk factors for childhood sexual abuse in women: National survey findings. *Child Abuse and Neglect, 23,* 579–592.

Volz, A., & Kerig, P. (2010). Relational dynamics associated with adolescent dating violence: The roles of rejection sensitivity and relational insecurity. *Journal of Aggression, Maltreatment & Trauma, 19*(6).

Wahab, S. P., & Olson, L. (2004). Intimate partner violence and sexual assault in Native American communities. *Trauma, Violence, & Abuse, 5*(4), 353–366.

Walby, S., & Allen, J. (2004). *Domestic violence, sexual assault and stalking: Findings from the British Crime Survey.* London, UK: Home Office.

Waldner-Haugrud, L. K., & Gratch, L. V. (1997). Sexual coercion in gay/lesbian relationships: Descriptives and gender differences. *Violence and Victims, 12,* 87–98.

Waldner-Haugrud, L. K., Gratch, L. V., & Magruder, B. (1997). Victimization and perpetration rates of violence in gay and lesbian relationships: Gender issues explored. *Violence and Victims, 12,* 173–184.

Walker, D. F., Reese, J. B., Hughes, J. P., & Troskie, M. J. (2010). Addressing religious and spiritual issues in trauma-focused cognitive behavior therapy for children and adolescents. *Professional Psychology: Research & Practice, 41*(2), 174–180.

Walker, D. F., Reid, H. W., O'Neill, T., & Brown, L. (2009). Changes in personal religion/spirituality during and after childhood abuse: A review and synthesis. *Psychological Trauma: Theory, Research, Practice, and Policy, 1*(2), 130–145.

Walker, E., Downey, G., & Bergman, A. (1989). The effects of parental psychopathology and maltreatment on child behavior: A test of the diathesis-stress model. *Child Development, 60,* 15–24.

Walker, L. E. A. (1979). *The battered woman.* New York, NY: Harper & Row.

Walker, L. E. A. (1993). The battered woman syndrome is a psychological consequence of abuse. In R. J. Gelles & D. R. Loseke (Eds.), *Current controversies on family violence* (pp. 133–153). Newbury Park, CA: Sage.

Walker, L. E. A. (2000). *The battered woman syndrome* (2nd ed.). New York, NY: Springer.

Walker, L. E. A. (2009). *The battered woman syndrome* (3rd ed.). New York, NY: Springer.

Walker, N. E., Brooks, C. M., & Wrightsman, L. S. (1999). *Children's rights in the United States: In search of a national policy.* Thousand Oaks, CA: Sage.

Wallach, V. A., & Lister, L. (1995). Stages in the delivery of home-based services to parents at risk of child abuse: A Healthy Start experience. *Scholarly Inquiry for Nursing Practice: An international Journal, 9,* 159–173.

Walsh, J. A., & Krienert, J. L. (2007). Child-parent violence: An empirical analysis of offender, victim, and event characteristics in a national sample of reported incidents. *Journal of Family Violence, 22,* 563–574.

Walsh, J. A., & Krienert, J. L. (2009). A decade of child-initiated family violence: Comparative analysis of child-parent violence and parricide examining offender, victim, and event characteristics in a national sample of reported incidents, 1995–2005. *Journal of Interpersonal Violence, 24*(9), 1450–1477.

Walsh, W. A., Cross, T. P., Jones, L. M., Simone, M., & Kolko, D. J. (2007). Which sexual abuse victims receive a forensic examination? The impact of children's advocacy centers. *Child Abuse & Neglect, 31,* 1053–1068.

Walters, M. L. (2011). Straighten up and act like a lady: A qualitative study of lesbian survivors of intimate partner violence. *Journal of Lesbian and Gay Social Services, 23,* 250–270.

Walton-Moss, B. J., Manganello, J., Frye, V., & Campbell, J. C. (2005). Risk factors for intimate partner violence and associated injury among urban women. *Journal of Community Health: The Publication for Health Promotion and Disease Prevention, 30*(5), 377–389.

Wang, M., Horne, S., Levitt, M. H., & Klesges, L. (2009). Christian women in IPV relationships: An exploratory study in religious factors. *Journal of Psychology and Christianity, 28,* 224–235.

Wanless, M. (1996). Mandatory arrest: A step towards eradicating domestic violence, but is it enough? *University of Illinois Law Review, 2,* 533–587.

Ward, K. J. (2001). *Mentors in Violence Prevention Program evaluation, 1999–2000.* Unpublished report, Northeastern University. Boston, MA.

Wareham, J., Boots, D. P., & Chavez, J. M. (2009). A test of social learning and intergenerational transmission among batterers. *Journal of Criminal Justice, 37,* 163–173.

Warner, J. D., Malinosky-Rummell, R., Ellis, J. T., & Hansen, D. J. (1990, November). *An examination of demographic and treatment variables associated with session attendance of maltreating families.* Paper presented at the annual conference of the Association for Advancement of Behavior Therapy, San Francisco, CA.

Waterman, C. K., Dawson, L. J., & Bologna, M. J. (1989). Sexual coercion in gay male and lesbian relationships: Predictors and implications for support services. *Journal of Sex Research, 26,* 118–124.

Wathen, C. N., & MacMillan, H. L. (2003). Interventions for violence against women: Scientific review. *JAMA: Journal of the American Medical Association, 289*(5), 589–600.

Wealin, J. M., Davies, S., Shaffer, A. E., Jackson, J. L., & Love, L. C. (2002). Family context and childhood adjustment associated with intrafamilial unwanted sexual attention. *Journal of Family Violence, 17,* 151–165.

Webb, M., & Otto Whitmer, K. J. (2003). Parental religiosity, abuse history and maintenance of beliefs taught in the family. *Mental Health, Religion, and Culture, 6*(3), 229–239.

Webb, N. B. (1999). Play therapy crisis intervention with children. In N. B. Webb (Ed.), *Play therapy with children in crisis* (pp. 29–46). New York, NY: Guilford.

Wegner, D. M., Schneider, D. J., Carter, S. R., & White, T. L. (1987). Paradoxical effects of thought suppression. *Journal of Personality and Social Psychology, 53,* 5–13.

Weidel, J. J., Provencio-Vasquez, E., Watson, S. D., & Gonzalez-Guarda, R. (2008). Cultural considerations for intimate partner violence and HIV risk in Hispanics. *JANAC: Journal of the Association of Nurses in AIDS Care, 19*(4), 247–251.

Weil, J., & Lee, H. (2004). Cultural considerations in understanding family violence among Asian American Pacific Islander families. *Journal of Community Health Nursing, 21*(4), 217–227.

Wenzel, S., Tucker, J., Elliott, M., Marshall, G., & Williamson, S. (2004). Physical violence against impoverished women: A longitudinal analysis of risk and protective factors. *Women's Health Issues, 14,* 144–154.

Wertheim, L. J. (2010). Why did Yeardley Love have to die? *Sports Illustrated.com.* Available at http://sportsillustrated.cnn.com/2010/magazine/05/11/virginia.lacrosse/index.html.

West, C. M. (2002). Lesbian intimate partner violence: Prevalence and dynamics. *Journal of Lesbian Studies, 6*(1), 121–127.

West, K. P., Bledsoe, L., Jenkins, J., & Nora, L. M. (2002). The mandatory reporting of adult victims of violence: Perspectives from the field. *Kentucky Law Journal, 90,* 1071–1082.

Whipple, E. E., & Webster-Stratton, C. (1991). The role of parental stress in physically abusive families. *Child Abuse and Neglect, 15,* 279–291.

Whitaker, D. J., Haileyesus, T., Swahn, M., & Saltzman, L. S. (2007). Differences in frequency of violence and reported injury between relationships with reciprocal and non-reciprocal intimate partner violence. *American Journal of Public Health, 97*(5), 941–947.

White, H., & Widom, C. (2003). Intimate partner violence among abused and neglected children in young adulthood: The mediating effects of early aggression, antisocial personality, hostility, and alcohol problems. *Aggressive Behavior, 29*(4), 332–345.

Whiteford, L. M., & Vitucci, J. (1997). Pregnancy and addiction: Translating research into practice. *Social Science and Medicine, 44,* 1371–1380.

Whitfield, C. L., Anda, R. F., Dube, S. R., & Felitti, V. J. (2003). Violent childhood experiences and the risk of intimate partner violence in adults: Assessment in a large health maintenance organization. *Journal of Interpersonal Violence, 18*(2), 166–185.

Widom, C. (1999). Posttraumatic stress disorder in abused and neglected children grown up. *American Journal of Psychiatry, 156,* 1223–1229.

Widom, C. S. (1989). Does violence beget violence? A critical examination of the literature. *Psychological Bulletin, 106,* 3–28.

Widom, C. S., & Brzustowicz, L. M. (2006). MAOA and the "cycle of violence": Childhood abuse and neglect, MAOA genotype, and the risk for violent and antisocial behavior. *Biological Psychiatry, 60,* 684–689.

Widom, C. S., & Kuhns, J. B. (1996). Childhood victimization and subsequent risk for promiscuity, prostitution, and teenage pregnancy: A prospective study. *American Journal of Public Health, 86,* 1607–1612.

Wiehe, V. R. (1990). Religious influence on parental attitudes toward the use of corporal punishment. *Journal of Family Violence, 5,* 173–187.

Wiehe, V. R. (1997). *Sibling abuse: Hidden physical, emotional, and sexual trauma* (2nd ed.). Thousand Oaks, CA: Sage.

Wiglesworth, A., Mosqueda, L., Mulnard, R., Liao, S., Gibbs, L., & Fitzgerald, W. (2010). Screening for abuse and neglect of people with dementia. *Journal of the American Geriatrics Society, 58*(3), 493–500.

Wilcox, W. B. (1998). Conservative Protestant parenting: Authoritarian or authoritative? *American Sociological Review, 63,* 796–809.

Wildeman, C., & Western, B. (2010). The demography of punishment in America. *Fragile Families, 20*(2). Available at http://futureofchildren.org/publications/journals/article/index .xml?journalid=73&articleid=535&sectionid=3685.

Wille, R., & Beier, K. M. (1989). Castration in Germany. *Annals of Sex Research, 2,* 103–134.

Willett, J. B., Ayoub, C. C., & Robinson, D. (1991). Using growth modeling to examine systematic differences in growth: An example of change in the functioning of families at risk of maladaptive parenting, child abuse, or neglect. *Journal of Consulting and Clinical Psychology, 59,* 38–47.

Williams, L. M. (1994). Recall of childhood trauma: A prospective study of women's memories of child sexual abuse. *Journal of Consulting and Clinical Psychology, 62,* 1167–1176.

Williams, L. M. (1995). Recovered memories of abuse in women with documented child sexual victimization histories. *Journal of Traumatic Stress, 8,* 649–674.

Williams, O. J., & Griffin, L. W. (1996). Elderly maltreatment and cultural diversity: When laws are not enough. *Journal of Multicultural Social Work, 4,* 1–13.

Williams, S. L., & Frieze, I. H. (2005). Courtship behaviors, relationship violence, and breakup persistence in college men and women. *Psychology of Women Quarterly, 29,* 248–257.

Williamson, J. M., Borduin, C. M., & Howe, B. A. (1991). The ecology of adolescent maltreatment: A multilevel examination of adolescent physical abuse, sexual abuse, and neglect. *Journal of Consulting and Clinical Psychology, 59,* 449–457.

Wilson, B. J., Smith, S. L., Potter, W. J., Kunkel, D., Linz, D., Colvin, C. M., & Donnerstein, E. (2002). Violence in children's television programming: Assessing the risk. *Journal of Communication, 52*(1), 5–35.

Winstock, Z., & Straus, M. A. (2011). Perceived neighborhood violence and use of verbal aggression, corporal punishment, and physical abuse by a national sample of parents in Israel. *Journal of Community Psychology, 39*(6), 678–697.

Wisseman, K. B. (2000). "You're my pretty bird in a cage": Disability, domestic violence, and survival. In W. Abramson, E. Emanuel, V. Gaylord, & M. Hayden (Eds.), *Impact: Feature issue on violence against women with developmental or other disabilities, 13*(3) [online]. Minneapolis, MN: University of Minnesota, Institute on Community Integration. Available at http://ici.umn.edu/products/impact/133/over1.html.

Wolak, J., & Finkelhor, D. (1998). Children exposed to partner violence. In J. L. Jasinski & L. M. Williams (Eds.), *Partner violence: A comprehensive review of 20 years of research* (pp. 73–112). Thousand Oaks, CA: Sage.

Wolak, J., Finkelhor, D., & Mitchell, K. (2011). Child pornography possessors: Trends in offender and case characteristics. *Sexual Abuse: A Journal of Research and Treatment, 23*(1), 22–42.

Wolak, J., Mitchell, K. J., & Finkelhor, D. (2007). Unwanted and wanted exposure to online pornography in a national sample of youth Internet users. *Pediatrics, 119,* 247–257.

Wolf, M. E., Ly, U., Hobart, M. A., & Kernic, M. A. (2003). Barriers to seeking police help for intimate partner violence. *Journal of Family Violence, 18*(2), 121–129.

Wolf, R. (2000). The nature and scope of elder abuse. *Generations, 24*(2), 6–13.

Wolf, R. S., & Pillemer, K. (1989). *Helping elderly victims: The reality of elder abuse.* New York, NY: Columbia University Press.

Wolfe, D., Fairbank, J. A., Kelly, J. A., & Bradlyn, A. S. (1983). Child abusive parents' physiological responses to stressful and non-stressful behavior in children. *Behavioral Assessment, 5,* 363–371.

Wolfe, D. A., Crooks, C. V., Lee, V., McIntyre-Smith, A., & Jaffe, P. G. (2003). The effects of children's exposure to domestic violence: A meta-analysis and critique. *Clinical Child and Family Psychology Review, 6*(3), 171–187.

Wolfe, R. S., Strugnell, C. P., & Godkin, M. A. (1982). *Preliminary findings from three model projects on elder abuse.* Worcester, MA: University of Massachusetts Medical Center, University Center on Aging.

Wood, W., Wong, F. Y., & Chachere, J. G. (1991). Effects of media violence on viewers' aggression in unconstrained social interaction. *Psychological Bulletin, 109,* 371–383.

Woody, G. E., Van Etten-Lee, M. L., McKirnan, D., Donnell, D., Metzger, D., Seage, G., & Gross, M. (2001). Substance use among men who have sex with men: Comparison with a national household survey. *Journal of Acquired Immune Deficiency Syndromes, 27,* 86–90.

World Health Organization. (2005). *WHO Multi-country Study on Women's Health and Domestic Violence against Women* [Electronic Version]. Retrieved from http://www.who .int/gender/violence/who_multicountry_study/en/.

Worling, J. (1995). Adolescent sibling-incest offenders: Differences in family and individual functioning when compared to adolescent nonsibling sex offenders. *Child Abuse and Neglect, 19,* 633–643.

Wright, C. V., Perez, S., & Johnson, D. M. (2010). The mediating role of empowerment for African American women experiencing intimate partner violence. *Psychological Trauma: Theory, Research, Practice, and Policy, 2*(4), 266–272.

Wright, P., Nobrega, J., Langevin, R., & Wortzman, G. (1990). Brain density and symmetry in pedophilic and sexually aggressive offenders. *Annals of Sex Research, 3,* 319–328.

Xu, X., Tung, Y. Y., & Dunaway, R. G. (2000). Cultural, human and social capital as determinants of corporal punishment: Toward an integrated theoretical model. *Journal of Interpersonal Violence, 15,* 603–630.

Yehuda, R., Rosenbaum, T. Y., Labinsky, E., & Schmeidler, J. (2007). History of past sexual abuse in married observant Jewish women. *American Journal of Psychiatry, 164*(11), 1700–1706.

Yick, A., & Agbayani-Siewert, P. (1997). Perceptions of domestic violence in a Chinese-American community. *Journal of Interpersonal Violence, 12,* 832–846.

Yllo, K., & Straus, M. A. (1990). Patriarchy and violence against wives: The impact of structural and normative factors. In M. A. Straus & R. J. Gelles (Eds.), *Physical violence in American families: Risk factors and adaptations to violence in 8,145 families* (pp. 383–402). New Brunswick, NJ: Transaction.

Yllo, K. A. (2005). Through a feminist lens: Gender, diversity, and violence: Extending the feminist framework. In D. R. Loseke, R. J. Gelles, & M. M. Cavanaugh (Eds.), *Current controversies on family violence* (pp. 19–34). Thousand Oaks, CA: Sage.

Yoshioka, M. R., DiNoia, J., & Ullah, K. (2001). Attitudes toward marital violence: An examination of four Asian communities. *Violence Against Women, 7,* 900–926.

Yuan, N. P., Koss, M. P., Polacca, M., & Goldman, D. (2006). Risk factors for physical assault and rape among six Native American tribes. *Journal of Interpersonal Violence, 21*(12), 1566–1590.

Zambrano, M. Z. (1985). *Mejor sola que real acomoanada: For the Latina in an abusive relationship.* Seattle, WA: Seal Press.

Zanarini, M. C., Ruser, T. F., Frankenburg, F. F., Hennen, J., & Gunderson, J. G. (2000). Risk factors associated with the dissociative experiences of borderline patients. *Journal of Nervous and Mental Disease, 188,* 26–30.

Zellman, G. L., & Fair, C. C. (2002). Preventing and reporting abuse. In J. E. B. Myers, L. Berliner, J. Briere, C. T. Hendrix, C. Jenny, & T. A. Reid (Eds.), *The APSAC handbook on child maltreatment* (2nd ed., pp. 449–478). Thousand Oaks, CA: Sage.

Zhai, F., & Gao, Q. (2009). Child maltreatment among Asian Americans: Characteristics and explanatory framework. *Child Maltreatment, 14*(2), 207–224.

Ziegler, R. G., & Weidner, D. A. (2006). Assessment and intervention with parents to stabilize children who have witnessed violence. *Journal of Family Violence, 21*(3), 209–219.

Zielinski, D. S., & Bradshaw, C. P. (2006). Ecological influences on the sequelae of child maltreatment: A review of the literature. *Child Maltreatment, 11,* 49–62.

Zierler, S., Cunningham, W. E., Andersen, R., Shapiro, M. F., Bozzette, S. A., Nakazono, T., . . . St. Clair, P. (2000). Violence victimization after HIV infection in a U.S. probability sample of adult patients in primary care. *American Journal of Public Health, 90,* 208–215.

Zingraff, M., Leiter, J., Johnson, M. C., & Myers, K. A. (1994). The mediating effect of school performance on the maltreatment-delinquency relationship. *Journal of Research in Crime and Delinquency, 31,* 62–91.

Zolondek, S. C., Abel, G. G., Northey, W. R. J., & Jordan, A. D. (2001). The self-reported behaviors of juvenile sexual offenders. *Journal of Interpersonal Violence, 16,* 73–85.

Zolotor, A. J., Theodore, A. D., Runyan, D. K., Chang, J. J., & Laskey, A. L. (2011). Corporal punishment and physical abuse: Population-based trends for three-to-11-year-old children in the United States. *Child Abuse Review, 20,* 57–66.

Zona, M. A., Sharma, K. K., & Lane, J. (1993). A comparative study of erotomanic and obsessional subjects in a forensic sample. *Journal of Forensic Sciences, 38*(4), 894–903.

Zorza, J., & Woods, L. (1994). *Mandatory arrest: Problems and possibilities.* Washington, DC: Center on Women and Family Law.

Zuravin, S. J. (1989). The ecology of child abuse and neglect: Review of the literature and presentation of data. *Violence and Victims, 4,* 101–120.

Zuravin, S. J., & DiBlasio, F. A. (1992). Child-neglecting adolescent mothers: How do they differ from their nonmaltreating counterparts? *Journal of Interpersonal Violence, 7,* 471–487.

Zuriff, G. (1988). A quick solution to the psychologist's problem of defining "psychological maltreatment." *American Psychologist, 43,* 201.

Index

About the Authors

Denise A. Hines, PhD, is a research assistant professor in the psychology department at Clark University, where she is also the director of the Family Impact Seminar Series and the codirector of the Clark Anti-Violence Education Program. She completed her doctoral degree in Psychology at Boston University, and then spent two years as an NIMH postdoctoral research fellow at the University of New Hampshire's Family Research Laboratory with Drs. Murray Straus and David Finkelhor. She is the author or coauthor of over 30 articles or book chapters, and two books published by Sage on issues of family violence. She has also been the principal investigator on six major grants, focusing on issues of the etiology of partner violence; prevention of dating violence, sexual assault, and stalking on college campuses; and the mental and physical health of male victims of partner violence and their children.

Kathleen Malley-Morrison, EdD, is a professor of psychology at Boston University. She has conducted considerable research on family violence since 1980 when she was a postdoctoral fellow on the family violence team at Children's Hospital in Boston. She regularly teaches undergraduate and graduate courses focusing on family violence. She is the lead author of the 1998 book *Treating Child Abuse: Family Violence in Hospitals,* along with Eli Newberger, Richard Bourne, and Jane Snyder. She also coauthored *Studying Families* (SAGE, 1991) with Anne Copeland, and *Family Violence in a Cultural Perspective* (SAGE, 2004), with Denise Hines. Her current focus is primarily on cross-cultural and international perspectives on family violence and abuse as well as on war and peace.

Leila B. Dutton, PhD, is an assistant professor in the criminal justice department of the University of New Haven. She received her doctoral degree in experimental psychology at the University of Rhode Island in 2004. She spent two years as an NIMH postdoctoral research fellow at the University of New Hampshire's Family Research Laboratory, working with Murray Straus on the International Dating Violence Study. Her research interests include stalking, partner violence, and sexual coercion. She has published her research in the *Journal of Interpersonal Violence, Partner Abuse,* and *Journal of Social and Personal Relationships.* She has written two book chapters on stalking. She is currently on the editorial board of the journal *Partner Abuse.* She is also the codirector of the University of New Haven's Institute for Social Justice and codirector of UNH's Campus Grant to Reduce Violence Against Women funded by the Department of Justice's Office on Violence Against Women.